Forbidden Knowledge

Inside Information *They* Don't
Want You to See

Editors

**Robert E. Bauman JD
Ted Bauman**

— Seventh Edition —

The Sovereign Society
55 NE 5th Avenue, Suite 200
Delray Beach, FL 33483
Tel.: 1-866-584-4096
Email: www.sovereignsociety.com/contact-us
Web: http://www.sovereignsociety.com

ISBN: 978-0-692-46550-9

Copyright © 2016 Sovereign Offshore Services LLC. All international and domestic rights reserved, protected by copyright laws of the United States and international treaties. No part of this publication may be reproduced in any form, printed or electronic or on the worldwide web, without written permission from the publisher, Sovereign Offshore Services, LLC, 55 NE 5th Avenue, Suite 200, Delray Beach, FL 33483 USA.

Notice: This publication is designed to provide accurate and authoritative information in regard to the subject matter covered. It is sold and distributed with the understanding that the author, publisher and seller are not engaged in rendering legal, accounting or other professional advice or service. If legal or other expert assistance is required, the services of a competent professional advisor should be sought.

The information and recommendations contained herein have been compiled from sources considered reliable. Employees, officers and directors of The Sovereign Society do not receive fees or commissions for any recommendations of services or products in this book. Investment and other recommendations carry inherent risks. As no investment recommendation can be guaranteed, The Sovereign Society takes no responsibility for any loss or inconvenience if one chooses to accept them.

The Sovereign Society advocates full compliance with applicable tax and financial reporting laws.

U.S. law requires income taxes to be paid on all worldwide income wherever a U.S. person (citizen or resident alien) may live or have a residence. Each U.S. person who has a financial interest in or signature authority over bank, securities, or other financial accounts in a foreign country that exceeds $10,000 in aggregate value must report that fact on his or her annual federal income tax return, IRS Form 1040. The Foreign Account Tax Compliance Act (FATCA) requires an annual filing along with IRS Form 1040 IRS Form 8938 listing specified foreign assets. An additional report must be filed by June 30th of each year on an information return (FinCEN Form 114, formerly Form TDF 90 22.1) with the U.S. Treasury.

Willful noncompliance of reports may result in criminal prosecution. You should consult a qualified attorney or accountant to ensure that you know, understand and comply with these and any other U.S. reporting requirements.

About the Editors

Robert E. Bauman JD

Bob Bauman, legal counsel to The Sovereign Society, served as a member of the U.S. House of Representatives from 1973 to 1981 representing the First District of Maryland. He is an author and lecturer on many aspects of wealth protection, offshore residence and second citizenship.

A member of the District of Columbia Bar, he received his juris doctor degree from the Law Center of Georgetown University in 1964. He has a B.S. degree in International Relations from the Georgetown University School of Foreign Service (1959) and was honored with GU's Distinguished Alumni Award.

He is the author of *The Gentleman from Maryland* (Hearst Book Publishing, NY); and the following books, all published by The Sovereign Society: *The Passport Book: Complete Guide to Offshore Residency, Dual Citizenship and Second Passports*; *The Offshore Money Manual*; *Panama Money Secrets*; *Where to Stash Your Cash Legally: Offshore Financial Centers of the World*, *Swiss Money Secrets*; *How to Lawyer-Proof Your Life*.

His writings have appeared in *The Wall Street Journal*, *The New York Times*, *National Review*, and other publications.

Ted Bauman

Ted Bauman joined The Sovereign Society in September 2013 and serves as the editor of *The Bauman Letter* (previously named *Sovereign Confidential*) and Plan B Club, specializing in asset protection and international migration issues. Born in Washington D.C. and raised on Maryland's Eastern Shore, Ted emigrated to South Africa as a young man. He graduated from the University of Cape Town with postgraduate degrees in Economics and History. During his 25-year career in South Africa, Ted served a variety of executive roles in the South African non-profit sector, primarily as a fund manager for low-cost housing projects. During the 2000s, he worked as a consultant, researching and writing extensively on financial, housing, and urban planning issues for clients as diverse as the United Nations, the South African government, and European grant-making agencies. He also travelled extensively, largely in Africa, Asia, and Europe.

In 2008, Ted returned to the U.S., where he served as Director of International Housing Programs for Habitat for Humanity International, based in Atlanta, GA. During that time, he extended his travels to Latin American and the Caribbean. He continued to research and write on a variety of topics related to international development. In 2013, Ted left Habitat to work full-time as a researcher and writer.

Ted has been published in a variety of international journals, including the Journal of Microfinance, Small Enterprise Development, and Environment and Urbanization, as well as the South African press, including the *Cape Times*, *New Internationalist*, *Cape Argus*, and *Mail and Guardian*.

Forbidden Knowledge

Inside Information *They* Don't Want You to See

Editors

Robert E. Bauman JD
Ted Bauman

Seventh Edition

Table of Contents

Preface 9

Chapter One: The Sovereign Life & How You Can Achieve It Starting Today 13

Chapter Two: Your Guide to Second Passports, Dual Nationality, Foreign Residence & Expatriation 57

Chapter Three: Little-Known Secrets of Offshore Banking, Insurance & Finance 141

Chapter Four: Offshore Trusts, Family Foundations & Other Wealth Preservation Strategies 195

Chapter Five: Real Estate 245

Chapter Six: Your Finances & Estate Planning 293

Chapter Seven: Your New Goal: Pay Zero Taxes — *Legally* 365

Chapter Eight: Tax Havens — International Asset Acquisition & Storage 435

Chapter Nine: Special Places for Business & Profits 471

Chapter Ten: Personal & Digital Privacy Secrets 587

Chapter Eleven: Unchain Your Personal and Civil Liberties 657

Appendix A: Council of Experts 689

Appendix B: About the Authors 697

Preface

"Just as the State has no money of its own, so it has no power of its own. All the power it has society gives it, plus what it confiscates from time to time on one pretext or another; there is no other source from which State power can be drawn. Therefore, every assumption of State power, whether by gift or seizure, leaves society with so much less power; there is never, nor can be, any strengthening of State power without a corresponding and equivalent depletion of social power."
— Albert J. Nock (1935)

"Knowledge itself is power."
— Francis Bacon, *Meditationes Sacrae* (1597)

In the age-old struggle for individual liberty against the power of the state, there can be no question which side has triumphed throughout most of the twentieth century.

The one interest the state willingly sacrifices to the "common good" is personal liberty "the freedom to produce and create, to buy and sell, to speak and publish, to travel, to live freely."

By diminishing liberty, government systematically subverts people's responsibility for their own lives. It robs those who produce in order to placate those who only consume. The result is economic stagnation, retrogression and political corruption.

Since the seventeenth century, in England, France and America, and more recently in Russia and Eastern Europe, revolutions against this tyranny of the state were fought on behalf of an alternative we can call "natural liberty."

At first successful, over time these revolutions cooled to complacency and hard-won freedom came to mean guaranteed entitlement to government largess.

True natural liberty means that each of us is the sole legitimate owner of our own life and destiny, free to act as we wish so long as we use no violence, fraud or other aggression against others.

That same freedom dictates a free-market economy enjoying peaceful production and trade. It opposes government control by self-serving politicians.

No activity of statist government has diminished personal liberty more than the unchecked power to tax. In the United States, the United Kingdom and Germany the effective rate of personal taxes far exceeds 50 percent of earnings. In some nations, such as France and Sweden, it is higher still. Business is taxed at even greater levels.

And everyone pays the ultimate price.

When government takes wealth from some and gives it to others, this forced redistribution diminishes the rights and well-being of the former, and often destroys the independence of the latter.

The issue of taxation involves nothing less than the human and natural right to own, use and enjoy private property, a "civil right" of the most basic kind.

Property and wealth determine personal power to control our own lives, to make decisions, to raise a family, to live free.

As Albert Jay Nock noted, every additional tax imposed diminishes our freedom. In an economic history of the Middle Ages, Paul Craig Roberts, the economist and columnist, showed that medieval serfs bound to the land and their masters rarely paid more than one-third of the value of their labors in taxes. For good reason: with very low productivity, serfs could not survive if forced to pay more taxes. With nothing to lose, they would revolt and kill the tax collectors.

Yet a half-millennium later, with capitalism's enormously increased productivity, we have even less right to our earnings than did those enslaved serfs. Says Roberts: "You are not free when you do not own the product of your own labor."

This book, *Forbidden Knowledge*, is a compendium of the acts and ideas of dynamic men and women who have exalted natural liberty in their own lives — and many do so to this day.

Albert Camus said, "Revolutionaries are men who say no!"

These authors have said an emphatic "NO" to Big Brother government. These practical people refuse to bow down to government, to submit to bureaucratic demands for ever higher taxes, greater controls and increased regulation.

In some cases, this has meant leaving the nation of their birth and moving to countries that still believe in and practice natural liberty. There are such places, as you will see.

Some individuals you will meet in these pages call no single nation "home," spending the changing seasons of each year in many places where they do business, and enjoy the new experiences and the pleasures life has to give.

Drawing on their experience, you too can have a life of natural liberty. You too can live, work, invest and do business without having to pay taxes to any government anywhere. And you can do this legally and with maximum personal security and financial privacy.

To knowledgeable people, true financial security means:

- the maximum possible legal tax avoidance
- the strongest possible financial privacy
- the greatest degree of asset protection
- the most profitable investments

These goals, and how to achieve them, are spelled out in *Forbidden Knowledge*.

Bob Bauman

Robert E. Bauman JD, Editor

Chapter One

The Sovereign Life & How You Can Achieve It Starting Today

On Becoming a Sovereign Individual 14
What We May Be 16
The "PT" Life…Is It For YOU? 17
What's Wrong with the U.S. Constitution? 19
A Declaration of Independence for Sovereign Individuals 22
Mirror, Mirror on the Wall, Where's the Freest Land of All? 24
Is It Un-American to "Go Offshore?" 26
Five Strategies to Maximize the Best Offshore Has to Offer 28
Atlas Shrugged: From Fiction to Fact in 52 Years 31
The Only Way to Avoid Wealth Confiscation 33
Property Rights Are Civil Rights 35
Revise the PATRIOT Act 38
Big Brother Is Watching and Listening 40
Police Militarization: The New Search and Seizure 43
The "War on Terror"— Surrender of Civil Liberties? 45
The Roots of Terrorism 48
Are You a Libertarian? 50
Obamacare is About to Get More Personal 53

Editor's Note:

We live in one of those times when civilization becomes "a thin crust over a volcano of revolution."

Unrecognized by most, the Old Order is dying, replaced by a new world economic structure built on free markets, massive technological change, instant communications, interlinked databases, electronic commerce and digital cash. These emerging systems inevitably weaken the power of traditional governments, even as they have the very real potential to increase individual freedom, financial choice and personal privacy.

Today's politicians saw what was coming and have been clawing desperately to stay ahead of the inevitable tide towards freedom. They'll fail, as did the corrupt leaders of a dying Soviet Union, brazenly trying to stop the spread of free ideas by outlawing fax and copying machines. And just as myopic nineteenth century Luddite workers failed to thwart the Industrial Revolution by destroying new labor saving machinery.

As evidence, consider how shared, instantaneous information contributes to the spread of economic collapse of national economies. The worst economic recession since the Great Depression of the 1930s may have been engendered by stupid government policies, mass irresponsibility in the part of American and European banks and greed in Wall Street and the City. But every nervous wave rippled hourly across time zones and stock markets as cable news covered the panic live and Internet trading went wild — yet another example of irresistible techno-advances forcing a totally new financial and banking reality, whether good or bad.

Consider the impact of the global recession. Stock of corporations whose billions in wealth existed only on paper or as future concepts that had rocketed up in price, even more quickly disappeared.

A select few people long ago anticipated the revolution now at hand. These are the Sovereign Individuals, voluntary citizens of the world-at-large, who seek freedom and fortune wherever they judge best.

Weary of oppressive governments and onerous taxes, of constant surveillance, they search the globe for greater personal liberty, for safe havens for their families, themselves and their wealth.

ON BECOMING A SOVEREIGN INDIVIDUAL
John Pugsley, *The Sovereign Individual*, June 1999

The late Chairman of The Sovereign Society traces the evolution of freedom from serfdom to democracy, and now to a modern slavery by government in the name of democracy.

Since emerging from the caves and jungles of antiquity, mankind has been engaged in an epic struggle to discover the ultimate design for social organization, one that would allow civilization to progress in peace and ever-increasing prosperity.

For thousands of years, the idea of monarchy reigned. The overwhelming majority accepted rule by an all-powerful government headed by a king appointed by God.

Then, about 200 years ago, an idea emerged that was to change the nature of government...the idea that all men and women were born with equal rights to life, liberty and the pursuit of happiness. In short, individuals were sovereign and had both the right and the responsibility to rule themselves.

The concept of the divine right of kings was cast aside and in its place democracy was born; citizens were free to elect their rulers. It was believed the era of oppressive government was over.

When democracy was embryonic, it seemed to work. Individual freedom from oppression led to a flourishing new world. Over the past few decades, however, there has been a steady growth of government as the masses of voters have learned that they can manipulate government to their advantage. They have found they can enrich themselves at the expense of the successful and thrifty.

This attack on the more affluent and productive individuals in countries such as the United States, Canada, Germany and the United Kingdom has had the same effect as the repressive policies of King George III had in the eighteenth century. It has led to a rising exodus of society's most productive people as they migrate to political environments that offer greater asset protection, privacy and lower taxation.

Many are moving only their assets offshore to countries that offer more financial privacy and low or no taxation. A smaller but rising number are electing to move themselves and their families offshore as well.

While a few officially disconnect from their nation of birth by renouncing their citizenship, others merely reside offshore while retaining their original citizenship. Still others acquire dual nationality by ancestral right or through financial citizenship programs offered by many countries.

A few adopt the so-called "PT" lifestyle and become nomads, never staying long enough in one place to become subject to its taxes, thus becoming "Perpetual Travelers" or "Prior Taxpayers." But all are united in seeking privacy, freedom of movement, low or no taxes, safety of capital and minimal connection with big government, and in being Prepared Thoroughly for the unexpected.

What We May Be

Robert E. Bauman JD, *The Sovereign Investor Daily*, December 2008

In "Hamlet" (circa 1601) William Shakespeare sagely noted: "Lord! We know what we are, but we know not what we may be."

Nevertheless, each New Year's the world media engages in a mild form of entertainment by attempting to predict events for the next 365 days.

I don't intend to join their prognostications except to say we are likely to suffer more of the same, based on all the current sad indications — more and bigger government, more and bigger taxes, spending, debt and deficits, more and greater depredations against our remaining, but rapidly, diminishing liberties.

The Chairman's Wisdom

I am indebted in many ways to my good friend, the Chairman of The Sovereign Society, the noted author, the late Jack Pugsley, but also for the following wisdom which he shared with us on New Year's Eve a few years ago:

"The Sovereign Society was conceived by a group of individuals who shared the conviction that peace and prosperity would be optimized when every individual's property is rightfully his or hers to keep, control, and dispose of.

"Having witnessed over our lifetimes the relentless expansion of government and the concomitant erosion of individual liberties, it was clear to us that the preponderance of aggression against private property did not come from criminals or from foreign nations, but from citizens' own governments and judicial systems."

As Voltaire summed up the process 240 years ago: "The art of government consists in taking as much money as possible from one party of the citizens to give to the other."

"Most still believe government is a protector, and it grows because people believe it will cure the social ills that plague us. In fact, it is the source of our problems. By restricting individual liberty, by preventing individuals from freely producing and exchanging goods and services, and by taxing and inflating, government has become the source of social conflict."

The Sovereign Society Credo

The Sovereign Society has grown to a membership of nearly 30,000 in many countries around the world. The principles around which The Society was conceived are built into its credo are even more relevant today:

- THAT individual liberty is the highest good in any society;

- THAT every individual has the natural right to keep, control, and dispose of his or her justly acquired property;
- THAT individuals are not the property of the government of the political jurisdiction in which they are born or reside;
- THAT individuals are sovereign unto themselves;
- THAT to whatever extent government interferes with the free exchange of goods or confiscates the property of citizens, it reduces the wealth of the nation;
- THAT when government takes from one to bestow on another, it diminishes the incentive of the first, the integrity of the second, and its own moral authority;
- THAT it is the right and responsibility of each individual to defend justly acquired property from unjust and arbitrary seizure, expropriation, and taxation;
- THAT the goal of The Sovereign Society is to encourage and help individuals achieve and maintain individual sovereignty over their own lives and fortunes.

THE "PT" LIFE…IS IT FOR YOU?

John Pugsley, *The Sovereign Individual*, February 2002

More than a decade ago, an interesting character with the nom de plume of "Bill Hill" penned a popular escape manual for freedom advocates titled PT — The Perpetual Traveler. Hill had spent much of his life traveling the world, visiting the continents, regions, countries, and cities that interested him, while carefully avoiding staying in each place long enough to be considered a permanent resident and therefore subject to such unpleasantries as taxes, military service, and other local rules and regulations.

Hill argued that in a world in which every spot on the globe is under the forcible control of one gang of politicians or another, the answer for individual sovereignty is to avoid their control by becoming a "PT," an acronym for a Perpetual Traveler, Prior Taxpayer, or Permanent Tourist.

The ability to become a full-fledged Bill Hill-style PT — i.e., living a life absolutely free of taxation, restrictions and obligations imposed by most governments — depends to a great extent on your citizenship. U.S. citizens, for example, are liable for taxes on their worldwide income, wherever they travel or live.

I've spent many years living outside the United States. But, because I haven't relinquished my U.S. citizenship (yet), living an expat lifestyle has provided very minimal tax advantages.

Most countries, however, impose tax on the basis of residency, not citizenship. Move abroad for at least a year or two and thereafter, the mother country ignores you, at least in reference to income tax. Therefore, for citizens of most countries, the PT lifestyle could legally eliminate income (and with proper planning, estate) taxes, along with achieving many other goals of individual sovereignty.

A dozen years ago I became friends with Paul and Vicki Terhorst, who could be considered a poster couple for the PT concept. Paul began his career as an accountant. After working his way up to a partnership in Peat Marwick, he and Vicki decided that what they really wanted in life was freedom from routine and the opportunity to travel. Paul retired at age 35, and for the past 18 years Paul and Vicki have made do on a modest income from their investments, while leisurely wandering the world.

After retirement they spent eight years in Argentina, then lived in Mexico, London, Thailand, Bali, Australia, Paris, and even had a couple short stints in the United States. Often they just hit the road for several months, revisiting their favorite countries or exploring new ones.

Since they've chosen to remain U.S. citizens, there are no significant tax advantages to their PT lifestyle. They file tax returns every year and meticulously declare all investment income, in spite of the fact that their investment accounts are offshore. And they are careful not to do anything that would constitute legal residence in any state with a personal income tax. Thus, they carry Nevada driver's licenses, and keep their financial records and mailing address in the state of Washington (several states including Nevada, Texas, Florida and Washington do not tax personal incomes).

To Paul and Vicki, the allure of the PT life has less to do with keeping out from under the scrutiny of Big Brother and minimizing taxes than with being free of the routines. Travel and exploration is their idea of the sovereign life.

If the PT life sounds attractive, it's probably more achievable than you might imagine. The communications revolution has dissolved the chains that bound many professions to urban offices. However, Paul and Vicki have demonstrated that if you're willing to trade the security of roots and possessions for travel and leisure, it can be done on a very modest income.

While not everyone will find being a perpetual traveler fulfilling, it still makes sense to increase our personal sovereignty by adopting any of the elements of the PT concept that fit. The full PT plan includes holding citizenship in one country; maintaining official residence in a second; if not retired, domiciling your business in a third; and keeping investment accounts in one or more others.

In each case, the country chosen should provide the best and most advanced laws for minimizing taxes, optimizing business and investment opportunities, and providing maximum privacy and legal protection from lawsuits. Then, if your business permits and you enjoy travel, you can live the PT life by spending your time in the most interesting places around the world in their prime seasons — London or Aspen in July and August, January and February in The Bahamas or New Zealand, April and May in Paris, and so on.

The goal of every Sovereign Individual is to maintain control of his or her life and property, which coincides nicely with the PT concept. These are goals for which members of The Sovereign Society can strive for and which we can help you to achieve.

What's Wrong with the U.S. Constitution?

John Pugsley, *The Sovereign Individual*, July 2009

The country's founding document is concerned almost exclusively with granting powers to the government.

The Bill of Rights partially counteracted that. Yet, today, the tendency towards big government surges almost unchecked. In his 1970 reprise of Rousseau's classic *The Social Contract*, author Robert Ardrey lamented, "Something, unconfined by national boundaries, undeterred by degrees of prosperity, unimpressed by political systems or ideologies, is wrong with human societies." As the world's nations struggle in the throes of a deepening depression, Ardrey's lament rings true.

A Long Train of Abuses and Usurpations

Unable to levy higher taxes to meet the rising demands of a populace that has become addicted to subsidy and promises, politicians worldwide have no solution to offer other than to drastically increase government borrowing in hopes of spending their way out of the credit contraction.

The U.S. leads the pack. This year and next the Treasury will sell more than $5 trillion in IOUs. Other countries are close behind, jostling each other to sell their IOUs to anyone who'll buy — other governments, institutions, pension funds, and individuals.

The Keynesian hypothesis posits that this torrent of government spending will resuscitate the world's economies, tax revenues will increase, and governments will be able not only to pay the interest, but to repay the debt. Unfortunately, both the evidence of history and common sense tells us that a nation's economy cannot be cleansed of bad debts by replacing them with even more bad debts.

The growth of government debt is but a symptom of the growth of government itself, and the growth of government is exactly what's wrong with human societies. This month, Americans celebrate the 233rd anniversary of the signing of the Declaration of Independence.

The signers, an assemblage of the brightest, most dedicated minds to come out of the Age of Enlightenment, believed this document would deliver the colonies from oppressive government. They recognized that preventing government encroachment on individuals' liberty was prerequisite to peace and prosperity. So they pledged their lives, their fortunes, and their sacred honor to the cause.

Revolts against despotic governments are a familiar pattern in history. With hardly an exception, every modern nation, from Mexico to the Philippines, from Zaire to the Ukraine, has its own national "independence" day, marking each country's emergence from some form of government tyranny. But it seems that no sooner is one oppressive government overthrown than each nation is delivered into the grip of another. Throughout history, independence and subjugation have chased each other around a revolving door.

Derived from the Consent of the Governing

Here we are again.

A nation in which government has grown from a mewling infant, seemingly tightly bound in its crib to restrain its growth, into a behemoth with debts approaching $100 trillion.

Yes, there is something wrong with our society, and sadly there is little that you and I can do to fix the problem. However, each of us can minimize the effects of the error on ourselves. To understand what we can do, it's necessary to examine the social contract and identify the flaw. The Declaration of Independence and the Constitution were bold attempts to limit government.

What did the Founding Fathers get wrong?

They signers of the Declaration of Independence took the unprecedented stand that individuals had "unalienable rights" and that the only function of government was to secure those rights. They challenged the authority of the British government to rule their lives, and went to war and won. Then they set about to fashion a "new" social contract — hopefully one that could protect them from the rebirth of tyranny.

Unfortunately, a different group of political aspirants with a different agenda from the original signers drafted the new social contract, the Constitution. The Constitution did not follow the principles set down in the Declaration of Independence. This was a huge shift over the peaceful Articles of Confederation where each state was free to pursue its own interests peacefully.

Rather, the new Constitution of the United States was little more than a sweeping grant of power to a new government. Article I delineated the powers granted to the legislative branch, Article II to the executive branch, and Article III to the judicial branch.

The word "power" appears 16 times within the Constitution, always referring to the power of government over individual citizens. The "unalienable rights" of individuals is never mentioned in the body of the Constitution.

It Becomes Necessary…

Only later, when critics demanded that the new document be amended to limit the power of the new government, were the first 10 amendments, the "Bill of Rights," inserted.

Sadly, time has proven that the Bill of Rights was not sufficient, as the federal government has steamrolled over what few protections individuals and states were granted. As we know today from the expanding power of government, the founders' quest for a social contract that would guarantee individual liberty has failed.

Why did the quest fail? What is wrong with the social contracts now governing human societies?

The mistake lies in any form of social contract in which one person is given power over another. To understand this, it's necessary to recognize that every individual is guided by a common human nature formed over millions of generations by relentless natural selection.

At the core of that nature lies self-interest. As E.O. Wilson, the father of sociobiology, noted: "Individual behavior, including seemingly altruistic acts bestowed on tribe and nation, are directed, sometimes very circuitously, toward the Darwinian advantage of the solitary human being and his closest relatives."

It is this self-interest which ensures that when put into a position of power over the lives and property of others, any individual's tendency will be to look through the lens of his own self-interest (and that of his immediate family, friends, and associates). As Lord Acton so famously put it, "Power tends to corrupt, and absolute power corrupts absolutely."

So-called political scientists can argue and even demand, as Karl Marx did, that individuals devote their lives to the common good. But neither persuasion nor indoctrination nor force can reprogram individuals to favor the welfare of strangers over their own.

To uncover the cause of today's social and economic catastrophes, we need only follow the self-interest of each individual involved. Whether banker, industrialist, entrepreneur, worker or bureaucrat, each follows an instinctive drive to benefit himself and the democratic process provides a mechanism to do so through government.

These Truths Are Self-Evident

To understand why the American Revolution failed to give birth to permanent liberty, we need look no further than the Constitution, and its grant of power to government. As we attempt to live our lives as sovereign individuals, we first must recognize that we have negligible influence over the direction of society, but by understanding the source of society's problems, we insulate ourselves and our assets.

This has been the focus of The Sovereign Society since its founding a dozen years ago. As the nation's economy withers under rising taxes, surging monetary inflation, and falling asset prices, The Society continues to be dedicated to developing new and better strategies for both defense and profit.

A Declaration of Independence for Sovereign Individuals

John Pugsley, *The Sovereign Individual*, July 2002

For Americans, July 4, 2002, will be a particularly emotion-filled Independence Day. The first one since last September's terrorist attack, it strums an intensely patriotic chord in most citizens.

That makes this an especially appropriate time to reflect on the principles of independence.

Revolts against despotic governments are a familiar motif of history. Almost all modern nations from Mexico to the Philippines and from Zaire to the Ukraine have their own national "independence" days, marking their emergence from under one group of tyrants and usually into the grip of another.

Throughout history, independence and subjugation have chased each other around a revolving door. In light of the destruction of freedom in America since 9/11, it seems assured that the hopes of the Founding Fathers that their sacrifices could end this cyclical process are being dashed.

Understanding why the struggle for independence must be waged again and again requires us to step back and examine the social contract in the light of human nature. The rising specter of devastation from weapons of mass destruction make it clear that man had better solve this conundrum, and quickly, or risk annihilation.

Homo sapiens is a mewling infant on the evolutionary scene, arriving a mere 100,000 to 200,000 years ago. Our species is not physically imposing and would have been at a serious disadvantage in the struggle for survival except for a single evolutionary difference that catapulted it to dominance: a powerful forebrain. A single species was equipped with cognitive powers immensely greater than those available to all other life forms. With this formidable weapon, our forebears quickly spread around the globe, reproducing and expanding until we colonized every continent, adapted to every climate, and overwhelmed every physical and biological obstacle.

They did it by using their new cognitive powers for discovery and invention. Somewhere in the prehistoric dawn early humans invented language, captured fire, learned to make spears, fabricated the wheel, conceived agriculture, developed metallurgy, domesticated animals, and originated writing.

Progress accelerated as they recorded instructions for making gunpowder, the catapult, the steam engine, electromagnetism, atomic energy, and the computer. Human "progress" has been built upon science and technology. We are the inheritors. But we are also faced with a terrible obstacle.

Our species has overcome all but one threat to long-term survival. As Pogo said, "We have met the enemy and he is us!" The urgent problem is to discover the social contract that will end the perpetual cycle of subjugation followed by independence once again leading to subjugation.

Man is, by nature, a social animal. Each individual is bound to his community, but is simultaneously bound by his genes to pursue individual survival and the well-being of his immediate kin. In the hunter-gatherer environment in which our ancestors evolved, the social contract was much simpler. In a tribal village of a few dozen members, everyone was kin, and although there were disputes over food and mates and other property, the resolution was simple. Everyone understood fairness. Everyone participated in the decisions.

In modern nations with millions of inhabitants, kin altruism does not extend even to the other side of the town, let alone to strangers across the country and certainly not to "foreigners." At the primal level of our brains, and in spite of all indoctrination to the contrary, strangers are non-kin, and are thus viewed either as potentially dangerous or to be exploited.

When political power is handed to distant persons, those individuals instinctively tend to use it to benefit themselves, their immediate kin, and those who support their power. Simply declaring independence from a distant tyrant, however, does not solve the problem of despotism if the political system remains intact. It merely leaves the seat of political power open to be grabbed by a new despot. Thus, man's natural bias toward self-interest, programmed into his brain by eons of natural selection, eliminates the possibility of creating a workable, enduring social contract that is founded on investing power in unrelated individuals or groups.

All individuals, by the authority of the nature of man, should sign a personal Declaration of Independence.

It should state that they are, and of right ought to be free, independent individuals, absolved from all allegiance to any of the arbitrary rules and restrictions forcefully imposed on them by politicians and bureaucrats who claim to be working selflessly in the public interest. Certainly, this is the right of Americans under the Declaration of Independence, although in the cycle of subjugation in which the United States is now mired, exercising our rights as "sovereign individuals" may bring retribution from an increasingly despotic government.

While nations will continue to pass in and out of the revolving door of independence and subjugation, the personal declaration of independence is for all time. It is the statement that you consider yourself a sovereign individual.

The day you sign your personal Declaration of Independence should become the most important holiday in your life.

MIRROR, MIRROR ON THE WALL, WHERE'S THE FREEST LAND OF ALL?

John Pugsley, *The Sovereign Individual*, January 2003

Each November, The Heritage Foundation and *The Wall Street Journal* release their annual "Index of Economic Freedom." Backed by voluminous comparative data on taxes, regulations, labor laws, property rights, judicial independence, sound money, international trade barriers, capital controls, etc., this index proposes to rank the world's nations in a descending order from most free to least free.

As has been the case in the past few years, Hong Kong received top billing as the world's freest nation; Singapore was second. The United States, usually rated around third or fourth, dropped to eighth. Heritage and the Journal are not alone in passing out freedom "Oscars." The Fraser Institute, a Canadian public-policy organization, cooperates with free-market research institutes in 56 countries to publish "The Economic Freedom Network Index," and the Cato Institute competes with its "Economic Freedom of the World" index.

It's a commendable effort, but unfortunately, as Pierre Lemieux, a member of The Sovereign Society Council of Experts, noted in a recent article in the Financial Post, "...in trying to measure it with simplistic index numbers, our friends unwittingly betray their cause...They give us a false sense of contentment...they provide our politicians and bureaucrats with another tool to persuade us that we live in 'the best of all worlds.'" The concept of indexing freedom has many flaws.

First, if polled, the hundreds of economists and other social "scientists" who compile these indexes wouldn't even agree on an exact definition of "freedom" let alone the way to measure it. As an example, at the recent Freedom Summit conference in Phoenix, Arizona, every speaker addressing the topic had a different definition for freedom. No science can progress without precise definitions of terms. If each auto manufacturer could make up its own definition of what constituted a gallon, or what length constituted a mile, each one would claim its vehicles got the best fuel mileage.

Nor does the principle of measurement apply to a condition such as freedom. One is either free or not free.

The late physicist Andrew Galambos provided the best and most precise definition of the word. He defined freedom as: "The societal condition that exists when every individual has 100% control of his own property."

There is no such thing as partial freedom. It's 100 percent or 0 percent. Nor are indexes or averages even useful to us in our quest for freedom. As Chris Mayer pointed out in a recent essay for The Mises Institute on price indexes, "To speak about average prices is like talking about average precipitation to a golfer. It either rains during a specific time period or it doesn't. There is no average that is in anyway useful for an acting human being on a golf course. The only information that counts is what it is doing right now while he is teeing off."

The same fallacy attaches to the idea of indexing freedom.

Over and over I hear that the United States is among the freest nations on earth. Perhaps that's true, but it's tragic that after 10,000 years of civilization that "free" citizens have almost half of all their earnings confiscated, almost all of their exchanges scrutinized and regulated, and let those in power control what they're allowed to put into their bodies, whether, where and what they're allowed to inhale, and what they are allowed to say.

There are no free countries, only competing political enclaves where authorities with guns use differing degrees of coercion against their populations. The organizations that purport to monitor the level of government control over private action would serve their purpose much better if they changed the names of their reports to "Coercion Indexes" so as not to give the impression that people are enjoying something akin to real freedom.

A general freedom index has no meaning for someone who is facing the decision about where to live, invest, or start a business. Such decisions are based on specific levels of coercion — what is the income or capital gains tax rate, what tariffs are levied on goods, what licenses are required, etc. At best, such indexes serve only the purpose of gaining publicity for non-profit organizations that seek to demonstrate to their contributors that they are doing something worthwhile in the promotion of freedom. It's doubtful that they even have any effect on the public policies they are meant to affect.

The rational individual understands that the quest is, as Harry Browne put it in his classic book, *How to Find Freedom in an Unfree World*. Freedom will not be found in any single nation, regardless of how high that country may rise in any index of the freest places on earth.

Finding freedom in this un-free world is a never-ending search for places and legal structures that provide the highest degree of privacy, asset protection, business and investment opportunity, and personal safety.

This quest is the real challenge to each individual who seeks sovereignty over his or her life, and is the purpose and mission of The Sovereign Society.

Is It Un-American to "Go Offshore?"
Robert E. Bauman JD, *The Sovereign Investor*, December 2009

You would think so — if you believed 2008 presidential candidate Barack Obama — or if you believe U.S. Senator Carl Levin, far left Democrat from Michigan, a "soak the rich" politician obsessed with the belief that any American with foreign financial business is somehow dodging taxes.

For an extreme example of this offshore phobia, take the case of White House National Economic Council Director Lawrence Summers. When good old Larry was President Bill Clinton's Secretary of the Treasury in 1994, he went off the deep end referring to American expatriates as "tax traitors." He was subsequently made to apologize by his boss for that over the top comment.

This idea that it is unpatriotic for otherwise good Americans to have foreign bank accounts, own foreign investments and real estate and live in foreign lands has long been the unspoken policy of the U.S. Internal Revenue Service and other government agencies.

Presumed Guilty

I once heard an assistant U.S. Attorney General publicly state to a conference of several hundred lawyers and bankers in Miami that at the Department of Justice anytime an individual had offshore accounts he or she was assumed to be engaged in something that was probably illegal.

So much for the rule of law and the presumption of innocence. But, as they say, "Old habits die hard."

Despite the occasional financial excursion abroad, human nature dictates that most folks prefer to make and save money at home. We tend to be comfortable with the familiar and less threatening domestic economy of our home nation, even if the government is near bankrupt as in America.

In 2009, only 74 million, or about 26% of Americans had passports (and another million Americans living near the Mexican and Canadian borders had "passport cards") — yet this was a historically high percentage.

Buy American or Bye-Bye America?

As one who believes in the principle of free international trade and its decided benefits for all parties, the political resurgence of "Buy America" under Obama and the Democrats should concern Americans.

The anti-offshore arguments of the America Left seem to fit into this "America First" theme, and both are wrong headed. I love my country too much to believe such nonsense.

Harry Binswanger, Ph.D. of the Ayn Rand Institute writes: "According to a recent poll, 80% of Americans think it their patriotic duty to give preference to American-made products. But 'Buy American' is wholly un-American in both its economics and its philosophy.

"America's distinction among all the nations of the world is that it enshrined political and economic freedom. Although we have departed greatly from our original laissez-faire principles, to the whole world America still symbolizes capitalism. Americanism means understanding that a free market, domestically and internationally, is the only path to general prosperity."

Practical Reasons

But beyond the principles involved, there are good and sufficient practical reasons why aware Americans now should "go offshore" financially — simple financial survival first among them.

At a time when the United States government is deeply in debt (nearly $13 trillion), with Obama's pending plans for higher income, capital gains and estate taxes looming, and with major and minor banks teetering on the brink, prudence dictates offshore planning and activity.

So-called "patriotism" does not require us to commit financial suicide when there are reasonable escape exits to better places.

Why go offshore?

The multi-faceted answer includes greater asset protection, stronger financial privacy, higher returns in carefully selected markets, more diversification of investments and among currencies, increased safety and security, both personal and financial, and deferred taxes on annuities and life insurance.

In contrast to Bank of America, CitiBank and AIG, the offshore banks and insurance companies The Sovereign Society recommends aren't exposed to the risky investments of third-world debt and Wall Street's esoteric derivatives.

These banks are located in politically neutral countries that don't employ interventionist foreign policy, making them much less likely to be terror targets.

Act Now

Unfortunately, too few Americans are taking advantage of the fruits of global diversification. I think you owe it to yourself and to your family to benefit from offshore advantages.

At the very least, you should hold a portion of your assets offshore — just in case.

Five Strategies to Maximize the Best Offshore Has to Offer

Robert E. Bauman JD, *The Sovereign Investor Daily*, December 2011

More than two decades ago, an interesting character with the nom de plume, "Bill Hill" wrote a popular escape manual for freedom advocates titled "PT—The Perpetual Traveler."

Hill outlined his PT ideas with a five-point plan "…for those," he said, "with courage enough to pursue freedom." He memorably illustrated his plan with something he called *The Five Flags of Freedom*.

Hill wrote: "People of intelligence and wealth owe it to themselves and their descendants to have more than one flag. No one with common sense should give all their assets or allegiance to just one."

Confiscatory income taxes and suffocating government regulations have caused many independent-minded Americans and their European counterparts to seek new flags.

They are discovering that, as business owners, expatriates or tax exiles abroad, they need not belong to any particular country nor participate in its senseless policies and politics.

An individual's relationship with government should be a matter of choice, an option. The passport you hold and the country where you live or were born need not determine your fate forever…

The Greatest Wealth Migration in U.S. History Has Begun

Today, millions of the wealthiest and most productive Americans are leaving home to relocate various aspects of their lives in the best possible places.

They view governments as providers of facilities and services, like hotel keepers. If they offer good accommodation and make you feel comfortable and prosperous, you stay. If your government becomes too demanding or too nosey, or if a competitor offers a better deal, you can move on.

A few years ago, *U.S. News & World Report* confirmed, "A wave of native born citizens are going abroad in search of new challenges, opportunities, and more congenial ways of life."

Some are seeking full-time residences… others find part-time tropical vacation homes where they can live like kings for $20,000 a year… while some move their businesses to slash their taxes.

No one government can or even should be trusted to control all your money. Experience shows us that government does not have your best interests at heart. Americans have learned with a vengeance how much politicians love to redistribute other's wealth. In the end, they also will succeed in redistributing taxpayers. The major portion of all liquid private wealth, the smart money, already should have been moved offshore. As Bill Hill would say, it has been "re flagged."

And these days, it's not just the wealthy jumping ship. Every day, middle-class folks are re-flagging themselves to get the government they want and to gain access to economic opportunities that no longer exist in America.

Individuals can remove themselves from the control and jurisdiction of any government by acquiring dual citizenship, investing internationally and becoming human multinationals.

In order to accomplish this, you have to arrange your assets according to the following simple outline:

Your Five Flags: A Strategy to Live as Close to Government-Free as Possible

Flag 1: Second Passport and Citizenship: You should obtain citizenship and a second passport from a country that does not tax non-residents on their worldwide income. The U.S. taxes its citizens without regard to where they live in the world. Your second passport should be issued by a country that is unconcerned about its offshore citizens and their outside activities. It can act as the ultimate insurance policy during times of war, persecution and political upheaval.

Flag 2: Business Base: You need a place in which you can form a corporation or limited liability company and invest and earn money with minimal restrictions. This should not be where you legally reside, thus it excludes your personal fiscal domicile. Some countries grant free land, interest free loans or tax holidays to promote new local business and jobs with minimal regulation. Such places include the Cook Islands, St. Kitts & Nevis, Uruguay and Panama. I write about these jurisdictions often in *Offshore Confidential*, a monthly research series that offers offshore wealth protection solutions to every day Americans.

Flag 3: Residence and Domicile: Obviously, the best place to live is where you're happy. But as a practical matter it also should be a place with a territorial tax system that does not tax outside income. You should live in a tax haven with good infrastructure and communication systems where wealthy, productive people can be creative, live, relax, prosper and enjoy themselves, preferably with maximum bank privacy and a stable government. Panama, Monaco, Andorra, Singapore, Hong Kong, Liechtenstein, Austria and Switzerland should be considered.

Flag 4: Asset Management: In spite of all the negative publicity, Switzerland remains the world's best place from which assets, securities and business affairs can be managed by proxy. It is one of the best for an offshore bank account, life insurance and annuities. The Swiss have highly competent independent financial managers, and there is little or no taxation of non-residents or non-citizens. Other possibilities include Austria, Luxembourg, Denmark, Liechtenstein and Hong Kong.

Flag 5: Playgrounds: These are places where you physically spend time, where quality of life is a top priority. Normally, because of legal restrictions on how long one can stay without being considered a resident for tax purposes, it is necessary to have several such places, although, depending on the place, legal and political deals usually can be made if you want to stay in one place. But for tax purposes, one should avoid spending more than 90 days per year in any one country. Factors here are matters of personal choice: climate, seasons, geography, leisure activities, culture, history, security and prices.

Stay Away from "Home" To Maximize the Benefits

One point to remember: governments only have power and jurisdiction over their citizens when they are within their home territory or colonies. For this reason, one generally should stay out of the country on whose passport one travels. Your major financial assets should be invisible and far away from the country in which you actually make your home. And keep your lifestyle as unremarkable and humble as possible, never flamboyant and attention-getting.

By using the Five Flag strategy, you too can get the most out of life. Once you have your new second passport and money enough to survive comfortably at your chosen destination, security is yours.

ATLAS SHRUGGED: FROM FICTION TO FACT IN 52 YEARS

Robert E. Bauman JD, *The Sovereign Investor Daily*, February 2009

"Many of us who know Ayn Rand's work have noticed that with each passing week, and with each successive bailout plan and economic stimulus scheme out of Washington, our current politicians are committing the very acts of economic lunacy that *Atlas Shrugged* parodied in 1957, when this 1,000-page novel was first published and became an instant hit."

So writes Stephen Moore, formerly of Heritage Foundation and later the senior economics writer for *The Wall Street Journal*.

Rampant Do-Goodism

As Moore notes about Rand's magnum opus: "…the moral of the story is simply this: Politicians invariably respond to crises — that in most cases they themselves created — by spawning new government programs, laws and regulations. These, in turn, generate more havoc and poverty, which inspires the politicians to create more programs…and the downward spiral repeats itself until the productive sectors of the economy collapse under the collective weight of taxes and other burdens imposed in the name of fairness, equality and do-goodism."

Having read Rand's book (long ago), I agree that the United States government and its self-styled political saviors in Washington have by now surpassed the worst case scenario Rand spelled out in her best-selling book. The similarities of the plot to the present are uncanny — and disturbing.

Traditionalist vs. Objectivist

In politically turbulent 1960s America, Rand spawned a cadre of young followers (not including me), brash and headstrong "objectivists" who were a part of the driving force in conservative organizations such as Young Americans for Freedom (YAF — which I headed from 1962 to 1965), the Intercollegiate Studies Institute (ISI), and the Young Republicans.

Our passion was real, and our commitment to liberty genuine. But in those ancient days, most of us were firmly in the anti-Rand "traditionalist" conservative camp. We agreed with the objectivists in the need for a revived capitalism, but not without what Randians called the "sentimentality" of religion.

Witness a Turning Point

The publication of Whitaker Chambers' *Witness* in 1952, and its phenomenal popularity, decisively shaped the conservative movement in America at a time when the movement could well have taken a different turn.

After *Witness*, American conservatism gained a religious dimension. I was a student at Georgetown University School of Foreign Service when I devoured the book. Its astringent treatment of capitalism, communism and faith clarified and solidified my nascent conservative philosophy.

Chambers was a man who recognized the absolute necessity of faith in God, and who argued that the collapse of such faith on all sides had brought about a crisis of civilization. His piety and sincerity spoke to Protestant, Catholic, and Jew alike.

A Masterpiece

Understanding this difference of attitude explains the famous controversy that followed the 1957 review of Rand's *Atlas Shrugged* that Whitaker Chambers wrote for my friend, William F. Buckley's *National Review*.

As Prof. Joseph S. Salemi, a poet and critic at Hunter College observed: "A masterpiece of polemical deflation, [Chamber's] review precipitated a major split in the conservative movement between traditional conservatives and their objectivist allies of expedience. A good number of the magazine's readers canceled their subscription to the journal, and both Chambers and Buckley became unmentionable pariahs in certain libertarian circles where Rand was seen as a bulwark of intellectual freedom and anti-collectivist energies."

Back to the Future

Never the less, the non-believer Rand was prescient in much of the plot of *Atlas Shrugged*.

As Stephen Moore notes, Obama's current economic strategy is right out of *Atlas Shrugged*: The more incompetent you are in business, the more handouts the politicians will bestow on you…With each successive bailout to 'calm the markets,' another trillion of national wealth is subsequently lost. Yet, as Atlas grimly foretold, we now treat the incompetent who wreck their companies as victims, while those resourceful business owners who manage to make a profit are portrayed as recipients of illegitimate 'windfalls.'"

Deadly Combination

"Ultimately, *Atlas Shrugged* is a celebration of the entrepreneur, the risk taker and the cultivator of wealth through human intellect. Critics dismissed the novel as simple-minded, and even some of Rand's political admirers complained that she lacked compassion. Yet one pertinent warning resounds throughout the book: When profits and wealth and creativity are denigrated in society, they start to disappear — leaving everyone the poorer."

Based on current events, one might venture the opinion that an even greater threat to personal and collective liberty results from a deadly combination of the stupidity and greed of entrepreneurs with the incompetence and idiocy of Big Brother government and its slavish advocates.

THE ONLY WAY TO AVOID WEALTH CONFISCATION
Ted Bauman, *The Sovereign Investor Daily*, March 2014

The politicians who created the bloated and growing $17.3 trillion U.S. national debt are now planning ways to confiscate your wealth to pay off their bill.

That debt comes out to $54,730 for every U.S. citizen and $150,641 for each U.S. taxpayer. (Almost half of all Americans pay no income taxes.)

Across the world, in nearly bankrupt countries (think bank "bail-ins" in Cyprus), politicians are talking openly about forced confiscation of wealth — and the Obama administration is more than sympathetic.

It was the U.S. Congress that adopted the Foreign Account Tax Compliance Act (FATCA), a mechanism that makes global wealth confiscation easier for all governments.

There is even discussion of the U.S. government taking over all private retirement plans, IRAs, 401ks and the like. And how about that "one time" wealth tax, where banks will be ordered to turn over to the U.S. Treasury a percentage of your deposits?

Make no mistake — we are all at risk.

Moreover, in an effort to pay down debt, countries typically adopt austerity programs that severely restrict public services and government salaries, and, at the same time, slow the economy.

This often prompts public unrest and political instability, further spooking the markets.

Thus begins a socioeconomic and political spiral that can lead to collapse and chaos. Argentina is a prime example. At least seven people were killed in Argentina in December 2013 during a week of riots.

My point is this: If wealth confiscation becomes a reality, it means that things here have gotten really bad. There will be civil unrest, and an even greater divide between the rich and the poor.

You'll want to take yourself out of harm's way.

It won't be chaos on a global level — it'll just be happening in the bloated Western nations.

Nobody expects the worst. But those who prepare for it are usually better for it.

Indeed, the signs point to wealth confiscation in the near future. With a little sensible preparation, you can be one of the few who weathers the storm.

How to Prepare

Before I show you how to prepare, let me ask you …

Is it worth taking a few really simple steps today to protect yourself and your family from potential danger, financial ruin and chaos?

I'm sure your answer is the same as mine.

But I only ask you this question because I am certain a major crisis in America is coming … and I want you to prepare *before* it strikes.

If you wait, it will be too late. Your money will be taken from you and it could put your family in danger unnecessarily.

That's why it's important to plan now — before the confiscation and chaos begins … so you can get out stress-free. Here's what I suggest you do:

- <u>Step 1</u>: Make sure your passport and vital documents are up to date.
- <u>Step 2</u>: Keep bank account balances to a minimum. The government can't take what isn't there.
- <u>Step 3</u>: Have cash on hand. In a crisis — cash is king.
- <u>Step 4</u>: Invest in transportable assets. Things like foreign currencies, gold, rare coins, stamps and art are easy to travel with.
- <u>Step 5</u>: Know exactly where you want to go. Pick the country you plan to escape to as soon as possible.

Follow these steps and you'll be ready to "get out of dodge" on a moment's notice should you need it.

But, here's the thing: There's more to it than this.

As an expat who left America 30 years ago, I can tell you I've met hundreds of people who have left the U.S. for various reasons.

And most have made costly mistakes when leaving.

They've alienated themselves from their families, had difficulty getting health care abroad, and one man I met was miserable after moving to a country he'd only seen online.

My point for telling you this is, I've seen it all when it comes to moving overseas.

I've seen successful moves and I've seen people head back to America with their tail between their legs.

That's why I've been working on creating a resource for Americans who want to know how to plan a move overseas. It covers every last detail, from telling your family you plan on moving to choosing a destination that's ideal for you.

Of course, I know many people won't actually move out of the country, but I also know that every *Sovereign Investor* reader I spoke with at the Total Wealth Symposium last fall wants a Plan B in place just in case they need it.

Property Rights Are Civil Rights

Robert E. Bauman JD, *The Sovereign Investor Daily,* November 2009

Several years ago the chairman of The Sovereign Society, **Jack Pugsley**, in a commentary entitled *"It All Starts with Property Rights"* wrote the following: *The feelings that drive us to defend ourselves against government oppression are an expression of our innate compulsion to control our own property. Each of us shares the feeling that it is unjust and an outrage for our hard-earned wealth to be taken from us without our consent.*

Jack went on to observe: *The Declaration of Independence suggests that the Founding Fathers sensed this aspect of human nature. It argued that all men "are endowed by their Creator with certain unalienable Rights; that among these are Life, Liberty and the pursuit of Happiness." Life, liberty and the pursuit of happiness, of course, are all aspects of property.*

The long train of abuses and usurpation that drove the Founding Fathers to rebel was triggered by the same genes that give rise to your rage when someone burglarizes your home, steals your car or defrauds you. Those genes are equally activated when that attack comes from government.

Kelo v. New London

Jack's sentiments were written two years before the U.S. Supreme Court, in a shocking 5-to-4 decision, greatly expand local governments' power of eminent domain to take private property for public use. The 2005 case, *Kelo v. New London*, was one of the most controversial property rights cases in years.

To the surprise of the great majority of Americans, the high court ruled that it was permissible for government to take private property, not only for *public use*, but to turn it over to *private* developers as part of a plan to bolster the local economy.

The decision was widely criticized, spurring lawmakers in 43 states across the country to adopt statutes to prevent similar uses of eminent domain in their states.

Joint Power Grab

The situation that gave rise to the *Kelo* case was a classic example of the little guys falling victim to the combined power of a major corporate business and politicians eager to please that company.

It seems government that bails out banks with trillions of tax dollars, can't keep the same banks and credit card companies from raping card holders, allows financial groups to pay billions in bonuses after getting tax bailouts, also has the right to take our homes and property and give it to political buddies.

The city council had created the New London Development Corporation to buy up the nine-acre neighborhood and find a developer to replace it with an "urban village" that would draw shoppers and tourists to the area.

Supreme Court Justice Clarence Thomas, one of the four dissenters in the case, called New London's plan *"a costly urban renewal project whose stated purpose is a vague promise of new jobs and increased tax revenue, but which is also suspiciously agreeable to the Pfizer Corporation."*

Economic development officials in Connecticut used that plan and a package of tax breaks and financial incentives to lure the giant drug company, **Pfizer**, to build a headquarters for its research division on 26 acres nearby.

With an agreement that it would pay just one-fifth of its property taxes for the first 10 years, Pfizer spent $294 million on a 750,000-square-foot complex that opened in 2001. Scores of citizens who lived in the adjoining nine-acre area were forced to sell to the city; their homes leveled, leaving what is now a waste land. Susette Kelo, a nurse, fought for her home all the way to the Supreme Court — and lost.

Pfizer Screws New London

Last week Pfizer announced it would pull 1,400 jobs out of New London within two years and move most of them a few miles away to a campus it owns in Groton, Conn., as a cost cutting measure.

It would leave behind empty the city's biggest office complex — and the adjacent swath of barren land that was cleared of dozens of homes (including Ms. Kelo's) to make room for a hotel, stores and condominiums that were never built.

"Look what they did," Michael Cristofaro, a resident, said. "They stole our home for economic development. It was all for Pfizer, and now they get up and walk."

Scott G. Bullock, senior attorney at the **Institute for Justice**, a libertarian group in Arlington, Va., that represented the landowners in New London, said Pfizer's announcement "really shows the folly of these plans that use massive corporate welfare and abuse eminent domain for private development. They oftentimes fail to live up to expectations."

Obama Proposals Confiscate Property

In many ways the Obama agenda seeks to confiscate wealth from earners and give it to non-earners.

The Obama health care bills impose several new taxes. The entire idea behind this "health care reform" is to have those who already have health insurance and are satisfied with it pay for health care for those who don't want it or can't afford it.

That single agenda item alone illustrates the Obama administration's antagonism to our most sacred of private property: our money.

And it is not just more taxes that confiscate our property. Now there is serious discussion about confiscating all private retirement plans, Keoghs, 401ks, Roths — and dumping them into a government managed scheme.

More Power to Seize

The pending financial regulatory bills Obama has proposed would give the U.S. government broad authority to seize private financial institutions supposedly on the verge of collapse to keep them from harming the economy.

The seizure power would extend to a broad array of financial companies, apparently including private hedge funds as well as bank holding companies. Is it not enough that under Obama the government (taxpayers) have become major owners of General Motors, Bank of America, Citibank et al?

A Different Kind of President

Throughout American history, our leaders have understood that private property rights are key to the survival of the individual.

If you take a person's property, you take away their livelihood. If you take property, you attack their spirit. From the day our nation was born, the preservation of private property has been considered a priority of law.

Through taxes and government controls Barack Obama appears to want to use the law to destroy private property.

This is what he means, when he openly attacks businesses large and small, when he insists that there must be limits on what you can earn and keep and pass on to your family when you pass away, when he makes political deals with insurance and drug companies to get their support for his health proposals.

This president wants his government to control your private property, your income and your assets.

The Sovereign Society Credo

One of the basic tenets in The Sovereign Society Credo states: "Every individual has the natural right to keep, control, and dispose of his or her property."

That fundamental natural right is now under serious attack, not just in the parochial New London city council, but in the highest offices of the White House and the United States Congress.

REVISE THE PATRIOT ACT
Robert E. Bauman JD, *The Offshore A-Letter*, September 2009

"He who sacrifices freedom for security deserves neither."

— Benjamin Franklin

It's been eight long years since attacks on the World Trade Center and the Pentagon inspired a sense of unbridled panic. Amidst this frantic chaos — with stock markets falling so fast that trading was halted for several days — the USA PATRIOT Act was quietly passed into law… and the American people were introduced to the worst legislative attack on the Constitution since President John Adams and the 1789 Alien and Sedition Laws.

Well, this week — eight years later — the U.S. Congress will hold hearings on extending three provisions of the USA PATRIOT Act that expire at the end of this year.

At the same time, civil liberties groups and some Democratic senators are pressing for changes to Bush era surveillance laws that might revive some of the Fourth Amendment protections the PATRIOT Act has all but destroyed.

The Act's name itself is a public relations acronym. It stands for the "Uniting and Strengthening America by Providing Appropriate Tools Required to Intercept and Obstruct Terrorism Act," Public Law No. 107-56.

Both the House and the Senate are set to hold committee hearings this week on re-authorizing sections that expanded the power of the F.B.I. to seize personal and financial records without a warrant and to eavesdrop without court approval on phone calls in counter terrorism investigations.

Restoring the Fourth Amendment?

A group of U.S. senators who support greater privacy protections introduced a bill, S.1686, last week that would impose new safeguards on the PATRIOT Act while tightening restrictions on other surveillance policies.

Senator Russ Feingold (D-Wis), the chief sponsor, was the only senator who had the courage to vote against the Act when it was first adopted in 2001. The measure is co-sponsored by nine Democrats, an independent and no Republicans.

Some want to use the extension bill to restrict the FBI's use of so-called "national security letters" — administrative subpoenas that allow agents to seize business records without obtaining permission from a judge, which, in the past, was required. Agents have used this device tens of thousands of times each year.

The Justice Department's inspector general issued two reports finding that FBI agents frequently abused these letters in obtaining bank, credit card and telephone records.

Remember, dear friend…it was presidential candidate Barack Obama who criticized the PATRIOT Act and promised, if elected, to reform it.

Rather than make improvements, Obama has since endorsed and adopted as his own questionable Bush policies of prolonged detention without charges, and surveillance of Americans without warrants or probable cause. Obama has indicated he may even go further, requesting new powers to arrest and detain people without charges, a direct violation of the Constitution.

Assault on Financial Privacy

The section of the PATRIOT Act (125 of 362 pages), that pertains to U.S. banking and finance is the greatest single governmental assault on personal and financial privacy in American history.

The net result was that American banks and financial institutions, indeed all U.S. businesses, by law now are required to spy on their clients, "know their customers" and report any "suspicious activity" to the government.

Understand that this Act, then and now, is still sold as being an "anti-terrorist" law.

In fact, the Act's police powers have been used broadly to investigate and prosecute all types of crimes, many having nothing to do with terrorism. In 2004, two federal judges secretly ruled that the Act could be used to investigate any criminal or other pending charges, even if unrelated to terrorism.

Strategies to Shield You

The PATRIOT Act's powers operate mainly within the United States.

That means you should arrange your investments, cash, assets, record keeping and financial information in a way that maximizes your privacy, including the use of structures located offshore. Three major moves to consider:

1. Move some of your assets to offshore jurisdictions that guarantee privacy by law. Foreign insurance contracts, annuities, foreign real estate and offshore precious metals holdings all are examples of legal investments that, even under the PATRIOT Act, are difficult for the U.S. government to seize.
2. Create one or more offshore legal entities, such as an asset protection trust or private family foundation. Pick a maximum privacy country and your name as owner is not a public record and can be kept confidential unless a local court orders otherwise. An offshore entity can also provide asset protection against frozen bank accounts or attempts at civil asset forfeiture.
3. Choose an offshore country as your base of business operations and possibly, as your home. In tax haven or maximum privacy nations such as Panama, Austria, Switzerland, Liechtenstein, Monaco, Andorra, Belize, Singapore, Uruguay and the Cook Islands, information is not surrendered automatically to demands by foreign governments or lawsuits, even under the newly imposed OECD tax information exchange rules.

We Can Help...

The Sovereign Society can advise you on tax and asset haven nations that have statutory protections for financial privacy, as well as professionals that can help. With the current political situation in the United States, the time to act is now.

BIG BROTHER IS WATCHING AND LISTENING
Robert E. Bauman JD, *The Sovereign Investor Daily*, July 2012

But do *you* even give a damn?

Folks I know often snicker when I tell them they should never, ever say anything on a phone that they would not want the police or the government to know about. *"You don't really think somebody is listening to everything we say, do you?"* they asked incredulously.

Yep, I sure do think that. If they're not listening at that moment, they may have a record of it for later review.

Just in time to celebrate the 236th anniversary of our national independence from the tyranny of King George III, the Administrative Office of the U.S. Courts last week released an annual report that cheerfully noted that American law enforcement engaged in 14% fewer phone wiretaps in 2011 than in 2010. That's only the fifth time in 20 years the count has fallen, bucking the government's trend of intercepting ever more of Americans' phone communications.

Really great news for freedom lovers — *not!*

Eavesdropping in Secret

Those in the know say that phony "drop" in reported phone taps doesn't mean less invasion of Americans privacy. Instead, it reflects how the government's spying now takes place in total secret, with no legal requirement that it be counted or reported to the public.

In 2011, law enforcement reported 2,732 phone wiretaps performed by state and federal authorities, down from 3,194 the year before.

But compare those numbers with the government's requests for users' data from Google, the only communications company that voluntarily reports how often it surrenders Web users' private information to the government in response to subpoenas or other orders.

The U.S. government asked for Google's data 12,271 times in 2011, and Google complied 11,412 times. That represents a 37% jump over 2010, and more than four times more Google surveillance than all the telephone company wiretaps the government legally reported.

Warrantless Surrender

An American Civil Liberties Union Freedom of Information report based on Freedom of Information Requests to police departments earlier this year showed that every major phone company provides call records and location data to law enforcement, often without requiring a warrant.

In some cases, phone companies even handed over "tower dumps," records of every phone user who had accessed a certain cell phone tower. With GPS now in almost every phone and even more accurate ways of locating users with cell tower triangulation, law enforcement doesn't need wiretaps anymore say experts. They only need a graph of a suspect's social connections and the places a person has been to build a conspiracy case.

A Sprint official in 2009 revealed that the company's location-tracking tool, an interface it offers to police so that they can track users without its Sprint employees' help, was used 8 million times in the preceding year.

Six months ago I explained on this page about how the U.S. National Security Agency (NSA) new America's largest-ever spy center in Utah will have the power to intercept every electronic communication in the world!

Your Taxes at Work

I also told you how the U.S. Department of Homeland Security had revived the discredited Total Information Awareness Program, a secret spy system of vast databases containing private information on Americans including phone conversations, personal emails, visited web sites, Google searches, text messages, credit card transactions, mobile phone GPS location data, travel itineraries, Facebook activity, medical records, traffic tickets, surveillance camera footage and online purchases.

It is no wonder that the annual Gallup poll last month measuring trust in institutions shows weak support for what are supposed to be the pillars of American society. The numbers are at or near record lows. Americans who say they trust the Congress are at 13% and those who trust the presidency and the Supreme Court at 37%, and even that seems too high.

A New Revolution Needed

I must believe that if the average American fully realized how his or her privacy has been totally destroyed by government, how naked we all stand before our official masters they would rise up in revolution in the streets, if not at the ballot box.

And the old, tired, phony excuses to violate privacy are always the same; 1) endlessly fighting the failed war on drugs; 2) anti-money laundering; 3) catching terrorist.

On June 4, 1788 in a speech before the Virginia Ratifying Convention, Patrick Henry was prescient in his remarks: "Show me that age and country where the rights and liberties of the people were placed on the sole chance of their rulers being good men, without a consequent loss of liberty! I say that the loss of that dearest privilege has ever followed, with absolute certainty, every such mad attempt."

And when it comes to protecting our precious right to financial and personal privacy the leaders of both parties always told us: "Trust us!"

We did ... and they screwed us.

Time for Action

Wake up, folks. Open your eyes. For all my long life, I have been a political conservative — but it is plain that America has become a police state and most people are either too dumb to know it or they just don't care.

Well, some of us do care and if we go down, it will be fighting for freedom all the way.

Face reality and take two essential immediate steps to protect yourself from an out-of-control government:

First, establish an offshore financial nest egg. An offshore bank account is a good start, and The Sovereign Society can assist by helping you find reliable banks that still welcome American clients.

Second, investigate places to live and do business outside the United States. We explain where and how this can be accomplished in several of our research articles.

The important thing is to do *something* before it's too late.

POLICE MILITARIZATION: THE NEW SEARCH AND SEIZURE

Ted Bauman, *The Sovereign Investor Daily*, July 2014

As World War I drew to a close in November 1918, over 2.5 million soldiers of the Imperial German Army remained in the field. They brought training, experience and battle-hardened attitudes with them as they streamed back across Germany's borders.

These *soldaten* soon found ways to deploy their skills at home. Supported by Minister of Defense Gustav Noske, right-wingers — including one Corporal Adolf Hitler — organized ex-soldiers into *Freikorps*, and armed them with surplus military weaponry. These militias brutally crushed Germany's nascent post-war democratic movement. For the next 20 years, they provided the core of the feared Brownshirts, street thugs who helped Hitler and the Nazis into power.

Fast forward 100 years. Another faltering empire in domestic political crisis, the United States, brings its own frustrated warriors and their weapons back home …

Brownshirts in America — far-fetched? Not at all. They're already here, this time dressed in black or camo. I've already told you about the militarization of our borderlands, using tactics drawn directly from the battlefields of Afghanistan and Iraq. I warned then that events there would soon affect you and me.

I was right. A few weeks ago, a police paramilitary unit raided a house not too far from my home in Atlanta, in search of a teenager suspected of dealing drugs. Upon breaking down the door, they lobbed a flash bang grenade into the crib of a two-year-old child, Bounkham "Bou Bou" Phonesavanh, blowing a hole in the infant's chest. The teenager they were searching for — a relative in the family — did not even live in that house.

This is the norm in today's America. The American Civil Liberties Union recently released a report documenting the explosive growth of paramilitary police forces like the one that assaulted Bou Bou. Originally intended for hostage situations and shootouts, police paramilitaries are now deployed tens of thousands of times each year, largely for routine jobs such as search warrants or municipal code violations — all within our own borders.

These boys have some really nasty "toys." Since the late 1980s, the Department of Defense's Program 1033 has transferred tons of military-grade weaponry, including machine guns, tanks and aircraft, to state and local police departments, free of charge. As our Middle Eastern wars degenerated into counterinsurgencies, these weapons have become more and more oriented to the sort of urban "combat" that SWAT teams seem to think is their mission.

None of this would have happened, however, if America's police hadn't embraced the opportunity to go military with such gusto. Indeed, America's police culture long ago abandoned any pretense at a Mayberry-style "Officer Friendly" approach. With few exceptions, police now see themselves as an occupying army, confronting a population where every individual is a potential "hostile." Police routinely refer to their daily beats as "tours," and to interaction with potential criminals as "combat."

What accounts for this radical change in attitudes? Where's Sheriff Andy Taylor? The influx of former military personnel into domestic policing jobs definitely plays a role. So too does the glorification of force that goes with being a militaristic empire surrounded by imagined enemies.

More important, however, is the profound change in the relationship between citizen and government in America since 9/11.

In everything that matters, we citizens are no longer treated as the "employers" of civil servants like police, to whom they are accountable, but as the object of government's efforts to impose its own independent will. From the National Security Agency to your local sheriff's office, a sense of impunity and utter lack of accountability reigns supreme.

Aiding and Abetting

Today's police are recruited and trained in a carefully cultivated atmosphere of us vs. them that treats the rest of us as potential threats to be neutralized, not as citizens to be served and protected. But every policeman in the country is theoretically accountable to representatives elected by the citizenry. If America's police are out of control, it's because those elected officials aren't doing their jobs. And that means we aren't, either.

Many citizens of interwar Germany's Weimar Republic craved "law and order" to such an extent that they were willing to overlook blatant abuses of basic rights and freedoms, as long as they were directed at "others." Political opponents were deemed not to be "real Germans." As political temperatures rose, the militaristic skills and attitudes developed on the Western and Eastern fronts of 1914-18 were increasingly substituted for democratic debate and process. Many Germans thought this was fine, because the ascendant forces seemed to favor their own interests.

Then came Hitler. As the courageous theologian Martin Niemöller wrote shortly after his release from a Nazi concentration camp,

> *First they came for the Socialists, and I did not speak out — because I was not a Socialist.*
>
> *Then they came for the Trade Unionists, and I did not speak out — because I was not a Trade Unionist.*

Then they came for the Jews, and I did not speak out — because I was not a Jew.

Then they came for me — and there was no one left to speak for me.

Americans would do well to meditate on Pastor Niemöller's words. Too many of us are guilty of looking the other way as our politicians allow America's police forces to morph into heavily armed, unaccountable paramilitary thugs.

Ultimately, however, it is unlikely that our political process will arrest this trend. That's why it's so important to emulate another group of Germans from the 1930s — those who left while there was still time — and escape America while you still can.

THE "WAR ON TERROR" — SURRENDER OF CIVIL LIBERTIES?

Mark Nestmann, *The Sovereign Individual*, September 2002

Terrorism has been part of daily life in many parts of the world for decades. On September 11, 2001, Americans discovered that they are not immune to such attacks, which are virtually certain to recur. It is only prudent to adjust your portfolio and the way you live to deal with their anticipated effects.

"Freedom and human rights in America are doomed. The U.S. government will lead the American people and the West in general into an unbearable hell and a choking life." — Osama bin Laden

Did Osama bin Laden win the "war" against the United States?

If "victory" means achieving his oft-voiced objective of removing foreign troops from the Mideast and ending U.S. support for Israel, the answer is no.

But if "victory" instead means ending the "American way of life," with its support for free markets, property rights and limited governmental powers, then terrorism has indeed triumphed.

In the wake of September 11:

- Hundreds of foreigners suspected of being terrorists or to have terrorist sympathies have been detained without being charged with any crime. The U.S. Department of Justice now asserts that U.S. citizens can also be held incommunicado as "enemy combatants."

- Military tribunals, operating in secret may be set up to try foreigners charged with terrorism.

- Millions of dollars in property have been confiscated from persons alleged to be terrorists, or to support terrorism. Most of the owners have not been charged with any crime.

- The FBI is eavesdropping on lawyers' conversations with clients, including people who have been not charged with any crime, when deemed necessary to prevent violence or terrorism.

- Restrictions on the FBI's ability to spy on religious and political organizations have also been relaxed.

- The FBI can monitor e-mail message "header" information (i.e., obtain source, destination and subject line information) and web browsing patterns merely by declaring that such spying is "relevant" to an ongoing investigation. The same authority applies to materials checked out of libraries.

- Police can conduct secret searches of homes and businesses and implant electronic surveillance devices without informing the occupants.

- Restrictions on data sharing between federal agencies have been significantly relaxed.

- Immigration controls have been tightened, and issuance of visas restricted.

- Other initiatives appear to have little relevance to terrorism, but are being justified as having an anti-terrorist purpose.

- The Treasury Secretary has the authority to unilaterally terminate all U.S. financial transactions with any country.

- The IRS is publishing the names of persons suspected of being engaged in aggressive tax avoidance strategies, smearing their reputations.

- A nationwide financial transaction-tracking network is under construction.

- Millions more businesses now must report "suspicious transactions" by their customers to law enforcement.

- Any person engaged in a trade or business must file the U.S. Treasury's Financial Crimes Enforcement Network if a customer makes one or more "related" currency transactions that exceed US$10,000.

- Carrying large amounts of cash has now become "bulk smuggling" and made a criminal offense.

- Persons living in low-tax jurisdictions who previously enjoyed visa-free travel to the United States now find it necessary to obtain a visa to do so.

One of the most disturbing aspects of these initiatives is the loose definition of "terrorism." Both the Declaration of National Emergency declared by President Bush in September 2001 and the USA PATRIOT Act (the primary legal authorities under which these initiatives have occurred) define "terrorism" as: "…

an activity that — (i) involves a violent act or an act dangerous to human life, property, or infrastructure; and (ii) appears to be intended — (A) to intimidate or coerce a civilian population; (B) to influence the policy of a government by intimidation or coercion; or (C) to affect the conduct of a government by mass destruction, assassination, kidnapping, or hostage-taking."

This incredibly expansive definition allows the U.S. government to label practically all forms of domestic protest as "terrorism." One could certainly conclude that the words "intimidate" and "coerce" could apply to any group or organization that actively disapproves of official U.S. policy. Indeed, it could be argued that many forms of organized protest are designed to "intimidate or coerce" a change in government policy.

But these erosions in civil liberties aren't sufficient to fight the War on Terrorism, we are told.

The Bush Administration now proposes:

Issuing all Americans a "tamper proof" driver's license from their state — a de-facto national ID card. Without the federal ID, you likely will not be able to obtain health care, get a job, conduct bank transactions, board an airplane, purchase insurance, or obtain a passport.

- Asking millions of American workers who in the course of their job visit homes or businesses to report any suspicion of illegal activities there to the police.
- Permitting any mail crossing a U.S. border to be searched for any reason.
- Using the military for domestic law enforcement purposes.
- Making the penalties for "attempting" to violate any federal law the same as actually violating it.

Nor is the United States acting alone:

- Throughout the European Union, Internet Service Providers must now install equipment that permits governments to monitor their client's e-mails and web browsing patterns.
- In Hong Kong, the government may now confiscate assets it believes are linked to terrorists. Anyone who has been wrongly accused must prove their innocence in court to reclaim their property.
- Citing terrorism as the cause, the United Kingdom has opted out of Article 5 of the European Convention on Human Rights, which bans detention without trial.
- The United Nations has proposed that every person in the world be fingerprinted and registered under a universal identification scheme to fight illegal immigration and terrorism.

In short, the "War on Terrorism" has been co-opted into a war against civil liberties.

Is there a better way to fight this war? Yes.

We have observed previously that it is the U.S. propensity to intervene in ethnic and religious struggles worldwide that makes it a terrorist target. Ending U.S. foreign intervention would dramatically reduce the terrorist threat against the United States and its allies.

Equally important is to narrow the focus of the fight against terrorism so that it does not require the wholesale destruction of civil liberties. Programs designed to collect information to administer taxes, for instance, should not come disguised in an anti-terrorist wrapper.

Obtaining the information about the financial activities of terrorists should have a higher priority than obtaining information for tax purposes.

THE ROOTS OF TERRORISM
John Pugsley, *The Sovereign Individual*, June 2002

June marks the beginning of the tenth month in the War on Terrorism, or as Doug Casey calls it, "the Forever War."

Forever seems to be an accurate description of war in general, as inter-tribal aggression has been a characteristic of Homo sapiens from the beginning. Anthropologists classify it as a general characteristic of hunter-gatherer social behavior.

Harvard professor Edward O. Wilson calls the practice of war "…a straightforward example of a hypertrophied biological predisposition. With the rise of chiefdoms and states, this tendency became institutionalized, war was adopted as an instrument of policy of some of the new societies, and those that employed it best became, tragically, the most successful." As a result, 6,000 years of recorded history appears as an endless series of wars interspersed with brief periods of recuperation and rearmament.

Terrorism is the easiest if not the only strategy of war left open to a group that cannot directly attack or defend against a superior armed force.

The U.S. colonists who were confronted with the superior army of King George III saw the futility of following the accepted rules of war. They fired from behind trees and walls, engaged in sabotage, tarred and feathered innocent Tories, and thus were denigrated as rabble terrorists by the British. In our day, the Israeli commandos who blew up the King David Hotel in Jerusalem in 1946 were called terrorists.

But the actors change costumes as power shifts. When 'terrorist' tactics succeed in overthrowing the incumbent power structure, terrorists are reclassified in the history books. Today Sam Adams and John Hancock are remembered not as terrorists but as heroic freedom fighters. Menachem Begin, who ordered the destruction of the King David Hotel, subsequently became Israel's Prime Minister and went on to win the Nobel Peace Prize.

The chameleon nature of "terrorists" and "freedom fighters" leaves politicians struggling to distinguish terrorism from their own strategies of aggression. The U.S. Department of Defense, for example, defines "terrorism" as "the calculated use of violence or the threat of violence to inculcate fear; intended to coerce or to intimidate governments or societies in the pursuit of goals that are generally political, religious, or ideological." It seems a perfect description of the U.S. military, or the armed forces of any major power.

Considering mankind's innate aggressive tendencies, can the War on Terrorism ever be won?

Can we end the Forever War?

Yes. But it will never be accomplished through military victory. The solution to all forms of war, including terrorism, will be found in a deeper understanding of man's biological programming.

We are each endowed with powerful primal instincts that natural selection perfected as survival mechanisms long before Homo sapiens was a twinkle in evolution's eye. All life forms require two things: an instinct for self-preservation and for procreation. Two powerful primal instincts that support self-preservation and procreation are territoriality and hierarchy.

Today, these instincts are permanently hardwired into all mammals. They dominate human behavior, and therefore hold the key to the solution of inter-tribal aggression.

The territorial instinct is the internal, subconscious program that urges almost all animals to mark the boundaries of their chosen habitats, defend against intrusions, and battle for food, lairs and mates. In humans, the territorial instinct pushes us to acquire property, and defend it against threats, theft, and trespassing. We "mark" our land with deeds, our bank accounts with name and number, and our mates with rings and contracts. We are angered and enraged when our property is taken.

The hierarchical instinct pushes us to seek approval, climb the social ladder, and achieve dominance among our peers. In the non-human animal world, it is documented everywhere from the struggle for the position of alpha male in primate groups to the pecking order of chickens. In human culture, the drive for status creates the endless battle for political power and the insatiable desire for property.

Viewed through the lens of these two primal instincts, the root of all conflict is the innate, subconscious drive in all humans to acquire and defend resources. When individuals feel their territory has been attacked, they instinctively feel rage and seek vengeance. As Wilson notes, under the sway of our primal instincts we are "…strongly predisposed to slide into deep, irrational hostility."

Contrary to the nonsense perpetrated in the media, suicide bombers don't sacrifice their lives in hopes of a sexual paradise in the afterlife. Their irrational hostility boils up from deep within the limbic system of their brains. Their primal instincts take control. Such instincts are not devils that can be exorcized through fear or punishment. As long as people feel their property has been stolen from them, their primal instincts will urge them to seek revenge at any cost.

The answer to minimizing human conflict, and particularly war, will be the design of a social contract that protects every individual's property. Our innate human nature leads directly to the conclusion that the Forever War will end when all of us are sovereign individuals, and we feel securely in control of our individual lives and property.

ARE YOU A LIBERTARIAN?
Vincent H. Miller, *The Sovereign Individual*, 1998

One of its American leaders recalls the history and growth of the Libertarian movement — and asks you to examine your own political conscience.

What is a libertarian?

The catch phrase, "Fiscally conservative; socially liberal," explains it — sort of. But simplifications often lose the essence of what they describe. Basically a libertarian is a person who believes in individual liberty, an unregulated market economy and social tolerance for diverse lifestyles. It's a "live and let live" philosophy.

The foundation of libertarianism is the Non-Aggression Principle, which states that no one may initiate force or fraud against others. This is sometimes stated as, "First, do no harm," or in the biblical turn of phrase, "Thou shalt not agress."

Many libertarians trace their roots back to the eighteenth and nineteenth century classical free trade liberals to England's Adam Smith, John Locke, John Cobden, Richard Bright, French philosopher Frederic Bastiat and others. Others look to nineteenth century American individualist anarchists such as William Lloyd Garrison, Lysander Spooner, and Henry David Thoreau.

The modern libertarian movement, however, has been most strongly influenced by the late Austrian economist Ludwig von Mises, and by Mises' protégé and Nobel Laureate, F. A. Hayek, and Nobel Laureate Milton Friedman of the University of Chicago.

Perhaps the most influential of all was the novelist and philosopher Ayn Rand, whose novels, plays, and essays strongly influenced the new wave of libertarians. The message of her epic novel *Atlas Shrugged* has been so powerful that a joint survey by the Book of the Month Club and the Library of Congress ranked Atlas Shrugged second only to the Bible as the book that had most influenced people's lives.

Although there have been pockets of libertarian influence throughout history, the modern movement began to gain momentum in the 1940s. With the founding of Leonard Read's Foundation for Economic Education at Irvington-on-Hudson, New York, and the near-simultaneous publication of Rand's *The Fountainhead*, Hayek's *The Road to Serfdom*, Isabel Paterson's *The God of the Machine*, Rose Wilder Lane's *The Discovery of Freedom* and Mises' *Human Action*, the modern libertarian movement took its first steps. It wasn't until the publication of *Atlas Shrugged* in 1957 that the Libertarian movement as we know it today regained its stride.

During those earliest years, a whole generation was inspired by Rand's libertarian message of individualism and uncompromising free-market capitalism. It was all the more amazing given that libertarianism began evolving during the era of President Roosevelt's socialist/fascist New Deal.

Libertarian pioneers such as author Rose Wilder Lane and H. L. Mencken, columnist for the *Baltimore Evening Sun*, vigorously attacked the socialism and collectivism of the New Deal and paved the way for a much larger and more influential movement which later developed.

A seminal moment of the modern libertarian movement was the 1969 convention of the pioneer young conservative group, Young Americans for Freedom (YAF) in St Louis, Missouri. Since the founding in 1960 of this association of young Barry Goldwater conservatives, there had been an uneasy peace between YAF's traditionalist conservative wing and the libertarian-Randian wing. Libertarian opposition to the Vietnam War, the military draft and other human rights issues finally erupted into full-scale political war. This confrontation resulted in a purge of the libertarians, who left en masse and met under St. Louis Gateway Arch to found a new movement.

Luminaries such as Karl Hess, author of the 1960 Republican platform and a former Goldwater-Nixon-Ford speech writer, Leonard Liggio, who would later become president of the Institute for Humane Studies, and most of the International Society for Individual Liberty's (ISIL) current board members were there.

At this time ISIL's sister organization the Society for Individual Liberty (SIL) was formed as an umbrella group for disenfranchised libertarians. From this new beginning the movement grew. SIL produced a comprehensive series of educational pamphlets which sold in the millions. They organized tax protest days, and created a network of activist student chapters in colleges and universities across the nation. In the years following the historic 1969 conservative/libertarian split, many of the movement's intellectual institutions formed: Laissez Faire Books, Reason magazine and the Reason Foundation, the Cato Institute, the Institute for Humane Studies, the Ludwig von Mises Institute and more.

Today libertarianism in America, if not a major success at the ballot box, is an intellectual force to be reckoned with.

One of the key contributions of the libertarian movement has been its critical examination and analysis of the proper role of government. This is a subject libertarians take very seriously. For many years the standard line was that since governments enjoy a monopoly on the use of force, its proper role should be limited to those agencies in which such powers seem appropriate (i.e., police, military and courts). Nothing else.

An impressive body of literature has arisen from the pens of libertarian scholars challenging the role of government in today's society. They have observed that it is difficult to find anything that government touches that is not eventually turned into a cesspool of corruption, patronage and mindboggling waste.

Competitive markets in a free economy, they assert, can provide most if not all the essential services currently provided by government.

Many in the movement, including David Friedman, son of Milton Friedman and author of a seminal book entitled *The Machinery of Freedom*, explain that virtually every function currently provided by governments can be provided better and more inexpensively — not to mention more compassionately — by competitive market institutions.

There are interesting arguments of great merit from both sides of this debate. How much better would it be, for example, if organizations like the United Way, churches or other charitable organizations handled welfare instead of government?

For example, in America the government wastes over 80 percent of its welfare dollars on mammoth bureaucracies and their palatial offices, whereas private charities reverse these figures. The Social Security system is bankrupt and inflicts a terrible tax burden on the younger generation. Why not take it out of the hands of corrupt politicians and privatize it? There is a vast library of literature on the privatization of most governmental functions by the world's leading scholars. For those interested, Laissez Faire Books can provide the proper research material. Their book service and informative catalogue is one of the treasures of the libertarian movement.

We believe that the world is in for a rough ride over the next decade, but that the twenty-first century holds the promise of a renaissance of freedom. Libertarians will remain on the front lines of the battle for free markets and free minds.

Obamacare is About to Get More Personal
Robert E. Bauman JD, *The Sovereign Investor Daily*, August 2013

"He has erected a multitude of new offices, and sent hither swarms of officers to harass our people, and eat out their substance."

That defiant statement was included in a list of 30 "facts" contained in the Declaration of Independence, rejecting the tyranny of King George III of England, proclaimed on July 4, 1776, by the Continental Congress in Philadelphia.

That revolutionary document contained a list of grievances against the British King that compelled the colonists to throw off the chains of oppression and form a new government.

Now, some 237 years later, the ghost of King George III is ready to haunt Americans again … in the form of IRS enforcement agents tied to Obamacare.

In 2009, the U.S. Congress passed the grossly misnamed Patient Protection and Affordable Care Act in an incredibly narrow vote. It became law with President Obama's signature on March 23, 2010.

Ever since, Obamacare has degenerated into what U.S. Senate Finance Committee Chairman Senator Max Baucus (D-MT) has described candidly as a "huge train wreck."

I served in the U.S. House with Max Baucus, and I know him to be a thoughtful legislator and a gentleman, but his "train wreck" comment was an understatement.

Baucus was referring to the messy implementation of Obamacare: missed deadlines, 10,000-plus pages of new rules and the solid opposition of a majority of Americans who support repealing the law — a number that keeps growing.

And there are other serious Obamacare failures that have received far less attention.

- Electronic health records (EHRs) were supposed to save billions of dollars in health care costs. But a *New York Times* report reveals what many health experts predicted: The only beneficiaries of EHRs are the companies that lobbied for this costly provision.

- A desperate Obama administration has spent a questionable $30 million in taxpayers' funds on public-relations contracts, trying to convince people they should like Obamacare. Even in the face of widespread opposition to it by state governments, businesses, insurers, doctors and, now, even the labor unions that originally supported it. The result has been massive amounts of waivers exempting select pro-Obama political groups and backers. Even the U.S. Congress and its staff have opted out. How's that for equality under the law? It's rank cronyism at its finest.

- Contrary to repeated Obama promises that everyone would save money, the cost of health-insurance premiums has exploded, some by 100% or more. Many insurers have declined to participate.

Yet, as bad as those developments are, there is something even more sinister afoot.

Your Privacy is Under Attack

Obamacare contains an "individual mandate" requiring every American to have some form of health insurance by March 31, 2014. If you don't have Medicaid, Medicare, or other public or private insurance, you must pay a fine as determined by thousands of new IRS agents who will administer financial tests to see if you have done what Dr. Obama has ordered.

This means that new health care exchanges must access your personal records from any applicable government agencies, including the IRS, the Social Security Administration, Homeland Security, the Veterans Health Administration, the Department of Defense and even the Peace Corps, in order to determine eligibility for exchange subsidies and penalties.

All of these personal records are being consolidated into government-accessible Obamacare information "hubs" — even though federal privacy laws forbid the release of such information to other agencies.

As the Obamacare crowd works against a totally unrealistic deadline of October 1, 2013, they have hired thousands of new bureaucrats, colorfully known as "navigators," to seek out Americans, demand their information and sign them up.

Florida Attorney General Pam Bondi and a dozen other state attorneys general sent U.S. Department of Health and Human Services (HHS) Secretary Kathleen Sebelius a letter underscoring a major looming privacy issue. They asked her to implement more stringent privacy requirements and safeguards on these so-called navigators.

The critical questions are these: Who is in charge of monitoring these navigators? Who will be liable if someone's identity is stolen? And who is responsible for alerting the American public about fraud prevention?

Bondi said that the HHS is making it easier for your private information to fall into the wrong hands by cutting back on employee background checks and eliminating a fingerprinting requirement for navigators and those that work with them.

"It's more than navigators," Bondi said. "It's people that assist the navigators. Now, these navigators will have our consumers throughout the country's most personal and private information: tax return information, Social Security information. And our biggest fear, of course, is identity theft."

Not to mention the theft of our personal, financial and medical privacy in the name of health care "reform." The tyranny of the Age of Obama continues unabated.

Chapter Two

Your Guide to Second Passports, Dual Nationality, Foreign Residence & Expatriation

Passports Explained 58
Five Routes to a Second Passport 61
Advantages of a Second Passport 63
Expatriation: The Ultimate Estate Plan Explained 65
Is Expatriation Right for You? 69
What It Really Costs to Expatriate 71
What is "Economic Citizenship?" 73
Economic Citizenship Choices 74
What it's Really Like to Expatriate 89
Practical Questions for Aspiring Expatriates 91
Diary of an Expatriate:
    1) A Search for Security 94
    2) A New Home 96
Countries that Offer Quick Residence 98
The Great Irish Opportunity 112
Malta Offers No-Wait Citizenship 122
Latin American Route to EU Citizenship 128
Six Ways to Escape from America — Now 129
Moving Abroad — Not as Hard as You Think 132
Rules Offshore Real Estate Buyers Must Know 135

Editor's Note:

Almost anyone with determination and the financial means can become an international citizen.

This is accomplished by acquiring a legal second citizenship, and along with that enhanced status you receive an official second passport. This new passport can expand your legal rights, allowing easier world travel unmolested by a curious border guard or nosy customs and tax officials. It also can open doors that otherwise would remain closed to you.

Best of all, a second citizenship/passport can serve as the key to reducing your taxes and protecting your assets — or even saving your life.

In Chapter Two, we explain how this second passport "magic" can work for you. You should consider this chapter in conjunction with Chapter Seven — Taxes.

Passports Explained
Robert E. Bauman JD, *The Passport Book*, 2014

The natural human tendency is to live life in the present and to forget much of the past. Most people don't realize how often that history does repeat itself, offering valuable warnings of what may come again.

On many occasions, history has proven the many flexible uses and powers of that official personal document known as a passport — and having a second passport can double those powers.

From serving as a life insurance policy that protects you from political violence at home and abroad…to guaranteeing a greater degree of liberty and security in the age of greedy governments and rising tax rates…a second passport has become an indispensable fact of life for millions of free individuals the world over. (An estimated 40 million American citizens currently may be eligible for a second passport.)

But it hasn't always been that way…

Passports — A Modern Invention

Foreign travel in the modern world means having to deal with all the inconveniences imposed by national sovereignty — international borders, customs officials, passports, visas, and identity documents. (Add to that the nuisances of rude security inspections, X-ray machines, sniffing dogs and luggage searches.) It means having to suffer officious customs and immigration agents, secret government "no fly" lists, bribe-seeking border guards and unreasonable, unexplained delays.

One of the most significant benefits of the European Union, for example, is that it comprises a common geographic area of 28 countries inside of which all such cross border difficulties are greatly reduced for those who hold an EU country passport.

Few realize that this modern liberal EU travel policy actually harkens back to earlier times before passports became the rule.

Until shortly before the First World War (1914-1918), most countries did not require their citizens to have official passports.

In those slower, less traveled times, document-free international travel was the general rule. Before the last century, passports were usually rare special travel documents used to protect official emissaries of nation states at war with each other, allowing safe conduct for surrender or peace negotiations.

The first modern travel document, known as the "Nansen Passport," was issued to White Russian faction refugees in the prolonged civil war that followed the 1918 anti-Tsarist Russian Revolution led by the Communist Bolsheviks.

That document took its name from Fridtjof Nansen, a Norwegian explorer (later a delegate to the ill-fated League of Nations in Geneva), who first proposed the passport concept.

That passport, administered by the League of Nations, successfully served hundreds of thousands of refugees as a travel and identity document until the outbreak of World War II in September 1939. The International Refugee Organization (IRO) replaced the defunct League's Nansen Passport Office from 1930 to 1945, but had no authority to issue refugee documents.

In a 1951 treaty, the "Convention on the Status of Refugees" (CSR), the United Nations (UN) attempted to define the rights of international refugees. Effective in 1960, after the required 35 countries ratified it, the UN CSR authorized signatory countries to issue travel documents for those they determined eligible for refugee status, applying the Convention's criteria.

But each nation interpreted the CSR in its own fashion, so the world soon became cluttered with hundreds of thousands of refugees fleeing from wars, ethnic conflicts, famine, and pestilence. These unfortunates were admitted by some countries, rejected by others, and the result was misery on a grand scale in places as diverse as the Balkans, Israel and Palestine, Iraq, Hong Kong, Vietnam, Cambodia, Rwanda, Somalia, Syria and numerous other countries.

On the subject of the right of persons to travel freely, the United Nations Universal Declaration of Human Rights states:

Article 13 — Everyone has the right to freedom of movement and residence within the borders of each state. Everyone has the right to leave any country, including his own, and to return to his country.

Article 15 — Everyone has the right to a nationality. No one shall be arbitrarily deprived of his nationality nor denied the right to change his nationality.

It goes without saying that these so-called "rights" of free movement, travel and residence have been, and are, systematically violated by almost every nation, including both dictatorships and democracies.

The United States and the United Kingdom are among the worst violators when it suits the political convenience of the government in power at the moment.

Since World War II domestic politics has dominated the history of world refugee problems.

In 1956 the U.S. government, under President Dwight Eisenhower, welcomed thousands of refugees from the failed Hungarian popular revolt against Russian-backed Communists, who at the time dominated Hungary. That revolt failed in part because President Eisenhower chose not to help the Hungarians militarily and avoided confrontation with Soviet Russia.

During more than four decades of the Castro brothers' regime in Cuba, the U.S. has repeatedly admitted tens of thousands of Cuban refugees, who — with their offspring — now constitute a large part of the Latino majority of U.S. citizens in South Florida.

In contrast, in what has been called a racist policy, the U.S. has turned away thousands of Haitian "boat people" trying to escape dictatorship and poverty in the last decade. In a shameful act, the British refused to give citizens of Hong Kong full U.K. citizenship rights when Communist China took over the colonial government in 1997, mainly because of a feared U.K. voter backlash against admitting more immigrants "of color." Before and during World War II (1939-1945) the U.S. government under President Franklin D. Roosevelt refused to admit to America thousands of European Jewish refugees trying to escape Hitler and Nazi persecution, many of whom died as a result.

Tribal wars in Africa and wars in the Balkans involving Serbia, Bosnia, Albania, and Kosovo, have produced hundreds of thousands of refugees whose fate seemed the least concern of many world leaders. More recently these scenes of refugee horror have been repeated in Syria and its neighbors, Turkey, Lebanon and Iraq.

Who Needs a Second Passport?

The English political philosopher Edmund Burke (1729-97) observed in another time: "Early and provident fear is the mother of safety."

That is still good advice for any potential world traveler. Having to be "politically correct" often means travel using a national passport that keeps the bearer as far away as possible from international controversy. It may be a fact of your political life that your home nation's passport provides you little or no safety margin, but another nation's passport will.

Some countries are more popular and accepted in the world than others. Some countries are respected in some parts of the world, reviled in others. Some countries are universally condemned and ostracized. Whichever categories your nation happens to fall into at the moment can determine when you present your passport.

Travel in the Middle East or the Balkans, parts of Russia or Asia using a U.S. passport can make you an instant target for terrorist groups. If your government is out of world favor at the moment, your passport could be confiscated, revoked or suspended at will, as happened to citizens of the Republic of South Africa during the apartheid years.

It's a fact of international political life that citizens of certain countries, the U.S. among them, find travel abroad difficult. For many reasons some countries impose strict visa requirements each time a foreign national wants to enter their country. It's their way of keeping out troublemakers and other supposed "undesirables."

Similar troubles can be expected by Americans who want to visit Cuba. For decades it has been illegal for U.S. citizens to visit Cuba because of the official U.S. embargo aimed at toppling the Communist dictatorship of the Castro brothers. Those restrictions are now easing however.

FIVE ROUTES TO A SECOND PASSPORT
Robert E. Bauman JD, *The Sovereign Individual*, July 2009

How you can become a citizen depends on a country's laws, but there are five main methods:

1. birth within the borders of a nation's territory
2. descent from a parent or grandparent
3. marriage to a foreign citizen
4. religion, as in Israel's Law of Return
5. formal naturalization by applying and qualifying for citizenship.

The naturalization process varies among countries, but on average, five years' residence is required before citizenship is granted.

Citizenship for Sale

The Commonwealth of Dominica and St. Christopher and Nevis, both Caribbean island countries, grant official citizenship in exchange for cash without any prior residency requirements — but both are expensive. These so-called "economic citizenship" programs offer a nationality quickly and simply for those who qualify.

Citizenship by Ancestry

A much easier path to second citizenship may lurk somewhere up in your family tree.

Several countries grant full citizenship based on the law of blood, *jus sanguines*, even without a descendant ever having lived in the country. All one needs is a parent or grandparent who is (or was) a citizen of that country.

Ireland: One the best of these ancestral programs is offered by the Republic of Ireland. Persons with one parent or grandparent born in Ireland are eligible for Irish nationality, with a passport valid for 10 years and renewable. As a result, with a population of only 4.1 million, Ireland has over 14 million current official passports in circulation.

Italy: The Republic of Italy offers a similar program. The children and grandchildren of former Italian nationals can qualify for citizenship on the basis of any of the following: 1) a father who was an Italian citizen at the time of a child's birth; 2) a mother who was an Italian citizen at the time of a child's birth after January 1, 1948; 3) the father was not born in Italy, but the paternal grandfather was an Italian citizen at the time of birth; or 4) the mother was not born in Italy, but for those born after January 1, 1948, the maternal grandfather was an Italian citizen at the time of the mother's birth. In addition, ethnic Italians who cannot qualify under ancestry rules can qualify for naturalization after only three years' legal residence in Italy.

Poland: Poland changed its laws a few years ago so that persons whose parents or grandparents were Polish citizens may be eligible to obtain citizenship. Citizenship can be claimed only by descendants of Polish citizens who left Poland after the country became an independent state in 1918. However, there can be no break in Polish citizenship between the emigrant ancestor and the descendant. Application for "Confirmation of Possession or Loss of Polish Citizenship" can be made through Polish embassies or consulates.

Other countries that offer citizenship based on the citizenship of parents or grandparents include Spain, Greece, Lithuania and Luxembourg. Spain also offers a reduced two-year residence before citizenship to citizens of any of several Latin American countries. Portugal and Brazil have a similar arrangement.

Immediate Residence

Several other countries, including Uruguay, are attractive because they offer immediate official residence under a variety of plans, some leading to citizenship. Both the Republic of Panama and its Central American neighbor, Belize, offer *pensinado* programs to retirees who have guaranteed annual incomes. Neither leads to citizenship, but Panama does have several investment programs that grant immediate residence and eventual citizenship after five years.

Advantages of a Second Passport
Ted Bauman, *The Sovereign Investor Daily*, June 2015

I get around. And it has made me popular with Uncle Sam.

My U.S. passport is the size of a small phone book, and my destinations include some decidedly non-touristy locales. So when I return from someplace like Cambodia, Haiti or Rwanda, the person who examines my passport inevitably asks a series of penetrating questions about my reasons for going there, the nature of my business, where I stayed, who I spent time with, whether I brought back any voodoo dolls, and so on.

I've learned to grin and bear these intrusive questions, although it can be difficult to maintain one's composure after a 24-hour flight from Bangkok. Or when a TSA agent confiscates a snow globe you bought your daughter in Frankfurt because it contains a liquid.

But for real fireworks, nothing beats being pulled aside for "special examination" — the dreaded *SSSS* (secondary security screening selection) designation on one's boarding card. I get this *a lot*. One day I found out why … and how to avoid it in the future.

Big Brother's Watching You

I have a second passport. It's useful for all sorts of reasons, including some that aren't always apparent at first … such as U.S. border formalities.

My experience with the U.S. Transport Security Administration (TSA) reflects the sort of country the U.S. has become. It's a massive intelligence and security state, with myriad bureaucracies that often operate independently, with little supervision. And our approach to constitutional law is exactly backwards: Instead of actively protecting our rights, our government ignores them until some courageous litigant challenges it, whereupon the Supreme Court reminds every one of those rights — if they're in the mood.

My TSA nightmares illustrate this. On several occasions, TSA goons have pulled up my "records" on their computer screens. They inevitably ask me about every country I've visited in the last few years: Nepal. Bangladesh. Kenya. Vietnam. Nigeria. Guatemala. Tanzania. Even Hungary and Slovakia. They know about all of my journeys and want to know more. (Which makes recent revelations even more ironic.)

My travel history, you see, qualifies me for some sort of "watch list." I've never done anything wrong, and yet I am watched closely by the U.S. government.

But there's a way around that.

Options, options…

U.S. citizens aren't the only people in the world fed up with our government. Plenty of foreign countries consider Washington to be a bully and a bad neighbor. Some of them retaliate against U.S. passport holders visiting their shores.

Brazil, for example, requires visas of U.S. visitors because the U.S. does the same to Brazilians. So do India, China, Russia, Pakistan, Vietnam, most of Africa … and Australia. In some cases, it's not a big deal, but sometimes U.S. citizens are subjected to intrusive and abusive examinations that are a clear response to our country's own practices. A U.S. passport is an invitation to a shakedown by customs officials and cops in many countries.

But I've visited almost all of those countries with no hassle. That's because my second passport is from a country that has good relations with them. They welcome me with open arms.

Even better … the U.S. government has no idea I've visited them.

After all, avoiding visas and anti-U.S. sentiment isn't the only reason a second passport comes in handy. Privacy is a huge bonus. I regularly visit countries that don't penalize U.S. visitors using my second passport. I do this specifically to avoid having entry and exit stamps in my U.S. passport, where TSA snoops can see and record them.

Doing Nothing Wrong … Except Seeking Privacy

My international travels are all for perfectly legitimate reasons. But so were those of Laura Poitras, a U.S. journalist and filmmaker who has been subjected to detention, confiscation of her personal effects, and other forms of harassment at the U.S. border — all because she is openly critical of the U.S. government's abuse of our constitutional rights. Her shocking experience is shared by many Americans.

Bob Bauman's *The Passport Book* tells you how to obtain residence and a second passport from many countries. Some aren't so easy, but many just require the right ancestry, a reasonable investment, or a willingness to spend some time abroad.

The way I look at it, with every day that passes — with every new violation of our liberties by the U.S. government — the relative value of a second passport increases.

After all, what price can you put on privacy?

EXPATRIATION: THE ULTIMATE ESTATE PLAN EXPLAINED

Bob Bauman, *The Sovereign Individual*, March 2007

American tax law, unlike that of almost all other nations, imposes taxes on U.S. citizens and resident aliens ("green card holders") no matter where in the world they actually live and without regard to where the sources of their income may be located. In this sense, the United States is unlike many other nations that enjoy "territorial tax tax systems" — meaning taxes are imposed only on income earned within their borders. Thus a Canadian or a Englishman can move out of their home country and legally avoid most domestic taxes.

But there is a legal, though complex way in which Americans can end their U.S. tax obligations.

It's called "expatriation" and it's also been called "the ultimate estate plan." It's a step-by-step process that can lead to the legal right for an American to stop paying U.S. or income taxes — forever.

In sum, it requires professional consultations, careful planning, movement of assets offshore and acquisition of a second nationality — a second passport. When all that's done, (and done exactly right), the plan calls for the person to leave behind his or her home country and become a "tax exile" with an established domicile in a low or no-tax jurisdiction. And, for U.S. citizens, this unusual plan requires, as a final step toward tax freedom, the formal relinquishment of citizenship.

A drastic plan? You bet. And in truth, there are many other perfectly suitable offshore strategies that can result in significant tax savings. These include international life insurance policies and offshore investments made through annuities and retirement plans. But for U.S. citizens and long-term residents who seek a permanent and completely legal way to stop paying all U.S. taxes, expatriation is the only option.

Blueprint to Ultimate Tax Freedom

One of the first tax experts to appreciate the potential tax savings of expatriation was my friend and colleague, Marshall Langer JD. Langer is an international tax attorney and the respected author of several major international tax treatises, but also the daring creator of a now out-of-print book, *The Tax Exile Report*. This title gained international notoriety when the late U.S. Senator Daniel Patrick Moynihan (D-N.Y.), red-faced and angry, waived a copy of the book at a televised Senate hearing, denouncing it as "a legal income tax avoidance plan."

In explaining why "expatriation" is so attractive to wealthy Americans (and others), a few years ago a Forbes magazine article gave the compelling arithmetic: "A very rich Bahamian citizen pays zero estate taxes; rich Americans — anyone with an estate worth US$3 million or more — pay 55%. A fairly stiff 37% marginal rate kicks in for Americans leaving as little as $600,000 to their children." Even though U.S. estate taxes have been reduced since then, an even more impressive part of the Langer plan is the ability to escape American income, capital gains and other taxes.

Becoming a tax exile is not without problems, but, so far, they are more political than legal.

The source of the current controversy over expatriation was a sensational article in the Nov. 24, 1994 issue of *Forbes* magazine, entitled "The New Refugees." Filled with juicy details (famous names, luxury addresses, big dollar tax savings), the story described how clever ex-Americans who became citizens of certain foreign nations, paid little or no U.S. federal and state income, estate and capital gains taxes.

Ever since, expatriation has been a favorite "hot button" issue kicked around by the American news media and "soak-the-rich" politicians. The Democrat controlled U.S. Congress elected in 2006 now is considering several proposals that would try to restrict and punish tax expatriation.

One would impose an immediate tax on unrealized capital gains on anyone who ends their U.S. citizenship. It uses an arbitrary test of net worth and/or income tax paid over a period of years to assume an ex-citizen is trying to escape income taxes. Similar net worth/income tax provisions have been the law since 1996.

It's understandable why politicians keep this political football in play. To the average uninformed U.S. taxpayer, expatriation seems like just another rich man's tax loophole. Before *Forbes* raised the issue, few people had even heard of the concept of formal surrender or loss of U.S. citizenship. Former U.S. Treasury Secretary Larry Summers went so far as to call tax expatriates "traitors" to America. He later was forced to apologize.

Right to Surrender U.S. Citizenship

As a national political issue, expatriation is hardly new.

In the Foreign Investors Tax Act of 1966, Congress decided to make an issue of expatriation. In that Act, lawmakers tried to impose onerous taxes on exiting wealthy Americans who relinquished their U.S. citizenship "with the principal purpose of avoiding" U.S. taxes, a highly subjective intention that was virtually impossible to prove. The IRS couldn't prove such "intent" and very rarely even tried.

A 1996 anti-expatriation law inspired by the Forbes article asserts limited U.S. tax jurisdiction for a period of 10 years over persons who renounce their U.S.

citizenship "with the principal purpose of avoiding U.S. taxes." Also covered by this law are permanent resident aliens ("green card" holders) or anyone else who has resided in the United States for any eight of the preceding 15 years.

For the purposes of this law, tax avoidance is presumed to be the true purpose if, at the time of expatriation, an expatriate's net worth exceeds US$622,000 or he or she paid an annual tax bill exceeding US$124,000 annually for the past five years, figures that are indexed for inflation. However, with proper planning, it is relatively easy to avoid U.S. taxes during this 10-year period.

The lengths to which politicians will go to penalize expatriates is demonstrated by a never-enforced provision of U.S. law, also enacted in 1996, that permits the Attorney General to bar from returning to the United States anyone who renounces their U.S. citizenship to avoid U.S. taxes. In this manner, Congress lumped individuals exercising their legal right to avoid taxes with narcotics traffickers and terrorists.

These Draconian laws set a dangerous precedent. They involve not only retaliatory government acts against resistance to high taxes, but poses possible human rights violations guaranteed by others laws and even the Human Rights Charter of the United Nations. It is worth noting that the U.S. Supreme Court has repeatedly affirmed the right of U.S. citizens to end their citizenship as well as the right to enjoy dual citizenship.

In reality, this political frenzy probably reflects collective envy more than any sense of patriotism by Americans or their congressional representatives. Expatriation is not as serious a problem as some pretend: fewer than 800 Americans, rich or poor, have formally given up their citizenship in recent years. Most expatriates give up their U.S. citizenship because they are returning to their native land or marrying a non-U.S. citizen.

Save Millions of Dollars, Legally

Amidst the controversy, there remain very substantial tax savings for wealthy U.S. citizens who are prepared to give up their citizenship. While only a handful of very rich Americans have legally expatriated, these individuals include some prominent names: In 1962, John Templeton, respected international investor, businessman and philanthropist, surrendered his U.S. citizenship to become a citizen of the Bahamas. This move saved him more than US$100 million when he sold the well-known international investment fund that still bears his name.

Other wealthy ex-Americans who have taken their formal leave include billionaire Campbell Soup heir John ("Ippy") Dorrance III (Ireland); Michael Dingman, (The Bahamas) chairman of Abex and a Ford Motor director; J. Mark Mobious, (Germany) one of the leading emerging market investment fund managers; Kenneth Dart (Belize), heir to the billion dollar Dart container fortune; Ted Arison

(Israel), head of Carnival Cruise Lines; and millionaire head of Locktite Corp., Fred Kreible (Turks and Caicos Islands).

How to Do It

Long before you formally give up your U.S. citizenship, you should reorder your financial affairs in such a way as to remove from possible government control and taxation most, if not all, of your assets.

Here are the steps you must take:

- Arrange your affairs so that most or all of your income is derived from non-U.S. sources
- Title your property ownership so that any assets that remain in the United States are exempt from U.S. estate and gift taxes
- Move abroad and make your new home in a no-tax foreign nation so you are no longer a "resident" for U.S. income taxes
- Obtain an alternative citizenship and passport
- Give up U.S. citizenship and change your legal "domicile" to avoid U.S. estate taxes

One of the most important decisions is the choice of a second nationality. Millions of Americans already hold a second nationality; millions more quality almost instantly for one by reason of birth, ancestry or marriage. For instance, in many countries (Ireland. Italy, Poland), having a parent or grandparent born in that country will qualify children or grandchildren for immediate citizenship and passport after presenting appropriate documentation.

Otherwise, you will need to qualify for alternative citizenship through prolonged residency (2-10 years) in a country in which you qualify for residency based on your economic status or investments you make there. For instance, both Panama and Belize have formal tax advantaged residency plans for foreign nationals who wish to make their home there. After five years, sometimes less, you can apply for citizenship.

Alternatively, you may choose to purchase economic citizenship, which can be obtained in a matter of months, but only at significant cost (US$225,000 or more). The only two legitimate economic citizenship programs still in existence [2007] are from two small Caribbean nations, the Commonwealth of Dominica and St. Christopher Kitts & Nevis.

Tax expatriation — it's complicated, but it could save you millions in taxes.

Is Expatriation Right for You?
Mark Nestmann, *The Sovereign Society Offshore A-Letter*, 2009

The United States is one of only two countries that imposes tax on a citizen's worldwide income, no matter where that citizen lives. (The other country is, of all places, Eritrea.)

For citizens of most high-tax countries, it's easy to legally avoid the obligation to pay tax on your worldwide income. You simply relocate to a lower-tax jurisdiction, or one that only taxes local income. After an extended period — normally 1-2 years — you become "non-resident" for tax purposes. You no longer have the obligation to pay tax on your worldwide income to the country that issued your passport. You may, however, still be subject to gift and estate taxes.

But *Not* in the USA...

To permanently disconnect from the obligation to pay U.S. income tax, U.S. citizens must not only leave the United States, they must also take the radical step of giving up U.S. citizenship and passport. This process (from a U.S. standpoint) is called expatriation. Before giving up U.S. citizenship, they must acquire citizenship and a passport from another country.

If you're wealthy, expatriating could result in big tax savings. The total combined state-federal income tax burden for highest earners is close to 50%. And President Obama promises to hike that burden to pay for his spending plans.

If you anticipate earning US$2 million over the next five years, expatriation could save you a cool US$1 million in income tax during that period. Not to mention millions more in the years ahead, and millions more again in estate tax savings.

Expatriation also eliminates the increasing difficulties that U.S. citizens face when they invest or do business overseas. Many non-U.S. banks and brokers now prohibit anyone with any connection to the United States from opening an account. This is a result of the U.S. government's intensifying crackdown against anything "offshore."

Foreign entrepreneurs may avoid joint ventures with U.S. citizens, for fear of U.S. tax or regulatory entanglements.

If you give up your U.S. citizenship and passport, you eliminate all of these problems.

But you're also taking on a whole new life in a different country and a different culture. Unless you've previously lived abroad or have family in another country, it can mean a major change in your life. As such, it's no surprise that few people — only some of which could be considered wealthy — actually choose to give up their U.S. citizenship annually.

Despite this reality, though, expatriates remain vulnerable to political bombast. The image of wealthy former U.S. citizens living tax-free in tropical paradises is an irresistible populist target.

Former Congressman Sam Gibbons, a Florida Democrat, once spoke of "the despicable act of renouncing allegiance to the United States." Former Congressman Martin Frost, a Texas Democrat, supported tax penalties on expatriates on the basis of "basic patriotism and basic fairness." The result has been a series of increasingly stringent laws penalizing expatriate Americans.

Exit Tax: "Legal Fiction" Targets Expatriates

Until 2008, it was relatively easy to circumvent these anti-expatriation rules.

But in June 2008, Congress replaced the existing law in its entirety with an "exit tax." The exit tax establishes a legal fiction that you sell all your worldwide property the day before expatriation. Never mind what we've learned from the stock market in the last year — that unrealized gains can easily be wiped out when the market takes a turn for the worse. If you're a "covered expatriate" (which I'll define momentarily), you must then pay tax on this fictional gain.

Unrealized gains in non-grantor trusts and some retirement and pension plans are exempt from the exit tax. Instead, payouts that would be taxable to a U.S. person are subject to a 30% withholding tax.

Only certain dual citizens and minors with few ties to the United States are exempt from these requirements. Long-term green-card holders must also pay the exit tax if they've lived in the United States for at least eight of the 15 years preceding expatriation.

How are you supposed to pay the tax without selling your assets? That's your problem! However, the law permits deferral by posting acceptable security with the U.S. Treasury and paying an interest charge on the amount deferred.

Fortunately, the first US$600,000 of unrealized gain isn't subject to the exit tax. This amount is adjusted annually for inflation, and for 2009 the exemption is US$626,000. The exemption doubles for a married couple, both of whom expatriate.

In addition, even if your unrealized gains exceed US$626,000, the exit tax only applies to you if you're a "covered expatriate." This means:

- Your average annual net income tax for the 5 years ending before the date of expatriation or termination of residency is more than a specified amount that is adjusted for inflation ($147,000 for 2011, $151,000 for 2012, $155,000 for 2013 and $157,000 for 2014).

- Your net worth is $2 million or more on the date of your expatriation or termination of residency.

- You fail to certify on Form 8854 that you have complied with all U.S. federal tax obligations for the 5 years preceding the date of your expatriation or termination of residency.

"Back-Up" Exit Tax

There's also a very sneaky substitute estate tax provision in the exit tax law. Let's say you expatriate, and then 20 years in the future make a gift to family members remaining in the United States. If you're a "covered expatriate" at the time you make the gift, U.S. recipients must pay a tax when they receive it.

And not at ordinary income tax rates, but on the highest estate tax rate existing at the time!

However, a covered expatriate can make annual gifts up to US$13,000 to any U.S. person without a tax consequence to the recipient. The US$13,000 exclusion is adjusted annually for inflation.

The best that can be said about the exit tax is that it offers a relatively clean break with the U.S. tax system as of the date of expatriation. Unlike prior law, there is no longer a 10-year period after expatriation during which punitive tax and immigration rules apply.

Is Expatriation for You?

The decision to give up U.S. citizenship is a serious one. It also requires substantial advance planning, including the acquisition of a second passport, if you don't already have one.

It's a step you should take only after consulting with your family and professional advisors. But it's the only way that U.S. citizens and long-term residents can eliminate U.S. tax liability on their non-U.S. income, wherever they live. And it's a tax avoidance option that Congress may eventually eliminate altogether.

What It Really Costs to Expatriate

Ted Bauman, *Sovereign Investor Daily*, February 2015

How much is it worth these days NOT to be a U.S. citizen? Quite a lot, apparently.

As an undergraduate in Economics 101, I was taught that supply and demand curves intersect at the "market-clearing price." That's where the number of buyers equals the amount of a product that sellers can profitably supply. Raise the price, though, and there are usually fewer buyers at the market-clearing point — only those to whom the product is worth a great deal.

What does it mean when the price of a product goes up by 422%, but the number of buyers *triples*? It means that product has suddenly become *a lot* more valuable to those people.

And that's exactly what's happened in the "market" to expatriate from the U.S. ...

Scrambling for the Exits

U.S. citizens can legally expatriate, a process of legally ending their citizenship.

Expatriation is formally known as "renunciation." You fill out a form. A State Department official subjects you to two interviews similar to those "retention specialists" who try to convince you not to cancel your cable contract. You settle accounts with the IRS, hand over your passport and leave. The next time you visit the U.S., you'll need a visa (which in some cases, isn't granted).

In 2014, the State Department raised its fee for this process from $450 to $2,350, claiming the previous price didn't fully capture the costs involved. But something funny happened. The number of citizens renouncing their citizenship more than *tripled* from the previous few reporting periods.

That suggests that the intrinsic value of ceasing to be a U.S. citizen has skyrocketed, enough that people are willing to pay a lot more to do it.

The real cost to expatriate, however, can be much higher than the State Department fee.

What You'll Pay

Uncle Sam will be sorry to see you go. So sorry, in fact, that he'll want to keep a part of you for himself.

To renounce U.S. citizenship, you must prove five years of U.S. tax compliance — all returns submitted and taxes paid.

But if you have a net worth greater than $2 million or an average annual net income tax for the five previous years of $157,000 or more (that's tax, not income), you'll pay an exit tax. It's levied at the prevailing capital gains rate, and calculated as if you sold your property the day before you cease to be a citizen, even if you don't. (Fortunately, the first $680,000 of these theoretical "capital gains" is exempted from the exit tax.)

On top of the exit tax, anyone to whom you give or bequeath any of your U.S. assets must pay tax at the prevailing gift/estate tax rate (they were unified under the American Taxpayer Relief Act of 2012). You can take the annual gift/estate tax exclusion ($14,000 for 2015), but the lifetime federal estate and gift tax exemptions ($10.9 million) won't apply.

Let's say you want to give $100,000 to your U.S. citizen child at or after your expatriation. The kid would have to pay $34,400 of your gift in taxes to the IRS (($100,000 – $14,000) X .40). Normally, there wouldn't be any tax at all unless you exceeded your lifetime limit, and even then, the tax would be less — and you'd pay it, not your child.

Even on the Way Out, You'll Need an Attorney

The U.S. has more lawyers per 100,000 persons than any other country on the planet. From birth to death, we rely on them to navigate the perilous waters of both private and public regulation and litigation. Failing to use an attorney can cost you, either by failing to comply with little-known rules or by failing to take advantage of similarly hidden opportunities.

Expatriation is no exception. If you ever decide that you want to take this step, you will need a good attorney who specializes in these matters. For example, the calculation of your exit tax will involve applying short-term capital gains rates to some assets and long-term rates to others. And there are ways to reduce gift and estate taxes, too.

There are plenty of reasons to expatriate in addition to the outrageous U.S. tax system. Over the last several years, we've watched the decimation of our privacy, the reduction of our civil liberties, the militarization of our police forces and the looming threat of a wealth confiscation as our country wallows in debt. Whatever yours might be, if and when you do, make sure you get help from the experts, such as those on our *Offshore Confidential* "Rolodex".

You'll be glad you did.

WHAT IS "ECONOMIC CITIZENSHIP?"
Mark Nestmann, *The Sovereign Individual*, November 2002

Economic citizenship is the granting of citizenship by a sovereign government in exchange for a financial contribution to that government.

The Sovereign Society recommends economic citizenship only from countries where a statute clearly authorizes it to be granted. "Unofficial" documents purchased from corrupt government officials can lead to the arrest and incarceration of the purchaser.

Why seek economic citizenship? A second nationality is a hedge investment against the unknown events of tomorrow. If you are a citizen of a currently or potentially politically unstable country, your physical survival and self-preservation may require you to leave, quickly.

In addition, any number of unanticipated events could make it necessary for you to leave your home country, including divorce, government corruption, violence, etc. Your passport is the property of your government and a local court could order you to relinquish it. And in many countries, a court is the last place to expect justice!

A second nationality gives you the right to reside in the country granting it. The concept of residence is critical in international tax planning, and in most cases, permanent residency in that country is sufficient to eliminate income and capital gains tax liabilities at "home." (U.S. citizens, no matter where they live, must take the additional step of relinquishing their citizenship to avoid future liability for U.S. taxes.)

You may be able to acquire a second citizenship based on your ancestry, your marriage to a citizen of that country or your religious affiliation. If you qualify under any of these grounds, you should take advantage of them.

If you don't qualify on any of these grounds, your options are limited to obtaining citizenship through prolonged residency (anywhere from 2-10 years) or purchasing economic citizenship.

In recent years, economic citizenship programs have come under heavy criticism. There have been allegations that documents are being sold to international organized crime figures and terrorists. These allegations are false. In the surviving programs (Dominica and St. Kitts & Nevis), applicants must pass through a rigorous screening process involving checks with Interpol and other agencies before citizenship is granted.

ECONOMIC CITIZENSHIP CHOICES

Ted Bauman, *Offshore Confidential*, December 2014

He smiled at me. I couldn't believe it. In all my travels, I'd never had a customs agent actually smile at me.

I'd just arrived on the Caribbean island of Dominica (not the Spanish speaking Dominican Republic, with which it is often confused). It was nearly midnight.

My flight from San Juan had been delayed by six hours, and neither the customs agent nor I wanted to be where we were right about then.

To top it off, it was raining, and I had dripped water onto his precious customs forms.

But still, he smiled at me ... when I told him I was there to learn more about "economic citizenship" — the process of acquiring Dominica citizenship and a passport by investing on the island, via its government.

"Sir, if you want to live here, you are most welcome," the agent said. "But I hope you brought a dry checkbook."

His was just the first of many smiling, welcoming faces I encountered on the tropical paradise that is Dominica.

Search for an Affordable Economic Citizenship

Economic citizenship offers a quick and easy way to acquire a second citizenship through an investment without requiring a lengthy residence. Dominica continues to be one of the best on the market, which is why I went there to see if for myself.

Dominica offers you a perfectly legitimate, cost-effective and easily-obtained second citizenship solution that's guaranteed to give you more in the future ... *even more than it does now, which is a lot* ... one that's ideal for us Americans. But I predict that this citizenship is about to become more expensive ... *a lot more.*

Dominica has long been the cheapest route to a Caribbean passport. But that is going to change soon — a year, maybe 18 months. Right now, a couple can obtain valuable Dominica passports for less than $200,000, including government and other fees. That's less than half the cost of any of the other options in the region.

But Dominica is about to achieve something that will make its passports much more valuable, as I'll explain below. This will change the game for Dominica. The price of its passport will go up accordingly — probably at least by double, maybe more.

And at the same time, that passport will be instantly more desirable.

Your Passport to Freedom ... Or Out of Disaster

Many people are conditioned to see second passports as something for crooks, thanks to the steady drumbeat of negativity from the U.S. government and the mainstream media. But they're not. I have one, and so do many of my friends and colleagues.

A second passport — a second citizenship — is one of the most important tools in any sovereign person's toolkit.

Unlike *permanent residence* in another country, a second citizenship confers the right of residence as well as all the protections of being subject to a foreign government. Nation-states are usually happy to extradite a permanent resident, for example, but not one of their own citizens.

That's an extreme example of the benefit of a second passport, one you're unlikely to ever need. But most people want second passports for more mundane reasons.

In fact, the demand side of the global market for second passports is made up of perfectly innocent people who happen to come from countries where citizens have a hard time traveling because of the visa requirements of other countries.

Seekers of second passports really want to be able to use that document to get around the visa requirements imposed on their compatriots ... especially for places like Europe's Schengen Area, a 23-country region where visitors can cross international borders without clearing customs, once they have been admitted to one of the member countries.

Americans also have good reason to want a second passport. In today's uncertain times, we never know when the powder keg that's the U.S. is going to blow. Wealth confiscation, political gridlock, rioting in the streets ... a second passport gives you an escape route to a friendlier clime.

And if and when the time comes, a second passport allows you to do what some people regard as unthinkable ... give up your U.S. citizenship, as tens of thousands are doing to avoid insanities such as the Foreign Account Tax Compliance Act (FATCA).

Why I Like the Caribbean Option

Some of the island nations of the Caribbean — Dominica, St. Kitts and Nevis, Antigua and Barbuda and Grenada — allow foreigners to become citizens through investment, also known as "economic citizenship." And when compared to other countries that offer this, such as Malta, Cyprus or Bulgaria, the West Indian countries have several distinct advantages.

They're close to the U.S., and thus to friends and family — if you ever decide to live there. The residents speak English and have familiar customs and culture. Economic citizens of these countries are generally accepted by the community of nations as perfectly legitimate.

These island countries are also part of the British Commonwealth of Nations, which means their citizens have certain visa rights to the rest of the Commonwealth ... such as the right to ask for diplomatic protection from the embassy of any Commonwealth country.

And citizenship there is faster and less expensive to obtain than in other countries in Europe and Latin America. We're talking several hundred thousand dollars as opposed to millions, and months rather than years.

It's true that prospective citizens from far-off lands, such as Russia and China, sometimes struggle with the logistics involved in obtaining citizenship on these West Indian islands. Over tea and biscuits, the Senior Inspector of Dominica's Economic Citizenship Unit told me stories of Chinese investors who were prepared to fly the entire government interview panel to China at their own expense to avoid having to come to Roseau, the capital, in person.

But for Americans, it's no obstacle at all ... just a few hours on a plane, and you're there, interviewed and on your way home.

I traveled to the Caribbean to get the inside story on this unique opportunity, and I'm going to tell you straight out: if you think you will want to purchase a second passport someday, the time to acquire one is now.

The Market is Heating Up

Let's put Dominica's citizenship-by-investment program in context, globally and regionally.

Citizenship by investment isn't the same as naturalization, where you get citizenship after a certain period as a permanent resident. And it's not the same as citizenship by marriage, ancestry or other family ties. It's an immediate grant of citizenship in exchange for some financial, investment, or other consideration to the host government.

Besides the West Indian island states I'm discussing here, a handful of other countries offer "instant" economic citizenship: Austria, Bulgaria, Malta, Macedonia and Cyprus. All other countries require a lengthy period of permanent residence first. (Many countries — including the U.S. — grant immediate permanent residence based on investment, but almost all of them require lengthy waits before giving citizenship and a passport.)

There's nothing wrong with obtaining citizenship by investment. It's a legitimate way to obtain a second passport. The dynamics of the market are tricky these days, however. That's due to the small proportion of bad eggs (think terrorists or criminals) who try to get second passports, as well as the increasing paranoia and greed of the tax-hungry developed countries, who hate the idea of people getting freedom somewhere else.

The locals I spoke to on Dominica, such as my driver Manny also worry about "bad guys" getting passports, although no one has ever seen any of them on Dominica itself. And government officials involved in the process swear that nobody wants to avoid granting citizenship to troublemakers more than they do.

Countries that offer economic citizenship don't release the number of applicants or approval rates, but informed observers such as Chris Willis of Henley and Partners in Basseterre, St. Kitts, estimate that between 15,000 and 20,000 people apply annually for second passports globally. Probably 15% to 20% of those applicants fail. So somewhere between 12,000 and 17,000 individuals — many with spouses and family members — obtain a second passport each year.

Dominica's program is one of the few where it's possible to estimate the numbers of economic citizens.

Bernard Wiltshire, a former Dominica attorney general, estimates there were around 3,000 economic citizens when he left government 10 years ago. The current attorney general, Levi Peter, approximates that Dominica earns about US$22 million a year from the program. That suggests about 200 new citizens a year. All things considered, there are probably about 4,500 to 5,000 purchased Dominica passports out there.

But second passports are becoming more difficult to acquire — not necessarily on Dominica, but all over.

Consider Malta. Last year, I wrote about the Mediterranean island nation's new product, which offers unrestricted access to the European Union — not just visa-free Schengen travel, but all the rights of residence and economic activity that go with EU citizenship. That made it pricey, but the people who signed up for it don't mind: mainly super-wealthy non-Europeans, including sports and Formula One auto racing stars.

But the EU in Brussels pushed back at the Maltese government in Valletta, forcing it to limit the number of new citizenships and to impose a stringent residence requirement. Something similar happened to Cyprus a few years ago as well. There were plenty of willing buyers, and Malta was willing to grant more citizenships, but other countries had an interest in the matter too, since they have to let Maltese passport holders into their own countries without visas.

The ripples of global scrutiny have also hit the Caribbean. In April, the U.S. Treasury Department's Financial Intelligence Unit (FinCen) issued an "advisory" to U.S. banks recommending extra scrutiny of St. Kitts and Nevis passport holders. And in October, Antigua and Barbuda announced a "limited time offer" on their program, lopping $50,000 off the base price and reducing the required residence period to five days in five years. Sales were evidently too slow at the previous price point.

I don't cite these examples to scare you off economic citizenship. I share them to illustrate the paradox at its heart: even though demand for second passports is rising, purveyors of citizenship-by-investment programs are finding it harder to market them ... because deep-pocketed prospective citizens aren't the only stakeholders they have to please. Foreign governments want to have their say too. And foreign governments are becoming more particular about how these programs operate.

Assessing Economic Citizenship

The little boy marched right up to me and said: "Sir, welcome to Dominica."

He was about four feet tall, with a blue school blazer and a straw boater hat. I met him on a side street in the capital, Roseau. He had spotted me coming down the street, and made a beeline toward me, ignoring the many tourists from the cruise ship at the quay. Clearly he had some criteria in mind when greeting foreigners ... he was selective. He got a dollar for his investment in me.

I'm selective too. And when it comes to economic citizenship, I have my criteria. Legitimacy. Reliability. Ease of application combined with strict due diligence to weed out the bad apples. Price. No strings attached, like mandatory or "approved" real estate investments. And for me ... but not for everyone ... a place I'd actually like to live someday, if it came right down to it.

That last point is important, and I'll admit it probably colors my thinking about Dominica, since I really like the place. I'm a sucker for reggae music, coconut palms, pastel-colored houses and turquoise blue seas.

But those aren't the criteria everyone uses. Purchasing a second passport is usually about a passport, not physical residence. "Few, if any, of the people who want to apply are planning on living in those countries," says Oleg Lemeshko of Elma Global, which helps Russians obtain economic citizenship. "Most of the clients simply wish to have the ability to travel visa free."

Mr. Lloyd Garraway, a businessman I met on Dominica who was familiar with the internal politics of economic citizenship, expressed the same view. "We don't see much of them (passport-seekers) except at the government interviews. That's fine with us, but they don't know what they're missing."

I agree with him wholeheartedly.

For many Americans, too, the initial impulse to invest in a second citizenship is also about the passport: we want to protect the freedoms and privacy that we've come to expect from the United States, but whose future is increasingly uncertain. I suspect that many Americans are more interested in the potential to live in a tropical paradise than say, Russians or Chinese. Now, the criteria you'd use to assess a *permanent residence* program — say, in Panama, or Uruguay — are different from those you'd use for a second citizenship. Residence is about lifestyle, culture, banking, distance from "home" and other issues related to living in the place.

For many potential citizens, on the other hand, citizenship by investment is about the cost, both in cash and in transactional hassle, of obtaining a passport. They want to do it discreetly; from the place they live now. They don't want to have to buy real estate they'll never use. They don't want to have to live in a place to qualify for its passport — many don't even want to travel there at all, ever.

But there's the paradox: the easier it is to get a passport at a distance, sight unseen, the more potential problems you're likely to have down the road with its legitimacy. That leads to some key differences in the way different countries design and operate their programs.

Citizen Options in the Caribbean

You want to know which of the programs represent the best value for your money. So a few weeks back, I did what I'm here to do ... I flew to the region to check out the various West Indian programs on your behalf. Here's what I found:

The Old Boy on the Block ... St. Kitts & Nevis

St. Kitts and Nevis is the Western Hemisphere's smallest nation, with about 35,000 inhabitants. It's an English-speaking member of the British Commonwealth of Nations, which means its citizens have certain visa rights to the rest of the Commonwealth, as well as the right to ask for diplomatic protection from the embassy of any Commonwealth country. (That applies to all the Caribbean options I'm discussing here, in fact.)

St. Kitts has the oldest economic citizenship program in the world. Established in 1984, it lets a foreigner qualify for citizenship in St. Kitts in one of two ways: with a donation to a government fund for retired sugar workers — a deal made when the government closed down the sugar industry at about that time — or with a real estate investment in an "approved" project.

A Dubai-based company is currently building a resort community on St. Kitts with a 200-room hotel, yacht marina and condominium units. Investors in the project get property and citizenship at the same time. By all accounts it will be a major boost to the island's economy. But it's pricey. And it may restrict your options if you ever decide to visit or live on the islands, because you are forced to invest in the approved project.

I spoke to Chris Willis of international migration specialists Henley and Partners, who is based in Basseterre, St. Kitts' capital. He was candid about some issues with the St. Kitts program. The quality of government administration of the Economic Citizenship Unit leaves much to be desired, he told me, contributing not only to lengthy waiting periods, but also due diligence problems. He speculated that this is why the country got a slap on the wrist from the U.S. Treasury Department a few months back.

Now, that track record doesn't threaten St. Kitts' citizenship-by-investment program, but it did convince me to keep looking.

- **Cost for individual:** $250,000 contribution to sugar fund or $400,000 investment in real estate; approximately $65,000 processing and due diligence fees; $25,000 agency fees
- **Residence requirement:** None
- **Processing time:** 6-18 months

Living the High Life: Antigua & Barbuda

Frustrated with problems in St. Kitts, Henley and Partners has turned much of its attention to a new economic citizenship program a few miles to the east. Antigua, home to about 87,000 people and also an English-speaking Commonwealth nation, is considered one of the most beautiful places in the world. Tourism generates around 60% of the island's income.

Owing to its popularity with tourists, Antigua is significantly more developed than either Dominica or St. Kitts, with more miles of paved roads, more hotels and restaurants, as well as a vibrant nightlife. Many famous celebrities (such as Eric Clapton and Oprah) have bought holiday homes on this charming island. Antiguans tend to see themselves as a cut above the rest of the West Indies.

Passing through the areas on my travels, I spent a couple of hours in the island's main airport. It was definitely the snazziest of those I saw on my travels. High-end goods from all over the world were on sale at hefty mark-ups. Sophisticated craft merchants offered high-quality local stuff I didn't see anywhere else. Thankfully, however, the beer was as cheap and tasty as it seems to be all over the West Indies.

Perhaps for these reasons, Antigua's economic citizenship offering, launched late last year, was initially priced significantly higher than the other islands. But recently announced changes to the program suggest that it was still too expensive for the market. The price of a passport was slashed by $50,000 two months ago, and government processing fees were reduced significantly. The residence requirement was reduced from 35 days to five days in the first five years after becoming a citizen.

Chris Willis of Henley and Partners is convinced that the upgraded Antigua program is a winner. Like St. Kitts, it offers packaged citizenship in conjunction with investment in approved resort projects.

But there are reasons to be wary of Antigua. The country got into trouble a while back when U.S. fraudster Allen Stanford got busted for a $7 billion Ponzi scheme operated from Antigua. Government officials were involved, and although they are now out of office, some stigma remains.

So I kept looking.

- **Cost for individual:** $400,000 investment in real estate; approximately $50,000 processing fees; $45,000 agency fees; due diligence varies

- **Residence requirement:** Five days in five years after obtaining citizenship
- **Processing time:** 6-12 months

Grenada: An Unspoiled Paradise

Some Americans will remember Grenada as the little island that Ronald Reagan invaded in 1983 to depose a "socialist" prime minister. Like its English-speaking Commonwealth neighbors to the north, Grenada is a West Indian nation (of 110,000) with few options for revenue. It is stunningly beautiful and much less developed than Antigua.

Grenada had a citizenship-by-investment program from 1995 until 2001, but it was suspended when it became "too risky" in the light of the 9/11 attacks. By all accounts, the program in those days was not well-regarded. P.T. Freeman, a former American and Dominican citizen who is also a citizen of the Dutch island of Aruba, told me about one incident when the Canadian government deported non-English speaking Chinese Grenada passport holders who arrived in Ottawa. The Canadians were not impressed, and imposed visa restrictions on the island.

Recently, Grenada's government announced a new economic citizenship program based on a single resort development, Mount Cinnamon. By buying shares in the company that plans to build and operate the hotel, you get citizenship as well as a dividend from any hotel operating profit.

The new Grenada offering is the brainchild of Mount Cinnamon's entrepreneur Peter de Savary, a controversial British real estate tycoon who is also Grenada's "Ambassador for External Investment."

His partner is Michelle Emmanuel-Steele, the wife of Grenada's Foreign Affairs Minister, Nicholas Steele.

This isn't de Savary's first attempt to market a development scheme in Grenada. In March, he lost a $1 million court case in Grenada's High Court to a British couple who had invested in a failed "hotel scheme" in which de Savary testified was not supposed to be a hotel, even though all the documentation specified otherwise.

I'm not 100% happy with that, and neither should you be. So I kept looking.

- Cost for individual: $311,750 investment in real estate; agency fees unknown.
- Residence requirement: None
- Processing time: claim 60 days, but currently unknown

Dominica: Where Everyone is a Neighbor

Manny could drive this route with his eyes closed, I thought to myself. I looked over at him just to make sure he wasn't.

I sat in a small metal box grinding its way across the lush tropical hills of Dominica. It was close to midnight, humid but pleasantly cool. Manny was at the wheel of his taxi. We had picked up a worker from the airport on her way home as well. The moon was waning, but still close to full. Periodically we crossed a stream that reflected the moonlight like pearls bouncing lightly on a trampoline.

Suddenly, we came out into the open: the road briefly hugged the beach, the vast Atlantic Ocean to our left. The moonlight on the ocean's surface was almost blinding. Over the sound of Manny's reggae CD, I could hear the surf crashing into the rocks just below the road to our left. I smelled the tang of seaweed and salt, so familiar to me from my second home on the beach in Cape Town. A little further on, we passed a small fishing harbor where sharp-prowed open boats bobbed in the light swell.

I was in heaven.

Not to be confused with the Spanish-speaking Dominican Republic, Dominica is an English-speaking Commonwealth nation of 74,000 at the junction of the Leeward and Windward island chains. It's geographically rugged and has few beaches. But it's extremely popular with adventure and eco-tourists, and cruise ships visit almost daily.

It also has one of the longest-lived populations on the planet, right up there with Okinawa and some of the Greek islands. Apparently the local diet, made up almost entirely of fresh produce, goat and seafood, is really good for you.

Dominica's economic citizenship program began in 1993 by act of Parliament under authority granted by the island's constitution. At $100,000 per person, it's long been the least expensive Caribbean passport — but also the only one that requires a personal interview on the island. It doesn't require any actual residence on the island, either before or after application. There is no real estate requirement, making Dominica the only Caribbean program without one.

I tracked down a local notable who had served on Dominica's immigration review panel in years past. His office was in a tidy old house in Roseau, overlooking the narrow, twisting streets of the town's French Quarter, dating to the 17th century. Windsor Park Stadium, where I'd seen West Indies play cricket dozens of times on TV, was right across the street. I could see the Chinese lettering on the plaque commemorating its construction with a $17 million "gift" from the People's Republic in 2007.

Mr. Bardouille (he prefers that I not use his first name) gave me an insider's view of the Dominica selection process. "Unlike the other islands," he told me, "Dominica asks 'why do you want this?' Are they running from something? We care because we love our island. I'm not saying the others don't, but we prefer to look an applicant right in the eye and get a close view of them. We're a small country so if a new citizen decide to live here, we want them to be the sort of people we'd like as neighbors."

He explained to me that Dominica has a higher rejection rate for economic citizenship applications than the other islands. That's due in part to the "eyeballing" — as he called the mandatory on-island interview — but also because Dominica is a feisty democracy with a vocal opposition party. Although he's confident the United Worker's Party would never cancel the program if they gained power (an election is scheduled for December 8), they keep a close eye on it to keep the incumbent Labour Party government honest. "The Chinese stadium you're looking at is a good example" he explained. Although it was all above board, that hasn't stopped the opposition from clobbering the government with allegations, just to keep the people's eyes open."

I reflected on Mr. Bardouille's words. I recalled something that P.T. Freeman, who is married to a onetime speaker of Dominica's small parliament, had told me before I left for the Caribbean:

"You clearly understand the global dynamics of economic citizenship," he said. "But the key factor that most people don't understand is the internal politics of the islands. In some cases economic citizenship programs have become corrupted by politicians, but the opposition parties on the islands don't let it get out of hand. They self-correct. Opposition politicians beat the incumbents over the head with allegations of impropriety. It embarrasses them. On Dominica especially, you can basically meet the Prime Minster at a restaurant and walk up to his table and tell him what for. It matters to him what people think because they're his neighbors. Of all the islands, Dominica is the one that keeps best to the straight and narrow."

Bingo. That's what I'd been looking for. A Caribbean economic citizenship program that would last ... because the good citizens of the country were firmly in charge, not foreign developers or less-than-competent bureaucrats.

- **Cost for individual:** $100,000 investment in real estate; $1,765 processing fees; $20,000 agency fees; due diligence varies
- **Residence requirement:** None
- **Processing time:** 4-12 months

Change is Coming

My call for you is straightforward.

If you think you'd like to purchase a second passport, apply for Dominica economic citizenship without delay. A combination of external and internal forces is going to change the cost and value of the Nature Island's passport soon ... dramatically.

Antigua, St. Kitts and Grenada all have economic citizenship programs based on a new hybrid model.

They are moving their programs away from "high-volume, low-margin" sales to non-residents, and toward deals that package citizenship with investment participation in (hopefully) job-creating real-estate/resort projects.

Increasingly, prospective citizens of these islands will be required to invest in a packaged deal that will result in both a passport and local property ownership, as in St. Kitts and Grenada. Prices will be much higher — since you're investing in a resort project, not just obtaining citizenship.

Call it timeshare with a passport.

The days of buying a passport from afar via middlemen in Moscow or Dubai will be over, and a small number of big players will put together passport/investment deals on behalf of island governments.

This will allow the islands to recruit "higher-quality" citizens with less potential "baggage," protecting their visa-free access to Schengen and beyond. It will create a stream of foreign investment funding into concrete projects that could well create sustainable jobs, fending off local suspicions that economic citizenship is all about envelopes stuffed with cash passed to crooked politicians under the table. And it will create an incentive for developers and other offshore entities to get directly involved in managing citizenship programs, and help to spread the administrative burden over multiple stakeholders.

Within this new paradigm, the competition is heating up. For example, Antigua and Barbuda just reduced its on-island residence requirement from 35 days to five days in the first five years after becoming a citizen. None of the other islands require any at all. The only island that continues to require a personal interview for all applicants is Dominica. The rest grant passports sight unseen.

But that tactic, driven by the demand side of the market, directly contradicts the other constituency these countries have to satisfy: the rest of the world. The more obviously a country's passport is just a commodity for sale, the less regard it receives from other governments. They can do as much arm's length due diligence as they like, but purveyors of passports who waive personal interviews and residence requirements create the risk that passport holders will lose visa-free access to places such as the Schengen area of Europe ... the Holy Grail of economic citizenship.

That's why I like Dominica's offering, and predict that it will outlast all the others. But the changes sweeping the Caribbean programs are going to affect Dominica as well.

During my stay in Dominica, a lively debate raged in local online chat forums between supporters of the incumbent Dominica Labour Party (nominally social democratic) and the opposition United Workers' Party (centrist). Both parties are dominated by powerful old island families and hardly populist. But Labour, which has ruled since 2000, was in charge when the Chinese made their loans and gifts, and when the global economy tanked in 2008.

According to the dynamic Bardouille, P.T. Freeman and others had explained to me, the UWP has made reforming the citizenship program part of its election platform. Anticipating this, Labour ministers and the PM have been hinting that they, too, have changes in mind. No matter what the outcome of the election on December 8, everybody I spoke to in Dominica expects things to change … soon.

And of course there's the little matter of full visa-free access to the Schengen area for Dominica passport holders. Dominica is on the list of countries approved by the European commission for visa-free access starting in 2015. Even if Dominica doesn't adopt an investment-based passport program, the price *will go* up because of Schengen access.

So my advice is this: if you want to obtain the world's least-expensive respectable passport — one that will also give you visa-free access to the entire EU as well as Commonwealth countries such as Singapore and Hong Kong — you have about six to 18 months to do it.

How to Do It

Applying for economic citizenship in Dominica is straightforward. At the end of this report you will find links to several agencies authorized to facilitate the process for you. You are required to use such services, and I strongly recommend The Nestmann Group for Americans, because they are based here in the U.S.

There are four "packages" for Dominica:

Package A: Single Applicant	A non-refundable investment of $100,000.00
Package B: Family Application One (applicant and spouse)	A non-refundable investment of $175,000.00
Package C: Family Application Two (applicant plus spouse and two children below the age of 18)	A non-refundable investment of $200,000.00
Package D: Family Application Three (applicant plus spouse and more than two children below the age of 18)	A non-refundable investment of $200,000.00 and $50,000.00 for every additional person below the age of 18

There is also an application fee of $1,000, a processing fee of $200, a naturalization fee of $550 and a stamp fee of $15 — all per applicant.

Applicants must be over 21 years of age and of "outstanding character." Applicants must also have a basic knowledge of the English language.

The investment must be made upfront, by deposit into the National Commercial Bank of Dominica. If the application is withdrawn or rejected the applicant will be refunded, but if this is because of false information or declarations or forged or fraudulent documents, the money is forfeit. Processing and other fees are not refunded. Documentation required includes:

- An Application Form, in duplicate, for all persons.

- Two original personal references for the investor, spouse and any child over 18 years old.

- One original Professional reference for the investor, from someone who has been acquainted with the investor's work for at least three years.

- One original recommendation from the investor's banker. The investor must have been a client of the bank for at least two years.

- Original Letter of Employment for the investor, or most recent audited financial statement if self-employed. A detailed resume is required of all applicants who are working adults.

- Original affidavit by investor stating source of funds.

- Marriage certificate where applicable. If an applicant is divorced and has remarried, then a notarized copy of the Dissolution of the Marriage is required.

- A letter of application addressed to the "Honourable Minister responsible for Citizenship" stating the reason(s) for applying for economic citizenship.

- Original police clearance certificates or similar documents showing absence of a criminal record for all applicants sixteen years and over from country of birth, citizenship and residence (for six (6) months or more), including a set of fingerprints.

- Four certified passport size photos notarized on the reverse side.

- Birth certificate for all applicants.

- Notarized copies of University/College diplomas.

- Completed medical for all applicants.

- Notarized declaration that the information submitted is correct.

- Any other document deemed necessary by the Minister.

Processing of applications for Dominica economic citizenship can take as little as two months but as long as a year, depending on the frequency of meeting of the interview panel.

Economic Citizenship at a Glance

	Dominica	St. Kitts & Nevis	Antigua & Barbuda	Grenada
Fee (individual)	$100,000	$250,000	$200,000	n/a
Fee (couple)	$175,000	$300,000	$200,000	n/a
Real Estate Option	n/a	$400,000	$400,000	$311,750 (more for spouse)
Govt. Fees	Procedural fees of $1,765; due diligence fees $4,000	$50,000 for applicant, $25,000 for spouse; due diligence fees $15,000	$50,000 (investment option only)	Included for main applicant, $5,350 for spouse
Agency fees	$20,000	$25,000	$45,000, plus due diligence costs; $22,500 for fast-track service	Unknown
Residence Requirement	None	None	Five days over five years	None
Interview	Yes	No	No	No
Visa-free access	90 countries including U.K., Switzerland, Hong Kong, Singapore	120 countries including U.K., Schengen, Hong Kong, Singapore	139 countries including U.K., Canada, EU, Hong Kong, Singapore	110 countries including U.K., Schengen, Hong Kong, Singapore

Contacts

All the countries discussed in this report require that you use an accredited agency when applying for economic citizenship. Although there are many agents on the islands themselves, we recommend that you use one of two that we know and trust, particularly since they have experience with obtaining requisite documents for U.S. applicants. They are:

The Nestmann Group, Ltd.
2303 N. 44th St. #14-1025
Phoenix, Arizona 85008
Tel.: 602-688-7552
Email: service@nestmann.com
Web: www.nestmann.com

Henley and Partners
Sugar Bay Club
Zenway Boulevard
Frigate Bay
St Kitts, West Indies
Tel.: 869-465-6220
Fax: 869-465-6221
Web: https://www.henleyglobal.com

WHAT IT'S REALLY LIKE TO EXPATRIATE
Mark Nestmann, *The Sovereign Individual*, October 2009

There are a lot more former U.S. citizens than there once were. Americans fed up with paying tax — and with their government — are voting with their feet. And they're doing it in much greater numbers than ever before.

Why might you wish to give up your U.S. citizenship? Primarily, because doing so is the only way that you can eliminate your lifetime obligation to pay U.S. taxes, no matter where you live.

Expatriation is a major decision. It means, for instance, that you no longer have the automatic right to enter or live in the United States. You'll need to get a visa to do so, unless your non-U.S. passport qualifies you for visa-free entry. In all cases, the Department of Homeland Security can deny you re-entry to the United States, and is under no obligation to tell you why.

However, the actual process of expatriation isn't as arduous as you might think. You're likely to encounter bureaucratic incompetence, unexplained delays, and rampant stupidity. But giving up your U.S. nationality is a legal right; one that even the inane employees of the Department of State understand.

Here's one account my colleague Bob Bauman recently received from a now-former U.S. citizen on how the expatriation process really works:

> As you wrote, the first step is to find alternative citizenship. After attending a Sovereign Society meeting, I decided that my best bet was to gain citizenship in St. Kitts & Nevis by purchasing a property there for an amount over $350,000. Then, I paid another $50,000 for two additional family members to apply for citizenship. This whole process, including closing on the property, application, review of paperwork, citizenship, then waiting for issuance of the passport, took about nine months.
>
> After moving all of my assets whose title I could change or move offshore, I purchased a home and moved to Panama. Then it came time to surrender my citizenship. From everything I could find on-line or in any books, I was expecting the surrender process to be rather grueling, including meeting one-on-one with a consular official sitting me under a bright light, interrogating me about reasons and taxes, then almost beating me with a rubber hose. We are all aware of the onerous threats of what the IRS can do if we have the nerve to try to escape the plantation.
>
> Bob, I was absolutely dumbfounded at how EASY it really was. No problems, no questions about anything, they were simply willing to cut me free. I had thought I

wanted an attorney with me, so I would have some idea which questions I legally had to answer and which I could refuse to answer. It was just not necessary. I believe the IRS and the State Department tries to scare the hell out of us so we won't even try to surrender citizenship. The process is far different than I envisioned.

There are a total of five forms needed. All are available on-line on the State Department website. The numbers for these forms are DS-4079 through DS-4083. You complete these forms, and then take them along with your U.S. passport, birth certificate, Social Security card and new passport to the embassy. If you are smart, you will also bring a typed letter explaining your reasons for wanting to expatriate.

Do not say ANYTHING about taxes. My reasons were that I abhorred socialism, loved the Constitution, but was unbelievably sorry that we no longer followed it. Then a clerk will re-type all the forms. This took about two hours because of numerous typographical errors. It is important to proofread every answer and every single line. It took something like 10-12 different efforts to get all five forms finally completed correctly.

A consular representative then came to the window, asked for my U.S. passport, asked me if I was really the person who wanted to expatriate, and whether I understood the consequences. Then he signed a few papers, took my passport and said good-bye. That was it! Oh, he also told me I should contact the IRS to inform them of what I had done. He said I would receive my certificate of loss of nationality in about four months. He never asked me ANYTHING about taxes or finances.

After a follow-up call to the embassy four months later, I was told I could return and pick up my official certificate of loss of nationality. They returned my U.S. passport with holes punched in it. The next day I returned to the embassy to apply for a 10-year, unlimited visit VISA to come to the United States. It was approved the same day. I also applied for Social Security because I was now old enough to receive it. You do NOT surrender your right to Social Security benefits by expatriating.

I thought it might be helpful to you to know what they ACTUALLY do to those who wish to surrender citizenship. Regardless of how intimidating they want you to believe this process can be, at least in my case, NOTHING happened.

I am now a free, sovereign citizen of the world. St. Kitts & Nevis charges me zero income tax, zero capital gains tax, and zero death tax. I don't even have to file a tax return any longer for ANYONE. Panama leaves me alone, so long as I pay my property tax and sales tax, and the U.S. no longer "owns" me.

My St. Kitts & Nevis passport gets me almost anywhere in the world that I could have gone with my former U.S. passport. With my 10-year visa, I can come back to visit the U.S. whenever I want. Believe me, I don't want or need to come back very often, and there are lots of other nice places to see in this world. And, if we are both on the same plane hijacked by terrorists, they'll kill you long before me.

I have the very best of all worlds. I live virtually tax-free in a beautiful country. I actually have more freedom and liberty as a guest resident of Panama than I did as a citizen of the United States.

I simply don't understand why there are not MILLIONS of Americans giving up their citizenship. If only they knew how EASY it is, how practical it is and how much better for their financial health, there would be lines around the block at every U.S. embassy from those who realize there are better choices than remaining a U.S. citizen.

PRACTICAL QUESTIONS FOR ASPIRING EXPATRIATES
John Sturgeon, 1998 *The Sovereign A-Letter*

Here's a practical "how to" and "what to expect" test for those considering expatriation to a new country. It's not a course for the faint of heart. I recently spoke with a colleague who resides in a continental European nation. The economy there is in a shambles and many young people have decamped to other parts of the world to seek better prospects. My colleague said he too would leave but he noted that an expatriate needs three things:

1. The ability to speak the language of his intended country;
2. To be able to work or have another source of income there; and
3. To have full family support for the move.

For my friend, these were all reasons not to leave. In my own experience, these perceived problems are easily overcome.

The Language Barrier

Life is easier when you're fluent in the tongue of your future home country. But that should not present an insurmountable barrier. A great many people have managed to learn the rudiments of a new language relatively quickly. Younger people, particularly children, are capable of learning a language very quickly if motivated. They don't suffer from the "I can't do it" syndrome, a condition that generally afflicts adults.

Instead of seeing a new language as a barrier, take it as a chance to enhance options and opportunities available to you. Colleges in most countries hold night classes in a variety of languages. After a few weeks, you will be surprised how quickly you have acquired a working knowledge of a language that seemed impenetrable.

Alternatively, there are numerous language courses on the market cassettes and supplementary materials enabling you to study at your own pace, in the comfort of your own home, office or car. Shop around and find a course you like. But the best way to familiarize yourself with a new language is to immerse yourself in it on a daily basis. You can do that when you're in the country where the language is spoken.

The Means Barrier

Employment or an alternative source of income is obviously important. A move overseas doesn't stop the bills coming in even if the cost of living may be cheaper in your intended destination. This needn't present the creative and flexible individual with a problem.

I've been impressed by how many expatriates, regardless of their origin, live in every country of the world. More than likely a group of expatriates from your current country already resides where you are going. This might be an ideal market for your skills, products or services or a source of leads for new work. Alternatively, it may be possible to work at your current profession on a long-distance basis. Modern communications, transport systems and sophisticated computer software make it possible to live in one country, retain clients and contacts in your old country, while developing new customers all over the world. With a portable office consisting of a laptop, an internet connection and a telephone, you are ready. Consequently, expatriation needn't adversely affect earnings potential and with organization and effort it can be enhanced.

The Family Barrier

It is true that if your family is not supportive, finding happiness in your new home is unlikely.

Too many guides on expatriation fail to acknowledge family problems. They wrongly assume that expats seek a better place on their own or for their sole benefit. Many of those who move overseas do so because they want a better place for their family to grow and thrive. Obviously, you should include the whole family in the decision-making process.

The prospect of leaving friends, family and present lives behind induces a certain amount of hesitation regardless of where you plan to live. Advantages and disadvantages should be weighed by the whole family.

A Million Dollar Question

Perhaps the most important question you must ask yourself is what you are seeking by moving to another nation. Naturally, personal preferences play a role in deciding where and how you wish to live. If you want to get away from "civilization" (i.e. crowds) there is no point considering large cities that offer little elbow room.

I recommend you commit your thoughts to writing as a means of clarifying your goals. Never assume that people and things function in another country in same way they do at home. Local customs and attitudes develop over a long period. Make sure your religious views are tolerated in the new country. Remember you are the foreigner. Once you are there you will be expected to abide by local customs.

Go on a Fact-Finding Mission

Having narrowed your selection, you and your family should travel to your prospective country before you actually move there. You will soon learn whether that country is acceptable to you, or whether alternatives should be considered.

When you visit, don't stay in a big hotel that is part of an international chain. That won't provide an accurate picture of the country, its people or customs. Instead, stay in a small local hotel or bed and breakfast to learn about the locals, their food and habits.

While there, things you should investigate include:

- Availability of housing. Are there any restrictions on property ownership? Speak to lawyers experienced in real estate. They know the pitfalls and the best ways of getting things done.
- The infrastructure. How does it affect the way you intend to make a living?
- Schools for the children. Do they meet your expectations? Is alternative schooling available? Most schools are happy to allow an inspection.
- Medical and dentistry services. How do they measure up? As an ex-patriate will you get free care? Be sure you and your family will be adequately served.
- Are shopping and recreational facilities suitable and sufficient to your anticipated needs?
- Does the country really look and feel as you thought it would? Or has it engaged in clever self-promotion that fails to reflect reality?
- How do local people receive you? Do you feel comfortable around them?
- Are you free to practice your chosen religion or engage in activities you consider important?
- What level of government restriction will you have to overcome?
- How do you obtain a residence permit? What do you need to do?
- How long will the process take? What will it cost? Will you be able to obtain a work permit (restrictions will apply for your employment by others as well as for self-employment)?

- Will you be able to bring your household goods, cars, pets, etc. with you and, if so, under what conditions?
- Cost of living issues. How much will a tank of gas, food, local taxes, cable TV, postal stamps, telephone cost? Will you save as much as you anticipated or will moving overseas result in additional household expenses?

Armed with this information you will be able to base your eventual decision on cold, hard facts. It is not bad to be overly critical about what you find in your chosen country, but realize no place on earth is perfect in every detail. Are you willing or able to overlook imperfections in light of what the country has to offer? Moving abroad is difficult but worth pursuing to obtain the lifestyle and standard of living you want.

DIARY OF AN EXPATRIATE:
1) A SEARCH FOR SECURITY

Ted Bauman, *The Sovereign Investor Daily*, May 2014

The United States has seen an increase in expatriation, which isn't too surprising. The health of the United States continues to decay, with first-quarter GDP coming in at a pathetic 0.1%. The anemic "recovery" is flagging and there is little hope of improvement when you consider the mounting debt the government is accumulating.

Americans are at a crossroads.

You stay and turn a blind eye to the continued downward spiral of our country.

Or you begin to formulate your contingency plan to protect yourself and your family …

As we pick up Part 2 of Brad and his wife's three-part story, they've made the decision to look into moving overseas. Brad and his wife have traveled extensively over the years due to Brad's work, and feel a bit like vagabonds as they lived in several states across America. They like the challenge of trying a new place, but they realized that it would require proper research and planning on their part for it to be successful.

They started with the goal of finding a place where they would live at least part of the time as a second home. One particular priority was that they wanted to be able to attain a second citizenship from their new home.

As they began their research, they met with people from the governments of Australia, New Zealand and Canada. They also visited Panama, Costa Rica and

St. Kitts and Nevis. Also as part of their planning and research phase, they met with attorneys and bankers from each of those places.

Brad described this as critical "boots on the ground" research that was key to answering the question: "Can we actually do this?"

Just prior to flying out to St. Kitts and Nevis to file their paperwork for citizenship there, Brad received information from The Sovereign Society regarding a unique opportunity in Uruguay. Long-time followers of Bob Bauman and The Sovereign Society, Brad and his wife decided to wait until after they attended the Uruguay conference before making any final decisions about where they would establish their second home.

While staying in a vacation home in St. Kitts and Nevis, they contacted The Sovereign Society, where they received more information about expatriation as well as contact information for Juan Fischer, who is a managing partner for a law firm based in Uruguay. Brad was impressed with the amount of information Juan was able to send them, allowing them to learn a great deal about the country and the requirements for gaining citizenship.

Upon returning to the United States from their stay in St. Kitts, Brad and his wife began pulling together information so they could apply for Uruguayan residency. During that process, they contacted Carla Piaggio, who is the director of residency and relocation for the Fischer & Schickendantz law firm, as well as Sancho Santayana (for residential real estate) and Sebastian Da Silva (for agricultural investment real estate).

Brad found everyone he spoke with helpful and knowledgeable. When they flew to Uruguay to meet with Sancho to look at different homes around Uruguay, Brad admitted that their biggest problem was choosing which they liked the best — the house near the water or out in the country?

While the United States continued to struggle, business was booming in Uruguay. During their first visit in 2012, Brad reported that he saw no fewer than 24 condo high-rise buildings under construction. And with mortgages a rare thing in Uruguay, there is no threat of a housing sector bubble developing — a reassuring thing after watching most of the world suffer through one not so long ago.

Expatriation: The Final Decision

After gathering more information about expatriation, taxes, investment opportunities, Uruguay and attaining citizenship while at The Sovereign Society conference, Brad and his wife decided to purchase a house in Uruguay. They loved the idea that they would not only attain a second citizenship in Uruguay, but by spending nine to 10 months in Uruguay and the remainder of their time in the United States, they would be living in perpetual summer.

Upon returning to the United States, they put their house in Florida up for sale and began the process of downsizing so they could more easily complete the transition to living in two countries.

And how has life in Uruguay been for Brad and his wife?

Well, you'll just have to come back tomorrow for the conclusion to this three-part series on becoming an expatriate.

Diary of an Expatriate: 2) A New Home

Ted Bauman, *The Sovereign Investor Daily*, May 2014

An average person doesn't become an expatriate. They don't have second homes in foreign countries.

It's too hard.
Too dangerous.
Too expensive.

We've all heard these excuses — and maybe even made a few ourselves — when it comes to establishing residency in another country and becoming an expatriate. We hear that only the extremely wealthy and movie stars having homes in far-flung places around the globe.

But what about an average guy from Ohio who just wanted to feel safe again…?

This week, we've followed the story of Brad Little and his wife. They were average Americans who realized that they needed a second home in another country so that they could live where they felt safer and free of a government that was controlling too much of their personal lives. After a period in which they completed research on a number of different countries, searching of the one that would best meet their needs, they decided to settle in Uruguay.

How has it gone for them?

"Things couldn't be better! It's so beautiful here, and safe. Our lives have changed so much in the last year. We're freer … more alive than ever," Brad reported.

Brad and his wife purchased a nice home at a fair price just outside of Punta del Este, and marveled at how much simpler the paperwork process was than buying a home in the United States. In addition, every one of the experts that The Sovereign Society recommended to them held their hands through every step: finding the home, getting residency, even getting checkups at the doctor's office and opening bank accounts.

Crime is low in Uruguay. Brad never feels as if he must look over his shoulder, worry about getting robbed, and he isn't concerned about the local government invading his privacy and rights. In fact, he told me he accidentally left his wallet and passport in the car and returned later to find them exactly where they had been left — no damage done.

During their time in Uruguay, Brad and his wife have made some wonderful friends. They meet expats from all around the world, and it seems as if people are more than happy to stay in Uruguay once they've arrived.

They've also found many things to do. Uruguay has lovely beaches, fishing — particularly surf fishing — and long relaxing rides in the country along smooth roads. Picnicking, hiking and biking are popular, as well as multiple cultural events throughout the year. There are excellent restaurants and shopping. Brad and his wife enjoy visiting a huge open market on Sundays that allows you to purchase anything from fresh vegetables to a puppy. In addition, they discovered great quality supermarkets in Uruguay that are comparable to what you'd find in the United States.

When Brad and his wife moved to Uruguay they didn't speak Spanish, but they still managed to accomplish a great deal during their first four months of living there — begin the immigration process, buy a house, renovate it, and have household items shipped down to Uruguay. While English is taught in the schools, most don't have a need to practice it so most people don't speak English. However, they have been able to get by with their limited knowledge. In fact, they've met several expats who have lived in Uruguay for several years who don't speak the language and don't intend to learn.

But Brad and his wife plan to make a serious effort to learn. Brad said that you shouldn't be afraid to try to speak the local language. Most people appreciate your effort and know that you are trying.

Besides the difference in language, there are other things that require some mild adjustment. Brad joked that he is still getting accustomed to the idea that the month of May is now in autumn instead of spring.

An American Expatriate Settled in a New Home

Despite being in Uruguay rather than the United States, Brad and his wife have settled happily back into retired living. "Living here gives us a feeling of freedom and empowerment like we used to feel back home. I can't describe it in words. It's something you just have to experience for yourself ... Which is a lot easier to do than you think," Brad commented.

Brad Little proves that with the right planning and research, you can easily establish a second home outside the United States that will allow you to enjoy the life you want without worrying about the growing threat posed by the government.

Countries that Offer Quick Residence
Robert E. Bauman JD, *Offshore Confidential*, October 2011

To state the obvious, the United States of America is going in the wrong direction.

U.S. fiscal and monetary policies continue to destroy our wealth and undermine our dollar. And a country that was once the economic engine of the world is now the largest debtor in world history.

If you want real peace of mind and to ensure your economic survival, your only solution is to look elsewhere. And acquiring a second passport is a crucial step in achieving that end.

There are places in the world where the concepts of liberty and freedom still mean what they used to here at home. Places where taxes are lower and government interference is less… and where your "dream home" is more than just a comfortable house, but a place where you feel safe and insulated from the world's problems.

You never know where you may discover your next home. Just keep in mind that building a contingency plan takes time…

No doubt you have heard these old proverbs… *Patience is a virtue. Slow and steady wins the race. All good things come to those who wait.*

There are a lot of sayings that advise the benefits of taking our time and not being in such a rush. Yet we live in a "New York minute" world that demands instant gratification. Even when it comes to acquiring status as an official resident in another country or a legal second citizenship and passport, one of the first questions I'm asked is, "How long will this take?"

Most countries require five years on average of official residence in the country before you can even apply for citizenship. (The Principality of Andorra requires 20 years of prior residence, but at the moment they are considering reducing that to 10 years).

So for this issue of *Offshore Confidential*, I've compiled a list of countries that provide immediate residence that can lead to full citizenship. If you and your family want to escape the very real problems facing this country, you must start planning now.

But first things first…

CHAPTER TWO: SECOND PASSPORTS AND DUAL NATIONALITY

Who Qualifies to Become a Dual Citizen?

Legal grounds that may allow a person to have or acquire dual citizenship include:

- Birth within the borders of a nation's territory. The 14th Amendment to the U.S. Constitution, for example, grants citizenship to any child born within American territory, regardless of the citizenship of the parents.

- Descent from a foreign citizen parent or grandparent, making blood ancestry a basis.

- Marriage to a foreign citizen.

- Religion, as in Israel and its Law of Return for Jews.

- Formal naturalization, which is applying and qualifying for citizenship status. The process for receiving the privilege of naturalization varies among countries. Usually, a certain period of residence is required (e.g., five years in the U.S. and most other countries), plus good character and an absence of any criminal record, among other requirements.

In this report, I reveal three countries that offer expedited citizenship if you can prove ancestral ties, as well as five countries that allow quick residence and whose naturalization processes take five years or less.

Citizenship by Ancestry

The easiest and quickest way to acquire second citizenship is through bloodline.

This legal principle, known as jus sanguinis (Latin, "right of blood"), describes citizenship resulting from the nationality of one parent or from earlier ancestors, usually grandparents.

On the basis of blood ancestry several countries, notably Ireland, Italy and Poland, positively encourage Americans and others to sign up for their citizenship. None of these countries require you to live there after obtaining ancestral citizenship.

- **Ireland:** Citizenship is available to those with Irish parentage or ancestry. If you were born outside of Ireland and either your mother or father (or both) was an Irish citizen at the time of your birth, then you are entitled to Irish citizenship. The same applies if at least one grandparent actually was born in Ireland. An applicant must prove this claim of Irish descent by submitting an ancestor's official marriage and birth certificates.

With three photographs, proper proof of Irish ancestry and legal residence in the country where you make your application, a 10-year renewable Irish passport will be issued in due course bearing the stamp of Ireland and the European community.

Now, finding proof of Irish ancestry can be a problem since many church and court records were destroyed in the long running Irish independence struggle against the British. But Irish consulates and embassies are adept at verifying affidavits and genealogical research and there are online services that specialize in this research.

- **Italy:** If you are the child or grandchild of former Italian nationals, you can qualify for citizenship if you meet any of the following criteria:

  1. Your father was an Italian citizen at the time of your birth;

  2. Your mother was an Italian citizen at the time of your birth after January 1, 1948;

  3. Your father was not born in Italy, but your paternal grandfather was an Italian citizen at the time of your birth;

  4. You mother was not born in Italy, but for those born after January 1, 1948, your maternal grandfather was an Italian citizen at the time of your mother's birth.

- **Poland:** If your parents or grandparents were Polish citizens, you may be eligible to obtain Polish citizenship based on that relationship. Citizenship generally can be claimed only by descendants of Polish citizens who left Poland after the country became an independent state in 1918. There usually can be no break in Polish citizenship between the emigrant ancestor and the descendant, but that general rule is not absolute. Application for "Confirmation of Possession or Loss of Polish Citizenship" can be made through Polish embassies or consulates.

Become an Immediate Resident

Even without ancestral ties, as an American, you have a legal right to retain U.S. citizenship and also become a citizen of another country — and that "dual citizenship" status could change your life for the better.

Whether they're eager to work or retire abroad, to be free of confiscatory taxes or simply establish a second home, an increasing number of Americans is obtaining a second, foreign passport as "insurance" against the time when economic or political storms arrive.

But as I mentioned at the beginning of this report, becoming a citizen of another country takes time. The process for receiving the privilege of naturalization varies among countries.

Usually, a certain period of residence — the legal right to live in a particular place — is required before you can apply for full citizenship, plus good character and an absence of any criminal record, among other requirements.

In the following pages, you will find information on five countries that offer immediate residence, although the naturalization processes still require five years' residence in order to qualify for full citizenship.

Quick-Residence Haven #1: Dutch Caribbean Islands

Visa Program: Under 1956 treaty and local law
Cost: Island fees vary
Time required: 4 months after application
Result: temporary, permanent residence

The Dutch Caribbean Islands (formerly known as the Netherlands Antilles) is one of the best-kept secrets in the world of offshore residence and second passports. Not many Americans know that the Kingdom of the Netherlands (a.k.a. Holland) long had a six-island Dutch colonial possession in the eastern Caribbean off the northern coast of Latin America. These semi-independent tropical islands are still an autonomous part of the Netherlands.

The Dutch Caribbean islands are in two groups: ABC — Aruba, Bonaire, and Curaçao, off the Venezuelan coast — and SSS — Saint Eustatius, Saba and Saint Maarten, located southeast of the U.S. Virgin Islands and Puerto Rico. While still associated with the Netherlands, the former Netherlands Antilles as a confederation was dissolved as a unified political entity in 2008.

Each one of these islands has its own character… from bustling St. Maarten to sleepy Saba. On some of the islands, Dutch is widely spoken. On others, English as well as a regional language called "Papiamento" that mixes English, Spanish and Dutch is more common.

Special Treaty for Americans

As a place that U.S. citizens can gain quick official residence, these islands are unique. Upon arrival Americans are eligible for six months of temporary residence under the terms of a 1956 "Treaty of Friendship, Commerce and Navigation between the Kingdom of the Netherlands and the United States of America."

Some treaty provisions no longer apply to the Netherlands itself but still do apply to the Dutch Caribbean islands. In 2010, a Dutch court confirmed that the treaty guarantees U.S. citizens the same rights in the Dutch Caribbean islands as those enjoyed by European Dutch citizens, including the right to stay for a continuous initial six months in the Caribbean territories.

This is an important first step if you are a U.S. citizen who eventually wants to acquire Dutch citizenship and a passport. If you maintain legal residence on one of these islands, there's a big payoff after five years of continuous presence there.

You are then eligible to apply for citizenship and a passport from the Netherlands, a member of the European Union, with all the rights that entails, including full access to the 27 EU countries. You can live or work anywhere in the EU, and a Dutch passport gives you visa free travel to more than 120 countries, including Canada, Mexico and the United States.

And unless you choose to live in the Netherlands, you won't be subject to Dutch taxes — although, each of the Dutch Caribbean islands has their own tax system. (Americans continue to be liable for U.S. taxes without regard to where they live offshore.)

Nevertheless, for U.S. citizens considering expatriation, once you clear the hurdles, a Dutch passport provides a first-class alternative travel document that can be used anywhere in the world.

Step 1: Residence Permits

For Americans, Dutch Caribbean residence for more than six months requires application for a residence permit, either in person or through a local agent. Most permits are valid for only one year and must be renewed annually.

To qualify, you must demonstrate good health, good moral character, and financial self-sufficiency. Since most application forms are in Dutch, it's helpful to have assistance from a professional intermediary.

Step 2: Dutch Citizenship

To qualify for Dutch citizenship after five years of uninterrupted legal residence either in Holland or the Dutch Caribbean islands, the "Kingdom Act on Netherlands Nationality" requires a record of good conduct, and "substantial integration in the community."

If you'd like to pursue Dutch citizenship, you must act quickly. Proposals in the Dutch Parliament are pending that will extend the period of legal residence required before citizenship application from five to 10 years, and it could soon become the law. My contacts in the Netherlands say there is no guarantee that those with current official residence will be "grandfathered" under a new law.

And the requirement for "substantial integration in the community" now is being interpreted to mean an applicant must be proficient in the Dutch language, not an easy language to learn or speak. There is also a "naturalization test" in Dutch. Given the political mood in the Netherlands, it is likely that even more restrictive immigration changes will become law.

Contacts

The Nestmann Group is experienced in obtaining Dutch Caribbean residence permits and can assist you in choosing the most appropriate island for residence.

The Nestmann Group, Ltd.
2303 N. 44th St. #14-1025
Phoenix, AZ 85008
Tel.: 602-688-7552
E-mail: service@nestmann.com
Web: http://www.nestmann.com

Royal Netherlands Embassy
4200 Linnaean Avenue NW
Washington, D.C. 20008
Tel.: (202) 244-5300
Web: http://www.the-netherlands.org

Dutch Immigration & Naturalization Service (IND)
Immigratie- en Naturalisatiedienst
Klantinformatiecentrum
Postbus 287
7600 AG ALMELO
Web: https://www.ind.nl/EN

Quick Residence Haven #2: Republic of Panama

Visa Program: *Pensionado*
Cost: $3,000
Time required: 90 days
Result: Immediate residence
Other Visa Program: Immigrant, cost varies
Time required: 5 years of permanent residence
Result: Citizenship

For years, we've recommended Panama as one of the best offshore residential havens in the world for a second home or retirement.

Only hours by air from the United States, Panama offers a variety of lifestyles and geographic areas with a century-long history of working closely with Americans. Panama's real estate boom has cooled, but the current multi-billion-dollar expansion of the Panama Canal contributes to the country's continued growth.

Panama is a country the size of South Carolina with a population of about 3.4 million. When you think of Panama, you think of one of the great technical wonders of the world — the Panama Canal. Located in southern Central America, Panama is bordered by both the Caribbean Sea and the Pacific Ocean, situated with Colombia on the south and Costa Rica on the north. It enjoys a major world strategic position on the isthmus that forms the land bridge connecting North and South America, including the Panama Canal linking the Atlantic Ocean via the Caribbean Sea with the Pacific Ocean.

In recent decades the government of Panama deliberately has positioned the country as a first-class retirement haven, with some of the world's most appealing programs of special benefits for foreign residents and retirees. Panama also offers a variety of visas for investors, persons of high net worth, wealthy retirees, small business and agricultural business investors and entrepreneurs, and those who simply want to immigrate and become Panamanian citizens.

You must travel to Panama in order to obtain any of the available visas and be present for the application filing and again when your visa is issued to you. The Pensioner Visa (*pensionado*) requires about 90 days to be issued and others about five months on average. Time spent in Panama as a *pensionado* does not count towards citizenship.

If you obtain one of the other visas to reside in Panama, but wish to live overseas, it is recommended that you visit Panama at least once a year, although legally you may stay out of the country for up to two years and still be considered as a legal resident with time counting towards the five years.

Once you obtain any of these Panamanian visas, even if you decide to live in Panama permanently, you are required to obtain a "multiple entry permit" should it be necessary for you to travel often or unexpectedly. The permit for multiple-entry is valid for up to two years, and to avoid paperwork and bureaucratic hassles, don't ever let it expire while you are out of the country.

Panama truly does offer probably the best quick residence deal in the world today in its *pensionado* program. For $3,000, the benefits are incomparable. And living in Panama offers an extraordinary financial opportunity. Property prices are continuing to climb — but at a much slower pace and you still have a chance to buy at comparatively low prices. And Panama has a sensible territorial revenue system that taxes only income earned within the country; offshore income is tax exempt.

Immigrant Visas

Under all visa programs other than the *pensionado* visa, if you've lived in Panama for at least five years, have a command of the Spanish language, are knowledgeable of Panamanian history, then you can apply to become a citizen of Panama.

A child under age 7, born abroad and adopted by Panamanian nationals, doesn't need a naturalization certification. However, he must declare his intention to elect Panamanian nationality no later than his 19th birthday.

The immigrant visa is provisionally granted for the first year. At the end of one year, a petition for permanent residence must be filed. Once this is approved, a permanent residence permit and a Panamanian identification card (*cedula*) will be issued.

Five years after obtaining a permanent visa, the holder is eligible to apply for and receive fully Panamanian citizenship. This next part is important…

The Panamanian constitution and laws don't recognize a citizen's right to hold dual citizenship. If you want to become a Panamanian, in theory you must renounce your American or other citizenship.

That said, according to Rainelda Mata-Kelley JD, a member of The Sovereign Society Council of Experts and a leading citizenship attorney in Panama, the government only enforces this law in rare cases when citizenship status becomes an extradition issue. When a foreign citizen is naturalized as a Panamanian citizen, government officials don't insist on any formal renunciation of foreign citizenship. Nor do they ask that you surrender your non-Panama passport.

Err on the side of caution when you're making the decision to naturalize. Be 100% certain that you are prepared to renounce your current citizenship should the Panamanian government insist on it.

Contacts

Rainelda Mata-Kelly JD
Suite 406-407, Tower B, Torres de las Americas
Punta Pacifica, City of Panama
Tel.: (+507) 216-9299
Email: rmk@mata-kelly.com
Web: http://www.mata-kelly.com

Embassy of the Republic of Panama
2862 McGill Terrace NW
Washington, D.C. 20009
Tel.: (202) 483-1407
Email: info@embassyofpanama.org
Web: www.embassyofpanama.org

Quick Residence Haven #3: Belize

Visa Program: Permanent Residency
Cost: $1,000 per person
Time required: One full year living in Belize
Result: Citizenship after 5 years

Belize is the only English-speaking country in Central America. It borders on the Caribbean Sea, between Guatemala and Mexico. Its mixed population of about 321,000 includes descendants of native Mayans, Chinese, East Indians, and Caucasians.

Independent since 1981, its language came from its colonial days when it was called British Honduras. Situated south of Mexico and to the east of Guatemala, Belize is on the Caribbean seaboard. It has the largest barrier reef in the Western Hemisphere and great deep sea diving.

Inland, visitors and residents enjoy ecotourism in lush tropical rain forests and exploration of countless Mayan architectural sites and sacred caves, with many yet to be discovered.

To the east, there's a sprinkle of Caribbean tropical islands included within the nation's borders, providing access to sport fishing in the lagoons and open sea. A member of the British Commonwealth, Belize retains many of the colonial customs and features familiar in places such as the Cayman Islands and Bermuda.

In the September issue of *Offshore Confidential* I told you all about a tax-free residence program for retirees known as the "Qualified Retired Persons" (QRP) Program. QRP offers immediate official residence within a matter of a few months.

Similar to Panama's *pensionado* program, time spent in Belize under the QRP program does not count towards the five-year residence required for citizenship for which you can apply only if you have been a resident of Belize for five years.

In order to obtain residential status in Belize, you will need to apply for residency. To qualify as a continuing resident, you must reside in Belize for a year and can leave the country for no longer than two weeks at a time during that first year.

The application process is best done in person. Here is a list of documents you will need to provide:

- A police report from the police department where you have resided for more than six months.
- A health certificate including an AIDS test, which can be obtained from any of the local doctors.
- 3 passport pictures.
- A statement from your bank or financial institution, if you are not employed or retired.
- Birth certificates for minor children, marriage certificate/declaration of support etc.
- A work permit or Trade License, where applicable.

After you submit your application, you will likely hear back from the department in eight to 12 weeks.

Contacts

For information and application forms, contact:

CitiTrust International
Joy Godfrey, Managing Director
35 Barrack Road, Belize City, Belize
Tel.: + 501-223-3738
Email: joy@cititrustintl.biz
Web: http://www.cititrustintl.biz
CitiTrust is a professional firm assisting foreign QRP applicants.

Government of Belize
Belmopan City, Belize
Tel.: + 501-222-4620
Web: http://www.belize.gov.bz

Belize Tourism Board
P.O. Box 325, 64 Regent Street, Belize City, Belize
Tel.: + 501-227-2420
Toll-free: 1-800-624-0686
Email: info@travelbelize.org
Web: http://www.travelbelize.org
See also: http://www.belizeretirement.org

Quick Residence Haven #4: Oriental Republic of Uruguay

Residence & Citizenship Program: Authorized by law
Cost: Nominal government fees
Time required: One-year residence before citizenship application
Result: Permanent residence, citizenship after 3 or 5 years

I am not going to spend a lot of time on the details about Uruguay because I devoted an entire special *Offshore Confidential* report in May 2011 to this delightful jewel of a country. You can go back and read at your leisure about all that it has to offer.

Uruguay is high on my list of countries that grant quicker than usual (less than five years) citizenship for qualified applicants. Until now I have been telling you about countries that allow immediate or very short-term waiting periods to become official residents.

The average residence required for most countries is five years. In Uruguay, that citizenship waiting period can be cut to just three years — and immediate residence is also the rule.

Popular Residence

In recent years' residence applications have tripled. The Immigration Department, with this increased inflow of applications, has noted three things it wishes to avoid:

1. People from lower income countries that come with fraudulent "proofs" of income.
2. People with gaps in their police record information.
3. People who obtain residence to later "buy" an illegal Uruguayan passport

Immigration officials now require:

1. Better documentation of proof of ability for self-support which may need to be updated periodically to ensure proof has not changed. For most American and European applicants, this is not a problem since the income requirement is only US$500 to $650 per month.
2. That if a person spends three months in Mexico (for example) between leaving their home country and coming to Uruguay, a Mexican police record must be produced.
3. That applicants for residence established a bona fide address and spend time in the country.

Unfortunately, these tougher verification requirements and the increased numbers have slowed the application process. That does not affect applicants who, from the moment they apply, are legal "temporary residents" and are issued a temporary *cédula*, the national ID card.

Uruguay has no immigration quota and it does not discretionally reject applications. Those who meet the basic requirements are approved for residence as a matter of official policy.

Once you arrive, acquiring Uruguayan citizenship starts by filing a residency application.

Quicker Path to Citizenship

What makes Uruguay stand out as a faster-than-average citizenship country is that full citizenship can be granted in final form, on average, within three to five years — three years (for couples or families) or five years (for single persons).

Immediate residency is easy to obtain with three key proof requirements:

1. a birth certificate (authenticated and stamped by the Uruguayan Consulate in the country of birth);
2. a home and any intermediate country clean police record, and;

3. proof that one can support oneself financially during the year of the residency process (known as the "income requirement") showing an annual income of at least US$6,000.

To acquire residence, one must enter Uruguay as a tourist and then file a formal request at the Immigration Authority (DNM). Once a foreign person applies for residency, they can stay in Uruguay indefinitely. They also can request a national identification card, which allows travel without a passport to neighboring Argentina, Brazil, Chile and Paraguay, a real convenience because the high volume of traffic among these nations.

Five years after filing for residency (three years in the case of families), the foreign resident can apply for citizenship. At this point one must have established Uruguayan residence and have had a permanent connection with the country and not have been absent for more than six straight months during the three/five-year period. Uruguay does allow dual or multiple citizenships.

Deal for Retirees

A special law expedites citizenship for foreign retirees with an annual official government pension of US$18,000 or more. In addition to the pension, the applicant must also own real property in Uruguay valued at US$100,000 or more. Under Law 16,340 the document granted to foreigners resident in the country appears the same as the one issued to any citizen, but in fact it is only a "travel document," not a passport. It states on p. 7 (where "Observations" may be listed) that "this passport was granted to a Uruguayan Permanent Resident with (named country) nationality." The blank is filled in with the individual's actual national citizenship.

The immigration law states that residency is granted to those "who show intent to reside in Uruguay." The government has tightened considerably its requirement that foreigners applying for residence and/or citizenship actually spend time in the country while their application is pending.

Applicants must have an established address in Uruguay (rented or owned) that may be randomly verified by the Immigration Department and also must show significant time residing in Uruguay. This does not mean that an applicant cannot come and go, or spend several months outside of the country during the application process.

After permanent resident status is granted, there is no longer any requirement to reside in the country. Residence status is maintained so long as the applicant does not stay out of the country for more than three years. In the permanent resident later seeks citizenship, continued presence in the country is a requirement although a person may come and go.

Contacts

Juan Federico Fischer Esq.
Managing Partner, Fischer & Schickendantz
Rincón 487, Piso 4
Montevideo 11000, Uruguay
Tel.: (+598) 2915-7468
Email: jfischer@fs.com.uy or info@fs.com.uy
Web: www.fs.com.uy

Embassy of Uruguay
1913 I (Eye) Street NW
Washington, D.C. 20006
Tel.: (202) 331-1313
Email: uruwashi@uruwashi.org
Web: http://www.uruwashi.org

Quick Residence/Citizenship Haven #5: Republic of Paraguay

Residence & Citizenship Program: Authorized by law
Cost: Nominal government fees
Time required: Three-years residence before citizenship application
Result: Permanent residence, citizenship after 3 years

Paraguay is a country of fascinating contrasts. It's rustic and sophisticated. It's extremely poor and obscenely wealthy. It boasts exotic natural reserves and massive man-made dams. It is a place where horses and carts pull up by Mercedes Benz cars. The 6.4 million people who live here have an average annual income of only US$5,200.

This small, landlocked country in central South America is surrounded by Bolivia, Brazil and Argentina. The Paraguay River runs north/south through the country forming an excellent commercial trade route. The country's history is marked by numerous border wars with its neighbors with great loss of life. Military regimes and dictatorships have been a more recent facet. Since 1989, democratic elections have been held, but problems continue with periodic military coups.

Paraguay prides itself upon its independence from influence by foreign powers. Extradition demands aimed at a resident foreign national are commonly ignored if the person sought has curried favor with Paraguay's political establishment. Paraguay does not recognize tax or currency crimes and has a reputation as a haven for political and tax refugees.

Citizenship Requirements

Acquiring citizenship by naturalization is relatively easy and requires only three years' residence in the country. You will be considered for citizenship if you have ties to Paraguay and declare your intention to become a citizen. You must also be at least 18 years of age, have exhibited good conduct during the three-year residence and have continued gainful employment.

That short three-year residence requirement makes the country, like Uruguay, a real possibility for a quicker second citizenship. The residence process requires you to travel to Asuncion and submit an application in person. You may be required to open a local bank account with a minimum deposit as evidence of self-support. Usual approval time is said to be four months unless you pay a local well-connected attorney. Government officials are notorious for taking bribes that can expedite almost any pending official action, including residence and citizenship applications.

The Paraguayan Constitution is very liberal in granting rights to foreigners. It proclaims all inhabitants have the right to develop their personal inclinations, trade and business. Nationals and foreigners are equal before the law, without discrimination. There are also no restrictions on property ownership by foreign nationals.

After about 30 days of processing in Paraguay, a Certificate of Residence will be issued, including a *cédula* or identity card. After three years of residence, a resident foreign national qualifies for naturalization. Paraguayan passport holders benefit from the 1995 Mercosur Agreement, which allows free entry to other member states, currently Argentina, Brazil, Chile, and Uruguay.

A Word of Caution

What I described above are the legal routes to acquire citizenship in Paraguay. That observation is made with good reason. Some in the government of Paraguay may well have been the inventors of instant passports as an easy income source from foreign nationals seeking second passports.

It is an established fact that, in recent decades, large numbers of this nation's official passports were sold illegally. As a result, other nations' border officials look closely at North Americans or Europeans who speak no Spanish and travel using a Paraguayan passport.

It is alleged that illegal "official" passports have become more difficult to acquire and investigations into "irregularities in the issuance of passports" have been reported. Since the nation's passport must be renewed in person every two years at a Paraguayan Consulate, past issued passports are being scrutinized more carefully.

Contacts

Editor's Note: *To avoid direct entanglement with Paraguayan government officials or local professionals, an intermediary who knows the scene and the players in Asuncion, but who is somewhat removed, is a better agent if you are interested in arranging truly legal residence and citizenship at a minimum cost. For that reason, I recommend you employ Juan Fischer who has agreed to act in this capacity for you.*

Juan Federico Fischer Esq.
Managing Partner, Fischer & Schickendantz
Rincón 487, Piso 4
Montevideo 11000, Uruguay
Tel.: (+598) 2915-7468
Email: jfischer@fs.com.uy or info@fs.com.uy
Web: www.fs.com.uy

Embassy of Paraguay
2400 Massachusetts Avenue NW
Washington, D.C. 20008
Tel.: (202) 483-6960
Email: secretaria@embaparusa.gov.py
Web: http://paraguay.usembassy.gov

THE GREAT IRISH OPPORTUNITY

Robert E. Bauman JD, *Offshore Confidential*, April 2012

A few years ago, the booming Irish economy was the envy of Europe. It earned the nickname "the Celtic Tiger" — and for good reason.

I can reveal that within this current Irish economic crisis there lies an opportunity for you — not only to profit financially, but to become a resident and eventually a citizen of a nation that has proven historically it has the resilience and resources for a comeback.

Forget the clichés about shamrocks, shillelaghs, leprechauns, lovable rogues and 40 shades of green. This is the land of literary giants James Joyce and W.B. Yeats.

It is the land of U2 and the Undertones, of Dublin, Cork and Belfast, of top-notch restaurants, party-on pubs and a foot stomping live-music scene.

It is a land of powerful politics and astonishing history — from countless medieval castles and early Christian monasteries to the largest concentrations of prehistoric monuments in Europe.

It is also a land of real beauty — lakes, mountains, sea, sky, and its lonely, wind lashed wilderness coastline — and, of course, the marvelous Irish people themselves.

The Celtic Tiger is at best hibernating. The rolling green hills of Ireland's countryside still touch crystal clear lakes and rivers. The wild Atlantic roars and crashes on towering cliffs and mile long sandy beaches. Surfers, golfers, walkers, musicians and fishermen travel from all over the world to be here. The frantic pace and stress of the last decade has given way to a return to a gentler, more neighborly Ireland.

And now there is the great Irish investment opportunity — but more about that in a moment. But first, let's take a look at the disaster that created this opportunity in the first place.

How the Opportunity Came About

What makes the current dire economic situation even more humiliating is that a few years ago the Irish seemed to be engaged in nothing short of a miracle.

In the 1990s, the Irish government instituted a number of incentives for investment, and introduced a low rate of corporation tax (12.5%, compared with 39.5% in the U.S.). It attracted companies, workers and investment from every corner of the globe.

Government-backed investment incentives, a low rate of corporation tax and a highly educated, young, flexible workforce, all combined to make Ireland the desired location for more than 1,100 overseas companies as a base for their European operations.

During this period, almost half a million new jobs were created in Ireland, a phenomenon which changed the outlook of its people and the profile of its society and economy.

Back then, EU citizens were swarming to Ireland for good paying jobs. Between 1995 and 2000, the Irish economy expanded at a phenomenal annual rate of 9.4%. And it continued to grow at an average rate of 5.5% until 2008, when disaster struck. Ireland, and much of the rest of the world, tumbled into a deep downturn. While that disaster has created an extraordinary opportunity — first, let's take a look at some recent Irish economic history..

Real Estate Bargains Galore

In 2009, in a further effort to save its faltering banks, the government set up the National Asset Management Agency (NAMA), now dubbed by the Irish people as the "Bad Bank."

NAMA took over an estimated US$100 billion in problem commercial property and development loans from the six institutions, the Bank of Ireland, Allied Irish Banks, Anglo Irish Bank, EBS Ltd., Irish Life and Permanent and Irish Nationwide.

Exact and reliable figures on the extent of the real estate situation in Ireland aren't available. But Ireland's "Bad Bank," NAMA, controls more than 10,000 properties including residential, commercial, resort and hotels, development land and even pubs. Few of these have been offered for sale. With each fire-sale auction taking bids on less than 100 properties, this activity is insignificant relative to the long shadow of unsold inventory that NAMA inventory casts over the market. A list of available properties can be obtained from NAMA on their website.

Glutting the Irish property market are thousands of these unsold foreclosed properties of the country's collapsed banks, now held by NAMA. These include thousands of apartments and houses, hundreds of hotels, development sites and golf courses. And that's just in Ireland.

Until now, NAMA has been selling off Irish bank real estate assets in the United Kingdom where a healthier market means they can raise cash. But Ireland's announced 2013 debt-reduction targets means NAMA must start selling off this Irish property soon. It's in this environment, with much inventory still left to go, that you could pick up real bargains.

All of these distressed numbers show just how much the Republic of Ireland needs help. And that's where your opportunity arises.

Investment Gets Immediate Residence

Perhaps as a mark of official desperation, or the politicians' universal urge to "do something" in a crisis, or both, under a new program that starts on April 15, 2012, the Irish government is offering special residence visas to foreign individuals willing to invest in the country.

This investment can eventually lead to full citizenship, and Irish citizenship opens the door to full personal and commercial access to all 28 countries in the European Union.

The Irish government's aim is to attract both money and wealthy individuals from outside the European Union, who wish to take advantage of one of several new and existing investor schemes and immigrate to Ireland.

These official proposals come as Ireland tries to rebuild its shattered economy and bolster financial markets after one of the largest banking collapses in history. The Irish government said it will even offer finders' fees of about €4,000 (US$5,332) for those who locate foreigners willing to create jobs in Ireland.

Under the new 2012 program, potential investor immigrants have these choices, (all numbers are required minimums):

- Make a one-time payment of €500,000 (US$666,000) to a public project benefiting the arts, sports, health or education.
- Make a €2 million (US$2.7 million) investment in a low interest immigrant investor bond. The investment is to be held for a minimum of five years. The bond cannot be traded but must be held to maturity.
- Invest €1 million (US$1.3 million) in venture capital funding in an Irish business for a minimum of three years.
- Make a €1 million mixed investment in 50% property and 50% government securities. Special consideration may be given to those purchasing property owned by the National Asset Management Agency (NAMA). In such cases, a single €1m investment in property may be sufficient. NAMA is stuck with real estate from bailed-out Irish banks and financial institutions.

Start-up Entrepreneur Program

This separate program is for foreigners with entrepreneurial ability, who wish to start a business in an innovation area of the economy with funding of at least €75,000 ($99,000). They will be given a two-year residence period for the purposes of developing the business. No initial job creation targets will be set, because it is recognized that such businesses take time to establish.

The plan looks for high-growth start-ups and is not intended for retail, personal services, catering or other businesses of that nature. The department's existing immigration "Business Permission Scheme" is available for this sort of enterprise.

Investors will be able to bring family members into Ireland on the resident visa. Successful applicants will be granted residence permission for two-years — renewable thereafter, provided the business is still operational and the applicant is earning a living without being a burden on the country. There will be no requirement to employ people for the first two years, but the business is required to be profitable at the two-year renewal stage.

More information is available at the Ministry of Justice webpage. Emails can be directed to investmentandstartup@justice.ie. But a word of warning from those on the scene who know; dealing with the NAMA bureaucracy is painfully slow and cumbersome. That suggests the need for professional help that can smooth the way. See Pathfinder in the contacts section at the end of this report.

Irish Citizenship by Ancestry

Aside from joining the country of your ancestors, as I noted before, there is a very practical use for an Irish passport. It entitles the holder to live, work, own real estate and a business and travel freely in any of the 27 countries in the European Union, of which Ireland is a member state.

Other EU countries that issue passports based on ancestry include Italy, Spain, Poland, Lithuania, Luxembourg and Greece. You don't need a work permit and after you work in an EU country for a certain length of time, you are entitled to unemployment compensation, health care and pension rights.

Even if you don't want residence in Ireland by investment under the new program just announced, you may be eligible for an official Irish passport because of your family blood lines.

"We are all Irish today." Those ritual words are repeated by American politicians each Saint Patrick's Day to identify with the 40 million citizens of the U.S., nearly 12% of the population, who can trace their ancestry to Ireland — more than 10 times the number who live in Ireland.

Many millions of Irish emigrated to the U.S., beginning well before America's Revolutionary War against Great Britain. In 1776, eight Irish Americans signed the U.S. Declaration of Independence, and 22 American presidents, from Andrew Jackson to Barack Obama were at least partly of Irish descent.

Ireland values its foreign sons and daughters. And to maintain their ties, Irish law grants citizenship based on parentage and grand parentage. As a consequence, an Irish passport is one of the most sought-after travel documents in the world. Remarkably, with a resident population of only 4.7 million, Ireland has many millions of current passports in worldwide circulation.

When asked about the total number of Irish passports in circulation in 2006, the Minister for Foreign Affairs told the Irish Parliament that he could not give an exact number. However, between 1996 and 2005, about 4.7 million passports were issued.

In part, this large number of passport holders stems from the principle of Irish nationality law that views blood lines as determining a birthright to citizenship — even without ever having lived in the country.

Citizenship is governed by the Irish Nationality and Citizenship Acts of 1956 and 1986. These laws confer Irish nationality:

- By reason of one's birth in Ireland;
- By Irish parentage or ancestry, and;
- By marriage to an Irish citizen.

Automatic citizenship by reason of birth within Ireland was limited in 2004 by a constitutional amendment that restricted that right to a child with at least one Irish citizen as a parent.

This reflected demands for limits on the many foreign immigrants, who came to Ireland to get welfare and other services for their born or unborn children. After January 1, 2005, citizenship and residence history of both parents and all grandparents was thereafter taken into account.

If you were born outside of Ireland, and either your mother or father (or both) was an Irish citizen at the time of your birth, then you are entitled to Irish citizenship.

There are two circumstances under which a great-grandchild is eligible to apply for Irish citizenship by descent:

- If the parent (the grandchild of the Irish born person) registered before the great-grandchild was born;
- If the parent (the grandchild of the Irish born person) registered before June 30, 1986 and the great-grandchild was born after July 17, 1956.

The Irish Consulate in New York explains that the parent would need to be registered in the "Foreign Birth Register," which is held at the consulate, a listing of Irish citizens born abroad, who are entitled to citizenship because their births officially were "registered."

Marriage to an Irish citizen also entitles a foreign spouse to Irish citizenship. To claim citizenship by marriage you must:

- Be married for at least three years;
- Have had one year of "continuous residence" in Ireland immediately before your application; and
- Have been living in Ireland for at least two of the four years before the one year of continuous residence.

A foreign-born person who marries a person of Irish birth or descent may become an Irish citizen after three years of marriage by formally declaring acceptance of Irish citizenship. The marriage must continue at the time of application and grant of citizenship. A married applicant must file a notarized form at an Irish Consulate or Embassy within 30 days of its execution. Once Irish citizenship is established, an application for an official passport can be filed.

The most difficult route to citizenship is through permanent residence in Ireland for a continuous five years, after which you may be entitled to naturalization if you are over 18-years-old and have no criminal record.

How to Breeze Through the Research and Paperwork

With three photographs, proper proof of Irish ancestry and proof of legal residence in the country where you make application, a renewable, 10-year Irish passport will be issued in due course bearing the stamp of Ireland and the European Community.

Finding proof of Irish ancestry can be a problem since many church and court records were destroyed in "The Troubles," the long running, often violent Irish independence struggle against the British. Irish Consulates and Embassies are adept at verifying affidavits and genealogical research. Numerous Irish genealogical sources can be found on the Internet.

Ireland also permits dual citizenship, as does the U.S. It does not require an oath of exclusive allegiance, and does not notify the country of origin of its new passport holders.

Contact the nearest Irish Consulate or Embassy for application forms and assistance.

The authoritative Genealogical Supplement is published by a company called *"Inside Ireland."* This book is available to subscribers of the Inside Ireland Quarterly Review available from *Inside Ireland*, P.O. Box 1886, Dublin 16, Ireland. Email: info@insideireland.com.

Even without Irish ancestry, it is also possible to obtain Irish citizenship and a passport after a five-year period of residence. Irish residence is not generally sought because of the nation's high income taxes.

According to Ireland's nationality law, a person is an Irish citizen at birth if "either parent was an Irish citizen, or would, if alive, have been an Irish citizen." Therefore, if you have at least one parent who was born in Ireland, you are automatically an Irish citizen at birth. As such, you would also be an Irish citizen, no matter where you were born. If this is the case, you can apply for citizenship directly to the passport office at your nearest consulate.

If you have at least one grandparent who was born in Ireland, he or she would have been a citizen. Moreover, one of your parents would have been automatically entitled to Irish citizenship, regardless of where they were born — and so are you. The process works a bit differently in this case. You must go through something called a Foreign Birth Registration.

Every applicant for Foreign Births Registration must provide certain documentation about the grandparent from whom the citizenship is being claimed. Specifically:

- Birth certificate including place of birth, date of birth and full name
- Marriage certificate, if applicable
- Copy of passport (if alive) or death certificate (if deceased)

Then you'll need some documentation on your parent through whom the citizenship is being claimed. Specifically:

- Birth certificate (indicating details of his/her parents)
- Marriage certificate, if applicable
- Copy of passport (if alive) or death certificate (if deceased)

And finally you'll need some documents for yourself, including:

- Birth certificate (including the details of your parents)
- Marriage certificate, if applicable
- Passport copy
- Two photographs
- Proof of address (bank statement, utility bill)
- Application form

All of the documentation, together with the application, must be submitted to your nearest Irish consulate.

If you have children and are claiming citizenship through your grandparents, your children can only become citizens if you registered them with the Irish government before their birth. Once you become a citizen through your grandparents, future children can also claim citizenship. If you're claiming citizenship through your parents, however, all of your children can claim citizenship.

You obtain these records from the Government Records Office (www.groireland.ie) directly. They have records of births, deaths and marriages since 1864. There are also services such as RootsIireland.ie and Irish-Certificates.ie that can help in accessing the records.

Others include the Irish National Archives website, census records, and a number of genealogy websites, including:

- General Register Office, Dublin: births, marriages, deaths since 1864
- National Library website: Church records
- Griffiths Valuation: Land and property records (1848-1864)
- irishgenealogy.ie
- rootsireland.ie
- *The Irish Times* Genealogy

A U.S. or other valid passport is necessary for travel to Ireland. A visa is not required for tourist or business stays of up to 90 days.

A Word about Irish Taxes

In Ireland, the taxation of individuals is based on mixed concepts of residence and domicile.

Irish residents domiciled in Ireland are subject to taxation on all of their worldwide income. Non-resident Irish citizens who live abroad are exempted from taxation.

Current official practice is to allow new citizens to declare formally that they don't intend to live in Ireland and are, therefore, not domiciled. They are then obligated to pay income tax only on income actually remitted to Ireland. This practice makes Ireland an attractive tax venue for naturalized citizens.

As in many countries, residence is based on presence in Ireland for more than half of a tax year, or for 280 days in two consecutive years. An individual's domicile is in the country where he or she maintains a permanent home.

Because of this days-in-days-out rule, it appears possible to structure Irish residence in such a chronological order so as to avoid taxes.

Domicile in Ireland is acquired from an Irish-domiciled father, but can be changed to another country by establishing a life there. Resident foreign employees will thus not normally be domiciled in Ireland. An individual resident domiciled in Ireland pays tax on his worldwide income; a resident who is not domiciled pays tax on his foreign income only if it is remitted to Ireland.

A non-resident individual pays income tax only on Irish-sourced income, and is liable for capital gains tax only on gains arising in Ireland or remitted to Ireland, unless he is domiciled in Ireland, in which case he is liable for all capital gains. Current residence rules require all visits to Ireland by non-residents to be counted for tax purposes against their permitted days in the country.

In Ireland, the main tax on individuals is income tax. There is also capital gains tax, capital acquisitions tax which includes an inheritance tax, property taxes and stamp duties on transfers of various types of property. As a member state of the EU, Ireland levies VAT of from zero to 21%, on a luxury scale.

The standard Irish income tax rate for individuals is 20% on the first €32,800 ($43,700) of taxable income, rising to 41%. See the website, Lowtax Global Tax and Business Portal on Ireland, for details. http://www.lowtax.net/information/ireland

There is another good reason to look to Ireland as an international business base — it has very low taxes on holding companies.

Many U.S. and British multinationals that have relocated here from Bermuda or the Cayman Islands pay little or no Irish taxes. Unlike most other countries, Ireland does not tax capital gains from the sale of subsidiaries. While it does tax the dividends of a multinational firm's holding company, it does not tax its global profits. These companies are also allowed to write off the cost of acquiring intellectual-property assets against taxable profits for 15 years.

Ireland is a common law nation with legal and commercial practice much like the U.K. It has excellent, modern telecoms systems and the corporate tax breaks offered in the Dublin Free Zone have drawn commercial operations from all over the world. The currency is the euro.

Under the European Savings Tax Directive, banks establish the identity and residence of beneficial owners of all new bank accounts opened in Ireland. Banks report details of earned savings income for taxation purposes to the Revenue Commission, which passes this information on to the tax authorities of the EU member state where a customer resides.

Contacts

Specialists in Irish & World Real Estate:

Pathfinder International
Ronan McMahon, Executive Director
Elysium House, Ballytruckle Road
Waterford, Ireland
Email: rmcmahon@pangaearealestate.net
Web: www.pathfinderinternational.net

Margaret Summerfield, Associate
Panama City, Republic of Panama
Email: msummerfield@pathfinderinternational.net
National Asset Management Agency
Treasury Building, Grand Canal Street
Dublin 2, Ireland
Tel.: +353 1 238 4000
Web: https://www.nama.ie/

Embassy of Ireland
2234 Massachusetts Avenue NW
Washington, D.C. 20008
Tel.: (202) 462-3939
Web: http://www.embassyofireland.org

United States Embassy
42 Elgin Road, Ballsbridge
Dublin 4, Ireland
Tel.: + 353 1 668 8777
Email: acsdublin@state.gov

Malta Offers No-Wait Citizenship
Robert E. Bauman JD, *Offshore Confidential*, October 2013

How would you like to live on a historic island in the middle of the breathtaking Mediterranean Sea while enjoying all the benefits that Europe has to offer?

Sound like a wonderful lifestyle? It can be. And now is a great time to pursue it.

Over the years, my special reports have focused on offshore wealth enhancement and asset-protection strategies. More recently, ominous signs of impending chaos in the U.S. have compelled me to write more frequently about obtaining a second (or third) citizenship to escape the domestic pitfalls. With a toxic mix of U.S. economic stagnation, political dysfunction, widespread violations of our constitutional rights and an ever-growing federal government, the second-citizenship option is more urgent than ever.

Which leads me to … Malta.

With a brand new no-wait citizenship plan being unveiled (joining a Maltese permanent-residence option released earlier this year), the island of Malta will now be offering desirable economic citizenship, or "citizenship-by-investment" with access to all of the benefits of the 27 European Union countries.

Besides its spectacular historical treasures, Europe boasts some of the world's most attractive lifestyle amenities. The continent's rail network is legendary, allowing residents to travel to Europe's world-class museums, restaurants, sporting events and recreational attractions, quickly, cheaply, and for those with citizenship or residency, hassle-free.

And, of course, Europeans' relaxed "live and let live" attitude is very mindful of privacy in both personal and financial matters, which is a far cry from the U.S., where the National Security Agency's domestic spying continues unabated and abominations like the Foreign Account Tax Compliance Act (FATCA) pass with solid bipartisan majorities in Congress.

With Malta's new "Individual Investor Programme" (IIP) in the final stages of approval, our inside contacts — including the firm contracted to manage the program, Henley & Partners — have given us a wealth of information we want to share with you before anyone else hears it.

But first, a bit about Malta — a place many have never heard of.

The Next Best Thing to Italy

Many of us are only slightly aware of Malta — indeed the most common reference point is the classic Humphrey Bogart vehicle, "The Maltese Falcon" (a remake of a racier version released in 1931).

In fact, Malta has been a crucial part of European and Mediterranean history since ancient times.

Malta is an independent republic within the British Commonwealth consisting of a small group of islands in the central Mediterranean, southeast of Sicily. It's been a cultural, economic and political stepping-stone between Europe, the Middle East and North Africa for more than 5,000 years. Accordingly, the Maltese language is closely related to Arabic, but almost all Maltese are Roman Catholic. English is the second official language.

In 1947, the British granted Malta self-government, and in 1964, after 150 years as a Crown Colony, the islands became independent. Malta became a republic in 1974, and has been a member of the European Union since 2004. It adopted the euro in 2008.

British traditions live on in Malta, including an efficient civil service, a Westminster-style parliamentary structure, a respect for the rule of law and a legal system based on English common law.

And yet Malta is a classically Mediterranean society. Hot, dry summers and mild winters produce a vibrant lifestyle similar to that found in Sicily, Greece or Spain, with youthful tourists from northern Europe in abundance. While Malta is a bit lacking in sandy beaches, it makes up for it with an energetic sailing culture, with numerous bays along the indented coastline of the islands providing good harbors.

Malta has an excellent infrastructure, with telecommunications, postal services, banking, and hospitals and health services all of high quality. Malta also offers a quick connection to Europe: Air Malta operates 35 routes within Europe and the Mediterranean region, and most major European airlines operate flights to Malta. There is a regular sea link with Italy.

Now that we know more about the place, let's dive right into the new programs …

Two Appealing Options to Experience all of Europe

When considering Malta's new programs, it's important to note the difference between residence and citizenship.

A residence permit entitles you to work, travel and study in that country. It does not, however, grant the right to vote, hold a passport and pass your status on to your children.

Citizenship, of course, makes you a full member of the national community, including the right to vote, hold a passport, and reside and work in the country at any time without any restrictions. It's good for a lifetime, is passed on to future generations and can't be revoked except by law under strict circumstances.

Residence

There are two routes to a Maltese residence permit for non-EU persons. One is the customary work/marriage/small investor/self-employment path practiced by many countries. It involves at least five years of continuous Maltese residence via annual permits, which in turn results in qualification for a five-year, renewable long-term residence permit.

Obtaining a long-term permit requires scoring at least 75% in a course on "the social, economic, cultural and demographic history and environment of Malta."

The other route to residence for non-EU persons is through Malta's Global Residence Program (GRP), adopted earlier this year. The GRP is based on the purchase or rental of residential property. The requirement varies from a €220,000 (US$301,000) purchase price (for properties on Gozo island and in southern Malta) to €275,000 (US$376,000) elsewhere, or from €8,750 (US$12,000) to €9,600 (US$13,000) annual rent.

Under the Global Residence Program, residents enjoy privileged tax status, and benefit from Malta's wide network of double taxation treaties — although, under certain treaties, limitations of treaty benefits apply. Such treaties protect an entity or individual from paying two separate taxes on the same property for the same purpose and during the same time period. And if you're not yet retired and still earning an income, the GRP gives you a flat 15% tax rate — subject to a minimum €15,000 (US$20,500) tax.

To obtain a residence permit under the Global Residence Programme (GRP), candidates must:

- Not be a Maltese, European Economic Area or Swiss national.
- Not benefit from any other special Maltese tax status.
- Hold a qualifying property, as above.
- Have stable and regular income sufficient to maintain a household without recourse to the social assistance system in Malta.
- Have a valid passport or other travel document.
- Have health-insurance coverage for the entire EU area for each member of the household.
- Be fluent in either Maltese or English.
- Be a fit and proper person.

Citizenship

To date, Malta's approach to immigration has been paradoxical. On one hand, the country encouraged residency via generous tax laws. On the other, for ordinary people, it appeared to make the path to citizenship somewhat challenging.

Part of the challenge existed because the Maltese minister for Home Affairs and National Security assumed absolute discretion to give citizenship by naturalization. It was neither guaranteed nor a mere formality. The minister needed to be convinced that applicants were of a "good character" or "suitable citizens." Some commentators estimated that 20 years of residence was a good rule of thumb before citizenship was feasible.

Now, all of that is about to change.

Barring any last-minute hiccups, the Maltese Individual Investor Programme's (IIP) offering of citizenship is set to take effect on November 1.

Now before I explain the details — since, as you'll see, the IIP isn't cheap — there's an interesting quirk of Maltese residency/ tax rules that you should know about. It's not automatic, but it is possible to become a Maltese citizen and continue to be regarded as domiciled in their country of origin for tax purposes.

Maltese tax authorities define "domicile" as the country where you were born, where you were married, where your will and other important legal documents are registered, and so on — in other words, where you're "from" and might one-day return. IIP participants who obtain Maltese citizenship and who can demonstrate that their "domicile" is elsewhere — not a problem if you maintain links to your other home — will pay a flat tax rate of 15% on Maltese and offshore income, but nothing on offshore investment income or capital transfers. In other words, they will be treated the same as permanent residents for the purposes of taxation.

To participate in the IIP, applicants must pay some fees (see below) and qualify under a strict due-diligence system, combining several different background verification procedures with a risk-weighted assessment of whether the applicant is suitable to be admitted as a citizen under the program.

Successful applicants must make a contribution of €650,000 (US$890,000) to a National Development Fund (for social projects), plus €25,000 (US$34,000) each for spouse and minor children, and €50,000 (US$68,400) each for dependent children 18 to 25 years or dependent parents above 55. For a family of four, the cost per person will be around €185,000 (US$253,000).

Regardless of the applicant's eventual success or failure, the Maltese government will also charge due diligence fees of €7,500 (US$10,300) for the main applicant; €5,000 (US$6,800) each for spouses, adult children and parents; and €3,000 (US$4,100) each for minor children; as well as passport fees and bank charges of €500 (US$685) and €200 (US$275) per person.

Finally, applicants will pay a professional service fee to Henley & Partners, an international firm appointed by the Maltese government to manage the application process.

To ward off domestic criticisms that it's "selling citizenship" — and to weed out bad apples — the Maltese government is stressing that "the due diligence to be applied to those applying for Maltese citizenship will be subjected to complete X-ray of applicants' and relatives' lives and the source of their riches."

Here's how our sources tell us it will work.

IIP candidates will have to have clean criminal records. They must also produce a medical certificate confirming that they and their dependents aren't suffering from any contagious diseases and are in good health.

Once an applicant has undergone Henley & Partners' initial due diligence process, a new government agency, Identity Malta, will subject applicants and their families to background checks. In some cases, a request for a personal interview may occur.

From there, Identity Malta will then produce a report on each individual with a recommendation detailing the rationale for approving or declining the application.

How Does Malta's IIP Stack Up Against the Competition?

It's clear that the Maltese IIP is aimed at the top of the citizenship-by-investment market. The fee structure and cost of compliance put the minimum cost of IIP citizenship at over $1 million. But the benefits are extraordinary: fast-track Maltese and therefore EU citizenship, without a prior residence requirement, with a relatively short application process, and low non-resident tax rates.

Just how valuable is it within the global market?

For some time, only three countries have offered relatively *fast* economic citizenship such as Malta's: Austria, the Commonwealth of Dominica and St. Kitts & Nevis. Those countries effectively offer passports for sale, since cash payments to their governments are one way to obtain them (for more information, refer to *The Passport Book*).

Unfortunately, Dominica's program spooked the U.S. and Canadian governments, concerned about the possibility of terrorists or international criminals taking advantage of it to gain access to their territories. Both lost their spots on the U.S. visa waiver list.

Within the EU, Austria, Cyprus, and Bulgaria also offer citizenship-by-investment. Compared to those programs, Malta's clearly comes out on top. Austria's program requires a $2,750,000 donation to an Austrian "public cause," or business investment of at least $10 million; it is notoriously difficult to qualify. And although Austria allows dual citizenship, it is on a case-by-case basis.

Cyprus' program is also expensive — requiring an investment of around $4 million — and the country is tarred by its serious financial problems. Bulgaria offers passports at just over $400,000, but even though it is part of the EU, it is outside the euro zone, and more importantly, its passport-holders are not yet eligible for unrestricted travel and resettlement in the rest of the EU.

At the other end of the market, St. Kitts and Nevis' cash-for-citizenship program is currently at least $250,000. This program is fine if your goal is a second passport, but it doesn't give you EU access.

Compared to these programs, the Maltese IIP will be the most respectable, easiest to navigate, and will offer the fastest-track, dual-citizenship-friendly program in the world.

So if you want a passport that opens up EU borders, Malta is the place to be.

A Welcoming Tax and Banking Atmosphere

Malta levies three types of direct taxes — private income, corporate income and estate taxes — but the government bends over backward to keep rates low for well-heeled foreigners and corporations. There are no property taxes. Interest and royalty income on local investments are entirely exempt from tax, as are capital gains on collective investment arrangements and securities (as long as the underlying asset is not Maltese real estate).

Some aspects of Maltese tax law flirt with "tax haven" territory. Foreign companies receive tax discounts of up to 85% on profits remitted to Maltese subsidiaries. And under some circumstances, individuals who are considered not *domiciled* in Malta — even if they live there — only pay a 15% tax on income earned in Malta as well as foreign income remitted to Malta.

More recently, the Maltese government has intentionally refashioned the country as an "international business center." The islands conform to EU and international anti-tax haven requirements, so living in Malta is no longer seen as a red flag to the global tax authorities.

Which Option is Right for You?

Malta is a beautiful country smack-dab in the middle of the Mediterranean, with all the cultural amenities of southern Europe and the political, financial, and legal stability and order of northern Europe. What's not to like?

Well, there is one possible drawback, and I'd be remiss if I didn't draw it to your attention. The fact that the Maltese government has amended its laws to keep IIP participants secret may raise red flags in the U.S., Canada, the U.K. and potentially even the EU itself. Although many countries don't publish the names of newly-naturalized citizens, the combination of secrecy and a fast-track process creates a unique challenge in this paranoid world of terrorism and over-reaching taxation.

Hopefully, the Maltese government's claim that its process will be the most thorough in the world, subject to external audit, and so on, will allay any fears of abuse.

If you are primarily interested in a second citizenship, you're looking for unrestricted access to the EU and have the resources to take advantage of it, the new IIP is a wonderful option. It represents a major breakthrough in fast-track economic citizenship.

On the other hand, if second citizenship isn't such a big deal, if you're primarily interested in living in Malta, and/or if the IIP price tag is too steep, the Global Residency Program is the best bet option for you.

Indeed, the IIP is really more about EU access than living in Malta per se. The greatest single benefit of the IIP is that successful applicants will become citizens of the EU, as well as Malta, which means visa-free access to the EU as well as the "right of establishment" in all 27 EU countries. This is a *very* big deal.

And, of course, as Maltese citizens, IIP participants will hold a Maltese passport and enjoy visa-free travel to more than 160 countries in the world.

Latin American Route to EU Citizenship
Robert E. Bauman JD, *The Passport Book*, 2014

Almost everyone wants a passport issued by one of the 28 European Union member countries.

With that document in hand, you're free to roam, live and do business in any of the EU countries, few questions asked. However, EU member-states don't grant citizenship easily, but some of their former colonies do. Few know it, but for those who qualify, the quickest backdoor route to EU citizenship is through several South American countries, long ago colonies of Spain and Portugal. A similar arrangement exists between Spain and another of its former colonies, the Philippines. In recent years, Spain has been much stricter on applicants using the "colonial route," who now must prove their personal origins in the country from which they seek to move to Spain.

One can apply directly for residence in one of the various 27 EU countries, but unless you qualify for either immediate citizenship or a reduced period of residence due to marriage or your ancestry, you won't become eligible to be an EU citizen for five to ten years.

Spain will grant citizenship within two years after application to persons of "Spanish blood" or descendants of Sephardic Jews. Spanish blood is normally taken for granted whenever an applicant is already a citizen of a former Spanish colony or has a Spanish surname and speaks Spanish. Latin American passport in hand, the next step is acquisition of a house or apartment in Spain and a Spanish residence permit. After the special reduced period of residence based on your Latin American second citizenship, you can apply for a Spanish passport.

An Argentine passport allows visa-free travel to 133 countries, including most of Europe and nearly all of South and Central America. It's also the first passport in South America that entitles its holder to visa-free entry into the U.S., although some post-9/11 restrictions now apply. Argentineans also qualify for a reduced, two-year residence period in Spain when seeking Spanish nationality.

A Guatemalan passport is good for travel to most countries in Europe without a visa, and dual citizenship is common in the nation. Most upper-class Guatemalans hold U.S. and Spanish passports. Spain gives special consideration to Guatemalans, who, by treaty, need only two years of residence in Spain to acquire Spanish citizenship or vice-versa. Both a Honduran and a Uruguayan passport entitle holders to Spanish citizenship after two years of residency in Spain.

Portugal also offers special considerations to members of its former colonies. Brazilian citizens qualify for Portuguese nationality after only three years of official residence; no visa is required to enter or take up residence in Portugal. Citizens of former Portuguese colonial enclaves in India (Goa, Daman and Diu); and parts of Asia, East Timor (a former Indonesian province), Macao in China, and Africa (Cape Verde, Guinea-Bissau, Angola, Mozambique, and São Tome-Principe) may also qualify for Portuguese citizenship. The same goes for Brazil, the biggest Portuguese ex-colony on the world map. However, Brazilian citizenship is not cheap. Any one of these former colonies could be your shortcut into the EU.

SIX WAYS TO ESCAPE FROM AMERICA — NOW
Robert E. Bauman JD, *The Sovereign Individual*, September 2009

Have things gotten so bad that freedom loving Americans need to escape from their own beloved country?

Howard Beale is a fictional TV news anchor in the 1976 movie *Network* played by the late Peter Finch, who won a posthumous Oscar for his role.

In the movie, Beale struggles with depression and insanity, but his producers, rather than give him the medical help he needs, use him to get higher TV ratings. The image of Howard Beale, in a beige raincoat with his wet, gray hair plastered to his head, standing up during the middle of his newscast hollering, "I'm as mad as Hell, and I'm not going to take this anymore!" ranks as one of the most memorable scenes in film history.

Galloping Socialism

Flash forward to 2009 AD, America's First Year of Obama.

Galloping cradle-to-the grave socialism is the dominant theme in Washington. As I write this, the Obama administration is projecting a budget deficit of $1.84 trillion, more than four times 2008's record-high. To put that number in context, that amount had never been spent by the federal government in a single year until 2000, let alone borrowed.

The Government Accounting Office (GAO) says the national debt per capita could exceed the gross domestic product (GDP) per capita by 2030. The national debt is now nearing $12 trillion. With the U.S. population at about 307 million, each citizen's share of debt exceeds $38,000. Almost 50% of that debt is owed to foreigners, $800 billion to the Communist Chinese.

These trillions in deficit spending guarantee Weimar hyper-inflation just down the road. The dollar is sinking faster than the Titanic. At historic levels, both home prices are down and unemployment up. Big government now controls auto, insurance and financial companies, with massive socialized government health care next.

Lost Trust

No sensible American places trust in bailed out banks or Wall Street fraudsters. And now a radical U.S. Congress is seriously considering imposing all sorts of unconstitutional restrictions on your traditional right to invest, bank and conduct business offshore. Greedy politicians want your cash kept at home where they can tax and take it.

Now your hard earned wealth may be confiscated by the IRS and "spread around" to finance leftist programs that reward deadbeats, illegal immigrants and labor union bosses.

Shared Pain

This time we're all sharing that exquisite pain Bill Clinton so glibly said he understood. The very existence of the doers and producers in our society, those who forged their own path to success, dollar by dollar, is now in question.

We've worked hard all our lives, only to have an unholy, bi-partisan alliance of politicians and their lobbyist buddies rob us of the value of our homes, our investments and — worst of all — our basic freedoms.

If you really understand what's happening to America, you must do more than agree with Howard Beale's lament. You may be frustrated and "mad as Hell," but you need to act now to change those things you can — while you still have the power to act.

Using the talents that got you this far, you need put in place your own plan to save yourself and those whom you love and who depend on you.

You need an escape plan.

Six Escape Paths

At least for now, for safety's sake, you or some part of your wealth, need to escape from America. Here's how:

1) Immediately move a portion of your wealth into a foreign bank account. While few tax savings are possible offshore, there is still a world of opportunity, safety and greater privacy to be found there. An offshore bank account offers protection from the dying U.S. dollar, letting you profit from currency fluctuations across the globe. It gives you access to international investments trading on the world's leading exchanges, plus the ability to acquire precious metals and tangible personal assets with real value.

Your offshore bank account is an important first step on your escape route. It can provide peace of mind against the weakened U.S. banking system — even if the Federal Deposit Insurance (FDIC) starts to buckle under the strain.

2) Create your own offshore asset protection trust. The APT is located far from your home place in an asset-friendly, higher privacy offshore jurisdiction. That makes it one of the best available legal structures for asset protection. Use it to stash your cash, securities, personal property and other moveable valuables.

The offshore APT is tailored to protect those who live in a distressed country and that need the foreigner-friendly laws of a more stable country where trust operations are based. The laws where the APT is registered govern, acting as a shield for your business and personal assets — and to discourage potential claims and lawsuits.

Offshore trusts are not just for the very rich any more.

3) Purchase an offshore variable annuity. This is one of the easiest routes to investing in foreign funds without having to pay immediate U.S. taxes. A properly diversified variable annuity gives you legally deferred taxes, much like an IRA, until funds are actually withdrawn. And annuity investments can be transferred from one fund manager to another with no immediate tax consequences, plus you achieve significant asset protection under foreign laws.

4) Acquire offshore life insurance. One of few remaining offshore estate tax planning opportunities, life insurance combines solid asset protection with tax deferral. Despite all the phony "estate tax reform" talk in the United

States, when an American dies without prior proper planning, combined income and estate taxes can consume 50% or more of a U.S. person's estate.

This estate tax rape can be avoided with various techniques, but only life insurance provides four key benefits: 1) tax-free buildup of cash value, including dividends, interest, capital gains; 2) tax-free borrowing against cash value; 3) tax-free receipt of the death benefit; and 4) freedom from estate and generation skipping taxes.

5) Buy and hold precious metals offshore, including gold, silver, and collectibles. The Perth Mint in Australia, NMG's My Swiss Gold in Zürich and your offshore bank account each give you the ability to buy and store your own physical gold and silver. Whatever happens to fiat paper currencies, your precious metals will have value.

If you bought $100,000 worth of gold in 2001, you got 384.6 ounces of gold at the then current price of $260/oz. In August 2009, gold was at $950/oz and has been as high as $973/oz. That 2001 gold is now worth almost four times your original investment.

You also can purchase foreign securities using your offshore bank account or trust. Properly structured foreign legal entities are not considered "U.S. residents, persons or citizens" so they enjoy an unrestricted right to buy non-S.E.C. registered securities.

6) Move your existing IRA or other retirement account offshore. Switch to a U.S. custodian who will help you to invest your account offshore in real estate and other more lucrative investments.

Moving Abroad — Not as Hard as You Think
Jocelynn Smith, Managing Editor, *Sovereign Investor Daily*, June 2014

Most Americans don't even think about leaving the country they call home. Who can blame them? Uprooting from your closest friends and family, the places that are like an extension to yourself. It hurts. It's *like* losing a loved one.

Even today the cultural myth continues that America is the land of opportunity. Immigrants flood into the country every day hoping to lead a better life than their home country could offer them. No wonder we don't think of leaving.

But people are. Expatriation is on the rise. Forces are pushing people over the edge, beyond the comforts and love of family, nationality, familiarity. The thought is rapidly beginning to creep into peoples' heads.

Chapter Two: Second Passports and Dual Nationality 133

Ted Bauman, a contributing editor to the *Sovereign Investor Daily* and editor of *Offshore Confidential* and *Plan B Club*, knows all too well the difficulty of leaving America. Today, I asked Ted to talk to us about the reasons why people decide to expatriate from their country, and how.

Jocelynn: What are some of the top reasons people consider when getting a second citizenship or having a home in another country?

Ted: I think the reasons can be divided into personal, economic and political. Most people go abroad because they enjoy it, and because they are at a time and place in their lives where they can do so. I did that when I went to South Africa. I didn't need to go. I didn't expect to get rich there. I just wanted to.

And I stayed because I loved the place and the people. It was never about money.

Another group of people go abroad to work or run businesses. Of course their motivations are also partly personal. Nobody in a rich country like the U.S. goes abroad as an economic refugee — at least not yet. So people who choose to work abroad are usually a bit adventurous. Then there are those who go abroad to retire or otherwise live on a fixed income because it's cheaper.

We talk about people going abroad for political reasons, and some do. But overall I think it's a small minority — but one likely to grow. I know there are limits to my own tolerance of the nonsense the U.S. government gets up to, and I'm not alone.

Jocelynn: Isn't having a home in another country limited to people with staggering wealth and movie stars?

Ted: Do I look like a movie star? I lived abroad for 30 years and still do, at least part-time. The jet set, as people used to call them, are basically trans-nationalized people who can go wherever they want and do whatever they want because of their money. We don't write for those folks. We write for people who have to make choices because their resources aren't unlimited. And one of those choices, a perfectly reasonable one, is to live overseas in a place where the cost of living may well be much less than the U.S. I think it's fair to say that you do need to have either some means, in the form of a fixed income or a successful business, or an ability to reinvent yourself, to move abroad. But you don't need any more money itself than you would to retire or live in the U.S.

Jocelynn: So, what you're saying is that there's hope for me without needing to land a big movie deal. I'm glad to hear it! But what are some of the common mistakes or important things people overlook when considering a country to which to move?

Ted: Culture and lifestyle preferences are the big one. People need to understand that you're going to someone else's place, and you can't and shouldn't expect them to adapt to you. It has to be largely the other way around. If you're the type of person who struggles to compromise and adapt, then either don't go abroad, or move to an expatriate enclave where you can live surrounded by Americans. But if you do decide to go abroad to live among the natives, make sure it's a place that suits you temperamentally.

The other mistake is to think that you're going to escape government entirely. We often write about how governments are less intrusive abroad, and that's broadly true of banking, tax, and other financial matters. But when it comes to daily life, all governments like to tell people what to do — it's what they do for a living. So it's important to check out the "blue laws" sort of stuff — the little regulations and laws that you have to abide by to get along in that place. Most countries are far less regulated than the U.S., but some have specific regulations that might irritate you — for example, some traditional Roman Catholic countries in Latin America have Sunday laws that reflect that.

Jocelynn: It's definitely the little things we so often overlook and take for granted. I've had friends warn me of Singapore's strictly enforced chewing gum ban. Should expats expect to find the same high quality health care abroad as in the United States?

Ted: Better, actually. The only thing that the U.S. offers that's unquestionably better than most other countries in the less-developed world is advanced care for serious issues like cancer and genetic disease. Otherwise, most countries are perfectly capable of providing excellent care for everyday ailments and chronic conditions such as diabetes, heart disease and the like.

One major difference is that medicine is far less corporatized in the rest of the world. It's still a family doctor sort of environment in many respects. You do have big insurance companies and hospital groups, but the front-line, every day care you get is far more likely to be with a doctor of your choice, on your own terms. That's a much better way to be treated, in my opinion.

Jocelynn: Does moving abroad mean giving up all the little things you love, such as American sitcoms, a morning copy of the *Wall Street Journal*, and junk food?

Ted: As long as you have Internet, you have it all! You can get at least past seasons of most American TV shows on Internet services. You can get U.S. sports on the websites of the MLB, NFL, NHL, NBA, etc. And other than my parents, I don't know anyone who still reads an actual physical newspaper. But even that can be arranged, at least for the big American papers.

Of course you won't find everything you're used to, but what you will find is that you'll learn to love new things over time. The things I crave are all South African because I lived there so long, so I'm essentially a South African expatriate (I'm a citizen, after all). I managed to find some of the South African essentials like Marmite (a yeast paste) and biltong (dried meat) at a South African importer, but it's hard to get the stuff I crave as often as I would if I still lived there. Now that I'm back in the States, I've developed a taste for American-style barbeque and Cajun food, to the point that now I'm just as good at cooking those things as most Americans.

If you go abroad, the same thing will happen to you, if you let it. You'll forget all about bagels and cream cheese and fall in love with something else — but you'll be able to get your bagel from time to time,to satisfy old cravings. After all, life would be boring if there were never any change!

Rules Offshore Real Estate Buyers Must Know
Robert E. Bauman JD, *The Sovereign Individual*, September 2009

For many, searching for real estate offshore, where different laws and customs apply, may be enough to slow or end the dream of moving abroad.

Yet the most common real estate pitfalls are easy to avoid, if you know what they are. Following these simple rules can save you thousands of dollars and hours of regret.

1. Beware of net commissions. In many countries, the real estate agent (rather than the property owner) sets the sale price. The seller specifies the minimum amount they want from the sale. The agent may try to sell for 50% or even 100% more.

In foreign markets, these deals are particularly dangerous for buyers, because there's no U.S.-style Multiple Listing Service. So there's no way to compare selling prices of similar properties. The easiest way to avoid this practice is to negotiate directly with the property owner, not an agent.

2. Title insurance is available for offshore real estate. Buyers will always be told by the seller and his attorney that the title is good and they'll do all the paperwork to register the property in your name.

Never, ever rely on verbal promises. Raising the question of title insurance early in the process will head off future problems. If the seller has something to hide and becomes confrontational, you should immediately look elsewhere.

Use a reputable, independent attorney to guide the transaction. Make sure the title is investigated and the final deal is registered with the Public Land Registry.

3. Always buy fully titled real estate, never "rights of possession." Rights of possession are found in some Latin American countries such as Panama. This legal status means you can get only possession of a property with the possibility that the full title may be obtained after a length of time — normally about 15 years. But your rights are subject to legal challenge by the titled owners of the land at any time.

If you ask, the owner or agent may tell you that rights of possession are just like a title. That's absolutely untrue. Walk away from any property being sold merely as rights of possession.

4. Beware of laws that restrict foreign ownership. When buying foreign real estate, you must know the local rules and laws governing foreign ownership of the specific land in which you are interested.

In some countries, foreign buyers are advised to purchase through a corporation. In others, such as Mexico, foreigners are not allowed to buy oceanfront or coastal property or in other designated areas. Calculate the expense of dealing with such restrictive rules to decide if you are getting a good deal. If foreign ownership limits are at issue, always get a written guarantee from local authorities.

5. Offshore real estate markets can be difficult to navigate. In many countries there are no multiple listings, no sales histories and often no real estate agents per se. For foreign buyers, the asking price may well be higher than for a local buyer because the seller assumes you don't know the market.

To avoid this, start with local realtors and get an idea of the general market. Visit areas of interest. Look for "For Sale — *Si Vende*" signs. Stop in local bars and talk with whomever you can. It helps if you have a reliable local contact or friend to act as your front person to be sure you're quoted true local market prices.

6. Learn the options of offshore financing. In Western Europe, Panama and Mexico, loans should be available through a local bank, especially if you're a resident of the country. Although European rates are low, you can't get the high loan-to-value loans that U.S. banks used to give before the 2008 crash.

Also, don't expect a 30-year mortgage; 20 years is more typical. In less-developed countries, your options may be limited to developers who offer direct financing with terms that are generally unappealing.

You might arrange a loan in the U.S. using U.S. collateral from a second mortgage. Some offshore private banks will lend money against the value of your investment portfolio placed with them in your choice of currencies, but watch the currency exchange risk. Banks in Uruguay, for example, are helpful in advising on real estate investing, both on residential and farmland.

7. Market price, not asking price, must be your guide. For real estate in developing markets, the asking price is just a starting point; there are no multiple listings or comparative sales lists. Sellers price a property based on what they'd like to make, momentary cash needs or how neighboring properties have sold, regardless of how those properties compare with their own.

Offer only what you believe the property really is worth, even if it's only half the asking price. What it is really worth, the market value, is determined by the prices at which similar properties have recently sold. Don't be afraid to haggle.

Always insist on English translation. Buy/sell contracts are usually in Spanish or another local language. Due to vagaries in translation, the English version may not always be interpreted the same as the foreign language version. Before signing, have your local lawyer explain contract terms in English and resolve any conflicts or ambiguities.

8. Protect Your Privacy. When abroad, live modestly, securely and guard your privacy. Remember that real estate is generally a matter of public record in a foreign jurisdiction.

You can purchase and hold real estate in a foreign country without disclosing your ownership by placing the title in an international business corporation (IBC) located in another nation, such as Panama, where a company is known as an SA. There beneficial ownership does not have to be disclosed except to your attorney, in non-public listings or by court order.

An IBC that holds title does not have to be registered in the same nation where the real estate is located, thus real estate located in Hong Kong can be owned by an SA registered in Panama or elsewhere.

Buy Offshore Real Estate Using Your IRA

Not generally known, one of the best ways to "go offshore" is to use your existing U.S. pension or retirement plan to purchase offshore investments, including real estate. It's legal under U.S. law, although finding a cooperative U.S. custodian willing to let you buy the offshore investment can be challenging.

This strategy works for self-directed IRAs and 401(k) plans, along with some defined benefit plans. It won't work if your plan prohibits offshore investments. However, the overwhelming majority of plans have no such prohibition; the plan administrator simply doesn't want to take the effort to provide an offshore option.

There are some limitations, but they're easily managed. The first is that you can't immediately live in property purchased through your retirement plan. You can rent it out, though, and any income generated accumulates on a tax-deferred basis. When you retire, you can make a distribution of the property to yourself and then live there, if you choose. This is a taxable event if you funded your plan with pre-tax dollars.

In addition, if the rental income during the deferral period exceeds maintenance and other ownership costs, you'll pay tax on that income as well, but then the offshore home is yours.

All U.S.-based retirement plans are required by law to have a U.S.-based custodian. However, the plan's administrator and the cash and other assets owned by the IRA and its brokerage or other accounts can be located offshore, outside the jurisdiction of U.S. courts and government. The main function of this U.S. custodian is filing annual government tax and reporting paperwork, giving the value of your IRA account, contributions and distributions.

Several firms in the U.S. act as custodians for retirement funds. California-based Entrust Group and Texas-based Gold Star Trust are open to alternative investments and we work with both. If you want to use your IRA to buy offshore real estate or to establish a new offshore retirement account, as a first step I recommend you contact our associate Josh Bennett (refer to Appendix A for his contact information).

The Tax-Friendly Swap

You can also save taxes when acquiring offshore real estate by utilizing something called a "1031 exchange." Named after the section of the U.S. Internal Revenue Code that authorizes it, this program is a method for selling one property and acquiring another property within a set time period. The process practically is the same as any sale situation, but unique because the transaction is treated as an exchange and not a sale. This allows a U.S. taxpayer to qualify for deferred gain tax treatment.

Section 1031 lets you defer paying federal capital gains taxes when you sell an investment property and buy another one of "like kind" through an approved exchange transaction. As a bonus, you may be able to deduct tax for depreciation on the new property, without needing to recapture depreciation on the one you sell. To have a fully deferred exchange, the property you acquire must be of equal or greater value to the property you sell.

These exchanges are amazingly flexible because almost any like-kind investment property can be exchanged: real estate, industrial equipment, business assets, art work, aircraft or vessels. For instance, you could exchange raw land for a shopping center, a condo for a coffee shop or an office building for an apartment complex.

Exchanged properties can be located within the U.S. and also offshore. Plus, exchanges can be done within your IRA.

Offshore Real Estate is Not Reportable

The so-called 2010 HIRE Act passed by the Democrat-dominated U.S. Congress in 2009 that contained the odious Foreign Financial Assets Report requires that U.S. persons annually disclose any foreign financial assets with a combined value exceeding $50,000 on a new IRS Form 8938.

To the surprise of many, when the IRS issued the rules implementing in 2012, two types of titled offshore real estate owned by Americans were exempted from reporting:

1. Personally titled offshore real estate owned by Americans directly
2. Real estate held through a foreign registered legal entity controlled by a U.S. person

However, the foreign entity (IBC, LLC, SA) itself must be listed as a "specified foreign financial asset" on Form 8938 and the maximum value of the real estate included for calculating the total value of a person's offshore holdings must be reported.

This means that direct ownership in your own name of real property in a foreign country is not reportable annually to the U.S. Treasury on Form TD F 90-22.1. But any income earned from offshore real estate is reportable as taxable income on IRS Form 1040, the annual U.S. income tax form.

Chapter Three

Little-Known Secrets of Offshore Banking, Insurance & Finance

Part One: Offshore Bank & Financial Accounts

The Simple Way to a Private & Secure Offshore Account 142

Private Banking — Not Just for the Ultra-Wealthy 145

Types of Accounts Available at Offshore Banks 147

Ultimate Wealth Protection Secret: Strategies for Guarding Your Assets Overseas 149

Achieving Maximum Privacy in Your Offshore Account 160

Part Two: Law, Privacy & Asset Protection

U.S. Government Secretly Grabs Offshore Cash in Secret 164

The Money Laundering Control Act of 1986 166

The Government Took Their Cash — Literally 171

The Financial Crimes Enforcement Network (FinCEN) 173

To Report or Not to Report… That Is the Question 175

Five Ways to Maintain Your Offshore Privacy 176

"Article 26" and the Demise of Offshore Banking Secrecy 179

Asset Protection: What You Can Learn from Squids 181

Part Three: Places for Banking

Two Top Banking Havens of the World 183

The New World of Offshore Private Banking 186

Editor's Note:

The prime requirement for achieving iron-clad financial privacy and asset protection is to get your cash and property out of what the late admiral of the U.S. Navy John Paul Jones correctly described in a military sense as "harm's way."

This simply means you must move a large part of your financial activity "offshore" — out of, and away from, the high-tax nation you call home, whether it is the U.S., the U.K. or any other state bent upon confiscating your hard-earned wealth.

Here we present information and ideas that explain how to establish and use accounts located in a bank or financial institution in a foreign nation. We also explain U.S. laws governing offshore banking, money laundering and reporting of offshore cash transfers, touchy matters under the current state of the law.

PART ONE: OFFSHORE BANK & FINANCIAL ACCOUNTS

THE SIMPLE WAY TO A PRIVATE & SECURE OFFSHORE ACCOUNT
Erika Nolan, *The Sovereign Individual*, October 2009

About four years ago, I accomplished my "freedom trifecta."

I was living in one country, banking in two others and I had a second passport. You see, I hate to be pinned down or restricted in any way.

Freedom is about having options.

I sleep better at night because I know I could abandon my life here in the U.S. if worse came to worst. I could provide for my family using our offshore savings. I could also rebuild my career more quickly than most by being able to legally work in 27 countries.

Of course, I hope it never comes to this. But, smart money should be prepared and well diversified because the U.S. is struggling. The deficit, rapidly growing government and our nation's dependency on foreign lenders will have a profound long-term impact on the stock market as well as the value of the dollar.

If you haven't already done so, you should consider putting 10-20% of your net worth in non-U.S. investments and hold them overseas.

Rules of the Game Changed

For years the main way to do move wealth offshore was to find an offshore bank and open an account.

Most banks in Europe and Asia warmly welcomed American clients. But the climate has changed in the past year as the IRS has put pressure on international banks to turn over their U.S. clients as they search for non-reported accounts.

Attacks from the U.S. government have made many banks decide that it's not worth the hassle to service American clients.

How quickly is it changing? In March 2009, I set up a relationship with a boutique Swiss bank in Geneva.

Their only other office is in southern Switzerland…they have no U.S. exposure. By July, they had increased the minimum account opening minimum from $25,000 to $800,000. In August, they raised the minimum for Americans to over $2 million. And in September, they called to tell me they would no longer accept American clients regardless of the account size.

The same thing happened with two banks in Singapore.

While searching for an offshore bank today is a much greater challenge, all hope is not lost. Rather than searching for a bank overseas that will accept American clients, look for a qualified asset manager instead.

Asset Protection, Not Tax Savings

Keep in mind that you will not save on U.S. taxes…that's not the point. Any agreement you make with an independent asset manager (or a bank) will be in full compliance with IRS and SEC laws. Given all the attention on American clients, most international firms will require you to sign an IRS Form W-9 so that any taxable gains can be easily reported for tax compliance.

Wealth Preservation Techniques

Of course, independent managers can implement traditional investment strategies based on broad risk levels. However, they will often create customized portfolios for individual investors starting at lower minimums than offshore banks.

Many of the managers I know will provide customized investment management for accounts starting at $500,000. Compare this to the private banks (assuming they will even speak to an American client) that require a $2 million to $5 million account for a tailor made portfolio.

Your independent asset manager will work with you to determine the appropriate investment strategy to enable you to plan for your future. Also, by selecting the asset manager, you no longer have to worry about selecting an offshore bank.

Let the Manager Work for You

Asset managers have preferred banks they work with and will select a bank that will take American account holders. Plus, they will assist you in completing the account paperwork and in most cases they will select a bank that can provide tax reporting for you so that you stay compliant with the IRS.

You see, many banks will accept U.S. clients if the account is managed by a registered advisor with whom they have a proven history. The bank uses the advisor as their point of contact on the account.

They bank has very little, if any, interaction with you directly and this is why they will accept the account, even if you're an American citizen.

In addition, you have the added benefit of getting personalized service from your manager with only a tiny increase in annual fees depending on the size of your account.

Enjoy Better Service

Another important benefit is that independent asset managers get to know you on a personal level. A good independent asset manager will call you every few months to report on their investment performance and share their vision for the coming months.

Also, working with an independent asset manager means you won't have unwanted turnover on the management of your account. Independent managers tend to hold positions for many years. Independent asset managers are operating their own business or are partners in the business, as opposed to being a bank employee. That allows you and your family to build up good communication, expectations and trust with the manager over years rather than having to break in a new account manager every few years.

When you decide to move money offshore, you are able to take advantage of several benefits. For many the benefit is as simple as holding liquid non-dollar cash outside of the U.S. in case things go from bad to worse.

But one of the big benefits of diversifying your wealth internationally is access to a skilled international advisor. An advisor based in Vienna, Zürich, Singapore or Copenhagen has a very different world view then a U.S.-based advisor. They can bring true diversification to your overall investment portfolio.

A list of recommended asset managers are listed in Appendix A.

Private Banking — Not Just for the Ultra-Wealthy

Robert E. Bauman JD, *The Sovereign Investor Daily*, April 2007

The term "private banking" is becoming so overused that it's lost some of the exclusivity that was once attached to the intensely secret dealings between a banker and his wealthy clients.

American banks, always chasing the almighty dollar, have recently been trying to sell their wholesale "private banking" as if it were a special service. This — from banks where you must stand in line forever to see a teller and where you can never get a human being, only a recording, on the phone.

Almost every bank with any pretensions to being international offers special rates of interest to wealthier private depositors under the heading of "private banking." Minimums in some cases start at entry levels of US$100,000 or much higher (US$500,000 in Swiss banks) before offering special treatment to their clients. The truth is, the more cash you deposit, the more private banking attention you get.

History Behind Private Banks

Private banking, for the most part, was an art developed offshore — in London, Zürich and Vienna. Over two centuries ago Mayer Amschel Rothschild (1743-1812), founder of the famous international banking dynasty, created private banking. The House of Rothschild filled a void, creating a profitable continental money system that influenced the course of European history by financing its rulers and wars. Now, that was private banking.

"Private banking" has come to mean investment management beyond offering a confidential relationship with a person to whom you entrust your money. Those personal relationships still exist in the traditional places such as The City in London. But they apply more to extremely rich people than to moderately wealthy people who want more personalized treatment than they can get from their local bank branch or on the Internet. In this case, private banking means investment management offered on a personalized basis by a bank to an individual (or his company, trust or family foundation) with disposable wealth of more than US$250,000 or more.

Until relatively recently, only the wealthiest investors could benefit from having any kind of offshore bank account. Only the richest of the rich could afford the fees and legal advice associated with going offshore. Now, after dramatic changes in international banking and communications, even a modest offshore account can be your quick, inexpensive entry into the world of foreign investment opportunities.

Only Law-Abiding Customers Welcome

Put aside the erroneous popular notion that foreign bank accounts are designed for shady international drug kingpins and unscrupulous wheeler dealers trying to avoid paying taxes. For some people, offshore accounts will always evoke images of spies from the U.S. Central Intelligence Agency or the U.K.'s MI-5. Although these cloak and dagger images are entertaining, they hardly relate to our present practical purposes: to build offshore financial structures to increase your wealth legally and protect your assets.

And private banking offshore is better because the cost of such special treatment is more than offset by the superior profits available with offshore investments. You can use a foreign bank account as an integral tool in an aggressive, two-pronged offshore wealth strategy. One goal is to increase your asset value by cutting taxes and maximizing profits. The other is to build a strong defensive asset protection structure. In other words, an offshore private bank account is not just a place for safekeeping cash.

One of the great advantages of an offshore bank account is the ability to trade freely and invest in foreign-issued stocks, bonds, mutual funds and national currencies that are not available in your home country. An offshore account is an excellent way to diversify investments and take advantage of global tax savings. You can have instant access to the world's best investment opportunities, including currencies and precious metals without concern about your home nation's legal restrictions.

Big Business — Worth Trillions in Overseas Assets

Offshore banking is big business worldwide. Recent estimates [2007] calculate that US$2 trillion to US$5 trillion is stashed in nearly 40 offshore banking havens that impose no taxes, have less onerous regulations, guarantee privacy and cater to nonresidents. One-third of the entire world's private wealth is stashed in Switzerland alone!

The Sovereign Society can recommend excellent banks that offer private management in many offshore financial centers — Switzerland, Panama, Liechtenstein, Austria, Hong Kong and Singapore. Other banking haven nations such as Monaco, Andorra, the Cayman Islands, the Channel Islands and the Isle of Man are also available.

If you want to protect and grow your wealth, an offshore private bank account should be a primary consideration.

Types of Accounts Available at Offshore Banks
Banking in Silence, Scope Books, 1998

The offshore banking industry offers a much wider range of account types than most onshore banking jurisdictions. The options vary from simple savings accounts to accounts designed for the sole purpose of tax avoidance to accounts where the bank invests and oversees your money on your behalf.

The various types of accounts can be grouped into a few categories. Although the names may change from bank to bank, the basic design behind each account type is more or less the same.

They are as follows:

Current accounts are the most common type of account. They generally come with a checkbook or debit card and can sometimes be linked with a credit card. The required starting balance is low, but the interest rate is also generally low. Some banks allow for multi-currency accounts, meaning that you can deposit and withdraw funds in any of a number of currencies. You can also easily change either all or part of your account into the currency of your choice.

Deposit accounts are generally a good place to store money over the slightly longer term. They offer higher interest rates, but restrict your ability to get at your money by requiring that you provide sufficient notice or sacrifice the interest earned. Starting balances are also generally higher with many banks requiring a minimum deposit of somewhere in the region of US$10,000. The interest rate depends upon the amount deposited, as well as the time period for which it will stay in the account. It also depends on the currency in which the account is denominated, stronger currencies paying less interest.

Twin accounts basically combine a high-interest deposit account with the convenience of a current account under one, all-inclusive number. The bulk of the funds on deposit is kept in the high interest account while a smaller amount is kept in the current account for day to day use. If you one day find yourself overdrawn, the bank would then merely transfer money from the deposit account into the current account. Thus, the need to maintain two different accounts is eliminated.

Fiduciary accounts allow you to invest anonymously in high-tax markets, even in your home country, by using your bank as a proxy investor. For example, if you maintain an account in a Liechtenstein bank but wish to hold part of your overall portfolio in German marks, you could instruct your banker to open an account in Germany on your behalf. The marks would be purchased in Frankfurt and then held there in the bank's name, although the interest earned is paid to you in Liechtenstein. For the record, it appears as if the bank is acting on its own initiative, meaning that if you happen to be German you would no longer be liable for German tax. Of course, the bank charges a fee, usually one quarter of one percent of your principal, for providing you with such anonymity. You also receive a slightly lower interest payment than you would if you made the deposit on your own.

Certificates of Deposit (CDs) are a way to earn much higher interest rates than those on offer through deposit accounts. In short, your funds are loaned to the Euro currency market at the current rate for the currency in which the CD is denominated. CDs usually come in bearer form, meaning that they can be freely and anonymously traded. They enjoy a large and active secondary market. They vary a great deal in terms of the maturity of the investment, ranging from almost overnight to up to five years. Best of all, banks do not withhold any tax on the CDs that they issue, meaning that with a little creative planning your money can earn hefty interest payments tax free.

Precious metal accounts allow you to invest in precious metals via your bank. The bank will then store the metal in its vault on your behalf. The advantage of opening up this type of account is that by combining your resources with those of other bank clients, you can purchase precious metals at a far more competitive price. Of course, such an account does not generate any income but should be seen as a safety net. The bank generally charges an annual storage fee usually in the region of one half of one percent of the value of the metals on deposit.

Investment accounts are usually only offered by larger banks. They allow you to invest your funds in commodity markets with the help of your bank. They usually take the form of a mutual fund in stocks, bonds and other commodities and are overseen by the bank itself. The required starting balance is somewhat hefty, generally US$50,000. These accounts usually come with rather high front-end costs as well as significant management fees. But as long as the markets are performing well a good investment account will on average prove to be more profitable than a simple deposit account.

Managed accounts work much like investment accounts but allow you to choose where to invest your funds. Instructions of what to buy and sell are sent to the bank by phone or fax. It is possible to hold the commodities purchased in the bank's name rather than your own for an extra layer of privacy. The price for such convenience takes the form of a minimum deposit requirement of at least US$250,000.

Safekeeping accounts allow you to deposit bonds, stocks and other valuables. The bank will then manage the overall portfolio deposited, redeeming the bonds when they mature and doing whatever need be done with the valuables entrusted to them. Of course, such convenience comes with a price tag, usually a fee of approximately .015 percent of the market value of the portfolio they are maintaining.

Ultimate Wealth Protection Secret: Strategies for Guarding Your Assets Overseas

Ted Bauman, *Offshore Confidential*, October 2014

Your wealth isn't safe. Trust me — I know.

As someone who researches and writes on asset and wealth protection, privacy, banking and electronic security issues, I make sure to get several bank balance updates every day. And just this morning, as I sat down to write this report, I noticed that the balance on my main transaction account was less than it should have been.

My Bank of America ATM card had been hacked.

Overnight, someone had conducted bogus Internet transactions at non-existent businesses in Florida and California. The pattern was classic, and a dead giveaway: first a small amount, then a bigger one, then a bigger one after that. They were probing to see if my card worked and how much I had in my account.

Luckily, I called the bank to cancel the card before they tested it a fourth time … which is typically when they clean you out.

Even an expert like me is at risk. All I did was buy something at corporate data breach victim Home Depot … or use the card at a gas station pump with a "card reader" surreptitiously installed … and boom! My money's gone.

You're at risk, too … but hackers may be the least of your worries.

Imagine you wake up one day to find that your bank accounts have been cleaned out, your credit cards frozen and your investment accounts blocked. You and your business have bills to pay. Your family depends on you for food and shelter.

And now you can't provide for them because someone has taken your wealth — or more precisely, they've taken the electronic data entries that represent the pieces of paper and coinage that represent your wealth. In the topsy-turvy world of 2014, where our government is obsessed with snooping on its private citizens, the biggest threat to your wealth isn't the mafia, Russian hackers, identity fraudsters or petty criminals surreptitiously inserting card readers into gas-station pumps.

The biggest threat is, in fact, the Internal Revenue Service and the U.S. Department of Treasury. These goons have constructed a web of legal and regulatory traps that can be used to justify stealing your wealth for a wide variety of reasons.

You don't have to do anything wrong … you just have to be "suspicious" or have your property unknowingly misused by a criminal, triggering asset forfeiture laws. That's all the "justification" our out-of-control government needs to set your net worth clock back to zero — or worse.

But as I wrote in February's *Offshore Confidential*, there's an even bigger threat looming on the horizon ... wealth confiscation in the form of a one-off tax.

One fine day you'll wake up to find that the government has taken your money out of the bank — just like the hackers did to me. Except that the government's theft will somehow be "legal."

I've got a special solution for you. It's legal, above-board, and within the financial reach of almost everyone. But it will lower your financial profile and go a long way to protecting you from wealth confiscation.

Bet on it: A Wealth Tax is Coming

Wealth taxes have been on many people's minds since the International Monetary Fund (IMF) first mooted the idea back in November 2013. They've been imposed already in Cyprus. The EU, the German Bundesbank and the Bank of England have been dropping hints ever since that a wealth tax could be coming soon to a country near you.

A "wealth tax" — or "bail-in" — is a one-off statutory procedure to seize a proportion of private wealth in order to reduce government debt rapidly. It could be imposed on households' net worth — including their shareholdings and fixed assets such as real estate — but this would pose liquidity problems for many people and enforcement problems for governments.

The scenario I predict is a levy on bank balances, as in the Cyprus case. Banks would simply be instructed to deduct a certain percentage of the balance — say, 10% — of each savings, checking or deposit account and transfer it to the government or central bank.

But the government could go one step further and order households to report the value of near-liquid assets, such as gold, and calculate the amount to take from your bank accounts based on that figure.

And if there wasn't enough in your bank accounts ... and those near-liquid assets were located in the U.S. ... the government could just seize them by court order.

There's only one sure way to stop this nightmare scenario from happening to you. You've got to convert some of your portfolio into physical assets that are hard to track, value ... and aren't reportable to our kleptomaniac Uncle Sam. But this isn't about hiding your wealth.

You're just taking advantage of legal provisions that allow you to keep your wealth in forms and places that aren't subject to offshore reporting requirements, such as the Foreign Account Tax Compliance Act (FATCA).

Some of the steps you need to take that we've discussed previously in *Offshore Confidential* include:

1. Keep cash, in U.S. dollars and select foreign currencies, in a home safe (February 2014 issue).
2. Maintain some asset in "quiet wealth" such as rare collectible stamps (March 2014 issue).
3. Set up a "dirt bank" of foreign land holdings (June 2014 issue).
4. Create an i-Account (http://i-account.cc/welcome) — an easy and legal way to keep some cash in an offshore account (July 2014 issue).

In this article, I'm going to reveal the ultimate wealth protection secret. These are strategies that anyone, even small investors, can take to protect themselves against financial intrusion from the biggest threat of them all ... our own government.

How Safe is a Safe?

A home safe is an essential part of your wealth protection strategy. If it's in your safe, it's not in a bank. This move helps to significantly lower your financial profile.

A home safe should be too heavy to move. It should be fire resistant, offering at least 30 minutes of protection against 350 degree Fahrenheit external heat, with a maximum internal temperature of 125 degrees (Underwriters Laboratories Class 125). It should be rated class UL TL-30 or above, which means that it will take a minimum of 30 minutes for someone to cut into it with most power tools. It should be waterproof.

But there's a bigger threat than fire, water and criminal elements: The U.S. courts.

As my dad, Bob Bauman, regularly points out, there's a massive loophole in every strategy based on keeping wealth inside the U.S., including physical assets in your home safe. If you're instructed by a judge to reveal your assets under oath, you must do so. And once you have, courts can order them seized — including the contents of your home safe.

Most of us are aware of President Roosevelt's infamous Executive Order 6102 of 1933, which ordered anyone holding gold to turn it over to the government at $20 an ounce. The order also made it a crime to hold monetary gold anywhere in the continental United States. But it's happened in other places, too.

In 1959, Australia used its Banking Act to outlaw the ownership of most gold, demanding it be turned over to the government. Not long after that, the British tried to shore up the pound by banning ownership of more than four gold coins.

The bottom line is that keeping gold or other precious metals in your own country is asking for trouble if wealth taxes are in the offing. That's why the strategies I'm about to reveal are all based on secure storage of physical assets in a vault located outside the U.S. but in economically stable regions so that your assets are highly unlikely to fall prey to confiscation. Of course, they're perfectly legal and above board in every way.

Assets in foreign countries are beyond the immediate reach of U.S. courts. Even if you have to tell a judge about them, you don't have to hand them over and the Feds can't just go get them. Instead, the U.S. government would have to pursue those assets in foreign courts under foreign rules.

Some countries might cooperate to seize and repatriate assets of U.S. citizens, but many won't. Even those that are inclined to do so would have to follow their own privacy and forfeiture laws, making it expensive and time-consuming for the U.S. government to go after most people's offshore physical wealth in the event of a tax grab.

Beating the Bank

So locating part of your physical wealth offshore is a key tactic. But there's some crucial information you must consider to help you decide how you're going to store your wealth offshore.

If your precious metals or other physical assets are kept in a safe deposit box or other storage facility operated by a bank or other financial institution, you must report them to the Treasury and the IRS. That's because secure storage with a financial institution is considered a "foreign financial account" … and therefore reportable.

If in any calendar year the total value of all your "foreign financial accounts" is more than $10,000, you must complete Part III of Schedule B of IRS Form 1040 when you file your U.S. federal income tax return, and FinCEN Form 114. (Report of Foreign Bank and Financial Accounts, or FBAR.)

And starting in 2013, under FATCA, U.S. persons are required to file an IRS Form 8938 along with their annual tax return, disclosing any foreign financial assets with a combined value exceeding $50,000. That includes bank-stored gold or other physical assets starting in 2014.

But here's the thing … if your offshore physical assets are stored in a non-bank secure facility … presto! They aren't reportable to Uncle Sam under current law. So he won't know to deduct a corresponding amount from your U.S. bank accounts in the event of a wealth tax.

The secret to maximum security and peace of mind in an anti-wealth tax strategy is therefore to own gold and other precious metals and valuable assets directly, in your own name, stored in a reputable non-bank institution outside the United States.

I have investigated your various options for overseas asset protection. Let me show you how to do it.

Offshore Vaults: The Basics

In what follows, I'm going to refer mainly to gold and other precious metals, since these are the most common forms of physical assets held offshore. But the principles apply to certain other storable, high-value assets, such as rare collectible stamps, which I discussed in the March issue of *Offshore Confidential*.

There are a variety of non-bank services around the world that can store your physical assets. They are extremely secure — that's what they're selling, after all. All holdings are subject to regular external audits and are fully insured, typically by Lloyd's of London or another reputable international insurer.

These services generally fall into two broad categories:

1. **Storage-only services** will accept and store anything of value, from coins to fleets of cars. These are typically high-end services used by seven- and eight-figure net worth individuals who have the wherewithal to arrange international asset transportation, negotiate customs, and deposit them with the vault company, to whom they pay a storage fee for strictly segregated storage (i.e., an individual vault or sub-vault). They are often used by people who have regular business in the storage country, and travel there regularly.

2. **Brokerage services:** These services help you buy and sell gold (coins and bars) and other precious metals as well as store it. These services are suited to individuals who may have no reason to travel to the storage country regularly, don't have existing gold or other hard asset holdings that need to be transported there and/or who may be in the process of accumulating such assets over time.

To meet the non-reporting requirement, such brokerage services must only facilitate the purchase, storage, and sale of precious metals and other assets. They charge you for these services. The gold or other assets they store for you aren't part of their own corporate assets, so the companies can't borrow or trade against them — they are yours and yours alone at all times. Brokerage storage services are further subdivided into two types:

   a. **Unallocated storage** means that you have an ownership interest in coins or bars that are part of a collective holding. You don't have title to specific coins or bars, but instead have fractional ownership of the total pool of metal, together with other investors. This lets you buy in smaller quantities at a more favorable price. Unallocated services usually charge lower storage fees here.

Vendor reputation is critical, as the relationship is based on trust that the metal will be there should you opt to take physical possession. When you do, you'll pay a "fabrication fee" — so-called because your personal holding has to be "fabricated" from the common pool. The Perth Mint is an example of this.

b. **Allocated storage** means that you own specific coins and/or bars within a total pool of metal. They may or may not be segregated from other people's holdings, but they are certified and audited in your name. Allocated storage allows you to take delivery of your metals anytime. An allocated storage service doesn't incur delivery fabrication fees, but storage charges are higher and vary as the price of (and cost to insure) precious metals varies. The Hard Assets Alliance is an example.

Two Key Tips for Global Storage

There are some caveats to non-bank offshore storage that I want you to know about for your protection.

1. If ownership of precious metals or other assets is held in the name of a legal entity, such as a corporation under your control, they must be reported as part of your interest in the entity, even if they are in a non-financial storage facility.

2. The Treasury Department defines a financial agency as "a person acting for a person as a financial institution bailor, depository trustee, or agent, or acting in a similar way related to money, credit, securities, or gold, or in a transaction in money, credit, securities, or gold." If you buy gold or other precious metals offshore and pay a company a fee to manage it, under this definition, it is probably acting as a financial agency. But if specific gold is owned in your name, and in a private vault facility to which you or your designee have access, it isn't reportable.

Which One is for You?

We're after a solution that maximizes your financial privacy and legally eliminates the need to tell the U.S. government about physical assets that you hold offshore, so they can't be used to calculate your net worth at wealth-tax time.

In this respect, the preferred option is allocated storage. That's because — although the rules on this post-FATCA aren't entirely clear — it appears that unallocated storage may meet the Treasury definition of a foreign financial institution, and therefore trigger reporting requirements.

If you buy gold or other precious metals offshore on an unallocated basis, you don't own specific metal, and you can't just show up and visit it or claim it. It's not being audited in your name as owner, but in the name of whoever manages the collective pool of metal. The transaction is more about the value of the gold than the gold itself — and hence could be seen as primarily a financial matter.

To be absolutely secure, your goal should be to own specific metals in your own name, which are audited on your behalf, in a private vault facility to which only you or your designee (such as power of attorney) have access.

Of course, not everyone is in a position to achieve this immediately, since it's only cost effective to store gold this way when you've got a fair amount of it. That's why I'm going to give you an option that gets you there a step at a time.

Choosing an Overseas Haven

Obviously, whether you opt for allocated or unallocated offshore storage, you're going to want to do business with a reputable company, such as those I'm going to recommend below.

But there's another issue to think about: in what country should your vault be located? Most storage companies give you options in this regard, and it's important to think carefully when choosing among them.

As I noted earlier, some countries are a little too close for comfort to the U.S. government and tend to cooperate when asked. And some European countries, such as Germany, France and Italy, have been talking openly about wealth taxes for some time.

Under the current global climate, I don't recommend using storage facilities in the Anglo countries — the U.K., Australia, Canada or New Zealand. London, Melbourne and Perth offer well-known storage and brokerage services, but for our purposes — maximum protection against potential wealth confiscation — their closeness to the U.S. government rules them out.

Instead, I want to focus on two countries with excellent secure storage facilities, strong privacy laws and respect for property and the rule of law more generally.

Safe in Singapore: Singapore is a safe and political reliable jurisdiction. That's why many of the world's wealthy households are moving their gold there. But it's also the result of a deliberate strategy by the island state. Singapore's government wants to be the global leader in offshore gold holdings.

Indeed, Singapore is on track to increase its gold deposits five-fold in just a few years. It did this by eliminating taxes on bullion purchases. Previously, bullion sales were taxed at the normal 7% Goods and Services Tax rate (VAT). It was possible to get around that by trading and storing metals at the Singapore FreePort by the airport, a tax-free zone where holdings are stored under lock and key. But that was only for big-money types.

On October 1, 2012, however, Singapore's government eliminated the GST tax on gold, so purchases of "investment grade" bullion are now tax-free. As a result, it is possible to buy and sell gold and other precious metals throughout Singapore at competitive international prices.

At the same time, Singapore made it easy to get gold in and out of the country. The government views precious metals as commodities, not as reportable currency. Singapore Customs doesn't even ask about the beneficial owner of precious metals when they pass through the airport.

With these changes in the regulatory environment, Singapore has sprouted numerous secure non-bank storage facilities. Some offer free storage for a time. Others charge competitive prices based on the volume of storage required, starting at a few hundred dollars a year.

Austrian Options: Because of local laws, renting a vault in Singapore does require the vault owner to know who you are, as well as the broad nature of what you're storing (e.g. "precious metals"). But if completely anonymous gold storage is what you're after, the place to go is Vienna, Austria.

Austria has long valued financial privacy. When EU banking regulators forbade anonymous bank accounts in 1984, Austrian banks were prohibited from offering anonymous safe deposit boxes too. So one Austrian bank with a large number of anonymous box holders sold its physical assets to a new company that turned the place into a private non-bank storage service — Das Safe.

It's one of the only offshore facilities that allows you to rent secure storage space anonymously. Das Safe is relatively inexpensive (the smallest anonymous box is about $580 a year). A personal visit is required to rent a box, however.

The advent of FATCA, which has prompted banks all over the EU and in Switzerland to drop American customers, has forced many bank-based box-holders to look for non-bank alternatives, putting pressure on the supply of Austrian storage space. As market forces usually do, this is prompting Das Safe to expand and other Austrian institutions to consider getting into the secure storage business.

Three Options for Wealth Security

The big question you're probably asking yourself is this: what's the best option for me? Let me spell your options out. But before I do, let's be clear: I'm not advising you on the financial and investment aspects of owning gold. That's the job of my esteemed colleague, Jeff Opdyke. My purpose here is to give you ways to own and store gold and other hard assets outside the U.S., in a secure, allocated non-financial facility, so you don't have to report them to the U.S. government.

Strategy #1: The Hard Assets Alliance

The Hard Assets Alliance (HAA), with whom we have an existing relationship, offers a handy way to build a precious metals position directly offshore, stored securely with its vault partner Malca-Amit in Singapore.

HAA's SmartMetal program allows you to invest toward ownership of bullion (gold or silver) each month (minimum $250) using an online interface. Once you've accumulated the equivalent of one troy ounce of gold (or 100 ounces of silver) you can convert it into a serial-numbered bar that sits in allocated storage under your title. (Precious metal is measured in troy ounces, unlike the avoirdupois ounces used to measure things like food; 16 ounces avoirdupois equal 14.58 troy.) At this point you are able to "take delivery" of the physical bullion, or simply leave it HAA's nonbank, and therefore non-reportable, Malca-Amit vaults in Singapore.

Until your account with HAA converts into a real bar of bullion, it's considered a "financial account" located inside the U.S., like any other bank or investment account. Because of this, it's not reportable as a foreign financial account (but it is traceable to you). As soon as HAA converts your account into a real piece of bullion, however, it becomes an allocated, and therefore, non-reportable physical asset located offshore — just what I've been recommending in this report.

For example, if the price of an ounce of gold is $1,250, you will own one ounce of non-reportable, fully-allocated offshore gold in five months at $250 a month with HAA. And throughout the entire process, your interest in the gold isn't reportable to the IRS or under FBAR.

It's worth mentioning that HAA has direct access to refiners, bullion banks and institutional level dealers, which helps drive its relatively lower global purchase premiums. Your order is bid out to this pool of institutions that compete for HAA's business, ensuring a great price.

Once the bullion is yours, HAA's current annual Singapore storage rates are (as a % of the value of your metal):

Up to $100,000 in assets:	0.70% gold, palladium, platinum; 0.80% silver
$100,001-$500,000 in assets:	0.65% gold, palladium, platinum; 0.75% silver
$500,001-$1,000,000 in assets:	0.60% gold, palladium, platinum; 0.70% silver
$1,000,001+ in assets:	0.50% gold, palladium, platinum; 0.60% silver

So, for example, storing $100,000 worth of gold with HAA in Singapore would cost you $700 a year.

Strategy #2: Coins in a Box … And Then Another Box

Roosevelt's 1933 confiscation order didn't apply to gold and silver coins with "a recognized special value to collectors of rare and unusual coins," a.k.a. "numismatic coins." You've probably seen adverts for such coins on TV.

The attraction of these coins is that they are likely to be exempted from any future gold confiscation (although it's impossible to be certain of that).

Among pre-1933 collectible gold coins, the "bullion coin" is of particular interest among investors. The coin is valued by its weight in a specific precious metal. Unlike commemorative or numismatic coins valued by mintage, rarity, condition and age, bullion coins are worth what the metal they contain is worth.

There are many pre-1933 bullion coins that trade at their bullion value and are protected by their pre-1933 status as "collectible." Those are the ones you want — the first part of a coin-based strategy. The second part of a coin strategy is to buy bullion coins — recently minted, non-collectible coins that trade for their weight in gold or silver. In most cases, purchases of bullion and are coins are not reportable to the U.S. government as many might fear. Yes, most sales of most bullion coins have to be reported to the government on a Form 1099-B, but only the amount sold. Not to whom the bullion or coins were sold.

The added good news is that there are some coins that don't need to be reported at all to the government. Coins that aren't on the list include: U.S. Gold Eagle and Gold Buffalo coins, Australian Perth Mint coins, Austrian coins, Canadian silver Maple Leafs, Chinese Panda coins and fractional bullion coins.

In addition, sales of less than 25 ounces of foreign bullion coins such as South African Krugerrands and British Sovereigns are also not reportable. Similarly, certain pre-1933 coins trade at bullion prices but are technically classified as "collectible." That means they aren't considered a financial asset, but rather as a numismatic coin, even though they carry no numismatic premium. Sales of such coins also don't have to be reported.

Finally, cash purchases of any bullion under $10,000 more than 24 hours apart or by check for higher amounts, aren't reportable either (although your bank may report a very large check transaction to FinCEN).

So if you want to go it alone, a good strategy is to accumulate a stock of pre-1933 bullion coins, contemporary non-reportable bullion coins, or small (one ounce) gold bars over time, being careful to ensure that the transactions aren't reportable.

You can store them in your home safe until you have enough to justify the expense of acquiring an insured private offshore storage facility such as Das Safe and shipping them to it by a secure courier, such as Brinks.

At a current price of about $1,250 an ounce, as few as 50 coins or ounce bars could do the trick.

Strategy #3: Straight to Das Safe

A third strategy is more direct, but requires more upfront investment and involvement on your part. It involves purchasing a larger quantity of bullion offshore and having it transferred to storage there, without ever involving the U.S. Here are some options:

- You can purchase a quantity of bullion via HAA and to have it immediately deposited in secure storage in Singapore with Malca-Amit. There is one catch, though. In order to "take delivery" of your bullion in Singapore, you actually have to go there, sign for it and make arrangements in advance with HAA to verify your identity.

  Nevertheless, for those able to purchase a significant amount of bullion (over $200,000), HAA can make special arrangements on an individual basis to facilitate delivery to their private vault in Singapore without your presence.

- You can purchase bullion through another dealer in Singapore and, if the amounts in question warrant it, even rent space in the Singapore FreePort.

- In Vienna, the most desirable option is Das Safe. As I've noted, however, Das Safe requires your presence to rent space initially, and the post-FATCA rush to get out of formal banks means such space may be limited. Other secure storage companies are planning to open in Vienna, and we will keep you updated as new opportunities arise.

- It's certainly possible to do this with fairly small amounts of gold or other metals, but again, this must be balanced against storage costs. Coins and small bars (one ounce) can be acquired as I have explained above, but if you have deep pockets, large bullion bars may be your choice. They tend to sell for the lowest premium per ounce. The top three weights are 1 kilogram (32.15 troy ounces), 100 ounces, and 400 ounces.

A Final Word

There are, of course, a myriad of ways to own gold and other precious metals, both in the U.S. and abroad. There are exchange-traded funds. You can own metals via an LLC, or even make a gift of gold to your children tax-free. But there is only one way to own gold that is completely secret from the U.S. government: In your own name, in a secure non-bank vault in a foreign country.

Fortunately, there are ways of achieving this that even people of modest means can achieve. For my money the most attractive is the Hard Assets Alliance. Not only is their product affordable and easy to use; HAA can also liquidate your bullion holdings for you. If you go it alone with bullion coins or a bigger offshore vault, you'll have to be more directly involved.

As with all other aspects of offshore asset protection, it's important to seek good legal and tax advice. For this reason, if you have any doubts about what you are doing, I would encourage you to seek expert counsel, such as our trusted friend Josh Bennett, whose contact details are listed in Appendix A. Additional asset protection services can also be found here:

Hard Assets Alliance
1325 Avenue of Americas, 7th Floor Suite 0703-2
New York, NY 10019
Toll-free: 877-727-7387
Internationally: +602-626-3022
Email: support@hardassetsalliance.com
Web: http://www.hardassetsalliance.com

DAS SAFE
Auerspergstrasse 1, A-1080
Vienna, Austria
Tel.: +43 1 406 61 74
Email: info@dassafe.com
Web: http://www.dassafe.com

Brink's Global Services:
Web: http://www.brinksglobal.com

Holdings
1801 Bayberry Ct.
P.O. Box 18100
Richmond, Virginia 23226-8100 USA
Tel.: +1 (804) 289-9600

U.S. Operations
555 Dividend Dr. (U.S. Operations)
Coppell, Texas 75019
Tel.: 469-549-6000 or 800-927-4657 x 3475
Email: servicequote@brinksinc.com

ACHIEVING MAXIMUM PRIVACY IN YOUR OFFSHORE ACCOUNT

Mark Nestmann, *The Sovereign Individual*, August 2003

In the minds of most Americans, there is nothing so mysterious, so enticing, as an "offshore bank account."

The very phrase, particularly among the wine and brie crowd, brings up images of exotic and possibly illegal financial dealings in a tropical setting, accompanied by absolute bank privacy.

The movie *The Firm*, which was popular a few years ago, greatly reinforced these stereotypes. It portrayed the Cayman Islands as a jurisdiction where you could simply land a plane stuffed with bags of cash and deposit that cash directly into a local bank account.

However, those days, if they ever existed at all, are long gone. The truth about offshore bank accounts is very different from what you hear at parties or see at the movies. In this article, I'm going to separate fact from fiction, and give you six recommendations that will allow you to legally protect the privacy of your offshore account.

The Truth about "Bank Secrecy"

For better or worse, the concept of "bank secrecy" has changed greatly in recent years. Thirty years ago, it was possible to hire an attorney in one of several offshore jurisdictions — including Switzerland, Liechtenstein or The Bahamas — and have the attorney open up an offshore bank account, in his name, and operate it for you without the bank knowing your real identity.

In those days, secrecy was virtually absolute. No one — including agents of the U.S. government — could penetrate it, except in very unusual circumstances.

All this began to change in the 1970s, when the United States signed its first "Mutual Legal Assistance Treaty" (MLAT) with Switzerland. This agreement obligated Swiss authorities to waive bank secrecy when the U.S. government presented them with evidence that money tied to a serious crime in the United States was held being in Switzerland. Tax offenses, with the exception of tax fraud, were not covered.

Since then, the United States has ratified nearly 50 additional MLATs, most with expanded provisions in comparison to the Swiss agreement. In addition, various international organizations, including the Organization for Economic Cooperation and Development (OECD) and its stepchild, the Financial Action Task Force (FATF), have prepared "blacklists" of countries in which "excessive financial secrecy" prevails, and tried to impose sanctions against those countries not agreeing to severely restrict it.

But bank secrecy has not been "eliminated," as some press reports would imply. The best way to view bank secrecy today is as a bulwark against prying eyes peering into your financial affairs, unless you are suspected of committing a serious crime.

No doubt, bank secrecy occasionally shields lawbreakers. But more often than not, it is used for legitimate purposes — to shield individuals and their families from retribution by corrupt or totalitarian governments; to give them access to investments forbidden or restricted in their own countries; or to hide wealth from kidnappers who typically target persons with visible wealth.

And today, even if some of the more powerful tools individuals and companies could once use to keep their financial affairs secret have been severely restricted, there remain opportunities for financial privacy "offshore" that simply don't exist domestically. You just have to be realistic in your expectations.

Offshore Bank Accounts and Privacy

While it's become more difficult to move money offshore, you can still take your domestic wealth off the radar screen to achieve practical, if not necessarily impenetrable, privacy.

The single best reason to move assets outside your own country is to protect yourself from the global litigation epidemic. The United States is unique in its approach to "tort liability," in which both sides in a lawsuit pay their own expenses, no matter who wins, and where lawyers are permitted to finance lawsuits, no matter how ridiculous the claim. In recent months, doctors have actually gone on strike in several states to protest skyrocketing malpractice premiums resulting from increased exposure to lawsuits.

However, truly frivolous litigation is no longer only a U.S. phenomenon. The U.K. and Canadian legal systems are also undergoing quiet, yet revolutionary transformations that dramatically increase the odds of being sued and losing.

An offshore bank account provides substantial protection from frivolous lawsuits. Since lawyers size up targets for lawsuits by looking for their money, someone considering suing you may decide to find a target with more visible wealth. Unfortunately, the availability of offshore bank accounts with low minimums is rapidly diminishing. This is a direct consequence of the escalating cost of banks performing "due diligence" on their customers to comply with new initiatives from the OECD and FATF.

Six Recommendations for Offshore Banking Secrecy

The advantages of dealing offshore — privacy, asset protection and investment diversification — remain in place, but only if you follow a few simple rules.

1. **Choose the right jurisdiction.** We believe the top offshore jurisdictions to be Switzerland, Panama, Uruguay and Hong Kong. First class offshore banking services are also available in Austria. Denmark offers low-cost offshore banking, but no privacy with regards to foreign tax authorities.

2. **Understand foreign "due diligence" requirements.** Along with the end of anonymous accounts in most offshore jurisdictions, most offshore banks now require prospective customers to prove their identity with a certified copy of their passport or other official document. You may also face questions regarding the origin of the funds you are placing into the account. Don't be afraid to answer these questions— the application for your account along with all documentation you provide is subject to whatever bank secrecy laws prevail in the jurisdiction you've chosen.

3. **Don't try to cheat the tax man.** Most high tax countries impose taxes on the worldwide income of their residents. While domestic tax authorities don't generally have the authority to go on offshore "fishing expeditions" to uncover unreported offshore income, the momentum is clearly toward greater disclosure. There's also little doubt that the tools that governments are giving themselves to fight "terrorism" will ultimately be used to augment tax collection. Our recommendation is to report the existence of the account to your domestic tax authorities and pay whatever taxes are due. Doing so will not generally raise a red flag and will not negate the privacy advantages of the account with respect to prospective litigants. At least in the case of the IRS, there have been many more prosecutions for failing to report an offshore transaction than for engaging in an allegedly illegal transaction that was reported.

4. **Don't open an account at the foreign branch of a U.S. bank or a foreign bank that has U.S. branches.** Either of these factors places the bank under the jurisdiction of U.S. courts, thus providing litigants with additional opportunities to penetrate offshore banking secrecy.

5. **Don't use offshore accounts to hold U.S. dollar denominated investments, including U.S. securities.** The USA PATRIOT Act gives U.S. authorities the right to demand to know the identity of individuals with interests in the U.S. "correspondent accounts" offshore banks maintain for their customers who maintain U.S. dollar investments. In addition, the U.S. government is beginning to confiscate the proceeds of such accounts under the notorious "civil forfeiture" statutes.

   IRS "qualified intermediary" (QI) regulations enmesh correspondent accounts in a maze of red tape. U.S. depositors in foreign banks who purchase U.S. securities and refuse to identify themselves to the IRS under the QI regulations are subject to a 31% withholding tax — not just on income from the account, but on their entire investment. So make sure to set up your offshore account(s) so that you can use them to purchase U.S. securities or other dollar denominated assets without actually holding them in U.S. dollars (sounds complicated, but it really is easy to do).

6. **Keep it simple.** It's a good idea never to get involved in an investment you don't understand, and this is doubly true for investments you make outside your own country. Ultimately, the value of offshore investing is to create a "nest egg" that can survive lawsuits; changes in public policy; even a collapse in the value of your domestic currency. You don't need complex investments to achieve these goals.

Part Two:
Law, Privacy & Asset Protection

U.S. Government Secretly Grabs Offshore Cash in Secret
Robert E. Bauman JD. *The Sovereign Individual*, July 2003

It gives me no pleasure to say we told you so. But what is happening was inevitable, given the blind reaction by the U.S. Congress to the terrorist attacks on Washington, D.C. and New York City in the aftermath of September 11, 2001.

On May 30, 2003, *The New York Times* reported: "The Justice Department has begun using its expanded counter terrorism powers to seize millions of dollars from foreign banks that do business in the United States... Officials at the State Department, however, have raised concerns over the practice, in part because most of the seizures have involved fraud and money laundering investigations that are unrelated to terrorism."

The Times explained: "A little noticed provision in the sweeping antiterrorism legislation passed in October 2001, gave federal authorities in such cases the power to seize money that passes through banks in the United States without notifying the foreign government. Most overseas banks maintain what are called 'correspondent accounts' in American banks, allowing them to exchange American currency and handle other financial transactions in this country. Section 319 of the Patriot Act, as the legislation that grew out of the Sept. 11 attacks is known, allows federal authorities to seize money from the foreign bank's correspondent account if they can convince a judge that the money deposited overseas at the bank was obtained illicitly."

So only now, for some uninformed people, is it becoming clear just how far reaching the PATRIOT Act is.

Small wonder since the Congress passed the law without even knowing what was in it. Less than six weeks after the terrorists' horror, Congress rammed through a 362-page law, sight unseen, with few members having the courage to oppose one of the worst attacks on the American liberties ever enacted into law.

Writing in our sister publication, The Sovereign Society Offshore A-Letter, on November 2, 2001, I said: "The 'USA PATRIOT ACT' — Public Law No. 107 56, signed by Pres. Bush on Oct. 26 — devotes 125 of its 362 pages to U.S. and offshore banking and finance under the banner of 'anti-money laundering.' In the wake of the Sept. 11 horror, 'anti-terrorism' is the patriotic fig leaf, but, as the fine print makes painfully clear, the real objective is massive expansion of the all-purpose prosecutorial crime of money laundering, with tax collection an equal, if unstated, goal."

Previously, on October 2, 2001, I had said: "Using the newly created terror imperative as their cover, leftist U.S. politicians are scurrying to hang their favorite anti-offshore nostrums on the catch all terrorist legislation about to sail through Congress…these opportunists want to ban much of U.S. offshore correspondent banking and give the Treasury power to cut off foreign nations from the U.S. banking system, a radical Clinton proposal that failed in Congress last year. These totalitarian proposals have as their true goals abolition of financial privacy and increased tax collection. The lie is that this is sold as fighting money laundering and terrorism."

So now, it is happening, and thanks to federal judges who seal the records of the pending cases, America knows little about these cash seizures from the U.S. correspondent accounts of foreign banks.

Law enforcement officials said the U.S. Justice Department had employed the new tool in about a half dozen investigations, seizing money from at least 15 bank accounts. Most of those came in recent months and involved alleged fraud and money laundering cases that had nothing to do with antiterrorism.

Here's How It Works

In one case, the U.S. government seized $1.7 million in funds from a correspondent account in the U.S. belonging to the Bank of Belize. A U.S. lawyer, James Gibson, was accused of bilking clients out of millions of dollars, then fleeing to Belize where he deposited some of the money.

Although the government of Belize initially agreed to freeze the money, a court there blocked the move, but U.S. prosecutors said they believed that Mr. Gibson and his wife were looting the accounts to buy yachts and other luxury items. After passage of the PATRIOT Act, the Justice Department moved within weeks in late 2001 to seize the money from the Belizean banks' correspondent accounts in the United States.

Using this drastic procedure, the U.S. government ignores mutual legal assistance treaties with other nations which they have used in the past and which do contain procedural safeguards. They do not have to prove guilt or even show probable cause. They simply demand that the U.S. correspondent bank hand over sums they claim to be the result of alleged illegal activity of someone who has funds in the offshore bank. Once the U.S. bank surrenders the cash, the offshore bank is left holding the bag. They either deduct it from the accused person's account, or sustain the loss. Banks in New York City that hold correspondent accounts for Citibank, Standard Chartered Bank, Deutsche Bank and HSBC Bank USA have all been hit.

We would not be surprised to see this unconstitutional tactic used in tax cases by the IRS. Until the Congress or the courts curb this wholesale money grab sans proof or due process, you can expect to see more.

These developments place even greater wisdom on our repeated advice; choose an offshore bank without any U.S. branches, which only makes seizures easier. Maintain your funds outside the U.S. dollar so that there is no need for the bank to maintain your funds in a U.S dollar correspondent account.

But with the inter-related world banking system as it is, this new government seizure tool confirms the Nazification of the U.S. financial system. The day has now come where government money police, on their say so, can loot banks of funds belonging to people who have never been tried or convicted of any crime.

Welcome to the new Amerika.

THE MONEY LAUNDERING CONTROL ACT OF 1986
Banking in Silence, Scope Books, 1998

In 1985 and 1986, it came to light that, in spite of the government's many and varied efforts, a large number of banks and financial institutions were simply ignoring the restrictive requirements of the Bank Secrecy Act and its accompanying legislation. Many individuals felt that the government really had no right to such information and proceeded according to their own beliefs rather than those of the bureaucratic system. Understandably, this practice caused a great deal of embarrassment for the federal government and inevitably led to a crackdown.

Banks were forced into compliance through the use of several highly publicized and large fines. The Bank of Boston was the first to fall, fined US$500,000. This was quickly followed by fines against Seafirst Bank for US$697,000, the Bank of New England for US$1.2 million, Crocker National Bank for US$2.25 million and the Bank of America for US$4.75 million. Banks across the country took notice; no longer was this myriad of regulations a matter to be taken lightly. The government's precious forms started to roll in and Big Brother found himself buried in an avalanche of paperwork.

Next came another decisive blow against financial privacy with the Money Laundering Control Act of 1986. This single act is responsible for the loss of more American liberties than any other piece of legislation. Again, to keep the public from realizing what was really going on behind the scenes, the actual provisions of the act were encoded in pretty language and political rhetoric.

The act set about dismantling the basic rights of Americans in three separate ways:

1. Money laundering was made into a federal crime for the first time anywhere in the world.
2. It became a federal crime to engage in any transaction involving the proceeds of any "specified unlawful activity."
3. Structuring transactions so as to avoid any federal reporting requirements was made illegal.

The fines and penalties for violations of this act are some of the harshest possible in all U.S. legislation. Money laundering, an activity that was legal in the U.S. until 1986, was put on a par with crimes such as murder, espionage and racketeering. The fines and jail terms handed down are often more severe than those given to rapists. Fines can be levied for up to US$500,000 or twice the value of the transactions involved.

Furthermore, the law provides Big Brother with powers to seize any property involved in or even related to an illegal transaction. If convicted of money laundering conspiracy, fines can reach up to US$25 million and can include forfeiture of all assets, not just those criminally derived. Often a money laundering conviction is linked with a charge under the Racketeer Influenced and Corrupt Organizations (RICO) Act, which permits the federal government to seize all monies "laundered" as well as all assets derived through these funds.

In addition, a fine of up to three times the amount laundered is permissible. For example, in 1988 when Lee Chan-Hong, an investor who went by the name of Fred Lee, was convicted of insider trading, he was fined a total of US$77.6 million, four times the US$19.4 million he supposedly earned from his specified illegal activity.

What Is Money Laundering?

The term "money laundering" is certainly not lacking in connotations. It brings to mind images of suitcases stuffed with cash carried by men wearing pin-striped suits who speak in raspy whispers.

In the eyes of the public, money laundering is one and the same with drug smuggling and violent crime. The government and the mainstream media foster this image. The truth is far less exciting, as money laundering is one of the most boring crimes on record.

The actual legal definition of money laundering is found in Section 1956 of the Money Laundering Control Act. It states that it is illegal to make any transaction with the proceeds of specified unlawful activity:

A. with the intent to promote that activity; or

B. knowing that the transaction is designed in whole or in part—

  (i) to conceal or disguise the nature, the location, the source, the ownership, or the control of the proceeds of specified unlawful activity; or

  (ii) to avoid a transaction reporting requirement under state or federal law.

What falls within the bounds of specified illegal activity? Of course tax evasion appears at the top of the list. Simply depositing or using money on which taxes have not been paid is now legally defined as money laundering. Opening a foreign bank account and establishing a small nest egg offshore without notifying the government of your activities can now be classified as money laundering.

Prosecutions for money laundering are soaring and often lead to confiscations of all funds concerned.

Prison terms of up to 20 years are frequently issued. Not to mention the fact that a conviction of money laundering all but ruins the reputation of the individual involved. Such tactics are clearly primarily intended to succeed in routing yet more money in the direction of the government. They are akin to a 100 percent tax on those individuals smart enough to realize that governments are not to be trusted.

The moral of the story? Do not be surprised if what originally appeared to be a simple tax investigation by the IRS turns into a money laundering conviction.

More alarming, the government does not stop there and goes on to define a host of other specified unlawful activities; at last count more than 150 such activities appear on the growing list.

Have you ever heard of the Emergency Economic Powers Act of 1977 or the Trading with the Enemy Act of 1917? Violating either of these acts could land you in jail for money laundering. Recently, even violations of environmental laws have been added to the list. In short, it seems that almost any activity that involves money and financial transactions, or in other words just about any business activity, could be linked to a money laundering charge. As a money laundering conviction tends to be easier to achieve and also manages to bring much larger sums into the government kitty, it is really no wonder that the list of prohibited activities just keeps on growing.

Furthermore, you need not even directly participate in any of these activities to take the fall. Merely doing business with or accepting cash or other monetary instruments from the public could also set you up for a conviction of money laundering. According to Section 1957 of the Money Laundering Control Act, it is illegal for a merchant to accept funds that he suspects have been derived from any of the growing list of specified unlawful activities.

[Ed. Note: It is estimated that there are now over 200 federal statutes and many more state laws that allow forfeiture of cash or property associated with prohibited criminal activities. The trend is to add on "money laundering" criminal charges against persons engaged in all crimes if evidence shows cash dealings as part of the criminal activity.]

If you would like an indication of the level of commitment expected from you in Big Brother's war, consider the comments of then Florida [and now Florida's attorney general, 2010] Congressman Bill McCollum (R-Fla.): "The corner grocer in a community is aware of the reputation of the local drug trafficker. That person comes to the store and buys five pounds of hamburger. The grocer has to know that he is coming in to buy groceries with what is indeed the money derived from a particular designated crime. I don't have any problem whatsoever holding the grocer accountable for money laundering."

Apparently McCollum had never heard of the idea of the right to a fair trial, or for that matter of the concept of innocent until proven guilty. Instead, he wanted the public to act as prosecutor, judge, jury and executioner. Businessmen and bankers have been instructed to discriminate against anyone who even appears to be guilty of a crime. If McCollum has his way, anyone unfortunate enough to be labeled as a criminal, whether correctly or not, will basically be sentenced to death without a trial. If no one is willing to do business with this individual or even sell food to him, he will be left with no alternative but to become destitute and homeless.

This is not such an unlikely scenario, as anyone not willing to participate in Big Brother's campaign risks forfeiture of his assets as well as up to 10 years in prison. Even more damaging is that the merchant need not even be aware that the activities of which the person is suspected of committing are criminal. According to Section 1957, the government need not prove that "the defendant knew that the offense from which the criminally derived property was derived was a specified unlawful activity." As already mentioned, this growing list contains many activities that most individuals would never even imagine could be linked with a money laundering conviction. Should every corner grocer in the U.S. consult a competent attorney on a weekly basis so that he can find out which customers he is allowed to sell hamburger to and which ones he must turn away? If he wishes to stay entirely inside the law, this is his only option.

Even criminal lawyers almost automatically risk entering into a criminal conspiracy just by agreeing to represent a client. Under common law, one must both have knowledge of an illegal activity and the intent to encourage it to be convicted of criminal conspiracy. Under Section 1957, neither is required, as one can be convicted of conspiracy for merely not taking a person's reputation into account before doing business with him. If an attorney even suspects that his client is guilty, he may well go to jail for merely representing him.

Placed under such restrictions, many attorneys will choose not to represent individuals solely because they are known to have a bad reputation. In other words, Congress has yet again succeeded in turning over a basic civil liberty, that of the right to legal representation as promised by the Sixth Amendment.

About the only saving grace is that Section 1957 only applies to amounts in excess of US$10,000. However, related transactions over a 12-month period that exceed US$10,000 are also enforceable. Be warned: many in Congress would like to further restrict American liberties and reduce the limit to only US$3,000.

What Is Structuring?

The new crime of structuring was brought into existence by the Money Laundering Control Act.

It came to the attention of the government that many individuals interested in laundering large amounts of money simply changed tactics to circumvent reporting requirements. They developed a process that became known as "smurfing." This procedure simply involved large number of couriers, known as "smurfs," making several deposits a day at various locations. Each smurf would deposit an amount just below US$10,000, meaning that in the end no CTRs would need to be filed. Over a relatively short period of time, very large amounts of cash could make their way into the banking system.

The Money Laundering Control Act brought an end to all of this. Transactions structured in such a way were made illegal. However, like most of the legislation introduced to curb money laundering and to snare drug traffickers, the act has failed miserably. Once smurfing became illegal, professional criminals changed their tactics again. Instead of using banks, today's launderers feed dirty money into the system through other financial operators, such as money exchanges, money transmitters and check cashing services.

In reality, the new legislation has succeeded mostly in stealing the assets of innocent individuals.

For the most part, those prosecuted for structuring first hear of the crime's existence when they are arrested. According to a 1991 Treasury Department analysis, over 75 percent of assets seized as a result of the anti-structuring laws were originally the property of individuals not involved in any illegal activities. In the modern, over-legislated world, the question of guilt or innocence increasingly seems to be a thing of the past.

The major problem with anti-structuring laws is that no underlying illegal intent need be proven by the government. Merely depositing US$9,000 in cash into an account on two consecutive days is now a crime. The penalties for such infractions are severe. The funds involved almost automatically become the property of the government. Criminal violations may well bring an additional fine of

US$250,000 as well as a five-year stint in jail. Civil penalties for "willful" violation are a bit less severe, but still claim either US$25,000 or the full amount of the funds involved, whichever is greater. You can be convicted of willfully violating the law even if you are unaware of its existence.

Finally, if you are convicted of structuring in conjunction with a violation of any other law, the fine can escalate to a cool half a million as well as 10 years in jail.

The Government Took Their Cash — Literally
Ted Bauman, *The Sovereign Investor Daily*, November 2014

Carole Hinders has run a moderately successful, financially well-managed restaurant business in Spirit Lake, Iowa for years. But now she's in debt up to her eyeballs and able to keep operating only on the goodwill of her suppliers and creditors. She can barely afford to eat, because she has to pour every cent she makes into her working capital.

Jeff Hirsch's distributorship business in Long Island has been successful and in the black for nearly 30 years. Now he's almost half a million dollars in the red and facing the loss of his family's business.

What's to blame for these sudden reversals of fortune? A sudden downturn in the market? Business bet gone wrong? Lawsuits? No — these were cases of asset forfeiture, as both of these small businesses had their bank accounts cleaned out without warning … by the federal government.

NOT Safe for Legal Tender

It's all about the cash.

In Carole's case, the government claimed that she "structured" her cash bank deposits to keep them under $10,000. Banks are required to report cash transactions in excess of $10,000 to the IRS. It's illegal to break up one's deposits or withdrawals — or "structure" them — for the purpose of evading those reporting requirements.

But it's not illegal to deposit less than $10,000 in cash when you have a legitimate business purpose for doing so. Carole takes only cash at her restaurant, and her insurance doesn't cover cash-on-hand amounts in excess of $10,000.

But the government grabbed Carole's money with no warning, no notice, and has held it for more than a year without any hearing before a judge. That's because "civil forfeiture," the process used to take her money, doesn't provide even the basic due process of a prompt hearing.

"The protections our Constitution usually affords are out the window," says Louis Rulli, a law professor at the University of Pennsylvania, a leading forfeiture expert. Property doesn't have the rights of a person. There's no right to an attorney and no presumption of innocence. People whose funds are seized who want to fight back often find that the cost far exceeds the value of their lost money. Washington, D.C., charges up to $2,500 simply for the *right* to challenge a police seizure in court, which can take months, or even years, to resolve.

Asset Forfeiture: Good Work if You Can Get It

Between 2005 — when it made 114 seizures — and 2012 — when it made 639 — the IRS seized $242,627,129 in alleged "structuring" cases like Carole's. The IRS held on to that money for an average of 356 days before it returned any of it. Only *20%* of the cases resulted in any charges. The median amount seized by the IRS was $34,000, according to an Institute for Justice analysis, while legal costs can easily mount to $20,000 or more.

The New York Times reports informed critics of this practice describe a "law enforcement dragnet, with more than 100 multiagency task forces combing through bank reports, looking for accounts to seize."

They do this because it's profitable: government agencies can keep a slice of seized funds or property to use as they please. Local police forces are known to sponsor internal competitions to see who can seize the most cash, which is then used for guns, to top up pension funds or for office Christmas parties.

Banks, of course, are deathly afraid of the consequences of failing to inform the IRS about "suspicious" patterns of deposits. But they are strictly forbidden from warning customers that their deposit habits may be illegal or educate them about structuring — unless they ask, in which case they are silently handed a boilerplate IRS pamphlet.

Enough, Already: Why You Should Buy a Safe

With your bank account vulnerable to the greedy and indiscriminate hands of the government, one of the best courses of action to take is to purchase a household safe and assemble a stash of physical cash. The amount should be at least enough to cover several months' expenses and should be in at least two stable currencies. This will give you a secure location outside the current banking system to protect your assets.

The first step accomplished will leave you confident to begin long-term planning for your protection, such as offshore investments and a second residence. This week I was on the lovely Caribbean island of Dominica doing some research for *Offshore Confidential*. The people weren't rich, but they were unfailingly cheerful, positive and proud of their little country. Perhaps that's because they don't pay any income tax. The government has tried, but they just refuse.

I couldn't help but admire the true freedom of these people, especially when compared to the feudal serfs we have become in the so-called "land of the free." It reminded me that there are plenty of places on the planet to be happy, prosperous and free … as long as you search them out and take steps to get yourself and your wealth there before the U.S. government robs you blind.

THE FINANCIAL CRIMES ENFORCEMENT NETWORK (FinCEN)
Scope Books, July 1994

Because you have lots of money, you are automatically guilty until proven innocent. That, at least, seems to be the view of FinCEN, the Financial Crimes Enforcement Network of the U.S. Department of the Treasury, a quasi-secretive federal sleuthing operation whose brief is to unearth money secrets.

The U.S. government is lining up the computer big guns ostensibly to defeat drug barons and criminals but, in reality, frightening links are being developed between the data systems of the IRS, the FBI, the Secret Service, similar policing groups and FinCEN.

The following scenario is an example of the capacity to delve into an individual's past. A drug dealer is found by police with the word "John" and a phone number scribbled on a piece of paper but no other evidence of the suspected drugs supplier.

The local police turned to FinCEN. When FinCEN received the request, the digital hunt was on. First, the telephone number was checked against listed businesses, and was quickly found to belong to a restaurant.

Next, the computer operator entered the Currency and Banking Database of the IRS to check currency transaction reports, which note all transactions of more than US$10,000. Within the database, the operator requested a list of "suspicious" requests made by banks and other institutions.

It came up with a number of suspect deposits in the area of the restaurant's ZIP code. The suspicious requests were made because a series of US$9,500 deposits, just below the official reportable threshold had been made. They were made by someone whose first name was John. Through one of those suspicious Currency Transaction Reports, the computer operator was able to ask for personal details on the depositor and the machine came up with data including a full name, social security number, date of birth, home address, driver's license number and bank account numbers.

When the IRS computer was accessed again, it came up with more suspicious and non-suspicious reports on John, who listed his occupation as being involved in a restaurant with a telephone number identical to that found originally.

Turning to commercial and government databases, John's restaurant was discovered to have a substantially smaller income than that being deposited on its behalf. Cross-checks found other suspicious transactions by John's other businesses. Within an hour of the first police inquiry, FinCEN had enough evidence to make a case against John on charges of money laundering and conspiracy to traffic narcotics.

Since its inception in 1990, under the auspices of the Treasury Department, FinCEN has become one of the world's most effective financial crime investigation units. Its 1993 tally of cases being probed totaled 40,000, plus longer-term reports on 16,000 other individuals or organizations.

Although its major successes have been in the field of drugs and money laundering, civil liberties activists worry about FinCEN's close links with the CIA and the Defense Intelligence Agency, which enable it to act with immense power and breadth of operation. The consummate ease with which computers can tap into linked databases can mean the world is an oyster ripe for opening — or a nest of vipers, depending on your viewpoint.

Operation Gateway is a new system implemented by the U.S. government in all 50 states. Gateway gives state and local law enforcement officers access to the federal financial database containing 28 years of records filed under the Bank Secrecy Act. The results from all queries are written into a constantly updated master file for cross-indexing purposes. The financial database contains only records on major money movements and is not a threat to individual privacy. However, there is worse to come.

When implemented, this computer system can be used to probe all 400 million bank accounts and their holders in the U.S. The government says it is wanted to assess the funding needed for federal deposit insurance, and to locate assets of individuals ordered by courts to make restitution for financial crimes.

The deposit tracking system has attracted civil liberties criticism at a high level. The federal law enforcement agencies and intelligence agencies see the system as a valuable addition to economic intelligence gathering, such as monitoring foreign financial dealings in the U.S. The present system has successfully identified previous unknown criminal organizations and activities because of deposit flows and patterns.

To Report or Not to Report…
That Is the Question

Erika Nolan & Shannon Crouch, *The Sovereign Individual*, October 2009

One of the most popular questions we receive is: "What do I need to report to the IRS?"

This is an extremely important one to answer, since it doesn't matter what kind of gains you achieve, if you're also running afoul of the taxman. Luckily, there are several types of investments you DON'T need to report to any U.S. regulatory agency.

1. **Offshore Securities:** A securities trading account at an offshore bank is reportable. You are required to fill out the U.S. Treasury form. However, if you purchase securities from an offshore bank, over the counter, without opening an account, and keep the certificates in your safe deposit box, the reporting requirement doesn't apply.

2. **Real Estate:** Direct ownership of real property in a foreign country isn't reportable per se. So you can own a vacation or retirement home with considerable privacy. However, you are required to report income from your real estate holdings — wherever they are located — so this provision does not apply to rental real estate.

3. **Valuables or Documents:** Valuables such as colored diamonds or rare coins as well as documents purchased outside of the United States and placed in an offshore non-bank vault don't constitute a foreign account. Of course, when you sell the diamonds or the coins you would pay tax on any gains.

4. **Physical Gold:** If you have certificates that represent ownership of precious metals or other commodities stored outside the United States in a non-bank vault, they are not reportable. This is true if you hold the metals in a segregated account. This means you own specific bars, coins, or bullion that is held in your name. Again, taxes are due on any gains when you sell the gold or metals.

Through these diverse vehicles, you can accumulate a portion of your offshore wealth in a more private and secure way — while in full compliance with U.S. tax laws.

Now…the second most popular question we get (though it often comes with a grimace) is, "Alright, what do I have to tell the IRS?"

The good news is, you only have to answer that question once a year. With the help of a professional tax advisor, it should be a snap.

What the IRS Wants to Know

The first and most basic rule of going offshore is: All accounts and most financial activities must be reported. Specifically, if you're a U.S. citizen (or permanent resident), you'll have to notify the IRS when the value of your foreign account(s) exceeds $10,000. This law applies to:

- Any type of savings, checking or deposit account with a financial institution, including accounts in which you own the monies deposited and those accounts for which you are an authorized signatory, such as a business account.

- Any bank, security or investment account held within a financial institution.

- Any accounts in which assets are held in a commingled fund and in which you hold an equity interest.

This is not a be-all-end-all list, but there are two IRS forms to which you should play close attention. Get these documents squared away and you can relax the other 364 days of the year, knowing you're on the right side of the law:

- Acknowledge foreign accounts on Schedule B of your federal income tax 1040 return due each April 15th

- File Form TD F90-22.1 (the foreign bank account reporting or FBAR form) with the U.S. Treasury Department (due each June 30th)

You can find the most recent forms and detailed information about filing as a U.S. citizen living abroad by visiting the IRS website: https://www.irs.gov. See also https://www.irs.gov/pub/irs-utl/2013_NTF_Foreign_Assets.pdf.

Keep in mind, you should not rely on the staff of an offshore bank to guide you through the reporting process. Naturally, they are not up to speed on every country's specific laws and regulations and are not likely to be experts on your home country's tax law.

Like most things in life, compliance is up to you. But with a little planning and the guidance of a tax professional, you can enjoy the effective (and surprisingly affordable) private wealth solutions and profit opportunities of the offshore world.

Five Ways to Maintain Your Offshore Privacy
Mark Nestmann, *The Sovereign Individual*, March 2009

In today's global economic turmoil, it's never been more important to hold assets outside your own country. And one of the most important reasons to do so is to enhance your financial privacy.

When you invest outside your own country, you reduce the threat of lawsuits, corporate espionage, and other financial threats. With an offshore bank account, annuity, or other foreign investment, you can take a portion of your wealth off the domestic "radar screen," where anyone with access to the Internet can assemble a remarkably detailed portrait of your finances.

Open the Closing Offshore Door

While offshore investments are a great way to obtain financial privacy, you shouldn't try to keep details of your dealings a secret from your government's tax authorities.

Beginning in the 1980s, the United States began enacting laws to force offshore banks to enforce domestic tax and securities laws. Other high-tax countries quickly followed. Since then, these efforts have only intensified. The unmistakable trend is toward greater disclosure of banking records in criminal inquiries and increasingly, in tax investigations as well.

As a result, offshore banks are increasingly leery of dealing with clients from high-tax countries, particularly the United States. When foreign banks do accept U.S. customers, they may impose stringent restrictions on their ability to trade foreign securities.

They may also require you to allow them to disclose details of your offshore earnings to the IRS. A handful of offshore banks have gone even further. They've ordered their U.S. depositors to close their accounts and move them elsewhere.

For instance, UBS, Switzerland's largest bank, is closing all offshore accounts of its U.S. clients — about 19,000 people in all. Fortunately, some offshore banks still accept U.S. clients.

Here are a few suggestions how you can act to open the closing offshore door:

1. **Be prepared to sign IRS Form W-9.** Many offshore banks now require U.S. clients to sign IRS Form W-9, which authorizes them to turn over information about your account to the IRS. Fortunately, this form only notifies the IRS about your offshore account, and no one else.

2. **Make a personal visit to open your account.** Many offshore banks now require prospective U.S. clients to open their accounts in person, rather than by mail. Even banks that claim to refuse all U.S. business may be receptive to a relationship if you visit them in person.

3. **Send correspondence and trading instructions from outside the United States.** Numerous offshore banks won't execute trading instructions originating in the United States. To avoid this restriction, ask the bank if it will comply with instructions sent from a non-U.S. address (or from a non-U.S. telephone

or fax number). Alternatively, have your offshore bank, or an independent manager, trade your offshore portfolio.

4. **Invest through an offshore legal entity.** Some offshore banks reduce investment restrictions if you invest through a foreign corporation, limited liability company, or trust. Ask the bank what structures are acceptable to operate the account before you decide which one to form. The foreign LLC option is usually the least expensive and has the most benign U.S. tax consequences. But consult with a qualified U.S. tax professional before you form any offshore entity.

5. **Establish a legal residence outside the United States.** Many offshore banks are more willing to accommodate non-resident U.S. investors than those living in the United States. If you can present proof of legal residence from a non-U.S. address, this may provide sufficient proof to the bank that you don't reside in the United States.

Yes, some of these recommendations can be inconvenient or even expensive. But the payoff is the opportunity to move substantial assets out of harm's way, and achieve substantial privacy while you're at it.

You Haven't Done Anything Wrong — It's Government

The reason that some offshore banks are reluctant to deal with Americans has nothing to do with you. It's the U.S. government that has done so, with initiatives such as:

- **The USA PATRIOT Act.** This law permits U.S. courts to confiscate the U.S. assets of foreign banks, without convicting the bank, or any of its depositors of any crime.

- **"Qualified intermediary" (QI) rules.** These rules impose a 30%-31% withholding tax on both income and gross sales proceeds of U.S. securities owned by foreign banks. The banks can avoid this tax only by entering into one-sided "QI agreements" with the IRS to enforce U.S. tax laws.

- **Securities laws.** Laws enforced by the U.S. Securities & Exchange Commission (SEC) allow offshore banks to execute "unsolicited" securities transactions with U.S. persons. However, the SEC interprets "solicitation" very broadly. As a result, many offshore banks refuse to honor even unsolicited orders of foreign securities by U.S. persons.

- **Treaties mandating disclosure.** The U.S. government is modifying its network of tax treaties by insisting that treaty partners consent to enhanced record sharing. In addition, the United States now has 21 "Tax Information Exchange Agreements" (TIEAs) in effect, mostly with offshore centers.

- **Crackdowns against individual banks.** Case in point: a criminal probe was launched by the U.S. Department of Justice against Switzerland's UBS in which one of UBS's top executives was charged with helping 17,000 Americans evade taxes by hiding their money in Swiss bank accounts.

What You Need to Tell the IRS about Your Offshore Dealings

When offshore banks first began asking U.S. depositors for Form W9, they used it only to report income or gain from U.S. investments held through the bank. Most offshore banks still only report this type of income to the IRS. Therefore, even if you give your offshore bank Form W9, the IRS will still likely rely on you to give them the details of your income or gain from your non-U.S. investment portfolio.

Naturally, you may not want to do so. But if you fail to report your offshore income, and the IRS suspects you've under-reported your income, it can probably use one of the treaties I've already described to extract the information from your offshore bank.

To report your account properly, begin with Treasury Form TD F90-22.1, which is due each June 30. Use this form to disclose offshore accounts you held for the previous year. You don't need to file this form if the total combined value of all your offshore accounts never exceeded US$10,000 at any time during the preceding year. Also, don't forget to check "yes" to the question about foreign accounts on Schedule B of your annual 1040 tax return.

If you held your account through some kind of offshore structure, you may need to report the existence of and activities of that structure to the IRS as well. For instance, if you formed an offshore LLC, you'll need to file a tax return for it. You may also need to file a form when you add money to, or remove money from, an offshore entity. Unless you're an expert, this is a job for a tax professional.

"ARTICLE 26" AND THE DEMISE OF OFFSHORE BANKING SECRECY

Mark Nestmann, *The Sovereign Individual*, June 2009

If you invest or do business internationally, you need to know about double taxation agreements, more commonly called "tax treaties." These agreements are designed to avoid, or at least minimize, double taxation. However, they have another, less publicized function: to facilitate information exchange between governments and to help enforce domestic tax laws.

One of the consequences of the political firestorm this year over bank secrecy laws in Switzerland and other offshore financial centers is that information exchange through tax treaties increasingly will become common.

Tax treaties are based on a model treaty prepared by the Organization for Economic Cooperation and Development (OECD). The OECD regularly updates its model treaty. Each successive model has provided tax authorities greater powers to retrieve financial information from the other signatory country. This is accomplished via the "Exchange of Information" provision in the model treaty; Article 26.

Early tax treaties gave signatories countries wide latitude to turn down requests for information under Article 26. Signatories could refuse requests for information under several different rationales, all based on the concept of "comity" (i.e., the recognition accorded by one nation to the laws and institutions of another).

For instance, a signatory could turn down an information request if it concerned a tax not imposed by that country ("domestic tax interest"). It could also invoke a "dual criminality" requirement: if the conduct in question wasn't illegal in both countries, the request wouldn't be honored.

However, in 2000, the OECD completely revamped Article 26 to expand the scope of information exchange. Bank secrecy laws, dual criminality requirements, and domestic tax interest requirements could no longer be invoked to prevent information exchange, all provisions that gradually have made their way into the international network of tax treaties.

Therefore, if a particular country agrees to implement information exchange arrangements "consistent with OECD standards," the laws you thought might have prevented your financial information from being disclosed to your domestic tax authorities may no longer apply.

Almost every country with strict bank secrecy laws, including Andorra, Austria, Belgium, Liechtenstein, Luxembourg, Monaco, Switzerland and Singapore, has announced it will comply with the expanded version of Article 26. Panama has not provided specific assurance on this point, but has made a vague commitment for "effective exchange of information" in accordance with OECD standards.

Still, there are limits to Article 26. The OECD model only requires treaty signatories to exchange information on request. That is, the country requesting information must know that a person's assets or accounts are in a particular jurisdiction — and likely, in a particular institution — before it can request information.

These limits are unlikely to satisfy the more rabid advocates of full disclosure. You can expect the next revision of the OECD model tax treaty to include a provision for mandatory "automatic" exchange of information between tax authorities.

In the meantime, the handwriting is definitely on the wall. Offshore bank secrecy laws will not protect you from having your account information turned over to your domestic tax authorities. If you have unreported offshore accounts, you need to deal with the problem now — not later. A good start would be a call to an attorney specializing in criminal tax defense.

Asset Protection: What You Can Learn from Squids

Ted Bauman, *The Sovereign Investor Daily*, October 2015

I spent last week in The Bahamas, at our annual Total Wealth Symposium (TWS), held at the Atlantis Resort on Paradise Island, just across the channel from Nassau Town.

No — since I know you're wondering — it wasn't all work and no play for me. In fact, I took my wife and daughter so they could benefit from a last summer fling before winter hits … my colleague Chris Orr predicts it may be a cold one.

On one of several father-daughter snorkeling dives between TWS sessions, we came across a shoal of Caribbean reef squid. There were seven of them, aligned in a disciplined row, always facing us, precisely equidistant from each other. They seemed far more aware of our presence than the ubiquitous jacks, parrotfish and sergeant-major fish nearby.

Besides being intelligent, reef squid are also masters of disguise. Thanks to the chromatophores in their skin, one minute they are an iridescent purplish-brown … then semi opaque … then gone entirely … only to reappear when it suits them.

We should all be like reef squid … and we can.

Hiding in Plain Sight

You don't have to be invisible to be hard to pin down.

Many of the attendees at this year's TWS were new to The Sovereign Society. Although they had the right instincts — that's why they were there! — some had yet to shed damaging mythologies peddled by unscrupulous wealth-protection "experts."

For example, during the Q&A portion of my panel discussion on the Foreign Account Tax Compliance Act (FATCA), one fellow asked why he should bother to go offshore if foreign banks were going to report his accounts to the IRS anyway. Isn't the point of banking offshore to hide one's wealth?

No, it isn't. The point of banking offshore — of adopting any asset-protection strategy other than plain vanilla, in-your-own-name fashion — is to be versatile and a difficult target.

Like reef squid. They're hard to pin down. Their coloration and patterning are constantly changing and adapting. It's hard to know exactly how far they are from you. If the need arises, reef squid can blend into their surroundings so well as to become almost invisible. But they're still there ... typically close to a nearby bolt-hole in the reef. Before you can get close to one, they seem to disappear.

Squids and Tall Weeds

In my early days as a liberty activist in Africa and Asia, older, wiser colleagues advised me not to be the "tall weed." Don't attract attention to yourself, they said, like a plant growing above all the others in the wheat field. Let other people do that. That way, the clumsy oafs from the government will chase after them and leave you alone, and you'll survive to grow into a tree too tough to cut down.

The ideal offshore asset protection strategy is a combination of the reef squid's wily misdirection and the hard hide of a sturdy oak tree.

Putting assets into vehicles other than your own name — such as a trust, limited liability company, family foundation or similar structure — allows those assets to appear differently from different angles. Potential litigants can never be sure what's really there, who owns what and how far they'd have to go to get at them. That makes pursuing them difficult and costly. So they go after someone else.

Of course, in this day and age, an adversary can follow the trail to your assets if they're really determined. That's why even more important than misdirection is to put them in jurisdictions that are too tough to crack. For example, a bank account owned for your benefit by a Cook Islands trust or a Nevis LLC is, for all intents and purposes, impossible to attack. Those jurisdictions just don't implement foreign judgments, period. They have to be retried from scratch under foreign law, with a new attorney in a courtroom before a foreign judge on a small, faraway island. That's why they almost never succeed.

But What About the IRS?

Fine, you may say ... but surely the IRS isn't going to let a little legalese get in the way of wealth confiscation when the time comes? What then? How is an offshore strategy going to help? Won't they just force foreign banks to send your money back to the U.S.?

Ultimately, that could happen. But the TWS lineup of speakers tells us something important about that.

Of the many presenters, only two were from financial institutions. Instead, the majority of TWS presenters offered wealth in other forms: metals, collectibles, diamonds. Even the financial folks at TWS specialize in highly secure vehicles that are worlds away from a simple, sizable bank account.

Want to protect your cash? Get rid of it. Diversify your wealth so it looks like the shimmering mirage of the reef squid. Store it in places that are as tough as old oak to crack open.

That's the secret to security.

PART THREE: PLACES FOR BANKING

TWO TOP BANKING HAVENS OF THE WORLD

Robert E. Bauman JD, Excerpts from *Where to Stash Your Cash Legally: Offshore Financial Centers of the World*, 2015

In our opinion these are two of the safest money havens in the world, used by the super-rich for decades. Your cash will be protected by some of the strictest secrecy laws in existence. Interest rates are competitive, and tough banking regulatory laws, for the most part, keep bankers honest.

To help you decide about where best to locate your offshore bank account, we regularly investigate and visit the world's banking havens. We have narrowed the choices down to the two safest and most stable havens.

1) Switzerland: The World's Best Money Haven

Switzerland is our choice as the best all-around asset and financial haven in the world. For centuries, it has acted as banker to the world and in that role has acquired a reputation for integrity and strict financial privacy. It is also a great place for the wealthy to reside. Switzerland may be neutral in politics, but it's far from flavorless. The fusion of German, French and Italian ingredients has formed a robust national culture, and the country's alpine landscapes have enough zing to reinvigorate the most jaded traveler. Goethe summed up Switzerland succinctly as a combination of "the colossal and the well-ordered." You can be sure that your trains and snail mail will be on time. The tidy, just-so precision of Swiss towns is tempered by the lofty splendor of the landscapes that surround them. There's a lot more here than just trillions of francs, dollars and euros.

Switzerland today still stands as the world's best all-around offshore banking and asset protection haven, despite the many compromises in recent years the Swiss have been forced to make under international pressure in 2009 the Swiss agreed to the exchange of tax information using the OECD standard. (See "Article 26" and the Demise of Offshore Banking Secrecy, earlier in this chapter.)

Although Switzerland has succumbed to U.S. pressure to loosen its strict secrecy laws, for safe banking it still rates as one of the top havens.

Technically, any depositor will still be protected by Switzerland's secrecy laws. These laws were first enacted in 1934 and call for the punishment of anyone who releases information on any Swiss bank account holder without authorization. Offenders can receive a fine of more than CHF50,000 and a six-month prison sentence.

However, Switzerland has entered into a number of treaties with other countries that allow for information to be released in cases involving a crime committed in another country that is also a crime under Swiss law. Tax evasion is not a crime under Swiss law but tax fraud is a crime and under OECD Article 26, foreign tax evasion is a basis for possible tax information exchange.

At the very least, if any creditor or government wanted to come after your money they would have to go through a complicated and expensive process to get at it. But if you want strict banking privacy, you are probably better off to go to a haven that does not have any information-sharing treaties with your country.

Having said that, Switzerland is still the yardstick by which all other financial centers are measured. Most Swiss bankers (UBS excluded) enjoy an international reputation that is second to none. The country has been economically and politically stable for centuries. It enjoys a low rate of inflation, and the Swiss franc is one of the strongest currencies in the world.

Swiss offer a full range of services to investors, as well as a wide variety of investment opportunities in stocks, bonds, precious metals, insurance and most other financial services.

Switzerland does impose a 35 percent withholding tax on all interest and dividends earned within its borders, but this can be easily avoided by investing money through a fiduciary account. Also double-taxation treaties may cancel out the tax.

According to the Swiss Bankers Association, in January 2016 there were 275 banks in Switzerland with total assets of US$3.25 billion. In addition, the banks had $6.6 billion in assets under management, 52% of them foreign owned. Thus Swiss banks held over 25% of the world's cross-border asset management. The best banks, however, require very large deposits (up to and over US$500,000) and also require personal recommendations. Anyone wishing to bank in Switzerland may do best to first go through a local advisor. We can recommend one if you wish.

2) Republic of Austria

Austria is not a haven in the sense of low taxes, but it is a "banking haven." That's because this nation has one of the strongest financial privacy laws in the world. That guarantee has constitutional protection that can be changed only by a national referendum of all voters. For a very few select of the foreign wealthy, Austria also offers low-tax residency, for those who you can qualify.

The Austrian Republic has long been a bastion of banking privacy strategically located on the eastern European border. From the end of World War II in 1945 to the collapse of Russian Communism in 1992, with the Soviet Union and the United States locked in armed confrontation, this convenient banking haven served as a willing Cold War financial and political go-between for both West and East.

Secrecy: It's the Law

When Austrian national banking laws were officially re-codified in 1979, the well-established tradition of bank secrecy was already two centuries old.

Notwithstanding the demands of the EU, current Austrian bank secrecy laws forbid banks to "disclose secrets which have been entrusted to them solely due to business relationships with customers." The prohibition is waived only in criminal court proceedings involving fiscal crimes, with the exception of petty offenses. The prohibition does not apply "if the customer expressly and in writing consents to the disclosure of the secret."

As an additional protection, Austrian law raises this guarantee of banking and financial privacy to a constitutional level, a special statute that can only be changed by a majority vote in a national referendum, a highly unlikely event. All major political parties support financial privacy as an established national policy of long standing.

As a member EU country, until 2009 Austria consistently strongly opposed European Union demands for compulsory withholding taxes and financial information sharing. In 2009, in a change of policy under pressure from the G-20 countries and the EU, Austria agreed to apply Article 26 of the "OECD Model Tax Convention."

This article recognizes "tax evasion" as a valid basis for foreign tax agency inquiries concerning their citizens with accounts in an offshore center. Under this OECD procedure, foreign tax authorities wishing to take advantage of tax information exchange agreements need to supply evidence of their suspicions (names, facts, alleged tax crimes) to the requested government. If there is sufficient probable cause to believe tax evasion has occurred, the requested government may supply the information.

Even with its agreement to share tax information using the OECD standard, Austria's financial and banking privacy laws provide great security. As a result, it's wise to keep Austria near the top of your potential banking list, especially if your major area of business interest is in Eastern Europe and Russia.

Absolute Bank Secrecy — A Myth

Note that nations with the strongest bank privacy laws, such as Switzerland or Austria, a bank account holder's true name is on record somewhere in an institution's files. Even if the account is in a corporate name, or the name of a trust or other legal entity, there's always a paper (or computer) trail to be traced to the beneficial owner, especially if government agents want to know about alleged criminals and their finances.

THE NEW WORLD OF OFFSHORE PRIVATE BANKING
Robert E. Bauman JD, *Offshore Confidential*, July 2013

Almost 25 years ago, the founder of The Sovereign Society, the late Bob Kephart, decided to spend a year abroad, part of it in Switzerland and Lichtenstein.

Soon after his arrival in Zürich, Bob, a pioneer in Internet use, emailed me: "Can you imagine? Most of these Swiss banks have no Internet connection and don't even know what email is!"

I understood what Bob meant. A short time before I had visited an old friend from the Eastern Shore of Maryland, a wealthy lady who also had a mountain-top home in Switzerland, a few miles from the famous tax haven, Campione d'Italia.

I needed to cash a check and my hostess assured me her local Swiss private banker would handle it. That meant calling her banker and making an appointment for me. When I appeared the next morning at the bank in a small but impressive building, I had to knock on the street-front, glass door. A conservatively dressed, older gentleman, who looked every inch a private Swiss banker, appeared and unlocked the door. In a few minutes, based on my hostess's assurances, my U.S. check was cashed for Swiss francs.

Well, the world has turned over many times since those ancient banking days.

All offshore financial centers (frequently referred to by our cash-strapped government as "tax havens") are now digitally connected in every possible way to almost every bank in the world through the Society for Worldwide Interbank Financial Telecommunication (SWIFT).

Today, we have a technologically-advanced, global system that offers huge financial opportunities based on instant communications, interlinked databases, electronic commerce and digital cash flows. And, in many ways, this system has shifted power from the monopolistic policies of the high-tax nation-state to the beleaguered individual citizen, greatly increasing personal financial freedom and the chance for profit — if you know how to navigate it.

The technology that makes these global systems available for our use is also being used by government authorities for constant surveillance in an attempt to track our every financial move, well beyond the numerous and redundant official reports we are required by law to file with the U.S. government.

But, there is a new legal way to beat the U.S. government at its own game — and to allow you free access to offshore investments and banking. With those come greater privacy, strong asset protection and better profits.

Another IRS Scandal

There has been a lot of deserved discussion about the IRS scandal that exposed the supposedly impartial agency's bias against conservative groups seeking the educational tax exemption allowed by the Internal Revenue Code.

But the Foreign Account Tax Compliance Act (FATCA) constitutes a different, stealth IRS scandal.

FATCA is a master of disguise. While the government pitches it as a way to catch all the tax cheaters who supposedly aren't paying their fair share … it is much more than that. By forcing U.S. tax law on every country around the globe — which of course is 100% illegal at its core — the U.S. government and the IRS have evoked just the reaction they intended.

That is to make current and potential American clients very unattractive to foreign financial institutions that do not want the headache of trying to make sense of the byzantine U.S. tax code.

As part of Big Brother's plans to control citizens and their money, we have seen that political leaders will use almost any excuse to attack and curb offshore financial activity. They want to keep cash and assets at home where they can be taxed and confiscated at will.

What happens when no one will take you as a client? You must keep your wealth at home. And you must hold your wealth in U.S. dollars. So, to me, FATCA is the government's way of implementing currency controls without the average voter taking notice.

The Heritage Foundation in Washington, D.C. notes that the Federal government debt has nearly doubled since President Barack Obama took office. It is now about $17 trillion. It concludes: "Under existing policies, federal debt is projected to increase another 50% over the next decade and then rise rapidly thereafter." Since the recession began to ease four years ago, the federal budget deficit has topped $1 trillion every year.

The annual deficit and national debt will continue to soar and the dollar will continually diminish in value. And it will be us — you and me as American citizens — who go down with the ship because all our financial exits have been closed off.

The New American Refugees

The impact of FATCA is slowly being felt. Untold numbers of foreign banks, financial institutions, insurance companies and investors avoid doing business with Americans, prompted by the trouble, cost and the very real legal threat of even accidental non-compliance with the imperial edicts of FATCA and its enforcers at the IRS.

I know from experience with our European, Asian and Latin American banking contacts that there is a continuing general alarm and deep-seated resentment at the imperial Obama administration for claiming that U.S. tax law now covers the world and that they must conform or risk being prohibited from clearing any U.S. dollar transactions.

Even those offshore banks and financial institutions that are still willing to work with American clients for self-protection have imposed a number of limitations.

Some have declined to deal directly with U.S. persons as individuals, but will accept accounts opened in the name of corporations, limited liability companies or trusts controlled by U.S. persons.

Others have agreed to continue only as custodians of private investment or retirement account funds, but have transferred management of the investments to independent investment managers.

New Face of Private Banking

As American clients are being asked to leave traditional private banks in Austria, Singapore, Switzerland and Denmark because of the onerous provisions of FATCA, they are finding better service and better investment advice from a boutique group of advisors — independent asset managers (IAMs). These investment managers aren't tied to a particular bank. Rather, they are tied to their clients — your needs come first.

Working with an independent asset manager comes with all the benefits of traditional private banking ... but without any of the negatives.

You see, private banking used to mean that unless your account carried a balance of $5 to $10 million, your bank-assigned asset manager could change at any time … without any notice. Likewise, the name of your customer service contact changed frequently as younger people at the bank were promoted or left for other opportunities.

You needed to know the names of at least five people in a private banking department. Why? Because most of the time the one person you wanted to speak with would be on vacation because of the six to eight weeks of leisure that employees enjoy in countries that are private-banking havens.

Few to none of those annoyances arise when you work with an independent asset manager.

Here's why…

Entrepreneurs Rule

Independent asset managers (IAMs) share your desire for maximum profits. If you don't profit, neither do they. Many went independent, creating their own businesses after years of experience in private banks or leading investment houses.

With a background at behemoth banks, such as UBS or Credit Suisse, they appreciate the markedly different needs of clients with lower account minimums and give the superior service that only smaller operations can provide. For example, most Swiss independent asset managers have professional teams of four or five experienced staffers, enough to respond to all their clients on a continuing basis.

Our experience shows that the typical IAM firm has less than $1 billion under management; their goal is not to be another UBS or Julius Baer. Knowing and serving the customer well is their highest priority. Fortunately, all the banking changes have given independent asset managers the chance to step in and cater to the Americans that large private banks have abandoned.

These managers are also creating confidence by registering with the SEC. Ironically, they continue to work with the very same private banks that dropped Americans for being too much trouble and cost. These private banks don't want Americans as investment clients, but they do provide back-office services for independent managers — holding the cash in custodial accounts, executing investment trades, compiling and sending IRS-compliant financial statements, and more.

Executive Publisher Erika Nolan summed it up this way: "IAMs provide all the efficiency of the big name banks without any of the hassles, and they provide personal service from an investment manager whose income is tied directly to how they perform for you — rather than for the shareholders. To me, that's exactly how it should be."

For Once, Thank You SEC

A big plus for the new IAMs is that most are registering with the U.S. Securities and Exchange Commission. This offers benefits unavailable in the old school days of private banking. In order to qualify to become a registered SEC investment adviser under Section 202(a)(11) of the Investment Advisers Act of 1940, the applicant and his professional firm must tell all in writing.

This complete transparency is perhaps the greatest advance for you. No more guessing about whether your adviser's choice is the right one; no more dependence on hearsay from well-meaning friends. Under SEC rules registration, each person or entity must file full information on their professional activity and business, the nature of their investments and the overall amounts. Investors can access adviser registrations and other company filings using the SEC electronic system known as EDGAR.

That SEC registration means the offshore manager understands relevant SEC rules and regulations. It also allows registered foreign advisers to contact freely and to visit American clients, working with them in a fully U.S.-compliant way. That includes the U.S. investor receiving all investment transaction documents on a regular basis, as well as the U.S. tax statements needed for IRS filings, all provided directly on a timely basis from the custodian bank where the client's investment funds are held.

Making Offshore Investments Easy

An offshore bank account definitely offers stronger asset protection than a domestic American account. The same rule applies to offshore account holders who live in any country. But the other major plus of an offshore account is the direct path it offers for better and more profitable and more diverse investments.

Self-management by a foreigner to produce profits from an offshore account obviously requires intimate knowledge about procedures, fees and rules in another country. An offshore investment account also requires constant supervision and instant information, almost forcing you to become a day trader. This is where an independent asset manager (IAM) can make all the difference to your investment success.

In Switzerland alone there are about 8,000 licensed IAMs that manage an estimated US$5.3 trillion. Other leading IAMs can be found in most major financial centers such as London, Copenhagen, Gibraltar, Singapore, Hong Kong, Montreal and the Cayman Islands. There are good reasons why some independent asset managers attract such large investment sums. It's because they are good at what they do and they provide a vital service.

Those with experience know that it is to an investor's advantage to work through your own personal independent investment manager, rather than trying to deal directly with an impersonal foreign bank and its possibly overburdened staff.

Based on my experience, here are six reasons why an independent asset manager enhances your offshore investment account:

- Most IAMs run small operations that are flexible, tailoring investments to the individual client. They don't insist on the usual bank customer investment categories of aggressive, nonaggressive or conservative, but they do offer service to fit your specific goals. They limit the total number of clients to that which their staff can assist readily without undue delay.

- A good IAM builds a personal relationship, understanding at the beginning exactly what a client is seeking and accommodating those goals on a continuous basis with periodic updating sessions. Working with an IAM greatly simplifies your investment life. Your manager handles opening your account at one of the leading banks with which they work. A limited power of attorney enables the manager to work with the bank on your behalf as you direct. And the IAMs we recommend work with offshore banks that welcome Americans as desired clients.

- With an IAM, you don't need to devote time to monitoring your portfolio on a daily basis.

- A good manager stays in regular contact with his client to build on their relationship, but that does not require constant contact.

- An offshore investment manager will free you from the drag of the U.S. dollar by choosing foreign investments that do not mirror domestic U.S. investments. The IAM will take advantage of the world of investments, many not immediately available to U.S. investors. That includes foreign stocks and bonds, national currencies, commodities and precious metals.

- Having an offshore bank account will enable you to invest in all of the above (and more) using one single account. An IAM and his associated foreign bank acts as your stock broker and foreign currency, commodity and precious metals trader. The IAM can also convert a domestic 401K or other retirement account to a foreign custodian for greater asset protection.

Change for the Better

Within the last year, under pressure from the pending FATCA enforcement, some of our banking associates have ended their investment advising for Americans and changed instead to the independent asset manager system.

In 2011, the Swiss-owned Valartis Bank in Vienna decided that FATCA compliance was too costly and discontinued investment management for American clients. The bank has continued to act as custodian for funds but, by mutual agreement, the management has been passed to independent asset managers, Rob Vrijhof and Eric Rosemen, both long associated with The Sovereign Society.

Our long-term partners at Jyske Global Asset Management (JGAM) in Denmark also decided to follow a similar path. As of September 13, 2013, JGAM will discontinue providing investment advisory services, but JGAM has partnered with SEC-registered and privately owned ENR Asset Management in Montreal, Canada.

Eric N. Roseman heads ENR. Sovereign Society members will remember Eric as our former investment director and editor of *Commodity Trend Alert*. ENR Asset Management will continue to use Jyske Bank in Denmark to hold the assets as custodian, record and account keeper and provide Internet access as well as IRS and other required U.S. reports.

In addition, ENR will have its own dedicated support desk at Jyske Bank. ENR is lowering the required account minimum by 50% to $100,000, about the lowest asset-management minimum now available. ENR is also lowering the annual management fee by 25% to just 1.5%. Thomas Fischer, the head of the investment committee for JGAM, will be the lead investment consultant for ENR at JGAM, bringing to bear his many years of wealth and foreign currency experience.

The Future Is Now

There is truth in that old saying that "out of every bad situation, some good can be found."

In that very category there has been a new development in response to all the many challenges to offshore financial activity.

As a result of FATCA and the U.S. government's imperial-world, tax-enforcement policies — a new, streamlined and fully legal system has developed that better serves American and other nations' investors.

Instead of diminishing American investment abroad, these new procedures should expand and multiply U.S. capital offshore.

The use of your own independent asset advisers as intermediaries working with reliable custodian offshore banks produces easier access, expanded personal advice, and, hopefully, will result in greater profits from world markets.

No longer will you be trying to talk to "the bank," but you will have your own personal investment manager.

Chapter Three: Offshore Banking, Insurance & Finance

I believe the independent asset manager is the solution for those of us who realize we must diversify our wealth quickly, removing at least some of it from U.S. official threats and spying.

Keeping all of your money in the U.S. banking system, especially in U.S. dollars, is akin to putting your life savings into a wallet, handing it to a crack addict on an inner-city street corner and telling them to only take out $10. Good luck.

The U.S. government's anti-wealth biased IRS and the big banks are going to take every last cent and they'll even pawn your wallet, and then bill you for their services.

That is exactly why the rise of the independent asset manager is a useful and profitable new link in offshore banking — one you should take every advantage of that you can.

For the IAMs and the custodial banks which they are associated, refer to the list of contacts in Appendix A. It also includes contacts for offshore banking in several jurisdictions.

Chapter Four

Offshore Trusts, Family Foundations & Other Wealth Preservation Strategies

Illegal Tender: The War on Cash	196
The "War on Cash" Spreads to Europe	198
U.S. Uses Roving Border Checkpoints to Escalate the War on Cash	199
Avoiding U.S. Exchange Controls	201
The Key to Safe Banking at Home and Overseas	203
Kick the Government Out of Your Retirement	213
What the Rise of Digital Currency Could Mean for You	215
Avoid the Next Global Financial Crisis by Investing in Gold	217
Suspicious Transactions	219
The $7 Billion Laundry Bill	221
The Future of Money: The Financial Secret That Banks Will Hate	222
How to Beat the Great Wealth Grab	230
Electronic Cash: The End of Privacy	240
The Coming Currency Conundrum	242

Editor's Note:

Cash is defined as "money or its equivalent." At one time, back in the last century, money meant paper currency backed by gold, or metal coins of gold or silver with intrinsic value. Today cash can be billions of binary digits controlled by computers that send it around the world via the internet with a speed once reserved for lightning bolts.

The Bible, in the First Book of Timothy, admonishes us, "The love of money is the root of all evil."

In the modern world the manner in which you handle your money can result in evils befalling you worse than all the plagues described in both the Old and New Testaments.

In this chapter, we survey the state of money and its many current equivalents in what can be called a "money safety course" — the new money regime you must master to survive.

ILLEGAL TENDER: THE WAR ON CASH
John Pugsley, *The Sovereign Individual*, December 2001

History teaches us that the most serious casualty of war is always liberty.

In "America's New War," this sad lesson is being demonstrated again. Each passing day we are told that in order to protect our freedoms we must relinquish them. George Orwell had a name for this: doublespeak.

Using the fear of terrorism as cover, world governments are cranking up an all-out assault on financial privacy. Their primary target: cash.

I'm old enough to remember when cash was the most common medium of exchange. Companies paid their employees in cash, and people used cash for most purchases, including large ones like cars and even houses.

Until the mid-20th century, bank accounts were the exception rather than the rule for individuals and even businesses worldwide. Credit cards were non-existent until the 1950s. The American Express card didn't appear until 1958.

Although wealthy individuals sometimes purchased stocks, for almost everyone else, savings were in the form of cash (or gold and silver coins) stashed "under the mattress." Cash was king.

Large bills circulated in most countries. In the United States there were $500 and $1,000 notes, and even $10,000 and $100,000 bills. They're long gone, although they are still sold as collector's items. Now the U.S. government is working to eliminate $100s, and $50s are likely to follow.

Chapter Four: Trusts & Family Foundations 197

Governments don't like cash. With cash, citizens can conduct exchanges without written records and in complete privacy. Cash leaves no trail. While we are told government is against cash because it facilitates crime, in fact they hate it because cash makes individuals, sovereign.

The objective is a "cashless society," where every financial transaction will be available for instant examination and comprehensive analysis in government-run data banks.

It has taken decades for governments to gradually lull the public into accepting the elimination of cash, but success is at hand. Citizens are learning through bitter experience that to accept, hold, transport and exchange relatively large amounts of cash is to risk forfeiture and even prison.

In bygone days, the danger in carrying cash was that you might be robbed. It still is. Only today the robber is most likely to wear a police uniform.

The early signs of this war on cash came with the passage of the 1970 Bank Secrecy Act, which made it a federal crime for anyone to cross the U.S. border with more than $10,000 in cash without filing a report with the U.S. Customs Service.

Today, government agents can basically empty your wallet of cash anytime they want. Most people whose cash is seized are never formally charged with a crime. Some 90% never get their property back.

In Florida, the "Impact" unit, a force of 50 officers backed by nearly a dozen police agencies, funds itself entirely through asset seizures, and it doles out millions more stolen dollars to area police departments.

A Vietnamese immigrant forfeited US$80,000 in cash he was carrying despite the fact he was never charged with a crime after agents seized money from him during a train ride from California to Boston.

In Wayne County, Michigan, police confiscate the cash that people bring in to bail out friends or family members, simply by having a dog sniff it, supposedly "alerting" to the smell of drug residues on the currency.

Such seizures continue, despite that numerous federal court cases have established that nearly all U.S. currency has enough such residues to excite a drug-sniffing dog.

Occasionally, the amount confiscated is large enough that the victim sues to recover it. In 1998, the U.S. Supreme Court said federal authorities could not keep the $357,144 in legally earned funds they had taken from Hosep Bajakajian for failure to declare it when exiting the country.

The Court, for the first time in its 200-year history, invalidated the forfeiture because it would result in a punishment grossly disproportionate to the underlying offense to which Bajakajian had pleaded guilty, which would have resulted in a maximum fine of only US$5,000.

Not willing to be bound by the U.S. Constitution or by justice itself, the Bush administration successfully lobbied to change the Bajakajian type of offense from "failure to disclose" to "smuggling," a crime with a much stiffer maximum penalty. This change is part of the new U.S. anti-terrorist legislation. In the future, someone like Bajakajian will not be able to recover his legally earned after-tax money and could be sent to prison for up to five years.

Is the war on cash likely to end? Not a chance.

The events of September 11, 2001 have given all major governments new justification for their war on cash.

Is there an answer for sovereign individuals? Yes.

The ongoing battle between the sovereign state and sovereign individuals is moving to the next evolutionary step in money: electronic currencies.

The largest operation in existence is called e-gold (www.e-gold.com). However, my preference is for GoldMoney (www.goldmoney.com), the patented cyber-gold payment system introduced this year by long-time gold advocate James Turk. This new concept completely eliminates the forfeiture and theft risks of transporting cash and is the perfect solution to moving money across borders. It also eliminates fraud and solves the collection problems and costs inherent with transferring money through checks, wires and credit cards. Best of all, GoldMoney (and e-gold) offer individuals the opportunity to bypass fiat currency.

As mediums of exchange fully backed by gold or other precious metals, these avant garde systems are based on tangible wealth — in contrast to the "dollars" issued by the Federal Reserve which are backed by nothing but the "good faith" of politicians.

Each of us, like it or not, is at war to protect our dwindling liberties. As sovereign individuals we don't assemble, arm ourselves and march against the enemy. Instead, we search for strategies and products that protect our property, and deny our resources to the State. Gold-backed electronic currencies are one more such tool.

The "War on Cash" Spreads to Europe
Mark Nestmann, *The Sovereign Investor Daily*, May 2007

In 1970, the United States for the first time imposed reporting requirements for persons moving substantial quantities of cash, or cash equivalents, across a

U.S. border. Current law requires that cash movements that exceed US$10,000 be reported via Form 105.

The original rationale for these controls was to help the IRS track the movement of cash to bank accounts offshore, where cash deposits were supposedly accepted with "no questions asked." But over the years, the rationale changed from "tax evasion" to the "war on drugs," and now, most recently, to fight "terrorist financing."

Now, the European Union has imposed its own reporting requirements for cross-border movements of cash, bank drafts and checks. Under the new rules, anyone traveling to a EU country from outside the EU, or from a non-EU country into a member state, must report if they are carrying more than €10,000 (US$13,500) with them. The regulations go even further than U.S. law in defining checks of any kind as cash — not just cashier's checks or traveler's checks.

Penalties for non-compliance with this regulation vary from country to country. In the United Kingdom, for instance, violations can lead to a fine of £5000 (US$9,900). Customs authorities may deduct the fine directly from the cash seized. However, these penalties are much less severe than the maximum sanctions available under U.S. law for failing to file Form 105 — a fine up to US$500,000 and imprisonment up to 10 years.

The real danger of this regulation is when it's used in conjunction with existing asset forfeiture legislation now in effect throughout the EU. For instance, under U.K. law, cash may be seized if there are "reasonable grounds to suspect that it is either the proceeds of, or is intended for use in, unlawful conduct." This includes not just terrorism or drug-related crime, but ANY crime.

It is undisputable that EU officials have access to data maintained by the U.S. Homeland Security Administration and other repositories of information. What's to stop the U.K. Revenue & Customs Authority, or the equivalent authority in other EU countries, from using information retrieved from U.S. "data mining" efforts to create "reasonable suspicion" that lawfully declared cash might potentially be connected to a crime, including one that's yet to be committed?

The answer, not surprisingly, is "nothing at all." And that's the real problem with "cash reporting" legislation, no matter how well intended it's dressed up to appear.

U.S. Uses Roving Border Checkpoints to Escalate the War on Cash

Mark Nestmann, *The Sovereign Investor Daily*, September 2009

I just returned to Phoenix from a week's vacation on the beach in San Diego. My all-too-brief holiday was very pleasant, with the exception of the time spent waiting in line at checkpoints manned by agents of the U.S. Border Patrol — five in all on Interstate 8 between Gila Bend, Arizona and San Diego.

I'm white as a ghost, and over 50, so I don't fit the profile of an illegal immigrant, terrorist, or drug smuggler. That allowed me to proceed unmolested after brief interrogations by hulking Border Patrol agents. But what shocked me was that at one checkpoint, agents brought out dogs to inspect each vehicle passing through. Presumably, if the dog had alerted to the presence of who-knows-what, I would have been subjected to a thorough search of my vehicle.

For decades, the Border Patrol has operated dozens of these interior traffic checkpoints. And in 1976, the Supreme Court ruled that warrantless stops and searches near the border don't violate the U.S. Constitution. But over the last decade the number of these checkpoints as proliferated.

Today, there are about 30 permanent checkpoints and numerous additional temporary or "roving" checkpoints along the Mexican border, and a few along the Canadian border. Apologists for the Border Patrol say warrantless searches of vehicles at these checkpoints is necessary to fight the War on Terrorism, the War on Illegal Immigration, and the War on (Some) Drugs.

However, organized criminal interests learned long ago to post lookouts near the permanent checkpoints. Whenever they're unmanned, they alert their colleagues that the coast is clear. In recent years, it appears from press reports that most arrests at these permanent checkpoints are tourists transporting small quantities of marijuana for recreational use.

Which brings us to the roving checkpoints, and the friendly dogs that inhabit them. These are more difficult for the professional smugglers to avoid, but hardly impossible. They simply send vehicles ahead of a major shipment of narcotics or illegal immigrants and then choose whatever route is unmanned at the time. Again, press reports indicate that most arrests appear to be of recreational drug users.

I personally think it's ridiculous for the government to prohibit anyone from indulging in their favorite libation, but there's also a much larger issue. What else are the dogs sniffing for?

It's my guess that it's cash, not drugs, immigrants, or anything else is what the Border Patrol dogs are after. Since more than 95% of circulating U.S. currency is contaminated with drug residues, it's a lead-pipe cinch for a dog to "alert" on any large quantity of cash you might be transporting in a border area. And that's backed up by numerous reports of cash seizures at these checkpoints, inevitably accompanied by a press release from the Border Patrol.

U.S. courts have repeatedly ruled that possession of a large sum of currency is "strong evidence" of a connection to trafficking in illegal drugs. Merely possessing currency provides the government with sufficient evidence to seize it, unless you can provide clear and credible evidence that it's NOT connected to illegal drugs. And even then, Border Patrol Agents — or any other law enforcement authority — can still seize it, and force you to sue in court to try to get it back.

The creeping militarization of our border areas gives me, well, the creeps. It's not effective at stopping illegal immigration or illegal drug trafficking. What it is effective at is establishing a de facto prohibition against moving any meaningful quantity of cash near a U.S. border.

AVOIDING U.S. EXCHANGE CONTROLS
Mark Nestmann, *The Sovereign Individual*, October 2009

Imagine for a moment that you're the most powerful person in the world. You have millions of men under your control. Your soldiers are stationed in more than 100 countries worldwide. Your naval forces include dozens of nuclear submarines, battleships, and aircraft carriers. And, you have the legal authority to take anyone's money with impunity.

Yet, you have a problem. To finance your empire, you've borrowed $10 trillion from investors. And it's still not enough. You need to borrow $2 trillion more each year to stay afloat.

If you can't convince your creditors to lend what you need, wouldn't you try to use your legal authority to stop your creditors from escaping with what's left of their money? After all, it's perfectly legal for you to take it.

Now, substitute "U.S. government" for "you." In a nutshell, this is the situation in which the United States now finds itself. And should buyers fail to pony up and buy the trillions of dollars of debt it needs to finance its borrowing appetite, the U.S. government just might resort to "unconventional measures." One such measure would be to restrict outflows of U.S. dollars abroad.

Why Exchange Controls Won't Work

Exchange controls always cause more problems than they solve. The controls permit the government to continue irresponsible financial practices far longer than market forces would otherwise permit. In addition, graft and corruption always accompany exchange controls.

Treasury officials and those with political connections always commit the most serious violations.

Exchange controls inevitably disrupt legitimate businesses. For instance, exchange controls in Venezuela bankrupted thousands of businesses because they could no longer obtain foreign currency.

Finally, exchange controls impoverish the countries that impose them. While Venezuela's foreign currency reserve position stabilized after it imposed exchange controls, remittances of foreign currency fell dramatically. This led to a steep decline in the standard of living for most residents.

If foreign exchange controls come to the United States, there's no reason to anticipate a different outcome. You can count on irresponsible spending to continue, increased corruption, and a decline in living standards.

How to Prepare for Exchange Controls

U.S. residents concerned about the prospect for exchange controls need to prepare for them now.

Here are some recommendations:

- Purchase a residence in a foreign country. The government can't force you to repatriate real estate if it imposes exchange controls. A foreign residence also gives you a place to live, at least temporarily, if the United States becomes politically or economically unstable.
- Start or purchase an offshore business. Again, it will be very difficult for the government to confiscate it.
- Purchase precious metals offshore and keep them in an offshore bank, safety deposit box, or private vault.
- Create an international structure in which you are a beneficiary of the underlying investments. An offshore trust and some types of offshore annuity investments provide this sort of protection. Beneficial interests are more difficult to confiscate than direct ownership interests, especially if held overseas. These structures may also protect against claims in civil litigation.

These precautions aren't foolproof.

The Treasury could force you to repatriate your foreign investments in exchange for dollars at the official exchange rate. This rate may be much less than the market exchange rate. Congress may also impose taxes on unrealized gains on foreign investments it can't force you to repatriate.

For this reason, the only strategy certain to be effective against exchange controls is to physically leave the United States. Take as much capital with you as is legally allowed. Set up residence in another country and watch the United States melt down from a safe distance.

Even this strategy may not be sufficient, since the United States taxes its citizens no matter where they live. Ultimately, the only way for you to protect yourself against exchange controls may be to give up your U.S. citizenship and passport and expatriate.

That's a big step, but it's the only way to free yourself permanently from U.S. legal authority.

THE KEY TO SAFE BANKING AT HOME AND OVERSEAS

Ted Bauman, *Offshore Confidential*, February 2015

The scene unfolded right before my eyes.

It was Christmas Eve. I was with my family in my second home of Cape Town, South Africa, for the holidays. So were tens of thousands of tourists, mostly from Europe, but also from the U.S. South Africa's Cape Province is an unbeatable destination in the Southern Hemispheric summer with beaches, mountains, vineyards and wildlife everywhere you go. Millions of dollars were being spent on all the usual touristy things, overlaid with the U.S.-style Christmas shopping frenzy that's finally reached this tip of Africa.

Upper Midwestern accents gave away a couple's American identity who were next to me in line for a bank of ATM machines at a shopping center in my oceanfront village. Like me, they carried the standard magnetic stripe ATM cards issued by most U.S. banks for the last 50 years.

Almost everyone around us, however — locals as well as Europeans — were using modern chip-and-pin cards that are virtually impossible to hack.

My U.S. countrymen took their turn at the ATM, husband and wife each withdrawing a wad of South African Rands. Just after they completed their transactions, however, the lady noticed a flapping sign that had been taped to the ATM but had come loose in the strong beachfront breeze. Turning it over, she read:

> *"This ATM machine has been compromised. It is NOT SAFE for use by magnetic stripe cards (e.g. from U.S. banks) as they will be hacked. Other cards may be used safely."*

The couple confronted a security guard at the bank's main entrance, asking why the machine was in use at all. The guard calmly explained that since the vast majority of ATM users weren't at risk, the bank didn't bother to fix machines that had been compromised with "card skimmers" — little inserts that copied magnetic stripe cards — until after the holiday crush. The posted warning signs were considered adequate, even though the notorious Cape Southeaster had rendered this particular one ineffective.

He recommended that they cancel their ATM cards immediately since they would almost certainly be cleaned out within hours. Naturally, this was of little comfort to the American couple, who now faced the prospect of trying to enjoy the remainder of their vacation in a foreign country where many smaller merchants accept only cash … without ATM cards to obtain it.

You're just as likely as this couple to come face to face with the fear and inconvenience that comes with being financially compromised while abroad … unless you carefully absorb the advice I'm about to give.

There are safe, simple solutions available to you that don't require complicated foreign banking arrangements and hassles. As a seasoned foreign traveler — 75 countries and counting — and a certifiable security and privacy nut, I'll show you how they can protect you and your wealth safely, cheaply and above all, simply.

And to top it off … I predict that these solutions — moving well beyond the chop-and-cards you've probably heard about — will be the norm in the U.S. itself within two to three years. So follow my advice and you'll be ready for them.

Protect Your Cash with E-Wallets

Needless to say, I didn't complete my Christmas Eve transaction at that ATM. Instead, I deployed a workaround that takes advantage of advances in transactional security that have largely bypassed Americans … until now. You can transact abroad with confidence and security if you learn the secret to using them.

I quickly searched for and downloaded a payment "app" on my Apple iPhone called Snapscan, developed by South Africa's Standard Bank. It's similar to apps used in the U.S. such as LevelUp or Square. I then used a U.S. credit card to purchase a prepaid debit card from a local bank that has a partnership with my U.S. bank, saving on foreign transaction fees. I entered its details into Snapscan, then walked in to the nearest Standard Bank branch, went to a Snapscan terminal, held up my phone to the screen with the app open, entered my desired amount, and voilà … out popped a pile of local bank notes.

I avoided having to use my vulnerable U.S. ATM card entirely. Afterwards, I was able obtain cash or even make purchases directly using this simple, secure cellphone app.

This illustrates the secret to safe banking abroad: "cloud computing." That's a fancy term for large "farms" of remote servers that allow centralized data storage and processing for a variety of always-available Internet-based services, like the one I used. Cloud computing has created endless opportunities for innovative, competitive software companies to develop and deploy new smartphone apps for paying for goods and services, without having to own and run their own expensive server farms.

Often called "e-wallets," these financial smartphone applications allow you to avoid the obsolete card technology still used by most U.S. banks when transacting abroad. They are actually safer than credit cards, including the advanced chip-and-pin cards used abroad. And as I'll explain, e-wallets have the happy side effect of often reducing or entirely eliminating costly foreign transaction fees (for you) and credit card terminal fees (for merchants).

Freedoms the Banks Will Hate — But You Will Love

In the August 2014 edition of *Offshore Confidential*, I called the Hong-Kong-based i-Account "The Financial Secret That Banks Will Hate." I went on to say:

> *Most of us think of a "bank" as a place, in a building, where bankers keep our money in account products they've sold to us. In almost all cases, those bankers make the rules governing our accounts, and we are locked into one currency. They decide under what conditions we can access our deposited funds or our credit lines, and since we're typically tied to our banks by a web of interlocking products '— transaction, credit, mortgage, investment and other accounts' — we have to tolerate whatever nonsense they decide to throw at us.*

It turns out that not all banks love such nonsense — at least not foreign banks.

During my recent visit to Cape Town, I met with Standard Bank's regional Consumer Technology Manager, whom I've known for years. Desiree Maarten has a unique ground-level perspective on the forces shaping retail banking in countries in Europe and Asia that are leapfrogging U.S. banks in technological terms. She basically agreed with my negative assessment of U.S.-style retail banking.

For generations, Desiree explained, most retail banks around the world have stored our money and/ or given us lines of credit, and charged us fees and interest. They've also supplied the means by which we access our money and our credit — debit and credit cards.

This amounts to a double-dip. That's because the systems required to use debit and credit cards — such as MasterCard and Visa — were created by the banks themselves. Merchants who accept bank-issued cards must pay fees to these networks.

These payment systems still rely mainly on telephone lines because they were built before the Internet. A critical element is the "terminal" that accepts your payment card at checkout — the "point-of-sale" (POS). They are usually provided by the bank to the merchant, for a fee.

The payment processor (e.g. Visa) charges the merchant a fee every time you use a POS terminal to make a purchase. A portion of these "swipe fees" is shared with your bank and the merchant's bank.

Busy merchants can generate thousands of dollars in fees every day. They're highly unpopular and have generated numerous lawsuits, but they're central to the business model of current U.S.-style retail banking systems.

There is another problem — besides the fees — with these archaic networks. With millions of terminals in use, changing technology to something safer — say chip-and-pin instead of magnetic stripe — is a wildly expensive proposition. Card processing companies expect merchants to pay for new terminals, but merchants don't want to. Resistance to mass replacement of merchant POS terminals is the main reason the U.S. lags so far behind the world.

But as well all know, the security weaknesses of magnetic stripe technology to store card data has been highlighted in POS system breaches at major U.S. retailers, including Neiman Marcus Group, Michaels, Lowe's, Supervalu, Albertsons, Target and Home Depot. That's created an incentive for change.

It's this combination of unpopular fees and restrictive, insecure technology that's created a gap for alternative smartphone-based payment systems that bypass the card terminals altogether — the key to safe transacting for you. A merchant can acquire a generic QR Code reader (for images like the code on this page) and connect it to the Internet, or even use their own smartphone or tablet to accept payments. Your payment is charged to your own debit or credit card, which they set up in the payment app as I did when I used Snapscan.

Daily, weekly or monthly, the payment app company transfers funds to the merchant — all without card swipe fees, saving the merchant — and you — lots of money. The app I use in the U.S., LevelUp, gives me a 7% discount on all purchases, for example. That really adds up.

So why, then, would a bank like the one Desiree Maarten works for invest in a smartphone payment app that undermines its own traditional business model?

"We recognized that we could make more money by attracting clients with advanced front-end banking services than taking fees from traditional POS machine transactions," she told me. "We lose a bit on the old-fashioned system but we more than make up for it by people banking with us so they can use our app for free." (Standard Bank currently allows clients of other banks to use their app too, but charges their bank a small fee which is inevitably passed on to the client — thus driving them to Standard itself.)

"Almost everyone in South Africa has a smartphone nowadays, so it made sense to piggyback on that. In any case the writing is on the wall for traditional card systems in Europe and Asia, and we wanted to be the first local bank to make the shift."

And it's not just in Africa. It's a play that's being replicated all over the world … one that creates opportunities for you.

But Is It Safe?

The question you're probably asking right now is whether this sort of system is safe, given the dangers lurking on the Internet — which is where banking is moving, after all. The answer is: it's safer than using a traditional debit or credit card. A lot safer.

That's because the payment apps I'm going to recommend don't actually store your debit/credit card details on your smartphone or on their own servers. Instead, they use a sophisticated encryption technique called "tokenization."

This involves converting your Primary Account Number (PAN, a.k.a. your card number) into a unique, randomly-generated sequence of numbers and/or alphanumeric characters. This "token" is stored in a special part of your smartphone's memory that's impossible to decode — even the phone's manufacturer can't read it.

When you make a purchase with a payment app, your card information is "tokenized," encrypted and sent to the bank, which decrypts it and authorizes the transaction. The token is never stored by either the merchant or the bank. This avoids exposing your real card information number to theft. You, the customer, never notice the difference in the way transactions occur.

Of course, all this encryption magic doesn't do you any good if your smartphone is lost or stolen … but if you have (a) a passcode to secure the device, (b) a PIN for opening your payment app and (c) a way to "wipe" all the data from your smartphone remotely, as I do with Apple's "Find My iPhone" app, you are as protected as you can be.

Of course, there are certain privacy risks — as distinct from financial risks — that come from using cellphones and their apps. Some apps can compromise your location and other private data, so it's important to use those that don't — as I'll discuss below.

Saving You Money

Besides convenience and safety, cellphone-based transacting abroad can save you a lot of money. Consider the fees when you use a conventional ATM card outside the U.S., or even inside it, when using another bank's ATM:

- **Flat fee from your bank:** This is a fixed fee that your bank charges for using ATMs outside of its network. These fees usually vary between $2 and $5.

- **Flat fee from the foreign bank:** You also have to pay a fixed fee to the foreign bank which owns the ATM you're using. This again is usually in the range of $2 and $5.

- **International transaction fee:** Instead of a fixed fee (or in addition), your home bank may charge a percentage fee for foreign withdrawals. These range from 1-3%.

- **Currency exchange fee:** The ATM interbank network — like Plus (operated by Visa) or Cirrus (MasterCard) — will also take a 1% cut.

Now consider the method I used. I bought a prepaid foreign debit card in a single transaction using my foreign credit card, on which I paid an international transaction fee of 1%. I then loaded its information into the local payment app, and from that point on, I paid no foreign transaction fees. Of course, I wouldn't have paid any such fees if I had used the foreign prepaid debit card directly, but then I would have lost the extra security of encrypted tokenization.

Payment Apps You Can Use Abroad

The wave of the future — and of the present in much of Europe, Asia, and Africa — is therefore a hybrid system in which banks provide money-storage and credit facilities, but independent application developers provide secure, Internet-based POS systems that largely bypass traditional credit card processors such as Visa and MasterCard. Where can you use them?

According to Netherlands-based payment processing specialists Adyen, Asia now has the second-highest proportion of mobile transactions globally, at 17% of total POS transactions. From August 2013 to August 2014, Asia experienced the strongest mobile payments growth of all regions, increasing by 58%.

Europe remains the leader, with mobile payments averaging 24% in 2014. Europe also experienced strong growth of 34% from August 2013 to August 2014. The UK leads Europe and globally, with mobile payments averaging 41%, followed by the Netherlands and Spain at 26%, France 18% and Germany 16%.

North America remains steady, at 16.7%, and Latin America remains below other regions, at 6% for the quarter.

The ease with which merchants can access these payment systems — often simply by downloading them to a tablet or laptop computer — means they can accept multiple payment systems in their store or restaurant, no matter how small. And since customers can simply download the app and set it up while they're on the go, any of us can access them as needed, recharging them with local prepaid debit cards, as I did.

So you're thinking about going abroad ... and you're wondering which app you need, where to get it, and how to set it up and use it. Let's review your options. Remember, I'm talking here about solutions that allow you to turn your vulnerable physical magnetic-stripe cards into virtual payment systems that require no card to be present.

Apple Pay

Globally, Apple-based payment apps are the most popular in every region of the globe. In most places, twice as many people use Apple-based apps than Android (which runs on most non-Apple smartphones). The only place where Android apps are close to Apple levels of usage is Asia. So it makes sense to start with Apple Pay.

Apple Pay works only on the iPhone 6 or the Apple Watch. You register your supported credit cards in the device's Passbook app. When you want to buy something from a retailer that supports Apple Pay, you point your device at the near field communication (NFC) payment terminal, and your payment information is delivered from your iPhone over a radio frequency connection. Then you do a fingerprint scan on your phone's TouchID sensor to verify your identity. If everything is OK, your phone vibrates and tells you the transaction was approved. Apply Pay also works form within other apps, such as when you wish to purchase a plane ticket using an airline's app.

Apple Pay uses tokenization, which I described, to keep your transaction safe. The token is stored on a special chip called a Secure Element. If the iPhone is lost or stolen, for instance, you can use "Find My iPhone" to suspend all payments from that device. There's no need to cancel your credit card, because the card information isn't stored on the device.

Apple doesn't get to know what you bought, how much you paid for it or any other personal details. The guy behind the counter doesn't get to see your name or your credit card number — all of which are potential weak spots of the current system, under which cards are occasionally cloned and ripped off.

- **Where:** Apple Pay is rolling out rapidly in the U.S., U.K. and Europe. Two things are required to use Apple Pay: the merchant must accept it and your bank must authorize use of your card abroad. As things stand, I expect most major and many smaller merchants in these regions to support Apply Pay by the end of 2015. Apply Pay is also making rapid inroads in Asia, but with the popularity of Android smartphones there, it may take a little longer. In those regions, you can use local payment apps in the meantime.

- **Pros:** The safest system of all, with end-to-end tokenization and no storage of your card or personal details on Apple servers.

- **Cons:** You must upgrade to iPhone 6 or an Apple Watch to use it. Also, not all countries allow prepaid debit cards to be loaded into Apply Pay.

- **Who it's for:** Essentially everyone who uses an Apple iPhone, especially in the U.S., U.K. or Continental Europe.

Google Wallet

Like Apple pay, Google Wallet involves tapping your phone on a POS terminal, entering your Wallet PIN and completing your transaction as usual. And like Apple Pay, Google Wallet uses tokenization — your real 16-digit card number is never exposed to merchants. But instead of securing the token in a chip on your phone, Google uses something called Host Card Emulation (HCE), which stores your token virtually in "the cloud." This makes Google Wallet compatible with any near field communication (NFC)-equipped Android phone. The app also lets you store club cards and gift cards as well as credit and debit cards.

- **Where:** Widely available in the U.S. and expanding rapidly in the UK and Europe. Not yet available in most of the rest of the world.
- **Pros:** Increasingly available in the U.S., U.K. and Europe. Also, Google Wallet is potentially compatible with highly secure Android-based phones such as the BlackPhone (although there are rumors that BlackPhone is developing its own super-secure payment systems).
- **Cons:** In order to use Google Wallet in stores, you'll need an NFC-capable Android phone, which is only 25% of Android phones on the market right now. Major players such as Samsung are rapidly adopting NFC technology. If you aren't an Apple fan, you should choose one of their phones if you'd like to use Google Wallet in future.

A second drawback is that the HCE technology Google has chosen requires that your phone be connected to your cell service to use, because the phone needs to retrieve its tokens from the cloud. That could be expensive if you're travelling abroad.

The biggest con, however, is that is that anything that operates in the cloud — instead of locally, on your phone, as with Apply Pay — is automatically more vulnerable to security attacks.

Who it's for: For security reasons, I would use Google Wallet only if you are resolutely against Apple.

PayPal

Like Apple Pay and Google Wallet, PayPal transactions are tokenized and encrypted, and merchants never see their customer's complete identity, personal information or financial data. Plus, if your phone has a fingerprint scanner (like the Samsung Galaxy S5), you can use that to authorize transactions.

- **Where:** Restricted to U.S. merchants at the moment, particularly on the west coast.
- **Pros:** Secure and widely accepted in the U.S. You also have the option to make purchases at credit card terminals using your phone number and a PIN code.
- **Cons:** Because it moved in early and missed some more recent technological innovations, PayPal has struggled to get merchants to sign on to its systems and is therefore likely to be eclipsed rapidly by Apple Pay. Like Google Wallet, you need cell service in order to use PayPal.
- **Who it's for:** People who already have PayPal accounts and for whom adding another payment option is essentially costless. But not for overseas travelers.

Other Apps

As I discovered, the reality is that in most countries outside the major markets of North America, Europe and Asia, you will need to use a local smartphone app to make payments. I was able to do this with SnapScan in South Africa using my Apple iPhone. As I explained, however, I was only able to do so because SnapScan allowed me to load a local prepaid debit card into the app. That might not always be an option stick with cash until your U.S. bank issues you a chip-and-pin card sometime in the coming year. Of course, if you have a bank account in a foreign country, you can probably use a compatible local app with their bank cards.

When using a foreign payment app, the key is to ensure that it uses tokenization to encrypt your card details. At the moment, the only sure way to know that (other than to research the app yourself) is to see whether it is compatible with all types of smartphones. If it is, it's probably not secure. Token-based apps only work with iPhone 6 and recent Android phones.

My Pick

Apply Pay. It's significantly ahead of the competition, and given the iPhone's wide and deep penetration in the U.S., U.K. and Europe, it will inevitably set the standard for smartphone-based payment solutions in those areas, even for non-Apple services.

The Key to the Puzzle

Throughout this report, I've written as if the question of where your money is ultimately stored is not a major issue. Only in the case of payment apps or countries that don't work with U.S.-based accounts does this become an issue, in which case I've recommended using a foreign prepaid debit card as a workaround.

But the ultimate source of your banking facilities does indeed matter, as we all know. For reasons of privacy, wealth protection and overall peace of mind, having at least some of your money in a secure offshore bank account that you can access via payment apps — or directly — is essential.

That's where the i-Account, which I wrote about in August, is the essential linchpin of your offshore transaction strategy. The i-Account is based on one of the world's safest and most private banking jurisdictions, Hong Kong. Funds are stored in a Chinese bank with the highest possible global ratings, far beyond the prying eyes of Uncle Sam. Even though you must report i-Account balances if you fall under FATCA and FBAR thresholds, the actual data related to your overseas transactions is entirely inaccessible to the U.S. government.

That fact alone makes the i-Account my preferred choice for the debit card I'd load into Apply Pay or another app for use when travelling. Besides the intrinsic security of your i-Account details, tokenization means even those i-Account details will be completely secure.

But there's another huge advantage to the i-Account that basically makes it the ultimate deal for global travelers like you and me.

You can hold your i-Account funds in any one of 10 currencies (USD, EUR, JPY, GBP, NZD, CAD, AUD, SGD, HKD, CHF), with more on the way. You can exchange among these currencies instantly with no added fees, at competitive rates. So instead of having to pay your U.S. bank currency exchange fees when using a payment app, either on every transaction or when purchasing a foreign prepaid debit card, you can simply load your i-Account with the appropriate foreign currency — say, euros — and away you go ... no currency conversion costs at all.

If you would like more information about opening and using i-Account, you can go to http://i-Account.cc/welcome. There you will learn more about funding your i-Account, the currencies available and even uses for corporate accounts.

My Prediction … With Payment Apps, the Future is now

Payment apps have already started to make inroads in the U.S., but mainly amongst merchants that cater to younger and more tech-savvy shoppers. That will change rapidly in the next 12 to 18 months as such payment options expand to nearly all merchants.

The recent Target data breach that exposed data on 40 million debit and credit cards has led to calls to adopt the chip-and-pin standard in the U.S. MasterCard and Visa have said they want merchants and banks to be ready to start accepting such cards, as well as smartphone-friendly NFC terminals, by October 2015.

MasterCard says that it believes half of those 12 to 15 million terminals will be upgraded to handle chip-and-pin by the end of 2015. After that, the liability for any fraud that occurs at POS sale terminals will shift either to the merchant or the card-issuing bank — MasterCard and Visa won't be responsible. That's a powerful incentive to change.

But third-party experts, such as consultancy Adyen, believe that many smaller U.S. merchants are going to resist paying for new chip-and-pin terminals, and will try to leapfrog straight to mobile and online applications to save money and hassle.

As payment specialist Mark Taylor puts it, with chip-and-pin, "Visa and MasterCard are hell bent on making the U.S. homogenous with the rest of the world. But the fact is that we're going to be the last guys in on an aging technology."

For this reason, I predict that all of us will be migrating to app-based payment solutions more quickly than anyone realizes, both in the U.S. and abroad. That's because smartphone apps and tokenization don't require merchants to make major changes to their current payment acceptance systems, like chip-and-pin does.

Be Safe, Bank Safe

So there you have it … the sovereign traveler's strategy for transacting securely and cheaply in foreign countries. Although this strategy is still expanding rapidly across the globe and hasn't reached everywhere yet, chances are that it will have reached your destination of choice in the next 12 to 18 months.

And that's true even if your destination is the U.S. itself … because as I've predicted, this will be the way you'll transact here soon. And thanks to *Offshore Confidential*, you'll be ready before almost everyone else.

KICK THE GOVERNMENT OUT OF YOUR RETIREMENT

Robert E. Bauman JD, *The Sovereign Investor Daily*, February 2014

One of the many quirks I share with my sons, James and Ted, is an appreciation for the absurdist humor of the 1970s-era British comedy troupe Monty Python's Flying Circus. Messrs. Palin, Cleese, Idle et al. had a knack for incisive political commentary dressed up as nonsense.

Perhaps that's why the first thing that came to mind when I read President Obama's State of the Union proposal for a new government-controlled retirement account system, called "MyRA," was a classic Python sketch. It involved a deadbeat Scottish poet named Ewan McTeagle, whom everyone mistook for a literary genius. He was actually a moocher whose primary theme was begging for handouts.

The President's latest proposal, too, masquerades as genius but is really nonsense. He plans an Executive Order to create an IRA scheme in which all workers not covered by employer 401(k)s would be automatically enrolled unless they opted out. Automatic monthly paycheck deductions would be invested in U.S. Treasury bonds — in other words, loans to the government.

In the fashion of cheap poetry, Obama's MyRA proposal is gussied up with many so-called advantages and enticements, such as tax-free earnings and a government guarantee. But like the proverbial lipstick on a pig, these bells and whistles don't change the real nature of this beast.

Let me show you what that real nature is …

Let me start by stating plainly that you must avoid this MyRA like the plague. But more importantly, you must treat it as a warning of worse to come, and make preparations to protect yourself.

The real agenda behind Obama's proposal isn't helping people save more for retirement. MyRA lays the groundwork for the eventual transfer of the bulk of the nation's private retirement savings to government control, something I wrote about in relation to Poland last year.

Government control over private pensions has two big attractions for big-government liberals like Obama. In the long term, it will make it possible to confiscate our wealth en masse — something that appears more and more likely with each passing day. And in the short term, it will help Obama to fund his annual budget deficits with our retirement savings.

There are good reasons for floating this scheme now. With the Fed not buying up as much government debt due to reduced Quantitative Easing, the bloated deficit will have to be funded another way.

You see, with the MyRA plan, the government is basically tempting millions of people to buy government debt with every pay check. The Treasury will take your money and spend any "surplus" funds — just like Social Security. Everything above the amount needed to pay out current MyRA benefits will be dumped into the government's general accounts and spent. And like Social Security, the MyRA system will rapidly become a bunch of IOU's from the government. But this time, the IOU's will be held by individuals instead of the Social Security trust fund.

So like Ewan McTeagle with his poems, Obama's MyRA plan is yet another honey-tongued ploy to part you and your money. It will start out voluntary, but will surely become mandatory for all IRAs and 401(k) plans one day in the not-too-distant future.

A Retirement Investment Protected from Government Spending

Luckily, there is a little-known, yet highly affordable offshore solution to retirement savings that can ensure your money won't be taken — offshore variable annuities.

Offshore variable annuities are a great alternative to traditional IRAs. They give you access to some of the world's best investment opportunities. Instead of the short list of U.S. equity funds in your typical 401(k), the manager of your offshore annuity can choose any investment, anywhere, unconstrained by your U.S. citizenship.

Offshore variable annuities are also tax-deferred, since taxes are paid only when a distribution is made to you or your beneficiaries. And in most cases, the companies who offer offshore annuities operate under strict foreign privacy laws. No internet search or phone call will reveal the existence of your policy.

In addition, variable annuities offer significant asset protection, especially in Switzerland, shielding your investment and the annuity income from creditors and other claimants. In addition, Swiss law exempts annuities from foreign court judgments including bankruptcy. The degree of asset protection afforded by Swiss insurance and annuities is unparalleled anywhere else in the world. Other offshore jurisdictions with a well-developed insurance sector provide statutory protection against creditor claims for insurance policies.

So it will take more than Obama's poetry to entice your money out of it. Offshore variable annuities are a great alternative to a traditional IRA and a wealth protection solution wrapped up in one.

What the Rise of Digital Currency Could Mean for You

Jeff D. Opdyke, *The Sovereign Investor Daily*, March 2012

Say goodbye to George and Abe. Andrew and Ben, too.

After nearly 1,400 years of use, paper-money is fading away. That means the men who populate your wallet — George Washington, Abe Lincoln, Andrew Jackson and Ben Franklin — are on their way out.

In their place, a new kind of currency is emerging — digital currency.

You don't see it yet on a widespread level, but digital currency is spreading rapidly across other parts of the world and will soon hit a wallet — and a cell phone — near you.

Living Your Financial Life Through Your Cell Phone

Consider Africa, for a moment. What Americans think of as a cauldron of famine, pestilence, corruption and genocidal war is also the birthplace of a financial revolution. You can see it in action every day at the Flomu General Store, in a village near Kenya's border with Uganda.

Each morning, when the shopkeeper opens the doors to his cinderblock stall, a group of local villagers is already standing in line.

They've not come for the flour, the sugar or the water.

They've come to do their banking … because while Kenya ranks among the world's 30 poorest countries in terms of per-capita GDP, it has become the epicenter of a digital-cash revolution on the verge of spreading globally.

Everyone in front of the Flomu General Store carries a cellphone and the store has become their ATM. Through a technology known as M-Pesa — M for mobile; pesa, the Swahili word for cash — the villagers are able to spend, receive and save money simply by sending a text message from their phone.

More than half of the country now uses mobile phones to complete some or all of their banking needs, and they are zipping among themselves a sum of money equivalent to as much as 20% of Kenya's annual GDP.

The company behind the M-Pesa technology — a company we own inside *The Sovereign Investor* portfolio — hired the man running the show in Kenya to take the platform global ... meaning that digital banking could invade India — one of the world's largest cell-phone markets — as early as this summer. Egypt is up after that ... and then the world.

Effectively, M-Pesa technology — and others like it — allow you to live a financial life through your cellphone, safely, securely and conveniently ... even when you're in the middle of nowhere in Kenya.

Technology that's Roaring Across Underdeveloped Nations

I first wrote about the digital currency phenomenon in June of last year, and today various media outlets like the BBC are picking up on the trend. The British news agency reported just last month that "whether you want to pay a friend or your window cleaner, [digital cash is] laying that foundation to enable mobile payments to become a mainstream option."

In short, digital currency will girdle the globe and become a service embedded in just about every cell phone in just about every country in the world. By 2015, global mobile transactions could exceed a projected $3 trillion annually.

As in Kenya, the death of hard currency has already begun in some places. Payment by cell phone has existed for years in countries such as Norway and Japan — where with a mobile phone held against a vending machine you can buy a soft-drink without ever touching a coin or a bill.

And though most Americans still rely on currency, even in the U.S. most of the cash is digital already. Just one of every $10 exists as a paper bill. In other words, the vast majority — 90% of the dollars created — are purely digital.

Even the money the Federal Reserve has been "printing" in recent years is more ethereal than physical. Ben Bernanke recently told CBS News: "People talk about the printing press. That's not what this is about." It's about creating virtual money that can be created and erased with keyboard strokes.

And, in a darker context, it's the ability of government to track money flows.

For instance, one of the biggest challenges Europe faces with its current financial struggles is that Greek and Italian individuals and businesses are notorious for shirking their tax obligations. No one can easily trace the all-cash transactions that are commonplace in both countries.

An Enormous Investment Opportunity

A digital currency makes that much easier. Prying government eyes can see exactly how much a consumer spends and at which store — allowing tax authorities to compare an individual taxpayer's spending pattern with reported income, and comparing a business's reported income with the electronic receipts created during the year.

Like it or not, though, digital cash is the future.

It's a global phenomenon, and an enormous investment opportunity.

Avoid the Next Global Financial Crisis by Investing in Gold
Jeff D. Opdyke, *The Sovereign Investor Daily*, January 2015

The state of the world today requires one commitment from you — a commitment to gold.

When you look around the world, there is a **hurricane of crosscurrents** blowing across the investment landscape — the stock and bond markets, developed and emerging economies, monetary policies taking shape in various countries, what's happening to oil and commodities, geopolitical machinations.

The ultimate conclusion to the events now unfolding will take the world in one of two directions: an economic meltdown, or a dramatic re-correction.

Indeed, we are on the precipice of a new global financial crisis, one that once again will be caused by America's actions, as was the crisis of 2007/08. And, as with the last go 'round, a crack in the system will see assets of all stripes struggle in unity, save for the U.S. dollar.

Gold, too, will struggle temporarily, if only because of the shock factor. But just as it did in the last crisis, gold will gather its bearings and prove to be a safe haven for shell-shocked investors and savers.

Then again, we could very well avoid the precipice all together if politicians and central bankers take certain actions. And if so, gold rallies hard as the dollar retreats.

Let me explain what I see and you will understand why investing in gold is mandatory in 2015…

A World of Turmoil

The U.S. reported 5% GDP growth for the third quarter. If you're going to lie, lie big!

There is no possible way the U.S. economy honestly grew at 5%. It grew at that rate through data manipulation largely tied to explosive health care spending (i.e. Obamacare mandates) but that's a topic for a different day.

Ask yourself this: How can America's GDP grow at such an explosive rate when A) the strong dollar is hurting exports, B) our major trading partners — Canada, Mexico, Japan, Germany — are all growing at between 0.4% and 2%, and C) U.S. consumer spending — a proxy for the domestic economy — is largely flat?

Something is amiss.

And it's amiss at a moment when the world in is political and financial turmoil, for several reasons:

- Russia is on the brink of a crisis that, if the U.S. allows it to happen, will spin through the global economy like a tornado ripping through a trailer park. (And at this point, Russia's direction is entirely a function of U.S. policy; even German leaders are worried about the unintended implications in Europe of the White House pushing too hard to bring an old foe to its knees economically.) The contagion will weaken European economies and rip apart emerging economies, which will haunt the U.S. economy and global stock markets.

- Japan has reached its end game and is printing more money than God as it tries to (futilely) save itself from the deadly effects of having put its faith in Keynesian monetary beliefs over these last few decades. That excessive liquidity (along with Japan's asinine cultural beliefs about immigration) is fueling a national crisis that, given Japan's role as the world's third-largest economy, will reverberate globally — and nastily.

- The European Central Bank is about to launch a round of quantitative easing that will pour even more currency into a global system bloated with money. Bad bad bad.

- The strong dollar is hurting emerging nations and their companies that have lots of dollar-denominated debt, and could cause a huge — huge! — currency crisis somewhere.

- The Federal Reserve finds itself in an impossible situation as it looks to normalize interest rates: Raising rates even 0.25% would strengthen the dollar even more, hurting U.S. exports/the U.S. economy even more and risking that currency crisis somewhere else. Don't raise rates, and the markets remain confused about Fed policy, while the easy-money stance expands the global asset bubble even more.

The list goes on — Greece is causing fears in European gains, China is (also) printing money like mad, oil has disconnected from reality…

If any one of those goes pear-shaped, it will knock over a string of dominoes globally. Investments around the world tumble as money rushes into the dollar

… and gold. It's the fear trade, potentially on steroids, depending on what event causes which dominoes to fall.

And if none of those go pear-shaped, if world leaders manage to navigate all those shoals … well, then gold rallies, potentially dramatically, because the dollar's strength abates as global sentiment brightens.

Prepare Now for the Coming Crisis

I have written many times that **gold is not an investment** but, rather, an insurance policy protecting you from political and monetary stupidity. And if nothing else is true in the world, it's this: Political and monetary leaders globally have spent the last three to four decades acting with the wisdom and acumen of roadkill.

The manifestation of any of the multitude of risks our world confronts now are globally destabilizing because of the interconnectedness of economies and investment markets, the unfathomably large quantity of currency that has been printed globally over the last decade, and global dependence on a single currency — the dollar — that is managed horrendously.

Gold is down because traders too often treat it as a commodity, and investors too often misunderstand its role in a portfolio.

Yet central banks around the world have continued to be large buyers of gold, regardless of price. They're loading up on insurance. They're preparing for a catastrophe that could shake the world far more violently than the global financial crisis.

Which is why I tell you at the start of the year: The state of the world today requires one commitment from you — a commitment to gold.

Suspicious Transactions
Mark Nestmann, *The Sovereign Individual*, March 2001

Welcome to the "Snitch Society."

In the United States and, increasingly, in other countries, your children are encouraged to report their suspicions to teachers that you might be using illegal drugs. Tax authorities pay generous rewards for turning in tax cheats. Anyone who forwards a lead to police that property was used illegally is eligible for a reward if it is forfeited.

These aspects of a snitch society, odious as they are, for the most part are voluntary. Yet with respect to our money, they are mandatory. U.S. law requires banks, casinos and money transmitting businesses to report "any suspicious transaction relevant to a possible violation of law or regulation" to the Financial Crimes Enforcement Network (FinCEN), the U.S. Treasury's financial intelligence unit.

These incredibly broad provisions, through the first half of 1998, led to 150,000 Suspicious Activity Reports (SARs) being filed. From these reports, a total of 337 money laundering, fraud, embezzlement, theft or narcotics prosecutions were initiated. More than 99.7 percent of these reports did not lead to a criminal investigation.

But the collateral damage is huge. In one case, a mistaken report caused the accounts of 1,100 innocent depositors to be frozen. And the reports keep coming: an additional 350,000 SARs were filed through October 2000.

SARs are available electronically to every U.S. Attorney's Office, 59 federal agencies and police in all 50 states. No suspicion of crime need be shown for disclosure. Since FinCEN is exempt from U.S. privacy legislation, it can maintain SARs indefinitely. In addition, SARs have been made available (illegally) to private investigators.

The more reports filed, the greater the chance for such foul-ups. Especially since FinCEN itself has trouble entering the data it gets accurately. A 1999 audit found that in one case, $5,000 was entered as $5 million.

But this is only the beginning. FinCEN notes approvingly the expansion of mandatory SAR requirements in other countries to all professionals that handle money as fiduciaries. U.K. law, for instance, requires lawyers to report transactions they believe are related to money laundering. Similar provisions are now in effect in many offshore centers.

FinCEN is already preparing new SAR rules for U.S. securities brokers and firms engaged in foreign trade. And it suggests extending the requirements to accountants, insurers and even appliance makers and consumer electronics stores.

It is possible that these new requirements will result in some crimes being solved that might otherwise have gone undetected. But at what cost?

The tradition of confidentiality in the conduct of one's financial affairs is more than 5,000 years old. The Code of Hammurabi, one of the first written system of laws, stipulated that the when persons entrusted their money to a banker, those transactions were not to be disclosed to outsiders.

The Justinian Code of the sixth century A.D. (that compilation of Roman Law on which most European legal systems are based) recognized that relationships between individuals and their lawyers should also be afforded secrecy. In English law, the principle was first mentioned in 1580.

The common thread in these traditions is that clients should feel free to make full disclosure, thus making it more likely that a professional advisor will provide good advice. Confidentiality makes us feel comfortable disclosing information that, if known to others, could be damaging.

But today, banks, attorneys and many other professionals owe their first duty to the state, not to their clients. We are rapidly approaching the Nazification of the global financial system, with our trusted advisors acting as spies against us in an illusory "War on Crime." We have no choice but to take responsibility for our own individual sovereignty.

THE $7 BILLION LAUNDRY BILL

Daniel J. Mitchell, Senior Fellow at the Cato Institute, *Forbes*, October 2006

According to *The Tampa Tribune*, a Florida convent recently had its bank account frozen because an 80-year-old nun did not have a Social Security number and photo ID on file with the bank.

Equally bizarre, *The Providence Journal* reports that a retired Rhode Island school teacher's attempt to pay off a credit card was held up because the transaction did not fit his usual pattern, and therefore raised a red flag.

These are not tales of heartless clerks or incompetent bank tellers. Instead, they are examples of the government's ill-designed fight against money laundering. Under proposed regulations not only banks but merchants, like auto dealers, real estate agents and travel agencies, are obliged to snoop on their customers in hopes of detecting whether money was obtained illicitly. Some of the snooping is inane, such as the costly requirement that banks file a report every time a cash transaction exceeds $10,000.

The original purpose of anti-money laundering laws was to reduce the incentive for illegal behavior by making it more difficult for crooks to enjoy their ill-gotten gains. From an economic perspective this made sense. Policies that increase the cost and/or reduce the benefit of criminal activity are likely to curb bad behavior.

Anti-money laundering laws do impose high costs, and that cost is borne by the financial industry and its consumers. The recent decision to reauthorize the PATRIOT Act, without any examination of whether it makes sense to extend some 30 onerous money laundering provisions, guarantees that costs will continue to rise.

According to the Financial Crimes Enforcement Network, institutions filed 14.8 million reports in 2004, including nearly 13.7 million currency transaction reports (for $10,000 plus transactions) and more than 650,000 suspicious activity reports. What constitutes suspicious activity? The government offers no guidelines, except to decree that depository financial institutions report "any instances of known or suspected illegal or suspicious activity." It's sort of like the late U.S. Supreme Court Justice Potter Stewart who, when asked to define hard core pornography, famously said, "I know it when I see it." Banks have privately complained that potentially suspicious transactions encompass a quarter of their business.

All this paperwork carries a hefty price rag — $7 billion in 2003, according to the Institute of International Economics. It is worth noting, though, that this does not include the cost of diminished privacy and disrupted lives for Florida nuns and retired schoolteachers in Rhode Island. Nor does it include the cost of driving poor people (whose limited assets and irregular financial transactions make them particularly costly to service) out of the banking system.

These costs might all be worth it if there were any proof that anti-money laundering laws lowered crime rates. But the laws don't even put a dent in money laundering. A Brookings Institution scholar testified before Congress that 99.9% of dirty money in the United States is successfully laundered. And the U.S. Sentencing Commission reported that only 715 people were sentenced in 2000 for the crime of money laundering (an additional 800 people were sentenced for money laundering plus another offense).

Lawmakers should give serious thought to junking the current anti-money laundering system and figuring out smarter ways to fight crime. Society would probably be safer if the $7 billion was reallocated to fighting terrorists and/or putting more cops on the street in poor neighborhoods.

This is not to say that all anti-money laundering policies should be tossed. A few of the laws and regulations that have been implemented over the past 20 years carry relatively little cost and promise some benefit. For instance, requiring financial institutions to maintain records on account holders is not terribly burdensome and can aid criminal investigations and prosecutions.

Another useful tool is a sensible provision of the Patriot Act that authorizes the government to send a limited list of suspect individuals to financial institutions. It makes a lot more sense for the government to actively monitor a few bad guys than it does to require banks to spy on all their customers.

THE FUTURE OF MONEY: THE FINANCIAL SECRET THAT BANKS WILL HATE

Ted Bauman, *Offshore Confidential*, August 2014

It was raining hard in Bratislava on the western border of Slovakia. And I was facing a cold, wet night on a park bench.

I stood in a pool of lamplight outside a warm, cheery hotel in the Old Town, just across the Staroměstská from the Castle. My flight from Paris had arrived in Vienna just before midnight, and after multiple layovers and a 45-minute bus trip, I was dog-tired.

But my client forgot to book and prepay the hotel, and the hotel didn't accept the credit card I had with me. My South African bank was closed for the weekend, and I had reached my overseas cash withdrawal limit under my country's foreign exchange control laws.

So I stood there with my bags, soaking wet, hoping for a "Hollywood" turn of events — maybe a passing Slovak girl who would take pity on me and take me to her place, inaugurating a weekend to remember. She never arrived. This is a worst-case scenario, one that's happened to me in multiple regions of the globe — some much worse than Central Europe.

Indeed, my years as a self-employed international consultant were plagued by mundane matters of travel finance. Foreign credit card machines that didn't work, or weren't compatible with my technologically backward South African bank cards. Banks that forgot to record my overseas travel plans, resulting in declined card charges at awkward times (to protect me from "fraud"). Foreign ATM and currency conversion fees that often exceeded 10% of my expenses, and which my clients refused to cover.

If only I'd had another option in those days that would have allowed me to get access to my money when I needed it. I'd even have preferred it to my imaginary Slovak *dievča*.

Safer Than a Bank

Most of us think of a "bank" as a place, in a building, where bankers keep our money in account products they've sold to us. In almost all cases, those bankers make the rules governing our accounts and we are locked in one currency. They decide under what conditions we can access our deposited funds or our credit lines, and since we're typically tied to our banks by a web of interlocking products — transaction, credit, mortgage, investment and other accounts — we have to tolerate whatever nonsense they decide to throw at us.

That's especially true for those of us who believe our money is ours. And for those of us who live and work as "global citizens." Permit me to share another personal example. I have a cottage in a seaside village near Cape Town, South Africa. For years, I've sent money from the U.S. to add to my monthly mortgage payment. I used a convenient online money transfer service. This service allowed me to send funds from my U.S. account directly to my South African account for under $5.

But earlier this year, my South African bank got into trouble with the national banking regulator for something to do with "anti-terrorist money laundering rules" demanded by the U.S. government.

So they decided to forbid all inward fund transfers, except those which came directly from "official" offshore banks.

No more cheap online money transfers for me. My only option was to pay my U.S. bank almost $100 per wire transfer, with a visit to a branch and wasted time in a line to boot.

Outrageous fees from my U.S. bank, unilateral changes in terms of service from my South African bank, topped off with stupid government interference: that's the behavior of dinosaurs, creatures who've ruled so long they think they're invincible. That's exactly what modern banks are — and why the product I'm going to tell you about is going to kill them dead in their tracks.

Your e-Money Passport to Security

Knowing that you have quick and easy access to your money is key to feeling secure — whether you are strolling down famed Russell Street in Hong Kong, cruising down the Seine in Paris or relaxing in your home. And with advances in technology, we've come to expect our financial transactions to be simple and efficient — just like so many other things in our lives.

I've found that the i-Account is international personal money management at its simplest and most efficient.

The i-Account is a transaction facility that you can use anywhere in the world, either at point-of-sale machines or via ATM withdrawals. The i-Account is offered through a Hong Kong financial services company using a large Chinese bank, providing you with an eMoney Passport that gives you access to your money anywhere around the world.

It's basically an international version of PayPal — but with some serious added benefits.

You fund this eMoney Passport, and then you can use it to transact anywhere in the world. And instead of dealing with a bloated, complex bank, you're dealing with a focused, cutting-edge financial services company whose goal is to make your personal international financial transactions as flexible, painless and cheap as possible.

If you're familiar with PayPal, you'll know that its main attraction is the ease with which you can receive and disburse funds anywhere in the world. As long as the other party has a PayPal account, you can transact without going through a bank, for a modest fee, and often for free.

PayPal's recent addition of a MasterCard-branded debit card means you can use your funds at merchants and ATMs too.

But PayPal is a typical American company: it relies primarily on market dominance rather than innovation and efficiency, so its features and global footprint are limited.

And as an American company, any money you keep with PayPal is still in the U.S. banking system, where it can be tracked, recorded — and potentially confiscated by a greedy government.

Not so with this eMoney Passport. In fact, the i-Account has features that make PayPal look positively antiquated:

- Anyone of any nationality can hold an i-Account, without restriction. There are no background or credit checks. Of course, the group does meet a standard of "know your customer rules" for international money laundering laws so that they can monitor for unethical activity. You can open more than one account: accounts in the name of a business, LLC, or other entity.

- You can hold your i-Account funds in any one of 10 currencies (USD, EUR, JPY, GBP, NZD, CAD, AUD, SGD, HKD, CHF), with more on the way. Furthermore, you can exchange among these currencies instantly with no added fees, at competitive rates.

- The i-Account operates entirely online, with a simple user interface. All transactions, including deposits, are done online. Funds can be transferred instantly, directly from and to your own bank accounts in the U.S. or any other jurisdiction.

- Funds from your i-Account can be transmitted to any Society for Worldwide Interbank Financial Telecommunication (SWIFT)-connected bank account in the world, online, at less than half the cost of most mainline banks.

- There are no monthly fees for average monthly balances above $2,000. What's more, most account transfers cost just $3.

- The linked i-Card MasterCard uses chip-and-PIN security technology, which is the global security standard, and is far superior to the magnetic stripe technology used on most U.S. cards. Whether in the U.S. 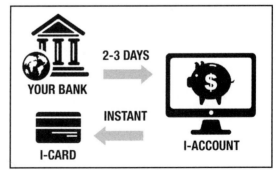 or overseas, the card can't be used without your private PIN number. And in the U.S., where the i-Card uses a magnetic stripe, you're covered by the same anti-fraud protections as all MasterCard or Visa cardholders.

- Even better, you can lock the card at any time by sending a text message from your mobile phone. You just send another text to unlock the card.

Monetary Peace of Mind

The i-Account is attractive for more than its snazzy features. Consider its most important quality of all: it's not a U.S. banking product.

We've written a lot lately about the growing threat of wealth confiscation from U.S. bank accounts.

The Sovereign Investor Daily website has been populated with articles by Bob and myself detailing how the government has snatched tax returns to cover so-called "old debts" and grabbed up dormant bank accounts. Stories of how the government is looking for new ways to grab your wealth are popping up with increasing frequency.

The massive debt the U.S. has accumulated is rising and the government is left with few options to pay it down. Wealth confiscation is close to becoming a reality for all Americans.

Against that day, we've made some specific recommendations, such as investing in rare collectible stamps and offshore real estate. And we've advised that you store cash in various currencies both in your home safe and in safe deposit boxes abroad. The more of your wealth you have stored offshore or in forms that don't require interaction with U.S. banks, the better.

The i-Account serves this goal — and at a much lower cost than many other options available to you. It allows you to move funds offshore, into a foreign bank account, but to access them cheaply and conveniently anywhere, including in the U.S. itself.

In terms of utility and convenience, it's indistinguishable from a U.S. bank account. It's an important part of your personal wealth-protection plan, but one that doesn't require any lawyers, accountants or complex offshore structures.

And you don't have to be a millionaire to use it. Just a few thousand dollars is enough to secure your private back-up plan.

Most Americans have never had to deal with the nightmare of currency controls, but they've already begun to sneak into our banking. Since late 2013, banks have come up with reasons not to allow us to access our funds. JPMorgan Chase established a policy of forbidding its small-business customers from withdrawing more than $50,000 per month, and banning foreign transfers. In the UK, HSBC began demanding explanations from people who wanted to withdraw large sums of their money. And it's only going to get worse.

Imagine the inevitable day when a bankrupt U.S. government imposes such rules here. Will you be prepared? How will you get access to your money?

With an i-Account setup — perhaps several — that is pre-funded, you'll have instant access to your money abroad and at home, without any interference from the government.

And instead of having to negotiate a tricky dance with an offshore bank, you can just whip out your i-Card — the MasterCard-branded debit card that goes with the i-Account — at any merchant or ATM anywhere on the planet, and have access to the full value of your money. You could even buy your plane tickets out of here with the swipe of a card.

We've learned to rely on banks to keep our money safe from thieves, but those same institutions have started to work against us, forgetting who it is that they are supposed to be serving once they have our money within their vaults. Too often banks have changed the "Terms and Conditions" of the money management relationship we have with them, but they never bother to update their customers. They trample customers' rights in an effort to keep you separated from your money.

An i-Account is more than easy international financial transactions. It's peace of mind … in your wallet.

This is a type of peace of mind most Americans haven't given much thought. Most Americans assume that they will always be able to withdraw their money from their bank. But what if you were faced with strict lock-downs by banks?

I know it might be hard to believe that something like that could ever occur, but I've already lived it elsewhere and I have little doubt that it will happen in the United States as well. During much of my time in South Africa, at a time of international sanctions against the apartheid regime, I lived under a system of extremely tight currency controls intended to prevent a mass run on the rand.

Not only were we forbidden from sending money offshore or purchasing goods and services from abroad; we were also severely constrained in using bank cards and other instruments when overseas.

A South African citizen had to apply for permission to spend money abroad, even while traveling on holiday, and any unused foreign currency had to be returned to the Reserve Bank immediately upon returning home.

Foreign transactions were subject to scrutiny, and you could be fined heavily for the slightest transgression of the rules. There was even a period when there were two "versions" of the South African rand with different values and rules, one for business use and the other for ordinary folk like me.

For all intents and purposes, our money was trapped in South Africa.

But an i-Account can circumvent those traps, keeping your money free and in your hands. And best of all, you can hold your i-Account balances in one of many currencies. You can easily escape and maintain a quality of life for your family with foreign currencies from this account, because you'll have your wealth safely held in the Hong Kong dollar or Swiss franc.

Not a Traditional Offshore Account

That's why the i-Account is imperative for people like you and me. Even if you don't travel abroad much, having an account at an offshore bank gives you the freedom, flexibility and peace of mind that comes with operating entirely outside the U.S. banking system, avoiding the dollar if you choose to do so. It's the ideal place to stash reserve or emergency funds, just as we recommended in our February *Offshore Confidential*.

The i-Account is not an offshore account in the traditional sense. It's the future of the internationalized financial world that most countries embrace. As Europeans or Asians know already, the idea of being restricted to one country's banking system is as antiquated as steamship travel or the telegraph.

Leveraging the extremely low costs of Internet-based banking, i-Account offers the same global advantages and levels of service that multi-millionaires get, but for everyday bank balances and budgets. In many ways, because the i-Account is no different from having a domestic account, it's even better than millionaire-level offshore banking.

The i-Account isn't a set of computer files on some vulnerable tropical island. It's built on the solid foundation of some of the world's best banking jurisdictions:

1. The company that offers the i-Account, Account Services (HK) Limited, is based in Hong Kong, one of the world's most popular and safest offshore banking centers.

2. In addition, i-Account funds are kept by Shanghai Pudong Development Bank Co., one of China's leading commercial banks. SPD is well-known and respected in domestic and overseas markets. Your funds are kept in a segregated account that is not part of the bank's own capital and never used for trading purposes.

3. The i-Card's MasterCard services are provided by a London-based company that provides transaction services to many financial services companies around the world.

If I'd had an i-Account

Let's revisit the situations I described earlier, to see how the i-Account could have made them turn out differently.

Stuck in Bratislava: My i-Account would allow me to transact at any ATM in the city, without restriction. Since the i-Card that goes with it uses chip-and-pin security, I wouldn't have to worry about having my card hacked, as is often the case with American-style magnetic stripe cards. And, of course, the hotel would gladly accept my i-Card too. **Result:** A dry night in a soft bed, dreaming of my Slovak *dievča*.

Reporting for the IRS

Like any foreign financial offshore bank account, the i-Account must be reported to the U.S. government if the amount you have in it exceeds certain thresholds.

If the total value of all your foreign accounts is more than $10,000, you must complete Part III of Schedule B of IRS Form 1040 when you file your annual U.S. federal income tax return.

You must file FinCEN Form 114, Report of Foreign Bank and Financial Accounts (FBAR) if the total value of all your foreign accounts exceeds $10,000 at any time during a calendar year. This form must be filed with the U.S. Department of the Treasury, not the IRS, by June 30 following the calendar year you are reporting. Filing must now be done electronically.

Under the provisions of the 2010 "Foreign Account Tax Compliance Act" (FATCA) U.S. persons living in the U.S. itself are required to file an IRS Form 8938 along with their annual income tax return disclosing any foreign "financial assets" with a combined value exceeding $50,000. The reporting threshold is higher for U.S. persons living abroad.

Slaying the dinosaurs: My i-Account would allow me to bypass both high-fee U.S. banks and South African "anti-terrorist" regulations. Since the funds in my i-Account are held at a reputable Chinese bank that does a great deal of business in Africa, I can just login to the i-Account site and transfer funds at will to my South African account — for less than half it would cost me at a U.S. bank. **Result:** I save money, time and hassle.

Protecting my wealth and financial freedom: Long before my country had imposed currency restrictions, I would have funded a variety of i-Accounts for myself, my family and my offshore trusts, LLCs and other wealth-protection structures. All of these accounts are held securely offshore, so even if the U.S. government knows about them (since I might have to report them), I'm still free to transact at will since the funds are held outside the U.S., or aren't held in U.S. currency at all. In other words, I'm in control of all these situations — not the bank, and not the government. That's the very definition of being sovereign. **Result:** I'm protected from wealth confiscation and currency controls.

A Final Word

Having an e-Money Passport protects your ability to access your money anywhere around the globe — even in the United States — when you want to, taking the power out of the hands of banks and the government. If you are interested in i-Account, they are going to be a sponsor of our Total Wealth Symposium in Panama this September as well as speaking at the event. There you will be able to get more information regarding the services they provide. Go to www.TWSPanama.com for a complete list of speakers and to reserve your seat before time runs out.

If you would like more information about opening and using an i-Account, you can go to http://i-account.cc/welcome. There you will learn more about funding your i-Account, quick remittance and even uses for corporate accounts.

How to Beat the Great Wealth Grab
Robert E. Bauman JD, *Offshore Confidential*, February 2014

I was adopted shortly after birth in 1937. My adoptive father, Carl, no doubt prompted by my mother, Floss, acquired a 16mm Kodak movie camera to record my early youth.

There is one entertaining sequence when Dad, camera at the ready, handed little Bobby a garden hose in our back yard and began filming. The spigot had already been turned on and the hose was pouring water. This early footage revealed me shaking my three-year-old curly head in earnest, saying: "No, no, Dada." I was assuring Dad I would never squirt him with that hose — just before the camera lens (and Dad) got drenched.

Think about all the times in life when you've been given ironclad assurances that something would or would not happen — either by family members or friends — or, more dangerously, by politicians. I know whereof I speak. I was once described by *The New York Times* as the "conscience of the House," because I attended every session and always questioned legislation that was proposed by "unanimous consent." I was lied to countless times by my congressional colleagues, who assured me there was nothing controversial in a bill they wanted me to vote for, sight unseen.

The biggest lie so far is currently making the rounds — the subject of this special issue of *Offshore Confidential* — and, in spite of repeated political assurances that it could "never happen here," America is on the verge of coordinated global wealth confiscation.

Think how many times politicians have lied to you — times you were told that something would never happen that eventually did. The daily news, the mass media, our government and history are replete with examples of lying politicians.

Back in 1909, for example, Senator Norris Brown of Nebraska proposed the 16th Amendment to the U.S. Constitution, which allowed the federal government to tax the income of Americans. Before it was ratified in 1913, Senator Brown made a few ironclad assurances — chief among them was the claim that this new income tax would only be needed during "national emergencies" or "when necessary to the life of the republic," echoing the language of previous temporary taxes that had been introduced to raise money during times of war.

Nonetheless, once the 16th Amendment was passed, the U.S.'s first permanent income tax law came into effect. It began by imposing a tax of 1% on income up to $20,000 and put in place a graduated surtax on incomes above that figure. The highest rate was 7% and applied only to Americans making more than $500,000 (almost $12 million in today's dollars).

A century later, American individuals with more than $400,000 in taxable income pay a tax rate of 39.6%. With the new Obamacare surtax, Americans earning over $450,000 are now forking out more than 44%.

So much for Senator Brown's promises …

Or think about President Richard Nixon. In 1971, he declared a "war on drugs" and, in doing so, he dramatically increased the size and presence of federal drug control agencies. Today, the Drug Enforcement Agency and associated bureaucracies have become multibillion dollar enterprises that thrive by grabbing private property via a device known as "civil forfeiture."

This device was sold to the public on the grounds that government would seize assets "used in the commission of a crime." The idea sounds wonderful, like Elliot Ness using tax law to bring down criminals, such as Al Capone. Indeed, since the early 1970s, police at all levels have seized at least $15 billion with the use of civil forfeiture laws. However, a little digging reveals more than 90% of the Americans forced to hand over that $15 billion were never convicted with a single crime.

The reason is simple — civil forfeiture has become a multibillion dollar cash cow. So much for Nixon …

And another excellent example of broken promises is the PATRIOT Act, which was rushed into law in the weeks after the September 11 attacks in New York and Washington, D.C. before a panicked U.S. Congress even had time to read it. This unconstitutional law and its extraordinary surveillance powers, according to its authors and President Bush, would be applied to terrorism and terrorists only.

Today, the PATRIOT Act serves as the basis for the NSA's massive spying operation on all Americans — our phone calls, emails, financial accounts and every aspect of our lives.

So much for the assurances of George W. Bush …

It should be no surprise to hear that the assurances of our elected officials are not worth a proverbial hill of beans.

While much of the concern over the forcible confiscation of wealth comes from Europe, the Obama administration has shown itself to be more than sympathetic. It's worth bearing in mind that it was the United States Congress that adopted the Foreign Account Tax Compliance Act (FATCA) — one of the mechanisms by which global wealth confiscation will be easier for all governments.

Make no mistake — we are all at risk.

Coming up in this issue, I will reveal six specific actions you can take to beat the coming wealth grab.

Why They Desperately Need Your Money

One undeniable phenomenon lies behind the coming wealth grab: skyrocketing and unsustainable public debt in every corner of the world. We are living through the greatest global debt bubble in modern history, one that stretches from developed nations, like the U.S., Japan and those in Europe, to emerging countries like China.

Public debt is essentially the money owed to all creditors by a central government to pay for the goods and services it provides. This debt comprises bonds and similar instruments. Included in the total public debt is also "implicit" debt — a government's future financial obligation, such as pension payments or likely bailouts for banks that are "too big to fail."

When a country's public debt reaches a critical point — typically 90% of its annual GDP — it is said to be in a "debt crisis." The country may be unable to "roll over" its short-term debts, or may face such high interest costs that it can't afford both debt servicing and normal government operations.

This is what happened in Cyprus and Greece recently, and to Argentina several times over the last few decades. Italy, Portugal, and Spain are currently expected to be at risk of a debt default.

As a rule, market sentiment about debt-critical countries deteriorates rapidly, raising interest rates, stopping the flow of investment, and thus undermining the growth needed to pay off debt. And so the crisis gets ratcheted up a notch or two.

Moreover, in an effort to pay down debt, such countries typically adopt austerity programs that severely restrict public services and government salaries, and, at the same time, slow the economy.

This often prompts public unrest and political instability, further spooking markets. Thus begins a socio-economic and political spiral that can lead to collapse and chaos. Argentina is a prime example. At least seven people were killed in Argentina in December 2013 during a week of riots.

Some countries, such as Japan, have carried high public debt for decades, as a result of earlier banking crises. In the aftermath of the 2008 financial crisis, many other countries' public debt rose rapidly, as tax receipts fell and unemployment benefits and other automatic welfare-state payments increased.

Most costly of all, however, many governments were forced to step in to assist domestic banks that faced collapse, and to increase deficit-financed "stimulus" spending in the hope of restarting stalled economies.

With public debt at historic highs — and still growing — and increasing government concern over the likely social unrest that will result from the growing gap between rich and poor, as well as deteriorating public services, it is no wonder that the International Monetary Fund has come up with a new and dangerous plan to repair the world's broken economies — global wealth confiscation.

Nefarious Plan Gathers Pace

Last November, the IMF issued its analytical monthly *Fiscal Monitor* report, in which it observed that while wealth taxes had fallen out of favor in recent years, they were attracting renewed interest in the post-2008 environment. Indeed, the IMF's wealth confiscation plan does not exist in isolation. The Bank of England and the U.S. Securities and Exchange Commission published a paper in 2012 proposing that funds, supposedly available to protect and guarantee savings in banks, might be seized to prop up a failing bank instead. The IMF report noted that "Iceland and Spain reintroduced the tax during the crisis" and added:

> The sharp deterioration of the public finances in many countries has revived interest in a "capital levy" — a one-off tax on private wealth — as an exceptional measure to restore debt sustainability. The appeal is that such a tax, if it is implemented before avoidance, is possible [as long as] there is a belief that it will never be repeated... The tax rates needed to bring down public debt to pre-crisis levels [are] about 10% on households with positive net wealth.

The uproar was fast and furious and the IMF subsequently issued a kind retraction, in which it said the IMF "emphatically does not recommend a wealth tax."

While IMF policy proposals have no legislative weight in individual countries, its influence is significant. Indeed, the IMF has a history of floating trial balloons to give cover to governments, which often cite them when enacting financial repression.

For example, in 2002, the IMF proposed a global accord on sovereign debt restructuring that would have made it impossible for individual creditors to opt out of negotiated deals for debt-critical countries. Although the accord wasn't enacted, its precedent has been cited in several legal cases, including one against Argentina involving U.S. hedge funds.

Moreover, economists at various leading institutions in Europe and the U.S. have recently presented a variety of theoretical and "moral" arguments in favor of wealth taxes. One, from the World Bank, comments favorably on a theory advanced by French economist Thomas Piketty that wealth confiscation aimed at top-earners is necessary to stabilize the global economy in all circumstances, not just during economic crises.

It is also clear that wealth confiscation would be a global effort, coordinated across all major economies, not just those with high public debt to GDP ratios. The IMF's *Fiscal Monitor* also noted:

> Financial wealth is mobile, and so, ultimately, are people... There may be a case for taxing different forms of wealth differently according to their mobility. Substantial progress likely requires enhanced international cooperation to make it harder for the very well-off to evade taxation by placing funds elsewhere.

In other words, don't think that Europe's troubles can't affect you. The U.S. government will likely impose a wealth tax on U.S. bank depositors, precisely in order to prevent Europeans from transferring their money here.

Uncle Sam couldn't very well refuse, given the tax-related demands the U.S. is making on other countries under FATCA — which also gives U.S. authorities the capacity to monitor your offshore wealth.

Meanwhile, the international funding organizations themselves, such as the IMF and World Bank, will benefit from global wealth confiscation. That's because their role is to backstop the financial systems of their member countries. Government wealth confiscation would relieve them of some of this burden.

The IMF, the lender of last resort to many nations, including most of the heavily-indebted, has a particular vested interest in spreading its risk. A wealth tax applied to ordinary citizens would mean the IMF wouldn't have to repeat an emergency bailout, like the one it implemented in Greece.

The European Central Bank also has powerful reasons to support wealth tax. The German Bundesbank is the main source of euro zone funds and the dominant influence in the ECB.

Wealth confiscation as the first-resort option at national level would allow politicians, such as German Chancellor Andrea Merkel, to tell their constituents that they had protected them from a hit to their own pocketbooks, which might result from future bailouts of EU member states. Unsurprisingly, Germany's council of economic experts, known as the "Five Wise Men," has come out in favor of wealth confiscation for Greece and other southern European countries.

Debt to GDP Ratios in 12 Major Nations		
Country	% of GDP	Per person (USD)
Japan	211.7%	77,577
Greece	156.9%	40,486
Italy	127%	37,956
Portugal	124.1%	27,531
Belgium	99.8%	37,948
France	90.2%	31,915
United Kingdom	88.7%	32,553
Spain	86%	25,931
Canada	84.6%	34,902
Germany	81%	31,945
United States	101.6%	36,653
Netherlands	71.3%	29,060
Poland	55.6%	11,298

Many private financiers and banks, too, favor wealth taxes, since much public debt is owed to them. Government wealth confiscation would allow these banks to continue carrying worthless assets on their books and to receive further government bailouts. In fact, the shaky banks of Europe probably have the most to gain from wealth confiscation.

At the same time, both the Federal Reserve and the big Wall Street banks would benefit greatly from having ordinary citizens pay off our government's debts with this extra injection of cash, rather than accept the consequences of their own reckless lending behavior. If European banks began to fail, the government would be tempted to implement a "TARP II" — but this time, using specifically "wealth tax" money to rebuild the balance of reckless banks. Indeed, the main threat to your pocketbook is coming from Wall Street, not Washington, courtesy of the enormous web of interests tying government and private finance together in the U.S.

How Wealth Confiscation Would Work

The proposed "wealth tax," as the IMF sees it, would be a one-off statutory procedure to seize a proportion of private wealth for the public treasury, a measure to reduce public debt rapidly and return a country's economy to a "sounder" financial footing.

Nonetheless, the idea is that a one-time, short-notice wealth tax, coordinated across all major economies, wouldn't disrupt markets too much, and rapidly pay for itself via resumed economic growth. But like the U.S. Income Tax of 1913, it would be just the beginning. And the groundwork for this sort of confiscatory action is being laid as I write.

The use of the phrase "wealth tax" is something of a misnomer. The IMF knows full well that even if 100% of the assets of the world's richest people were confiscated, it would not even come close to funding the gap between what governments spend and the cash they have to pay for it. As the IMF itself indicated, that means it's not just the wealthy who are at risk; it means everyone with a positive net worth — everyone with home equity, savings or even a reasonably well-paid job — could have their assets plundered, under the IMF plan.

A wealth tax could be imposed on the net worth of all income-positive households. Because this would pose serious liquidity problems for many people, and equally serious enforcement problems for governments, the more likely scenario is a "levy" on personal bank balances.

Such a mandate would be quick and easy to enforce. Banks would simply be instructed to deduct a certain percentage of the balance of each savings, checking, or deposit account and transfer it to the government or central bank. To get around deposit protection laws, such as the Federal Deposit Insurance Corporation, only bank balances above the insured threshold would be targeted — at least, in the first instance.

You may well argue that such a radical and drastic move by the federal government would require an Act of Congress. But consider that President Obama repeatedly has issued scores of "executive orders" that have bypassed Congress and changed statutory law, in effect imposing new "presidential laws."

Indeed, we've already seen wealth confiscation like this in Cyprus last April. In that case, the Bank of Cyprus unilaterally converted 37.5% of deposits exceeding €100,000 ($136,350) into shares of the bank, with an additional 22.5% held as a buffer for possible conversion in the future. A further 30% was frozen. This made for confiscation of a grand total of 90% of all deposits over €100,000 — the cut-off for the European Union's deposit protection laws.

But Cyprus is the tip of the iceberg. Also in 2013, Poland moved to forcibly transfer to the state many of the assets held by private Polish pension funds. Last year, European Union finance ministers also approved a plan for future bank bailouts, requiring bondholders, shareholders and depositors with more than €100,000 to be the first to suffer losses when banks failed. Closer to home, the Canadian government's "Economic Action Plan 2013" proposed to implement a depositor-funded "bail-in" process for that country's important banks in an emergency.

Make no mistake about it, wealth confiscation on a grand scale is coming to America. But you don't have to take it lying down. There is no need to be a lamb to the slaughter. I have researched a number of ways in which you can prepare and protect your hard-earned assets.

Six Ways to Beat the Cash Grab

Solution #1: Keep Your Bank Funds to a Minimum

The easiest way for the government to steal your money is simply to instruct banks to slice off a percentage under the guise of a wealth tax or some other ruse. Your bank accounts are easy targets.

Everyone, no matter your net worth, should take steps to reduce their bank balances, both U.S. and foreign — checking, savings, and Certificate of Deposit (CD) accounts.

And be careful where you keep the money you do leave in a bank. If a bank pays a better rate of interest, as a number of online overseas banks do, it is often because it has to pay more to attract capital, suggesting balance sheet weakness. A stronger bank can afford to pay less.

Of course, removing funds from bank accounts raises the question of what to do with the money now …

Solution #2: Get a Good Home Safe

Forget the proverbial mattress. Step number two — which should occur simultaneously with step one, if not before — is to acquire a sturdy and serious safe. I don't mean a small one that some opportunist might be able to carry off on his shoulder, but rather a built-in and bolted down safe that would require a team of horses to move.

Your safe should be fire-resistant, offering at least 30 minutes protection against 350 degree external heat, with a maximum internal temperature of 125 degrees (Rating: Underwriter's Laboratories Class 125). It should be rated class UL TL-30 or above, which means that it is will take a minimum of 30 minutes for someone to cut into it with most power tools. Underwriters Laboratories (UL) is a non-profit organization that tests hundreds of thousands of manufactured products to ensure they perform at high security standards. Absolutely steer clear of cheap equipment with "manufacturers" or "non-independent" ratings. Your safe should also be waterproof.

And it should be big enough to contain what I'm going to recommend you put into it …

Solution #3: Convert Your Bank Balances into Cash

Many of us are so conditioned to banking and electronic transactions that we've forgotten that cash is king. Cold, hard cash should be a key part of any wealth protection strategy. With real interest rates on U.S. bank balances in near-zero to negative territory, keeping cash isn't a wasted opportunity.

Indeed, you could easily argue that the risk-mitigation value of keeping cash outweighs any lost low-interest earnings. And the risk mitigation value rises as the threat of confiscation increases.

As with any wealth protection strategy, a portfolio approach is best. In addition to the U.S. dollar, keep cash in other stable currencies as well, such as the Canadian dollar, Swiss franc, Singapore dollar or Danish krona. Remember, the goal here isn't to earn a return on these currency holdings, but to hold cash that is reliably stable over time as part of your risk-mitigation strategy.

The ratio of greenbacks to other currencies in your cash portfolio should be based on your personal "exit strategy." If you envisage moving abroad in response to the coming wealth-confiscation threat, you should have enough U.S. dollars to finance that process — buying plane tickets, shipping goods and so on — as well as some funds to cover your expenses until you depart — say, two to three months' worth. You can calculate this easily and quickly by getting quotes for flights and global household-moving services.

On the other hand, if you envisage remaining in the U.S., your U.S. dollar holdings could be proportionately higher, since you want to cover your expenses for a longer period — say, six to 12 months.

Bear in mind, though, that the greenback is likely to depreciate rapidly against other currencies if wealth confiscation occurs here, as people scramble to acquire other currencies and offshore assets. So besides acting now — before the rush — you must also stock your safe with non-currency assets ...

Solution #4: Select and Transportable Physical Assets

In addition to multiple currencies, your safe could contain gems, rare coins, rare stamps, gold, valuable artworks, and even physical shares in stable companies. Again, the goal isn't necessarily to own items that tend to appreciate in value (although this is a good thing), but rather things that have a high and stable value to size/weight ratio, and are easy to convert into liquid cash. For example, it will be easier and less obvious to take small gems discretely abroad with you than gold bars.

Our associate Geoff Anandappa of Stanley Gibbons, a London-based stamp and rare coin dealer in business since the 1850s, points out that collectibles were an investment that beat the stock market during the 2008 to 2009 crises by appreciating a solid 38.6%.

Solution #5: The Safety of Offshore Vault

The next step up the ladder of "physical" wealth protection is to store gold, silver, gems, or other valuable physical items in a secure offshore vault. Many countries now host secure storage facilities that can accept anything from a handful of diamonds to a fleet of fancy cars. Most of these are located in tax-free customs zones, so assets within them are not taxed until they are removed. Those are an option — but our goal here isn't tax minimization, per se, but rather security and ease and speed of access.

For example, Miles Franklin Precious Metals of Minnesota, a company on which I have carried out due diligence, can arrange the purchase, transfer, and storage of precious metals, coins, and other items in a secure Brink's facility in Canada. All holdings are subject to semiannual external audits performed by the Inspectorate division of Bureau Veritas, one of the world's most experienced vault auditors, and insurance coverage that is provided by Lloyd's of London. This company can ship your existing holdings or purchase new items and transfer them to your Brink's account without customs or duties, because it has an import/export account with the Canada Revenue Agency.

When the time comes, Miles Franklin can either liquidate your items (sending you a wire within 48 hours of receipt) or have them shipped nearly anywhere in the world, via Brink's or UPS.

Solution #6: The Offshore Dirt Bank

The ultimate wealth protection strategy is to put some of the assets into an offshore "dirt bank." In other words, invest in land holdings in countries with stable, pro-individual governments and investment-friendly legal systems. There are two reasons for this:

Firstly, land is one of the most resilient of all assets, typically maintaining its value over long periods of time. In some cases, such as agricultural land or land in desirable urban areas, its value can appreciate rapidly. And there is always a ready market for land, especially in countries that have strong traditions of protecting property and other individual rights.

Secondly, foreign land holdings are not reportable to the U.S. government. Foreign real estate is not a "specified foreign financial asset" under IRS Form 8938 required by the Foreign Account Tax Compliance Act (FATCA) or the annual Form TD F 90-22.1, report of Foreign Bank and Financial Accounts (FBAR).

If foreign real estate is held through a foreign entity, however, such as a corporation, partnership, trust or estate, your interest in that entity is reportable — but the real estate itself is not. That means that although Uncle Sam might know that you have interests in land abroad, and how much they are worth, they don't necessarily know where they are.

Some countries that grant immediate residence status to foreign persons that purchase residential real estate or invest in other forms of real estate include, in Latin America: Bolivia, Brazil, Costa Rica, Ecuador, Dominican Republic, Dominica, St. Kitts & Nevis, Panama, and Uruguay; in Europe, Croatia, Ireland,

Latvia, Malta, Portugal, Slovak Republic, Switzerland, and Campione d'Italia; and in Africa, Mauritius.

Contacts

Stamps, Rare Coins, Gemstones:
Geoff Anandappa, Investment Portfolio Manager
Stanley Gibbons Investment
UK Address: 399 Strand, London, WC2R 0LX
Tel.: 0845 026 7170
Email: ganandappa@stanleygibbons.com or investment@stanleygibbons.com
Web: www.stanleygibbons.com and http://investment.stanleygibbons.com

Purchase and Secure Storage:
Andrew Schectman, President
Miles Franklin Precious Metals
1118 East Atlantic Ave. Suite F
Delray Beach, FL 33483
Tel.:1 (800) 255-1129
Email: Aschectman@milesfranklin.com
Web: http://www.milesfranklin.com

Offshore Real Estate:
Pathfinder International
Ronan McMahon, Executive Director
Elysium House, Ballytruckle Road
Waterford, Ireland
Email: rmcmahon@pangaearealestate.net
Web: www.pathfinderinternational.net

Margaret Summerfield, Associate
Panama City, Republic of Panama
Email: msummerfield@pathfinderinternational.net

ELECTRONIC CASH: THE END OF PRIVACY

Ted Bauman, *The Sovereign Investor Daily*, June 2014

Imagine cash never existed. There are only electronic records of all our financial transactions. Then imagine the reaction from the government if cash were to be introduced.

They'd be horrified. They'd fear financial collapse. They'd consider cash a weapon of mass destruction launched against law enforcement. They'd claim that because cash is anonymous and untraceable, it's only of interest to criminals, drug cartels, terrorists, prostitution rings and money launderers. They'd demand a licensing procedure for individuals or businesses that plan to use cash, limiting it to trustworthy individuals who keep detailed, auditable records of all their cash transactions, in order to keep America safe from criminals.

Sounds crazy, right?

Not so fast. The pressure to eliminate cash — and to turn you and anyone else who prefers it into a presumptive criminal — is growing fast.

Cash — coins and paper money — is only about 10% of the aggregate U.S. money supply, or M2. The rest is just entries on the balance sheets of banks. Nevertheless, plenty of people want to get rid of this remaining bit of real currency.

For example, Kenneth Rogoff, a professor of public policy and economics at Harvard University, recently published an article in the Financial Times headlined, "Paper money is unfit for a world of high crime and low inflation." He proposes that "it is time to consider whether … phasing out currency would address the concern that a significant fraction, particularly of large-denomination notes, appears to be used to facilitate tax evasion and illegal activity."

Plenty of pointy-headed intellectuals agree with Rogoff. Matthew Yglesias believes that "Already, a movie character depicted as carrying a large quantity of cash can be reliably assumed to be doing something illegal," and therefore looks forward to the day when "cash will be left with its rump use as a medium of exchange for drug dealers, tax evaders, and other shady operators and we can expect countries to start banning it altogether."

Apparently, cash is only of interest to pimps, thieves and fraudsters. But there's more. In a cashless society, governments could easily force people to spend their wealth by decreeing a negative interest rate for all electronic deposits: use it or lose it.

Left-wing economists salivate at the prospect of "privatized Keynesianism." There'd be no need to run government budget deficits to spur economic activity; just force people to spend their own virtual "money." Under a negative interest rate, "money" would be like a hot potato, as each person who receives some in exchange for goods or services tried to spend it as quickly as possible to avoid loss of purchasing power that would come from storing it in a bank.

Or what if the United States decided to implement a Cyprus-style wealth confiscation one night to ease the tremendous burden of its national debt? An all-electronic cash system would make it incredibly easy for the government to reach into your bank account and take what it needs to avoid financial collapse, leaving you with…? Nothing.

Indeed, a growing number of economists and technocrats want all money to be virtual, and therefore under the control of government and corporate financial institutions. Of course, that would mean the elimination of financial privacy once and for all. In 1976, in U.S. v. Miller, the Supreme Court decreed that there is no legitimate expectation of privacy in any financial transaction that involves a third party. Every electronic transaction involves a third party, such as bank or credit-card processing company.

No cash = no privacy.

Damned if We Do, Damned if We Don't

Cash allows private peer-to-peer transactions. It decentralizes power in society, and preserves a space where government and corporate elites can't monitor and control everything. That's why, for those elites, cash has simply got to go. And it's why we have to fight for our right to use cash.

There's a certain irony in that. After all, most cash in use today is issued by governments, and remains their property. They retain control over it and can manipulate its value at will. They can even declare it invalid and launch a new currency, as has happened numerous times in recent history. So in fighting for the right to use cash, we're fighting for one form of enforced dependence on government (state-issued cash) as opposed to another (electronic currency).

Plenty of people have tried to escape that contradiction. The most recent attempt is Bitcoin, the "virtual currency" that captured everyone's attention late last year, and then collapsed in the face of hostility from a variety of governments, including China's.

The problem with Bitcoin is that it lives in the electronic ether. It's just as vulnerable to interference as a sovereign currency like the dollar or the euro. All it takes is a government decision to do so.

That's why the only real escape from the slowly closing circle of government domination of our financial lives lies in hard assets — foreign real estate holdings, gold, gemstones, rare collectible stamps, art and other valuable items.

And that's why The Sovereign Society exists — to help you learn how to make your own escape from government.

THE COMING CURRENCY CONUNDRUM
Jeff D. Opdyke, *The Sovereign Investor Daily*, December 2014

Everybody's doing it.

The Japanese do it so frequently you'd think they'd be tired of it by now. Europeans like to do it while the Germans watch, knowing they get so angry. The British do it, but with a stiff upper lip because it's not something they really like doing at all. Chinese do it more than anyone else, but they don't want you to know just how much they do it. The Americans do it, too — we just love to do it online and pretend like it's not cheating that way.

Like I said, everybody's doing it … they're printing money as though money was going out of style.

And that will not end well for those who aren't prepared for the reckoning.

Flooding Our World with Fiat Currency

Our world is awash in cash.

Central banks in the five most important economies — the U.S., Britain, the European Union, China and Japan — have cumulatively increased the supply of money by 81% in dollar terms. It's the equivalent of nearly $24 trillion, roughly one-third the size of the entire global economy.

That's an incomprehensibly large sum of money.

At this point you should be thinking that I'm now going to tell you about the inflation that's baked into our cake at this point in our economic history. And, yes, inflation is a risk. Actually, it's the end game of every central bank in those five leading economies. They want — how desperately they want! — inflation so that they might inflate away their debts, regardless of the damage it does to me and you and our spending power. People are never as important as a government's lust for ensuring its own survival.

But I'm not here to tell you about the disaster of runaway inflation when the central banks screw it up … and one or more of the four central banks is bound to screw it up. History shows that the odds favor a fumble somewhere.

Instead, I'm here to tell you about the debt that the banks want to inflate away … and especially the interest rates on the debt.

As much as central bankers want inflation, they realize they can't allow inflation to reach a level that pushes up interest rates more than a few fractional points. Rising rates drive up the cost of debt repayment. And if the rates rise goes too far or too fast, it can threaten the viability of a country's fiscal and monetary system, leading to the same kinds of cataclysmic financial and social failures that befell Zimbabwe most recently, Sweden in the early 1990s and the Roman Empire of antiquity.

No central banker wants that.

Marching Toward a Currency Crisis

Bankers will do all that they can to keep interest rates low, even as they try to stoke some degree of inflation by printing gobs and gobs of money.

Just last week, Mario Draghi, who leads the European Central Bank, told the world — to the great consternation of Germans who fear a 1930s redux — that the bank would do whatever it takes to raise inflation, which implies dumping more euros into the Continental money supply.

China announced a new stimulus plan as well ... and Japan is at a point where it might start sacrificing virgins atop Mt. Fuji to jump start an economy in which decades of money printing have done exactly bupkis to save the nation from its impending doom. And we all know what our own Federal Reserve has been doing for the last seven years.

Politicians and central bankers aren't hurt by their actions. They operate in a theoretical space, moving chess pieces around in hopes that some monetary theory — tested or not — will get them out of this mess they've both had a hand in creating.

The people hurt are you and me. We're the ones forced to play in markets that central bank actions manipulate either directly or indirectly. We must take on more risk, though without necessarily earning larger reward, as it traditionally would be.

We have no place to go for income anymore, except the stock market and risky corners of the bond market.

And the worst part of it all ... the solution doesn't rest with the central bankers, despite all their efforts. The solution rests with the market, as it always has throughout history. And the market's solution, at some point, will be a financial crisis centered on currency — most likely our dollar or Japan's yen.

Success Favors the Prepared

Our solution as investors is simple: Be diversified! Broadly and deeply.

Own exposure to multiple countries and multiple currencies. Own exposure to multiple sources of income, from highly stable stocks and corporate bonds to Master Limited Partnerships. And own exposure to multiple asset classes, including alternative assets such as gold and silver coins and other collectibles.

While the future is unknowable, probability leans toward a crisis. Overly indebted societies that have ballooned their money supply typically face a major and painful reckoning to right the imbalances. Success in that future favors the prepared.

So, prepare.

Chapter Five

Real Estate

Calling All Real-Estate Owners: Your Assets May be at Risk
The Most Cost-Effective Way to Protect Yourself 247
How to Protect Your Dollars with a Dirt Bank 255
Harvesting Income Under the Southern Cross 265
Profiting From a Hedge City 276
Foreign Real Estate: More Than a Second Home 279
7 Rules for Buying Overseas Real Estate 281
A Real Estate Opportunity You Don't Want to Pass Up 284
The One Asset the Feds Can't Confiscate 286

Editor's Note:

With the U.S. government out of control at all levels — from the Oval Office down to local beat cops — it's important to hold some assets the government can't confiscate. There are three good reasons why you should consider investing in foreign real estate:

- *Foreign real estate — also known as a "dirt bank" — is one of the safest and most reliable forms of wealth preservation. Many things can happen to stocks, bonds, currencies, and commodities, but land and housing are always in demand.*

- *U.S. persons don't have to report to the U.S. government foreign property owned in your own name (i.e. not via an LLC or other vehicle) under the Foreign Account Tax Compliance Act (FATCA). That makes it last in line for official wealth confiscators.*

- *Foreign real estate is the ultimate escape plan — a place to go if you need it when that time comes.*

Given extensive (and frankly, invasive) reporting requirements to the IRS and the U.S. Treasury Department, it is critical to own financial assets that legally are not reportable — and therefore, not factored readily into your net worth. If a U.S. person opens a financial account offshore and has more than $10,000 in it at any time during the calendar year, they must report it on your annual income tax IRS Form 1040, as well as IRS Form 8938. Same goes for your interest in any foreign investment fund, corporation, LLC, trust, or other entity. Armed with this information, the government money-grabbers will know how much you've got and where to go when confiscation time comes, no matter where your money is located around the globe.

But because foreign real estate in your own name isn't a "specified foreign financial asset" under U.S. tax law, you don't have to report it at all. Like gold or gems in a vault in Montreal, artwork in a Swiss duty-free warehouse, or rare stamps in a safe deposit box in Guernsey, foreign land can be your own perfectly legal secret. It's a way to park your wealth in a place and form that can't be touched by the government under current U.S. law. With all that's going on in the U.S. and other countries today, you should consider owning real estate in more secure places such as Uruguay or Panama. Foreign real estate still is one of the simplest, most private and safest ways of securing your future and protecting your wealth. In this chapter we tell you the where, how and who of offshore real estate.

Calling All Real-Estate Owners: Your Assets May be at Risk
The Most Cost-Effective Way to Protect Yourself

Robert E. Bauman JD, *Offshore Confidential*, November 2013

The collapse of the U.S. real-estate market in 2008 has produced both winners and losers. Savvy investors, including many Sovereign Society members, have bought up distressed properties, generating significant income streams from rentals.

And it's no wonder. Real returns on rental investments in many U.S. cities are in the double digits. After all, the people whose former homes are on the foreclosure market need a place to live.

Being a landlord seems like an easy way to earn a good return, right?

It is — but it carries hidden risks.

The biggest risk of all is rooted in the fact that landlords are expected to take "reasonable care" to ensure that their properties are safe and secure from "foreseeable threats" to tenants.

Terms like "reasonable care" and "foreseeable threats" are catnip to trial lawyers, who just love to drum up business from aggrieved tenants. If a plaintiff's attorney can convince a jury that you've failed to exercise reasonable care — that you've been "negligent" — you're in big trouble. Your personal wealth could be at risk — a wealth that's far in excess of the value of the property in question.

Indeed, you can't go more than a mile or so along Interstate 95 in South Florida, where I live, without seeing billboards showing a happy tenant and the lawyer who got him or her many hundreds of thousands of dollars in damages from an unlucky landlord.

Many property investors are well aware of this threat, of course, and seek protection for their assets through various means — liability insurance, offshore trusts and the like.

The problem is that most of these methods fail to provide the right balance of protection, cost and simplicity when it comes to protecting U.S. real estate. The last thing you want is to spend a lot of money and time setting up something you think is going to work, only to find that you're still on the hook if one of those billboard lawyers comes after you.

You need to protect your real estate in such a way that if tenants attempt to sue, your personal wealth is protected.

Better yet, you want a strategy that discourages them from ever filing that lawsuit.

And the best way to do that is via a special legal structure that's actually based right here in the U.S.

Of course, your plan must be in place before any threat arises. Once the horse has bolted, closing the barn door will make no difference. In other words, you need to act now!

Let me tell you how ...

Four Principles of Asset Protection

Asset protection involves legal techniques to shield a debtor's assets from creditors' claims and lawsuits. In any asset-protection strategy, you want to accomplish four basic things:

1. **Segregate yourself from your asset.** You want a legal structure that you control, either directly or indirectly, in which you vest ownership and control of the assets. As long as those assets remain legally under the separate entity, it's as if you didn't own them at all — which, of course, you don't: You own the entity that does. The entity can operate as if you retained direct ownership and control of the assets in question, but without exposing you to undue risk.

2. **Manage your personal liability.** Your asset-protection structure must be subject to a different set of rules than you would be personally. Most important, claims against you from creditors and lawsuits shouldn't be transferable to the entity holding your assets, and vice versa. You want protection from claims arising from the use of your assets, and you want to protect your assets from claims against you.

3. **Be hard to find.** Your structure should be registered and operated in such a way that your ownership of it may not be revealed without prohibitive expense and effort.

4. **Keep it simple and cheap.** Make use of the right strategy for the circumstances. If you're primarily interested in protecting your primary residence or other real estate, a U.S.-based vehicle may be just as effective as an offshore one. You want a level of protection from liability and creditor claims that is appropriate to the circumstances, and not overly complicated or expensive.

Pick the Right Strategy the First Time

So, what's the best way to adhere to these four principles?

I recommend an inexpensive and easy-to-achieve strategy based right here in the U.S. — the limited liability corporation (LLC). To see why the LLC is the right vehicle for the job of protecting your U.S. real estate from litigation-happy renters, let's consider the problems with some common alternative strategies.

Let's say you're going overseas for a while, and you plan to rent out your primary U.S. residence. You've never had a major accident in your house, so why should your tenant be any different?

In that case, you might think liability insurance will cover you against any eventuality.

Think again. The fact is that liability insurance actually encourages a tenant to file a lawsuit against you. It tells their attorney that your insurer can pay lots of money if they win in court. All they have to do is convince a jury that you've been negligent in some way.

And, of course, like all insurance, liability insurance is subject to a maximum benefit — which could easily be exceeded, particularly if you live in a state where civil awards are made by pro-renter juries. To get the right level of protection, you could end up paying through the nose in premiums.

The bigger problem is that you never know how much protection is going to be enough.

Consider the case of one Arizona couple who rented out their home and were hit with a lawsuit after a workman hired by the tenants — without the couple's knowledge or permission — was severely injured when a garden retaining wall collapsed on him.

The couple had a landlord policy that included $1 million in liability coverage, costing $1,500 a year. They had also purchased $2 million in umbrella liability insurance for another $600 a year, taking their total liability coverage up to $3 million, at a cost of $2,100 a year.

The injured workman successfully sued for $5 million. The couple not only lost their house, but were forced to liquidate the bulk of their retirement savings, as well.

By contrast, an LLC structure, which would probably have forced the plaintiff's attorney to settle for much less, would have cost them $50 to $200 a year.

A U.S. LLC is the Secret to Optimal Protection

Here's why: It's always better to stop potential litigants from filing lawsuits against you in the first place.

If you can do this cheaply and easily, so much the better.

And when it comes to U.S. real estate, an onshore asset-protection strategy like an LLC is generally the most cost-effective — paradoxically, doing a better job than many offshore strategies.

For example, many people title their homes in the name of an offshore asset protection trust (OAPT), believing that it's therefore protected by the foreign jurisdiction of the trust.

Unfortunately, that's completely untrue. U.S. real estate will always fall under U.S. law because it sits on U.S. soil. A foreigner who commits a crime in the U.S. can't escape prosecution just because he's a citizen of another country.

Imagine going through the hassle and expense of placing your properties in an OAPT, only to find that you were no better off than if you'd left it in your own name.

That's where U.S.-based LLCs come in. Set up the right way — and above all, in the right state — an LLC can stop litigation in its tracks.

The reason is simple: The chances of success against a proper U.S.-based LLC are low, and the costs of litigation are high. And since most contingency-fee lawyers get paid only if the client collects, cases brought against LLC-protected assets are very unattractive to them.

Discouraging Lawsuits by Limiting Creditors' Options

LLCs combine features of a corporation and a partnership. With an LLC, you enjoy the corporation's legal segregation and limited liability, along with the partnership's easy-to-manage "pass-through" taxation.

That means that if your real estate is owned by an LLC, you can't be held personally liable for anything that happens to tenants. Moreover, your rental income can pass directly through to you and be reported on your own tax returns, with no corporate tax filing required.

Like partnerships, LLCs are based on "members" — they are the owners who act as managers and directors. LLCs can be formed by any number of members. Anyone can be a member, and many people form LLCs with family members and trusted friends.

There is no general rule. It's all about trust and the ability to work together through thick and thin.

It is possible, and even desirable, to have a domestic living trust as a member of an LLC. The two entities work together to protect your assets. They can be created at the same time or independently of one another, and both can be modified or dissolved at any time by the owner. Given the advantages of these legal entities, they are frequently used by real-estate investors to benefit themselves and their heirs.

A living trust contains your instructions for the distribution of your assets after death. Because a person's assets are transferred to the trust during their lifetime, the complicated and lengthy probate process is avoided entirely. After the person who established the trust dies, the successor trustee(s), usually the adult children or relatives of the trust creator, simply distribute the trust assets to the designated beneficiaries. Because the trust eliminates probate and can greatly reduce estate taxes, it may be possible to pass on a much greater portion of your assets to your heirs, and that includes your LLC interests.

The underlying legal principle of the "limited liability" part of the LLC is that innocent partners shouldn't suffer consequences from another partner's personal activities. Because of this, the remedies available to personal creditors of a single LLC partner are severely limited. Basically, remedies that would impose substantial harm on the innocent partners are ruled out.

"Limited liability" doesn't mean "no liability," however. An aggrieved tenant can still get a judgment against the LLC that owns your property. And your ownership stake in an LLC can still be awarded to a creditor who obtains a judgment against you.

But if your LLC is based in the right state, there is little the tenant or the creditor can do to enforce those judgments. They could spend thousands of dollars in legal fees and still be unable to get their hands on your property or your money.

Consider the case of Rita Métier …

Rita lives in New Orleans. She owns several rental properties in Palo Alto, California, that she inherited from her father. They are titled in the name of a Nevada-based LLC, which she owns with her two brothers.

In December 2011, one of Rita's tenants attempted to sue the Nevada LLC for negligence after falling down a badly-lit stairwell. And in January, Rita lost a breach-of-contract lawsuit brought by a supplier to her personal business in Louisiana. The supplier threatened to have her California properties liquidated.

Two years later, Rita's properties are secure and her supplier hasn't seen a penny from her real-estate holdings. Let's see how she worked her magic.

Segregating Multiple Properties

To begin, Nevada LLC law allowed Rita to put all her properties into a serial LLC. Each property has separate financial records and bank accounts, but they're all owned by the same LLC. Despite this, the properties are fully segregated from each other in terms of liability. Judgments against the LLC for one property can't touch the others.

Her tenant lived in the least valuable property. His attorney knew he couldn't get a court order to liquidate the others, so his earnings from the lawsuit would be meager. At best, he'd get a fraction of the proceeds from the sale of the house.

He therefore declined to take the case.

All Dressed Up with No Recourse

Then there was the lawsuit from Rita's business supplier in Louisiana. Even though the supplier prevailed in a Louisiana court, his attorney knew that, thanks to the Nevada LLC statute, his client couldn't actually force the LLC to sell any of Rita's properties, or even to hand over her share of the LLC's rental income.

That's because, even though the supplier might have obtained a Nevada court order to attack Rita's interest in the LLC (known as a "charging order"), under Nevada law all he would get is Rita's share of the proceeds from the LLC's operation. The limited liability principle would protect Rita's brothers' shares.

But as long as the LLC didn't distribute any proceeds to Rita, the supplier would get nothing.

To make matters worse, the supplier's attorney knew that once his client obtained Rita's "financial rights" in the LLC, the U.S. Internal Revenue Service would hold him responsible for taxes on Rita's share of LLC profits. Normally, Rita would pay personal income tax on her share of the LLC's income, but if the LLC never distributed that income to her, the LLC would have to pay the taxes instead. And since the supplier would "own" Rita's share, he'd have to pay those taxes out of his own pocket. If he tried to force the other LLC members to pay them on his behalf, he'd be outvoted.

Finally, the supplier's attorney knew that in Nevada, unlike some other states, a non-enforceable charging order against Rita's share of the LLC would be the only remedy available to him — a feature written into the Nevada LLC statute itself.

So, just like the tenant's attorney, the supplier's counsel advised him to not bother bringing a suit against Rita's Nevada LLC.

Choosing the Best State

You don't have to form your LLC in the state where your property is located or where you live. You can form an LLC in any state, and the formation state's LLC laws will govern your LLC. As Rita Métier's case shows, this gives you powerful options for asset protection.

But which states are the best? This is where my four asset-protection goals come in handy. Let's use them to assess your options.

Segregate Yourself from Your Asset

The purpose of creating an LLC is to have a legal entity that's separate from you. When you set up an LLC with partners, your rights and liabilities are joined together. The underlying legal principle is that one partner's personal activities shouldn't harm the other partners. As I mentioned before, this severely limits the remedies available to creditors of a single partner.

What if you're the only member of your LLC?

Here you need to be careful. Courts in Florida, Colorado, Texas and Utah have ruled that single-member LLCs aren't entitled to the benefits of a multiple-member LLC, since there aren't any other members to protect. Most other state courts have yet to rule on the single-member issue, so there's no way to be sure whether multiple-member LLCs would prevail.

By contrast, **Nevada**, **Wyoming** and **Delaware** have explicitly amended their LLC statutes to say that single-member LLCs are subject to full limited liability protections. If for any reason you plan to be the only member of your LLC, it should be based in one of those states.

A related issue is the internal segregation of assets. We saw above that Rita's Nevada serial LLC helped ward off a lawsuit because the plaintiff would only be able to attack one of her properties. The other properties are protected in "cells" within the LLC.

Serial LLCs originated in **Delaware** in 1996 (and are still sometimes called "Delaware series LLCs"). Besides **Nevada**, other states permitting them include **Iowa**, **Oklahoma**, **Illinois**, **Tennessee** and **Utah**.

Manage Your Personal Liability

In Rita's case, in addition to protecting her other properties, basing her LLC in Nevada prevented her tenant from pursuing her personally for damages. It also discouraged her business supplier in Louisiana from pursuing claims against her California properties.

That's because Nevada explicitly limits creditors to the charging order as a remedy for the personal debts of an LLC member. And as we saw, having nothing more than a charging order meant that the potential plaintiffs couldn't be sure when they would ever see any proceeds from their lawsuits — but they could be sure that they would be on the hook for Rita's share of the LLC's tax liabilities in the meantime.

The best way to understand the importance of charging order-only LLC statutes is to consider the alternative. Basically, limiting plaintiffs to a charging order says to them: "Our courts will not consider any attempt to pierce the veil of corporate identity, so don't bother trying."

"Piercing the veil" is legalese for a successful attempt to convince a court that an LLC has been formed strictly to avoid liability, and not for a legitimate business purpose. If a plaintiff can convince a judge of this, all bets are off — you are faced with full personal liability. It's as if the LLC didn't exist.

Plaintiffs who attempt to pierce the veil typically argue that an LLC hasn't been run "properly." They will cite the absence or inaccuracy of LLC records; failure to observe formalities in terms of meetings, documentation and the like;

non-functioning LLC officers and/or directors; or treating the assets of the LLC as your own.

In a reversal of the logic of using the LLC format to discourage lawsuits, the purpose of attempting to pierce the veil is often to make defending against it so bothersome that you'd prefer just to settle. Indeed, plaintiffs' attorneys love to demand voluminous evidence that your LLC is run like a business. Especially for a real-estate-oriented LLC, this can be a real burden: Do you really have the minutes of all your internal management meetings?

This places a premium on holding formal meetings, authorizing actions and keeping full records of all that the LLC does.

Given the importance of charging order-only LLC statutes, I recommend that real-estate LLCs be based in one of the states that make the charging order the only remedy available to creditors — **Nevada**, **Arizona**, **Delaware** or **Wyoming**.

Is Anonymity Worth It?

As I've said already, forget about total anonymity. If you're asked in court whether you own interest in an LLC, you have to tell the truth. But some states do make it possible for you to discourage pursuers. **New Mexico**, for example, doesn't require the LLC owners' names to be listed publicly in any of the founding paperwork or on annual reports and tax filings.

Of course, because of the tax "pass-through" status of LLCs, a determined adversary could theoretically find out where the LLC's income was going, but that would involve going to the IRS, a lengthy and expensive exercise. The law says the IRS cannot release taxpayer-filed information, but who trusts the IRS?

For the purposes of warehousing your property, anonymity isn't all that it's cracked up to be. The most important thing is limiting your personal liability.

Keep It Simple and Cheap

The beauty of the LLC is that it limits your liability but avoids all the hassle and expense of a corporation status. An LLC is a "disregarded entity" to the IRS — for tax purposes, it pretends your LLC doesn't even exist. You can elect to have your LLC taxed as a separate corporate entity, but for real-estate purposes there's really no point in that since you lose the favorable and less complicated "pass-through" tax status.

Most states charge a fee when an LLC is registered, as well as an annual fee. It's important not to let those annual fees go unpaid, because doing so means the LLC ceases to exist, and that opens a window of liability for its members. Some states, such as California, charge hundreds of dollars annually, but others are quite reasonable. Your goal should be to balance those annual fees against the liability protection your chosen state affords.

And the Winner Is ...

Based on the considerations above, my recommendation is straightforward: **Your first choice for real-estate-oriented LLCs is either Nevada or Delaware.**

Here's why:

- Both states limit creditors to the charging order as a remedy by statute.

- Both states permit serial LLCs, which is critical for multi-property operations. Even if you currently own only one property, setting up an LLC in one of those states sets you up for that eventuality.

- Setting up an LLC is cheap. Delaware charges a $90 filing fee and Nevada's is $75.

- Both states are low-tax. Delaware LLCs are required to pay an annual franchise tax of $250. Nevada levies an annual $200 business license fee.

- Annual state reporting requirements are minimal and can be accomplished online.

The runners-up in the LLC race are **Wyoming and Arizona**. Although neither state provides the serial LLC solution, both practice the charging order-only rule, so they would be suitable for single-property LLCs. Both are inexpensive, too: Wyoming charges $100 to set up an LLC and a $50 "annual report license tax." Arizona charges $60 up front and requires no annual report or franchise fee.

As always, I recommend that you consult a qualified attorney who specializes in domestic asset protection, and not try to go at it alone. There are far too many variables to consider. Any of these recommended attorneys can handle LLC formation in any state.

For a list of recommended attorneys, see Appendix A.

HOW TO PROTECT YOUR DOLLARS WITH A DIRT BANK

Ted Bauman, *Offshore Confidential*, June 2014

The newest and biggest blockbuster book on the bedside tables of the world's presidents, prime ministers and high-level government policymakers isn't Hillary Clinton's latest memoir. It's French economist Thomas Piketty's *Capital in the Twenty-First Century*, whose proposal to use wealth confiscation to address global inequality has added to the growing global clamor on the subject.

Unlike the International Monetary Fund, the Bank of England and the Securities and Exchange Commission, all of whom have proposed a wealth tax, Piketty's book puts real meat on the bones. *Capital in the Twenty-First Century* argues forcefully and convincingly for a global tax of up to 10% per year on all assets.

Piketty's powerful but simple argument about wealth, democracy and inequality under capitalism might anger many, but, like it or not, the popularity of wealth confiscation is a growing phenomenon and the idea is spreading like wildfire through dry brush.

The IMF suggested recently in Taxing Times that the only way that deeply indebted countries could ever hope to crawl free of their crushing debt was through a massive, one-time overnight surprise wealth confiscation.

People snickered and said it was impossible. But maybe they forgot about the wealth grab in Cyprus a few months earlier.

Make no mistake about it, Piketty's idea of a global wealth tax is gathering notice. His book has spent nine consecutive weeks on *The New York Times* bestseller list for hardbacks and his U.S. publisher is struggling to keep copies in stock. During his U.S. tour, he spoke at Harvard and MIT, and met with Treasury Secretary Jacob Lew. You may call a wealth tax impossible, but people are listening.

U.S. debt is still growing. The income inequality gap is still expanding. Despite the skeptics and the wishful thinkers, a wealth confiscation tax is closer than ever to becoming a reality in this country. So, if you don't think you need a defense strategy, think again.

We call this safe-haven option a "dirt bank."

Park Your Riches in Foreign Real Estate

Open some financial accounts overseas and have more than $10,000 in them at any time during the year, and you've got to report it to the IRS and U.S. Treasury Department on your annual income tax return. Don't forget to include the same information in detail on a little horror-show called a Form 8938. Same goes for your interest in any foreign investment fund, corporation, LLC, trust or other entity.

Armed with this information, the government money-grabbers will know how much you've got and where to go when the time comes to rob you, no matter where your money is around the globe. It won't matter if it's in an offshore bank. They'll probably just say, "You've got X in foreign accounts and we can't touch it directly, so we'll take more out of your U.S. accounts to compensate."

But under current rules personally owned foreign real estate can be held with no reporting requirement, so the Feds won't know about it at all.

That's because foreign real estate isn't a "specified foreign financial asset" under U.S. tax law. Like gold or gems in a vault in Montreal, artworks in a Swiss duty-free warehouse, or stamps in a safe deposit box in Guernsey, foreign land could be your own little — perfectly legal — secret.

Owning foreign real estate, also known as a "dirt bank," is a way to park your wealth in a place and form that can't be touched by the government under current U.S. law. And since you don't have to report it, the taxman can't use it to calculate your net worth for the purposes of potential wealth confiscation.

Foreign land holding isn't a wealth preservation vehicle in the same way as an asset protection trust (APT) or family foundation — strategies designed to maximize your privacy and protect your assets from private litigation. Instead, its primary role is as a hedge against the risk of potential wealth confiscation by government, as well as the collapse of the U.S. dollar.

For this reason, some of the traditional rules of portfolio investment don't apply when you use foreign property as a wealth-preservation hedge.

For example, although appreciation in the value of your land holdings is desirable, it's not the prime consideration. You don't want to see values fall, of course, but the main goal is to stabilize and protect your wealth in a form that isn't vulnerable to easy confiscation. As long as the overall value of your investment remains stable, that's success.

That means you must be prepared to trade some asset value appreciation for greater security.

In fact, that's what many foreign investors are doing — such as Chinese millionaires who buy property in the West as a hedge against the unpredictable policies of their nominally Communist government or Russian oligarchs who buy in London.

How to Dig Up the Best Dirt Bank

These considerations — risk-hedging versus asset protection and wealth generation — help identify the key variables you'll want to use when searching for investment property abroad. Here's my list of the main issues any investor looking for asset value stability in land should consider.

- **Restrictions on Foreign Ownership:** This is obviously important when you purchase property for the first time, but it could also be critical if and when you decide to sell it to realize its value. Unrestricted foreign ownership rights mean you're operating in a *global* market, not just a *national* one. You can sell to other foreigners as well as locals.
- **Market Stability and Liquidity:** Obviously, you want to invest in places that will maintain the conditions that prompted you to buy there in the first place. It's impossible to predict the future, but there are many countries that

can boast decades of stability on the issues that matter — property rights, taxation, openness to foreigners, and so on. That's where you want to invest in property. But you also want to be sure that you can liquidate your property holdings when the time comes, so choosing a country with an active property market is important too. The good news is that the two factors — stability and liquidity — tend to go hand-in-hand.

- **Property values:** Owning property is analogous to owning a business. You can invest in a big business that makes a good profit, or many smaller businesses that collectively earn the same. But the hassle of owning many small businesses may make it a more difficult route to wealth. The same goes for property. Whether to invest a big sum in a single piece of agricultural land or the same in 10 different residential parcels — even in different countries — depends on your desire to be involved in managing your foreign property assets. And some countries land values are such that any investment at all would constitute too big a chunk of your portfolio.

- **Title Security:** Some countries with great upfront property deals also have weak titling and deeds registry systems. This can come back to haunt you if someone comes along with a stack of old paperwork and claims that your land was actually stolen from his grandfather. Even if it isn't true, it can tie your property up for years.

- **Buying Costs:** Every country levies some form of tax or duty at the time of a real estate transaction, which are usually shared by buyer and seller. Some can be in the double digits, so it's important to anticipate this cost so you can balance it against expected land value appreciation and other cost factors.

- **Property Tax:** Some countries don't levy any property tax. But most do, and like transaction taxes, these need to be taken into account when working out how much of your wealth you're going to be preserving, and how much you're going to be giving to the foreign taxman for the privilege.

- **Capital Gains Tax:** Capital gains taxes on property sales vary widely, and some countries don't levy any at all, or tax it as ordinary income. But some — including some of the most popular expat destinations — have capital gains rates in the double digits. You want to know up front if you're going to be trading low transaction and property taxes now for a big capital gains hit when you sell, and vice versa. But bear in mind that the IRS is going to tax you on any gains from foreign property sales, so the most important thing is to ensure that the foreign rate is below or equal to U.S. rates, which are 15-20% for most households. That way you can deduct the foreign capital gains tax from your U.S. tax obligations and come out even. If you invest in a country with a capital gains rate above the U.S., you will pay more in taxes.

A Safe Haven for Your Wealth

The South American nation of Uruguay is an increasingly popular destination for foreign property investment — largely because it scores well on all the variables I mentioned above. What would it take to invest there as a hedging strategy? I spoke to Juan Federico Fischer, Managing Partner of Fischer & Schickendantz, a leading Uruguayan law firm. What he told me provides an excellent example of the issues you'd need to consider when investing in foreign property. Uruguay has some of the best farmland in the world. It has a mild climate and ample annual rainfall, and the seaports along the mouth of the River Plate make it easy to ship grain, beef, pulpwood and soybeans all over the world.

International interest in Uruguayan agricultural land has driven its price up an average of 20% a year since 2002, when you could buy excellent land for $3,700 per acre. Now land costs $17,000-$32,000 per acre for prime crop land (soya, corn, wheat), and $7,000-$15,000 per acre for good cattle pasture. Operational returns for farming in Uruguay are typically in the 3-5% range.

Uruguay's average farm is only 1,000 acres, which reflects the high productivity of its land, so you can expect to pay from $7,000,000 to as much as $32,000,000 for an average farm. But better deals on smaller farms are available — Fischer told me that you could find worthwhile opportunities for as little as $600,000 if you know where to look. But that's the minimum. To invest less than that in farmland means buying into a syndicate. But if you do that, you'll have to report on your interest in that syndicate to the IRS, since it's a "specified foreign financial asset."

As an alternative, Fisher told me that excellent residential property in Montevideo could be had for as little as $100,000, where rental yields are from 6-8%. If your "dirt bank" needs to be in smaller chunks, residential property would be your best option. It would offer not only a place to store a portion of your wealth outside the notice of the IRS, but rental property could also yield a nice, steady income as well.

The purchase process is simple in Uruguay. You appoint an *"escribano,"* or conveyancing attorney, like Fischer & Schickendantz. They draft a *boleta de reserva* (intent to purchase agreement), inspect and verify the title, draft the purchase agreement, set up the escrow account, and record the purchase at the national *Registro de la Propiedad*, or Property Registry.

All of this would cost you about 8% of the purchase price, or $8,000 per $100,000 in property purchased. You'll also pay property tax of 0.25% per annum. If and when you sell the property, capital gains tax will be 12% (under current law).

So, sticking with a hypothetical $100,000 residential investment, here's how your "dirt bank" hedging strategy would work out, assuming a 15-year ownership with 5% per annum increase in property values, which is actually quite conservative given Uruguay's recent market performance:

Purchase price	**$100,000**
Transaction costs	$8,000
Property tax (15 years)	$5,664
Capital gains tax	$12,947
Sale price	$207,893
Profit	$81,281
Average annual return	**5.4%**

A pretty good deal, I'd say.

If you rent out the property, you'd need to open a Uruguayan bank account, which isn't difficult (but keep in mind you must keep its balance below $10,000 at all times). You'll pay tax of about 12% on that income, but it can be offset against your U.S. tax without revealing the source of that income — i.e., the existence of your "dirt bank."

The Best Places to Look

So how does one go about identifying places to build your "dirt bank?" I've done some research on various countries based on the variables I identified, and compiled it in the table below. I selected the countries based on their overall fit with my variables, as well as the existence of robust and open property markets that are known to appeal to foreigners.

Country	Restrictions on Foreign Ownership	Title Security	Average Buying Costs	Property Tax	Capital Gains Tax	Stability
Belize	None	Medium	6.5%	1.00%	0%	High
Cayman Islands	None	High	7.5%	0.00%	0%	High
Costa Rica	Minor	High	5.0%	0.25%	0%	High
Dominica	Minor	High	21.0%	0.00%	0%	High
Dominican Republic	None	Medium	5.0%	1.00%	29%	High
Ecuador	Coastal	Medium	3.0%	0.25%	35%	Medium
Malta	Minor	High	12.0%	0.00%	0%	High
Mexico	Coastal	High	3.0%	0.28%	30%	High
Nicaragua	None	Medium	6.5%	0.25%	20%	High
Panama	Minor	High	2.3%	2.10%	10%	High
Turks and Caicos	None	High	10.0%	0.00%	0%	High
Uruguay	None	High	8.0%	0.25%	12%	High

Except for Malta, they're all in the Western Hemisphere. The reason for that is largely by default: Europe is too tax-heavy; Asia is generally unfriendly to foreign property ownership, and Africa, with some possible exceptions such as South Africa and Kenya, isn't stable enough.

The tables don't include an estimate of each country's property value appreciation prospects, since these vary widely by region and type of property, and are unpredictable for many countries. Nevertheless, you'll notice one thing most of these countries have in common: they're small — several are islands — so land is in relatively short supply. That generally means values will go up.

Some insights from this table:

- Ownership restrictions on foreign property are either non-existent or minimal. In some cases, such as Ecuador and Mexico, they restrict ownership of coastal or borderlands, except by investing in a corporate structure, which defeats the purpose of a dirt-bank strategy. In others, such as Costa Rica, Dominica, Panama, and Malta, they involve either special applications or extra fees for foreign land purchase.

- Purchase transaction costs are generally low, except for Dominica, Malta, and Turks and Caicos, where extra fees for foreign land purchase add to the normal real estate transactions taxes and fees.

- Some countries have relatively high property taxes — such as Belize, the Dominican Republic, and Panama. But in these places there is a tendency to undervalue property for tax purposes, so the tax actually paid is generally low.

- Only three countries have higher capital gains taxes than the U.S. — the Dominican Republic, Mexico, and Ecuador.

- Regarding title security: some countries are rated as "Medium," but mainly because of weak administrative capacity, not because there is a significant threat of challenges to ownership. In these places title research and documentation is largely a function of a good attorney, who can provide just as much — if not more — security than many governments.

The Top 5 Factors to Consider for Foreign Real Estate

Here are few things to bear in mind when considering investing in foreign real estate for hedging purposes.

1. When buying foreign real estate, make sure you know the rules and laws governing foreign ownership of the specific land you want, since they often vary within the country — say near coasts or borders, as in Mexico or Ecuador. If foreign ownership limits are an issue, always get a written guarantee from the authorities.

2. Make sure you can use your property for your intended purpose. This includes:
    a. *Build requirements*. If you're buying a residential lot, you may have to build a home within a certain timeframe. Check the style of house you're allowed

to build, the height, size and any other rules you'll have to comply with. In some countries foreigners have to build a house of a certain size and value within a relatively short time of buying a lot.

b. *Usage.* If you're buying land for farming, get an expert in to carry out a soil analysis test and give you a full report on land usage. It should cover climate, water access and the quality of the soil. That way you'll know if the land is suitable for growing wheat or raising cattle. Sometimes there are restrictions on the use of property (if it's classified as protected, for example); get your attorney to check the deed with the local municipality.

c. *Infrastructure.* Check out the standard of the water supply and sewage systems. Ask if they comply with local regulations. If the land doesn't have access to water or sewage, figure out how much it will cost to install them. Find out how reliable the electricity supply is — will you need a back-up generator? If you need to install it, how much will that cost and how long will it take? If you want cable or high-speed Internet or cell coverage, make sure you can get it on your property.

d. *Access.* If access is via a right-of-way make sure that it's recorded in the deed. And investigate to see if anyone else has access to your land. If they've used it to get from A to B or lived on it for long enough they may have acquired legal rights to carry on doing so.

e. *Boundaries.* Get a proper survey done to establish your boundaries. The survey will tell you how much land you're getting. That's very important if you're buying a big parcel of land and paying a price per acre. You need to know you're getting all the acres you're paying for.

3. Always focus on market price, not asking price. In many countries, the real estate agent sets the sale price, not the property owner. The seller specifies the minimum amount they want from the sale, but the agent tries to sell for a lot more to make a profit. There's often no U.S.-style Multiple Listing Service that allows you to compare what different agents might be asking. The easiest way to avoid this is to negotiate directly with the property owner. But if you can't do that, never offer more than what you believe the property is worth, based on the prices for similar properties that have changed hands.

Start with local realtors and get an idea of the general market. Visit areas of interest. Look for "For Sale/Si Vende" signs. Stop in local bars and talk with whomever you can. It helps if you have a reliable local contact or friend to act as your front person to be sure you're quoted true local market prices. Don't be afraid to haggle. And make sure you have a good local attorney to haggle for you.

4. Always buy fully titled real estate, never "rights of possession," which are found in some Latin American countries such as Panama. "Rights of possession" gives

you possession with the possibility of full title after a number of years. But your rights could be subject to legal challenge at any time. The seller may tell you that rights of possession are just like a title, but that's absolutely untrue — never, ever rely on verbal promises.

Title insurance is available for offshore real estate, either in the country where you're buying or from a U.S. insurer. Raising the issue of title insurance early in the process will often reveal whether the seller has something to hide.

Use a reputable, independent attorney to guide the transaction. Always be sure the title is investigated and the final deal is registered with the Public Land Registry. If the land was previously confiscated or held in any type of communal ownership your attorney should go through past title transfers and see if they were done correctly. Also check for taxes and liens. Your attorney should ensure that you're getting the land free and clear of any mortgages or debts owed by the seller.

5. If you earn any rental income from your property, it must be reported on your personal U.S. income tax return (Form 1040, Schedule E), regardless of the amount and regardless of whether you are required to report the existence of the property itself to the IRS.

If you open a foreign bank account to facilitate the purchase of the property, or to receive rental income, and that account has more than $10,000 in it on any one day of the year, then you also must report the bank account on IRS Form 1040 and on FinCEN Form 114 (which has replaced Form TD F 90-22.1), commonly referred to as the FBAR or Foreign Bank Account Report.

If you want to avoid filing the FBAR, when you purchase the property, wire funds from your U.S. account directly into escrow, and always keep less than $10,000 in the operating account.

Loophole the IRS Wants to Keep Secret

What if you don't want to hold foreign real estate in your name? What if you prefer the privacy, security and protection of a corporation?

Under some circumstances, even if you purchase foreign real estate via a corporation, trust, or other structure, you might not need to report your interest in it on IRS Form 8938. That's because Form 8938 applies to those with "significant" assets outside of the United States. You don't need to file Form 8938 if:

- You are resident in the United States, are a married couple filing a joint tax return, and your reportable foreign financial assets on the last day of the year do not exceed $100,000, and are not more $150,000 on any day of the year; or if you are single or married filing separate, and your reportable foreign financial assets on the last day of the year do not exceed $50,000, and are less than or equal to $75,000 on any day of the year.

- You are *resident abroad*, are a married couple filing a joint tax return, and your reportable foreign financial assets on the last day of the year are not more than $400,000, and do not exceed $600,000 on any day of the year; or if you are single or married filing separate, and your reportable foreign financial assets on the last day of the year do not exceed $200,000, and are not more than $300,000 on any day of the year.

Being "resident" abroad is based on a combination of factors, but essentially it means that your home, business, and income are all in non-U.S. locations, so if you maintain a home or business in the U.S., but live largely abroad, you'll need to act as if you were a U.S. resident, because legally that what you are.

The upshot is that you might be able to hold non-reportable foreign property worth up to $100,000 in a single corporation trust, or other vehicle if you are a U.S. resident, and up to $400,000 if you're resident abroad. That means you could possibly even participate in a property syndicate, as I explained when discussing Uruguay.

But beware that Form 8938 kicks in based on the value of all your foreign financial interest taken together — so if you have other offshore financial interests, the threshold for the value of your interest in a property-holding vehicle will be correspondingly lower.

A Final Word

As I've stressed repeatedly in this report, building a "dirt bank" isn't the same thing as buying property to live in overseas. Nor is it the same as investing for profit. The goal is to protect a portion of your wealth by converting it into a form that you're not obliged to tell the government about.

As the risks of government wealth confiscation grow, hedging investments like this are becoming more and more important. Don't just say to yourself "that would be a nice thing to do. Maybe someday ..."

Consider doing it now before it's too late.

Contacts

The Sovereign Society has many friends and associates around the world who can help you with property acquisition abroad. I mentioned Juan Fisher previously. He can be reached at:

Juan Federico Fischer
Managing Partner, Fischer & Schickendantz
Rincón 487, Piso 4 - C.P: 11.000
Montevideo, Uruguay
Tel.: (+598) 2915 7468 x 130
Email: jfischer@fs.com.uy or info@fs.com.uy
Web: www.fs.com.uy

For a global perspective on property markets, I recommend Pathfinder International. Pathfinder works with a number of real estate agents and developers in many different markets.

Pathfinder International
Ronan McMahon, Executive Director
Elysium House, Ballytruckle Road
Waterford, Ireland
Email: rmcmahon@pangaearealestate.net
Web: www.pathfinderinternational.net

Margaret Summerfield, Associate
Panama City, Republic of Panama
Email: msummerfield@pathfinderinternational.net

For expert advice and placement for title insurance for properties in Central and South America we recommend a veteran American attorney licensed in California and Colorado, Turalu Brady Murdock JD, based in Nicaragua.

In 2010, "Tuey" retired after 34 years from First American Title Insurance Company to start an independent consulting business, "TCS," for people and companies buying foreign property. Her experience, including 13 years specializing in transactions in Latin America and the Caribbean, gives her a unique perspective on the pitfalls of buying foreign property. Tuey also has worked for many years with our sister group, International Living.

Turalu Brady Murdock JD
Attorney and Title Coordinator,
Title Coordination Services (TCS)
Apartado Postal A-41, Managua, Nicaragua
Nicaragua cell: + 505-8930-2609
Email: tueymurdock@gmail.com
U.S. Vonage: 305-394- 8878

Harvesting Income Under the Southern Cross

Ted Bauman, *Offshore Confidential*, January 2015

When I was a kid growing up on Maryland's Eastern Shore, our house was wedged in between three parcels of rich alluvial farmland and a brackish tributary of the Miles River called Glebe Creek.

On either side of the half-mile dirt driveway to our home, the seasons expressed themselves through a steady cycle of corn, soy and winter wheat. Further off in the distance, dairy cattle munched on Ireland-green grass, visible through groves of bamboo surrounding a miniature Mount Fuji planted by an eccentric, Japan-obsessed neighbor.

But even at my tender age, inklings of the economics of farming managed to seep into my adolescent mind. I understood that not all land was the same. Just over the fence on the west of our property was a place my siblings and I simply called "The Field." It was a triangular tract on a slight bluff positioned between our land and an offshoot of the creek. Periodically, someone ... rarely did we know who, since it never seemed to be the same man or tractor ... ploughed it up and planted something, rendering it off-limits until harvest season.

We heard constant rumors that The Field would be sold, but it never happened while I was there. Years later, I learned that The Field had finally become the site of a residential house.

I also learned that it had been regarded as one of the choicest pieces of farmland in our area. Local farmers lamented its loss greatly. I once asked our old neighbor, Mr. Covey, why he'd never bought it outright instead of renting it year after year from its absentee owner. "We thought nothing would ever change," he said. "It took us by surprise when it was sold. I figured I could keep renting it forever."

For those reasons I'm going to explain, farmland is one of the world's hottest commodities. But as good as it is, land in Maryland isn't the opportunity I want to show you. It's in a great little South American country called Uruguay.

Before we dig in, let's get one thing straight — I'm not suggesting you move to Uruguay to become a farmer. There's no need for that (although you are welcome to give it a try). My goal is to show you how owning Uruguayan farmland — even from afar — can provide you with potentially unparalleled returns. There are plenty of opportunities to make use of Uruguay's extensive infrastructure in farm management and land-lease systems, designed to support the absentee owner.

Enjoy Steady Gains from This Hot Commodity

My colleague Jeff Opdyke thinks Uruguayan farmland is one of the 21ST century's hottest commodities, and I agree with him. Where else are steady annual returns from 4% to 12% possible in this day and age?

In the last 15 years, 18.5 million acres of Uruguayan farmland changed hands, for more than $10 billion. That's 44% of Uruguay's total arable farmland. Farm sales amount to more than $1 billion every year.

Why? Because Uruguay has 42 million acres of arable farmland — enough to meet the needs of more than 50 million people, 16 times Uruguay's own population. So it has land to spare, making agricultural exports a natural growth sector for the country. That's why this little country is the world's fourth largest exporter of rice, fifth largest exporter of dairy products, sixth largest exporter of soybeans, and responsible for 5% of global beef exports.

But there's more: it's not just the quantity of land available; it's also the quality.

Uruguay's farmland is uncommonly "good." The soil isn't degraded from decades of fertilizer and chemical abuse, like the U.S. or Europe. Rainfall is predictable and steady, so irrigation is seldom required. And if it is, Uruguay sits atop the world's largest aquifer, which remains largely untapped. The temperate climate means two crop cycles per year.

But none of that would matter if the world didn't need more food.

There are many ways to tell the story of global food demand, but here's my favorite, because it's simple.

Every day the planet's net population increases by 200,000 people. Each human being requires an average of 1.8 acres of agricultural land. So we need to add at least 360,000 acres of land to production every day — or to increase farming productivity — just to keep up.

According to the World Food Organization, global agricultural output will need to double by 2050.

Improved farming productivity, however, is only a short-term solution, because it often depends on chemicals that hurt the soil in the long-run. Farm yields in the developed world have peaked.

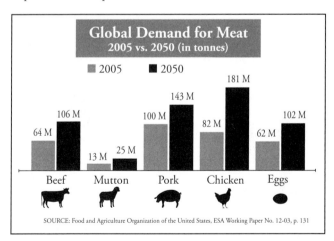

So the world's population needs more high quality raw farmland — something Uruguay has in abundance.

Uruguay is blessed with the type of farmland the world wants. One of the key drivers of food demand is economic development in the Middle East and South and East Asia, where increasing incomes translate into demand for beef, chicken and other proteins, and therefore for feed grains.

As it happens, Uruguay is perfect cattle and grain country — long prized for its output since the 19th century, when Uruguay became a key player in the supply of beef products to Europe through venerable companies such as Fray Bentos.

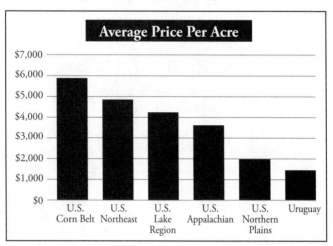

Most importantly, Uruguayan farmland is undervalued compared to regions that produce similar agricultural commodities, such as the United States. As food demand grows, so too will demand for the land used to produce it ... as will price for that land.

A Dirt Bank That Pays Healthy Dividends

As any investor will tell you, when you invest in farmland, as with any non-depreciating asset, there are two things to consider. One is the operational return to farming activity — how much you'll profit every year from farm operations. The other is appreciation of the value of the land itself.

With that in mind, here's why I see Uruguayan land as a great opportunity for you:

1. The average annual net operational return to Uruguayan farming is on the order of 4% to 6% of land value per annum. Every year. Some activities, such as forestry, enjoy annual returns of up to 10%. Compare that to the interest you're probably getting on money in the bank, such as 0.02% on a three-month T-bill or 0.5% on a two-year Treasury note, in this crazy environment of super-low interest rates. Meanwhile, the S&P 500 Index annual dividend yield is only 1.88%. In terms of steady return on investment, Uruguayan farming beats most options right now.

2. The value of Uruguayan farmland has appreciated 8% to 11% a year over the last five years. In some years prices have risen by as much a 20%. I predict that it will continue to rise, in the 8% to 12% per annum range, as demand for this valuable land remains high.

Applying these numbers to a hypothetical Uruguayan investment of $150,000 (I used 5% for operational return and 10% for asset appreciation), in the table below you can see what you could earn.

It looks even better when you compare the cost of U.S. and Uruguayan farmland used for similar purposes, as illustrated in the table below.

| \multicolumn{3}{c}{Farming at a Discount} |||
Year	Return From Operations	Asset Value
1	$7,500	$165,000
2	$8,250	$181,500
3	$9,075	$199,650
4	$9,983	$219,615
5	$10,981	$241,577
Total	$45,788	$91,577
Return	31%	61%

| \multicolumn{4}{c}{Solid Gains from Uruguayan Farmland} ||||
Region	Average Price Per Acre	Principal Crops	Uruguayan Discount
U.S. (Corn Belt)	$5,880	Grains, including feed grains	56%
Uruguay (Soriano)	$2,567		
U.S. (Northeast)	$4,850	Fruits, vegetables, vineyards, forestry, dairy	49%
Uruguay (Colonia)	$2,460		
U.S. (Lake Region)	$4,240	Groundnuts, dairy	43%
Uruguay (San Jose)	$2,418		

But Will It Last?

There are always naysayers who specialize in shooting down opportunities on the grounds that it can't last. Uruguay is no exception. Some people will tell you that Uruguayan land is just another South Sea Bubble or Dot-Com boom waiting to burst, and that prices have risen too fast. I don't agree with that. Those bubbles were based on anticipated returns on unproven products that weren't essential to human existence. Land that grows food — whether for animals or for us — is crucial for our survival.

It's true that Uruguayan land prices have stabilized in recent months. Economic growth in China is slowing, reducing demand for foodstuffs somewhat. The end of Quantitative Easing by the U.S. Federal Reserve is slowing the flow of finance for global investment ever so slightly, moderating asset prices.

But I believe that Uruguayan farmland values will roar back into double-digit appreciation soon. And the reason is simple.

Global demand for food is rising inexorably. But the export-suited farmland that has already been brought into production in North America, Europe, Asia and other developed regions is almost certainly near or even past its peak output. According to University of Nebraska researchers, one-third of rice, wheat and corn producing regions globally have experienced "yield plateaus or abrupt decreases in yield gain." In those places science has managed to extract as much as the earth can give, and further applications of chemical fertilizers and other productivity-enhancing techniques such as genetically modified crops won't help. Overuse of farmland in the U.S., for example, means that we are losing an average of almost 10 acres of land every minute, of every day to erosion, increased soil salinity or exhaustion of soil nutrients. That adds up to a loss of almost 0.5% of U.S. farmland every year.

To make matters worse, serious water shortages are looming or already present in these areas. As Jeff Opdyke explained in a recent edition of *Sovereign Investor*, we are seeing a rise in battled waged around the United States over water rights due to shrinking supply. From Florida to Canada, and Oregon to Michigan, the country is desperate for water.

This means that no matter what happens to the global economy, food prices are going to rise. In fact, they already are — global food prices rose an average of 2.7% a year for the last 10 years, reaching approximately 4% annualized in the first quarter of 2014. But if demand for food is increasing with a fixed — or declining — supply of farmland, then the value of high-quality raw farmland, as in Uruguay, must increase as well.

Increases in product prices raise the price of scarce factors of production. The more people are willing to pay for food, the more farmers will be willing to pay for farmland, because there's nothing else that can produce the former. It's an iron law of economics … a law that will work in your favor, if you let it.

And that one restriction? Well, in 2013 the Uruguayan government adopted a law that prevents sovereign wealth funds, state agricultural companies, and other government-based buyers from participating in Uruguay's farmland market. It didn't want the Chinese or Saudi governments to end up owning the whole place and using it to feed their own people, like they do in some African countries.

That means the Uruguayan farmland market is effectively reserved for individual and other private investors. It's as if the maître d' of the world's most prestigious restaurant has reserved a table for you.

Why Uruguay?

Uruguayan farmland is great stuff, but so too is land in Peru, Colombia, Chile, Myanmar and other foreign countries. What makes Uruguay special is … Uruguay.

Uruguay is unique in several important ways. In addition to having no restrictions on individual ownership of land by foreigners, it's one of the only countries on the planet whose constitution guarantees foreigners the right to become citizens. Obtaining residence and then citizenship is quick and easy. (Of course, you don't need to invest in land there, but it's great to have the option.)

Uruguay is unique in the Latin American context as well. It's strongly middle class. The wealth gap is narrow, so there's no social unrest or crime fueled by angry have-nots. People work hard and there's no "mañana" attitude. Democracy and the rule of law are well-entrenched. Government is stable and transparent. There's no need to pay bribes. The government is economically conservative, but also the most socially progressive in Latin America (marijuana use is legal, for example, as is gay marriage). Voters just elected another president from the well-regarded ruling party, Tabare Vazquez of the Broad Front. The Broad Front also controls both houses of the legislature, meaning no U.S.-style gridlock.

Uruguay's banks are among the strongest in Latin America. You don't have to live there to open an account, and there are zero capital controls or limits on how much money you can bring in or take out. Dollars and euros can be used freely and local accounts can be denominated in them. And privacy still counts … banks in Uruguay will release information only with a court order. Taxes are low and apply only to Uruguayan source income.

As my colleague Erika Nolan has put it, "The country is clean and tidy. The beaches are beautiful, many wild and often empty. The national highways are first world and well maintained. … You want a real vision of Uruguay — picture California's La Jolla, Newport Beach or Laguna Beach. That's what Punta del Este and the surrounding beach towns resemble … Only, they resemble the best of coastal Southern California circa 1970, before the traffic, congestion, masses of people, and overabundance of strip malls and cookie-cutter homes overran the place."

But perhaps the single most important feature of Uruguay is the organization, stability and liquidity of its land markets.

After all, you want to invest in a place that will maintain the conditions that prompted you to buy there in the first place. Uruguay is politically and legally stable, but it also has a highly-developed legal framework and institutional infrastructure for land sales and ownership — something often sorely lacking in other countries. Title security is strong, so nobody is going to come along with a stack of old paperwork and claim that your farm was actually stolen from his grandfather. Lawyers, bankers and other agencies can be trusted.

In addition, Uruguay offers land investors a unique tool to assess their options: the "CONEAT" system. Every property in the country is mapped, available online (www.prenader.gub.uy/coneat), so potential investors can verify a property's soil types and "productivity index." The productivity index of a property correlates with the price of the land, and it is easy to compare properties and determine their fair value, as well as their optimal uses. This produces a uniquely transparent market for farmland, perfect for the offshore investor.

And, of course, the demand for Uruguayan farmland is not going to disappear, so you can liquidate your property holdings easily at any time.

Winning Strategies for Uruguayan Land Investment

Let's get down to brass tacks.

Uruguayan farmland costs from $1,000 to 4,500 per acre depending on the region, the type of farming for which it is suited, and the land's productivity. The average Uruguayan farm is 1,000 acres, so you can expect to pay from $1 million to as much as $4.5 million for that "average" farm. That's good for those who have that kind of money to invest.

Nevertheless, Juan Federico Fischer of Fischer and Schickendantz in Montevideo told me that good farms can be bought for as little as $450,000 if you know where to look.

But that's the absolute minimum if you're interested in owning an entire farm. Anything less than that means you'll have problems achieving economies of scale with the equipment and services required to run the farm (tractors, irrigation equipment, farm managers, etc.). And as Juan explained, small farms tend to get served last by Uruguayan ploughing, crop-dusting and harvesting services, which increases your risk at each of those critical stages.

And don't forget that owning an entire farm makes you responsible for its management. Although you can hire local firms to do the on-the-ground work for you, individual ownership does carry some additional responsibilities that might not suit everyone, such as insurance liability.

Nevertheless, it's entirely possible to make profitable investments in Uruguayan farmland for much less ... as little as $100,000 ... and to get favorable tax treatment to boot.

Option One: Syndicated Ownership

One way to benefit from Uruguayan farmland ownership is to join a syndicate based on that country's version of a limited Liability Company (LLC). Each member of the syndicate receives a pro-rata share of operational income and asset appreciation.

Operational management of syndicated farms is typically undertaken by a specialist firm in return for a fee as well as 10% equity in the syndicate. Although this cuts into profits somewhat, the high perational and asset returns of Uruguayan farming more than make up for this when compared to alternative investment options. Often the same firm that assembles the LLC (such as Fischer and Schickendantz) provides the support for ongoing farming operations and LLC management.

A typical farm syndicate might have anywhere from a few to as many as 20 members. It is possible for such syndicates to acquire large, multi-million dollar farm properties, but a unique feature of Uruguayan tax law makes smaller syndicates well worth it, too.

For starters, property taxes in Uruguay are low — about 0.2% or even less — so your share of property tax on a $150,000 syndicate membership would be around $300 a year (although it would obviously rise as land value does). On top of that, there is no value-added tax (VAT) on most farm supplies and machinery, or on sales of farm products (except a 1% municipal sales tax on livestock sales). In addition, farm machinery is exempt from Uruguayan personal property tax.

But small farms get an additional benefit. If the farm is valued at less than $2 million, its owners pay a "small farmer tax" capped at 5% of net operational income. So some Uruguayan brokers put together syndicated LLCs limited to under $2 million in total value — for example, 20 partners of $100,000 each — specifically to benefit from this low tax rate. Farms with operational income under $238,000 per year pay even less in tax — about 2.5%. Both rates are far below the top Uruguayan income tax rate of 25%.

The U.S. and Uruguay do not currently have a tax treaty, and you will pay U.S. tax on your Uruguayan earnings. Nevertheless, despite the lack of a tax treaty, Uruguay gives full credit for any U.S. tax paid, eliminating double-taxation.

As I'll show in an example below, even after you take these taxes and costs into account, your average annual returns on Uruguayan land ownership are very good. Crop farms will return 4% to 9% per year; cattle 3% to 6% per year and forestry 6% to 10% per year — all after management cost and taxes.

And of course, the value of the land itself will appreciate too.

Option Two: Buy to Rent

If you want to own your own land free and clear, perhaps because you aspire to retire on the range one day, you'll want to consider another land-ownership opportunity.

It's entirely possible to buy a small parcel of land that you can then rent to a farmer, just like the land next to my childhood home in Maryland. This is especially suited to less capital-intensive farming, such as livestock and forestry, where no irrigation or regular cultivation is required. It also works for cropland when the parcel in question is reasonably close to other parcels being farmed by the same farmer.

There are even ranch parcels in the eastern part of the country that are right on the oceanfront, making them ideal to convert to a residence or to sell at a gain for subdivision when housing development reaches the area.

Fortunately, owning Uruguayan farmland to rent is just as easy — in some ways, even easier — than buying into a syndicate. Firms like Fischer and Schickendantz combine research and sales of such land parcels with an in-house management arm that finds renters and manages the entire process, for a fee.

Of course, if you rent out your farmland, you don't get the operational profit from its use. But as per Uruguayan practice, you do get the entire year's rent paid up front. And, of course, you benefit from appreciation in the value of the property.

Average annual returns to rental land in Uruguay are about 4% per annum after taxes and costs. You might miss some of the high operational returns available to syndicates and direct ownership, but it's a great way to get into the Uruguayan market if you have a limited amount to invest.

How to Make Your Land Purchase

I mentioned earlier that Uruguay is an exceptionally easy place to do business.

The land purchase process is simple in Uruguay. You appoint an "escribano," or conveyancing attorney. They draft a "boleta de reserva" (intent to purchase agreement), inspect and verify the title, draft the purchase agreement, and record the purchase at the national "Registro de la Propiedad," or Property Registry. You don't even need to have a bank account in your own name, since you can use the conveyancer's escrow account.

All of this would cost you about 8% of the purchase price, or $8,000 per $100,000 in property purchased. You'll also pay property tax of 0.25% per annum. If and when you sell the property, capital gains tax will be 12% (under current law). Although you'll also pay U.S. tax on capital gains, Uruguay will give you full credit for those taxes, eliminating double-taxation.

So, using the hypothetical $150,000 investment I mentioned when discussing syndicated ownership, here's how the strategy would work out, assuming a 15-year ownership with 5% per annum increase in property values, which is quite conservative given Uruguay's recent market performance:

What You Could Earn in Uruguay	
Purchase price	$150,000
Purchase transaction costs, property tax (15 years), and capital gains tax (when you sell)	$39,917
Sale price	$311,839
Sale profit	$121,922
Operational profit (15 years)	$162,000
Average annual return (profit plus capital gain)	12.6%

Now, this is only an example. Your returns can vary … but there's a reason why people are rushing to get into Uruguayan farmland … and this is it.

Don't Forget Uncle Sam

As a U.S. citizen, your investment in Uruguayan farmland will be part of your tax and other reporting to the U.S. government. Your interest in syndicated ownership of a Uruguayan farm via an LLC must be reported to the IRS and to the Treasury Department as part of your annual 1040 tax return and your FBAR report of foreign financial assets.

If you own the land outright, in your own name, however, you do not need to report that ownership.

You must report your earnings from Uruguayan farming on your annual U.S. tax return. Uruguay and the U.S. currently do not have a double-taxation agreement. Nevertheless, Uruguay will give you a tax credit equal to any U.S. taxes you pay on your farm earnings, thus eliminating a double tax.

If foreign real estate is held through a foreign corporation, partnership, LLC, trust, or estate, then your interest in the holding entity is considered a "specified foreign financial asset," and therefore reportable to the U.S. government for tax and other purposes, such as the Foreign Account Tax Compliance Act (FATCA). Land owned directly in your own name, on the other hand, is not.

If you own Uruguayan farmland outright in your own name, you may also exclude a portion of your farm profit under the U.S. Foreign Earned Income Exclusion. If you are part of a syndicate via an LLC, however, your Uruguayan income may be taxed by the U.S. as passive investment income.

Firms such as Fischer and Schickendantz are well-acquainted with the interplay of U.S. and Uruguayan tax law, and can optimize your investment to minimize your tax across both jurisdictions.

Secure Income the Right Way

One of the things that bothers me about the U.S. today is the fact that so much economic activity is just shuffling money around and extracting rent. I grew up in an America where people actually made things and produced food for ourselves and for export. It was something of which we could be proud.

That's why places such as Uruguay excite the inner economist in me. Like China, Uruguay is place where economic value is actually being produced by making and growing useful things that people need and want and will pay for. That's by far the most sustainable way to wealth creation. You can shuffle all the money you want, paying middlemen in the process, but for real returns … you need to produce the real goods. And food is a good that never goes out of fashion.

I'm convinced that there's only one thing that can stop the flow of remarkable returns to investment in Uruguayan farmland … when that market is fully subscribed and land prices have reached their equilibrium. In the meantime, you have the opportunity to earn double-digit combined returns on farm operations and land value appreciation … if you get in early.

We're not there yet, but those savvy investors who get on board now will be glad they did.

PROFITING FROM A HEDGE CITY
Ted Bauman, *The Sovereign Investor Daily*, June 2014

Standing on the edge of an inlet is a gem of a neighborhood, filled with gleaming high-rise condos and enormous homes with long driveways that wind past expertly manicured lawns. But there are no cars in the driveways. Motion-sensor lights snap on and off as private security guards patrol the quiet streets, but there are few signs of life behind drawn shades and curtains, besides cleaners. The owners of these luxury homes and condos are nowhere to be seen.

Welcome to Coal Harbour, the most expensive and luxurious residential neighborhood in Vancouver. And the hottest real estate market in North America for those who are interested in their financial freedom.

The big question real estate investors are asking themselves is, where is the next Coal Harbour going to be? You should be asking yourself the same question …

Vancouver isn't home to a major industry, and it isn't exactly a global cultural center (unless you consider native Bryan Adams a musical icon). Instead, Vancouver is comfortable and, above all, secure, making it what Andy Yan, of the Vancouver-based firm Bing Thom Architects, calls a "hedge city."

A hedge city is a place where wealthy people in booming but unstable societies — think China, Russia, the Middle East, and similar areas — pile into local real-estate markets, driving up values and supporting a luxury-construction boom. Unlike London, notorious for its Russian oligarchs, the typical hedge city is innocuous, offering privacy and seclusion as well as social and political stability.

Essentially, rich people around the world concerned with financial freedom are looking for places where they can invest some of their wealth and feel safer about it than they would at home. The phenomenon isn't new. London house prices track turmoil in southern and Eastern Europe. Miami's residential property market, hit hard by the 2008 collapse, has rebounded at the high-end based on an influx of money from Venezuela. Chinese investors are hot for Sydney and Melbourne. Hong Kong millionaires prefer Auckland.

But unlike London or Miami — and perhaps even Sydney — Vancouver is located in a stable, welcoming, unaggressive, reasonably liberty-respecting country. Historically, the city's been a magnet for the Chinese, since it developed largely as a result of Canadian trade with the Far East, and there are a myriad of existing connections. The first big Chinese influx followed Hong Kong real estate developer Li Ka-shing, who targeted Vancouver during the panic prior to the transfer of sovereignty over Hong Kong from the U.K. to China. Indeed, the ups and downs of Vancouver's real-estate market tend to track those of the Chinese economy.

Hong Kong has turned out just fine — so far. Nowadays, Vancouver benefits from the uncertainty inherent in making and keeping big fortunes in a country ruled by a (technically, at least) Communist Party. So even if property values eventually subside in the Canadian city, it's a great investment for wealthy Chinese. As architect Yan says, "If the choice is between losing ten to twenty per cent in Vancouver versus potentially losing a hundred per cent in Beijing or Tehran, then people are still going to be buying in Vancouver."

Searching for Return in All the Right Places

Unlike many busted U.S. real estate markets, those in hedge cities like Vancouver don't reflect an irrational bubble based on greed and perverse regulatory incentives. Wealthy foreigners are paying what they think it's worth to hedge in other countries against risk at home. In other words, from a global viewpoint, the *fundamentals* are good. There's genuine demand.

But because these hedge cities thrive on being out of sight and mind, many people have no idea they exist. Moreover, most of us non-oligarchs probably don't see the value in finding out more about them.

But consider this: if you knew about a city where *global* real estate market fundamentals are likely to push up values, wouldn't you want to invest there? After all, direct foreign property holdings aren't reportable to the IRS or Treasury, as a bank or investment account would be. And you don't have to move there to live — just hold on to it and rent it out until the time comes to sell and take your gains.

I spent some time thinking over my own travels, and came up with a few places that are potentially good candidates for "hedge city" status sometime in the future. Now remember, these aren't necessarily places *you'd* want to live, and the tax and regulatory environments aren't always ideal. They're not all like Uruguay, where all the stars are aligned for the perfect expat life. But from the perspective of future global buyers looking for a safe place to live — and thus for speculative property investment — they could be just right:

Somerset West, South Africa: not far from Cape Town, between the slopes of the Helderberg and the warm waters of False Bay, this town is home to a large European expatriate community. Chinese investment in Africa is starting to generate a demand for South African residential property. Hong Kong-listed Shanghai Zendai Property Ltd. has just inked an $8 billion property investment deal near Johannesburg. I'm betting that more than a few Chinese investors are going to start looking at Somerset West's spacious homes, which still go for under $150,000 on average, compared to the millions of dollars needed to buy a property on Cape Town's Atlantic seaboard.

Birżebbuga, Malta: This EU-member island state in the Mediterranean Sea recently launched a passport-for sale program, as we mentioned in the October issue of *Offshore Confidential*. As expected, it's attracted a lot of attention from Arab oil sheiks, Russian "businessmen," and Chinese billionaires. But to qualify, candidates have to own property in Malta, with special preferences given to the underdeveloped southern region. Birżebbuga is a seaside resort not far from Marsaxlokk in south-east Malta, approximately eight miles from the capital city of Valletta. Apartments, condos, and even freestanding homes can be had for under $150,000.

Mauritius: Another island state, this time in the Indian Ocean, Mauritius, has historical ties to China, just like Vancouver. It is also a critical financial hub for the Indian Ocean basin. Chinese buyers are beginning to sniff around properties available under the Integrated Resort Scheme, which allows foreigners to invest in homes in resort complexes around the island. Prices start at about $300,000, but are expected to rise substantially given Chinese residential interest, as well as Mauritius' proximity to Africa.

Now, none of these are "sure things," but they demonstrate the logic behind hedge cities. Look for places that are likely to attract serious buyers with stability, security and relative anonymity. Look for the links to others things that interest those buyers, like regional economic investment activity. Look for low prices.

And then get in early.

Foreign Real Estate: More Than a Second Home

Ted Bauman, *The Sovereign Investor Daily*, January 2015

Pretoria, South Africa — As I wrap up my month-long visit to my second home here at the southern end of the great African continent, my thoughts have turned to goings-on in the United States — endless political dysfunction, arrogant cops in open revolt against elected authorities, and riots in the streets.

As I often tell subscribers to my Plan B Club — a group I established to help and advise people on how to move overseas — spending time abroad is one of the best ways to gain perspective on one's "home." That's why I own foreign real estate, and why I've spent a good chunk of my time working on my lovely seaside cottage south of Cape Town — a property I snapped up 20 years ago for about $15,000. (It's now worth over ten times that.)

But this property, for me, is more than just a place I can go to re-charge and re-collect.

The knowledge that I own a second home outside the U.S. is also a source of great comfort to me and my family. That's a feeling you can share with me … and 2015 is the year to do it.

Why You Should Invest in Foreign Real Estate

With the U.S. government out of control at all levels — from the Oval Office down to New York beat cops — it's important to hold some assets the government can't get its hands on. I can think of three good reasons why 2015 should be the year you consider investing in foreign real estate:

Foreign real estate — also known as a "dirt bank" — is one of the safest and most reliable forms of wealth preservation out there. Lots of things can happen to stocks, bonds, currencies, and commodities, but land and housing are always in demand.

You don't have to report foreign property owned in your own name (i.e. not via an LLC or other vehicle) under the Foreign Account Tax Compliance Act (FATCA). That makes it last in line for the wealth confiscators.

Foreign real estate is the ultimate escape plan — a place to go if the time comes.

My South African property checks all three boxes, and I'm happy as a clam.

I ended up owning South African property for unique reasons that wouldn't apply to everyone. Chances are if I were starting out today, I'd look to own foreign real estate in the South American nation of Uruguay. Excellent residential property in Montevideo, the seaside capital city, can be had for as little as $100,000, where residential rental yields are from 6 to 8%. And Uruguay is one of the most immigrant-friendly countries on earth, with strict financial and personal privacy laws.

Purchasing property in Uruguay is simple and cheap. The transaction would cost you about $8,000 per $100,000 in property purchased. You'd pay property tax of 0.25% per annum. If you sell the property, capital gains tax would be 12% under current law).

So, for a hypothetical $100,000 residential investment in Uruguay, assuming a 15-year ownership with 5% per annum increase in property values (which is quite conservative), your profits would look something like this:

Protection in More Ways Than One

Given extensive (and frankly, invasive) reporting requirements to the IRS and the U.S. Treasury Department, it is critical to own financial assets that aren't reportable — and therefore, not factored into your net worth.

If you open a financial account overseas and have more than $10,000 in it at any time during the year, you have to report it on your annual income tax IRS Form 1040, as well as a little horror-show called Form 8938. Same goes for your interest in any foreign investment fund, corporation, LLC, trust, or other entity.

Armed with this information, the government money-grabbers will know how much you've got and where to go when the time comes to rob you, no matter where your money is around the globe.

But because foreign real estate isn't a "specified foreign financial asset" under U.S. tax law, you don't have to report it at all.

Like gold or gems in a vault in Montreal, artwork in a Swiss duty-free warehouse, or stamps in a safe deposit box in Guernsey, foreign land could be your own little — and perfectly legal — secret. It's a way to park your wealth in a place and form that can't be touched by the government under current U.S. law.

Simply, it's a no-brainer.

With all that's going on in the U.S. today, make 2015 the year you go beyond resolutions … to action. Owning foreign real estate in a place like South Africa is one of the simplest and safest ways of securing your future and your wealth.

7 Rules for Buying Overseas Real Estate
Bob Bauman JD, *The Sovereign Individual*, June 2013

Each day, over 10,000 baby boomers turn age 60. That's a rate of eight per minute.

Within 20 years, over 100 million baby boomers from the U.S. and Canada will retire. Scores of them are now seriously considering the purchase of international real estate as a vacation or investment home. And, many are looking for an international destination to be their primary home during retirement.

For many, the math is simple. *The New York Times* recently reported that "With life expectancies growing — and pension plans diminishing — baby boomers are doing the numbers and concluding that moving overseas makes more sense than aging in place."

But what holds most people back from making the leap to international living is that they don't know how to take the first (and most crucial) step — securing a place to live.

It's challenging enough to buy real estate in your home city, let alone another country. For many, replicating the process offshore — where different laws may or may not apply — might be more than enough to put the brakes on their dream of moving abroad.

The most common real estate pitfalls are easy enough to avoid, if you know what they are. Today, I'll reveal the offshore real estate rules you must know before you book your family's flights. Following these simple rules could save you thousands of dollars and hours of regret down the road.

7 Rules Any Offshore Real Estate Buyer Should Know

Before you buy property overseas you need to know what you're doing. Here are seven fundamental guidelines for investing successfully in overseas real estate, each critically important, especially in emerging and undervalued markets.

1. **Beware of net commissions.** In many countries, real estate agents (not the property owners) set the sale price. The seller specifies what amount he wants to make but tells his agent: "Sell the place for whatever you want." The agent may try to sell for 50% or even 100% more.

   In foreign markets these deals are particularly dangerous for buyers, because there's no U.S.-style Multiple Listing Service. So, there's no way to compare selling prices of similar properties. The easiest way to avoid this practice is to negotiate directly with the property owner.

2. **Title insurance is available for offshore real estate.** Buyers will always be told by the seller and his attorney that the title is good … that there is no need to worry … that they'll do all the paperwork to register the property in your name.

   Never, ever rely on verbal promises, especially since almost anywhere you can buy a title insurance policy almost identical to what you'd find in the U.S. Raising the question of title insurance early in the discussions will head off future problems. If the seller has something to hide and becomes confrontational, you should look elsewhere.

3. **Always buy fully titled real estate, not "rights of possession."** Rights of possession are found in some countries like Panama. This means you get only possession of a property with the possibility that the full title may be obtained after a length of time (normally about 15 years). But such rights are subject to legal challenge by the titled owners of the land.

   The owner of the land trying to sell his rights of possession and his agent may not tell you that the land is not titled. If you ask, they may tell you "rights of possession are just like title." That's untrue. Walk away from any property being sold merely as rights of possession.

4. **Beware of laws that restrict foreign ownership.** When buying foreign real estate, you must know the local rules governing foreign ownership of the specific land in which you interested.

   In some countries, foreign buyers must purchase through a corporation. In others, foreigners are not allowed to buy oceanfront or coastal property or in other designated areas. Calculate the expense of dealing with such restrictive rules to decide if you are getting a good deal.

5. **Offshore real estate markets can be difficult to navigate.** In many countries there are no multiple listings, no sales histories, and often no real estate agents. For foreign buyers, the asking price may be higher than for a local because the seller assumes you don't know the market and that you have more money to spend.

   To avoid this, start with local realtors and get an idea of the general market. Visit areas of interest. Look for "For Sale" signs. Stop in local bars and talk with whoever you can. It helps if you have a reliable local contact to act as your front person to be sure you're quoted true local market prices.

6. **Learn the options of offshore financing.** In Western Europe, Panama and Mexico, loans should be available through a local bank, especially if you're a resident of the country. Although European rates are low, you can't get the high loan-to-value loans that U.S. banks used to give before the crash. Also, don't expect a 30-year mortgage; 20 years is more typical. In less-developed countries, your options may be limited to developers who offer direct financing with terms that are generally are not appealing.

You might arrange a loan in the U.S. using U.S. collateral (a second mortgage). Some offshore private banks will lend money against the value of your investment portfolio held with them in your choice of currencies, but watch the currency exchange risk.

7. **Market price, not asking price, must be your guide.** For real estate in developing markets, the asking price is just a starting point; there are no multiple listings or comparative sales lists. Sellers price property based on what they'd like to make, momentary cash needs or how neighboring properties have sold, regardless of how those properties compare with their own.

Bottom line: Offer only what you believe the property really is worth, even if it's only half the asking price. What it is really worth, the market value, is determined by the prices at which similar properties have recently sold.

Don't Forget about Reporting

Until now, U.S. law has not required that direct ownership in your own name of real property in a foreign country be reported per se to the IRS. At the moment, a U.S. person can own an offshore vacation or retirement home with considerable privacy.

However, U.S. persons are required to report income from real estate holdings, wherever they are located, so this privacy does not apply to rental real estate income.

But non-reporting of foreign real estate may be about to change.

The so-called 2010 HIRE Act contained the "Foreign Financial Assets Report" (FATCA) that requires that U.S. persons file an IRS form with their income tax return to disclose any foreign "financial assets" with a combined value exceeding $50,000. It appears that personally owned offshore assets, such as real estate or business assets that are not owned by a legal entity, might be excluded from this new report.

Start looking for your offshore haven, and take your time to find the right realtor, lender and, most importantly, the right home where you'll spend not just your retirement money, but perhaps your retirement itself. International living is easy if you know the ropes.

A Real Estate Opportunity You Don't Want to Pass Up

Ted Bauman, *The Sovereign Investor Daily*, December 2014

Knysna, South Africa — Most people know South Africa as the land of gold mines, Nelson Mandela and the Big Five wild animals. But did you know that it also has the highest concentration of seaside golf estates in the world? Or that it's a world leader in swimming pool design and technology?

Since it's my second home, many *Sovereign Investor* readers and Plan B Club members ask me about South Africa as a potential offshore residence destination. Not only do I recommend it as a place to live, it's also one of my preferred destinations for international real estate.

More specifically, there is an opportunity in luxury real estate on the country's south coast, in a region most people have never heard of.

The town of Knysna is located on South Africa's southern coast, between the major cities of Cape Town and Port Elizabeth. Knysna lies along what is known as South Africa's "Garden Route," a stretch of the coast named for its scenic beauty and oceanic temperatures. It's a lovely place, famed for the tricky "narrows" leading from the sea, yellowwood furniture, art galleries and farmed oysters. And it's at the heart of one of the most unusual real estate opportunities in the world.

The "Southern Cape," as the wider region is known, is where Africa comes to an abrupt end. The coastline is marked by high bluffs overlooking wide white beaches with warm, pounding surf. The next stop isn't until Antarctica, some 2,500 miles to the south.

The region is unique in South Africa in that there are no "ancestral homelands." When Europeans arrived in the 17th century, it was inhabited by bands of cattle herders and hunter-gatherers spread out across the countryside with no fixed homes. As a result, it hasn't been subject to the complex post-apartheid land claims brought by peoples in other parts of South Africa. Many farms established by Dutch settlers hundreds of years ago remain, but much prime coastal land has been converted to high-end residential and recreational uses.

Investors started developing coastal golf courses and residential estates along the Garden Route in the late 1990s, due to South Africa's combination of natural beauty, a moderate climate and property security. Famed South African golfers like Gary Player, Ernie Els and Retief Goosen provided design input, and some of these courses are now famous in their own right for their spectacular views and unique layouts. Major global tournaments are held here annually.

Interspersed between the golf estates, coastal towns like Plettenberg Bay, Wilderness and Sedgefield boast numerous beachfront hotels and condominium developments. They're also home to many artists and other creative types, drawn by the inspirational environment and relaxed pace of life. There's even a beachfront castle or two, built by eccentric gold-mine barons from Johannesburg in the late 19th century.

No Barriers to Paradise

South Africa is a relatively open country for investor-immigrants. There are large colonies of European vacation homeowners and retirees, where snowbirds from England, Germany and other northern countries spend some or all of the year.

There are also populations of Portuguese and Greek immigrants and their descendants. This has given the southwestern part of the country a distinct Mediterranean feel, reinforced by a climate strikingly similar to the south of France. Vineyards, orchards and olive groves are everywhere.

Obtaining permanent residence here is easy. If you can demonstrate a net worth of $650,000, pension or other ongoing income of $1,750 a month, you're welcome to move on in. There are no barriers to foreign ownership of residential property.

Vacant plots in coastal estates can be had for under $150,000. Finished houses with plots can be had for $250,000 to about $850,000. Or, if you don't want to own a home outright, there are fractional ownership (i.e. timeshare) opportunities. Loans for up to 50% of property value are also available locally, and ownership via non-South African trusts, LLCs and other corporate vehicles is possible.

Note, though, that if you obtain permanent residence in South Africa, you will become subject to exchange control regulations, which will limit how much you can take out every year if you decide to sell your property. Non-residents can take their sale proceeds (minus capital gains tax) out without obstacle.

Returns on the Horizon

The key opportunity is that South African properties are being sold for less than they're worth at the moment. The South African luxury property market in particular has been weak for some time, due to diminished foreign demand thanks to severe economic conditions in Europe — but we know these economic conditions won't last forever.

This presents a unique opportunity for Americans to invest in real estate here. You could purchase a fabulous beachfront home or condo for a song, use it as a second home, with the potential for major returns once the European economy rebounds, as it must eventually.

I've never regretted my decision to become part of the South African community — and if you decide to spend your money or time here, you won't either.

The One Asset the Feds Can't Confiscate
Jeff D. Opdyke, The Sovereign Society, 2015

As you know, I believe our monetary system based on the U.S. dollar will break down soon. When that happens, our government will go broke. And they will do anything to get their hands on your wealth.

Well, one of the best ways to hedge against Washington's coming cash-grab is foreign real estate.

After all, land is hard to repatriate. And since it's a hard asset priced in a foreign currency, it's likely to maintain its value when the dollar collapses. Plus, it can offer rental income. That's why I scour the globe in search of places that welcome Americans, have a high standard of living and have the most profitable real estate. My "boots on the ground" research has provided me with the inside track to the unique real-estate opportunities out there.

Invest in One of the Freest Countries — Uruguay

You know you're not in America as soon as your plane lands at Montevideo's sun-drenched, gleaming, white, ultramodern Carrasco International Airport.

Unlike the long, mind-numbing lines that snarl the U.S. Immigration and Customs process at just about every American airport these days, you are whisked through the Uruguayan entrance routine in a matter of minutes. Outside, you are greeted by bright sunshine and a brisk breeze off the South Atlantic Ocean.

Welcome to Uruguay. Spend a few days here and you will no doubt be impressed by the friendly citizens, and soon you will also realize that this is not just a place to invest and bank, but you might also want to live here.

I've visited more than 44 countries, and Uruguay remains the top of my list for most livable places. It not only offers the complete package for investors and retirees, it's also the perfect place for freedom-seekers looking for a better quality of life abroad.

There is very little poverty, a high standard of living and a large middle class. It also has the most equitable income distribution in Latin America, which equals a low crime rate and a very livable society.

In Montevideo, Uruguay's capital, you'll find a beautiful opera house, the oldest in the Americas, as well as numerous top-ranked restaurants and shopping districts. And Uruguay has a great infrastructure, with safe public transportation, smooth roads and a nearly brand-new international airport. There is also a strong European feel ... so much so that you'd be forgiven for thinking you're in Spain.

And political and labor conditions are among the freest in Latin America.

Besides being a safe haven for investing money, banking is also a breeze in Uruguay. With good regulations and oversight, opening an account here could give you peace of mind. There are also a few private banks that will work with Americans on asset management and other private banking services.

Largely non-forested, flat and water-rich, the country is an often-overlooked agricultural giant and effectively a vast farm. Fertile soil fed by abundant rivers blankets much of the southwest and is home to soy, wheat and other crops. Plus, you don't have to worry about hurricanes, volcanoes or earthquakes.

Worry-Free Property Investments

The country's housing market offers anything you could want. In Montevideo's city center, you can find modern, newly constructed apartments hidden inside architecturally elegant brick and stone buildings from the early 20th century. You'll find leafy, tony suburban neighborhoods like Carrasco that are not unlike Lake Forest, Illinois, or southern Connecticut. Drive along the coastal highway through Punta del Este and La Barra and you'll see beautiful homes that look transported from the English countryside and post-modern apartment and condo towers made of steel and glass.

Punta has true international demand and attracts investors from across Latin America. Most coastal real-estate sales are in and around Punta del Este.

Traditionally, some 80% of property buyers in Punta del Este came from Buenos Aires. But booming agricultural exports from Uruguay (meat, grains, seeds, oilseeds, dairy products) and the country's strong economy swung the balance.

Today, around 50% of the buyers in Punta del Este are Uruguayan. While this playground for much of South America is not cheap, lower-priced investment opportunities abound just a few blocks from the boardwalk.

And in some of Uruguay's lesser-known beach towns, such as Piriapolis, La Paloma and La Pedrera, your realestate dollar will stretch even further.

The country imposes no restrictions on who can buy property, and no types of property are off limits.

You won't find a very active mortgage market, though one does exist. So be prepared to spend cash if you want to buy a home. In Montevideo, you can find newly built, modern apartments with all amenities starting in the $150,000 to $200,000 range. While in Punta, you'll find 1,200-square-foot, three-bedroom, two-bath bungalows with a view of the ocean for just $200,000 ... as well as $3 million, 10,000-square-foot homes right on the sand. In between is everything from traditional middle-class neighborhood homes to chic ocean-view apartments starting at $250,000.

During my previous visit to Uruguay, I had my friend, Sancho Santayana, show me what these kinds of properties look like. And they're all very nice — places I could happily live. If you want to know more about Uruguayan real estate, I suggest you reach out to Sancho, the managing director at 360 Terra International Reality in Uruguay at info@360terra.com or by going to the website at www.360terra.com.

An Easy Way to Invest Directly

While one of the most profitable investment opportunities in Uruguay is for foreigners to invest in second or vacation homes, one of the easiest ways to invest directly for profit is to buy farmland. This is a safe, turnkey investment with high appreciation potential and good returns.

Uruguay is ideal for agricultural pursuits. It is estimated that 46.4% of soils worldwide now have depleted biological functions — from water and wind erosion, changes in soil composition and physical degradation — and 15% of that total is in Latin America.

However, almost all of the soil in Uruguay is non-degraded and productive. The climate is temperate and there is rainfall year-round. The country also sits atop the world's largest aquifer, a wet underground layer of permeable rock from which ground water can be extracted. These factors all combine to make the country a competitive producer and exporter with no government interference in the market.

Principal crops include soybeans, wheat, rice, cattle and sheep ranches, and dairy farms. Forestry includes growing eucalyptus and pine trees and there are many vineyards, olive groves and fruits.

Foreign investors may work directly or have a farm management company handle all aspects of operation. There is also an active market for crop-land rental.

Overall, the Uruguayan property market has been safe and stable. For example, farmland prices have increased in value by a multiple of nine times since 2002 from US$385 per hectare to US$3,500 in 2013.

All of Uruguay's land was mapped some decades ago, and each plot was rated according to its productivity. The rating system is called CONEAT and it assigns a numerical rating to all land. The rating can be accessed by anyone, online, making it very easy to determine the fair value of land in this transparent market. Most of the prime agricultural land lies along the western edge of the country, near the Uruguay River near the Argentine border.

Never buy without knowing the CONEAT rating. An agronomist can tell which crops are best under any given rating.

And for the non-farmer investor, investing in farmland is easy: Uruguay has widespread expertise to help manage a farm, and the decisions are simple: You will usually plant what the global market dictates, typically soybeans in the summer and wheat in the winter.

Insider tip: If you are buying land for recreational, development or personal use, then you do not need a high CONEAT rating. If the rating is high, the land may be overpriced for your purposes.

If you're interested in farmland, I recommend contacting Juan Fischer at jfischer@fs.com. His law firm (Fischer & Schickendantz) has a specialized unit helping put together farmland investments, you can check out the website at www.uruguayfarms.com.

Not only does Uruguay welcome the right people — and clearly they are coming in steady numbers — it offers a delightful lifestyle and a myriad of real estate and land investment opportunities.

A Huge Wealth-Building Opportunity Just Two Hours From Miami

I've seen a lot of real estate over the past several years — from a true Galt's Gulch in northern Argentina and income-producing farmland in Uruguay to high-end Alpine living in Andermatt, the only place in Switzerland a foreigner can easily buy property. But I have fallen in love with a new destination — the southwest coast of Nicaragua.

Many people associate Nicaragua with Sandinistas and the 1980s civil war, in which the U.S. was involved. But that image of a war-torn country is no longer accurate. In much the same way that central air-conditioning revolutionized the Florida coast, technology and improving infrastructure has transformed Nicaragua into a budding — soon to be booming — tourist destination.

Imagine living inside a national forest, with the Pacific Ocean right outside your front door. I spent a week investigating real-estate opportunities two hours outside of Managua … in particular, a 2,700-acre luxury development called Rancho Santana. It's a rolling, forested patch of land from which is springing a community of homes and condos owned by people who see the opportunity in buying "frontier" property before it goes mainstream and values double or triple or rise even further.

The reserve boasts more than two miles of Pacific Ocean coastline and five district beaches, three of which are landlocked in the community. The development also boasts oceanfront dining, nature trails, an authentic horse and ranch atmosphere, a clubhouse, oceanfront restaurant, gym, spa, yoga center with an ocean view, horseshoe pits and tennis courts.

And the ease of purchasing land, low crime and a laid-back lifestyle make this stretch of coast even more appealing.

Big, Sweeping Views Available for $150,000 or Less

Ocean-view lots — with big, sweeping views — are available for $150,000 or less. Building costs for an exquisite property run about $100 a square foot. The clubhouse/restaurant/conference center is first-rate. The food — particularly the ceviche — is fresh from the ocean just a few steps away or the local produce garden on site. The poolside cabanas overlook breaking waves that attract surfers from all over the world.

The motto at Rancho Santana is "no asphalt, but a ton of WiFi."

And they've accomplished that. Roads are unpaved, but easy to drive, cutting through a hardwood forest canopy, where iguanas and howler monkeys roam. Yet, from the condos to the clubhouse ... from the restaurant to the pool cabanas, your laptop and smartphones remain connected. That technological connection is to me, the ultimate freedom. I can easily move between my office in Louisiana and the wild, breathtaking coast of Nicaragua while running my business — and my family life — without a hiccup.

But here's where the story for Rancho Santana really gets interesting ...

The second-richest man in in Latin America is building a massive new development just down the road, with an exclusive $500-night hotel and premium-priced lots that millionaires and billionaires will snap up. He's bringing in a new airport a few miles away that will one day service international flights that will be just two and a half hours from Miami and Houston. A new paved road is already under construction. And there's talk that a branch of a Managua hospital affiliated with Johns Hopkins will open up just 20 minutes away.

If you understand what all of this means, you will instantly recognize the huge wealth-building opportunity that's now unfolding at Rancho Santana. Some very smart people with some very deep pockets are spending some very serious cash — meaning hundreds of millions of dollars, and likely more — to transform Nicaragua's Emerald Coast.

There is Real Money Behind Rancho Santana

I know the people and investors behind this project personally. The development is an offshoot of Agora Publishing, the parent company to The Sovereign Society. For over a decade, I've watched this project develop from a remote stretch of wild beach only accessible by horseback to the vibrant first-world oasis it is today. Unlike so many resort projects, this entire development has been built with cash. No lines of credit here. Just smart money that knows there is a future in this part of the world.

I was first here in 2003, when there were only a dozen houses and a small, white-washed clubhouse. At the time I could appreciate the natural beauty but I missed the infrastructure. A couple of years ago, I was invited back for a publishers' meeting. Frankly, I was dreading it, but I was dead wrong. The event was amazing … from the food to the private firework display and the bonfire on the beach.

I was so impressed that I immediately booked another trip.

The Emerald Coast Will Not Stay Wild Much Longer

It wasn't too long ago that Cabo San Lucas, Mexico, was a barren community of surfing junkies along the Baja California coast. Today, that former frontier market is a tony preserve of million-dollar homes and a thriving tourist town. Early investors there have made actual fortunes.

Nicaragua's Emerald Coast is on the same path … and Rancho Santana is a leading player in the transformation. It's still rough right now in this part of Nicaragua, no doubt. But property values are already moving up sharply because of what's taking shape. It may be one of the last times that the Emerald Coast is this untouched. Five years from now, life along this frontier will be much different … and by then, much new wealth will have been created.

You can't go wrong with luxury living amongst rolling hillsides, dramatic cliffs and spectacular beaches.

If you are interested in acquiring your own slice of Nicaragua's Emerald Coast, we have negotiated a special deal where you can receive a 15% discount on the purchase of a lot. For more information, contact Marc Brown at 530-587-4929 or MarcB@RancoSantana.com. You can also visit RanchoSantana.com.

It's Time to Invest Offshore

The U.S. is rapidly declining — open a newspaper and you can see that for yourself. Every day brings more bad news for our country. That's why I'm urging you to protect your future and the assets that you've worked hard for by going offshore. And it's never been easier to invest in these thriving markets. If you are looking for a beautiful and secure second home with solid banking and financial institutions, all of the investments I've recommended offer luxury living in flourishing real-estate markets.

But don't just take my word for it. No one should buy property without an on-site visit. So it's time to start making travel arrangements, because demand for these properties is high, and they won't last forever. And with a little planning, you can own a luxury-filled, secure investment in one of the most beautiful places in the world. So start planning today.

Chapter Six

Your Finances & Estate Planning

Unintended Consequences: Why Government Intervention Destroys Wealth 294

Three Ways to Secure Your Inheritance 296

Bankruptcy Demystified: When Worse Comes to Worst 299

Foreign Trusts — Ultimate Offshore Asset Protection 302

Your Passport to Offshore Banking 307

Family Foundations: Lock Your Assets in the Safest, Private Vault — and Keep the Key 317

Lawyer-Proof Your Properties 326

Your Last Line of Defense Against Bankruptcy, Lawsuits, & Creditors 335

Charitable Giving: Tax Avoidance, Asset Protection & Dynastic Wealth Control 337

The Liberated Individual Retirement Account: Why the Self-Directed IRA is Your Key to Long-Term Prosperity 341

How to Protect Your Home Place from Legal Predators 351

U.S. Social Security: The Greatest Swindle Ever Sold 354

America's Tax System is a "Kludge" 357

The Savviest Way to Protect Your Assets 359

Editor's Note:

In this chapter we describe the available legal mechanisms that are useful in protecting your wealth and conducting business, such as the offshore asset protection trusts and other trust forms, the international business corporation and the limited liability company.

Most important, we present the philosophy and thinking of some people of wealth, some tycoons who have made it and who "have it made."

And we tell you who the experts are and how to contact them.

UNINTENDED CONSEQUENCES: WHY GOVERNMENT INTERVENTION DESTROYS WEALTH
John Pugsley, *The Sovereign Individual*, June 2009

It is a great mystery to most Sovereign Individuals as to why, in spite of all the passionate rhetoric about the evils of big government, and all of the promises of political candidates to stop it, that growth continues unabated.

Decade after decade, century after century, the number of laws increase, taxes increase, deficits increase and crises increase.

Yet when viewed through the lens of evolutionary biology, these universal and worldwide trends are no mystery at all. All the economic problems that bedevil the world are rooted in human nature in the way in which we are programmed to pursue our own self-interest.

Biologically Rational

Biologist E.O. Wilson explained our selfishness in his 1978 Pulitzer Prize winning book *On Human Nature*: "Individual behavior, including seemingly altruistic acts bestowed on tribe and nation, are directed, sometimes very circuitously, toward the Darwinian advantage of the solitary human being and his closes relatives."

Self-interest, however, is not necessarily the root of all evil. All human progress is a direct but unintended consequence of individuals pursuing their own self-interest.

As Adam Smith observed in The Wealth of Nations: "Every individual necessarily labours to render the annual revenue of the society as great as he can. He generally, indeed, neither intends to promote the public interest, nor knows how much he is promoting it…He intends only his own gain, and he is in this, as in many other cases, led by an invisible hand to promote an end which was no part of his intention."

How is it possible then, that the pursuit of self-interest, which has guided us from the cave to the moon, is also the source of the unrelenting growth of government?

The root of the problem is government intervention, in the freedom of individuals to make voluntary exchanges. Basically, the problem is interference with free trade.

Striking at the Root

In common usage, the term "free trade" refers to trade between individuals and businesses in different nations. Intervention in such trade is known as "protectionism," as its objective is to "protect" domestic industries from foreign competition. Today's political leaders tend to oppose protectionism because memories are fresh of the effects of The Smoot-Hawley Tariff Act of 1930.

U.S. tariffs were raised to record levels, which caused other countries to retaliate and raise tariffs on U.S. goods. The unintended consequences of intervention in free-trade were to reduce American exports and imports by more than half, and ultimately plant the seeds of world war.

Clearly, interference in free trade between nations has disastrous effects. Unfortunately, the disastrous effects of interference in free trade among individuals within a nation are almost never understood. Each law controlling your choices, whether in the currency you use, the products you buy, your choice of what investments you buy, who you are permitted to buy them from, where you are allowed to invest, and the price at which you are allowed to exchange your property for that of others, is destructive to your wealth and that of your nation. But that isn't all.

Government Interference Distorts the Human Condition

Homo sapiens are a problem-solving species; we are ingenious at overcoming obstacles that block us from pursuing our self-interest. Any intervention in our ability to freely exchange the fruits of our efforts for those of others immediately compels us to find a way around the intervention. The moment we find a 'loophole' in the law or regulation, we exploit it, and soon others find the loophole, and the government responds by passing another law to close the loophole, and the cycle continues.

The unintended consequences of this process are a relentless growth of government intervention.

For example, the consequence of drug prohibition is that legal drugs become illegal drugs; then, drug transactions move to black markets. The consequence of black markets is violence, such as gang warfare and murder.

The consequence of violence is restrictions on defensive weapons, rendering citizens helpless against lawbreakers — and their own governments. Each intervention leads to the need for another intervention.

Each law leads to the need for another law.

Rationally Circumvent Interference

We are now engaged in a deep recession that is the unintended consequence of government intervention in free exchange.

Laws giving the government monopoly power over money and the rates at which it could be lent led to excessive credit expansion and speculation, which in turn led to collapse, which led to the government further expanding credit, which led to more laws to control banks and speculators.

And the government leviathan continues to grow, shifting the blame for its prior failures onto the free market itself.

What can you do about changing the persistent, unrelenting growth in government intervention? On the larger scale, nothing.

Concerned activists have battled the growth of the leviathan, and wound up only stimulating that growth, and being corrupted along the way.

Your only rational choice is to strive for individual sovereignty. You must act in self-defense. You can conduct your own affairs in a way that does not interfere with the exchanges of others.

The founding principle of The Sovereign Society is that individuals should strive to be sovereign unto themselves and The Society's mission is to find and develop new personal defenses against the ever-expanding interventions of the state.

THREE WAYS TO SECURE YOUR INHERITANCE
Mark Nestmann, *The Sovereign Investor*, July 2009

Millions of Americans — baby boomers in particular — are expecting or have recently received an inheritance. Whatever its size, you should take steps to protect it once you receive it — or ideally, before.

Greatest Gift Parents Can Give

The best way to protect your inheritance is to have your parents leave it to you in trust, rather than giving you money directly. If your parents are working with a competent estate planner, that individual may make this suggestion. But if not, you should.

Yes, this can be an awkward conversation. You're asking your parents to spend money now to ensure that your interests — and possibly those of your siblings — are protected later. But it's important to have this discussion.

It's especially important if you're being sued, expect to be sued, have already suffered a judgment, or simply have an occupation prone to lawsuits (e.g., physician). If you point out that this simple precaution could protect their hard-earned assets from going to legal predators once your parents are gone, they'll likely be receptive to the idea.

Not just any trust will do: your parents should establish a discretionary trust for you and others they may wish to provide for in their estate. The trust will hold your inheritance for the remainder of your life.

A discretionary trust you don't fund and that names you as beneficiary provides extremely strong asset protection. (This is known as a non-self-settled trust.) Based on nearly a thousand years of case law in England and countries that inherited English common law — including the United States — it's almost impossible for a creditor to seize assets in such a trust. Nor can a creditor force the trustee to make a distribution that the creditor might then seize.

Wealth Preservation Techniques

The one downside is that you will never actually own or control those assets.

The trustee of a discretionary trust has complete discretion concerning how much income or capital you or other trust beneficiaries receive. Indeed, the trustee can completely exclude you from any distributions whatsoever. But since you have no legally enforceable right to any of the income or assets in the trust, neither do your creditors.

However, you can make a non-binding request for a distribution anytime. If there are no legal "storm clouds" on the horizon, the trustee will ordinarily comply.

One potential problem with discretionary trusts is the most recent version (2005) of a model act called the "Uniform Trust Code." The UTC diminishes the ability of a discretionary trust to shelter assets from a beneficiary's creditors. In most cases, your attorney should draft the trust under the laws of a state that hasn't adopted the 2005 UTC.

Discretionary Trust Protects You

A properly drafted discretionary trust protects assets from virtually any creditor — even the IRS!

Let's say the IRS sends you a notice of tax deficiency for $100,000. If you have that amount in your bank account, the IRS can simply seize it. But if the assets are in a discretionary trust, even the IRS has no right to force a distribution.

Then there's divorce. If your parents leave you a few million dollars and you have the misfortune to marry a greedy spouse, guess who receives a big chunk of the money if you later divorce? With a discretionary trust, since you have no rights to a distribution, neither does the greedy spouse in a divorce settlement.

What about bankruptcy? You're still protected! Courts have held that bankruptcy trustees can't seize a beneficiary's interests in a non-self-settled discretionary trust.

Best Time to Begin Asset Planning — Now

But what if you've already received your inheritance, without a trust in place? Don't worry. Assuming you have no creditors waiting in line, this is the best possible time to begin asset protection planning. This is because no creditor can make a claim that you engaged in any kind of "fraudulent conveyance" in setting up your asset protection plan.

In essence, fraudulent conveyance laws in effect in all 50 states stipulate that if property is transferred to "hinder, delay, or defraud" an existing obligation or known future obligation, the courts can void that transfer. If no creditors exist when you create the asset protection plan, it's almost impossible for a creditor to later prevail in a legal argument to prove you created the plan in order to defeat the creditor's legitimate claim.

Here are some options you and your professional advisors may wish to consider:

Offshore asset protection trust (APT). Trusts are one of the oldest asset protection instruments devised, however, with a domestic trust that you fund (self-settled trust), you can't generally be a trust beneficiary and also obtain solid asset protection. The best way to obtain asset protection is to form a trust in a foreign jurisdiction that has enacted appropriate "asset protection trust" legislation.

Offshore variable annuity. Offshore trusts are great for asset protection, but don't generally have any tax advantages. If your inheritance or other windfall is large enough that you don't need the income right away, consider investing part of it in a tax-deferred instrument such as an offshore variable annuity. Income earned within an annuity is tax deferred until you cash in the contract or receive payments from it. And if you purchase your annuity in a jurisdiction such as Switzerland, which has very strong asset protection laws for insurance and annuities, your annuity will be sheltered from lawsuits as well.

Offshore life insurance. Life insurance enjoys uniquely preferential treatment under the U.S. Tax Code. Not only do earnings and gains accumulate within the policy on a tax-deferred basis, but the death benefit can also pass through to your heirs tax-free. Indeed, with proper structuring, the proceeds can flow to beneficiaries free of both estate and generation-skipping taxes. Combine that with rock-solid asset protection in a jurisdiction such as Switzerland, and you have one of the most flexible estate planning solutions available.

What's the best time to begin planning? Well, you never know when you'll be sued or experience other financial misfortune. That means there has never been a better time to begin preparations…than now!

Asset Protection from a Trust You Create Yourself

If you create a trust for your own benefit, you have established a "self-settled trust."

To prevent individuals from creating trusts to defeat their own creditors, English courts — centuries ago — declared that a trust can't protect a beneficiary who also created the trust. Most countries that inherited English law follow this rule, along with most U.S. states.

However, there are exceptions. Beginning about 25 years ago, numerous offshore jurisdictions amended their trust laws to provide asset protection to someone who creates a trust for his own benefit. Several states enacted similar laws including Alaska, Delaware, and Nevada. These "domestic asset protection trust" (DAPT) laws sound good in theory, but most asset protection lawyers still believe that if you want asset protection in a self-settled trust, you should form the trust offshore.

Bankruptcy Demystified: When Worse Comes to Worst

Mark Nestmann, *The Sovereign Investor*, February 2009

Now is a great time to go broke.

History shows that ancient governments were far less forgiving. The Roman Empire was known to sell debtors and their families into slavery. And as recently as the 19th century, English citizens who fell deeply into debt were executed!

Fortunately, that's not the case today. Yet the prospect of bankruptcy remains terrifying for many. The truth is — bankruptcy law doesn't merely exist to protect creditors. It's there to protect you. As a last resort, it can safeguard your home… your inheritance…and your business.

But only if you prepare for it in advance.

Bankruptcy: A Fast Unfolding Epidemic

Today, record numbers of Americans are falling behind. Bankruptcies were up 33% in 2008 — and all signs point to a worsening outlook for 2009.

As the economy continues to unravel, small business owners, entrepreneurs and other high earners are increasingly at risk. No one wants to file for bankruptcy — but that's no excuse to be unprepared.

The good news is, once you file bankruptcy before a state or federal court, creditors can no longer try to collect on your debts. That means no more harassing phone calls, threatening letters, lawsuits, or foreclosures.

Instead, the bankruptcy court appoints a trustee to oversee payment to creditors. Because it allows you to delay, reduce or even eliminate debts, the mere threat of bankruptcy can often keep creditors at bay.

Which Chapter is Right for You?

Under Title 11 of the U.S. Code, several kinds of bankruptcy exist. Here are the most common:

Chapter 7: A complete settlement of all debts, except for certain non-dischargeable debts. These include child support, alimony, most student loans, most tax obligations, and debts incurred through fraud.

Chapter 11: Allows an insolvent business to continue operating while paying off a portion of its debts.

Chapter 13: Reschedules repayment of debts. (This may allow you to keep property that you would otherwise lose in a Chapter 7 proceeding, such as a mortgaged house or car.)

Still confused? I don't blame you. This topic is riddled with myths and assumptions. Most people don't understand what bankruptcy can or cannot protect. So let's set the record straight…

Bankruptcy Myths

Myth: Bankruptcy Will Threaten Your Retirement Plan

Fact: Federal bankruptcy laws protect all retirement plans that are "ERISA-qualified" and up to $1.095 million of assets in an IRA or similar "nonqualified" plan. Therefore, one of the most important strategies you can use to protect your assets in bankruptcy is to build up your retirement plan.

Myth: You Will Lose Your Home

Fact: Not necessarily. While most states protect only a few thousand dollars of home equity, six states (Florida, Iowa, Kansas, Oklahoma, South Dakota and Texas) forbid creditors (with a few exceptions such as mortgage-holders) from seizing the equity in your home, with no limit to its value. However, under federal bankruptcy laws, state homestead protection is limited to $136,875 if you purchased your home within 1,215 days (approximately 3.3 years) of filing for bankruptcy.

Myth: Life Insurance and Annuity Contracts Are Endangered

Fact: Many states exempt assets in life insurance and annuity contracts from creditor claims. These protections vary widely. For instance, Florida law protects the cash value in life insurance policies and annuities from most claims. Note: You can obtain even greater protection by purchasing life insurance or annuity policies in a suitable offshore jurisdiction. Nevis, Liechtenstein, Switzerland, and a few other countries won't enforce repatriation orders in foreign bankruptcy proceedings from properly configured insurance contracts.

Myth: Say Goodbye to Your Company's Assets

Fact: You may be able to protect business property by transferring it into a limited partnership (LP) or limited liability company (LLC). But keep in mind — your creditors can still seize any distributions. In addition single-owner LPs or LLCs provide little if any asset protection, especially if they hold only passive investments.

Myth: Bankruptcy Courts Cannot Touch Offshore Trusts

Fact: An offshore trust can only protect your assets from "claw back" if it was formed 10 years before you file for bankruptcy. If you can't retrieve these assets, the bankruptcy court can deny your petition for discharge of your debts.

Note: If you declare bankruptcy, you must make a full disclosure of your assets and any planning you did to protect them. If a transfer of assets made you unable to pay your debts, the bankruptcy trustee can invalidate that transfer, or deny your petition for discharge of your debts. The bankruptcy court can enforce the trustee's order with fines, foreclosures, property seizure, and occasionally, even criminal contempt citations (i.e., pay the creditor or go to jail).

Minimize Your Risk of Bankruptcy — for Less Than $300 a Year

Of course, the best strategy is to avoid bankruptcy altogether. One of the most common causes of bankruptcy is the exhaustion of renter's, homeowner's or auto liability policies. One of the best ways to prevent this is to carry enough liability insurance to pay off any reasonably anticipated claim. Since the typical limits on most liability insurance policies max out at $500,000 or even lower, consider buying an "umbrella" policy. Premiums are surprisingly low. (In most states, you can purchase a $1 million limit umbrella policy for less than $300/year.)

Bankruptcy is not a Do-it-Yourself Job

Keep in mind, federal and state bankruptcy laws are diverse and complex. Depending on your circumstances, they can significantly strengthen — or weaken — your financial position. Bottom line — don't file bankruptcy without first consulting a licensed attorney who specializes in this area.

With the right help and smart planning — you can minimize any claim on your wealth and put your life or business back on track.

FOREIGN TRUSTS — ULTIMATE OFFSHORE ASSET PROTECTION
Robert E. Bauman JD, *The Offshore Money Manual*, 2000

Offshore trusts — especially the asset protection trust — can place your wealth beyond the reach of claimants, creditors, irate ex-spouses and even the government of your home country.

If you ever ask a lawyer to define a "trust," your eyes may glaze over as you listen to something like this:

A trust is a legal device resulting when a person who creates the trust (variously called the "grantor," "donor," "trustor," or "settlor") conveys all and every legal and equitable right, title and interest that he or she holds in certain real property (the "corpus") to a second party (the "trustee"), perhaps a faithful friend, professional financial manager or a bank trust department, who holds the assets for the benefit of one or more named persons or entities known as "beneficiaries," according to the terms of the grantor's basic trust contract, called a trust "declaration."

Impressive. Overwhelming. At least it wasn't in Latin.

Simply put, a trust is a three-way legal device. It allows one person (the trustee) to take title and possession of any kind of property to be held, used, and/or managed for the benefit of one or more other persons (the beneficiaries). The person who creates the trust (the grantor) decides what it will do and donates property to fund it. More simply: the grantor gives money to the trustee to administer for the benefit of a stated beneficiary, being careful all the time not to attract gift and capital gains taxes.

The possible variations on this basic theme are endless. There can be any number of grantors, trustees and beneficiaries. Two parents can entrust four people with money intended to benefit their six children.

The assets placed in the trust can also be varied. You can choose cash, stocks, or any other vehicle you possess.

Whatever the arrangement, the trust must have a reason for being. To create a trust, the grantor signs a lengthy written declaration or indenture describing what he or she has in mind. This document spells out specific details of trust operation including income distribution and trustee powers. These instructions are binding both during and after the grantor's lifetime.

Thousands of court rulings have given unique definition to almost every word and phrase used in a trust declaration. Drafting one correctly requires expert legal advice. Before creating a trust, all estate planning must be coordinated and reviewed; the right hand must know what the left hand is doing.

What a Trust Can Do

A trust may be created for any legal purpose that does not run counter to public policy. That is a broad spectrum by any standard. The government constantly attempts to narrow the choices, but the fact remains: you can create a trust for almost any purpose.

A trust can conduct a business. It can hold title to and invest in real estate, cash, stocks, bonds, negotiable instruments, and any other kind of property. Trusts are often created to care for minor children or the elderly. Others are established to pay medical, educational or legal expenses. Again, the possibilities are endless.

For our purposes, there is one very important role a trust can serve, especially an offshore trust. In carefully arranged circumstances, trusts can serve as excellent wealth and asset protection devices.

Trusts Go Way Back

Before explaining how you can benefit from a trust, let's take a look at the history and progression of this all-important investment device.

Trust arrangements stretch all the way back to ancient Egypt. Ancient Germanic and French law recognized the trust as well. From the time of Mohammed, it was a fundamental principle of Islamic law. In the Middle Ages, the quasi-religious order of the Knights Templar acted as international financiers. They used trusts to help royal and ecclesiastical investors shield their financial activity from the public and one another. Citizens of sixteenth-century England used them to avoid feudal taxes on property inheritances and restrictions on land transfers. In fact, the trust is probably the world's oldest tax shelter.

Over centuries, the trust has been refined repeatedly by practical use and development, especially in England. This process was later carried on in the British Commonwealth nations and in the United States. American judges have played a large role in perfecting modern domestic trusts, producing significant beneficial legal and tax consequences for U.S. citizens.

Trusts are now used most often in personal estate planning. They allow you to pass property title to heirs while minimizing probate court costs, legal fees, and inheritance taxes. Nationally, probate fees (exclusive of taxes) average from one percent to 15 percent of estate value, a substantial chunk. Probate in some states like California can drag on for years while legal fees pile up and beneficiaries are left in limbo.

The Foreign Asset Protection Trust

In recent years, an asset-protection device in trust form has gained worldwide popularity.

The foreign asset protection trust (APT) is a personal trust created and based in a foreign nation. It will shield your assets better than any domestic trust ever can, simply because it is located outside the United States. Distance makes the trust grow stronger. This trust shields business and personal assets against demanding creditors, litigation and other unpleasant financial liabilities.

The key to creating such a trust is simple: planning. The APT must be planned and created long before you really need it, at a time of personal financial calm. As a belated response to an imminent financial crisis, it will achieve little. Last minute attempts to create an offshore trust can lead to civil liability for concealing assets or fraud under the "Fraudulent Conveyers" legislation found in American bankruptcy law. In litigation-crazed America, you should not wait for trouble before taking offshore precautionary measures.

As a practical matter, placing title to property in the name of an offshore APT cannot really protect any assets that physically remain within an American court's jurisdiction. Assets actually transferred to the APT's foreign jurisdiction, like funds moved to an offshore bank account, are usually safe from a U.S. creditor, even if he knows the account exists.

Locating Your APT

Certain countries tailor their laws to welcome foreign-owned APTs. Although these nations may be diminutive in geographic size and total population, their capital cities have well-developed, efficient banking and legal communities. Banking and legal officials understand APT law and finance. More importantly, they want your business and are eager to please.

There are established APT havens all over the world. From the Cayman Islands to the Isle of Man, investors looking for the perfect investment location have a wide variety of options.

Strong Creditor Deterrent

While the APT concept may be new to you, thousands of American citizens have successfully followed this international road to wealth protection. Here's what makes an offshore APT so attractive:

Start Over: Courts in asset-haven nations usually don't honor or even recognize the validity of U.S. court orders. A foreign creditor trying to collect must re-litigate the claim in a local court, use local lawyers and obtain another judgment. Sheer legal complexity and cost are likely to produce a quick and satisfactory compromise with all but the most determined adversaries.

Minimal Needs: To operate an APT, you'll need little more than a trust account in a local or multinational branch bank. The bank can provide trustees and working staff experienced in trust matters. With modem communications, conducting business will be much like having an account in another American city. Most banks offer US dollar-denominated accounts, often with better interest rates than American financial institutions offer.

More Control: As grantor of a foreign asset-protection trust, you can exercise far greater control over assets and income than American trust law permits. U.S. rules that discourage you from creating a trust for your own benefit do not apply in these countries. In all 50 states and the District of Columbia, a trust with the grantor as beneficiary won't protect against creditors. It will in these foreign jurisdictions.

Fast Acting: Foreign law usually does not support strict application of U.S. fraudulent conveyance and bankruptcy laws. Some countries have a strict statute of limitations on creditor suits; a claim must be filed within two years from the date the APT was established. The Cook Islands has a one-year limit. It may take a creditor longer than that just to discover the existence of an offshore APT.

Investments: An offshore APT is great for diversified international investments. Your trustee handles the paper work, while you give long-distance directions. You can take advantage of the world's best investment opportunities without worrying about restrictive U.S. securities laws.

Flexible: An APT provides added flexibility in the case of personal disability, when transferring assets, or avoiding domestic currency controls. Your foreign APT trustee can even make your mortgage payments and other personal bills on a regular basis.

No Insurance: An APT is a good substitute for, or supplement to, costly professional liability insurance. Such a trust can even be used as an integral part of a prenuptial agreement.

Quick Change: Often the trust declaration contains a force majeure clause that allows the situs, or location, of the APT to be changed at any time. Originally meant to be used in time of war, civil unrest or major natural disasters, this clause can also be activated if the offshore haven decides to change its APT-friendly laws. A complimentary feature in many APT-haven countries is a provision that allows instant acceptance of a transfer of an existing APT from one country to another with no break in legal operation. This can be done merely by filing a registration form and paying a filing fee.

Creating an APT

The legal structure of a foreign APT differs little from an American trust. You, as grantor, create the APT, transferring title to assets that are administered by an offshore trustee according to the trust declaration for the named beneficiaries. In some nations the law requires the naming of three trustees, two located in the grantor's home country, and one independent managing trustee located in the offshore country. Most countries do not permit the grantor to serve as a trustee, but they do allow a grantor to retain an unrestricted right to remove the trustees at will. This assures that trust administration reflects your wishes.

Foreign trust law, unlike strict American "arm's length" requirements allows you to be a beneficiary while maintaining effective control over the investment and distribution of the trust principal. The trust declaration can give the grantor a large measure of control, including the right of prior approval of investments or distributions.

Many of these nations require appointment of a local "trust protector." This individual acts as a neutral party who ensures trust objectives are met and the law is followed. A protector does not manage the trust, but can veto trustee actions in some cases.

Privacy is Paramount

Most of these countries require very little information about an APT at the time it is registered with the government. The terms of the trust agreement and the parties involved need not be disclosed, and any information filed is not available as part of a public record. The only public record is a registry of the APT by name, date of creation and the name of the local trustee. In these privacy-conscious countries, a trustee is allowed to reveal information only in very limited circumstances, and then usually only by local court order. This offers a distinct privacy advantage over offshore corporations (usually called international business corporations, or IBCs). At least one person involved in organizing a corporation must be listed on the public record. So must the corporate name and address. Some countries require corporate directors to be listed as well. This gives privacy invaders a starting point.

Another issue that worries most people is physical distance.

How can you rest easy when your money is thousands of miles away, in a foreign nation, controlled by an unrelated trustee? This concern is justified, but can be easily overcome. The trick is to choose reliable people to manage your trust. The experts in the legal and banking industries in these nations have extensive experience with APTs. References are in order, and each one should be checked carefully.

We suggest a few reliable contacts below. Call them, and they will be able to set you on the right path.

One thing is certain: your offshore trustee should have no connections that might subject him to pressure from U.S. courts. If you are considering an international bank trust department as your trustee, ask them bluntly what their policy is in such situations. It is better to go with a local, in country bank or trust company. These will be less likely to buckle under pressure from a U.S. court.

What Do You Put into Your Foreign APT

While you need not physically transfer your assets offshore, it is wise to do so. If you don't, it will be easy for U.S. courts to seize them. The best vehicles for trust investment are cash and evidence of intangible assets. Easily portable assets, such as precious metals, coins, jewelry or gem stones also can be transferred offshore for storage in the APT's name. But remember, if you transfer something other than cash, and you are not the beneficiary, you run the risk of attracting substantial gift and capital gains taxes. Be sure to consult with a professional before moving your assets.

We repeat: simply transferring title to real estate or a business located in the United States to an offshore trust does not remove those assets from the reach of American creditors and courts.

Your Passport to Offshore Banking
Ted Bauman, *Sovereign Confidential*, August 2015

The note from my old friend Zannos was expected ... but jarring nonetheless.

He'd come face to face with the consequences of keeping one's nest egg in a single country, and the specter was horrifying.

He sought my urgent advice ... but it was already too late.

I first met Zannos in Cape Town, South Africa, where he was a successful recording engineer, with his own studio overlooking the sea. His wealthy parents had immigrated to the Fairest Cape in the '60s, leaving behind a successful trading business in the Greek port town of Piraeus. Their ongoing ownership interest in that business had accumulated tens of millions of euros in Greek banks, which had helped Zannos fund his studio and a small olive farm on his mountainside property south of Cape Town.

And now those millions were inaccessible, and about to evaporate into thin air…

I'd told Zannos over the years that he needed to diversify. National banking systems are like organisms, I'd said. When they get sick, they can die. When they do, other countries' banking systems — like any survival-oriented animal — will isolate them ruthlessly to prevent contagion. Greece's fundamentals were like a man with serious heart disease, I said. He looks fine, but one day he'll keel over.

Zannos hadn't believed me.

When the inevitable Greek financial crisis peaked a few weeks ago, he flew overnight to Athens to see if he could transfer some of his money to other European banks. It was too late. All he could get was a measly 60 euros a day from an ATM … if he could find one that wasn't empty. He couldn't even get to his safe deposit boxes, since they had been seized under government order.

Today, I know about the importance of international banking diversification than I did when I first met Zannos. And banking itself is much easier now … you can do it from your living room. It leads me to say to you, now: If most of your money in the U.S., it's in a very sick animal — and you've got to get some of it out … IMMEDIATELY.

The Four Massive Benefits of an Offshore Account

My friend Zannos needed a safe haven for his money as the Greek financial system disintegrated.

Indeed, that's the main attraction of an offshore bank account. Protecting your wealth by keeping it safely overseas is just as important as being able to invest abroad.

Consider this: The International Monetary Fund (IMF) reports that "stability reasons" — not bank secrecy — help foreign havens like Switzerland attract almost a third of the world's offshore wealth in any given year.

Sovereign individuals use the simple yet effective tool of a foreign account to protect their wealth against domestic creditors, shaky domestic banks and declining currencies.

1. **Protection from shaky U.S. banks:** The 2008 financial crisis showed that the U.S. banking system no longer relies on sound financial principles like deposit reserves. Instead, it takes advantage of its corrupt relationship with

Washington to rely on de facto government guarantees of bailouts in times of trouble. Whereas most foreign banks keep up to 30% reserves, U.S. banks routinely operate with a tiny fraction of that, and are leveraged to the hilt. The only way to stop such banks from failing is to keep printing money, which presents problems of its own.

2. **Protection from litigation:** The U.S. is one of the most litigation-happy societies on earth. We have more lawyers per capita than any other nation, and each of us has a 1-in-12 chance of being sued in any given year. Having money in an offshore account means it is under the jurisdiction of another country's laws. Except for France, the U.K. and Canada, which have special agreements allowing U.S. accounts to be attached, all other countries require that a litigant redo their case in a foreign court, at great expense. That deters frivolous lawsuits.

3. **Protection from the declining dollar:** Printing money leads to currency devaluation. Since 1913, the dollar has devalued by 95%. From 1976 to 2009 alone, the U.S. dollar lost an average of 73% of its purchasing power against most major currencies. That means $100,000 in 1976 would only be worth $27,000 in buying power today. Yet, if you had held your "cash" portfolio in Swiss francs during that time, your portfolio would be worth $165,000.

Unlike most U.S. banks, offshore banks offer "multi-currency functionality." That is, they give you the ability to invest and transact business in your choice of strong currencies that appreciate while the U.S. dollar sinks.

4. **Offshore investment opportunities:** Of course, there's another benefit to banking abroad: you can do business directly with foreign investment institutions. Having a foreign bank account simplifies the process of investing abroad, and opens up opportunities that are entirely inaccessible from the U.S. You can invest in stock and bond markets that just aren't available via U.S. brokers.

Exploding the Myths

You have probably heard horror stories about banking abroad, especially recently, with the Foreign Account Tax Compliance Act (FATCA) wreaking havoc on Americans. So before I show you the specific offshore banking opportunities available to you, I want to address some myths and give you the basic rules of offshore banking. They don't stop you from exercising your right to bank outside the U.S.

There are a lot of myths out there about offshore banking. One is that it's illegal. That's just false.

Another is that it's only for the super-rich. That is also false.

But the most pervasive myth is that you can "hide" money in an offshore bank account.

An offshore bank account is not a tool for legally avoiding tax. As an American citizen or "green card" holder, the IRS taxes you on your worldwide income. No matter where you earn your money or how, you'll owe U.S. taxes.

Now, in years past, it was possible to put money into a "numbered account" in a foreign bank and have it be your own secret. This depended entirely on the willingness of foreign banks to maintain strict secrecy about the ownership of such accounts, and on foreign governments to enact and respect financial privacy laws. There were high-end jurisdictions (Switzerland) and dodgy ones (some of the Caribbean islands).

All of that ended due to two catalysts and one long-term trend.

The first catalyst was the 9/11 attacks on the U.S., which depended on international financial transfers for its planning and execution. Financial privacy was thus unfairly associated with terrorism.

The second catalyst was the discovery, in the mid-2000s, of hundreds of U.S. client accounts at Swiss banking giant UBS, which led to a federal lawsuit, massive fines, and the end of Swiss banking secrecy. Uncle Sam wanted his cut, and Swiss banking secrecy was in the way ... so it had to go.

But just as important was a long-term shift in the way the U.S. government understands its relationship with individual citizens and the rest of the world. Traditionally, government is supposed to be a servant to its citizens and an equal member of the community of nations.

By the early 21st century, the U.S. government had come to see itself as lord and master of all Americans and of all other nations. Its prerogatives superseded any quaint considerations of "privacy" or "national sovereignty." The result was a shift in the way existing U.S. law was enforced, and a new law:

- The **Report of Foreign Bank and Financial Accounts (FBAR)**, which had been around since 1970 but only sporadically enforced, requires every U.S. person with an interest in, or signature or other authority over, financial accounts in a foreign country to file an annual report to the government if the aggregate value of such accounts at any point in a calendar year exceeds $10,000. This is now strictly enforced.

- The **Foreign Account Tax Compliance Act (FATCA)** of 2010 requires U.S. persons — including those living outside the U.S. — to report non-U.S. financial accounts over a certain threshold to the IRS ($50,000 per individual, higher if you live abroad permanently). It also requires all foreign financial institutions to report the assets and identities of U.S. clients to the U.S. government. Failure to do so results in the effective ejection of the foreign bank from the global financial system.

The results of these two laws are that (a) it is no longer legally possible to maintain offshore financial accounts with more than $10,000 in them without reporting them to the U.S. government and (b) that many foreign banks are reluctant to do business with American clients … unless you have the right connections.

Three Great Options for Offshore Banking

As I will show you, it is still possible to bank abroad, as long as you know the rules and plan accordingly. Such accounts offer a variety of benefits besides those I've already mentioned. You can transact remotely, using web-based interfaces. You can get debit and credit cards that you can use anywhere in the world. They might even come with safe deposit boxes that you can use to store foreign currency, valuables and other items offshore.

But as with anything, there are levels of engagement with the offshore banking system. They vary in purpose, complexity, cost and the requisite size of the account. They are:

1. **Option One:** A personal offshore account.

2. **Option Two:** Foreign bank accounts owned by a foreign entity that you control.

3. **Option Three:** A personal independent asset manager who opens a foreign account for you and manages investments using the funds therein.

Let's look at each of these in turn.

Option 1: A Personal Offshore Bank Account

Let's be honest: Opening a foreign bank account isn't as easy as it used to be.

But isn't it worth it to jump through a few extra hoops now to protect your wealth rather than see it sucked away by a spendthrift government, broken banking system or frivolous litigation?

Now, if you live in the U.S. and just want to move some money abroad for currency diversification, you can do that with a multinational bank such as HSBC or Citi that has a U.S. presence. If you have enough money, they'll open a "Premiere" account for you in a U.S. branch. You can then open attached accounts in other countries. You'll get a personal banker in each country and no fees when transferring money through their system.

But … and this is a big but … if you take this route, you won't be protected from U.S. litigants or from potential wealth confiscation by the U.S. government. Your foreign accounts will be as vulnerable as the U.S. base account.

On the other hand, you can still open a personal bank account in places such as Panama, Hong Kong, Uruguay, Switzerland, Liechtenstein, and so on ... as long as you have the right contacts. Those contacts are crucial. Let me explain why.

If you are resident in the U.S. and want to open a private account in a foreign bank, you'll need to show that your business will be worth it to the bank. That means you will likely have to provide a minimum deposit, which will be from $20,000 to $100,000. You'll also have to show why you want to bank in that jurisdiction, and prove that you aren't a criminal, terrorist or money launderer. The bank will want a lot of paperwork and someone to vouch for you.

For these reasons, the best way to open a foreign bank account nowadays is to go through a local professional contact — like the ones I'll list at the end of this report — who specializes in helping U.S. citizens with local banking.

For example, we have contacts throughout Latin America and the Caribbean, Europe and East Asia who can help you open a bank account for a fee. This fee basically pays for the good reputation the contact has with the local banking system ... because without it, you won't get your account ... and helps pay for preparation of the paperwork involved in regulatory compliance.

If you go this route, you may be able to open the account remotely, but it is possible that you'll need to visit the country at least once, so the bank manager can "eyeball" you, and to sign various documents. Remember, the single most important thing to a foreign banker considering a prospective American client is to know that the costs and benefits of the relationship are right for the bank.

No matter how you apply, you'll be asked to provide the following:

1. A notarized copy of your passport and possibly other ID documents.
2. A recent utility bill that confirms the details of your permanent home address.
3. A reference letter from your domestic bank letterhead, or on a form provided by the offshore bank, stating you are a reliable customer.
4. A professional letter of reference from a lawyer or accountant in the U.S.
5. A letter describing the source of funds you will deposit initially and subsequently, and your projected banking patterns.
6. An IRS Form W-9, which allows the bank to share information with the IRS and, in some cases, acts as a waiver of the foreign country's bank secrecy laws.

Remember, no matter how much effort this seems to be, it's nothing compared to the risks associated with keeping all your wealth in U.S. banks ... where it's threatened by lawyers, currency collapse, and wealth confiscation.

Option 2: An Offshore Entity and Bank Account

A less direct approach to offshore banking is to create an offshore legal entity, such as a trust or limited liability company (LLC), and have it open a foreign bank account (or more than one) in its own name.

Again, it is critical to go through a trusted contact who knows U.S. law and has all the contacts required to open and manage the entity and its bank accounts … as I'll show you below.

Now, you may have seen offers for such arrangements on the Internet. **Don't use them.** There are plenty of scams out there that promise to get you a foreign LLC and offshore banking facilities cheaply and entirely online, but that's just not good enough for me. It is critical to talk to an actual person who can assess your situation and needs, and give you the best possible solution for both asset protection and investment growth. Mistakes can be costly.

Here are two legitimate, safe offshore entity options that you can set up at relatively low cost through my own trusted contacts.

OFFSHORE LIMITED LIABILITY COMPANY

A limited liability company (LLC) is a separate legal entity that you create and own, which in turn can own anything you give or sell to it. That includes cash and other financial instruments. The basic principle of the LLC is the same as for any corporation: There is a legal "veil" between you and the LLC, shielding you and it from legal action against the other party.

An offshore LLC can own foreign bank accounts using money that you place under the LLC. The LLC's accounts — there can be more than one — can be in many different currencies, in different jurisdictions.

These accounts don't have to be in the same country as the LLC itself.

Because they involve specialist assistance to set up, an offshore LLC can therefore be a shortcut to an offshore bank account. The attorney who sets up the LLC can open the bank account for you at the same time, and handle much of the paperwork the foreign bank would have to do under FATCA, for a consolidated fee. Like the personal contacts you need to open up a personal account, such attorneys have longstanding relationships with foreign banks, and can open a foreign account under the LLC's name with relatively small initial deposits. The attorney will then appoint an LLC "manager" in the foreign jurisdiction to act as its local representative for regulatory purposes, for a few hundred dollars a year.

Besides its low cost — it can be done for under $3,000 — the great advantage of an LLC is that you can operate it yourself just as you would your own accounts. As long as you follow certain basic procedures that the attorney who sets it up will explain, you can access the foreign bank accounts of an offshore LLC the same way as if it were a personal account — debit and credit cards, online banking and so on.

Choice of jurisdiction for an LLC is crucial, since the specific legal framework shapes asset protection. Nearby jurisdictions with good LLC laws include Nevis (part of St. Kitts and Nevis in the Caribbean), Panama and Belize. Of the three, Nevis provides the best value for money — you can get started for only a few thousand dollars — although if you want to create a bank account in the same jurisdiction as the LLC, Panama would be my preference, given the robustness of its domestic banking system.

OFFSHORE ASSET PROTECTION TRUSTS

A trust is a three-way legal device recognized in many countries' legal systems — many more than the LLC, which is a relatively recent legal development. The person who creates the trust (the grantor) decides what the trust will do, and donates property to fund it. The "trustee" takes ownership of that property, to be held and managed for the benefit of other persons (the beneficiaries). It's more complex than an LLC, but can open up even more banking opportunities than the former, since the legal "distance" between a trust and its grantors and beneficiaries is much greater than in an LLC.

Like an LLC, a foreign asset-protection trust (APT) can be used as an offshore banking platform with its own bank accounts in a variety of nations. Unlike an LLC, however, the grantor of an APT generally cannot access and manage the trust's assets directly, including its bank accounts. Trust law is quite strict about ownership and control, and violating it can make the trust invalid.

On the other hand, the trust's beneficiaries — say, your spouse and kids — can access the trust's ac-counts directly, as long as the terms of the trust deed allow them to do so.

An APT is a good bet when you have significant amounts to move offshore and you want to grow your wealth for your retirement, or for your family's inheritance. Besides bank accounts, an APT can own other foreign legal vehicles like an LLC, or financial contracts like offshore annuities. Good jurisdictions for APTs include the Cook Islands, Panama, Nevis, Belize and various British dependencies.

My personal favorite is the "Savvy Trust," a specialized product developed by my contacts in the U.S. and the Cook Islands, which can be created for as little as $5,000.

One critical thing about both LLCs and APTs is their strong asset protection features. If someone sues you in a U.S. court, the money in your LLC's or APT's foreign bank accounts isn't just in a foreign country ... it isn't even yours. That means a huge extra-legal step for any litigant, discouraging most before they even try.

There's one more benefit: Having accounts in the name of an LLC or APT means your name isn't on the bank's record on the account. Now, foreign banks are still going to want to know who the "beneficial owner" of the LLC or APT actually is, and they will still have to report on that account to the IRS under the terms of FATCA. But it does give you vastly increased privacy vis-à-vis private parties.

Option 3: An Independent Asset Manager

An offshore bank account, with or without an offshore entity, definitely offers stronger asset protection than a domestic account. But another major plus of an offshore account is the direct path it offers for more diverse and potentially more profitable investments offshore. A foreign account can be used to invest directly in foreign stock markets and other venues that simply aren't available to U.S.-based investment accounts.

Of course, investing offshore in this way on your own would require you to become an expert in foreign markets and operate like a day-trader. But that's not necessary. An independent asset manager (IAM) can be a useful route to offshore banking.

An IAM is a private advisor — often a former employee of a big Swiss or other European bank — who specializes in helping U.S. clients set up and operate offshore investment accounts. In fact, IAMs can help you in two ways: by facilitating the creation of an investment account at a foreign bank and by managing the investments themselves.

IAMs aren't tied to particular banks. They are tied to their client, i.e. you. An IAM provides personalized service, and can get you accounts at banks that normally don't deal with Americans directly.

You can expect two tiers of service from IAMs. Typically, an IAM will set up an offshore account that is invested into a portfolio based on your funding and risk threshold. For lower amounts — say, $100,000 — they will be standardized portfolios with limited options. At higher levels, (usually starting at $500,000), a personal portfolio manager will custom-tailor a bespoke investment solution suited to your specific needs.

This flexibility is critical. Because they are independent, IAMs can create portfolios that have gold-only stocks or bonds only, for example, depending on your needs and wishes. They don't have to "push" what's on someone's sell list for any given day. IAMs also get to know you on a personal level — a good one often calls each client at the end of every quarter, tells them how their investments have performed in the past months, and shares what their vision is for the next quarter.

In order to play their role safely and legally, the IAMs I work with register with the U.S. Security and Exchange Commission. In order to qualify to become a registered SEC investment adviser under Section 202(a)(11) of the Investment

Advisers Act of 1940, IAMs must "tell all" in writing ... providing complete transparency for you. It also means IAMs can prepare and file the U.S. tax statements needed for IRS filings.

Reporting

Whether you have a personal bank account, an offshore LLC with a bank account, or an investment account manager by an IAM, you are legally obligated to report this account under FBAR and FATCA (Form 8938). For FBAR, you meet the reporting threshold if:

1. You had a financial interest in or signature authority over at least one financial account located outside of the United States; and

2. The aggregate value of all foreign financial accounts exceeded $10,000 at any time during the calendar year to be reported.

For FATCA, the threshold is different:

1. If you live in the U.S. and have foreign accounts you must file a FATCA report if the total value of all of your foreign accounts exceeds $50,000 ($100,000 for couples) on the last day of the year, or exceeded $75,000 ($150,000) at any time during the year.

2. If you live abroad, the FATCA reporting threshold is $200,000 ($400,000 for couples) on the last day of the tax year, or more than $300,000 ($600,000) at any time during the tax year.

Remember, these thresholds refer to your accounts at foreign banks ... not foreign PLUS U.S. bank accounts.

But What About Costs?

Every option I've presented here has its own cost structure.

It's important to be aware that the fees at offshore banks are higher than those for similar U.S.-based accounts. While fees vary bank to bank, based on the amount of assets under management and the amount of your personal account, the fees and commissions you should anticipate paying offshore are estimated below:

- Currency conversion fees: 0.1% to 0.5%

- Trading commissions: 0.15% or more for each bond trade and 0.3% or more for each stock purchase. Commissions on precious metals are around 1%.

- Custodian/Safekeeping fees: To accommodate for administrative costs such as providing account statements, in-house research, collecting dividends on your securities, etc., you may be charged between 0.25% and 0.5% per year.

- Portfolio management fees: Should you elect to have your money invested by a professional at the bank, the typical portfolio management fee is 1% per year on the total amount of the account, excluding fees or commissions for trades on the account. You may qualify for a reduction in the portfolio management fee depending on the size of your account.

Find the Safe Haven That's Right for You ... Right Now!

My old friend Zannos had it easy. He had money in Greece, which is part of the European Union (at least as I write!), so he could have moved his euros to another bank effortlessly ... say, Austria or Luxembourg. And he had plenty of warning: from me.

You, on the other hand, have to do a little legwork and planning to put your wealth into a safe haven abroad, with stable currencies, stable policies and stable banks. But you can ... and should ... do it, as soon as possible, using the guidelines I've given here.

You never know when the U.S. dollar is going to collapse ... or special taxes are levied by the IRS ... or a lawsuit lands on your doorstep. The contacts provided will help you navigate the obstacles the international banking system set up so that you can effectively protect your wealth.

Like Zannos, you've had warning from me. But you're also getting something more than I could give him ... the accumulated experience and expert advice of the people I've met since those days, including some of the world's foremost offshore asset managers, attorneys, trust managers and bankers.

So what are you waiting for? Let's go offshore!

Refer to Appendix A for a listing of Offshore Banking contacts.

FAMILY FOUNDATIONS: LOCK YOUR ASSETS IN THE SAFEST, PRIVATE VAULT — AND KEEP THE KEY
Robert E. Bauman JD, November 2014

Secure Your Financial Future Permanently with a Strategy So Powerful You May Never Need Another

Your future and the future of your family are in danger. The war on terror, the largest budget deficit in U.S. history and increasing taxes amounting to wealth confiscation are threatening to destroy everything you worked so hard to preserve.

Even your privacy is compromised every day. Government snoops at the National Security Agency (NSA), the FBI and even local police, now are looking at your phone calls, emails, online trans-actions, banking activity, purchasing habits and travel history. In a claimed effort to discover and arrest terrorists, the U.S. government has resorted to massive spying on all Americans, profiling with secret "no-fly" lists and seizing allegedly suspicious property — cash, investments, homes, cars, and bank accounts.

This whole mess is dangerously reminiscent of Soviet Communism or even Hitler's Germany.

Never has it been more important to protect yourself and your wealth by "going offshore" with your assets by investing in foreign stocks, bonds, funds and currencies. But it's not enough to acquire a solid, foreign portfolio — you also need to shield and protect your investments.

The rich and famous have been successfully and secretly protecting their wealth for generations. It was once thought this practice was *only* for those with bulging bank accounts, a yacht, an exotic motor car collection and multiple homes. That may have been the case long ago, but now protecting what's yours isn't just for the wealthy. There is a very affordable option overseas you can take advantage of right now — whether you're a millionaire or not.

This unique strategy dates back to the Roman Empire and the early Catholic Church, but only in the last 80 years has it become one of the most effective ways to safeguard your assets for yourself and for future generations. In these pages you'll learn exactly what this strategy is, what it could mean for your portfolio and why you may well want to use its proven ability to protect and defend your wealth.

This unique legal entity is known as called a "family foundation" or a "private interest foundation."

We'll explain why this solution could erase threats to your financial future, and we'll describe the two best countries where you can establish your foundation for a cost less than you might think.

Traditionally in the United States, a "foundation" conjures up an image of a tax exempt, non-profit charitable entity with tax deductions for donations to churches or other philanthropic organizations — think Rockefeller or Ford. You could almost call the family foundation we are discussing here a charity as well. It is similar in the way it is formed and managed, but to be more accurate you would have to say that this foundation is a "charity" for you and your family — and far from non-profit.

The secret power of a private foundation is that all assets transferred to it become the property of the foundation. Should a lawsuit be filed against you personally, assets within your foundation cannot be touched by claims or law suits because those assets are no longer in your name. More about that later, but first let's start at the beginning, the origins of foundations, how they developed and why they have become one of the safest, most private ways to build and protect your wealth.

History of the Last Word in Asset Protection

Conceived in ancient Rome, the prototype of the family foundation was created by the Catholic Church. These first "foundations" were created and designed to administer the Church's wealth for the benefit of the religious community. The idea that a foundation could be used to benefit individuals or specific families did not surface for many centuries until the Principality of Liechtenstein changed the concept, creating the modern foundation.

On January 20, 1926, Liechtenstein enacted the Law on Persons and Companies or *Personen-und Gesellschaft Recht* (P.G.R.). The law took the Roman idea of a foundation and fashioned it into a most effective private interest device. Thus was born the family foundation, a special vehicle for the benefit of one or more families linked by blood or marriage.

A foundation is a hybrid, successful cross between a trust and a corporation. It can hold title to any real or personal property — cars, homes, stocks, bonds or investments.

Once formed, a foundation takes on its own separate personality and becomes an active legal entity. Everything a foundation acquires becomes its property — to invest and distribute profits as originally outlined by the founder.

Here are the structural parts of a foundation

- *The founder* (or founders) — establishes the foundation using the services of an attorney. Only the deed that creates the foundation is registered with the government and it may only contain the name of the foundation's attorney and council members (see below). The founder and beneficiaries can remain secret. The founder does not manage or control the foundation directly. He simply forms it for the beneficiaries he chooses and the founder can also be a beneficiary.
- *The council* — manages the foundation and its members can be chosen by the founder. In a company this council would be similar to the board of directors. The members of the council can be replaced at the discretion of the protector.
- *The protector* — controls the foundation and its assets. The protector is appointed by the council when the foundation is formed and, once appointed, has the power to replace council members or beneficiaries at will. The protector should be a trusted family member, since total control is in his hands. This process allows the founder, to maintain control over the foundation through the protector — privately and anonymously — since the protector carries out

the founder's wishes. Since the protector is appointed by the council, he or she can be removed and replaced by the council, usually in consultation with the founder whose representative he is.

- *Beneficiaries* — are chosen and described by the founder formally in the foundation bylaws. The beneficiaries can be designated to receive all or any part of the foundation income or assets at any time. Only the founder and any family member related by blood or marriage can be a beneficiary. That a foundation's beneficiaries must be related by blood or marriage is an important difference from a trust, where the grantor can designate any beneficiaries or groups of beneficiaries he or she wishes.

- *Bylaws* — are a formal statement of the purpose, investment objectives and beneficiaries of the foundation. Should the protector die or become incapacitated, the bylaws also provide for the foundation's continuance or dissolution.

- *A letter of wishes* — is an express indication by the founder of the manner in which he or she wishes the protector to exercise discretion in relation to investments, beneficiaries and other matters.

International Business Company

When searching for an asset protection device with the greatest protective power, privacy and investment flexibility are a top priority. There are many different legal entities that claim to be best. But which should you choose? One of the more popular choices is an international business company (IBC). As with a trust, there are advantages and disadvantages to having an offshore company.

The use of an offshore IBC is usually recommended if you are engaged in an active business outside your home country. In Panama, for example, you can form an IBC at a cost of less than $1000, with annual maintenance costs even lower. More importantly for privacy, the IBC can be formed by nominee directors who hold the organizing meeting and turn over control to you. There is no requirement that the true beneficial owners be listed in public. IBCs are not as good a tool for asset protection as a foundation or trust, since the IBC is liable for its debts. Corporate beneficial ownership need only be disclosed to the attorney creating the IBC. That information is not made public unless a Panamanian court orders disclosure based on illegal corporate activities.

Panama has a territorial tax system. So long as your Panama IBC conducts its activities outside Panama and does no business within the nation (except minimal housekeeping chores), you are completely free of Panamanian taxes. Your home nation may have tax and other reporting requirements with which you must comply if you have an IBC. For example, if a U.S. person controls an offshore IBC or a bank account that must be reported to the IRS annually. Payments from an offshore IBC must be reported to the IRS as annual income by you as controlling owner. But an offshore IBC may also allow payment of legitimate travel and business expenses, deferral of certain home nation taxes and it shelters your business from home country law suits.

You should know that there are some unwelcome U.S. tax consequences to having an offshore IBC, so you should check with an expert tax attorney before you act to create an offshore IBC.

Beware of the IRS — *"Per Se"* List

For U.S. persons who control the shares in a foreign corporation there are major limitations on U.S. tax benefits that would otherwise be available to a corporation formed in the United States. That is because the foreign corporation may be on what is known as the IRS "per se" list of foreign corporations, which appears in IRS regulations, section 301.7701-2(b)(8)(i).

The listed per se corporations are barred from numerous U.S. tax benefits. This means that U.S. persons cannot file an IRS Form 8832 electing to treat the corporation as a "disregarded entity" or a foreign partnership, either of which is given much more favorable tax treatment.

Under IRS rules, the foreign corporation that engages in passive investments is considered a "con-trolled foreign corporation," which requires the filing of IRS Form 5471 describing its operations.

U.S. persons also must file IRS Form 926 reporting transfers of cash or assets to the corporation.

A U.S. person who controls a foreign financial account of any nature that has a balance of $10,000 or more at any time during a calendar year must report this to the IRS on Form TD F 90-22.1. There are serious fines and penalties for failure to file these IRS returns and criminal charges can also be imposed. As a general rule, U.S. persons can be guilty of the crime of "falsifying a federal income tax return" by failing to report offshore corporate holdings.

Any eventual capital gains an IRS-listed per se corporation may make are not taxed in the U.S. under the more favorable capital gains tax rate of 15%, but rather as ordinary income for the corporate owners, which can be much higher. There is also the possibility of double taxation if the foreign corporation makes investments in the U.S., in which case there is a 30% U.S. withholding tax on the investment income. Under U.S. tax rules, no annual losses can be taken on corporate investments, which must be deferred by the U.S. owners until the foreign corporation is liquidated.

However, compared to these IRS restrictions, there may be offsetting considerations, such as complete exemption from foreign taxes, which may be more important in your financial planning. Therefore, it is extremely important that U.S. persons obtain an authoritative review of the tax implications before forming a foreign corporation for any purpose, including holding title to personal or business real estate.

As you can readily see from this discussion, an IBC is far different than a family foundation and has far different objectives, the least of which is asset protection, something a foundation does allow.

Strength of a Trust — Flexibility of an IBC

A foundation combines the most useful aspects of both a trust and a corporation. It melds both entities together and makes the sum better than its parts.

- As with a trust, foundation assets are not in your name. Unlike a trust, you, not a trustee, maintain a high degree of control over the assets and you can be a beneficiary of the foundation.
- As with a trust, the jurisdiction in which you locate your foundation may not acknowledge foreign judgments.
- As with a company, a foundation will keep your assets private, but unlike a company or partnership, a foundation need not be dissolved if a party dies.
- As with a trust, a foundation will shield virtually all of your assets offshore.
- As with a company, you have control over the distribution of your assets.

The Principality of Liechtenstein and the Republic of Panama

While the laws of the Unites States do recognize foreign legal entities such as the family foundation, the foundation must be formed in a country whose laws permit foundations. Several countries now permit foundations but two principal counties are leaders. There are some minor variations between the foundation laws in the two countries which might make a difference when it comes time for you to choose an appropriate home for your foundation.

The Principality of Liechtenstein

We've already mentioned Liechtenstein, a country that is managed like a family business. Prince Hans Adam, the absolute monarch, and his son, Prince Alois, know what it takes to make a business, and a small country, succeed.

Liechtenstein is perhaps the safest haven in which to set up a foundation, where it is known in the local German as a *Stiftung*. It was here that the modern family foundation was invented and perfected. But it's also the most expensive. Foundation creation costs are about US$25,000 in legal fees. A 2011 revised tax law eliminated inheritance and gift taxes. To establish a foundation in Liechtenstein, there is formation tax based on the original capital contribution paid into the foundation or a minimum of CHF30'000 Swiss francs (US$31,000). The formation tax is 0.2 per cent of the original capital contribution or a minimum of CHF200 (US$207.00). In addition, there is a registration fee. The majority of Liechtenstein foundations are established by foreigners and do not require registration.

The law in Liechtenstein is based on the Napoleonic "civil law," also called Romano-Germanic law, as compared with the English/American "common law" system. The common law was developed in England from judicial decisions based on customs and precedent, constituting the basis of the present English, British Commonwealth, and U.S. legal systems. Liechtenstein has a unique system which blends both civil and common law in many respects and allows foreigners to choose the national law they wish to apply to the legal entities they created there, in so far as it is applicable.

Liechtenstein's concept of a foundation is unique. Although Americans associate the idea of a foundation with a non-profit, tax-exempt organization, in Liechtenstein a foundation is an autonomous fund consisting of assets endowed by the founder(s) for a specific, usually non-commercial purpose.

The purpose can be very broad in scope, including religious and charitable goals. One of the more common uses is as a so-called "pure family foundation." These vehicles are dedicated to the financial management and personal welfare of one or more particular families as beneficiaries. The foundation and a beneficiary's interest therein cannot be assigned, sold, or attached by personal creditors.

The foundation has no shareholders, partners, owners, or members — it has only beneficiaries. It can either be limited in time or perpetual. This means that the founder can direct in the bylaws whether the foundation is to exist for a limited time ("until the deaths of all of my children") or "in perpetuity", meaning the foundation will continue forever.

Only foundation assets are liable for its debts. The governing board can consist of one or more persons or entities, at least one of whom must be a resident of Liechtenstein. The founder(s) name(s) need not be made public. Foundations may be created by the execution of a written document called a "deed," under the terms of a founder's last will and testament, or by a common written agreement among family members. Local Liechtenstein taxes on a foundation are low and are based on the total amount of paid-in capital and are payable on an annual basis. Actual creation of a foundation is accomplished by registering the foundation document with the Public Register in Vaduz or in Panama at the corporate registry.

The Republic of Panama

In 1995, Panama adopted the Liechtenstein foundation in its laws but made it more affordable. There you can create a foundation for about US$10,000 fee and a local annual tax of $250. In Panama there is an initial registration fee of US$250.

Panama has become a leader in blending common law and civil law legal entities, giving their clients an advantage. In keeping with this trend is Law 25 (1995) that created a "private interest foundation" statute, modeled after the popular family wealth protection and estate planning vehicle originated in and long used in the Principality of Liechtenstein.

Under Law 25, a Panama private interest foundation can be a highly flexible tool for estate planning. Unlike a trust, it does not require the founder to surrender management of donated and earned foundation assets but it does provide a high degree of asset protection.

When used for the benefit of the founder and his family, the Panama foundation is rather like a discretionary asset protection trust, and is generally referred to as a "family foundation." This tax-free family foundation can be used for investment, tax sheltering, commercial business share ownership, and private activity, with the founder retaining lifetime control of the foundation and its assets. Foundation assets are managed by a council named by the founder and have the duty to accomplish the objectives stated in the foundation by-laws.

Considered as a legal entity, the foundation acts in many respects like a trust, but operates like a corporation, although it cannot engage directly in business. Although its purpose cannot be commercial profit, the foundation can own assets, such as shares in active companies, which do generate profits.

The Taxman Cometh

"There is nothing sinister in arranging one's affairs so as to keep taxes as low as possible... nobody owes any public duty to pay more than the law demands. Taxes are enforced exactions — not voluntary contributions." —Hon. Learned Hand, Judge of the U.S. Court of Appeals, New York, *IRS Commissioner v. Newman*, 159 F2d 848, 851 (2nd Cir 1947)

Notwithstanding the many benefits of an offshore family foundation, for Americans there are important tax and reporting requirements imposed by law. This is a major reason why you must have competent American professional legal and tax advice before and after you form your foundation. You also need the same professional advice in the country where you locate your foundation. Get all this advice before you sign anything.

Keep in mind that Americans are taxed on all income earned anywhere in the world. Moving offshore or having offshore legal entities does not avoid that tax obligation, or the requirement to file reports. Indeed, there is very little in the way of tax savings offshore for Americans.

What follows here is only a general guide and should be treated as such. In order to assure absolute compliance with the tax law you must consult with the professionals described above.

First, you need to understand the difference between legal tax "avoidance" and illegal tax "evasion." With the muddled U.S. Internal Revenue Code there is often a fine line between the two. Evasion can be something as obvious as willful failure to file tax returns and reports, or even an innocent omission of a required form or report. Therefore, we cannot stress enough the importance of getting expert U.S. tax advice at every turn. These reporting requirements have become even more complicated because of the 2011 Foreign Account Tax Compliance Act (FATCA) that applies to all U.S. bank and other financial accounts held by UI.S. persons.

Because a family foundation has aspects of both a trust and a corporation, U.S tax law allows an option of having it taxed as whichever is most advantageous at lowering taxes. It is generally agreed that electing to have a foundation taxed as a trust is more beneficial.

U.S. tax rules state that a founder must pay taxes on annual income received by the foundation regardless of whether it is distributed during the tax year. This foundation income is reported on the founder's IRS Form 1040. Certain other IRS reports must be filed by the foundation itself, so consult your U.S. tax advisor to be certain you and your foundation are in compliance.

U.S. Tax Implications

Under U.S. tax law and IRS rules unless a foreign foundation is used exclusively for charitable purposes, it is classified as one of the following: 1) a trust; 2) an association taxable as a corporation; 3) a partnership; or 4) a disregarded entity. This classification determines the tax reporting requirements for a U.S. founder of an offshore foundation.

Once it is determined that an organization formed by one or more persons is classified as an entity for U.S. tax purposes, what is called "check the box" entity classification IRS rules apply. If the entity is an "eligible entity," it may be necessary to file an IRS Form 8832 in order to choose the U.S. tax classification most advantageous for the foundation. The Panamanian foundation, if classified as a business entity and not a trust, will qualify for U.S. tax classification purposes, as a partnership, corporation, or a disregarded entity. If entity classification is not selected by filing Form 8832 for an eligible entity, then "default" classification rules apply.

As you can, there are numerous drafting and tax issues to be consider when creating a foundation. Once again, we strongly advise that you first consult with a qualified tax attorney or accountant in your home country in order to determine your own potential national tax liabilities.

Set It and Forget It — A Solid Foundation to Build Your Future

We have discussed the history, details and benefits of establishing a family foundation. Let's quickly review:

- The family foundation concept began in the early Catholic Church and was used to transfer inheritances among Roman citizens
- Liechtenstein adopted the concept into law and applied it to families
- Panama copied the Liechtenstein law adding its own refinements
- The foundation has become a popular asset protection and estate planning vehicles for wealthy people in the know

If you've decided to create a family foundation, refer to Appendix A for a list of recommended professional contacts.

LAWYER-PROOF YOUR PROPERTIES
Ted Bauman, *Sovereign Confidential*, July 2015

I like to bowl tenpins. It's an old-school activity that's starting to make a comeback in the U.S., thanks to the "hipster" generation's reverence for everything "vintage."

But cultural cachet isn't the reason I like bowling. And I'm not sure I qualify as vintage just yet.

I like it because I like throwing things. I enjoy knocking things down, blowing them up or shooting them full of holes. Maybe it's a male thing. Whatever the reason, since my rural childhood on Maryland's Eastern Shore, where I could indulge such habits, I've been partial to knocking things into other things.

Bowling has a special attraction, though, because of the physics involved. Your target is a collection of disconnected objects. If you hit the pins the right way, the first ones to fall topple other ones. A strike is a sequence of events in which a single blow causes an entire set to collapse.

Now, when it comes to your real estate holdings . . . would you rather be the ball or a pin? Are your properties just pins sitting at the end of an alley waiting for another pin to knock them down?

Without a properly designed asset protection plan, they may well be.

The Hidden Risks of Property

In discussions with *Sovereign Confidential* subscribers by email, at our conferences or on one of our special calls, I've learned that many people have invested much of their wealth in U.S. real estate.

Indeed, real estate is one of the safest long-term investments you can make — they don't say "safe as houses" for nothing — and there have been opportunities galore to acquire it cheaply since the financial meltdown of 2008.

I have taken advantage of those opportunities myself. I bought one house for about $15,000 that's now worth a quarter of a million, and another that has tripled in value in just four years.

A typical property portfolio might include one's home, a vacation home, a parcel or two of undeveloped land and perhaps some houses and/or apartments put out to rent.

Such a portfolio generates wealth by value appreciation on some properties, and boosts your current income by rentals and the associated tax write-offs.

Whatever your personal strategy, the value of your property probably constitutes a big chunk of your net worth.

And every one of those properties is a bowling pin poised to get knocked down, and it will take the others down with it — such as your vacation home, or even your retirement savings — when that bowling ball comes rolling down the lane.

What is that bowling ball? A real estate crash? A natural disaster? A fire?

None of the above . . . I'm talking about a lawsuit.

One lawsuit can ruin a person's life. And they are a very real threat.

In his book, *Lawyer-Proof Your Life*, my father Bob Bauman states that 70% of the world's attorneys are located right here in the United States. The numbers are staggering: Every day 41,095 Americans are hit with a lawsuit. That means that every hour of every day, over 1,700 people are being sued.

But here's the great news.

There are simple steps you can take right now to prevent your properties from toppling over. You just have to put a plan in place. And you need to do it immediately, if you haven't already done so.

As the saying goes, once the horse has bolted, closing the barn door will make no difference.

I can't stress this enough, if you have assets of any reasonable size or no assets at all — you need to act now. Let me show you why.

If Frank Lost Everything, So Can You

Based on the figures above, you have a 10% chance of being sued in any given year. One year it was Frank's turn.

Frank inherited some farm and other property from his dad, acquired some during his career in the Navy and bought some more when he retired. He was in the habit of buying a house to live in when stationed for a few years in places like Hawaii, Southern California or Norfolk, then rent them out to fellow officers when he was reassigned. That way he augmented his service income and built a nest-egg for his retirement and his kids' future.

As a landlord, Frank was legally expected to take "reasonable care" to ensure that his properties were safe and secure from "foreseeable" threats to tenants. That wasn't always easy to do, especially when he was on sea duty. Sure enough, during a cruise to the Persian Gulf, a guest of one of his tenants — a civilian — was injured when a set of wooden basement stairs collapsed, resulting in the amputation of one leg above the knee.

The guest sued, and Frank was held personally liable for his medical costs and damages … all because of some rotting wood. The damages award significantly exceeded the value of the house in question, and the court ordered that several of his other houses and some of his pension funds be liquidated as well.

"Reasonable care." "Foreseeable threat." Terms like those are catnip to trial lawyers — those guys who set up billboards on highways to drum up business and have phone numbers like 1-800-INJURED. If a plaintiff's attorney can convince a jury that you've failed to exercise reasonable care — that you've been "negligent" in looking after your property — you're in big trouble.

Like Frank.

A Personalized Asset Protection Strategy

To beat this threat, savvy property investors adopt an asset protection strategy.

Imagine a scenario where that bowling ball comes flying down the lane, but the pins are shielded from each other. It's as if there were a force field between each of them and the others. The most that can be knocked down is one pin — and is some cases, it's nearly impossible to knock any of the pins down no matter how well the ball is bowled.

With the right asset protection strategy, that scenario can be very real.

An asset protection strategy involves legal techniques to shield your wealth from creditors' claims and lawsuits. It's based on three principles:

1. **Segregate yourself from your assets.** You want an impermeable "veil" between you and your assets. Your property should be held in a legal structure that you

control, not in your own name. That way they can't be touched to enforce any claim against you as an individual. And any claims against your property — like Frank's house with the dodgy basement steps — can't harm your personal assets.

2. **Be hard to find (legally speaking).** Your asset protection structure should be registered and operated in such a way that your ownership of it is hard to discover without prohibitive expense and effort. That will discourage frivolous lawsuits. Complete anonymity is impossible, but the harder it is to find you, the more money a lawyer will require upfront from a litigant looking to sue you.

3. **Match your strategy to the circumstances.** There's no one-size fits all. If you're primarily interested in protecting U.S.-based real estate from lawsuits, a U.S. legal vehicle is just as effective as an offshore one.

Remember, even if you vest ownership of your property in the name of an offshore asset protection trust or company, U.S. real estate will always be vulnerable to seizure from U.S. courts because it sits on U.S. soil.

Your Solution: Form a Limited Liability Company (But Not Just Any LLC)

One inexpensive and easy-to-achieve U.S.-based strategy is the Limited Liability Corporation (LLC).

An LLC is like any corporation. It has a separate legal identity from its owners. Any liabilities incurred by the LLC are for it alone, and do not pass on to you, the owner. If an LLC is sued, the most a claimant can get is the net value of the LLC — its assets minus its liabilities. And even that can be incredibly difficult for a creditor to achieve.

LLCs can be formed in most U.S. states. Property anywhere in the U.S. can be owned by any LLC in any state — they don't have to be the same state. A vacation home in Florida, for example, can be vested in the name of an LLC formed in Wyoming. Since LLC laws vary from state to state, that allows you to shop around for the best mixture of asset protection, cost and privacy.

One of the most attractive features of LLCs is that many states offer what's known as "charging order" approach to lawsuits against owners of LLCs. A court in a state that offers only the charging order remedy prevents the member of the LLC from losing the investment assets within the LLC if he or she gets sued personally. A charging order is basically a lien on the sued member's interest, but one that only comes into play if funds are distributed out of the LLC. If that happens, the holder of the charging order is entitled to the grab the distribution. But charging orders don't allow the holder to participate in the LLC to force the distribution. That way assets held in an LLC can be held safely indefinitely — which is powerful disincentive to sue someone to get what's in their LLC.

Some property investors rely on landlord's insurance to protect them, thinking it can protect them against a lawsuit. That is false. Landlord insurance covers claims only up to a certain amount, but an LLC can't be held liable for anything over and above the value of its own assets. And an LLC is actually cheaper in many cases than comparable insurance coverage.

LLCs are much better than landlord's insurance for protecting against liability arising from the property inside the LLC, too, as in Frank's case.

Consider the case of one couple I know personally, who rented out a property and were hit with a lawsuit when a workman hired by his tenants — without their knowledge or consent — was killed when a garden retaining wall collapsed on him. They were in the mid-30s, with two young kids, living a few years on the west coast for work reasons, and renting out their home here in Atlanta in the meantime.

The couple had a landlord policy that included $1 million in liability coverage. That cost them $1,500 a year. They had $2 million in umbrella liability insurance for an additional $600 a year, taking their total liability coverage up to $3 million, at a cost of $2,100 a year.

But the workman's family sued successfully for $5 million.

Because of this, the couple not only lost their property — they were forced to sell their own home and to liquidate a large proportion of their retirement savings as well. An LLC structure, on the other hand, would have forced the plaintiff's attorney to settle for the value of the property at most. And it would have cost them only a few hundred dollars a year.

An LLC . . . Warren Buffett Style

But there's a scenario that even the ordinary LLC can't prevent. If your properties are like a set of bowling pins — all housed under one LLC — you could lose them all in the event of a large lawsuit against any one of them.

That's because there's nothing to stop a court from ordering the liquidation of any property held in an LLC's name to satisfy a judgement against it . . . even if the property had nothing to do with the judgement in question.

For example, if Frank had had all of his properties in a single LLC, the judge could have attached his other properties to settle the guest's claim against the one property that injured him. The only advantage of an LLC in this case would have been that Frank's personal pension would be safe, since it was shielded by the legal "veil" between him and the LLC.

One way to prevent this scenario would be to form and maintain a separate LLC to hold each property in your portfolio. That way only the assets owned by a specific LLC would be subject to claims or lawsuits arising against that LLC.

The problem is that the costs and administrative burdens associated with properly forming, registering and maintaining several separate LLCs can be substantial. Here are the things you have to do for each LLC in any state:

- Choose an available business name that complies with state LLC rules.

- File paperwork with the Secretary of State, usually called "Articles of Organization," and pay a filing fee (ranging from a few hundred to about a thousand dollars).

- Appoint and compensate someone resident in the state where you form your LLC who can receive official communications — the "operating agent." This is often the attorney who helps you set it up.

- Appoint "members" to the LLC — the people who control it. This is usually you and one or two other people you trust completely, such as a spouse, attorney or relative. (You can have a single-member LLC, but many courts disregard these when it comes to personal liability, so I don't advise it.)

- Create and file an LLC "Operating Agreement," which sets out the rights and responsibilities of the LLC members.

- File annual regulatory reports and state and federal tax forms, and comply with other state and federal regulatory requirements as needed.

For one LLC, that's not such a big deal. But for three, four, even six . . . that's a lot of expense, paperwork and hassle. For example, if you formed a single LLC that owned a number of other LLCs — so called "parent and subsidiary" set-ups — you'd still have to do all the paperwork associated with each LLC.

But there's a special type of LLC that functions like a the portfolio holding company, where an umbrella firm like Berkshire Hathaway owns others that are legally independent and do not share liability. You can put Warren Buffet's strategy to work for you.

That's because some states allow you to form an LLC that has multiple "series." Each "series" can own distinct assets, incur separate liabilities and have different managers and members. A series LLC pays a single annual state fee and often files one set of official reports each year.

Most importantly, liability incurred by one series doesn't cross over and jeopardize assets titled in or allocated to other series of the same series LLC. A lawsuit brought by a tenant of one property cannot threaten other properties under other series — even though they are owned by the same LLC. In Frank's, his properties would have been like bowling pins with a force field around each of them.

The legal doctrine of "limited internal liability" provides that the debts, liabilities, obligations and expenses relating to a particular series — whether contractual or in relation to lawsuits — are enforceable against the assets of that series only, and not against the assets of the LLC or any other series, on two conditions:

1. The Operating Agreement of the LLC includes an "enabling statement" allowing series; and
2. Separate and distinct records are maintained for the series, and the assets of the series are held and accounted for separately from the other assets of the LLC and any other series.

The series LLC sounds radical, but it's really just an extension of standard legal practices in the corporate sector. The basic concept was first introduced to help the mutual fund industry avoid filing multiple Securities and Exchange Commission (SEC) filings for different classes of funds. SEC filings would all be under one corporate umbrella, but each individual fund's activities could still be conducted separately — separate profits, separate losses.

Your LLC Pays No Tax

What about taxes?

If you own 100% of your series LLC and each series is owned 100% by the LLC, with no partners, you can treat each series as a "pass-through" or "disregarded" entity. That means the LLC and its constituent series pay no income tax directly, although they do have to submit a federal return. Instead, the profit from each series "passes through" to you as personal income, and you pay taxes on it at individual rates.

U.S. Code 26 CFR 301.7701-1 provides that each series in an LLC is treated as a separate entity for tax purposes, regardless of whether the series is considered legally distinct under local law (as in the Florida example above). That means you file state tax returns (if applicable) for the series holding property in that state only. (Prior to that, some states tried to tax the entire LLC on the operations of all its series, even if the some of the properties in question weren't located in the state.)

Location, Location, Location

The first state to adopt the series LLC was Delaware in 1996. Since then numerous states have done the same, albeit in different ways. The District of Columbia, Illinois, Iowa, Kansas, Minnesota, Montana, Nevada, North Dakota, Oklahoma, Tennessee, Texas, Utah, Wisconsin and Puerto Rico all have adopted provisions for series LLCs.

Only three — Delaware, Nevada and Montana — allow the formation of separate LLC series without the legal rigmarole of registering each one. Overall,

I recommend Delaware as your jurisdiction of choice for a series LLC. Let me explain why.

Clarity

Delaware law has always been exceptionally friendly to the formation of corporations of all types. Delaware is like a small foreign country that seeks to encourage business by making its laws investor-friendly. It works hard to maintain this reputation and is unlikely to change its laws unless there is a compelling reason. That's a good thing, because it increases your security.

Initially, Delaware series LLC law didn't clearly state that each series could sue, enter into contracts and be sued on its own, without the entire LLC being named in the lawsuit. But the Delaware legislature soon clarified that a series can enter into contracts, hold title to assets, grant liens and security interests and sue or be sued separately from the rest of the series in an LLC. That's what you want — internal "veils" between the series.

In Delaware, Nevada and Montana, the procedure for adding and deleting LLC series is uncomplicated. You can form or dissolve additional series without any public filing by simply amending the LLC's "operating agreement" — something you can do with an attorney. By contrast, some states (such as Illinois) have restricted your rights to create new series by requiring a public filing when you do. This eliminates some of the savings of a series LLC. Illinois also doesn't treat series as separate entities or allow them to enter into contracts or sue or be sued … which doesn't help much.

Privacy

One of the great benefits of using a separate legal identity as an asset protection strategy is that you can make it very difficult for a potential litigant to identify who actually owns and controls your LLC. Some states, such as Delaware, Nevada, Wyoming, Alaska and New Mexico, don't require the identities of an LLC's members and managers to be listed on the public register of companies.

Now, complete anonymity is impossible — don't let anyone trick you into thinking otherwise. For example, because of the "pass-through" tax status of LLCs, a determined adversary could theoretically find out that an LLC's income is paid to you by going to the IRS for public tax records. And if you are asked by a court under oath to state your assets, you must include any LLCs that you control.

But such strategies of discovery are expensive and time-consuming. The point of legal asset protection is to make it difficult to identify you — so difficult that a litigant, or (more likely) the litigant's attorney, will do their sums and decide that their lawsuit isn't worth it. That's why Delaware and Nevada are the two states with series LLC laws that pass muster — Montana doesn't offer the same protections.

But Google Says It's Too Good to Be True!

If you Google series LLCs, you'll find plenty of people who warn against series LLCs on the grounds that they are too new and untested in states' courts to be reliable. They're usually attorneys who make money by forming and managing stand-alone LLCs and for whom series LLCs are therefore a threat.

The question of reliability arises because LLCs are governed by state, not federal, law. If you create a series LLC, will the separate series and internal liability protection be respected in the state where the property is located, even if that state doesn't have statutes allowing for series LLCs? There isn't any case law on the question yet. It also isn't clear whether a series is a "person" with the right to file a bankruptcy petition separate and apart from the LLC and its other series. Finally, many banks aren't familiar with series LLCs, and you may have to search for one that is comfortable opening different bank accounts for each series (although your attorney can do that if he or she is familiar with serial LLCs).

On the other hand, tax treatment of series LLCs is much clearer. The IRS has stated that the federal tax classification of each series — i.e., whether it is a disregarded (pass-through) entity, partnership or taxable association — is determined for each series as an independent unit (Private Letter Ruling 200803004, January 18, 2008). This led to a number of state tax rulings that reinforce the independent nature of series.

For this reason, I believe the efficacy of series LLCs for the purposes of real estate liability protection comes down to two things:

1. **The character of the operations of each series:** If the law of the state under which you formed a serial LLC says you have to do certain things — like maintain separate records and keep separate finances for each series — and you do this diligently; then, courts in that state have no reason to second-guess your intentions. Courts in other states would look at this matter carefully from the perspective of the other state's laws and would be loath to disagree.

2. **The quality of notice given to potential creditors that a series is a separate entity:** Above I mentioned several steps that you should take when establishing a series to hold a property in a state other than the one where you registered the series LLC. You register the series, not the LLC, with the state as a "foreign" LLC. This may involve a filing fee and in some cases, an annual maintenance fee. You also tell the county deed office where the property is located that it is titled in the name of the series — NOT the parent LLC. Your lease agreements, utility bills and other contracts are similarly titled. Finally, lease agreements with tenants specify the series as the owner of the property and that it is subject to the laws of the state where your serial LLC is registered.

If you do those things, you have told the entire world in no uncertain terms that your property is legally distinct from any others in the parent LLC, and that it is the only asset potentially attachable in a lawsuit. A court would have to violate practically every rule of interstate legal ethics to go against that.

Conclusion

At *Sovereign Confidential*, I look beyond the tried and trusted solutions. I'm looking for cutting-edge developments. Serial LLCs have moved a bit beyond cutting edge, and are poised to become mainstream. For the purposes of tax law, they already are.

My recommendation is that you seriously consider a Delaware series LLC for your property holdings if the following apply:

- You are a small or casual property investor who can benefit from the reduced cost and complexity of the series LLC form. Two or three properties, especially if they are in the same state, could probably use separate LLCs for each one. But larger numbers of properties and properties in different states are a good candidate for a series LLC.

- You, your attorney and your accountant are conscientious and prepared to maintain and document the operational distinctions between the different series and properties in your LLC.

- You do not anticipate unusual risks to your properties and are not aware of pending lawsuits. Forming any type of LLC in anticipation of a lawsuit renders the LLC meaningless to courts.

To further explore the benefits of a series LLC, contact Council of Experts member Josh N. Bennett, Esq. He can be reached at josh@joshbennett.com or at www.JoshBennett.com.

A series LLC is a great low-cost solution to a problem that is facing more and more of us. Do your research, consult a good attorney (as always) . . . and let them bowl away at you. I'm convinced your property pins will stay standing.

Your Last Line of Defense Against Bankruptcy, Lawsuits, & Creditors

Marc-André Sola, *The Offshore A-Letter*, January 2007

You may have heard that if you buy U.S. insurance or annuity contracts in states like Florida or Texas, then these assets are protected from your creditors. But, regardless of what domestic laws promise, real asset protection can only be found abroad. It's simple: if you protect your assets in a jurisdiction where a U.S. judge has no authority, then U.S. creditors won't be able to reach them.

The most effective and strongest asset protection can be achieved by investing through policies in Switzerland and Liechtenstein.

If you establish an annuity or insurance policy under Swiss or Liechtenstein laws, the policy is fully protected from your creditors. Once you've set up your policy correctly, a U.S., Canadian, or other foreign judge can order that your policy to be seized and still your policy remains protected. Both Switzerland and Liechtenstein have laws in place that will protect your policy regardless of what a foreign judge says.

In earlier articles, I've focused on the legal aspects of Swiss and Liechtenstein policies. I've commented on how the policies need to be established and about fraudulent conveyance rules. So today, I want to share with you some real life examples of how an annuity could work. The following stories were experienced by two of our clients.

A CPA in Florida

In the early 1990s, a CPA from Florida came to our office and purchased a Swiss Annuity. At that time, this CPA was very successful in his business and he advised only the wealthiest clients. In 1995, the CPA decided to retire, but he kept advising some of his largest and most affluent clients.

But disaster struck in the late 1990s. The CPA gave incorrect counsel to one of his clients. It was entirely his fault and he was certainly negligible since he had failed to keep abreast of legal changes in his profession. The CPA's client took him to court and the retired CPA lost his assets in the suit that followed.

Of course, creditors also tried to seize his Swiss annuity. I say "tried" because they tried and failed to liquidate and seize the assets safely housed in his annuity policy.

To this day, the Floridian CPA lives off the income from his intact Swiss annuity policy.

The Hotel Owner in Canada

In the late 1990s, we had a client domiciled in Canada. This client was a wealthy woman, who owned several hotels. Unfortunately, at a certain point, her business turned sour and she had to file for bankruptcy. The Canadian judge decided that her Swiss policy was part of the bankruptcy estate. So the Swiss insurer was informed and asked to immediately liquidate the policy.

Even though the policy document was appropriately presented, the Swiss insurer did not divulge any information. The insurance company fully protected the hotel owner's privacy and responded to inquiries only in generic form. The creditors were informed that the insurer was not allowed to give out any information to third parties.

The insurance company didn't even confirm that a person bearing this name or title was a client at the insurance company. Furthermore, the insurer subsequently wrote that in the event of bankruptcy (of a policy owner), Swiss law protects fully the policy because ownership was transferred to the beneficiaries automatically as documented in the accord. Any instructions from the original policy owner subsequently forced upon her could no longer be recognized. Only her beneficiaries, as the new owners of the policy, could give instructions to the insurance company.

Early Action is the Key to Success

If you're looking for solid asset protection, you must go abroad. Swiss and Liechtenstein policies provide utmost asset protection, as long as you set up your plan correctly.

Foreign courts have no authority in Switzerland or Liechtenstein. Even under duress, insurers will not liquidate your policy for creditors. Foreign insurance companies won't even give away details about your policy, because under Swiss and Liechtenstein law, your policy is fully protected.

Creditors usually drop their attacks on your wealth once they discover how little foreign insurance companies will do for them. Most stop their ridiculous witch hunts. But if a creditor relentlessly continues to seize your wealth, he'll have to file with the local Liechtenstein or Swiss court. And then the court will tell him the policy is not a sizable asset.

Remember, you must plan early. Your policy may NOT be protected, if you file for bankruptcy or your creditors try to seize your wealth within 12 months after you establish your policy. The key is to act now.

CHARITABLE GIVING: TAX AVOIDANCE, ASSET PROTECTION & DYNASTIC WEALTH CONTROL
Mark Nestmann & Robert E. Bauman JD

The old saying, "you can't take it with you," is true.

Yet, using both domestic and international charitable structures, you can do the next best thing: set up a pool of wealth that will not only survive your death, but support whatever lawful cause in which you believe passionately.

Many of the world's wealthiest people already know this. For instance, Microsoft founder Bill Gates has already transferred a staggering US$40 billion to the

Bill and Melinda Gates Foundation. Depending on where you live, charitable giving can generate huge tax savings. Charitable giving can also provide you and your loved ones a lifetime income virtually immune to attack by creditors.

Larger estates can form their own charitable structures so that after death, families have the opportunity to control the disposition of wealth over generations, while minimizing ongoing tax liabilities. The use of a charitable structure doesn't necessarily mean that your heirs will receive a smaller inheritance. Combining the charity with a life insurance structure can replace what was "lost" in making the original charitable contribution.

In most countries, the social function of charities makes them relatively non-controversial to tax authorities, an important virtue when tax collectors are aggressively seeking new sources of revenue to fund the soaring cost of the welfare state. The United States, reflecting its long tradition of private responsibility, is particularly generous in the tax breaks it provides to charitable giving.

The law allows income tax deductions for cash donations up to 50% of your adjusted gross income (AGI). Generally, a deduction for full fair market value of property, such as stock, with no capital gains tax paid, allows a deduction of up to 30% of adjusted gross income. Nationwide, there are about 700,000 "qualified" nonprofit charitable groups. Charitable gifts also reduce the size of your estate for estate and gift tax purposes.

Blockbuster Charitable Trust

Trusts offer an efficient means of passing property title to your spouse, heirs or your favorite charity. At death, a trust avoids lengthy and complicated probate court procedures required when the estate must be administered under a will. A properly written trust declaration can avoid payment of most estate, gift or inheritance taxes.

One of the most useful charitable trusts is a charitable remainder trust (CRT). The trust takes its name from the fact that the charitable entity (called the "remainderman") eventually gets title to the trust property when the trust ends.

The CRT is also called a "life income" or "wealth accumulation" trust, because the grantor who creates the CRT (as well as other possible beneficiaries) receives continuing lifetime payments from this trust.

Here are some of the benefits a CRT gives back to its creator:

- Achieve personal philanthropic goals
- Take a large charitable deduction (for the value of the donated assets) against your current year income tax liability
- Avoid all capital gains taxes on donated appreciated property, regardless of the original cost basis

- Guaranteed retirement income for life (your choice, immediate or deferred). For instance, you can convert your low yield real property into a high income investment guaranteed to provide you and your spouse (the "non-charitable beneficiaries") financial security. You can also have your CRT serve as a legal recipient for "roll over" of your qualified pension plan or individual retirement account, which will boost both your retirement income and tax savings.

Nor is there any need to deplete the size of the estate that you leave your heirs. For instance, your estate can purchase life insurance coverage for your life or for you and your spouse's joint lives to replace the monies going to your favorite charities.

The one CRT drawback is its complexity; in order to be certain your structure qualifies under tax laws an expert should draft it. Our experts say that the donated CRT start up assets should be valued at least at about US$50,000 to make the plan feasible.

A CRT trust is an irrevocable living trust. The "living" refers to the time when it is created while the grantor is alive (as compared to a testamentary trust created in a will). It is "irrevocable" because your control over the donated assets ends once the trust is created and the assets are formally transferred.

As in any irrevocable trust, the CRT also serves as an ironclad asset protection device. Once the trust gets the assets, the grantor no longer has title to nor any ability to reacquire those assets. A timely placement of assets into a CRT, well in advance of any claims against you, is an absolute defense against claims from future unknown creditors.

Once you have created your CRT, the institutions or groups lucky enough to be the objects of your generosity might want to reward their benefactor with a seat on their board of trustees. The CRT possibilities of immortality carved into stone are endless: libraries, hospitals, the arts, museums, symphony halls, campus buildings, etc.

An Immediate Tax Deduction

With interest rates near historical lows, some experts recommend the use of a charitable lead trust (CLT) rather than a CRT. One is The Sovereign Society Council of Experts member Gideon Rothschild. A CLT produces an immediate tax deduction and helps the charity of your choice for an extended period. It eventually passes assets to family members with a minimum payment of estate and gift taxes. Because the present value of the charitable interest at the time of the donation is deductible, gift or estate taxes are significantly reduced.

The resulting income or estate tax savings depend on when this technique is used:

An immediate income tax deduction is available to a grantor who establishes a CLT during his or her lifetime, the deductible amount being measured by the present value of the income stream going to the charity for the stated period.

If the CLT takes effect at the grantor's death, his or her estate receives a charitable deduction for the present value of the future income that will go to the charity.

The CLT is established when a donor transfers income producing property to a trust. The trust, in turn, will provide the charity with a guaranteed annuity or annual payments equal to a fixed percentage of the fair market value of the trust property that is computed each year. When the specified period ends, the remaining property is returned to the donor, or it goes to a non-charitable beneficiary of the donor's choice, often an heir or other younger family member.

Charities as Part of an International Estate Plan

As with many other aspects of long term financial planning, setting up an offshore charitable structure can provide additional benefits. The primary benefit is that an offshore configuration provides greatly improved prospects for setting up a dynastic structure that can control the disposition of wealth over generations, in contrast, e.g., to the laws of the United States.

Wealthy individuals usually have more assets and income than they need. However charitably minded they are, they may not wish to give up family control over the assets, both in life and after death. This may be true, as in the case when the assets being donated are shares in a private company owned by the donor.

In the U.S. context, a domestic irrevocable trust such as a CRT generally will not permit such a degree of control to be exercised. Additionally, in the many U.S. states and foreign jurisdictions with an English common law background that have not eliminated the "rule against perpetuities," dynastic control through a trust may not be possible, as the trust will eventually be required to dissolve.

In contrast, by using an offshore charity, the stock can be donated to the charity perhaps one established by the donor. The charity is so structured as to ensure that, in perpetuity, the control of the charity remains in the hands of the donor and his descendants. Not only can the charity (which is not subject to any rule against perpetuities) be used to perpetuate control, but it will also take the assets concerned outside the tax net.

According to Charles Cain, who heads up Skyefid Limited, an Isle of Man based international financial consultancy, "For a U.S. person to create a dynastic structure, an overseas charity is more effective than a U.S. charity. This is particularly true if the U.S. person wishes to avoid the very tight U.S. rules that effectively prevent the donor of assets into a charity from controlling that charity, or deriving benefit for his family from that charity. Nobody else has such strict rules."

Along with the benefit of greater control, there are potential drawbacks to an international charitable structure, the most significant one being that more complexity and higher costs. One source of complexity is the need, often using some rather esoteric mechanisms, to create a structure where a U.S. donor can both obtain a charitable deduction and shift the assets into an overseas charity.

Obviously, structures of this type require sophisticated planning by experienced international tax practitioners. This is not a job for an amateur.

For More Information

If you plan to name a domestic charity as a beneficiary of your estate, that charity may be able to provide assistance. Most major charities have "planned giving" departments eager to provide extensive help to your lawyer or CPA.

The National Committee on Planned Giving is an association of varied professionals active in planned gifting advice with 78 local chapters.

233 McCrea Street, Suite 400
Indianapolis, IN 46225
Tel.: 317-269-6274
Email: info@pppnet.org
Web: http://www.pppnet.org

Two attorneys, both members of The Sovereign Society's Council of Experts, who have extensive experience setting up the charitable remainder trusts described in this article are Michael Chatzky and Gideon Rothschild. You can find their contact information in Appendix A.

The Liberated Individual Retirement Account: Why the Self-Directed IRA is Your Key to Long-Term Prosperity

Ted Bauman, *Offshore Confidential*, May 2015

I'm a do-it-yourself (DIY) sort of guy. It's taught me something I want to share with you.

In my personal life and in my research and writing, I'm biased toward solutions that give me maximum choice and control. I like to service my own motorbike. I do my own basic electrical repairs and plumbing. I file my own taxes … unless they get really complicated, in which case I know where to draw the line and bring in an expert. DIY doesn't mean do it alone.

I've learned — often the hard way — that trusting big, remote institutions to make decisions or do things for me is asking for trouble. Retirement planning is an excellent case in point.

For a few years I had a 403(b) plan from a previous employer. It offered a fixed range of investment options. Some of them were superficially attractive, but once I took into account plan fees and the costs associated with specific funds, it became clear that I'd do better by ending my participation in the plan, paying tax on the compensation that would have gone to contributions, and investing it myself.

That's why I now manage my own retirement funds ... with the help of the right experts.

The fact is that most garden-variety institutional retirement plans — including Individual Retirement Accounts (IRAs) — are designed to gather people's retirement savings and direct them to U.S. stock markets. An entire "food chain" has grown up around the U.S. retirement system, that more or less guarantees that you won't do any better than inflation, even if the underlying investments occasionally do.

But the biggest problem with conventional retirement plans is a lack of investment options. Why should you have to limit yourself to someone else's choices, made for their own convenience and profit? You don't. You don't have to limit yourself to dollar-based U.S. equities and bonds. You can pursue almost any investment option imaginable ... real estate, business start-ups, intellectual property, precious metals ... you name it.

You want more for your IRA. And you can have it ... a lot more.

Take Control of Your Future ... and Your Present

There's about $17.5 trillion in all U.S. private pensions. More than 25% of it in personal IRAs. For a clever few, some of that money is in "self-directed" IRAs ... about 2% of the total. Those are the folks who have found that a more flexible approach to retirement planning provides the best returns and asset protection.

A self-directed IRA is a critical tool, regardless of how "DIY" you are. It's legal, profitable and can be as simple or as complex as you'd like it to be. And it can open up offshore opportunities for your retirement investment that are unavailable any other way. A self-directed IRA is just like a conventional IRA in all the important ways:

- You can have multiple IRAs, so a self-directed IRA can co-exist with others.
- Capital gains, dividends, and interest earnings within the account incur no tax liability.
- Contributions are tax deductible (subject to conditions).

- Distributions are taxed as ordinary income, and can begin when you turn 59 ½ or if you become disabled.
- You can withdraw funds for qualified unreimbursed medical expenses that are more than 7.5% of your adjusted gross income (AGI), or for qualified higher education expenses for yourself, your children and grandchildren.
- When you die, your spouse can roll both of your IRA accounts into one IRA account.

The big difference is that with a self-directed IRA, a specialist IRA "custodian" permits you actively to choose and design investments far beyond everyday stocks, bonds and mutual funds. You can invest in real estate, private mortgages, private equity, precious metals, intellectual property … and much else.

You can reap incredible gains, tax-free, both the income from your investments and their underlying appreciation … gains that go way beyond what a conventional IRA custodian can provide.

And if you like, you can do it *outside* the U.S.

Who's Who in the IRA Zoo

In strict legal terms, a "self-directed" IRA is a bit of a misnomer. In most cases — with one important exception that I'll show you — your IRA assets will actually be held by a custodian, like the trustee of a trust. The Internal Revenue Code requires a custodian for all IRAs — and they must be based in the U.S.

The custodian is responsible for records management and safe-keeping of your IRA, processing transactions, filing required IRS reports, issuing statements and other administrative duties on your behalf. Custodial firms generate revenues from fees, not from trading your money for themselves. In fact, your IRA funds must be "segregated" from the firm's own funds, so they're safe if the company goes bust. That's their core business, and they do it for millions of Americans.

But some provide a lot more value for that service than others. In fact, there are two types of IRA custodians.

One offers garden-variety securities, such as stocks, bonds and funds. This is what you'll get if you have an IRA with most big U.S. commercial custodians, such as Fidelity, American Express, Entrust or T. Rowe Price. Although you can choose from a variety of investment profiles, most of these plans are focused on the plain-vanilla U.S. market. You can forget about most "alternative" investments … especially if they are located outside the U.S.

The other type of IRA custodian, often called "self-directed custodian," is willing to entertain alternative investments that you choose yourself. They add value by helping you to decide what your IRA going to invest in, and if you wish, put them in safe offshore jurisdictions. There aren't many of them, but I watch them carefully to make sure you can access the best of them.

Self-directed IRA custodians allow you, the IRA owner, to choose and design specific investments, or have it done by an independent asset manager (IAM) of your choice, either in the U.S. or abroad. That's the key to supercharging your IRA, DIY-style.

But the U.S. Internal Revenue Code places some restrictions on IRA investments, as I will show. Most mainstream IRA custodians impose additional restrictions of their own, limiting you to garden-variety U.S. investment funds. That's because their job is to generate mass investment in U.S. equity markets, not to allow for customization.

But customization is exactly what you need. That's why self-directed IRA custodians, on the other hand, allow alternative investments, and embrace the increased complexity involved.

What sort of alternative investments are we talking about? The range is enormous … and most of these investments can be in the U.S. or abroad.

In fact, the Internal Revenue Code doesn't describe what a self-directed IRA can invest in, only what it *cannot* invest in. Let's start with some of the things people *have* invested in successfully.

Real Estate

A self-directed IRA can purchase any type of real estate, including residential and commercial properties, farmland and raw land — both U.S. and foreign. It can be new construction or renovation of an existing property. Your self-directed IRA funds can be used for purchase, maintenance and expenses such as taxes and utilities. When the property generates income, either from rental or sale, those funds go back to your IRA, tax-free. They can then be used to invest in other assets.

For example, your IRA could buy a home now that you'd plan to use in retirement. Your rental income goes back to your IRA and is used to maintain it, and to fund other investments.

Unlike an annuity or private insurance policy, where you can't self-direct your investments, with a self-directed IRA you can select the property and negotiate the terms of the deal yourself. You just direct your self-directed IRA custodian to pay for the purchase. The custodian must be the legal owner, so all documents associated with the offer and purchase, as well as anything associated with the ownership of the property, must be in the name of the custodian, albeit specifically referencing you as the IRA owner, such as "XXX Company Custodian for Benefit of (Your Name) IRA."

CHAPTER SIX: YOUR FINANCES & ESTATE PLANNING   345

If you wish, real estate purchased in a self-directed IRA can even have a "non-recourse" mortgage against the property (i.e. one where neither you nor the custodian have personal liability for the mortgage — only the property as collateral). That can help leverage your self-directed IRA funds. However, according to Section 514 of the Tax Code, if you do this on a real estate investment, some of the income from the property will be subject to Unrelated Business Income Tax (UBTI).

Bear in mind that an IRA-owned property won't qualify for tax deductions for property taxes, mortgage interest or depreciation. Also, neither you nor any "disqualified person" may live in or vacation in the property. You can make decisions about how the property is maintained, but you can't do the work yourself. (A "disqualified person" is basically you and your descendants, as well as any entity that you control. Investments involving your self-directed IRA must always be handled in a way that benefits your retirement account and not you or others close to you right now. Your self-directed IRA has to avoid any investment that would appear to involve *immediate* benefit for you, any descendants, or any entity in which you hold a controlling equity or management interest.)

One of the interesting aspects of real estate in a self-directed IRA is that you could purchase a retirement home for yourself with it. You'd have to avoid any involvement in the property while it is in your IRA, but you could rent it out and use the income to fund renovations and improvements in anticipation of moving in one day. When you do, taking title of the house will count as a "distribution" from your IRA. You will then pay ordinary income tax, on the appreciation of the house's value since the IRA purchased it, at the current rate.

For example, let's say you establish a self-directed IRA LLC with $100,000 to purchase a house. Assume you operate the LLC open for 10 years and that it appreciates at an average annual rate of 8%. Your rental income is all tax-free, since it all returns to the IRA. After 20 years your $100,000 investment would be worth $215,890, and you'd pay income tax on the $115, 890.

Business Investments and Private Equity

Self-directed IRA funds can be invested in private companies. Ownership is usually expressed as a percentage or number of shares of stock. A self-directed IRA can even fund a start-up business or other venture, as long as it's managed by someone other than you or a "disqualified person." This is especially attractive if the start-up does well: Your IRA's value will increase along with the fair market value of the company. And of course, it's all tax deferred.

The IRS does put a few restrictions on private equity investments by a self-directed IRA. It can't purchase stock that you already own. In most cases, neither you nor any disqualified persons can be employed by the company while the IRA has an equity position in that company. Also, the IRA cannot be a general partner in a limited partnership, nor can it invest in an S-Corporation.

Private Loans

The IRS also allows self-directed IRAs to make private loans. You can choose the borrower, the principal amount and interest rate, length of the term, payment frequency and amount of the loan, as well as whether or not the loan will be secured. The IRA custodian, of course, makes the actual loan in its name, for benefit of your self-directed IRA. (Such loans cannot be made to yourself, or to prohibited persons.)

Other Investments

You can choose self-directed IRA investments based on your own expertise. Depending on your area of specialty, you could direct your self-directed IRA to invest in currencies, commodities, hedge funds, commercial paper, royalty rights, intellectual property or equipment and leases. Self-directed IRAs have invested in golf courses, race horses and mineral rights.

Precious Metals

I know that metals are of big interest to people like us. You want them, and you'd prefer them to be offshore. That's smart thinking these days.

Fortunately, self-directed IRAs are an ideal way to hold part of your retirement kitty in precious metals. A self-directed IRA can hold gold, silver, platinum, platinum and palladium. The Taxpayer Relief Act of 1997 created this option for you.

The rules for taking distributions from a "gold IRA" are the same as those for a regular IRA. You can liquidate your IRA metals for cash or take physical possession of them. Both actions are equivalent to taking a taxable IRA distribution.

Your self-directed IRA can hold coins — as long as they aren't considered collectibles — and bullion.

- Coins: In order for coins to be held inside a self-directed IRA, they must be 99% pure (or better). They must be "bullion coins," not "collector's coins." That rules out Krugerrands, older Double Eagle gold coins and numismatic coins. Allowed bullion coins include one, one-half, one-quarter or one-tenth ounce U.S. gold coins; other gold coins, such as the Australian Kangaroo/Nugget, Austrian Philharmonic, Canadian Maple Leaf, Australian Kookaburra, Mexican Libertad, Isle of Man Noble and Australian Koala; one-ounce silver coins minted by the Treasury Department; or any coin issued under the laws of any U.S. state.

- Bullion: Your IRA can hold bullion, such as gold, silver, platinum or palladium in bars, as long as it's of the requisite fineness.

What about storage? Unless you opt to use an LLC as the vehicle for your IRA assets (see below), your bullion coins or bars must be in the physical possession of an IRS-approved trustee, which must be a U.S. bank or approved depository — not a foreign bank. The one exception is the American Gold Eagle coin. Because these are legal tender — like the paper U.S. dollar — they can be held in an offshore account.

Of course, there are other options for including metals in your self-directed IRA:

- The Hard Assets Alliance (HAA), a group I've written about before, offers you the ability to own gold, stored internationally, inside a pre-existing IRA without having to go through a complex process. That's because they use the American Gold Eagle, which is considered a form of U.S. currency.

- Another IRS-approved option is to buy shares of an exchange-traded fund (ETF) that tracks the value of particular precious metals.

- You can have your self-directed IRA buy stock in a mining company.

LLCs and IRAs

I'm sure you're wondering about the safety of keeping your IRA metals inside the U.S. After all, the federal deficit is about the same amount as the total U.S. retirement savings. That's an ominous thought.

The answer to this threat is an offshore IRA LLC.

In this structure, your self-directed IRA exclusively owns an offshore LLC, and you as the IRA owner become the manager of the LLC. This gives you the ability to manage your retirement funds directly, as long as you play by the "rules."

By forming the LLC offshore, you can hold metals offshore, open brokerage accounts in foreign countries, hold or trade foreign currencies, and make more aggressive investments. Plus, you get the added benefit of having your assets securely offshore as an extra layer of protection from the greedy U.S. government.

When you form an offshore IRA LLC, no one has access to or control over your investments but you. Your custodian is merely responsible for moving your IRA assets into your new LLC, and for reporting your offshore LLC to the IRS, since it's your only self-directed IRA asset. All the other assets are under the LLC itself.

From there, it's up to you — as a member of the LLC — to determine how and where to invest, including in offshore gold or other precious metals. As an added benefit, the custodian will no longer charge a transaction fee on your investments in the LLC, saving you a lot of money.

When it comes to precious metals offshore, offshore LLCs are critical. Several European banks and other financial institutions are willing to hold American

IRAs, offering a variety of precious metal storage programs as well. But to access them, you must have an offshore LLC — IRS rules prohibit your U.S. custodian from doing this on your behalf.

Sounds too good to be true? Don't worry: It's perfectly legal.

Getting Expert Help

I mentioned that although I'm a DIY guy, I know when to trust the experts. For example, before I start soldering the circuit board on my precious Fender Deluxe Reverb guitar amplifier, I run my plans by a trusted specialist in Seattle who knows a lot more than I do about such matters.

The same applies to your self-directed IRA. Whether your IRA is managed by your custodian or by you via an LLC, you are welcome to use the services of an Independent Asset Manager (IAM) to help you plan and execute your investments. For a fee, the IAM can help you decide what to instruct your custodian to do with your self-directed IRA assets.

This is especially useful — even essential — when it comes to offshore investments, especially via an offshore LLC. IAMs in Europe, for example, have well-developed relationships with European banks and other institutions that can host LLC accounts and arrange precious metals transactions and storage. And of course they know European markets much better that most U.S. advisors.

With the European economy looking up these days, an offshore IAM can help you take advantage of the rising tide.

Play by the Rules

The IRS has rules about IRA investments, and you don't want to break them. They're not too complicated, but it's critical to be aware of them … especially if you take the offshore LLC route with your self-directed IRA.

Here's why: If the IRS decides that there's been a "prohibited transaction" under Internal Revenue Code Section 4975, your IRA loses its tax exempt status. The entire fair market value of your IRA is treated as a taxable distribution, subject to ordinary income tax.

You'd also pay a 15% penalty as well as a 10% early distribution penalty if you're under the age of 59 ½.

You don't want that to happen. But it won't, if you know the rules and obtain and follow good advice from a qualified tax attorney like the ones I recommend.

There are three types of prohibited transactions: those involving specific investments, those involving "disqualified persons" and self-dealing.

Prohibited Investments: Your self-directed IRA can't invest in life insurance. It can't invest in collectibles such as artwork, rugs, antiques, gems, stamps, alcoholic beverages or collectible coins (there are exceptions, as I explained above).

Disqualified Persons: This is based on the premise that investments involving your self-directed IRA must always be handled in a way that benefits your retirement *account* and not you or others close to you right now. Basically, your self-directed IRA has to avoid any investment that would appear to involve immediate benefit for you, any descendants, or any entity in which you hold a controlling equity or management interest. That means things such as:

- Borrowing money from your IRA
- Selling property to your IRA
- Receiving compensation for managing your IRA
- Receiving compensation from a disqualified entity, such as a company your IRA owns
- Personally guaranteeing an IRA loan
- Using your IRA as security for a personal loan
- Using it to pay for a personal expense
- Living in a property owned by your IRA

Self-dealing and Conflict of Interest: This is when the IRS can show that you or a disqualified person received some indirect personal benefit from your IRA. Examples include issuing a mortgage on a residence purchased by a disqualified person, or buying stock from yourself, from any entity in which you have a controlling equity position or from a disqualified person.

Fortunately, there are excellent tax attorneys who specialize in staying on top of the rules and case laws involving prohibited transactions ... they are an essential part of your self-directed IRA strategy.

How to Convert Your IRA to a Self-directed IRA

Moving money from your existing IRA (or even from a 401(k) or 403(b)) to a self-directed IRA can be done in two ways. They're both legal and tax-free, as long as they're done the right way.

- A **transfer** is the method used to move your retirement funds from your existing IRA to a new IRA. In a direct transfer, the distribution check is not sent to you. Instead, your IRA's assets are transferred from your old custodian directly to the custodian of your new self-directed IRA. You can choose to transfer your existing plan at any time, tax-free.

- A **rollover** is used to move your retirement funds between two qualified retirement plans, such as from your current 401(k) to a self-directed IRA. With a rollover, the distribution from your existing retirement plan is paid directly to you. This distribution is tax-free as long as you re-deposit your funds into your new IRA within 60 days. It is important to note that if the 60-day period is exceeded, you will be liable for taxes and penalties on the funds withdrawn. You may rollover funds from an existing IRA tax-free once per year.

Choosing a Custodian

Self-directed IRA custodians aren't responsible for your investment choices … you are. If you tell them to invest in something that doesn't work out, it's not their problem. Indeed, most IRA agreements clearly state that investors are solely responsible for making investment decisions in connection with their funds.

Some investment promoters seeking self-directed IRA business require exclusive use of certain custodians. With a few exceptions, I'm wary of such arrangements. The exception is when an offshore Independent Asset Manager has an existing relationship with a trusted U.S. custodian, and prefers to work with them.

On the other hand, an investment scheme that says "you can buy in as long as you use custodian 'X'" should be treated with caution.

Needless to say, it's critical to choose the right self-directed IRA custodian. Here are some of the things to consider:

Specialization: Make sure you work with an IRA custodian that genuinely specializes in alternative investments. A few IRA custodians will custody both types of investments. An IRA custodian who specializes in traditional investments typically won't be the best choice also to custody your alternative investments. The reverse holds true as well. When you work with a self-directed IRA custodian, you want one whose specialty matches up with your needs. Remember, you can have more than one IRA.

Fees: Every IRA custodian charges fees for their services. They are often surprisingly low — several hundred dollars to set up and between $100 and $150 a year thereafter. Nevertheless, there are two fee models — either a per-transaction fee model or an asset-based percentage fee model. Make sure the custodian's fee schedule aligns with your investment strategy. Your choice will affect the total returns of your self-directed IRA. The bigger your account, the more negotiating room you'll have when it comes to fees.

Service: This is really the key, and why due diligence is so important. You want to consider your custodian's depth of knowledge, timeliness of response, precision, consistency of a process, speed of resolution of any issues, and willingness to adapt to a changing environment. Remember, investing in a piece of real estate inside a self-directed IRA requires the custodian to process all documentation associated with the property (e.g. paying taxes, expenses, insurance, maintenance personnel, or other expenses). If the service team at the custodian isn't experienced at this, or are slow in their response time, or are sloppy with their documentation processing, your investments could be negatively affected.

Contacts

There are many potential custodians who specialize in self-directed IRAs. I've recently come into contact with NuView IRA, who impresses me with the range of options available, including real estate, precious metals, and even more exotic and profitable options such as tax liens. They can be contacted as follows:

NuView Orlando
Tyler Carter, Director, Business Development
Tel.: +1 877-259-3256
Email: tcarter@nuviewira.com or info@nuviewira.com
Web: www.nuviewira.com

One of the attractions of NuView is their rate schedule. They charge just $50 to open an account. It costs $95 to fund an entity such as an LLC through the IRA, $50 for international wire fees, and $295 as an annual maintenance fee for the account.

If you decide to transfer your existing IRA to one of these alternative custodians, known as a "rollover," it's critical to work with an experienced legal professional, such as:

Josh N. Bennett, Esq., P.A.
440 North Andrews Avenue
Fort Lauderdale, FL 33301
Tel.: 954-779-1661
Mobile: 786-202-5674
Email: josh@joshbennett.com
Web: www.joshbennett.com

How to Protect Your Home Place from Legal Predators

Mark Nestmann, *The Sovereign Individual*, June 2009

Even with the collapse of real estate values across the United States, the equity in your home may remain your most valuable asset. Protecting it from lawsuits can pose a difficult challenge. After all, unlike financial assets, there's no way to move your home somewhere else.

With few exceptions, neither federal nor state laws provide much protection to home equity. For that reason, the most effective way to safeguard it is to transfer ownership of your home to a protective structure and then mortgage or otherwise encumber it. These techniques ensure legal predators no longer find your home equity attractive.

One ingenious strategy is to set up and fund an international structure and use it to issue you a mortgage. The structure then reinvests the mortgage payments, producing potentially tax-deferred income or gains for your future benefit. I'll tell you more about this strategy in a moment.

But first, I'll explain why it works…

Limits of Traditional Home Protection Strategies

Homestead statutes. Most American states have laws in effect that may protect part or all of your home equity if you lose a judgment or declare bankruptcy. However, limits are very low in many states with only a few thousand dollars protected. Numerous exceptions also apply (e.g., tax claims).

Tenancy by the entireties. About two dozen states protect property, usually real estate, jointly owned by a married couple, generally with no limit to value. Only judgments against both spouses are enforceable. There are obvious shortcomings; for instance, the unexpected death of the "low-risk" spouse may place the "high-risk" spouse in a vulnerable position. Again, numerous exceptions apply.

Limited partnerships (LPs) and limited liability companies (LLCs). Most advisors now caution against transferring a personal residence into one of these popular estate planning structures. To get any asset protection, you'll have to pay market rent to the LLC, and you may lose the tax benefits of the $250,000 tax-free gain (per taxpayer) on selling a home ($500,000 for married taxpayers filing joint tax returns).

More Protection with Irrevocable Trusts & Private Annuities

Domestic irrevocable trusts. One of the best domestic strategies to protect your home is to sell it to a special irrevocable trust called a non-qualified personal residence trust (NQPRT) in exchange for an installment note. You must pay rent to the trust as long as you live in the home. As long as you receive installment payments from the trust, they should cover a substantial part or all of the rent you must come up with to pay the trust. While the installment payments are generally attachable, you can structure the sale to make the arrangement very unattractive to a future creditor. At your death, the home passes to the trust beneficiaries with no gift or estate tax consequences.

Private annuities. Another protective strategy is to sell your home to your children or a third party in exchange for a life income annuity. The children or third party then rents the residence back to you.

While the sale of appreciated property to a private annuity is generally taxable, you can again exempt up to US$250,000 of gain per taxpayer (or $500,000 per married couple) from the sale of your primary residence. This arrangement may also have important gift and estate tax advantages.

Equity Stripping Your Home Makes It Worthless to Creditors

Borrowing against your home equity or otherwise "equity-stripping" it can also make your home unattractive to creditors. A commercial mortgage is the most common way to strip the equity out of your home. But if things ever get rough financially, it may be difficult to make the mortgage payments, and the bank may foreclose on your property. What's more, your home equity builds back up as you make mortgage payments. That equity then becomes available to your creditors.

Nine Steps for Home Equity Protection

1. You fund an offshore private annuity (OPA) using after-tax dollars.

2. At your request, the OPA administrator sends some of these funds to a U.S. company it owns or controls. (Your request must be non-binding; otherwise you could be deemed to "control" the OPA and lose tax deferral within it.)

3. You apply for a mortgage from the U.S. company.

4. Assuming state laws permit it to do so, the U.S. company grants the mortgage. The mortgage is tailored to make the property as unattractive to creditors as possible.

5. You place the proceeds of the mortgage back into the private annuity (or another asset protected investment).

6. The U.S. company places a lien against your home.

7. You make mortgage payments to the U.S. company. Interest on those payments may or may not be tax-deductible, or be partially deductible.

8. The U.S. company that issues the mortgage files a U.S. tax return. Depending on how it elects to be taxed, it may need to pay income tax on its profits.

9. Your OPA's share of the U.S. company's after-tax profits goes back into your OPA for your future benefit, and accumulates on a tax deferred basis.

This arrangement can be costly to set up, but provides very effective asset protection. It works because a properly executed lien generally takes precedence over any future liens. Assuming you own your home free and clear, and then pledge most of its equity to satisfy a lien, future liens are essentially worthless.

A creditor that examines the arrangement will see a lien from a U.S. company, not from a foreign entity.

There's no indication of an offshore connection, an increasingly important factor as the Obama administration's "War on Offshore" heats up.

This strategy also can successfully deal with some of the problems posed by a conventional mortgage:

You're depositing the mortgage proceeds back into a protected structure.

If you can't pay the mortgage, you're dealing with a company tied to your offshore structure. Assuming no creditor claims are pending, you may be able to renegotiate the terms of the mortgage — although there are potential tax pitfalls to avoid if you do. In the unlikely event that the lender forecloses on your home, your interests remain protected, because most or all of your home equity is in the OPA.

Because of the complexity involved in setting up the various structures and relationships, it's essential to obtain assistance from a qualified tax attorney to set up an offshore equity stripping arrangement.

U.S. SOCIAL SECURITY: THE GREATEST SWINDLE EVER SOLD

John Pugsley, *The Sovereign Individual*, May 2009

Since the Bernie Madoff scandal broke last year, the press has been filled with names and pictures of his victims. The front page of my local newspaper showed a photo of a woman joyfully cheering. The caption read: "Miriam Siegman of New York, who said she lost her retirement money with Bernard Madoff, celebrated yesterday upon leaving a Manhattan courthouse, where Madoff was ordered jailed."

We celebrate with the victims when a swindler like Madoff is brought to justice.

Yet there is a vastly larger fraud being perpetrated on all Americans, and it's unlikely that any of the perpetrators will ever be jailed for their crime.

Bernard Madoff defrauded a few hundred clients of some $65 billion. Yet his scam pales next to the swindle being perpetrated at this moment on hundreds of millions of Americans who have been told they have accumulated more than $40 trillion in future retirement benefits.

The Scam Is the U.S. Social Security System

Those who conceived the Social Security swindle promised that it would end the plight of the aged and disabled by guaranteeing them "security" — a steady income in disability and old age. It was promoted as a life raft that would carry everyone safely through to the end of his or her days.

Today, 74 years later, Americans continue to be told that regardless of what happens to the economy, the government will never renege on this promise. As the population has aged, Social Security beneficiaries have become the biggest political lobby in America. To get elected, any political candidate must participate in the swindle. Both as a candidate and now as President Barack Obama has consistently maintained that the Social Security program's financing is basically sound, and can be assured far into the future. He's lying.

I became aware of the technique of the fraud in 1975 when Arthur Andersen & Company published a lengthy report titled "Sound Financial Reporting in the Public Sector." It disclosed both the magnitude of the crime, and the simple accounting subterfuge used to disguise the fraud.

Cash Accounting Hides Rising Liabilities

The report pointed out that the government keeps its books using the "cash basis" method of accounting rather than the "accrual basis." The cash basis is what you use to balance your checkbook. If you deposit $50,000 in your account for the year and write $49,000 in checks to cover your expenses, your checkbook will show a $1,000 surplus for the year.

However, this does not tell the true story. If you took a vacation in December and ran up $5,000 on your credit card, but the payment didn't come due until the following year, your true expenses for the year were $55,000. You actually ran a $4,000 deficit which didn't show up in your checkbook. Every rational business owner knows that to track the true condition of the business he must add in the cost of purchases he made but must pay for in future years. Sound businesses always use the accrual method of accounting.

In its 1975 report, Arthur Andersen reviewed the U.S. federal budgets for fiscal years ending 1973 and 1974, and came up with shocking figures. Using the cash basis of accounting, the government had reported federal deficits of $14.3 billion for 1973 and $3.5 billion for 1974.

Recalculated according to the accrual method and including future Social Security payments and government pensions, the true 1973 deficit jumped from $14.3 billion to a staggering $86.6 billion. The 1974 budget was even worse, jumping from $3.5 billion to just over $95 billion. The government underreported its deficits by more than $160 billion in a two-year period.

Peter G. Petersen, former Chairman of the Federal Reserve Bank of New York, began sounding the alarm on this looming financial catastrophe more than a decade ago. In his 1996 book, *Gray Dawn: How the Coming Age Wave Will Transform America and the World*, he pointed out that if federal law required Congress to fund Social Security the way private pensions must be funded, the annual federal deficit in 1996 would have instantly risen by some $675 billion. Add in lavish and unfunded federal employee pensions and the deficit would have risen by $800 billion. Add in Medicare and it would have risen by more than $1 trillion.

The cash and accrual deficits that Arthur Anderson discussed in his 1975 report seem trivial compared to last year's federal deficit of $454 billion, and especially compared to this year's [2009] projected deficit of $1.8 trillion. Decade after decade the total of the swindle has been inexorably rising, until today the estimated shortfall owed Americans is an incredible $40 trillion. Nor has it stopped. The total continues to rise at a rate of $2 to $3 trillion per year.

Charles Ponzi Would Be in Awe

Bernie Madoff was able to get away with his fraud by using the same technique as Charles Ponzi did in the 1920s. He sold fictitious securities, promised a high return, and paid off old investors out of monies taken in from new investors. It collapsed when new victims could no longer be found to support withdrawals from old victims.

The Social Security swindle has worked exactly the same way. It receives "contributions" in the form of FICA taxes, pretends to place those funds in trust, and pays benefits to current retirees out of taxes collected from current workers. Just as in the case of Madoff, there is no trust, there is no income to the non-existent trust, and the payments are simply made from current collections. Madoff's scheme lasted 20 years before collapsing. The Social Security swindle is now in its 74th year...the end is near.

It's clear that Social Security cannot fulfill its promises to future retirees, but the casualties will not be limited to those victims, like Miriam Siegman, who find there is no life raft to carry them safely through retirement. In order to continue the fraud, politicians have no alternative except to issue more promises. Retirement checks will come, but they will be financed by more federal borrowing. Cash basis deficits will rise. Treasury IOUs will be converted by the Federal Reserve into dollars. As the monetary inflation morphs into price inflation, the victim list will swell to include everyone who doesn't see it coming.

Last year, former Comptroller of the Currency, David Walker, teamed up with Addison Wiggin of Agora Financial to produce an eye-opening movie, IOUSA, which documented the stunning financial swindle being perpetrated on the nation. This compelling addition to Petersen's disclosure of the government's financial fraud is being widely shown, and has just become available on DVD.

Unfortunately, we will never enjoy the sight of the politicians responsible for the Social Security swindle being sent to jail, but we can protect ourselves from their fraud.

What is the smartest way for prepare for retirement? The best retirement manual in existence today is the publication you are holding in your hands. If you have been pondering setting up offshore bank and investment accounts, do it now. If you have been considering establishing dual citizenship, start the process. If you want to protect yourself from the collapse of purchasing power of the dollar, listen to our currency experts and our recommendations on gold and select commodities.

Internationalize yourself, your family and your assets.

America's Tax System is a "Kludge"
Ted Bauman, *The Sovereign Investor Daily*, December 2014

Cape Town, South Africa — The U.S. tax system has been aptly described as a "kludge," a programmer's term for software that's been amended and modified so many times that it's lost coherence and no longer performs efficiently or effectively.

Unfortunately, since a kludge is the basis for so many other essential systems, it becomes an indispensable part of the system, difficult to change without massive disruption and cooperation by a wide variety of actors with differing interests.

As a structure that is so convoluted only tax attorneys can understand it, the U.S. tax system is the ultimate kludge. It's like one of those old cartoons by Rube Goldberg, where some simple task — say, pouring a cup of coffee — is performed by a multitude of complex maneuvers involving balls rolling down tiny tracks, swinging mechanical arms, pulleys and the odd chicken. It's so complex that even those responsible for its design and implementation, the members of the U.S. Congress, have little idea what's in it.

But at least in the United States there is some pretense of legality, propriety and public purpose in the way our tax money is raised and spent. That isn't true everywhere.

The One Exception to their Ignorance

Every Senator and Congressman is keenly aware that every year, a complex set of tax provisions must be renewed by majority votes in both Houses.

These provisions are a grab-bag of individual and corporate exemptions, indulgences and other gifts added to the tax system over the years. They are meant to encourage or discourage various economic behaviors, while rewarding or punishing classes of voters or corporate donors. They include:

- Deductions for state and local general and sales taxes
- Mortgage insurance premiums
- "Educator expenses"
- Business tax deductions, such as those for research and development or depreciation of capital investment

These business tax deductions are especially meant for energy companies — many of whom end up paying no tax at all, or even get tax refunds, as a result.

Every part of this unwieldy collection of "tax expenditures," as they are known, has become essential to the functioning of modern American life — at least in the eyes of those who benefit from them. But because of the dysfunction of our political system, neither party is willing to go on record making them permanent, thus creating the need for annual renewal, in a kabuki dance of public feints and backroom negotiations.

Brinkmanship at Your Expense

As anticipated, the House of Representatives has renewed most of these provisions, which will cumulatively save individual and corporate taxpayers almost $42 trillion over the next 10 years (assuming they are extended every year or made permanent). And as happens every year, some provisions have been amended or dropped, and new ones have been created.

Hooray. But the annual waiting game over the extenders complicates everyone's tax preparations. Will you be able to deduct R&D expenses for your business, making them more worthwhile? Who knows. Can you rely on a tax credit for your local property taxes, or the cost of your children's education? Maybe, maybe not.

Get a Good Tax Attorney

This annual silliness reinforces a critical rule every sovereign person should follow: Find and keep a good tax accountant and/or attorney. If the U.S. Congress can't keep track of what's in and out of the tax code, you won't be able to either. You need an expert who does nothing else.

The tax code just changed, whether you know it or not. Those changes could save or cost you thousands of dollars or more. As the annual personal tax battle approaches, make an appointment to see your personal tax champion now, before it's too late. The sooner you can make preparations, the more of your wealth you can protect from Uncle Sam's greedy hands.

The Savviest Way to Protect Your Assets
Robert E. Bauman JD, *Offshore Confidential*, January 2014

This is big.

It has been months in the making, but now I can share what we believe is one of the finest — and most affordable — ways to protect your wealth since the asset-protection trust became popular 50 years ago.

Working with a leading U.S. attorney and a top trust company located on an idyllic cluster of islands half way between Hawaii and New Zealand, we have created one of the most secure and highly affordable offshore trusts in the world.

While thousands of people pay seriously high fees for similar protection, this new trust solution comes at a cost of 50% less than anything comparable. Those who opt for this service will not only be able to take advantage of a new, iron-clad trust structure, but they can also have an offshore bank account titled in the trust's name, as well as receive thorough reporting advice for tax professionals to ensure 100% compliance with U.S. tax laws.

And this trust makes a successful assault very difficult for plaintiffs, claimants, creditors and almost anyone else who wants to get their hands on your hard-earned assets.

Before I tell you about the Savvy Wealth Protection Trust and all its unique benefits, let me explain a little about why the establishment of an offshore trust has never been more important.

Why You Need an Offshore Trust

The United States is, far and away, the world's most litigious society. At the last count, there were more than 317 million Americans, of whom well over a million are lawyers.

No other nation on earth has so many lawyers. According to the American Bar Association, the number of U.S. lawyers increased by 300% to 1.2 million from the early 1970s to 2013. And most of those lawyers file lawsuits — about 17 million civil cases were filed in state and federal courts over the last three years.

Comparisons with other countries are telling: America now has some 361 lawyers for every 100,000 people, compared with 94 per 100,000 in the U.K., 33 per 100,000 in France and just seven per 100,000 in Japan.

In 2013, the Association of Trial Lawyers of America estimated that the total cost of civil lawsuits to the American economy at no less than $233 billion annually. That's an individual cost of $809 for every person in the country.

Consider this: Lawsuits are not filed against the poor or those with few assets; they are filed against those with "deep pockets."

But asset protection is not a necessity only for the wealthy. Working people with a nice home and a couple of cars are also at risk of being sued. Certain professionals — lawyers, doctors, architects and engineers — who are well off, but far from rich, are at a higher risk, simply by the nature of their work. Let's face it, we are targets.

You could be sued as the result of medical bills or a car accident, or so-called social-host liability, which means you could be liable if you have a party, serve alcohol, and a guest causes an accident or injury after leaving. If your business partner or employee gets in an accident, you could also be sued.

And children who inherit money from parents or grandparents can also become targets for lawsuits.

The Beauty of a Trust

A trust is one of the most flexible, yet efficient, legal mechanisms recognized by law. Compared to the alternatives, it can provide superior asset protection and can assure that your bounty will be distributed exactly as you see fit.

Even though the concept of a trust goes back centuries in legal history, using the offshore trust format as a way to protect assets has gained much popularity in recent decades.

A trust is highly flexible in operation. It can hold title to and invest in real estate, cash, stocks, bonds, negotiable instruments and personal property. Serving as an international investment platform, it can also increase wealth many times over.

At the same time, it can provide care for minor children or the elderly. It can pay medical, educational or other expenses. And it can provide financial support in an emergency, for retirement, during marriage or divorce and even carry out premarital agreements.

The savviest individuals choose to create foreign-asset protection trusts in offshore financial centers such as the Cook Islands, because the added distance and the strict privacy laws of the land protect trust assets from claimants.

Locating the trust in the Cook Islands places your assets virtually beyond the jurisdiction of the U.S. government and American courts.

You should also set up your trust well before any challenge or claim is made on your assets. Once a claim arises it is probably too late.

The Savviest Trust Out There

This article focuses on how to get the most trust for your money in the inviolate Cook Islands.

This new trust will protect your money from lawsuits and other claims. While allowing you to achieve your asset-protection goa ls with an affordable, special, individually drafted offshore asset protection trust. Registering the trust in the Cook Islands means you have chosen one of the best jurisdictions in the world for modern asset-protection law.

In considering a name for this trust, we have decided to call it The Savvy Wealth Protection Trust.

We chose the word, "savvy," because it describes practical understanding, intelligence and common sense. Indeed, this unique trust is crafted for shrewd, experienced people, who are well informed.

The central legal protection of Savvy Wealth Protection Trust, as with all trusts, is the fact that all property that you, as the trust creator, properly donate to your trust ceases to be your property. You don't own it any more. It becomes the property of the trust itself.

Of course, the trust must be created before claims arise against you. However, once it is in place, a Cook Islands trust is the safest, low-cost trust in the world.

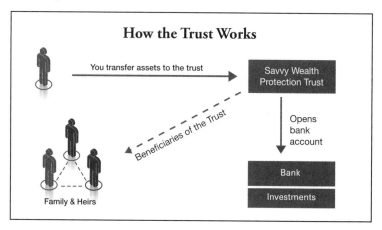

Although I have written before about the virtues of the Cook Islands as a trust haven, this is the first iron-clad trust vehicle available at such a low cost. With fees for the Savvy Wealth Protection Trust at just over $10,000, you can protect your assets up to a recommended $250,000.

Forget about promises to create a reliable trust for a few hundred dollars — that's not possible. Only the Savvy Wealth Protection Trust has made the right connections for you — the lawyers, the legal entities and the realistic costs associated with removing your assets from U.S. government scrutiny, the impact of frivolous law suits and any other attempt to rob you of your hard-earned savings.

Tailored to Your Needs

The Savvy Wealth Protection Trust is not an "off the shelf" prefabricated trust. One size does not fit all. The trust will reflect your individual asset-protection needs and your personal circumstances.

This trust is recommended specifically for U.S. persons, who have a net worth of $250,000 or less. Those with a higher net worth or numerous beneficiaries with special requirements, probably will need a more complex trust at a higher cost.

The Savvy Wealth Protection Trust comes with an immediately accessible professional maintenance staff to assist and answer questions. Both Josh Bennett and Ora Fiduciary managing director Puai Wichman Esq. can be contacted via U.S. phone telephone numbers and via email. Details are provided in the final section of this issue.

Essentially, those who create the Savvy Wealth Protection Trust get the complete trust structure, a bank account titled in the trust's name and all the reporting advice for their tax professional to ensure 100% compliance. If you add in the value of the bank account and the tax reporting advice, worth up to $3,000, the true cost of the Savvy Wealth Protection Trust is only around $9,000.

Forbes magazine reported in 2010 that a domestic U.S. trust, including attorney's fees, typically costs $10,000 or more to establish, and a creation of a foreign trust is twice as costly. Annual trust administration and accounting fees typically are $5,000 for a domestic trust and $7,000 for an offshore trust — and these costs are rising rapidly.

For more about trusts in the Cook Islands, see "The Cook Islands: Far Out" in Chapter Nine.

Your Resource Guide

Josh N. Bennett, Esq., P.A.
440 North Andrews Avenue
Fort Lauderdale, FL 33301
Tel.: 954-779-1661
Mobile: 786-202-5674
Email: josh@joshbennett.com
Web: www.joshbennett.com

The Savvy Wealth Protection Trust is registered and administered by Ora Fiduciary Ltd., one of the six officially licensed trust companies in the Cook

Islands. Ora Trust will act as trustee. Puai Wichman, Esq. a respected member of the New Zealand and Cook Islands' bars has spoken at The Sovereign Society events in the United States and has assisted many of our members.

Puai T. Wichman Esq., Managing Director
Ora Fiduciary (Cook Islands) Limited
Global House, Parekura, Tutakimoa Rd
P.O. Box 92, Avarua, Rarotonga, Cook Islands
Tel.: (682) 27 047
Mobile: (682) 55 418
USA Direct Tel.: (734) 402 7047
Web: http://oratrust.com
Email: puai@oratrust.com

The trust bank account will be held by Capital Security Bank Ltd (CSB), the only full-service private bank operating exclusively in the Cook Islands. Account applicants must meet due diligence requirements, but need not visit the bank personally. CSB also has online banking and offers accounts in numerous currencies.

Capital Security Bank
P.O. Box 906, Centrepoint
Avarua, Rarotonga, Cook Islands
Tel.: 682 22505
Web: https://www.capitalsecuritybank.com/en
Email: info@csb.co.ck

Working with Josh Bennett, CSB has developed three optional investment funds for Savvy Wealth Protection Trust beneficiaries, based on rates of risk with commensurate management fees. Funds are administered by CSB as a custodian bank together with Kaiser Partner Financial Advisors, based in Switzerland. The group is SEC registered.

Kaiser Partner Financial Advisors
Zollikerstrasse 60
8702 Zollikon (Zürich) Switzerland
Tel.: +41 44 752 51 52
Web: http://usa.kaiserpartner.com/en

We have performed due diligence on all the professionals associated with the Savvy Wealth Protection Trust.

Chapter Seven

Your New Goal: Pay Zero Taxes — Legally

Part One: American Taxes

How Government Steals from You 366

The Eight-Way Tax Grab 368

Tax Evasion = Jail Time 373

Tax Avoidance vs. Tax Evasion 375

The Annual IRS Fear Campaign 378

What to Do if You're on the Wrong Side of the IRS 380

Live Offshore: Two Can Earn, Tax-Free 382

ABCs of FATCA Regulations 385

The Only Way to End U.S. Taxes 393

4 Strategies for Beating the IRS 396

Beat the IRS From Six Feet Under 405

Part Two: International Taxation

Why Tax Competition Is Good for You 417

How to Invest Offshore and Legally Avoid the IRS 419

United Nations Seeks Global Tax Authority 422

Tax Haven Nonsense & Deception 425

Slippery Stepping Stones 427

Negotiate Your Own Tax Bill in Switzerland 428

The Ex-PATRIOT Act and America's Fading Freedoms 430

Government's Double Standard 432

Editor's Note:

No one needs to be reminded about what a burden taxes have become.

"Soak the rich" has been a popular slogan for political demagogues at least since the French Revolution.

Today the tumbrel and guillotine have been replaced with the tax audit and grim tax collectors who slice off half of your income to finance their beloved Nanny State.

Citizens complain about high taxes but few do anything about them. Whether out of ignorance or fear, sheep-like taxpayers allow themselves to be herded through government shearing programs that strip them of most of their hard-earned wealth.

Here we give you firm examples of how bad taxation has become, what can be done to change this official robbery and specific, legal steps you can take to cut your losses, perhaps even down to zero. And we do emphasize — legal steps!

You should consider this chapter in conjunction with the related taxes explained in Chapter Two, especially the U.S. "exit" tax.

PART ONE: AMERICAN TAXES

How Government Steals from You
PT2, 1997, Scope Books

Taxes can be considered straightforward theft by government.

The tax-and-spend growth rate of most western governments during the past 60 years has been phenomenal. From a base of nearly zero, close to two-thirds of all wealth generated in western democracies is now spent by politicians, not by the people who create or earn such wealth.

Worse still, the percentage of wealth being confiscated continues to grow. At present, government spending grows faster than national income, personal income and per capita income when adjusted for inflation or taken as a percentage of gross national product. In grossly overtaxed Europe, it seems clear that the new bureaucracy of the EU will only succeed in adding yet another layer of parasitic new taxes.

The growth of government budgets diminishes your personal freedom. If more and more of your earnings and assets are taken, your liberty is limited by just that much. In most industrialized countries citizens can no longer choose how to spend, invest or bequeath their own money. If any other institution practiced such profligacy while offering such inferior services, it would collapse. Because governments command the police and control the jails, they get away with this continued fraud.

You must take legal tax avoidance action, first by understanding the various forms of taxation employed by Big Brother, many hidden from the people who must pay the bills.

Income Taxes & Hidden Taxes

Hidden taxes, such as sales taxes, import duties and Value-Added Taxes (VAT), are reflected in raised prices. Sales taxes are generally believed to have a greater impact upon the poor since wage earners and state-supported individuals tend to spend more of their earnings on consumer items. In France, much more money is raised from sales taxes than from income tax, most likely because wealthy Frenchmen hardest hit by income taxes now live abroad.

Government Borrowing

This is a deferred tax, and it is unclear who will eventually have to foot the bill.

In an expanding economy with moderate inflation, an increase in national debt can be healthy, if the debt is used to pay for infrastructure like highways and communications systems that facilitate commerce and generate funds to retire the debt. In an ideal world, users of improved facilities would pay for them.

However, more typically, funds raised by government borrowing are squandered. They end up being exported. The poor buy imported consumer goods. The wealthy invest abroad. The country ends up impoverished, and living standards drop.

Who then must pay the debt? No one and everyone!

With a debt that becomes too large to service with taxes, the country can no longer simply roll the debt over by issuing more paper to pay off the interest and capital on bonds which have matured.

In such a situation, the government is faced with a hard choice. It can end the game with a default, as many third world countries are allowed to do from time to time; or, more likely, it can issue ever-more worthless currency to cover its debts. Russia has taken this rampant inflation route.

In this scenario, the burden of both the borrowing and default falls on those who did not have the financial ability or good sense to ship their assets abroad.

How much money has been sent abroad to offshore money and tax havens? Recent figures indicate that more American dollars have been deposited abroad in secret accounts during the past 30 years than the total amount now on deposit in all banks in the United States.

This amazing situation means that more than half the U.S. national wealth has been exported. That's the obvious response of smart money to the growth of a rapacious government. The U.S. situation is not unique and many Europeans engage in the same practices. Most liquid wealth in the industrial countries is now beyond the reach of the tax collectors, regulators and planners.

Printing Worthless Paper Currency

This is historically the most common form of taxation.

New currency by law must be accepted in payment of all debts, public and private. This running of the printing presses results in inflation and the erosion of the value of creditors' holdings, thereby reducing or eliminating government debt. It also raises general price levels.

This imposes a tax on those with assets in the form of cash, bonds or secured or unsecured debts due from others. Inflation shifts wealth from the creditor class who are owed money to the debtor class who owe money. It eventually erodes all wealth and brings about instability in the overall economy.

In times of inflation, no one can make long-term plans or invest in plant or equipment; even a farmer can't safely raise a crop of cattle or pigs. The creation of real wealth, economic growth, always declines when there is double-digit inflation.

THE EIGHT-WAY TAX GRAB
Marshall J. Langer JD, *The Tax Exile Report*, 1997

The octopus is a fearsome sea monster that uses eight uncoordinated tentacles to reach out and ensnare its hapless victims. Swimmers grabbed by any one of this beast's tentacles have a serious problem. Only if the victim has a knife sharp enough to cut all eight tentacles, does he win.

Similarly, any of eight different criteria can subject you to tax liability in your present home nation. Each test is used by some countries, most apply a few and the U.S. uses all eight. To avoid these taxes legally, you must eliminate each of these tax tentacles, one by one. They are: residence, domicile, citizenship, marital status, source of income, location of assets, timing and status of beneficiaries.

Residence

In many countries you are counted as a resident for tax purposes if you actually are present within the country for more than 182 days in any tax year. However, you are not necessarily a nonresident for tax purposes just because you spend less than half the year in that country. In the latter case you may still be taxed depending on factors other than time. In such countries, there is always a risk government will claim you are a taxable resident.

Many countries impose income tax on worldwide income based upon the residence of the taxpayer. In some, mere residence is sufficient to tax an individual on both his domestic and foreign source income. In others, taxation of worldwide income is imposed only on taxpayers who are permanently resident (or domiciled) in the country.

You may be able to escape your present country's taxes by changing your residence to a country that does not tax its residents on their worldwide income. You may even be able to escape residence anywhere by moving around from place to place as a perpetual tourist (PT).

Domicile

The concept of domicile is significant in English common law nations. Domicile is not necessarily the same as residence. Your residence for tax purposes is usually determined each tax year, while your domicile is generally more permanent — the place to which you intend to return and where you have your roots.

Under British and American law everyone begins life with a domicile of origin. This can be changed to a domicile of choice, but not easily. Merely moving to a new place does not automatically change your domicile. The domicile concept made better sense 100 years ago than it does now. Picture a 20-year old Englishman in the days of Queen Victoria. He might take a job in India and live and work there for 40 years before returning to retire and die in England. While in India he was clearly resident there. But in the eyes of the law he remained domiciled in England because he always intended to return there.

It is often difficult to determine an individual's domicile in today's jet-set era. One major problem is that the taxpayer always has the burden of proof. Each government is likely to claim you are domiciled there if that means you or your heirs have to pay them taxes.

In the U.S., your place of domicile is determined by state law rather than federal law, so there are over 50 different sets of rules. Your domicile for federal tax purposes depends on the law of the state where you are domiciled. There have been a number of cases in which more than one state has claimed to be a particular taxpayer's domicile. Similar rules apply in other countries such as the U.K. where a person is domiciled in England, Scotland or Wales.

Domicile is very significant in determining U.K. tax liability. Those who are both resident and domiciled in the U.K. are taxed on all their worldwide income. A U.K. resident not domiciled in the U.K. need not pay income taxes on foreign-source income unless it is remitted to the U.K.

In most civil-law countries, there is little or no difference between residence and fiscal domicile.

Domicile rules can be very erratic. A government may claim you or your heirs owe taxes even though you abandoned living there years before. Under U.S. rules, domicile can't be abandoned without establishing a new one somewhere else. One who tries to live as a PT may find themselves still domiciled in some U.S. state many years later. Under U.K. rules, if you abandon your domicile of choice without establishing a new one, your domicile will revert to that of your domicile of origin.

Citizenship

The U.S. is the only major country in the world that imposes income tax solely due to citizenship, but a few others levy estate taxes based on citizenship. The U.S. also imposes its gift and estate taxes on American citizens regardless of where they live or where they are domiciled. A U.S citizen cannot escape U.S. income taxes merely by moving abroad. An American citizen does get some income tax benefits when living and working abroad, but these are of relatively little value to U.S. taxpayers with substantial annual income.

An American who wants to become a tax exile must not only change his residence and domicile but also must surrender U.S. citizenship. Since no one wants to become a stateless refugee, another nationality in a suitable country that does not impose taxes based on citizenship must be acquired first.

Some Americans qualify as "dual nationals." They already have the legal status as citizens of one or more other nations. That is no help tax-wise since a dual national is still an American citizen for U.S. tax purposes.

Like most Americans, you probably do not have a second nationality. The first step towards tax exile is to acquire a second citizenship. The U.S. officially concedes that a U.S. citizen may voluntarily acquire another citizenship and the second passport that goes with it, without automatically losing U.S. citizenship.

The second, more dramatic step is giving up U.S. citizenship. An American who relinquishes U.S. citizenship may be able to obtain a multiple entry visa permitting visits to the U.S. the same as any other foreigner. However, a so-far-unenforced 1996 law authorizes the U.S. Attorney General to exclude from re-entry into the United States any individual who renounces U.S. citizenship to avoid taxes.

Marital Status

Your marital status may affect tax liability.

Not only whether you are married or single, but also where and how you were married and where you and your spouse have lived since marriage. Many countries have community property rules under which each spouse is entitled to a half interest in all property acquired by the other spouse during the marriage. These rules apply in virtually all civil-law countries and in some common-law jurisdictions, including nine states in the U.S.

Places as diverse as California, Texas, Quebec, the Channel Islands, Italy and Argentina all apply community property rules. For anyone married in, or with a marital home in, a community property jurisdiction, special planning to become a tax exile is needed.

Your marital status may also be significant even if you have not lived in a community property country. Example: a married woman's domicile may be the same as that of her husband, whatever her wishes may be. The U.K. permits a married woman to adopt a domicile separate from her husband. Less clear U.S. rules permit a married woman's separate domicile for some designated purposes, such as filing an action for divorce, but not for more mundane activities, such as taxes.

Source of Income

Most countries apply a source test that imposes income taxes on all income derived within that country whether the person earning it resides within the country or not. Income paid to non-residents may be subject to a withholding tax, and the entity paying the nonresident must pay the tax directly to the government. Withholding taxes are generally imposed at a flat rate on gross income derived by foreigners from domestic sources. The withholding tax rate is set by law but is often reduced by treaty.

For example, the statutory U.S. withholding tax rate on dividends paid to nonresidents is 30 percent, but portfolio dividends paid to a Canadian resident are subject to only 15 percent U.S. withholding tax under the income tax treaty between the U.S. and Canada. Some countries, including many in Latin American, impose taxes only on a territorial basis. Applying a source test, they tax all income derived from domestic sources and exempt all foreign source income.

Location of Assets

Most countries impose property taxes on real estate and other assets physically situated within their borders. Many nations impose capital transfer taxes on the disposition of property by a lifetime gift or at death because the property is located in that country. Taxes may be assessed on your worldwide assets because the government deems you to be a resident or domiciled there or because you are a citizen.

A tax exile must remove as much taxable property as possible from his high-tax home country to chosen places that do not tax assets merely because of their location. Personal property can be moved from one country to another. Real property cannot be moved but it can be sold or mortgaged and the proceeds can be moved abroad.

Timing

The taxation of income may depend on when it is considered to have been earned. Thus timing can be significant when moving from one country to another. A tax exile should postpone receiving income until after he leaves his high-tax country. In the U.S., for example, large tax-free gifts can be made between spouses only if the recipient spouse is a U.S. citizen when the gift is made.

It may be possible for a resident of a country to exchange domestic real estate for foreign real estate in a tax-free transaction while he is still resident. Or a former resident may be able to transfer domestic assets to a foreign corporation or sell foreign assets without tax liability after he ceases to be a resident.

Status of Beneficiaries

Not all members of one family usually become tax exiles. Frequently, one or both parents leave a country but their adult children and their grandchildren remain. Knowing this, a high-tax country may seek to impose taxes, interest and even penalties when assets are eventually distributed to remaining relatives. Careful planning at the outset can avoid these tax problems. Obviously, the planning is much easier when the children leave with their parents.

All of the Above

The U.S. uses all of the foregoing criteria to impose its federal taxes. Both U.S. citizens and resident aliens are taxed on worldwide income as citizens or as residents. Domicile is not necessary but if they are domiciled in the U.S. they are subject to U.S. gift and estate taxes on their worldwide assets and residence is immaterial. In cases where spouses have been married in a community property jurisdiction and one spouse is a U.S. citizen and the other is a non-resident alien, the U.S. may apply community property rules to tax the citizen spouse on half of the income earned by the nonresident alien spouse.

The U.S. taxes non-resident aliens on their U.S.-source income. It taxes non-domiciled aliens when they give U.S. situs property by lifetime gifts or by transfers at death. If all other attacks fail, the IRS may demand taxes by claiming the income was earned before the tax exile left the country.

The IRS also may impose transferee liability on beneficiaries over whom it retains jurisdiction. The answer to all these attacks is careful planning. If you plan to become a tax exile, do it right or don't do it at all.

TAX EVASION = JAIL TIME

Robert E. Bauman JD, *The Sovereign Investor Daily*, April 2008

In his *Thoughts on Government*, the second U.S. president, John Adams of Massachusetts, sagely observed that: "Fear is the foundation of most governments."

Based on its tax enforcement policies, the U.S. Internal Revenue Service could easily adopt that as its official agency motto.

Exhibit A: A "very sorry" Wesley Snipes, Hollywood star of the "Blade" movies, was sentenced to three years in prison for willfully failing to file U.S. income tax returns for 1999 through 2001. Snipes was convicted on three misdemeanor tax evasion counts.

U.S. District Judge William Terrell Hodges handed down the maximum sentence and said he felt it was important to create a general deterrent against tax defiance. Prosecutors said Snipes had earned more than $38 million since 1999 but still had not filed tax returns for the years 1999 through 2001 nor paid any taxes.

"I am very sorry for my mistakes and errors," Snipes told the judge. "This will never happen again." Sorry Wesley. Too little, too late!

Co-defendant Eddie Ray Kahn, a longtime tax protester who coached clients of his American Rights Litigators on supposedly how to beat the tax system, was sentenced to 10 years in prison. Co-Defendant Douglas Rosile, whom prosecutors called a "defrocked certified public accountant," was sentenced to 4-1/2 years for his part in the scheme. Both were convicted of conspiracy and tax fraud.

Fear Factor

As in the tax evasion case of the late hotel millionaires, Leona Helmsley who went to jail, with Snipes the IRS wanted a show trial so that taxpayers would be scared into unquestioning obedience to the laws "by pursuing a few prominent cases, making examples of those it judges to be violators" as *The New York Times* noted.

As a libertarian and a conservative I view taxes as, at best, a necessary evil.

I believe that when government takes wealth from some and gives it to others, it diminishes the rights and well-being of the former, and often destroys the independence of the latter. The issue of taxation involves nothing less than the human and natural right to own, use and enjoy private property. Property and wealth determine personal power to control our own lives, to make decisions, and to live free. Every additional tax diminishes our freedom.

Nevertheless, the 16th Amendment to the U.S. Constitution granted the Congress the power to "... lay and collect taxes on income, from whatever source derived, without apportionment among the several states and without regard to any census or enumeration."

And, oh boy, the politicians have had a wonderful time ever since, laying and collecting taxes.

Enforced Exactions

Notwithstanding the 16th Amendment, it should be balanced against the statement of the late, distinguished Judge Learned Hand of the U.S. Court of Appeals in New York.

In a memorable tax case dissent, Judge Hand offered these timeless remarks: "There is nothing sinister in arranging one's affairs so as to keep taxes as low as possible... nobody owes any public duty to pay more than the law demands. Taxes are enforced exactions, not voluntary contributions." *Commissioner v. Newman*, 159 F2d 848, 851 (2nd Cir 1947).

Charles Cain, editor of *Offshore Investment*, in an editorial rightfully charged that "the line between tax avoidance and tax evasion is purposely being blurred by governments, with honest people (and their tax advisors) being jailed for failed attempts at tax avoidance while tax evasion is put down on a moral level with heroin and cocaine pushing."

A great deal of time and effort on our part goes into exploring and explaining legal ways by which you can avoid, minimize, and defer taxes — I repeat — legal ways.

In the first page of every one of our book publications the following statement appears:

> The Sovereign Society advocates full compliance with applicable tax and financial reporting laws. U.S. law requires income taxes to be paid on all worldwide income wherever a U.S. person (citizen or resident alien) may live or have a residence. Each U.S. person who has a financial interest in, or signature authority over, bank, securities, or other financial accounts in a foreign country that exceeds $10,000 in aggregate value, must report that fact on his or her federal income tax return. An additional report must be filed by June 30th of each year on an information return (Form TD F 9022.1) with the U.S. Treasury. Willful noncompliance may result in criminal prosecution. You should consult a qualified

attorney or accountant to insure that you know, understand and comply with these and any other reporting requirements.

The Biblical admonition to "render unto Caesar" does not mean we have to surrender unto Caesar, and we shouldn't.

TAX AVOIDANCE VS. TAX EVASION
Mark Nestmann, *The Sovereign Individual*, July 2001

Every taxpayer has a right to try to avoid taxes. But when does complete legal tax avoidance turn into illegal tax evasion?

The answer seems intuitive: evasion is driving around a tollbooth to enter a toll road without paying. Avoidance is taking an alternate free route.

This fundamental difference couldn't be clearer. And courts in many countries have repeatedly stated: Tax avoidance is legal. Tax evasion is not. Justice Felix Frankfurter of the U.S. Supreme Court wrote: "As to the astuteness of taxpayers in ordering their affairs as to minimize taxes, we have said that, 'The very meaning of a line in the law is that you intentionally may go as close to it as you can if you do not pass it.' This is so because nobody owes any public duty to pay more than the law demands. Taxes are enforced extractions, not voluntary contributions."

In the House of Lords, the highest court of the United Kingdom and many other countries, Lord Clyde stated: "No man in this country is under the smallest obligation, moral or other, so as to arrange his legal relations to his business or to his property as to enable the Inland Revenue to put the largest possible shovel in his stores. And the taxpayer is entitled to be astute to prevent, so far as he honestly can, the depletion of his means by the Revenue."

Yet despite this ringing legal affirmation of tax avoidance, in practice, it's not always easy to tell the difference between evasion and avoidance. The line changes with amendments to tax laws, so that yesterday's legal avoidance easily converts to today's tax evasion.

Not knowing the difference can cost you dearly.

For instance, non-domiciled residents of the United Kingdom can arrange their affairs so that virtually all their offshore income is tax-free, except for that repatriated for living expenses. This scheme is perfectly acceptable from a U.K. perspective.

But residents of most other members of the Organization of Economic Cooperation and Development (OECD) are liable to tax on their worldwide income

— whether generated personally, or through a partnership, trust or as a shareholder in a corporation. There are narrow exceptions to these rules, but by and large — this is the law. Persons who fail to report their worldwide income, and pay tax on it, risk prosecution for tax evasion. And under U.S. law, if efforts are made to conceal the income, tax fraud or even money laundering charges are possible.

It is true that audit rates are relatively low so many tax evaders are never caught. But no matter what the odds, the penalties for non-compliance are unforgiving.

Too many offshore promoters ignore the law, or don't realize it has changed, and continue to promote tax-defective schemes:

- "Abusive trusts" in which the individuals forming and funding the trust are told by the promoter that the trust is "non-taxable" and "non-reportable."
- "Secret" and supposedly non-reportable offshore bank accounts.
- High-yield investment programs in many cases with your "profits" diverted into a supposedly "secret" offshore account.
- "Un-tax" schemes that claim by declaring yourself a "sovereign citizen," you are no longer subject to federal, provincial or state legislation, courts or taxes.

Hundreds of similar scams exist. Robert Bauman, The Sovereign Society's legal counsel reports: "Recently I saw an advertisement in major airline magazine touting purchase of an offshore 'how to' investment book. A bit of checking turned up the fact that the author is accused in an SEC lawsuit of masterminding a $14 million stock fraud using a U.S. firm he founded."

Does It Pass the Common Sense Test?

The common element in these schemes is that they promise something that defies common sense — that is too good to be true.

Common sense dictates that if you live in a country that imposes an income tax on your worldwide income, you can't eliminate your liability to that tax by signing a piece of paper purportedly revoking your Social Security number, Social Insurance number or driver's license number.

Common sense dictates that it's not possible to generate "risk-free" returns of 500 percent or more each year on any investment, offshore or otherwise.

Common sense dictates that an offshore banker or trust promoter is not going to give you unbiased or knowledgeable advice about tax liabilities in your own country relative to their proposed structure.

In short, a simple benchmark to determine the difference between legal tax avoidance and illegal tax evasion is: "If I were to read about this technique or instrument in the newspaper, or hear about it from a friend, would I be skeptical, or not?"

We advise members to stay away from tax schemes that fail the common sense test or that otherwise promise benefits that appear "unreal."

Many Legal Ways to Save Taxes

Fortunately, there are many completely legal tax avoidance strategies of which you can still take advantage. If you are a U.S. citizen, for instance, Vernon K. Jacobs, CPA, CLU (www.offshorepress.com) points out the following completely legal tax avoidance strategies:

1. U.S. persons who live and work outside the United States for at least 330 days in any consecutive 12 months can exclude up to US$91,400 in [2010 amount] foreign source earned income from their U.S. income taxes.

2. U.S. companies engaged in export sales may be able to save some taxes (although the law relating to this issue is being changed).

3. The foreign source income of a foreign trust after the death of the grantor (settlor) of the trust (and his or her spouse) is exempt from U.S. taxes until distributions are made to a U.S. beneficiary. This provides estate tax benefits for your heirs but no income tax benefits for yourself.

4. A small amount of currency gains from non-investment and non-business purposes is excluded from tax.

5. Tax deferral is available for profits from a foreign corporation owned by U.S. persons if it has no significant investment income and if most of its income and assets are utilized in earning profits from a foreign based corporation conducting a trade or business located outside the United States. However, there are numerous complicated restrictions on this principle and it must be pursued with qualified advice.

6. When a U.S. citizen expatriates by giving up his or her citizenship, future income from sources outside the United States is not subject to U.S. taxation and non-U.S. source assets are not subject to U.S. estate and gift taxes.

Jacobs lists more than a dozen additional legitimate tax avoidance techniques. Why pursue exotic and potentially illegal tax cutting strategies when there are so many legitimate ones to choose from?

These legitimate tax avoidance strategies get a bad rap in the mainstream media. Witness the comments of self-proclaimed offshore expert, Jack Blum, to a *New York Times* reporter: "There is no legitimate reason for an American citizen to have an offshore account. When you go offshore, you are doing so to evade rules, regulations, laws or taxes."

Blum takes his mistaken cue from government policies that deliberately blur the distinction between tax avoidance and tax evasion. Charles A. Cain, editor of *Offshore Investment* magazine, charged in a 1998 editorial that "the line between tax avoidance and tax evasion" is purposely being blurred by governments, with honest people (and their tax advisors) being jailed for "failed attempts at tax avoidance" while "tax evasion is put down on a moral level with heroin and cocaine pushing."

The blurring of these lines makes it all the more important for you to follow proven and prudent tax avoidance strategies, and not cross the line into illegal, and potentially dangerous, tax evasion.

THE ANNUAL IRS FEAR CAMPAIGN
Robert E. Bauman JD, *The Sovereign Individual*, April 2008

About this time each year, the IRS antics bring to mind the late, unlamented Josef Goebbels. In case you're unfamiliar with the name, Dr. Goebbels was Adolf Hitler's infamous minister of propaganda.

It was Dr. Goebbels who observed: "Propaganda has only one object; to conquer the masses. Every means that furthers this aim is good; every means that hinders it is bad."

Fear was the Nazi stock in trade. They used fear as a potent psychological weapon in their efforts to direct and control the German masses.

And each year, as dependable as the arrival of spring, the fear mongers at the IRS launch into their annual campaign to scare the American public.

The annual campaign begins with a barrage of press releases. The PR specialists at the IRS start sending them three months before the annual income tax filing date, April 15th (a week from today). The press releases are more than just friendly "please file your taxes" reminders. They announce (or you could say "brag" about) the convictions of an assortment of alleged tax evaders. This scare tactic has become a ritual to frighten U.S. taxpayers into paying up.

Based on his many years of experience my friend Vern Jacobs, CPA, notes: "Many of these press notices are announcements about successful prosecutions of tax evaders — all carefully timed to coincide with the first three months of the year when folks are working on their taxes or having them done by their accountants. Because tax prosecutions are relatively rare, an unquestioning news media dutifully picks up the press releases and runs them with large headlines."

IRS Brags about their Conquests

Criminal prosecutions for tax evasion are only worthwhile to the IRS because of publicity value. These cases take a long time and cost the IRS far more in time and effort than the added penalties they can possibly collect. In addition, in a criminal prosecution, the IRS has to be able to prove to a jury that the accused taxpayer knowingly and willfully failed to pay their taxes. That's what got actor Wesley Snipes partially off the IRS tax hook.

This has been a bad year for the IRS propaganda machine. In February, the IRS came out on the short end. A federal trial jury failed to find actor and tax protester Wesley Snipes guilty on several tax evasion counts.

The action movie actor was convicted on three misdemeanor counts of willfully failing to file a tax return. He faces up to three years in prison when he is sentenced on April 24th. The IRS went after Snipes for his high profile. And they undoubtedly will prosecute others with "large numbers or loud voices because they're spreading the anti-tax cause," says J.J. MacNab, a writer who monitors tax resisters.

Another "New" Dirty Dozen List

For several years now, the IRS has trotted out its ancient "Dirty Dozen" list — as some sort of keynote to its annual campaign. The list supposedly contains the top 12 worst tax frauds du jour. Quite frankly, the list is pretty entertaining — considering it's the same every single year.

Once again this year, the IRS put offshore financial activity on the list — although offshore has moved down to #5 on the list.

Without offering any proof, the IRS claimed that Americans are hiding trillions in taxable income offshore. That's a ridiculous claim at best — used for dramatic effect. Of course, legitimate international investing and banking is a normal part of doing business offshore.

Also, even in the midst of their glorious tax campaign, the IRS was forced to admit that it's legal for Americans to have offshore bank accounts, credit cards, investments and businesses. (If the IRS can spread their propaganda, then allow me to call attention to that, considering I'm sure few news organizations bothered to report that fact.)

Funny Numbers Game

These bogus claims about "trillions offshore" are part of the larger IRS "numbers game." Here's an example of how the IRS plays the game.

When he quit in 2002, then IRS Commissioner Charles O. Rossotti claimed the IRS had identified 82,100 taxpayers using offshore accounts to evade taxes. He also estimated the government lost US$447 million when tax evaders failed to pay their share. That's less than US$7,000 per taxpayer.

But only a year earlier, in 2000, under Rossotti, the IRS estimated that 505,000 taxpayers were using offshore bank accounts to evade taxes (that's about 400,000 MORE than Rossotti said two years later).

By early 2002, the IRS upped that number to two million. It was the same Commissioner Rossotti who, in May 2001, demanded federal court subpoenas for offshore credit card records. In 2001, he claimed offshore tax evasion was costing the government US$20 billion to US$40 billion in 2000 alone! (That's a long way up from US$447 million.)

Meanwhile Jack Blum, a Washington lobbyist and paid IRS propagandist on tax evasion, estimated that offshore evasion cost government US$70 billion annually.

If Only We Could Audit the IRS…

Apparently the IRS Commission can't figure out whether they lost US$447 million or US$70 BILLION (that's only a difference of US$69.5 BILLION). He also can't quite put his finger on whether supposed offshore evaders number 82,000 or 505,000 or two million. That's completely consistent with the way the IRS mishandles most matters. Talk about needing an audit!

The real IRS gap is not one of lost taxes, but the collective one between their ears.

So try and have fun with your Form 1040 and paperwork this week. Don't pay attention to the IRS's scare tactics. Simply fill out your forms as usual, and be done with it.

In fact, the most annoying thing you can do is fill your forms out correctly — then they won't have any PR material for next year's campaign.

What to Do if You're on the Wrong Side of the IRS

Erika Nolan, *The Sovereign Individual*, February 2009

The right offshore legal structure can offer many benefits: asset protection, financial privacy, tax savings and access to a wider world of investments. Yet if you're structure is not "compliant," you risk losing these benefits and worse. You could face significant fines from the IRS and, in the extreme, even jail time.

So, we're going to make sure you're doing all that you need to do — to make sure your offshore structure is helping you build and protect your wealth and not putting you in legal jeopardy.

Five Steps to Make Sure Your Offshore Structure is in Good Standing

The truth is, it's all too easy to run afoul of the U.S. taxman by under-reporting and misfiling the proper returns. So a key principle to keep in mind is that if you should suspect your offshore structure may not be compliant, take quick action to correct any mistakes BEFORE the IRS comes a knocking. Here's a quick check list to help you do that…

1) Have Your Offshore Structures Reviewed Annually

Put as much emphasis on your annual financial review as you spot because the tax code has changed — impacting your offshore structures — while you are left in the dark. And don't assume that a non-U.S. professional will remember which U.S. IRS forms must be submitted. It is up to you to ensure that the taxman gets everything on time and accurately filed.

2) Work with an International Tax Attorney — Not a CPA or Accountant

If you have any concerns about reporting requirements, work with someone who specializes in international structures and tax reporting.

Make certain your offshore structure is 100% compliant. It's never a good feeling to realize you've run afoul of the taxman. But the fate of your finances is in your hands. Rather than run the risk of increased penalties or the threat of an IRS shakedown — be proactive. Chances are, your structures are in good standing. But it pays to know for sure. Obtain the expertise of a licensed professional as well as the time honored principle of attorney-client privilege.

3) If You Discover Under-Reported Income — Seek Criminal Tax Counsel Immediately

U.S. citizens and U.S. resident aliens are required to report their world-wide income annually. If your international tax consultant believes you have inadvertently violated IRS reporting requirements, seek criminal tax counsel as soon as possible. (Under no circumstances should you, yourself, go to the IRS directly to resolve your situation!)

Criminal tax attorneys understand the necessary process to resolve most reporting mistakes. Their job is to represent you before the IRS and to work quickly and efficiently to ensure that your structure is fully compliant.

If you can prove reasonable cause and/or the absence of willful neglect for your failure to file the returns, you may be able to avoid penalties. In a best-case scenario, all you'd be liable for is back taxes plus interest. (Keep in mind, income must be reported in the year it was earned.)

4) Have Your Legal Counsel Hire an Accountant

By allowing your legal counsel to hire a CPA — you will greatly streamline the reporting process. In most situations, you will be required to provide documentation for up to three years (or as much as six years if you have made any mistakes that could be construed as tax fraud).

For example, say you established an offshore trust in 2003. You believed that your offshore trustee was filing the IRS Form 3520A each year. Yet four years later, during a routine conversation, you discover (much to your surprise) that they never filed the form. In order to correct this mistake, you would need to go back to the 2003 tax year and file all the necessary documents from that point forward.

Keep in mind that failure to file the form 3520A or 3520 could lead the IRS to assess a 35% penalty against the value of your trust assets.

5) Don't Liquidate an Offshore Structure Until You Take Care of Delinquent Tax Forms & Penalties

Disbanding an offshore structure will not help you avoid trouble. If the IRS discovers that you've closed a non-compliant structure without first getting it compliant, they could bring criminal charges against you.

But there is a silver lining…The government wants to encourage voluntary tax compliance. So even though the IRS has the right to file criminal charges against anyone who is non-compliant, you can minimize this threat by initiating contact with the agency.

LIVE OFFSHORE: TWO CAN EARN, TAX-FREE

Mark Nestmann, *The Sovereign Individual*, October 2009, Updated 2013

The United States is one of only two countries in the world that taxes its citizens no matter where in the world they live. Even U.S. citizens who haven't set foot in the United States in decades must pay tax on their worldwide income as if they never left.

Ridiculous? Yes.

Fortunately, the U.S. Tax Code contains one escape clause that allows you to earn up to $99,200 annually tax-free (2015, adjusted annually for inflation) if you live and work outside the United States. If your spouse accompanies you overseas and also works, you could double this exemption and jointly earn up to $198,400 free of U.S. tax obligations.

This tax break is known as is the "foreign earned income exclusion" (FEIE).

What it Takes to Qualify

You can't just run off to Mexico for a few months to qualify for this tax break. You must be a bona-fide resident of another country to qualify for the FEIE under one of two tests:

- Bona-fide residence test. You must have established legal residence in another country for an uninterrupted period that includes at least one "tax year" (generally Jan. 1–Dec. 31).

- Physical presence test. You must be physically present in a foreign country or countries for at least 330 full days during any period of 12 consecutive months. Under either test, you must have a new "tax home" outside the United States. That means a jurisdiction that can tax your income on the basis of residence or other ties. However, there is no requirement that you live in a country that actually imposes an income tax.

You must also file a U.S. tax return every year, along with IRS Form 2555 (https://www.irs.gov/uac/About-Form-2555). While you can take either a tax credit or deduction for any foreign income tax you pay, you can't credit or deduct foreign taxes on income exempt from tax under the FEIE.

Housing Expenses Count

You can also exclude taxes on additional income from your employer that are used to pay housing expenses.

In most cases, the maximum housing exclusion is about $13,000 (adjusted for inflation). If you are married and working offshore only one spouse can take the housing expense exclusion unless you maintain separate households. Still, that adds to the income each year that you can legally exclude from U.S. taxation.

What's more, benefits that are non-taxable to a U.S.-based employee are also non-taxable overseas.

Your employer can pay for health insurance or contribute to a retirement plan with no additional tax liability.

These exclusions apply if the company is domiciled in the United States, or if it's one you have a material interest in and one you incorporate yourself. Again, to qualify you have to live overseas.

Passive Foreign Income is Taxable with One Exception

If you're working for an employer abroad, the company will pay you a salary, a housing allowance, and possibly other benefits. You can exclude a substantial amount, if not all, of this income from U.S. taxes.

However, the FEIE provides no exclusion for unearned income. This includes rents, royalties, interest, dividends, and capital gains. But you may be able to convert "unearned income" into "earned income" if you follow the IRS rules carefully.

Here's what you need to do, step-by-step:

Step 1: Form a foreign corporation (such as an international business company or IBC) in a jurisdiction such as Nevis. The foreign corporation must file IRS

Form 5471 each year. You must also file Treasury Form TD F 90-22.1 annually to report foreign "bank, securities, and 'other' financial" accounts.

Step 2: Transfer capital to the foreign corporation. You must generally report this transfer by filing IRS Form 926.

Step 3: Move abroad for a length of time sufficient to qualify for the FEIE.

Step 4: Pay yourself (and your spouse if you're married and your spouse accompanies you abroad) a reasonable salary for the services you (and your spouse, if applicable) provide to the corporation.

The corporation may also pay for your housing and other benefits up to applicable limits.

Step 5: File IRS Form 2555 annually with your U.S. tax return to claim the FEIE and foreign housing exclusion. You won't need to make Social Security or Medicare payments, as long as you're living in a country that doesn't have a social security totalization agreement with the United States. (Under a totalization agreement, if a U.S. worker has some U.S. coverage but not enough to qualify for benefits, SSA will count periods of coverage that the worker has earned under the Social Security program of an agreement country.)

The Fine Print

The IRS could challenge this strategy if it believes the salary is unreasonably high. Therefore, you must show that the salary the corporation pays for your services is what you'd receive from an "arm's length" employer.

You might be able to justify a higher salary if you're certified as a portfolio manager, or the IRS classifies you as a "professional trader." But if you're not, you can still be compensated for services to the corporation, although the "reasonable" salary you receive would likely be lower.

Your attorney should prepare a written agreement between you and the corporation documenting the services you provide. You also need to keep detailed records to document performance of these services and maintain whatever records are required in the local jurisdiction.

If the foreign corporation generates more profits than you pay yourself as a salary, it's unlikely you'll be able to defer U.S. tax on the income. You won't be able to deduct losses for the corporation or be eligible for the 15% tax rate on qualified capital gains or dividends. But that's a small price to pay for being able to legally avoid U.S. income tax.

Finally, it's important to ensure that the tax or immigration laws of the country you're living in don't restrict this strategy, or make it uneconomical.

Know Before You Go

You must choose to elect the FEIE and the determination whether to elect it should be made only after you consult with your professional tax advisor. If you're paying yourself a salary for managing your own money, it's important to prove that your salary is reasonable as discussed above. For more details about the FEIE, see www.irs.gov.

ABCs OF FATCA REGULATIONS: IN LESS THAN 20 MINUTES YOU'LL KNOW MORE THAN YOUR CPA

Robert E. Bauman JD, *Offshore Confidential*, January 2012

As a savvy member of The Sovereign Society, you will be well aware of the odious U.S. law called the "Foreign Account Tax Compliance Act" (FATCA).

This law was rammed through the U.S. Congress in March 2010 as part of the so-called "Hiring Incentives to Restore Employment (HIRE) Act" and now it's on the books as Public Law 111-147.

As with most major U.S. legislation, a careless U.S. Congress delegated the power to write FATCA rules to the government agency charged with enforcing the law, the beloved U.S. Internal Revenue Service.

What is not yet widely known is that these new IRS rules, now in effect, apply to any taxpaying U.S. person who was engaged in just about any form of offshore financial activity during 2011. (The term *"U.S. person,"* as a matter of law, includes both citizens and resident aliens).

If you fit that broad definition, it means that this coming April you must file a new IRS Form 8938, "Statement of Specified Foreign Financial Assets," along with, and in addition to, your familiar annual income tax IRS Form 1040 for 2011.

First Rule: Don't Panic

Unlike your friendly IRS agent, I really am here to help you. This special report will explain how you can get through the process with a few relatively simple steps, by yourself or in cooperation with your tax advisor and accountant.

I am going to explain the fundamental issues posed for you by these new FATCA reporting requirements and Form 8938, how you can deal with this practically, and how you can comply with the law in ways that will help you avoid costly mistakes.

In fact, your tasks will be simple, if somewhat time consuming, and will include:

- compiling an inventory of your offshore financial activity and holdings
- determining the values of those offshore holdings
- applying IRS income "thresholds" to see if you must file the new Form 8938

A this point you may want to take a look at IRS Form 8938 on the IRS website in order to understand what this is all about. When you read it, if you are Mitt Romney, you might faint.

But if you only have an offshore bank account or a foreign-based IRA, life insurance or annuity — it's not too bad.

I assume that any U.S. person with offshore financial activity has relevant records that can be compiled and consolidated, although more offshore activity will mean more work.

Now, please understand that I am not minimizing the importance of your need to comply with this new FATCA reporting.

Failing to file Form 8938 could result in a $10,000 penalty, with an additional penalty up to $50,000 for continued failure to file after IRS notification.

On top of that, a 40% penalty on any understatement of tax owed on non-disclosed assets can also be imposed.

The statute of limitation is six years on failure to file, if the resulting tax liability is $5,000 or more.

But don't worry about that. Those penalties won't touch you. When you finish reading this Special Report you will be in no danger, so long as you do what is necessary — although, depending on your offshore holdings, it may require some effort.

Who Must Report

There is a possibility you will be able to avoid reporting, so check to see if the "thresholds" explained below apply to you. One group of U.S. persons that will be caught in the FATCA reporting net includes American expatriates living and working offshore.

But FATCA also ensnares any U.S. person with financial connections offshore, be it shares in a Caribbean resort investment or a bank account in Europe.

FATCA requires that a U.S. person files the new IRS Form 8938 when the total value of their foreign assets exceeds certain thresholds. The IRS answers the question of who must file on its website, but these answers are subject to change.

The filing thresholds vary, ranging from $50,000 in total foreign financial assets for U.S.-based taxpayers to $400,000 for U.S. taxpayers filing jointly who live abroad.

Reporting thresholds vary based on whether you file a joint tax return or reside abroad, and they are higher for married couples and taxpayers who qualify as foreign residents.

Here are the "thresholds" for filing Form 8938:

1. Unmarried and married taxpayers living in the U.S. and filing a joint income tax return if the total value of foreign financial assets is more than $50,000 on the last day of the tax year or more than $75,000 at any time during the tax year;

2. Married taxpayers filing separate income tax returns and living in the U.S., if the total value of foreign financial assets exceeds $50,000 on the last day of the tax year or more than $75,000 at any time during the tax year;

3. Taxpayers living abroad:

    a. Filing anything other than a joint return if the total value of foreign assets exceeds $200,000 on the last day of the tax year or is more than $300,000 at any time during the year; or

    b. Married filing a joint return and the value of foreign assets exceeds $400,000 on the last day of the tax year or more than $600,000 at any time during the year.

Married individuals who file a joint annual return must file a single Form 8938 that reports all of the foreign financial assets in which either spouse has an interest.

What Must Be Reported

I am reasonably certain that you share my opinion that it's none of the IRS's damned business and they have no right to force you to bare your financial soul just to satisfy their bureaucratic inquisitiveness.

But remember FATCA was the idea of a Democrat-dominated Congress in 2010 and had the enthusiastic support of President Barack Obama. Its repeal probably depends on the outcome of the 2012 U.S. elections.

Here's what those political worthies demand be reported:

1. offshore bank and brokerage accounts, retirement accounts, hedge funds, private-equity funds, annuities and life insurance.

2. the above includes foreign financial accounts, foreign assets held for investment, such as foreign stock and securities, financial instruments, foreign contracts with non-U.S. persons, and any interests in foreign legal entities (corporations, partnerships, limited liability companies, private family foundations).

What Not to Report

1. foreign assets used in a trade or business are exempt.
2. accounts maintained by a U.S. branch of a foreign financial institution, or a foreign branch of a U.S. financial institution;
3. assets reported on certain but not all other IRS forms;
4. assets held by residents in U.S. territorial possessions, (American Samoa, Guam, the Commonwealth of the Northern Mariana Islands, the U.S. Virgin Islands, and Puerto Rico).
5. a beneficial interest in a foreign trust or a foreign estate if it is unknown to the beneficiary;
6. a beneficiary of a domestic U.S. bankruptcy trust or a U.S. fixed investment trust is not required to report any foreign asset held by the trust.

Duplication

The Form 8938 filing requirement does not replace the obligation to file an FBAR (Report of Foreign Bank and Financial Accounts) by June 30, 2012. Under FBAR, a U.S. person with foreign "bank, brokerage, or other" financial accounts with a value of $10,000 or more, already must make two annual disclosures.

The first is to the IRS on Schedule B of IRS Form 1040, where you are asked to check "yes" or "no" if you have any direct or indirect control over a foreign financial account. The second report is to the U.S. Treasury is the above mentioned FBAR Form TD F 90-22 1 by June 30, 2012.

And FACTA reporting will result in still further IRS duplications. U.S. persons with real estate overseas held in the name of a foreign entity will also have to file a FATCA form, on top of the IRS Form 5471 already required if a foreign corporation holds the property.

If the asset is in a foreign partnership, the FATCA form will be required in addition to IRS Form 8865 for partnerships.

Here is a helpful chart published by the *Wall Street Journal* that summarizes all these FATCA and FBAR reporting requirements:

	Form 8938, Statement of Specified Foreign Financial Assets	FinCEN Form 114, Report of Foreign Bank and Financial Accounts (FBAR)
Who Must File?	Specified individuals, which include U.S citizens, resident aliens, and certain non-resident aliens that have an interest in specified foreign financial assets and meet the reporting threshold	U.S. persons, which include U.S. citizens, resident aliens, trusts, estates, and domestic entities that have an interest in foreign financial accounts and meet the reporting threshold
Does the United States include U.S. territories?	No	Yes, resident aliens of U.S territories and U.S. territory entities are subject to FBAR reporting
Reporting Threshold (Total Value of Assets)	$50,000 on the last day of the tax year or $75,000 at any time during the tax year (higher threshold amounts apply to married individuals filing jointly and individuals living abroad)	$10,000 at any time during the calendar year
When do you have an interest in an account or asset?	If any income, gains, losses, deductions, credits, gross proceeds, or distributions from holding or disposing of the account or asset are or would be required to be reported, included, or otherwise reflected on your income tax return	Financial interest: you are the owner of record or holder of legal title; the owner of record or holder of legal title is your agent or representative; you have a sufficient interest in the entity that is the owner of record or holder of legal title. Signature authority: you have authority to control the disposition of the assets in the account by direct communication with the financial institution maintaining the account. See instructions for further details.
What is Reported?	Maximum value of specified foreign financial assets, which include financial accounts with foreign financial institutions and certain other foreign non-account investment assets	Maximum value of financial accounts maintained by a financial institution physically located in a foreign country
How are maximum account or asset values determined and reported?	Fair market value in U.S. dollars in accord with the Form 8938 instructions for each account and asset reported. Convert to U.S. dollars using the end of the taxable year exchange rate and report in U.S. dollars.	Use periodic account statements to determine the maximum value in the currency of the account. Convert to U.S. dollars using the end of the calendar year exchange rate and report in U.S. dollars.
When Due?	By due date, including extension, if any, for income tax return	Received by June 30 (no extensions of time granted).
Where to File?	File with income tax return pursuant to instructions for filing the return	File electronically through FinCENs BSA E-Filing System. The FBAR is not filed with a federal tax return.

	Form 8938, Statement of Specified Foreign Financial Assets	FinCEN Form 114, Report of Foreign Bank and Financial Accounts (FBAR)
Penalties	Up to $10,000 for failure to disclose and an additional $10,000 for each 30 days of non-filing after IRS notice of a failure to disclose, for a potential maximum penalty of $60,000; criminal penalties may also apply	If non-willful, up to $10,000; if willful, up to the greater of $100,000 or 50 percent of account balances; criminal penalties may also apply
Types of Foreign Assets and Whether They are Reportable		
Financial (deposit and custodial) accounts held at foreign financial institutions	Yes	Yes
Financial account held at a foreign branch of a U.S. financial institution	No	Yes
Financial account held at a U.S. branch of a foreign financial institution	No	No
Foreign financial account for which you have signature authority	No, unless you otherwise have an interest in the account as described above	Yes, subject to exceptions
Foreign stock or securities held in a financial account at a foreign financial institution	The account itself is subject to reporting, but the contents of the account do not have to be separately reported	The account itself is subject to reporting, but the contents of the account do not have to be separately reported
Foreign stock or securities not held in a financial account	Yes	No
Foreign partnership interests	Yes	No
Indirect interests in foreign financial assets through an entity	No	Yes, if sufficient ownership or beneficial interest (i.e., a greater than 50 percent interest) in the entity. See instructions for further detail.
Foreign mutual funds	Yes	Yes
Domestic mutual fund investing in foreign stocks and securities	No	No

That 30% Tax

What many folks have concentrated on, rightfully so, is the 30% FATCA withholding tax.

I know there has been a good deal of confusion about FATCA's effective dates, and that's because in July 2011, after massive protests worldwide, the IRS bowed to reason for once and changed its bureaucratic mind. It announced then that the original January 1, 2013 FATCA target date would be delayed.

But FATCA reporting has not delayed for individual U.S. persons. Nonetheless, you may be involved in the reporting for a foreign financial institution (FFI), which can include banks, stock brokers, hedge funds, pension funds, insurance companies and trusts.

If an FFI does not comply with this reporting, FATCA allows the IRS to impose a 30% withholding tax on all the FFI's international transactions concerning U.S. securities, including the proceeds of sale of securities.

This 30% withholding tax on income transferred oversea from the U.S., such as dividends and interest, has been the rate for collecting taxes under most existing double-taxation treaties signed between the U.S. and other countries.

FATCA imposes a new 30% withholding on capital transfers on all U.S. source transfers to non-compliant foreign financial institutions, including interest, dividends and sales proceeds.

Basically, this amounts to the IRS holding ransom foreign companies' U.S. based income until they and their FFI surrender information about their U.S. clients.

As one commentator has said: "This puts a gun to foreign banks' heads… Any bank with U.S. clients must either enter into a costly information-sharing agreement with the IRS, or be subject to a 30% withholding tax on US-sourced capital flows."

Naturally enough, the reaction of most foreign banks was summed up in a document sent to me by the client of a leading Luxemburg bank: "FATCA: Turning US persons into toxic liabilities."

Untold numbers of foreign banks already have acted to avoid doing business with Americans because of the trouble of compliance with FATCA. Existing American accounts have been cancelled and new applications rejected.

Possible Intended Consequences

FATCA and other similar restrictions may be calculated to keep American investors — along with their cash and assets — at home, where we can be controlled (and our assets confiscated) at will by government. That threat includes the possible government confiscation of private pension and retirement plans.

There is no getting away from the reality that FATCA rules impose unjust penalties — especially on thousands of innocent American expatriates suddenly caught in a new jungle of paperwork they had no idea existed.

There are an estimated five to six million Americans living offshore and another 39 million immigrants in the U.S. who face similar IRS issues with overseas disclosure if they have foreign bank accounts. (Interestingly, in 2009 there were only 534,043 FBARs filed, according to a report by the Treasury Inspector General for Tax Administration). That's one consequence.

Another is that growing numbers of Americans living abroad are renouncing their U.S. citizenship because of FATCA and complex IRS reporting obligations that now come with the threat of financial and even criminal penalties.

The U.S. is one the few nations in the world that requires its citizens living abroad to pay income taxes.

The only way to end that U.S. tax obligation is to terminate U.S. citizenship.

The latest statistics reveal that more than 1,500 Americans living offshore did just that in 2011. According to the Federal Register, that's up from 743 people in 2009 and 235 in 2008.

Jackie Bugnion, director of American Citizens Abroad, a Geneva-based group, says the exodus is a backlash on the part of U.S. expatriates and the offshore financial sector to the radical IRS claim that its jurisdiction extends to every bank and financial institution in the world. Indeed, the backers of FATCA blithely assume the U.S. government and the IRS have jurisdiction over all the world's financial institutions.

This unprecedented extraterritorial claim bothers even the editors of the liberal *New York Times*, who have warned against the excesses of FATCA, asking: "Would the United States accept the same demands for information from the tax authorities in other countries — say Russia or China?"

What Benefit?

Dan Mitchell, chief tax expert at the Cato Institute raises the issue of what possible "benefit" could result from FATCA, which he sees as another "transfer (of) more money from the productive sector of the economy to the government."

Obama argued during his 2008 campaign that cracking down on "tax havens" with proposals such as FATCA would give politicians lots of additional money to spend. But when the legislation was approved in 2010, the Joint Committee on Taxation estimated the new law would raise only $8.7 billion over 10 years — not the $100 billion that Obama claimed could be collected every single year.

The IRS claimed a few weeks ago it had collected more than $4.4 billion from offshore tax amnesty programs in 2009 and 2011. Even if the IRS really did collect $4.4 billion— and that's debatable — that's just 0.16% the $2.7 trillion total tax take in 2009.

Meanwhile the figure that the IRS didn't publicize was how many millions it spent collecting that magnificent sum, which, at best, might finance the running of the U.S. government for a few hours.

FACTA is colossal mess. Complete repeal by Congress is necessary. Much hinges on the outcome of the 2012 U.S. presidential and congressional elections, not least of which is the freedom of Americans to do business where they choose.

Contacts

If you need assistance in complying with FATCA, our members of The Sovereign Society Council of Experts can help. You can find these professionals contact information in Appendix A.

Josh Bennett has more than 23 years' experience in law with extensive work in all aspects of international tax, estate, and gift tax planning for U.S. citizens, resident aliens, and non-resident aliens.

Michael Chatzky specializes in U.S. and international taxation and wealth protection with an emphasis on business, estate and asset protection planning. For 36 years Michael has helped clients establish a variety of wealth preservation structures.

Gideon Rothschild is a nationally recognized authority on offshore trusts and other planning techniques for wealth preservation. He is an Adjunct Professor at The University of Miami School of Law Graduate Program, and a Fellow of The American College of Trust and Estates Counsel.

THE ONLY WAY TO END U.S. TAXES

Robert E. Bauman JD, *The Sovereign Investor Daily*, February 2013

Take a look at these names and you will know what unites this disparate group:

- Pop icon Tina Turner
- Facebook co-founder Eduardo Saverin
- French movie star Gerard Depardieu

These three individuals have in common good sense and a keen grasp of the bottom line on a profit and loss sheet.

And they all recently have been in the spotlight for ending their native citizenship and moving their residence elsewhere. They were sensationalized by the news media and accused by politicians of unpatriotically avoiding high taxes at home.

Tina Turner has gone to Switzerland, and has been joined by Gerard Depardieu, and Saverin, a native Brazilian, went to Singapore.

They also joined an illustrious list of fellow expats, such as Bill Clinton buddy and Clinton Library donor Denise Rich; rock star Johnny Hallyday, tennis star Amelie Mauresmo, racing driver Alain Prost, singer Charles Aznavour; Canadian Shania Twain; Italian actress Sophia Loren; British pop star James Blunt and rock star Phil Collins; German Michael Schumacher, former Formula One race car driving world champion (all Switzerland); and grand slam German tennis star, Boris Becker went to Monaco.

Then there was Swede Ingvar Kamprad, founder of Ikea and one of the richest men in the world (Switzerland); billionaire Campbell Soup heir John ("Ippy") Dorrance III (Ireland); Michael Dingman, chairman of Abex and Ford Motor director (The Bahamas); J. Mark Mobious, leading hedge fund manager (Germany); Kenneth Dart, heir to the billion dollar Dart container fortune (Belize); Ted Arison, head of Carnival Cruise Lines (Israel); and millionaire head of Locktite Corp., Fred Kreible (Turks and Caicos Islands) — to name but a few.

One of the forerunners of this phenomenon, the late Sir John Templeton, respected international investor, businessman and philanthropist, surrendered his U.S. citizenship in 1962 to become a citizen of The Bahamas and the U.K. as well. That saved him more than $100 million when he sold the well-known international investment fund that still bears his name (Franklin Templeton) and that also saved his heirs millions more in estate taxes.

Chasing Away Success

This sentiment was echoed by classic comic book hero Superman, who also declared his plans to renounce his U.S. citizenship in 2012 in *Action Comics*. "'Truth, justice, and the American way' — it's not enough anymore" after both the Iranian and American governments criticized him for joining a peaceful anti-government protest in Tehran.

Common sense dictates the right not to pay more taxes than you owe; and also the right to escape taxation when it becomes confiscation. That escape is called expatriation and it is a legal right upheld by the U.S. Supreme Court.

The late Judge Learned Hand, of the U.S. Court of Appeals in New York, was a progressive who believed fervently in judicial restraint. Called one of the greatest judges in American history, in a memorable tax case dissent, Judge Hand wrote: "There is nothing sinister in arranging one's affairs so as to keep taxes as low as possible... nobody owes any public duty to pay more than the law demands.

Taxes are enforced exactions, not voluntary contributions. To demand more in the name of morals is mere cant."

Keep in mind Judge Hand's description of the right to avoid taxes by all *legal* means when you hear politicians weep and wail about U.S. persons who choose formally to end their citizenship — the only way by which Americans can end their tax obligations.

The Long Arm of the IRS

Unlike almost every other major nation, U.S. taxes follow American citizens wherever in the world they go. Most other nations only tax the income of their citizens from sources within their borders. When a Frenchman, a Canadian or an Englishman leaves and makes a new home in another country, most of their home country tax obligations end.

Radical leftists like Michigan U.S. Senator Carl Levin prefer U.S. style worldwide taxation because it undermines tax competition among countries, removing individuals' and companies' ability to escape high taxes by shifting activity to jurisdictions with better, lower tax policies. That is why they back the imperial Foreign Account Tax Compliance Act (FATCA), an attempt to extend the jurisdiction of the U.S. Internal Revenue Service over every country in the world.

Indeed, as Cato's Dan Mitchell says, this is why politicians from high-tax nations, like Levin and President Obama, are so fixated on trying to shut down so-called "tax havens." It's difficult to enforce bad, high-tax policy, after all, if some nations have strong human rights policies on financial privacy.

This same common sense geographic re-ordering based on taxation levels is occurring within the United States on a grand scale.

Higher Taxes Equals Less Revenue

The recent feeble complaint of golfer Phil Mickelson, a man worth $100 million, about California taking 65% of his income is only a symptom. The more famous Tiger Woods is worth more than $1 billion. He left California in 1996 because of high taxes and has saved millions in result.

In his book, Travis Brown, author of *How Money Walks*, writes that from 1995 to 2010 Americans moved about $2 trillion in wealth from California, Illinois, New Jersey and other high-tax states to states such as Florida, Nevada, Arizona and Texas that impose no income tax.

The 2010 U.S. Census showed these four low-tax states had the fastest population growth. The states that lost people were all high-tax states like California, New York, New Jersey, Connecticut, Maryland, and of course, President Obama's home state of Illinois.

But "Big Brother" politicians everywhere think they can bleed the rich dry. They're wrong.

In 2009, when the Labor Party in the U.K. raised the top income tax rate to 50%, two-thirds of the country's 16,000 £1 million earners disappeared from British tax rolls. In 2010, HM Revenue and Customs reported only 6,000 remained. Rather than increasing revenue, the tax actually cost the U.K. £7 billion ($11 billion) in lost tax revenue.

Similarly, in France, when Socialist President Francois Hollande imposed a 75% tax on 400 to 500 families worth more than one million euros ($1.3 million), a flood of top-end properties were put up for sale and Monsieur Depardieu headed for lunch with President Putin and a new citizenship.

When Presidents John F. Kennedy and Ronald Reagan reduced income tax rates, the result was much more revenue. As long as there are ships, autos, trains and planes, high taxes will only drive the highest earners elsewhere.

4 Strategies for Beating the IRS
Ted Bauman, *Sovereign Confidential*, December 2015

My wife is a teacher, specializing in pre-kindergarten kids. They're 4 to 5 years old, just as sweet as can be. Their experience of the world so far is almost entirely defined by the warm embrace of the families who love them and who put their needs before anyone else's.

Their whole lives are ahead of them, so they haven't yet experienced the pains and disappointments that led Henry David Thoreau to refer to adulthood as "lives of quiet desperation."

And yet the most popular phrase in my wife's classroom is "No fair!"

I've always been fascinated by the fact that every generation of kids enthusiastically adopts this little phrase as soon as they venture out into the world. Once they leave the bosom of home and interact with their peers, kids instinctively know that maintaining a stable society depends deeply on fair play.

And they know it when they see it.

Scientists have even demonstrated that many animals have such a sense. When two monkeys or crows are rewarded differentially for having performed the same task, they object.

The experience of unfairness is hardwired. We can detect it … unless it's hidden.

That's probably why the Standard Federal Tax Reporter, the annotated form of the U.S. tax code used by lawyers, is over 75,000 pages long. It grows by more than 10,000 pages a decade.

That's the only way the fundamental unfairness of the U.S. tax system can be kept hidden from us.

Leona Helmsley, a hotel chain executive who was convicted of federal tax evasion in 1989, was notorious for having said that "only the little people pay taxes."

Indeed, Leona! Forget about theoretical tax rates. Did you know that:

- The richest 100 or so individual U.S. taxpayers pay less than 15% effective income tax?

- The effective tax paid increases as you go down the income scale ... 20% for households earning between $100,000 and $1,000,000, 25% for those earning between $80,000 and $100,000?

- Many profitable U.S. corporations not only pay almost no tax at all ... they even get billions in tax refunds?

You see, one function of the complex U.S. tax code is to ensure that we "little people" remain unaware of the fundamental unfairness of the system ... not to mention what our taxes actually pay for.

The U.S. tax code contains thousands of little-known tricks designed to benefit special interests that can afford lobbyists and lawyers to manipulate the politicians who control it. But it also contains tricks that can help you.

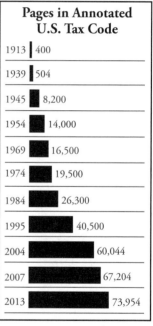

Pages in Annotated U.S. Tax Code

Year	Pages
1913	400
1939	504
1945	8,200
1954	14,000
1969	16,500
1974	19,500
1984	26,300
1995	40,500
2004	60,044
2007	67,204
2013	73,954

As you read on, I'm going to review some of the strategies that every American taxpayer should use to minimize what goes to Uncle Sam. They are perfectly legal and typically not very difficult to implement.

Your Golden Rule of Taxes

Adjusted gross income (AGI) — i.e. your taxable income — is a key element in determining your taxes. The tax code creates opportunities to reduce your AGI by diverting some of your gross income to certain uses.

The golden rule of your tax strategy is to reduce your AGI for the calendar year. You do this by taking advantage of certain pre-tax deductions, called "adjustments to income" or "above the line" deductions.

Here are four tactics you can deploy to achieve this.

STRATEGY ONE: Often Overlooked, But They Add Up ... Generic Deductions

- **Self-employment tax**

  The 15.3% self-employment tax is composed of a 12.4% Social Security tax on the first $118,500 of net self-employment income, and a Medicare tax of 2.9% on all net self-employment income. You can deduct half of this from your AGI.

- **Self-employment health insurance**

  If you are self-employed, a general partner in a partnership, a member in a limited liability company (LLC) treated as a partnership or an employee of an S-corporation who owns 2% or more of the S-corporation's stock, you can deduct the cost of medical, dental and long-term care insurance from your AGI.

- **Health savings account deduction**

  You can deduct up to $3,350 per individual, $6,650 per family (rising to $6,750 for 2016) and $1,000 per year in catch-up contributions for previous years from your AGI. In addition, you can deduct all contributions from January 1, 2015 to April 15, 2016 from your 2015 AGI.

- **Tuition and fees deduction**

  You can deduct up to $4,000 from your AGI if you pay the qualified tuition and fee expenses for an eligible student, which can be you, your spouse, one of your children or any other dependent who you claim. (If you or your spouse were considered a non-resident alien during any part of the 2014 tax year, you cannot claim this deduction.)

  You must have a modified adjusted gross income of $65,000 or below if single ($130,000 if married filing jointly) to receive the full $4,000 deduction, and $80,000 or below ($160,000 married filing jointly) to claim a maximum deduction of $2,000. People with higher incomes do not qualify.

  Expenses are deducted at the time of payment, not when the classes begin. Payments made in December 2015 for the first semester of 2016 are deductible in 2015.

- **Student loan interest deduction**

  You can deduct up to $2,500 from your gross income for this expense, but it is subject to phase outs once you reach $130,000 in modified adjusted gross income (see below).

- **Moving expenses**

    If you relocated to start a new job at least 50 miles further away than your current job, or to seek work in a new city, you can deduct moving expenses from your AGI. Qualifying expenses include costs for packing and shipping your household goods and personal property, and costs for travel and lodging. Active duty military who move due to change of station also qualify.

- **Educator expenses**

    If you are a grade school or high school teacher, aide, instructor, counselor or principal, and worked in a school at least 900 hours during the school year, you can deduct up to $250 for non-refunded expenses from your AGI.

- **Performing artists, National Guardsmen and Reservists, and certain governmental officials**

    If you paid for job-related expenses out of your own pocket, you can reduce your AGI up to the amount of those expenses.

STRATEGY TWO: Max Out Your Retirement Contributions

One of the most important ways to reduce before-tax income is to max out your retirement contributions. The 2015 annual contribution limits for Roth IRAs, 401(k)s, 403(b)s and simple IRAs won't change in 2016, but the limit will change for SEP-IRAs. Here are the numbers for 2015 and 2016:

- **Employer-based plans — $18,000**

    The 2016 elective contribution limits on Section 401(k) and Section 403(b) plans (and similar plans) are currently $18,000, and will remain at this rate for 2016. Catch-up contributions for those 50 and older are $5,500 for 2015, but will rise to $6,000 for 2016.

- **Individual Retirement Accounts (IRAs) — $5,500**

    You can contribute up to $5,500 to an IRA in 2015, which jumps to $6,500 if you are age 50 or older. If you also have an employer retirement plan, however, the tax deduction for your IRA contributions is phased out if your modified adjusted gross income is between $61,000 and $71,000 ($98,000 and $118,000 for couples).

    If only one spouse has a retirement plan at work, the deduction is phased out if your combined income is between $181,000 and $191,000. This will rise to $184,000 to $194,000 in 2016.

    Note that unlike 401(k) contributions, which generally need to be made by the end of the year, IRA contributions can be made up until the tax-filing deadline in April 2016.

- **Roth IRAs — $18,000**

    You can contribute up to $5,500 to a Roth IRA in 2015. If you're over age 50, there's a $1,000 catch-up contribution. Your eligibility to make Roth IRA contributions is phased out once your individual income is between $116,000 and $130,000 in 2015 ($183,000 to $193,000 for couples). These limits will go up by $1,000 in 2016.

- **SEP-IRAs — 25% of income up to $53,000**

    If you're self-employed and have a SEP-IRA plan, your maximum contribution has increased by $1,000 per year from last year. The amount is limited to the lesser of 25% of your income or $53,000; so if you make over $265,000, the most you can contribute is $53,000. There is no provision for catch-up contributions, but you have until April 15, 2016, to max out your contributions for this year. Note: If your business has employees, you are required to contribute the same salary percentage to a SEP-IRA for all your employees.

- **Pension plans**

    The 2016 annual benefit limit under a defined benefit plan will remain unchanged from 2015 at $210,000. The combined contribution limit for defined contribution plans will remain unchanged at $53,000.

STRATEGY THREE: Give Money to Someone Other Than the Taxman

You can reduce your AGI by giving money away to people or registered charities you want to help. You can deduct cash contributions of up to 50% of your AGI. Non-cash contributions, such as clothing, property or stock, can be deducted up to 30% of AGI. Charitable contributions are itemized on Schedule A of your Form 1040.

An excellent tactic is to give the gift of appreciated securities. Got a stock that has increased in value, but you don't want to recognize a taxable capital gain? Give it to charity and you can take a tax deduction for the full fair market value of the stock.

At the same time, you'll avoid tax on the stock's embedded capital gain. The appreciated property must be held by you for more than one year to qualify for favorable tax treatment in this scenario. This tactic also works for mutual funds.

Here's an example: Let's say you own shares in a mutual fund and you realize you are paying too much in annual fees. You own $2,000 of shares in the fund, with a cost basis of $900. If you sold the shares outright, you'd have to report a capital gain of $1,100, taxable at 20%.

However, if you give the shares to charity, you can claim a charitable deduction of $2,000, and you don't have to pay any capital gains tax.

Note that giving stock or mutual funds with embedded gains to charity reduces your taxes, but only if you've owned the stock for more than a year. If you have short-term capital gain stock, the charitable deduction is limited to your cost basis.

For example, six months ago you bought a stock with a basis of $1,000. The stock is now worth $10,000. If you were to sell the stock, you'd have a short-term capital gain of $9,000, taxable at your ordinary income tax rate. If you were to give the stock to charity, your charitable deduction would be only $1,000, and you still must pay tax on the $9,000 gain. If you held the stock for more than a year, you can give the stock to charity and take a deduction of $10,000, all while avoiding paying tax on the appreciation of the stock.

STRATEGY FOUR: Juggle Income and Expenses

One of the easiest, but often overlooked, ways to reduce current-year AGI is to shift income into the following year or next year's expenses into the current year.

For example, if it's possible to do so, defer some 2015 income until 2016 — such as a bonus or commission, consulting income, self-employment income, real estate sales, gain on stock sales, other property sales and retirement plan distributions.

On the expense side, you can prepay 2016 state and local income taxes, take losses on stock sales (up to $3,000 in net losses) and prepay 2016 real estate taxes, anticipated mortgage interest, margin interest and charitable contributions.

For example, you could make your January mortgage payment in December and take an extra month's interest deduction this year.

Taking investment losses now is another way to offset gains realized earlier this year, or to stockpile losses for future years. Unlike in the case of charitable giving, it doesn't matter if the asset sold has been held for less than one year.

Capital losses in excess of capital gains can reduce your AGI by up to $3,000; any loss above that is carried forward for use in a future year. Remember that if you sell stocks at a loss, the rules bar deducting a loss on a security when a virtually identical one is purchased within 30 days of the sale.

Estate Taxes

Unfortunately, you can't deduct gifts to friends and family to reduce your AGI. But you can use such gifts to reduce your estate taxes. I write about this in detail in the September 2015 issue of *Sovereign Confidential*, but here's a recap.

The federal estate tax is an "excise tax" your estate is expected to pay to the IRS voluntarily before it distributes your assets to your heirs. The maximum estate tax is currently 40%. The administrator of your estate calculates and pays it. If the IRS disagrees with the calculation, it can and will come after your heirs to claim any shortfall.

That's why estate tax planning is doubly important. First, it is the single most effective thing you can do to maximize the assets that pass on to your heirs. Second, getting it right means that process will be easy for those heirs ... easier than a nasty fight with the IRS.

Your taxable estate is basically your assets minus your liabilities, including any income tax from the year of your death, debts, funeral expenses and the expenses of administering your estate, and bequests to your surviving U.S. citizen spouse, or to charity (these are currently unlimited; the exclusion from tax on a gift to a spouse who is not a U.S. citizen is $147,000).

That means you can pass everything on to your spouse, or reserve some for your children or other heirs. In 2015, if your estate's worth more than $5.43 million, the administrators of your estate must pay federal estate taxes. It will rise to $5.45 million in 2016. This is known as the unified lifetime credit, because it rolls together both estate and gift tax limits into one figure.

The unified lifetime credit is why managing the size of your estate is so important: If you can reduce your taxable estate to less than that, there won't be any estate taxes. There are four ways you can do this:

1. Your surviving spouse can add the unused portion of your exemption to his or hers. For example, if a deceased husband only used $2 million of his $5.43 million in lifetime credit, his wife could move the unused $3 million into her estate at his death, tax-free, for a non-taxable estate of $8.43 million.

2. The first $14,000 per person (or $28,000 per married couple) that you gift to someone each year doesn't count toward your unified lifetime credit.

3. A trust can be created under your last will and testament (a testamentary trust), and come into existence only after your death. Your children can be the beneficiaries. The transfer to the trust that takes place at your death is not subject to estate taxes.

4. You can pay tuition or medical costs for someone without cutting into your unified lifetime credit. You can also contribute to Section 529 education-savings plans up to the annual exclusion amount.

Note that if you gift anything other than cash or marketable securities, you need to get a professional appraisal at the time you make the transfer, especially if it's a hard-to-value asset, such as real estate or a share in the family business.

If you plan to do this, you can make one gift late this year and another early next year, using the same appraisal for both — saving on appraisal costs.

Also be aware that there are different rules when it comes to the "tax basis" of property in your estate — i.e. its "starting value" to be used to calculate capital gains. For example, if your child inherits your property, the tax basis would be the fair market value of the property on the date you die. That means all appreciation during your lifetime becomes tax-free.

If he or she receives the property as a gift from you, however, the tax basis is whatever your tax basis was. That means your child will owe tax on appreciation during your life, just like you would have if you sold the asset yourself.

For example, let's say you have a house with a tax basis of $60,000. The fair market value of the house is now $300,000. If you give the house as a gift, your beneficiary's tax basis would be $60,000.

If you bequeath the house and pass away in 2014, the tax basis would be $300,000, its fair market value. If your beneficiary sold the house for $310,000 shortly after he or she got it, the taxable gain on the sale if it was a gift would be $250,000 ($310,000 minus $60,000). By contrast the taxable gain if it was inherited would be $10,000 ($310,000 minus $300,000).

Alternative Minimum Tax

The alternative minimum tax (AMT) is the minimum amount of tax the federal government expects you to pay. If your income exceeds the AMT threshold, certain exemptions fall away and many regular deductions are disallowed or allowed over a longer period of time. Tax rates under the AMT are also different.

If your regular tax is less than the AMT, the IRS will add the difference between the two rates to the tax you owe. The AMT exemption for 2015 is $83,400 for joint filers and $53,600 for single filers.

Because the income used for AMT calculations is based on regular income, the calculation begins with your adjusted gross income (if you claim a standard deduction) or your adjusted gross income less itemized deductions (if you itemize). You then add or subtract any AMT adjustments to determine your final income subject to AMT.

For this reason, if you suspect you're in AMT territory, you need to get to your tax accountant ASAP before the end of the year. You can avoid AMT by staying out of the $150,000 to $415,000 income range. For example, you might be better off realizing a $1 million capital gain all in one year rather than dividing it into two or three years.

Offshore Tax Issues

The foreign earned income exclusion in 2016 will be increased by $500 to $101,300.

The average annual net income tax for determining whether a taxpayer must pay an "exit tax" will increase in 2016 by $1,000, to $161,000. The amount that can be excluded from "gross income" for purposes of calculating the "exit tax" will increase by $3,000, to $693,000.

If, as a U.S. citizen or a permanent resident, you have interest in (or authority over) any foreign accounts with a cumulative total value of more than $10,000 at any one time during the calendar year, U.S. law requires you to report it. You need not report anything if the aggregate value of the accounts does not exceed $10,000. There are at least three separate reporting obligations you must meet:

1. You must acknowledge foreign accounts annually on Schedule B of your federal income tax 1040 return (due April 15 of each year or June 15 if you reside outside the United States). You can apply for a six-month extension of this deadline.

2. You must file Financial Crimes Enforcement Network (FinCEN) Form 114, Report of Foreign Bank and Financial Accounts (FBAR), annually with the U.S. Treasury Department. The deadline for filing is June 30 for foreign accounts held the previous year. Information requested on the FBAR includes how many foreign accounts you hold, their maximum value, the name of the financial institution where the accounts are held, the account numbers, etc.

3. Under FATCA, U.S. taxpayers holding financial assets outside the United States must report those assets to the IRS on Form 8938, Statement of Specified Foreign Financial Assets. If the total value of your accounts is at or below $50,000 at the end of the tax year, there is no reporting requirement for the year, unless the total value was more than $75,000 at any time during the tax year. The threshold is higher for individuals who live outside the United States, and different for married and single taxpayers.

The offshore reporting requirement doesn't apply to real estate and other non-financial, i.e. physical, assets outside the U.S., as long as they're held in your own name. You must report any income from such assets, however. You also must report if such assets are owned by foreign corporations, partnerships or other entities that have foreign bank accounts.

Contacts

When it comes to protecting your wealth from the grasping hands of the U.S. taxman, it is critical to have the knowledge and experience of someone who has spent years specializing in asset protection on your side. Below is a short list of attorneys who focus on asset protection and estate planning:

Josh N. Bennett, Esq.
440 North Andrews Avenue Ft. Lauderdale, FL 33301
Tel.: 786-202-5674 [cell]
Email: josh@joshbennett.com

Michael Chatzky, JD
Chatzky & Associates
6540 Lusk Boulevard, Suite C121
San Diego, CA 92121
Tel.: 858-457-1000
Email: mgchatzky@aol.com

Gideon Rothschild, JD, CPA, CEP
Moses & Singer, LLP
1301 Avenue of the Americas
New York, New York 10019
Tel.: 212-554-7806
E-mail: grothschild@mosessinger.com

William M. Sharp, Sr. JD
Sharp Kemm P.A.
4890 W. Kennedy Boulevard, Suite 900
Tampa, Florida USA 33609-1850
Tel.: +1 813 286 4199
Email: wsharp@sharptaxlaw.com

BEAT THE IRS FROM SIX FEET UNDER

Ted Bauman, *Sovereign Confidential*, September 2015

Everyone knows the old saw about death and taxes, the only certainties in life.

Attributed to founder and sage Ben Franklin, the aphorism neatly sums up the critical importance of estate planning for each and every one of us — if you don't plan well, your heirs will get less than you intend. More of the wealth you worked for all your life — up to 40% — will end up with the IRS rather than your family.

The government is constantly figuring out ways to ensure the IRS benefits, not your descendants ... after all, as comedian Will Rogers once said, "The only difference between death and taxes is that death doesn't get worse every time Congress meets." Will Rogers was only partly right, though: the biggest threat to your estate isn't Congress ... it's the bureaucrats at the IRS who are empowered to interpret the rules ... as they are doing right now (I'll get to that in a bit).

And it's up to you to beat them, legally and effectively, with my help.

As a father, I know that wealth passed on from one generation to the next is the single most important factor in my child's life success. As the executor of a loved one's will, I know it's an important role.

If you value your children's future prospects as much as you do their lives today, estate planning is every bit as important as any other form of wealth protection.

Needless to say, estate planning involves anticipating and arranging for the disposal of your estate during your life. Afterwards is too late. I know it's hard, but the decisions you make now about where your assets go after your death can affect people's lives profoundly.

And making arrangements can be a liberating experience ... and relieving your families of the burden of having to deal with it after you're gone is a demonstration of love.

Surely you love them more than the IRS?

The IRS has the upper hand here. The federal estate tax is levied on the transfer of property to your heirs when you die. It isn't a burden just because of its high marginal rates ... but also because it taxes many assets you might not consider taxable or even valuable.

Your gross estate is determined by including the fair market value of all property, real or personal, tangible or intangible, to the extent of your interest in that property at the time of your death.

Do you know what that figure might be?

In this edition of *Sovereign Confidential* I'm going to review the basic elements of estate planning, focusing on steps you can take right here in the U.S. I and other members of the Council of Experts will soon extend this to include offshore estate planning strategies.

Bear in mind that this is an introduction to a complex topic ... so don't forget to consult some of the experts and resources I list at the end.

Estate Planning 101

The primary purpose of an estate plan is to preserve the wealth you accumulate during your life, so that you can pass it on to your chosen beneficiaries. Estate planning thus involves making arrangements for administration of your estate when you're gone, and maximizing its value by minimizing taxes and other expenses.

Estate Taxes — A Tax YOU Can Control

Other than making sure you have a valid will, there isn't a lot you can do to alter the expenses associated with the winding up of your estate. The debts you have when you die are what they are. There will be funeral costs.

But there's one thing that influences the value of your heritable estate over which you can have a great deal of control ... estate tax.

The federal estate tax is an "excise tax" — one your estate is expected to pay to the IRS voluntarily before it distributes your assets to your heirs. The maximum estate tax is currently 40%. The administrator of your estate calculates and pays it.

If the IRS disagrees with the calculation, it can and will come after your heirs to claim any shortfall — just when they will be grieving.

That's why estate tax planning is doubly important. First, it is the single most effective thing you can do to maximize the assets that pass on to your heirs. Second, getting it right means that process will be easy for those heirs … easier than a nasty fight with the IRS.

So remember what I'm about to share with you is fundamentally about tax planning — minimizing the estate tax due when your estate is wound up.

Your Gross Estate

Let's start with No. 1: What is your estate? Everyone has one. If you own something of value that you will pass on to someone else upon your death, you have an estate.

Fundamentally, your estate is the sum total of your material assets and liabilities. The difference between the two is your net worth — the total value of what you own, minus the total amount you owe to creditors. Determining your net worth involves several processes, some simple, and some more complex.

On the asset side, you can begin with bank and investment accounts (such as mutual fund accounts and retirement plans). That's the simple part — it's usually just a matter of adding together the numbers.

Estimating of the value of tangible property, such as real estate, is more complicated. A proper determination of your net worth involves professional appraisals of the fair market value of personal property (such as art, antiques and other valuables), and any real estate you own. These should be regularly updated. The same is true for and business interests, especially when you are a partner in a corporation.

On the liability side, you simply add together what you owe on credit cards, mortgages, tax bills, business loans, and any other form of indebtedness.

One thing to be aware of in calculating your net worth is contingent assets and liabilities. They are assets and liabilities that don't yet exist, but likely will, given time or a specified event occurring. For example, your life insurance death benefit doesn't exist when you calculate your net worth, but you should include it when thinking about how much to leave behind.

Your Taxable Estate

Now that you have an estimate of your gross estate, it must be adjusted to determine your taxable estate. Deduct your liabilities (including any income tax from the year of your death, debts, funeral expenses and the expenses of administering your estate) from the total amount of your assets.

The next set of deductions is any gifts you make to charity. Bequests to legitimate charitable, religious, scientific, literary or educational purposes reduce the value of your taxable estate correspondingly. These are currently unlimited.

Then come any transfers to your surviving spouse (the marital deduction). Because married couples are considered to be a single person for tax purposes, these are entirely tax-free if your spouse is a U.S. citizen. You can pass everything on to your spouse, or reserve some for your children or other heirs. It's up to you. Note, however, that the exclusion from tax on a gift to a spouse who is not a U.S. citizen is $147,000 … any amount above that is subject to estate tax.

What's left after the marital deduction is your taxable estate. After any estate tax due is paid, the remainder of your estate can be distributed to your heirs.

Now, here's the kicker: if your estate's more than $5.43 million, the administrators of your estate must pay federal estate taxes. If it's less than $5.43 million, your estate isn't liable for any taxes. That's why managing the size of your estate is so important, as we will see.

Priority: Avoiding the State's Estate Plan

Whether you know it or not, you have an estate plan. The law provides one for you if you don't get around to designing one of your own. It's called the probate process, and involves a judge, fees, public disclosure of personal affairs and protracted delay in transferring ownership of your estate to your heirs.

In probate, everything is distributed according to the laws of the state in which you are a resident at death, or the state in which your property is located. That may or may not bear any resemblance to your wishes. To make matters worse, in some states, probate judges are elected, and may have little or no legal training. The probate judge will choose an "administrator" of your estate, the value of which soon will be diminished by probate fees, appraisals, administrative costs and compensation for services, ranging from 5% to 25% of the value of your estate. In extreme cases, costs can actually consume an entire small estate, leaving nothing for heirs.

Some states (notably California, Florida and New York) impose high fees and costs on intestate estate administration. Even with a will, probate may require months, even years, before the process is final and heirs are able to enjoy what's left of their inheritance. You don't want any of that. You want a real plan that goes beyond a simple will.

Remember, if the total size of your taxable estate falls below the estate and inheritance tax levels — currently $5.43 million — you may not need fancy estate tax avoidance features. Similarly, if there aren't any unusual businesses or capital gains involved, then your plan may not need the relevant tax savings features.

But if you own any corporations — such as a limited liability corporation (LLC) — trusts, annuities or individual retirement accounts, they may have specific tax requirements of their own. That's why you still need to plan with an estate professional, even if you expect that your estate will be under $5.43 million.

Such a professional will probably recommend transferring some of your assets out of your personal ownership long before your death as a way to avoid excessive estate taxation and probate delays. By its very nature, a simple will can't accomplish this ... but there are other techniques that can. Let's look at the basic will first, then turn to these more advanced techniques.

An Effective Last Will and Testament

A "last will and testament" is a written document in which you say how you want your estate to be distributed or disposed of after death. A will may also name a guardian for any surviving minor children. The person making a will (the testator) must be 18 years or older, of sound mind, and must act without undue influence by others.

State law governs validity of a will, but generally they must:

- Be in writing
- Meet the statutory requirements imposed by the state of residence
- Be intended by its maker as a will
- Dispose of property after death
- Remain revocable during the maker's lifetime

A will may be revoked at any time until the testator's death. The only exception to this is when two parties simultaneously make mutually "irrevocable" wills in which they name each another as their respective beneficiaries and expressly surrender the right to revoke their wills. Otherwise, a testator may revoke by destroying it or by obliterating the signature. A new valid will revokes a prior will.

In some states remarriage after execution of a will automatically revokes that will's provisions that concern the ex-spouse and children. In such an event, the prior spouse and children are entitled to the same rights in the estate as if the testator had died without leaving a will. That's why it's important that your will be reviewed periodically. Marriage, the birth of a child, divorce or a change in economic status can all outdate will provisions.

A testator can change the terms of an original will, revoke part of it or add new provisions by executing a "codicil," an additional document involving all the formalities of the original will. Any part or the whole of the will may be revoked by a codicil. If changes are extensive, however, it's best to write an entirely new will.

Distribution of estate property doesn't occur until the will has been "probated." This is formal court proceeding after notice to the heirs and next of kin. At this point, the interpretation of the terms of a will may be disputed. When a will is ambiguous, a probate judge will determine the testator's true intentions.

Each state has different restrictions on a testator's disposition of property by will. In some states, a will may not exclude a surviving spouse, and the rights of the spouse vary from state to state. Most states, however, permit a person to exclude their children from any benefits from the estate.

Even if you adopt some of the other strategies I'm going to review below, you still need a will to serve as a "catch-all" distribution mechanism for other property, such as personal possessions.

A will also contains your wishes about who is to serve as executor of the estate and/or as guardian for minor children. This is often called a "pour over will" because it catches and distributes things other strategies might miss.

For example, a provision in a will may gather together any remaining assets and "pour over" these assets into a previously established trust, to be distributed under the trust terms rather than by probate court.

The bottom line is this: Everyone should have a will, but it plays a relatively minor role in a modern asset protection and estate plan. A will is only one part of an effective estate plan and always should be used in conjunction with other more flexible and property transfer devices, to which we now turn.

Estate Planning Opportunities

Now let's review some of the techniques professional estate planners use to minimize the tax burden on your estate. These all function in the same way ... by removing certain items from your estate by transferring them to another entity or by adjusting their taxable valuation. And they all operate before you pass away, so you can be sure that they do what you intend.

Gifting

The federal tax code allows you to make tax-free gifts that reduce the value of your estate. The idea here is to give away parts of your estate now so that the amount left at your death is below the estate tax limit.

But there are limits to this. For 2015, you're allowed to make lifetime gifts of up to $5.43 million per individual and $10.86 million per couple without paying federal gift tax. And thanks to the American Taxpayer Relief Act of 2012, your lifetime exclusion is "portable" to your spouse, who can use any of your unused gift tax exclusion when you're gone.

For example, if a deceased husband used $2 million of his $5.34 million in lifetime exemptions, his wife inherits unused $3 million into her lifetime gift exclusion at his death, increasing hers to $8.34 million.

To make things ever better … bear in mind that the first $14,000 ($28,000 per married couple) that you give away every year — called the annual exclusion amount — doesn't count toward this lifetime limit. It's over and above it.

To be tax-free, a gift must not be for "future interest." A future interest is any gift that is "limited to commence in use, possession or enjoyment at some future date or time."

A qualifying "present interest" gift is one that's "an unrestricted right to the immediate use, possession and enjoyment of property or the income of property." That means, for example, that you can't "give" an asset to your kids but stipulate that they only get it when you're gone. It has to be available to them right away.

If you make a gift of anything other than cash or marketable securities, you need a professional appraisal at the time you make transfer, especially if it's a hard-to-value asset, such as real estate or a share in the family business. That's another place where a good estate planning lawyer comes in handy.

If you want to make gifts and not have to bother to keep track for gift tax purposes, you can make gifts for medical, dental, and tuition expenses for as many relatives (or friends) as you'd like if you pay the provider directly. These gifts don't count toward any of the lifetime or annual gift limits.

Another tactic is to fund a 529 college savings plan for your children or grandchildren. There's a special rule — the five-year election — that lets you put five years of annual exclusion gifts in a plan at once. You could put $70,000 in an account for your grandson. You'd have to file a gift tax return, but there would be no gift tax, assuming no other gifts to that child over those years.

As you can imagine, the federal estate tax exemption changes almost every year, as Congress fiddles with it. For that reason, attorneys often use a "formula clause" in trust documents and wills rather than stating a specific dollar amount to be left to certain individuals. For example: "I leave to my children the maximum allowable amount that is not subject to federal estate tax, with the remainder going to my wife."

Trusts

One of the best devices for hassle-free property transfer for estate planning is a trust. It's an effective means to pass a title to property, while completely avoiding probate and most federal and state inheritance taxes ... and it can serve as a wealth preservation vehicle during your lifetime as well.

A "trust" is a legal device allowing title and possession of property to be held, used and/or managed by one person, the trustee, for the benefit of one or more other persons, the beneficiaries. The "grantor" is the person who creates and donates assets to the trust. You sign a trust declaration, conveying legal title to your assets to the trustee.

Ownership of this property immediately passes from you to the trust, remaining there until the trust is formally dissolved. The trustee is usually a close friend, a professional financial manager or attorney who manages and invests the property for the benefit of the trust's beneficiaries. A properly drawn trust has the legal capacity to do many things, including:

- Hold title to and invest in real estate, cash, stocks and bonds
- Hold negotiable instruments and all sorts of personal property
- Provide care of minor children or the elderly
- Pay medical, educational or other expenses
- Provide financial support in retirement, marriage or divorce
- Assist in the execution of a premarital agreement

A trust can be created under your last will and testament (a testamentary trust), and come into existence only after your death. The disadvantage is that it must go through the probate process as part of the will which creates it. But if you established a trust while you're alive, it can avoid the muddle of probate and the burden of inheritance and estate taxes.

To create a non-testamentary (living) trust, you sign a written declaration setting forth the details of trust operation and income distribution, during your life and afterward.

Drafting a trust declaration requires expert advice, as well as full coordination with all other estate plans you might have made. There have been innumerable court and IRS decisions interpreting trust documents — investing nearly every clause with special connotations — and only an experienced attorney will know them all.

There are several types of trusts, each characterized by different variables to meet your goals, and each with its own advantages and tax results. Let's review them.

The Living Trust

While a "testamentary trust" is established by your will, a living trust, is created while you are alive (known as an *inter vivos* trust). These are typically "revocable" — you can undo them.

In a revocable living trust arrangement, you as the grantor will typically serve as trustee during your life, to be replaced by a previously-named trustee at death. You retain the power to vary the trust terms, withdraw assets or even end the trust entirely.

But this comes with certain drawbacks — a revocable living trust by itself is doesn't reduce your estate or income taxes. Since you still control its assets, the IRS doesn't consider the trust as an individual, separate entity.

Instead, for tax liability purposes, the IRS considers the assets and income of a revocable living trust as part of your personal estate. That means you must report all trust income on your annual Form 1040. This also means living trusts are subject to federal and state estate taxes, since the trust forms part of your gross estate valuation.

However, if you expressly say so in a "pour-over" will, the assets in your revocable living trust can be transferred to a second, "residuary" or "marital" trust when you die, without liability for estate taxes, by taking advantage of the marital deduction. Upon the death of your spouse, its assets are included in his or her estate for estate tax purposes, and also benefit from his or her estate tax exemption. That can help preserve your estates value for your heirs.

The big advantage of a revocable living trust is that they are excluded from your estate for probate purposes. That alone has significant value, since it means your heirs will get:

- Immediate income from trust assets without interruption
- Title to property without the delay of probate
- Uninterrupted operation of a family business placed in trust
- No public scrutiny of personal financial matters

Be aware though, that a revocable living trust offers little or no asset protection when you are alive, because you control and benefit from the trust. That means creditors can attach the trust's assets as if they were your own.

The Irrevocable Trust

A living trust may also be "irrevocable," which means you as grantor have no control over the assets you transfer to that trust. That solves the threat of creditor attachment of assets during your lifetime. You no longer have title to the assets, nor any ability to reacquire it, so they are safe from creditors.

But irrevocability is also a disadvantage. If circumstances change, you can't change the trust to accommodate them. That makes it less attractive as an estate planning vehicle.

Life Insurance Trusts

A life insurance trust is an irrevocable, non-amendable trust that is both the owner and beneficiary of one or more life insurance policies. It is similar to the private insurance policies I've written about previously. Upon your death, the Trustee invests the insurance proceeds and administers the trust for one or more beneficiaries, such as the non-insured spouse and children.

As grantor, you can make periodic gifts or loans to the trust so that it has sufficient funds to pay the insurance policy premiums. Such a trust can also own "survivorship" insurance, which only pays when both spouses are deceased, leaving your children as the beneficiaries.

A life insurance trust is one of the most useful wealth protection strategies around. That's because the life insurance proceeds are owned by the trust, and therefore excluded from the valuation of your estate at death, thus avoiding estate taxes on the payout amount. This can mean significant tax savings.

By contrast, the proceeds of any life insurance policy in your own name are included in your estate for tax purposes. This can inadvertently increase the value of your estate enormously, well beyond the estate tax exemption … so be careful here.

To be effective, the wording of the insurance trust must clearly take irrevocable title to your life insurance policies, and also be the beneficiary of those policies. Your heirs are thus beneficiaries of the trust, not the life insurance itself.

Life insurance trusts can also be used in conjunction with other vehicles. They can be designed to provide heirs with enough immediate cash to pay estate taxes due on the balance of an estate, with the rest coming from other sources. This saves your heirs from having to sell off assets under duress just to pay estate taxes.

Establishing an insurance trust is a little more expensive than most trusts — about $2,500 — because the language must be just right in order to pass muster with the IRS. If the policy you are buying offers high-dollar coverage, however, some insurance companies are willing to pay the legal fees to establish your insurance trust.

Family Limited Partnerships

For truly advanced estate planning, consider a family limited partnership (FLP). It can serve both asset protection purposes and reduce estate and gift transfer taxes. But any type of partnership involves some of the most complicated areas in the Internal Revenue Code. This is not a "DIY" option.

A FLP permits two spouses to retain control over their assets as managing general partners of a legal partnership. At the same time, the FLP reduces their combined estate value through the gift or sale of property to children who thereby acquire limited partnership interests. This can help you to reduce your estate to below the estate tax threshold.

Under U.S. law, partnerships can have both "general" and "limited" partners. Limited partners cannot take part in the management of partnership assets, but general partners can. This creates a unique tax opportunity.

A family limited partnership is formed when two spouses transfer their estate assets, such as stocks, bonds or real estate to the FLP in exchange for a 1% general partnership interest (one-half of the 1% owned by each spouse), which guarantees them management rights. As general partners, the parents control the partnership assets, including any distributions.

The remaining 99% FLP interest is also owned by the spouses, but as limited partners. Eventually, part or all of that 99% will be gifted to their children over a period of years, consistent with the annual $14,000 gift tax exclusion available to each parent. This allows them to give $28,000 worth of FLP interest annually to each of their children (and grandchildren) without having to pay gift tax.

After assets are transferred into an FLP, the parents/creators are in effect both general and limited partners. This split ownership causes the property to become "fractionalized," which lowers its value. Now, under IRS rules, fractionalized FLP interest is heavily discounted for tax valuation purposes — sometimes as much as 50 or 60%. That's because fractionalized interests can't easily be sold, and so lack an easily determined sale value.

When an FLP is created, a professional valuation expert who is familiar with IRS fractional interest discounts determines the discounted value of the limited partnership interests.

If this is done correctly, at their death, the limited partnership interests owned by spouses will be substantially discounted for federal estate tax purposes. Assets whose "real" value are much higher can sometimes even be brought below the $5.43 million estate tax threshold, and bequeathed to heirs tax-free.

Valuation discounts provide a significant leveraging increase of the amount that can be transferred out of the parent's estate through annual gifts. For example, a parent may give a child limited partnership interest whose fractionalized value is only $14,000 — the annual gift exclusion — but whose market value is actually $28,000.

As an added benefit, the recipients of family limited partnership interests — whether children, grandchildren or one or more trusts established for the benefit of such persons (a trust can also be a limited partner) — also enjoy strong asset protection. If a limited partner is sued for any reason, including a divorce action by a spouse, the plaintiff or creditor cannot attach any of their interest in the partnership's assets. That's because, as in the case of an LLC, a creditor only has the right to income actually distributed to the limited partner against which the claim is made. A creditor may obtain a "charging order" against future cash distributions to the limited partner they are suing … but this is a hollow victory, since the general partners completely control distributions of cash to the limited partners, and they cannot be compelled to distribute anything.

Which One Is for You?

The choice of estate planning vehicle depends on the interplay of the many variables of your personal and economic life. There is no one size fits all solution, which is why having a good attorney is so important. Nevertheless, I can give you some guidelines.

- Needless to say, you need a will, even if it is of the "pour-over" variety. A will is especially handy if you have a lot of personal property such as art, vehicles or other collectibles that you want to keep out of a trust and distribute directly to your heirs.
- If your estate is likely to be less than the estate tax exclusion, and you are not concerned about the threat of current creditors, a revocable living trust that pours over to a residual trust for your spouse at death can be a great option. It is less expensive and ensures you avoid probate. It also gives you maximum control over your assets during your lifetime.
- If you are concerned about potential — not existing — threats from creditors during your lifetime, and direct control over assets isn't critical, an irrevocable trust can be useful for some of your assets. This is especially good for passive investment assets such as brokerage accounts that you do not manage personally.
- If you qualify for high-value life insurance, a life insurance trust is the ideal solution, since it leverages your existing wealth and increases it tax-free for your heirs. Such a trust can be used in conjunction with other vehicles to give your heirs immediate access to cash whilst the others are wound up.
- If you have numerous business interests, a family limited partnership may make sense. But be aware of the importance of proper valuation of the partnership's assets, since getting it wrong can lead to tax penalties. It is also more expensive to set up and maintain that the other options.
- The importance of proper, IRS-approved valuation also applies to real and personal property, as well as any property held in partnership with another person or persons.
- Always consult a good lawyer!

Conclusion

That's the best way I can think of to drill home the one main recommendation of this report ... whatever you do with your estate planning, do it properly, legally, with a qualified and experienced attorney. It's worth every penny.

That's going to be especially true when we turn to the specific application of these estate planning principles to offshore opportunities, such as trusts, annuities and private insurance policies.

Recommended estate planning experts you may want to consider contacting are Josh Bennett, Esq., Michael Chatzky, Esq., and Gideon Rothschild JD. Each's contact information is provided in Appendix A.

PART TWO:
INTERNATIONAL TAXATION

WHY TAX COMPETITION IS GOOD FOR YOU
Robert E. Bauman JD, *The Sovereign Investor Daily*, December 2007

What is "tax competition" and why should you care about it?

In a nutshell (which is where Will Rogers said all economic theories originate), tax competition exists when national governments lower taxes, specifically to encourage investments and cash flow or to urge financial resources to stay at home.

Usually this means a government creates an official strategy to attract foreign direct and indirect investment into the country.

The government also might invent tax incentives to attract high value human resources (bankers, investment firms) to the country. These tax incentives might include low corporate and individual income taxes and/or special tax preferences for foreigners. And low taxes keep locals at home.

The Birth of Tax Havens

Thus "tax havens" were born. All over the world, tax havens are places where foreigners can house their assets, do business and pay little or no taxes.

Good example: Panama, a nation that has a "territorial tax" policy. Panama only taxes business and personal income actually earned within its borders. You can base your business in Panama, but you and your business can earn tax-free income from offshore sources.

Other no or low tax jurisdictions include Monaco, Andorra, Belize, Singapore, the Channel Islands and the Isle of Man. And, for foreigners only, the United States and the United Kingdom are also tax havens.

Prudent individuals look at taxes as a business cost that either adds to subtracts from their desired profits. Thus smart folks looking for more profits go where there are no taxes or low taxes.

Let the Tax Competition Begin

Two good examples of tax competition were in the news this week.

From Amsterdam, a new poll showed that many wealthy Dutch residents want to move elsewhere in 2008 to escape the higher income taxes. At least 4% of those polled are considering leaving and becoming a taxpayer in another, lower tax country.

The Netherlands is an EU member state, so Dutch citizens have the option to make their home in any other EU nation. And some EU states, like Ireland and Cyprus, have much lower taxes.

Among the wealthiest Dutch polled, almost 10% say they are considering moving to avoid the proposed new taxes. (This relocation tactic won't work for U.S. persons, because U.S. income tax laws apply to all income, no matter where the U.S. person lives.)

The second example comes from Washington, D.C. The U.S. Treasury Department released a report alleging that American-owned companies that use tax havens are shifting "substantially all of their income out of the United States."

While this is legal under U.S. tax law, the report to Congress claimed that a dozen companies are using a technique known as "earnings stripping" to avoid or minimize taxes on their U.S. profits.

The study looked at companies that have their headquarters in offshore tax havens, while also continuing to operate out of the United States. Of course, the U.S. imposes one of the highest corporate taxes (35%) in the world. No doubt these higher corporate taxes inspired these tax-saving offshore moves.

In both cases, tax competition attracts smart folks to go where taxes are lower — as well they should.

Furious Tax Collectors

Naturally, this tax competition and taxpayer mobility infuriates tax collectors in the socialist welfare states, including the U.S. IRS.

The leftist big spenders claim that what we all need is "tax harmonization." In other words, they want high taxes everywhere for everybody.

For example, the paid propagandist, the Organization for Economic and Community Development (OECD), claims, "tax should not be the dominant factor in making capital allocation decisions." The OECD also says that low-tax policies "distort the location of capital and services."

Instead, the OECD wants nations to have the power to impose taxes on worldwide income. In doing so, tax collectors could ensure that taxpayers always face the same tax rate regardless of where they earn their income or where they live.

European nations generally have very high tax burdens. (One nation, Ireland, has very low taxes and has the greatest prosperity as a result.) Government spending consumes nearly half of economic output in EU countries, compared to one-third of GDP in the United States.

Not surprisingly, this translates into a higher tax burden, which means jobs and investment capital generally flee Europe. Tax harmonization is an attempt to stop labor and capital from escaping by creating, for all intents and purposes, a "fiscal fence" to force tax slaves to stay at home.

A Positive Good

For U.S. persons (citizens and resident aliens), there are minimal tax savings by going offshore — but there are some. There is also far better asset protection and financial privacy guaranteed by the local's laws.

That's why tax competition is a concept to be encouraged — only because it forces all nations to keep taxes lower than they would be otherwise.

HOW TO INVEST OFFSHORE AND LEGALLY AVOID THE IRS
Mark Nestmann, *The Sovereign Investor Daily*, January 2011

These days, there's little you can legally keep secret from the tax-man. That statement rings doubly true when it comes to investments you hold outside the United States.

Like most wealthy industrialized nations, the United States taxes the worldwide income of its citizens and permanent residents. Unlike nearly every other country, the U.S. also taxes the worldwide income of non-resident citizens (and non-resident green card holders, too).

Unfair? You bet! Especially when you consider that some U.S. corporations avoid taxes by going offshore. But it's the law, and when a U.S. citizen living abroad challenged it nearly 90 years ago, the Supreme Court upheld the right of Congress to tax non-resident U.S. citizens.

Americans must also comply with extensive reporting obligations when it comes to their offshore investments.

So what's reportable? What's not? If you invest offshore, you need to know the answers.

To stay compliant, there are three reporting laws you absolutely must know … plus, three offshore investments you don't have to report.

Reporting Laws You MUST Know

Whether you're a U.S. citizen or resident, or a foreigner doing business in the United States, here's what you need to know about reporting your offshore investments.

The Bank Secrecy Act effectively ended bank secrecy in the U.S. It requires you to file a report each year acknowledging any "foreign bank, brokerage, or 'other' financial accounts" you hold.

There are three separate reporting requirements:

1. **You must acknowledge foreign accounts with an aggregate value exceeding $10,000** each year on Schedule B of your federal income tax return.

2. **June 30 is the deadline for filing a Foreign Bank Account Report (FBAR) form with the U.S. Treasury.** This form — cryptically named "Form TD F 90-22.1" — gives the Treasury a bird's-eye look at any foreign bank, brokerage or other financial account you held during 2010.

3. **A special reporting regime has been instated that could affect your tax returns** if you hold more than $50,000 of assets outside the United States. A law passed in 2010 requires Americans to file a new IRS form along with their income tax return that discloses any foreign financial assets valued over $50,000.

These reporting obligations apply to any American, anywhere. The tax penalties for failing to comply are draconian! You could end up paying a $10,000 fine *per* unreported account. Far worse, if you "willfully" fail to file the FBAR form, you face fines of up to $250,000, five years' imprisonment … or both. Penalties are doubled if you violate any other U.S. law. Failure to file the form authorized in the 2010 law may be punished with a $50,000 fine.

Three Offshore Investments You Don't Have to Report

It's not always easy to figure out whether you need to file the FBAR form or not. And recently, Congress, the Treasury Department and the IRS have expanded the definition of what constitutes a "reportable" foreign account. As I said earlier, there's little you can keep secret from the tax-man.

Here are three offshore investments that won't set off any alarms…

1. **Securities or precious metals purchased directly from an offshore bank, securities issuer, dealer, or individual.** You won't trigger the reporting requirements if you purchase securities or precious metals without opening an account — as long as the total value of these foreign financial instruments or investment contracts doesn't exceed $50,000. Otherwise, you must disclose these holdings. Moreover, gold and other precious metals held in any "account" are reportable.

2. **Safekeeping arrangements.** Valuables purchased outside the U.S. and placed directly into a non-U.S. safety deposit box or private vault to which only you have access shouldn't trigger the reporting requirements. Again, if the total value exceeds $50,000, you must disclose these holdings.

3. **Real estate.** Direct ownership in your own name of real property in a foreign country isn't reportable. But you must report income from your real estate holdings, wherever they're located.

Other Advantages to Offshore Investing…

Despite the ongoing efforts of the Obama administration and Congress to shut down any tax advantages of investing offshore, you can still achieve substantial non-tax advantages by investing outside the United States.

These include…

- Access to investment and business opportunities not available in the United States.
- Protection from the falling U.S. dollar.
- Reduced portfolio risk.
- Protection from professional liability and other claims.
- Increased privacy.
- Investment continuity in the event of disruptions in U.S. markets.
- The ability to create a financial lifeboat for individuals and families threatened by totalitarian governments.

Investing offshore offers you an asset protection strategy you can't acquire in a country overrun with issues of privacy, legality and constitutionality. Besides, many of the best investment opportunities in the world exist outside the U.S., anyway.

So what are you waiting for?

United Nations Seeks Global Tax Authority

Daniel J. Mitchell, PhD, The Cato Institute,
The Sovereign Individual, July 2006, revised 2010

The United Nations recently issued a report attacking international tax competition and national fiscal sovereignty.

There are four main recommendations in the report: an international tax organization, global taxes, emigrant taxation and a back door form of tax harmonization or information exchange.

Every one of these initiatives would undermine individual liberty and encourage statist economic policy. Like the Organization for Economic Cooperation and Development (OECD) and the European Union (EU), both of which are pursuing similar agendas, the UN seeks to prop up inefficient, high-tax welfare nations by making it difficult for taxpayers to escape oppressive tax systems. Leaders of all low-tax nations, particularly the United States, should block the UN's radical scheme.

A key United Nations panel recently put forth a series of initiatives that would radically change national and international tax policy. Chaired by Ernesto Zedillo, former President of Mexico, the "High-level Panel on Financing for Development" endorsed the creation of an international tax organization, recommended the imposition of global taxes, and called for a form of tax harmonization known as information exchange.

If implemented, the proposed changes would undermine the right of sovereign nations to determine their own tax policies. Yet the attack on sovereignty is minor compared to the likely effect on global economic performance. The report seems designed to prop up inefficient welfare states and promote more government spending. The report openly condemns tax competition, for instance, and repeatedly endorses expanded efforts to redistribute wealth and income.

But contrary to what is asserted in the UN report, tax competition is a desirable force in the world economy. Because it is increasingly easy for resources to cross national borders, politicians must exercise at least a modest degree of fiscal discipline in order to attract jobs, capital, and entrepreneurship.

The UN proposals would undercut this liberalizing process and therefore erode the economic advantage of all low-tax nations, including America. The President and Congress should reject this extremist agenda, and this rejection should be echoed by all nations that believe in freedom and prosperity.

The UN report contains four major initiatives. Each one of these proposals is bad tax policy. All of the proposals undermine national sovereignty, and most of them represent an assault on the right to privacy. The unambiguous result of these policies is that governments around the world would be shielded from competition and politicians would have much less incentive to be fiscally responsible.

Creation of an International Tax Organization

The UN report endorses the creation of an International Tax Organization. This new body would have some relatively mundane responsibilities, such as collecting statistics and monitoring developments in tax policy, but facilitating bad tax policy seems to be the number one objective. The Zedillo report explicitly states that the International Tax Organization should help countries tax income earned outside their borders, and it also argues that such a body could "take a lead role in restraining tax competition."

At no point, however, does the report demonstrate any harm caused by fiscal rivalry between nations. Instead, readers are supposed to blindly accept the assertion that this competitive process is bad. But if competition is good for banks, pet stores, and car companies, then how can competition be bad for governments? The answer, of course, is that competition is good, but it is good for taxpayers and national economies rather than politicians.

A global bureaucracy, by contrast, almost certainly would represent the interests of politicians. Like parallel efforts by the Organization for Economic Cooperation and Development (OECD) and the European Union (EU), it would create a cartel-like environment for purposes of undermining competition. Governments should not conspire to keep taxes high, and they certainly should not set up a supra-national institution to pursue a statist agenda.

An International Tax Organization is a threat to the best interests of all low-tax nations, including the United States. It also is bad news for taxpayers in high tax jurisdictions like France. Without tax competition, it is quite likely that many nations would impose even heavier burdens on their people. As such, any effort to restrict the tax-motivated flow of global capital would undercut the ability of all taxpayers to climb the ladder of economic opportunity.

Turning People into Government Property

Perhaps the most radical proposal in the report is an initiative to give governments permanent taxing rights over their people.

This taxation of emigrants is supposedly necessary to protect nations from economic loss when productive citizens emigrate. The report states that the enforcement of such a scheme could be one of the responsibilities of the new International Tax Organization.

This idea implicitly assumes that people are a form of chattel, the property of a government even if they seek opportunity elsewhere. To be sure, there are jurisdictions that suffer from "brain drain." French citizens have been fleeing to England in record numbers and Canadians often make their way to the United States. In a world that values individual sovereignty and personal liberty, this would not be an issue. And even if some governments think emigration is a problem, perhaps they should put their own houses in order before seeking to make their citizens perpetual tax slaves.

Back-door Tax Harmonization

Not only does the UN want to impose taxes on a global basis, it also wants to help individual governments to tax income on a global basis. This is why the report endorses "information exchange," which means every government would be expected to collect private financial data on individual taxpayers and then share that information with other governments. High tax nations would then use this information to tax any income their residents earn in other countries. This initiative is very similar to the information exchange schemes being pushed by the OECD and the EU.

Information exchange makes sense, but only for jurisdictions with oppressive tax systems. Politicians from high-tax nations like France, for instance, get upset when taxpayers shift their savings and investment to jurisdictions with lower tax burdens and they desperately want the ability to continue taxing any income these assets generate. But this should be a matter for the French government and French taxpayers.

Low tax nations should not be forced to suspend their financial privacy laws and act as vassal tax collectors for Europe's welfare states. Indeed, information exchange violates an important principle of international law, dual criminality, by seeking to force low-tax countries to put the laws of other nations above their own.

While this proposal will probably get the least attention of the report's four major recommendations, it could be the most dangerous. Information exchange is a back door form of tax harmonization since individuals would be taxed at the same rate regardless of where they earn their income.

This initiative is a dagger aimed at the heart of U.S. financial markets since people from all around the world invest in the U.S. economy, but many would withdraw their funds if financial institutions were forced to act as informers for foreign tax collectors. *[**Ed Note:** During 2009 almost all "tax havens" agreed to a limited tax information exchange under pressure from the OECD and the G-7 major nations. See the "Article 26 and the Demise of Offshore Banking Secrecy" in Chapter Three].*

Conclusion

In addition to the specific proposals discussed above, the report calls for a doubling of foreign aid, more social welfare spending, higher taxes, and international bureaucracies that would interfere with the ability of sovereign nations to determine their own labor and environmental policies.

Combined with the UN's recent pro-gun control meeting, it seems the organization is still wedded to an anti-American, anti-freedom agenda.

In the final analysis, motives do not matter. Regardless of whether the UN's behavior is driven by knee-jerk anti-Americanism or by hard-core socialist ideology, the organization's tax agenda would cripple the global economy. Low tax nations like America, the U.K., Switzerland and the so-called tax havens would suffer the most.

The good news is that the UN cannot move forward with its radical proposal without full support from the world's major governments. This means that the United States has effective veto power. To protect the interests of American taxpayers and to preserve prosperity and opportunity around the globe, Congress and the President should tell the bureaucrats at the U.N. to take a long walk off a short pier.

For more information: The UN Report is online at www.un.org/esa/ffd/a55-1000.pdf. The Center for Freedom and Prosperity Foundation is a public policy, research, and educational organization operating under Section 501(c)(3). It is privately supported, and receives no funds from any government at any level, nor does it perform any government or other contract work. It is the research and educational affiliate of the Center for Freedom and Prosperity (CFP), Tel.: 202-285-0244, Website: www.freedomandprosperity.org.

TAX HAVEN NONSENSE & DECEPTION
Vernon K. Jacobs CPA, CLU, *The Sovereign Individual*, April 2007

There seems to be a huge amount of nonsense and outright deception about the impact of tax havens and their alleged abuse. The following comments are offered as an attempt to provide some balance to the arguments of those who rail against U.S. persons with foreign income, particularly in so-called tax havens.

The U.S. imposes an income tax on the world wide income of our citizens and permanent residents, regardless of where the income is earned. If it is earned in a country that also imposes income taxes, the U.S. provides for a tax credit to avoid double taxation. But if the income is earned in a country that has no income tax (or a low rate of tax), the U.S. collects a tax on that income as if it were earned in the U.S. The law does allow a limited "foreign income exemption" from U.S. tax for earned income in foreign countries — but most of the U.S. citizens who work outside the U.S. pay substantial taxes to foreign countries. The tax credit is not allowed on foreign excluded income, so that apparent tax break doesn't really cost the U.S. any significant loss of tax dollars.

U.S. corporations that operate in multiple countries are permitted to defer tax on income earned in a low tax country, so long as the income is re-invested in the business and not used as passive investments. This is done to compensate partially for the disadvantages imposed on U.S. companies in competing with companies based in other countries where corporate taxes are lower.

Many decades ago, it was legal and possible for Americans to move assets offshore and to invest them on a tax-free basis until the money was returned to the U.S. But various laws have removed those tax breaks. If a U.S. investor opens a foreign bank account and buys offshore investments, the U.S. investor is obligated by law to pay taxes on the income earned from those investments. U.S. investor are encouraged to put assets into a foreign corporation or an international business company (IBC) and to make the investments through the corporation or IBC. But U.S. tax law requires the U.S. shareholder of a foreign corporation to pay taxes on the income of a foreign investment holding company or a foreign corporation controlled by U.S. persons.

Some people seem to believe that the use of a foreign trust is some kind of tax shelter, but it's not a legal way to avoid taxes. The U.S. person who puts assets into a foreign trust that has any current or future U.S. beneficiary is obligated by law to report the income earned by the foreign trust and to pay taxes on that income.

Virtually every other country in the world imposes income taxes on a territorial basis. Income earned in those countries is taxable. But income earned outside those countries is not taxable. But the U.S. insists on taxing the income of its citizens, permanent residents, corporations, partnerships, trusts and estates — no matter where in the world the income is earned.

Those American politicians who rail against alleged losses of tax revenue because of tax havens are either not aware of the scope of the U.S. tax laws, or are intentionally dispensing nonsense to pander to the public's lack of awareness of the current tax system. The only people who are evading taxes offshore are outright crooks or those not concerned about complying with the U.S. tax laws. More laws will have no impact on those who choose to ignore existing laws. Claims that closing up tax haven loopholes will somehow generate revenue to be used for domestic spending is political propaganda that is totally contrary to the facts.

We don't need more laws to prevent tax evasion offshore. We have more than enough laws already.

SLIPPERY STEPPING STONES

Robert E. Bauman JD, *The Sovereign Individual*, November 1998

Do what the big boys do: use a multi-layered set-up of offshore corporations to legally reduce your corporate tax burden.

Smart offshore business operators, large and small, often avail themselves of a multinational tax break allowed under U.S. tax law. It's called "stepping stones" by international tax experts, "treaty shopping" by a disdainful IRS.

This generous tax break, for which most Americans can't qualify, proves that the U.S. can be a tax haven for foreigners, if they play their cards very carefully.

The creative tax strategy takes advantage of international bilateral tax treaties. It requires at least minimal business operations in two or more countries. You simply base a defined part of your business where taxes are lowest for just such operations. The total business gross volume need not be large, but the net should be big enough to justify the accounting and legal expenses. But the tax savings can be enormous.

Because it has a worldwide network of tax treaties, the Netherlands is a favorite base for stepping stone business operations by companies from all over the world. Low taxes make the Netherlands ideal for passive interest or royalty income and for financing operations.

Once incorporated in the Netherlands, you're covered by the U.S.-Dutch tax treaty that requires no U.S. withholding taxes on interest and dividends paid from the U.S. to a Dutch company. A Dutch company in turn can make payments without tax withholding to a German, Canadian or other nation's firm.

The IRS hates such arrangements. To them it's tax evasion using phony affiliates of businesses operating within the U.S. Fortunately for astute taxpayers, if it's done right this system is legal and it works. The one key requirement is strict adherence to proper form and no corner-cutting.

The moral: There are ways to save taxes offshore, but do it right and be damned sure you know what you can and cannot do.

Negotiate Your Own Tax Bill in Switzerland

Marshall J. Langer JD, *The Tax Exile Report*, 1997

Did you know that Switzerland, widely known as a banking and tax haven, is also a place where a resident foreigner can negotiate with government officials the amount of tax he would like to pay?

Despite its fairly high taxes, Switzerland is an attractive destination for many tax exiles. You may be able to obtain both a residence permit, and a lump-sum tax arrangement, especially if you are retired. Obtaining a work permit is more difficult, but not impossible.

Switzerland has long been a favorite haven for rich and famous tax exiles from all over the world. It is not the easiest country in which to acquire residence, but if you are retired and have sufficient income, resident status in Switzerland is possible.

Foreigners living in Switzerland pay fairly high income taxes on their worldwide income. Federal, cantonal and local income taxes are levied on all income, except that derived from foreign real estate or a personally owned foreign business. There are also cantonal and local wealth taxes on capital. Despite this, Switzerland is an attractive destination for tax exiles, primarily because it is one of the world's safest and most stable countries.

Switzerland may be suitable for you if:

1. You already have a satisfactory citizenship and passport, since it takes from 12 to 15 years to obtain either in Switzerland.
2. You are a wealthy retiree over 60 years of age who has never worked in Switzerland.
3. You want a new permanent residence and are willing to reside in Switzerland at least part of each year.
4. You are prepared to pay a prearranged lump-sum tax to the Swiss each year.

A Negotiable Lump Sum Tax Deal

Wealthy foreigners of retirement age can negotiate a lump-sum tax arrangement, called a *forfeit fiscal*, with local cantonal tax administrators. The tax amount varies considerably depending on where in Switzerland you choose to live. Under the forfeit deal, 1n 2014 foreigners paid an average 75,000 Swiss francs

(US$77,400) in annual taxes, producing more than US$710 million per year in revenue

The smaller cantons will ask less, and you will pay considerably more in the larger, better-known cantons. Although one can apply for residency status at any Swiss embassy, I urge you to negotiate directly, and in person, with the authorities in the canton where you want to live. In any event, they are the ones who decide whom to admit as residents, and how much tax will be paid. Employ a competent local professional to work out the best deal.

Visit Annually

Despite recent changes, you can still visit Switzerland for up to three months each year without obtaining a residence permit and without having to pay Swiss taxes. As a visitor, you must observe the time rules faithfully. Swiss authorities keep records of exactly how much time each foreigner spends in the country.

Under tax rules, one is treated as a Swiss resident for tax purposes if 1) a person stays in Switzerland without working for more than 90 days in any year; or, 2) a person works in Switzerland for more than 30 days in any year.

In either case, you are deemed to have been resident from the first day of your stay in Switzerland. It doesn't matter whether you stay in one place or in several different places.

Moreover, brief absences from Switzerland do not suspend your residence. It used to be possible for a foreigner to "visit" Switzerland twice each year, for up to three months each time. That is no longer possible. A suggested program under the new rules: You can visit one of Switzerland's excellent winter resorts for about a month each February or March and one of its equally marvelous summer resorts for about a month each July or August. You can also spend a few days visiting your bankers at the beginning and end of each stay. It's a great life, if you can afford it.

An alternative is to obtain a "B permit" authorizing you to live and work in Switzerland. About 17,000 renewable B permits are available each year, most issued by cantonal authorities. Each canton has a small annual quota of permits allocated to it. Annual renewals are routinely approved. I have had success in obtaining permits for clients from the Canton of Neuchatel under its program to attract new business. Neuchatel offers special tax programs on an individual case basis for new residents.

Pros and Cons

Switzerland is clean, orderly, safe, stable and prosperous. Everything works and most things work well.

Everything in Switzerland is expensive. If you become a Swiss canton resident, you will be liable for Swiss inheritance and gift tax purposes. These taxes vary considerably from canton to canton but are not imposed by the federal government. Switzerland now has a value-added tax (VAT), but at a rate much lower than most other European countries.

The Ex-PATRIOT Act and America's Fading Freedoms

Robert E. Bauman JD, *The Sovereign Investor Daily*, May 2012

If the last 30 years of accumulated assaults on the constitutional rights of U.S. citizens have not convinced you to make plans to escape America, perhaps the reactionary political demagoguery surrounding Eduardo Saverin will do the trick.

Saverin, the billionaire Facebook co-founder, recently ended his U.S. citizenship as a legal means of avoiding U.S. taxes.

As I have explained many times, U.S. laws, unlike most nations, impose taxes on "U.S. persons" (citizens and resident aliens), no matter where in the world they live and without regard to their income sources. Terminating citizenship is the only way to avoid U.S. taxes.

The vast majority of other national tax systems impose taxes only on income earned within their borders. A Canadian or British citizen, for example, can move offshore and legally leave most domestic taxes behind. A Panamanian is taxed only on income earned within his country, none offshore.

The Perfect Target for Politicians

The leading publicity hound in the U.S. Senate, Charles E. Schumer (D-NY), and his PR apparatchiks regarded the Saverin news as a great chance to make headlines and they pounced.

On May 17, "ultra-liberal" Schumer and the usually reasonable Sen. Bob Casey (D-PA) unveiled the Ex-PATRIOT Act (Expatriation Prevention by Abolishing Tax-Related Incentives for Offshore Tenancy Act). This legislative disaster would impose a 35% tax on U.S. earnings on anyone who ended U.S. citizenship during the last 10 years.

To add juice to the story, Saverin's 4% stake in now publicly traded Facebook was estimated to be worth $3 billion to $4 billion. This made him the perfect target for politicians — an ungrateful tax-dodging billionaire skipping out on America and its suffering taxpayers.

Indeed, by ending U.S. citizen status, Saverin probably saved hundreds of millions in eventual estate and gift taxes. If he remained a citizen, he would not have owed U.S. capital gains tax on his income until he sold his shares. Wealthy American shareholders often borrow against their shares and live tax-free off the unrealized appreciation for years.

Anyone in Saverin's position would be insane not to act legally to save all the taxes possible, and that's just what he did. As it is, he will probably pay $150 million because of the Exit Tax the U.S. imposes on expatriates.

Saverin, 30, who was born in Brazil, came to the U.S. as a teenager and became an American citizen, reportedly to avoid being kidnapped from his wealthy parents. Exercising his legal right as an American, he filed to surrender his U.S. citizenship in January 2011 and it became official last September. He also was among the 1,780 Americans who ended U.S. citizenship last year.

He now is a resident of Singapore, where, unlike the U.S., the government welcomes wealthy foreigners with low taxes and eventual citizenship. Saverin will benefit from major tax savings by becoming a permanent resident of Singapore, which imposes no capital gains taxes.

Perhaps the most atrocious part of Schumer's proposal is the attempt to bar re-entry into the U.S. forever. This ban would be retroactive and apply to anyone who ended citizenship during the 10-year period before 2012.

The only other regimes to have adopted similar punitive laws are Nazi Germany, the Soviet Union under Stalin and apartheid South Africa.

Perhaps Schumer needs to be reminded where he is and whom he was elected to represent.

It is ironic that back in 1996, Chuck Schumer was a U.S. congressman from Brooklyn and his Democrat leader was the distinguished senior Senator from New York, Daniel Patrick Moynihan.

Are You Ready to Face Facts?

On October 4, 1996, in the last hours before final adjournment of the 104th U.S. Congress, Senator Moynihan rose to speak in the Senate, his face flushed with anger over the so-called Reed Amendment, a radical provision sponsored by Rep. Jack Reed of Rhode Island (now a U.S. senator).

He said: "Enacting an ill-advised provision to punish tax-motivated expatriates by banishing them from the land does not reflect well on a free society. It is our duty to act with special care when dealing with the rights of persons who are despised."

Is America a "free society" today? Are you ready to face facts and act accordingly?

Government's Double Standard: A Closer Look at the "HSBC Files" Scandal
Ted Bauman, *The Sovereign Investor Daily*, February 2015

Here's a quick quiz. Which of the following activities can get a bank in trouble with the U.S. government?

- Lying to clients about the value of assets sold to them?
- Conspiring to manipulate markets?
- Bribing public officials?
- Helping U.S. citizens with tax evasion?

The answer is (d). Getting involved with tax evasion is about the only thing the U.S. government seems to care about when it comes to the behavior of "too big to fail" banks. And even then, such tax evasion penalties that result lead to minimal consequences.

That's because despite all the public hoo-ha, the banks aren't really the government's primary concern — they're more worried about you and me. After all, when a former tax official says something like "There are very few reasons to have an offshore bank account, apart from just saving tax," individuals with offshore interests can rest assured that the system is biased against us … and only us.

Case in Point: The "HSBC Files"

You've probably heard about the scandal erupting around the "HSBC files," with the bank's Swiss subsidiary involved in some offshore dealings.

In 2007, a computer technician at HSBC's Swiss subsidiary hacked into his employer's files and extracted evidence that the bank was helping individual depositors avoid tax in their home countries. He then fled to France, where he turned the files over to tax officials. The French then shared them with other countries, including the U.S., UK, Greece, Spain, Belgium and Argentina.

Some U.S. clients were involved. Although the IRS has never admitted that it is scrutinizing individual taxpayers based on the HSBC files, investigations by the British newspaper The Guardian suggest that several U.S. residents have been convicted and penalized for hiding assets and income via HSBC accounts.

But here's the odd thing ... the U.S. has known about the HSBC files since 2010. In an unrelated case, the U.S. levied a $1.9 billion fine against HSBC in 2012, widely regarded as a slap on the wrist. But the deferred prosecution agreement concluded at that time didn't mention tax evasion or the bank's Swiss banking division ... even though the U.S. had received the "HSBC files" two years earlier.

Call This Fair?

That suggests that the U.S. government is much more concerned about the behavior of U.S. taxpayers than that of the banks that help them evade taxes. The IRS uses its legal powers to scare people wanting to bank offshore, not to punish the banks. For the IRS, it's enough that the banks stop accepting American clients, which is what HSBC's Swiss subsidiary did.

Our position on taxes is unequivocal: Pay what the law requires you to pay, no more and no less. Complying with U.S. tax laws means reporting all of your worldwide income as well as your offshore financial accounts. By all means fight the tax system legally and politically, but don't break the law.

But it's becoming more difficult to sustain that ethical stance. It's increasingly obvious that U.S. tax enforcement is biased against individual taxpayers. Consider the following:

- U.S. taxpayers must declare and pay income tax on their worldwide income. U.S. corporations, however, are exempted from income tax on foreign earnings until they are brought into the U.S.

- The IRS is more likely to prosecute and penalize individual taxpayers than corporations (or banks). For example, Foreign Account Tax Compliance Act (FATCA) penalties can amount to significantly more than the entire value of undeclared foreign assets — not just the tax due.

- Knowingly assisting a U.S. taxpayer to hide income and evade taxes is a violation of U.S. law. Yet no HSBC employees were charged by U.S. authorities as a result of the "HSBC files," which have been in the Justice Department's possession for at least five years.

Don't get me wrong: We don't support confiscatory taxation. But it's increasingly clear that the coercive power of the U.S. government is being directed selectively — against individual U.S. taxpayers who choose to bank offshore. Corporations and banks, however, get a pass. That is fundamentally unjust, which adds insult to the injury of excessive taxation.

How to Invest Offshore and Avoid Tax Evasion Penalties

If you're a U.S. citizen or resident, it's legal to have an offshore bank account, an offshore asset protection trust or family foundation, or an international business corporation. It's also legal to purchase offshore life insurance and annuities that allow deferred taxes, and to invest in offshore mutual and hedge funds, precious metals, valuable collectibles and real estate.

But do any of these things while trying to protect your privacy, and you immediately become the target of suspicion. The bankers, on the other hand, get off pretty much scot-free. That's because the goal of U.S. tax enforcement is clearly to discourage individual U.S. taxpayers from exercising their legal rights to bank and invest offshore.

Don't let their lies scare you. Get yourself a good attorney who specializes in offshore investing, and go right ahead — exercise your rights. We support you all the way.

Chapter Eight

Tax Havens — International Asset Acquisition & Storage

Part One: Tax Havens Explained

Why Go Offshore? 436

How to Choose an Offshore Haven 437

Four Types of Tax Havens 441

A Haven for You 444

The U.S. as an Offshore Tax Haven 445

Part Two: Havens Under Siege

Big Government's War Against Harmful Tax Competition 447

Here's What You Need to Know About FATCA 449

Blacklisting Tax Havens 455

Offshore Bullying from the World's Largest Tax Haven 458

Where Are the Real Money Laundering Havens? 460

Acts of War 462

Preposterous Law 463

Don't Believe the Smear… Offshore Tax Havens Are Legal 467

The IRS's New Offshore Settlement Tax: Are They Getting Reasonable? 469

Editor's Note:

For those who know the ocean or enjoy the beach, "offshore" may bring back pleasant memories of far-off vessels passing on a blue horizon, of a leisurely sail cutting through the waves in your own sturdy vessel.

In this chapter "offshore" takes on a whole new meaning — a different, expanded definition that, once understood, potentially could change your life forever.

Here "offshore" refers to sovereign nations with laws that protect your financial privacy, your assets and your cash. Countries where the welcome mat is always out for foreign citizens weary of high taxes and government snoops back home.

We explain how the offshore system operates, what is legal and what is not, and how you can use this system to your own advantage. We also give you an up-to-date battle report on the tax hungry, major nations' war against havens.

Keep in mind that in this area events change with great speed and what is accurate one day has changed the next. You will need to supplement your reading with keeping a close eye on current events in tax havens in general, and specific places in particular.

PART ONE: TAX HAVENS EXPLAINED

WHY GO OFFSHORE?
John Pugsley, January 1999

True financial security must include: 1) the maximum possible tax avoidance allowed by law; 2) the greatest possible financial privacy; 3) the highest level of asset protection; and, 4) access to the most profitable investments available.

I often have said that voters in the wealthy industrialized democracies seek to transfer benefits to themselves at the expense of the successful and thrifty. This attack on affluent and productive individuals in the United States, Canada, Germany and the United Kingdom has led to a rising exodus of both assets and individuals to political environments offering greater asset protection, privacy and lower taxation.

Through taxation and regulation, the executive branch of government excels in attacks on wealth, but the judicial system is now becoming an equal enemy of prosperity. Especially in the United States, courts are clogged with hundreds of thousands of civil suits demanding enormous sums for imagined or statutorily-concocted injuries such as sexual harassment or psychological discrimination.

Contingent fee lawyers whip up billion-dollar class action suits against persons or corporations deemed a ripe target, meaning one with enough ready assets to finance big judgments and outrageous jury awards.

It is a truism to say statist government has diminished personal liberty with its unchecked power of taxation. In the United States, the United Kingdom and Germany the effective rate of personal taxes far exceeds 50 percent of earnings. In some nations, such as France and Sweden, it is much higher. Business is taxed at even greater levels. And everyone, as consumers, pays the ultimate price imposed by taxation.

How can a person of wealth defend against such ferocious attacks?

As James Dale Davidson and Lord William Rees Mogg said in their book *The Sovereign Individual*, one cannot transport hard assets, farms or factories out of a high tax or politically oppressive jurisdiction. But the most important capital assets today are knowledge, experience and information which no political boundaries can contain.

Sovereign individuals understand these trends and take advantage of them. We chose our residence for its quality of life and will not be tied down by an accident of birth. We select haven nations for placement of our assets according to the relative safety and privacy such places guarantee by law. Those who move all or a portion of their assets offshore simply recognize reality, that government is engaged in a systematic destruction of its citizens' right to financial privacy, what's been called the "Nazification of the economy."

Sadly, we must look to foreign lands for the sort of economic freedom once guaranteed by our homeland.

How to Choose an Offshore Haven
John Pugsley, The Sovereign Individual, June 2003

Since its inception, The Sovereign Society has guided members through the minefields of international law, and this has chronicled the accelerating decline of financial privacy in many jurisdictions once considered secure, private havens for personal assets.

At the root of this pernicious erosion are the hyped-up "wars" on drugs, money laundering and terrorism. The war on drugs gave birth to money laundering laws, and together these legal weapons are being used to destroy privacy and bank secrecy. Rising terrorism (inspired by a rising resentment of American intervention in the politics of foreign nations) engenders the need for random searches, wiretapping and 24/7 surveillance.

Where two or three decades ago there were numerous haven nations where privacy was expected and delivered, the high-tax nations have pushed, cajoled and threatened until the field of choices has been dramatically reduced.

How do individuals interested in privacy and security choose the best haven for their wealth?

To begin with, you should understand that each "offshore" haven is unique. A country that provides the best banking regulations won't necessarily be the best place for incorporating a business, just as the best jurisdiction for privacy won't necessarily be the best for an offshore trust.

Yet, there are general guidelines for choosing an asset haven that apply across the board. The following are the more important considerations.

Is the haven a completely independent sovereign nation? Or is it a territory, dependency or colony of a larger country?

While the government of a dependency or territory may enact favorable legislation to attract foreign investment, such legislation will be hostage to the political and economic environment prevailing in the mother country.

Nothing illustrates this point more than the recent events in the British Virgin Islands. An overseas territory of the United Kingdom, beginning in the late 1970s, the BVI, with U.K. encouragement and funding, developed one of the world's largest and most sophisticated offshore financial sectors. Indeed, it became second only to Hong Kong in the formation of international business companies, registering nearly 40,000 new corporations annually. With a land area smaller than Washington, D.C., and a population of 21,000, providing a home for almost 400,000 companies provided substantial revenues both to the government and the country's financial sector, along with ending the BVI's historical dependence on U.K. foreign aid.

A key provision of the law that made the BVI so attractive as a corporate domicile was that shares in an IBC could be issued in "bearer" form. This meant the actual ownership of the corporation could be kept confidential. However, beginning in the late 1990s, escalating pressure from the U.K. Home Office and international organizations threatened the BVI's ability to offer bearer shares and enforce other aspects of its laws protecting privacy and wealth. Indeed, the U.K. Home Office threatened to use an arcane provision of colonial law called an "Order in Council" to enact binding BVI legislation, over the heads of the local elected representatives, if the BVI government failed to dismantle its favorable laws on its own.

Faced with this overwhelming pressure, the BVI recently re-wrote their laws regarding IBCs. One of the casualties was the ability of IBCs to issue bearer shares. The BVI is only one of the U.K.'s overseas territories. The others — Anguilla,

Bermuda, the Cayman Islands and the Turks & Caicos Islands — were subject to similar pressure from the U.K. Home Office.

Closer to the United Kingdom itself are several jurisdictions with a different constitutional status than overseas territories, but still subject to substantial interference in their financial affairs by the U.K. government. These "Crown dependencies"— the Isle of Man, Jersey, Guernsey and Sark — have also been forced to dismantle many of their favorable laws designed to attract foreign capital.

Does the haven respect privacy? And is privacy built into its law? Under what circumstances can creditors or the government obtain information about your wealth, or even seize it?

Financial privacy has gotten a bad reputation in recent years. The prevailing attitude is, "if you're not committing a crime, why do you need privacy?"

This attitude ignores the very real need for privacy in a nation such as the United States where there exist very few legislative protections for it. It is worth noting that a sue-happy lawyer or identity thief, armed with nothing more sophisticated than a personal computer, can in a few minutes unearth a great deal of financial information about whatever U.S. assets you own.

This is the reason why strong privacy laws are a must in any haven that you might consider. Some countries have a tradition of secrecy but no legal requirement enforcing it; others have laws that allow the local government access to information while pretending that the government is sworn to secrecy. Others have bank-secrecy laws but frequently ignore them, or have laws filled with exceptions.

Ideally, secrecy should be built into the legal code and violations should be prosecuted with civil or criminal sanctions. However, even in jurisdictions with the best privacy laws, it's foolish to violate tax or money-laundering laws of your home country. In their search for tax-evaders, big governments have a history of illegal espionage, bribery and coercion to get the information they seek.

Moreover, you may wake up one morning to find the haven nation's have laws changed and your "secret" records are in the hands of your home government. Make sure you comply with the laws in your home country!

From the standpoint of the tradition and legal basis for banking secrecy, the four countries that stand out are Austria, Liechtenstein, Luxembourg and Switzerland.

Austria has strict bank secrecy laws calling for the prosecution of any bank employee who divulges any information on a client's account, and its banking tradition is more than 200 hundred years old.

Liechtenstein has some of the strongest bank secrecy laws in existence. Since Liechtenstein is one of the five richest countries in the world in per capita income and personal wealth, it is unlikely to be swayed away from privacy by promises or threats.

Luxembourg is one of the fastest growing financial centers in the world and has seen a massive influx of capital in the last decade due to its liberal banking and tax laws. Although its secrecy laws only date back to the early 1980s, it has maintained a long tradition of banking confidentiality. Information will only be released to foreign governments if the depositor has been charged with a crime that is related to the account that is also a crime in Luxembourg.

Switzerland has been economically and politically stable for centuries, enjoys a low rate of inflation and the Swiss franc is one of the strongest currencies in the world. It remains the model from which all other financial centers are compared. Although Switzerland has succumbed to the pressure of the U.S. government to loosen its strict secrecy laws, for safe banking it still rates as one of the top havens.

How long a tradition has the haven had?

A country like Switzerland with centuries of traditional respect and protection of privacy, or like Luxembourg with decades of stability, are unlikely to change for transient reasons. The longer and stronger the traditions of law and privacy, and the more stable the economy, the better chance that those traditions will continue.

Political stability is a major consideration. During the last half of the 20th century, Hong Kong was a bastion of financial stability, growth and privacy. Hong Kong achieved this in spite of being a dependency of the United Kingdom. But when the U.K.'s lease on the territory ran out in 1997, control returned to China, casting a deep shadow of doubt about Hong Kong's future as an asset haven, a fact underscored by the continued exodus of wealth from the country.

Do the citizens support the haven's offshore status?

In some havens, such as The Bahamas, the local citizens are not the primary beneficiaries of banking secrecy. Since taxes are low to non-existent and the local legal eagles have not evolved into predators, locals have little interest in privacy laws or bank secrecy. This contrasts with Switzerland, Austria and now Panama, where privacy laws and traditions affect a significant segment of the citizenry.

Is the haven important to your government?

The United Arab Emirates, because it is a "friendly" nation in an unstable region, enjoys the favor of the U.S. government. Haven income is important to it and Washington won't want to lean too hard on it over a "non-strategic" issue. And, since the CIA uses Liechtenstein for its financial transactions, the U.S. won't seek to wipe out its haven status.

Another example is Panama, with its strategically important canal linking the Atlantic and Pacific Oceans. The Cayman Islands, on the other hand, has little or no strategic value to Washington.

Does the haven wave a "red flag?"

Public dealings with high-profile havens may raise a "red flag" for tax collector's around the world. The Cayman Islands, Switzerland and Liechtenstein are examples. Panama, Austria and Luxembourg are another step below that level. Bermuda is lower still, though it doesn't offer the secrecy the others do.

How efficient and convenient are the services? Are competent personnel available to serve your needs?

How well do they speak English? How easy is it to visit the place? Nothing substitutes for personal contact with the people who are trusted with your assets. It's best to visit your money periodically, and so much the better if it's in a place that you enjoy visiting.

What taxes are levied on the haven's users? The first requirement of a haven is to offer capital preservation. Nonetheless, to include a haven country which scores heavily in capital preservation but which also has high withholding, corporate, estate or other taxes, is to ignore an important consideration.

As I've written before, true financial security must include: the maximum possible tax avoidance allowed by law; the greatest possible financial privacy; the highest level of asset protection; and access to the most profitable investments available.

Sovereign individuals select haven nations for placement of assets according to the relative safety and privacy such places guarantee by law. Those who move all or a portion of their assets offshore simply recognize the reality that governments in the major nations are engaged in a systematic destruction of their citizens' right to financial privacy. Sadly, we must look to foreign asset havens for the sort of economic freedom once guaranteed by our homeland. The number of safe havens is dwindling, but they still exist.

FOUR TYPES OF TAX HAVENS
Robert E. Bauman JD, *Fundamental Tools of Wealth Protection*, 2001

Simply stated, a tax haven is any country whose laws, regulations, policies and, in some cases, treaty arrangements, make it possible for a foreign national to reduce overall personal or corporate tax burdens by voluntarily bringing one's self within the country's jurisdiction.

Usually this is done by establishing a residence in that nation. This general definition covers all four major types of tax haven nations, each categorized by the degree of taxation imposed, and it's important to understand the differences.

1) No-Tax Havens

In what are known as "pure" or "no-tax havens," there are no income, capital gains, or wealth taxes, and a foreign national can quickly and easily incorporate, form a trust and register to do business immediately.

The government in a pure tax haven nation earns revenue from the volume of registration and annual maintenance fees paid by foreign corporations and trusts doing business within its borders.

"No tax" means there is no tax levied on income or profits from corporate business operations, but there are minor taxes including stamp duties on documents of incorporation, charges on the value of corporate shares issued, annual registration fees, or other fees not levied directly on income.

Examples of this type of country include the British Overseas Territories of Bermuda, the Cayman Islands and the Turks & Caicos Islands, plus independent nations such as The Bahamas, St. Kitts & Nevis (primarily the latter of the two-island federation), all located in or near the Caribbean basin, and, in the south Pacific, the Cook Islands and Nauru.

2) Foreign-Source Income Havens

These havens use a domestic "territorial" approach, taxing only income actually earned within the country. They exempt from tax any income earned from foreign sources involving no local "in country" business activities — apart from simple housekeeping matters. Often there is no tax on income derived from the export of local manufactured goods, as compared to the domestic manufacture itself, which may be taxed.

These nations also could be called "no-foreign-source income tax havens," and they are divided into two groups.

The first group allows a person or a corporation to do business both internally and externally, taxing only the income earned from internal domestic sources. These nations include Costa Rica, Ecuador, Guatemala, Honduras, Israel, the Philippines, Thailand and Sri Lanka.

The second group requires corporate organizers to decide and elect at the time of incorporation whether the business will limit itself to domestic activity, with consequent local tax liabilities, or to do only foreign business that is exempt from taxation. Primary examples in this category are Panama, Liberia, Jersey, Guernsey, the Isle of Man and Gibraltar.

These jurisdictions and countries are particularly well suited as a location for a US-owned holding company, foreign trading corporation, or a foreign investment corporation.

3) Tax Treaty Nations

The third group of jurisdictions can be called "tax treaty nations" because their law does impose taxes on corporate or trust income, wherever earned worldwide.

However, these governments have adopted reciprocal double-taxation avoidance agreements with other nations, especially ones with which they have extensive trade, such as the United States, France, Germany or the United Kingdom.

These mutual agreements may reduce significantly the national withholding tax imposed on income derived from abroad by domestic corporations, usually giving full credit against domestic tax liability for taxes paid by a local business to a foreign government.

These nations may be less attractive as a base for an American seeking asset protection, since international tax treaties permit the free exchange of information between national taxing authorities, allowing far less financial privacy. Cyprus, the Netherlands, Belgium and Denmark are primary examples of tax treaty nations.

4) Special Use Tax Havens

In the fourth and last category are countries that impose most taxes with which Americans are all too familiar, but the government has a policy of granting special tax concessions, tax holidays or rebates to designated types of business enterprises they wish to attract and promote.

These concessions typically include corporate tax credits for job creation, tax exemptions for manufacturing and processing of exports, or special tax benefits for international business or holding companies, offshore banks, or other selected industries.

A primary example of a special use tax haven is the independent south Pacific nation of Samoa. All entities operating under its 1987 Offshore Banking, International Trust, and International Companies Act, and its 1988 International Insurance Act are exempt from Samoan income, stamp, and withholding taxes, and any other direct or indirect levies, as well as exchange and currency controls, foreign exchange levies, central bank restrictions, and domestic Samoan legislation.

Although the fact is largely unknown to their own citizens, both the United States and Canada offers such tax break incentives to foreigners who establish businesses within their borders, so long as certain minimal amounts are invested and local jobs result.

A Haven for You
Robert E. Bauman JD, October 2006

Sometimes in public perception a combination of words takes on a wider meaning than the individual words themselves. Indeed, slogans dominate political campaigns, advertising and even our colloquial speech.

Thus it is that a phrase we often use here at The Sovereign Society, "tax haven," has for us, a definitely good connotation.

On the other hand, the U.S. Internal Revenue Service has done their best to paint tax havens as unpatriotic, tax evading, money laundering criminal enterprises — which they are not.

In fact, a tax haven is nothing more than a country or other jurisdiction that offers foreigners lower taxes or no taxes, especially attractive to those of us who live in high tax nations. That various places offer lower taxes, produce healthy tax competition and keep taxes everywhere generally lower.

But consider the original meaning of the word "haven." The dictionary tells us that the word originated with mariners who plied the sea — to them it was a safe harbor or port where their vessel could be sheltered during a storm. Thus "haven," in the wider sense, has come to mean a place of shelter, safety, refuge, asylum, a place of sanctuary and rest; a place where you, or your assets, are protected from danger.

In that sense, we often speak not only of tax havens, but of "asset havens," countries that have enacted special laws to protect your cash and investments. Often one nation combines both aspects and becomes particularly attractive, as in the case of the Republic of Panama.

Based on almost a decade of experience, The Sovereign Society looks at five major factors when we examine each potential haven:

1. **Government/political stability:** How long has the current system of government been in place and is the jurisdiction politically sound?

2. **Favorable laws, judicial system:** Does the country have a well-established legal tradition? Does its legal and judicial system have a reputation for "fair play" with regard to foreign investors?

3. **Available legal entities:** Does the jurisdiction have a sufficient variety of legal entities, trusts, family foundations, international business corporations, to satisfy the average person seeking estate planning or business solutions?

4. **Financial privacy/banking secrecy:** Does the place have financial privacy and bank secrecy laws? How strictly are they applied? What exceptions exist?

5. Taxes: Does the haven impose taxes on foreign investors or residents? Can these taxes be avoided legally? Are there tax treaties or tax information exchange agreements in effect?

Based on all these factors there are four countries that we choose as the leading places for you to consider creating your personalized offshore plan: the winners are Switzerland, Panama, Liechtenstein and Hong Kong.

- **Switzerland** today still stands as the world's best all-around offshore banking and asset protection haven, despite the many compromises in recent years that the Swiss have been forced to make under international pressure. It's not really a tax haven, but it doesn't enforce tax laws for most other nations.

- **Panama** combines maximum financial privacy, a long history of judicial enforcement of asset protection-friendly laws, a strong anti-money-laundering law, plus near total tax exemptions for foreigners. Thanks to its unique historic relationship with the United States, it also exercises a high degree of independence from outside pressures, especially those from Washington.

- **Hong Kong.** Even though the Communist government in Beijing controls it, Hong Kong remains relatively free, a reflection of Beijing's need for it to be its financial powerhouse. Hong Kong retains a strong set of common law statutes governing banking and finance. If you're doing business in Asia, especially in China, this is the place to be. It is home to thousands of foreign businesses, traders and investors.

The jurisdictions I've named above are the leaders, but by no means the only tax and asset havens.

For example, Singapore has recently adopted a bank secrecy law based on the Swiss law. It has also revised its trust laws and reduced taxes on foreigners, making it a close rival to Hong Kong. And there are other tax havens too, such as the Channel Islands of Jersey and Guernsey, the Isle of Man, Bermuda and even the Cayman Islands. Each has it own pluses and minuses and differs in some respects.

Be assured, however there's one or more havens that will suit your needs and we will be pleased to help you choose.

THE U.S. AS AN OFFSHORE TAX HAVEN
Robert E. Bauman JD, *The Offshore Money Manual*, 2002

Few hard-pressed American taxpayers realize it, but the United States is a tax haven for foreign investors. There is a whole host of laws that provide liberal U.S. tax breaks that apply only to foreigners.

While Americans struggle to pay combined taxes that rob them of more than 40 percent of their total incomes, careful foreign investors can and do make money in the United States tax free.

Even so, the U.S. is not a straightforward "no-tax" haven like Panama, even for foreigners. Instead, a haphazard array of complex provisions in the Internal Revenue Code, coupled with a host of international tax treaties, provide rich opportunities for the foreign investor. Assisting these investors is an elite group of high-priced American tax lawyers and accountants known as "inbound specialists." They specialize in structuring transactions to minimize taxes and maximize profits.

Q. Why does the U.S. allow foreign investors to get off tax-free?

A. The U.S. government desperately needs foreign investment.

The U.S. Treasury needs it to provide capital to bolster the national economy and, more importantly, to finance the huge government budget deficit. A large portion of foreign investment goes directly into short-and long-term U.S. Treasury securities. This enormous cash inflow keeps the government afloat from day to day. Billions of dollars of the much-talked-about national debt is owed directly to European and Asian investors. The communist government of the Peoples Republic of China is one of America's largest individual creditors by virtue of their investments in U.S. government debt securities.

One other scary fact: the annual interest paid on this $5 trillion government debt now exceeds all other federal budget program costs, except the Defense Department. Some 38 percent of the entire budget is for interest payments alone, and most of it goes to foreign investors. We're talking very big money here!

Net interest on the U.S. public debt was approximately $240 billion in fiscal years 2007 and 2008. This represented about 9.5% of all government spending. Interest was the fourth largest single cost category, after defense, Social Security, and Medicare.

To give credit where it's due, foreign companies operating in the U.S. do pay corporate income taxes on some of their U.S. earnings. According to a report by KPMG Peat Marwick, they pay plenty.

Q. Do these foreign investors have power over the U.S.?

A. You bet they do.

Congress imposed a 30 percent withholding tax on all interest payments to foreign residents and corporations doing business in the US. Foreign investors bluntly let it be known they would take their money elsewhere if the withholding tax remained. Not surprisingly, the IRC is now riddled with exceptions to the 30 percent tax.

The biggest U.S. tax break for many foreigners comes from a combination impact of domestic IRC provisions and the tax laws of the investor's own country. The United States taxes its citizens and residents on their worldwide income. But non-citizens and non-residents are allowed to earn certain types of income from within the U.S. tax free. As you can guess, droves of smart foreign investors take advantage of the situation.

Q. Can Americans get in on this foreign investor tax-free gravy train?

A. The answer is a qualified "yes."

In the right circumstances, a U.S. citizen or resident can benefit from this same tax-free income that makes so many foreign investors wealthy. The qualifying process is complex, so it's not for everyone, but the laws offer clear possibilities and you can use them to your advantage.

Part Two: Havens Under Siege

Big Government's War Against Harmful Tax Competition
Mark Nestmann, *The Sovereign Individual*, January 1999

In recent months, world governments have unleashed a parade of special investigations, groundbreaking reports, and multilateral actions with a single goal severely curtailing or even wiping out the world's burgeoning offshore financial sector.

Three recent components of this war are the Organization for Economic Co-operation and Development's (OECD) report on tax competition; the Edwards Report on the Channel Islands and the Isle of Man; and the Cook Initiative on U.K. Overseas Territories, from U.K. Foreign Secretary Robin Cook.

War on Drugs Begets War on Tax Avoidance

In an April 1998 report entitled "Harmful Tax Competition," the OECD called for "severe countermeasures" against countries used by persons or companies trying to reduce taxes. The report proposed that domestic taxes be enforced internationally, using the anti-drug and anti-money laundering regime constructed in recent years as a model.

Many of us have long predicted that the "War on Drugs" was nothing more than a smokescreen to construct an international tax collection authority. We were right. Lost in the OECD's hand wringing over unfair tax competition is the fact that taxes are merely another cost of doing business. An individual or business that lowers its tax burden will be more successful than one that doesn't.

Wake Up, OECD: Marxism Doesn't Work!

In most OECD countries, a person or company pays tax according to their vulnerability to coercion by special interest groups that receive transfer payments according to their "needs." This is, of course, the Marxist model that was a colossal failure in the Soviet Union. Now the "kinder and gentler" version of Marxism that has flourished in the social democracies of Western Europe and the United States for decades is also in collapse.

However, the OECD is not merely delusional, but also schizophrenic. Around the same time, it released *Harmful Tax Competition*, it also published Policy Brief No. 9: *Fostering Entrepreneurship*.

A key factor in fostering entrepreneurship, of course, is reducing regulatory and tax barriers to success.

Once that is done, history has proven time and again that markets will establish themselves, a fact forgotten by the OECD.

OECD Members Lead in Harmful Tax Competition

The OECD defines a tax haven that conducts "harmful tax competition" as any nation that:

- Imposes nominal or no tax on income.

- Offers preferential treatment to certain types of income at no or low tax rates.

- Offers, or is perceived to offer, nonresidents the ability to escape taxes in their country of residence.

- Permits tax-related planning in activities that lack substantial economic (non-tax) advantages.

Under this definition, almost every OECD country is a tax haven. Indeed, OECD members Switzerland and Luxembourg, two of the world's largest offshore centers, refused to endorse the report.

Virtually every other OECD member uses tax competition to attract foreign investment or wealthy residents. For instance, the United States does not tax many types of income earned by nonresident investors. The United Kingdom and Ireland invite wealthy foreigners to live there, essentially tax free, through their "resident but not domiciled" rules. Even Germany has enacted recent legislation that makes it much more attractive tax wise for holding companies.

Economic Warfare

But the hypocrisy goes even deeper. While the OECD is prepared to tolerate tax competition among its members, it threatens "severe countermeasures" against nonmembers. It has in effect declared economic war against some of the world's most impoverished countries that, in the absence of their offshore industries, would have few if any opportunities to advance economically.

The OECD campaign is a concerted effort by the world's richest nations to hamper the development of some of the poorest ones, disguised in the rhetoric of "fairness."

The politicians governing the world's high tax democracies know that they cannot continue to tax and spend forever. But they will hang on to power until they are forced to abdicate because, to a politician, power is everything.

There will be major confrontations with "out of favor" offshore centers that do not at least pay lip service to the idea of applying anti-money laundering laws to tax crimes. Indeed, such a confrontation is already occurring in the U.K.'s Caribbean overseas territories.

HERE'S WHAT YOU NEED TO KNOW ABOUT FATCA
Ted Bauman, *Offshore Confidential*, April 2014

Let's get this out there, right off the bat — The Sovereign Society is outraged by the imposition of the Foreign Account Tax Compliance Act, or FATCA, as it has become known.

We have been in the forefront of the opposition to this nefarious piece of legislation since its inception.

In fact, my father warned you about this odious law a month before the IRS first published its draft proposal for FATCA regulations back in February 2012.

Now it is upon us, and we abhor its assault on our rights to freely conduct our banking where we please, and invest offshore. FATCA breaches both of these rights — and more, including our right to personal and financial privacy.

FATCA has been presented as the U.S. government's response to some U.S. citizens' attempts to evade tax by holding bank accounts overseas. After several high-profile cases, involving mainly Swiss banks, the U.S. Congress decided to shift the onus for discovering U.S. tax evasion away from the IRS and private whistle-blowers to the foreign banks and firms that hold the accounts.

These overseas institutions have been forced to cooperate in spilling the beans on U.S. account holders or lose their access to the U.S. financial system entirely.

As my father points out in the preface to this piece: "The IRS ... claims the imperial power to control and set rules for every foreign financial institution in the world. Not since the Roman Empire has such an imperious claim been made."

Of course, the real purpose of FATCA is to make offshore banking so difficult that people won't even try to do it — even if it is their right to do so.

Barring any last-minute changes on the part of the U.S. government, FATCA is happening. And aside from continuing to fight for its repeal, there is little we can do to stop it.

That means we are left with one defense strategy — preparation.

With so much misinformation out there, this special issue of *Offshore Confidential* is dedicated to telling you what you need to know — and do — about FATCA, which takes full effect on July 1, 2014.

FATCA — The Basics

So let's deal with facts as they are ... FATCA is a formal law, passed by Congress, and applies to all "U.S. Persons" with accounts at foreign banks and other financial institutions outside the U.S.

Don't let the terminology fool you. "U.S. Person" is government-speak for all U.S. citizens and green card holders. It also includes U.S.-based entities, such as corporations, partnerships, limited liability companies, trusts and estates. And it includes the estimated 7.2 million U.S. expat and dual citizens living abroad permanently, most of whom have had foreign bank accounts for years, as I do in South Africa.

While FATCA is aimed specifically at Americans with bank accounts abroad, its modus operandi is via foreign financial institutions, or FFIs, which include overseas banks, mutual funds, hedge funds, private equity funds and insurance companies that offer annuities.

However, it is worth noting that foreign branches of U.S. financial institutions aren't considered FFIs under FATCA.

The purpose of FATCA is to force FFIs to report the account numbers, balances, names, addresses and taxpayer identification numbers of all their U.S. person clients each year. It makes no difference whether the FFIs want to do this or even if it's against their own country's financial privacy laws.

FATCA doesn't mean that you're going to have to pay a 30% tax on any money you send offshore. That's a silly rumor doing the rounds, and it's based on a misreading of one of FATCA's enforcement techniques, which we'll get to in a moment.

The point is that if you have a foreign bank account and the bank doesn't comply with the rules of FATCA, all will be subject to a 30% "withholding tax."

As my father says, this is *Imperium Romanum* stuff, folks.

To accomplish this, the Obama administration has concluded agreements with 48 countries, with more in the pipeline. Most of these agreements require foreign governments to collect information from their own banks and pass it on to the IRS. Only two countries — Japan and Switzerland — have signed agreements allowing their banks to report information directly to the IRS.

A little known fact is that in concluding these agreements, the U.S. has promised foreign governments it will reciprocate by providing tax information on the other country's citizens' accounts in the United States. But this has not yet been authorized.

What You Need to Know

People have been up in arms about FATCA and there's a lot of misinformation about it out there. The truth is that for most individuals, FATCA isn't really a significant additional reporting burden, compared with what's already on the books.

While FATCA is gathering information via the foreign banks in which you hold your cash and investments, this new law has also imposed a few new reporting requirements on Americans with overseas bank accounts.

Starting with your 2013 U.S. income tax filing, FATCA imposes new reporting requirements on any American with a foreign bank account. You now must submit a Form 8938. That's in addition to the other reports you already have to file about your offshore accounts and assets.

Once the IRS gets the information of your overseas accounts, FATCA has its own penalties to impose on individual account holders — starting at $10,000, with an additional penalty of up to $50,000 for failure to file after IRS notification. A 40% penalty on any understatement of tax can also be imposed.

To get FATCA working, the U.S. government has forced many countries to amend their financial privacy laws to allow their banks to report on U.S. clients. That way the FFIs themselves don't need to interact with the IRS. The current list of agreements can be found on the FATCA website.

Nonetheless, if you're above board and not trying to hide anything from the IRS, you don't really have anything to worry about — although there are a few exceptions.

How FATCA Applies to You

I'm going to run through the most common scenarios, and tell you exactly what you need to do — if anything. All of these scenarios assume you have at least one foreign bank account.

- **If you live in the U.S.:** If you live in the States and have foreign accounts, you'll have to file a FATCA report on all your accounts, if the total value of all of them added together exceeds $50,000 ($100,000 for couples) on the last day of the year or exceeded $75,000 ($150,000) at any time during the year.

- **If you live permanently abroad:** The reporting thresholds for people who pass the IRS foreign residence test are significantly higher. To pass this test, you must live abroad most of the year, must not have made an official declaration that you are not a resident of that country, and must be subject to that country's income tax laws. The FATCA reporting threshold for foreign-resident couples filing jointly is $400,000 on the last day of the tax year or more than $600,000 at any time during the tax year on all accounts at foreign banks (not foreign PLUS U.S. bank accounts — only the foreign ones).

- **If you are married to a foreigner:** Americans married to a foreigner must report their spouses' foreign bank accounts under FATCA, even if the spouse isn't a U.S. resident or taxpayer. This is the case whether you live in the U.S. or live abroad.

As you might imagine, this has caused some domestic complications. As one American living in Switzerland put it: "My Swiss husband is furious. He says it's none of their business what he has in his account. He's absolutely right, but if I don't report, it's a criminal act." A black eye for Cupid, courtesy of the IRS.

If you're married to a foreigner, I recommend three courses of action:

a) Be prepared to report all of your non-U.S. bank accounts and investments under FATCA, for both yourself and your spouse;

b) Make sure all the foreign banks where you and your spouse have accounts are aware of your marriage and their obligation to report on both of you under FATCA;

c) If you haven't filed your U.S. tax returns, get ready to do so for the current year as well as previous years. This will require the assistance of a specialist legal counsel. REMEMBER: Never approach the IRS yourself.

- **If you're a dual citizen:** FATCA applies to people who hold dual citizenship, whether you live in the U.S. or not — or even whether you're aware of your U.S. citizenship status. (Remember, all it takes is to be born in the U.S., or abroad to a U.S. parent.) This has also caused some problems.

You can be a U.S. citizen even if you don't take any steps to claim it. Many Canadians, for example, were born in U.S. hospitals near the border. All of them are required to report under FATCA, as are their Canadian banks. And, of course, FATCA reporting applies to their Canadian spouses as well.

So how do they know you're an American, anyway? Well, it might be your accent — but the real answer is it doesn't matter. Either way, if you are a U.S. person, you and your overseas bank are still obliged to comply with the law. Many foreign banks don't ask for proof of citizenship when you open an account at a branch.

The same applies to dual citizens. I opened my bank accounts in South Africa with my South African ID number. As far as I know, these banks have no idea I'm also an American. Millions of people are in the same situation.

It's tempting to advise U.S. residents and dual citizens living abroad, who have no more than a few basic bank accounts and perhaps a mortgage on their foreign home to ignore FATCA. But this would be a mistake — and too great a risk.

U.S. Entities and FATCA

As I mentioned above, FATCA also applies to entities formed under U.S. law, such as corporations, partnerships, limited liability companies, trusts and estates. FATCA reporting applies to them just as it does to a natural person.

However, an important distinction here that FATCA applies only to entities formed under U.S. law. FATCA has no jurisdiction over foreign-based entities — unless, of course, they are owned by in whole or in part by Americans.

If you have financial interests in an offshore trust, company or other vehicle formed under foreign laws, you must report your financial interest in those entities as an individual. On the other hand, if you are a substantial owner (10% or more) of a U.S. entity with foreign financial assets, the entity itself does the reporting.

Moreover, if you are a substantial owner of a U.S. entity with foreign accounts, make sure the management of your company, trust, or other vehicle is aware of the FATCA reporting requirement and intends to comply.

Expats and Expatriation

Americans who live overseas and either haven't known about the need to file U.S. taxes every year or have ignored it, as I did in South Africa, are under immediate threat from FATCA.

Because FATCA requires foreign banks to report to the IRS on their U.S. clients, any Americans overseas who haven't been filing their annual Form 1040s have to start this year — and they have to catch up on past years, just as I did.

There is a growing exodus of Americans who have decided they are better off cutting official ties with the U.S., largely Americans who have lived and worked abroad for years, because of intensifying government pursuit of foreign assets. In 2013, there was a 221% increase over the previous year in the number of Americans who gave up their citizenship.

Unfortunately, expatriation isn't necessarily a better deal financially.

Renouncing your U.S. citizenship requires that you pay an expatriation tax. It applies to those who have a net worth of $2 million, or five-year average income tax liability exceeding $139,000.

The tax treats expats as if they have liquidated all of their assets on the day prior to expatriation. That means, any theoretical "capital gain" greater than $600,000 is taxed as income in that calendar year. And the tax applies whether you actually liquidate your assets or not. The law also applies to deferred compensation 401(k), 403(b) plans, pension plans, and stock options.

Moreover, a U.S. taxpayer seeking to expatriate must certify U.S. income tax compliance for all previous years as part of the expatriation process. So giving up U.S. citizenship isn't going to make the IRS ignore you.

Coming Clean

When I came clean to the IRS in 2007, I paid no penalties — partly because I benefited from the Foreign Earned Income Exclusion, and partly because I did this before the IRS decided in 2012 to impose massive penalties on U.S. filers abroad you try to "come clean."

Under the Offshore Voluntary Disclosure Program, you can come clean to the IRS, but you have to pay off all back income tax, a 20% penalty, interest, and 27.5% of your highest single-year foreign account balances.

Great way to get people to cooperate, IRS! No wonder many American expats have told Uncle Sam to get stuffed, and have renounced their citizenship.

Final Word

In a 2012 report to Congress, the National Taxpayer Advocate explained that there are 7,332 pages of instructions, 16 IRS publications, and 667 pages of tax forms applicable to overseas U.S. citizens. And now comes the abomination of FATCA.

As my father explained in the preface, FATCA is the product of a political effort to scapegoat innocent Americans, who want to exercise their right to live, invest and bank overseas. It is an overkill that will cost the taxpayer more than it will bring in.

FATCA will basically make the United States a global tax enforcer for all the major developed countries.

It's true there are a few Americans who have tried to evade U.S. taxes by banking overseas. But it's also true the U.S. government's financial difficulties, the enormous national debt and budget deficits are in no way related to these individuals. It has even less to do with the activities and finances of citizens who live and work abroad.

FATCA is nothing more than an attempt to divert our collective attention from the true causes of America's financial collapse — mismanaged federal budgets.

Playing to the jingoistic sentiments of the average American, FATCA is a direct attack on the freedoms of those who choose an international life but are unorganized and vulnerable.

Comply, but don't stop resisting.

Contacts

If your financial affairs include any of the scenarios I've sketched out above — especially if you're one of the millions of Americans abroad who haven't been keeping up with your IRS filings — the time to seek specialist counsel is now.

See the Appendix A for a list of tax professionals we recommend who will assure you are in FATCA compliance.

BLACKLISTING TAX HAVENS
Robert E. Bauman JD, *The Sovereign Indvidual*, July 2008

A "blacklist" is defined as a list of persons or entities to be shunned or banned because they are said to be under suspicion, disfavor or censure. Of course blacklisting is in the eye of the beholder, and one man's blacklist is another man's Honor Roll; some see groups as terrorists, while others see them as freedom fighters.

I was mildly surprised to learn that the first recorded use of this word denoting such *odium* dates way back to 1692, the same year of the Salem, Massachusetts, Witch Trials. In those quaint times what passed for due process meant that five women were burned at the stake for the offense of being witches.

Perhaps that's why blacklists and witch hunts seems to operate in tandem.

In American history, one of the most famous examples of blacklisting stemmed from an investigation in 1947 by the U.S. House of Representatives Un-American Activities Committee (HUAC) into the Communist influence on the motion picture industry.

Some in the industry were blacklisted because of their refusal to provide evidence to HUAC, including a group known as the "Hollywood Ten," most of them screen writers who were members of the U.S. Communist Party, a Moscow-dominated group that advocated the forceful overthrow of the U.S. government.

Involved in this episode was an actor named Ronald Reagan, who later said he was not very concerned about Communism until he returned from the U.S. Army after World War II to resume his movie career and became head of the Screen Actors Guild. It was a time of bitter controversy about Communist blacklisting. Reagan, under threats against his life, assisted in exposing the Reds and gained a lifelong suspicion of the Evil Empire that one may suggest contributed to the eventual downfall of Communism.

Phony Blacklists Exposed

What got me to thinking about blacklists was an article by Dr. Marshall Langer, the distinguished senior offshore attorney and a retired member of The Sovereign Society Council of Experts. In the May issue of Offshore Investment magazine, Dr. Langer exposed the stupidity and political prejudice of tax collectors from various nations who have decided to blacklist — of all things — tax havens.

Dr. Langer points out that so blind and irrational has been the hatred of some national tax collectors that they even have issued official blacklists of non-existent places (the "Pacific Islands," "Damask" and "Patau") and one nation, Venezuela, even issued a blacklist with itself on the list.

Fortunately, the United States under the Bush administration has refused to go along with tax haven blacklists, but Senator Barack Obama, the likely Democratic presidential nominee, is the proud author of a Senate bill that would not only blacklist scores of countries (Switzerland, Panama, Monaco, et. al.), but would curtail the rights of Americans freely to do business there.

Tax Competition Is Good

You would think that few sensible people would object to tax havens — countries or other jurisdictions that impose no taxes or very low taxes on foreigners who do business there. After all, tax competition among nations helps keep taxes lower everywhere, provides jobs, cuts costs and increases profits from business and investment.

But "sensible" does not include the Organization for Economic Cooperation and Development (OECD), a cabal that has often played bully and villain in its ham handed attempts to crush tax havens and force a uniform system of high taxes worldwide. In pursuing its dictatorial goals, the OECD is simply doing the bidding of its 30 member nations, many of which, like France and Germany, are high tax, socialist welfare states bent on wringing every last dollar, pound or euro out of domestic taxpayers in order to finance continuing deficits and statist economies.

And you guessed it — the OECD publicity instrument of choice in this pro-high tax campaign has been the phony "harmful tax competition" blacklist.

In the twisted OECD view, if a country freely chooses to impose no taxes, that policy choice is "unfair" to high tax countries that choose to soak taxpayers for all they can get. The OECD has created this smokescreen because they know that sensible people take their business to where taxes are low or non-existence.

Dirty Money/Terrorism Ploys

To lend drama to their demands the OECD spun off a subgroup, the Financial Action Task Force (FATF). These worthies claim to be devoted to fighting money laundering, (and, more recently, countering terrorism), but in fact their goal has been to destroy financial privacy. Both groups want unrestricted, automatic government access to any and all financial accounts anywhere in the world; again, doing the work of their tax collecting masters.

The irony in all this is that the OECD is nothing more than a paper tiger based on agreement of its members. It's not a government or international agency, even in the sense that the United Nations has legal standing.

The OECD presumes to tell the people and governments how they should conduct themselves by, as they claim, "setting standards and creating values for the entire world." These folks think they set the "ground rules for good behavior by multi-national enterprises and corporate governance principles." (A lazy world media trumpets every OECD press release, unctuous documents that always hawk the liberal, elitist, pro-tax line.)

A tall and very presumptuous order for the OECD's nearly 2000 bureaucrats, the salary of every one of whom is tax exempt because of their coveted diplomatic status. Housed in a fine Parisian mansion with a wine cellar that once belonged to the Rothschild family, the Château de la Muette, the OECD's annual budget is over $300 million (£200m), with U.S. taxpayers footing 25% of the total cost.

The Black Beast

At least for the time being, Americans still can and should avail themselves of their freedoms to bank and invest offshore.

In the meantime, I have an appropriate phrase to describe the OECD and the other blacklisters of tax havens — the French bête noire, "the black beast," first used in French literature in 1844 and still applicable today.

The phrase refers to someone or something unwanted or even hated, a pet peeve or strong annoyance — just like the OECD.

Offshore Bullying from the World's Largest Tax Haven

Mark Nestmann, May 2009

The devil is in the details.

My father, who practiced medicine for nearly four decades, often repeated this truism when confronting a difficult diagnosis. And the same truism applies in other areas — including "tax information exchange agreements" (TIEAs).

If you have mercifully avoided TIEAs thus far in your life, you may not be able to avoid them much longer.

That's especially true if you invest or do business offshore. The reason: supposedly to establish a "level playing field" for international investment, high tax countries have forced low tax jurisdictions to sign dozens of TIEAs in recent months. These agreements make it much easier for revenue authorities in high tax countries to obtain banking records and other financial records in numerous low-tax jurisdictions.

The Organization for Economic Cooperation and Development (OECD) leads this ongoing jihad against low tax jurisdictions. As they labor in a sumptuous palace in Paris, OECD bureaucrats enjoy diplomatic status. Unlike most of us, they receive a tax-free salary and benefits. And while working tax-free, they prepare lists of countries they deem insufficiently cooperative with revenue authorities in OECD — and mostly high-tax — countries.

"Grey List" Standoff

Earlier this year, the OECD issued its latest "grey list" of countries that have promised to boost cooperation in tax investigations, but have not yet done so. One of the most important demands the OECD made to countries on this list is to ratify at least a dozen TIEAs with other nations.

Countries that fail to do so may eventually find themselves on an OECD "black list."

And that could result, according to the OECD, in potential isolation from the global financial system. (Think North Korea or Iran.) Not surprisingly, countries on the grey list are trying to get off of it as quickly as they can.

OECD efforts to end what it calls "harmful tax competition" began back in the 1990s. But it wasn't until 2009 that their efforts came to fruition. Citing the need to uphold OECD "standards," several high-tax countries pressured Switzerland

and other offshore havens on the grey list to amend their laws to require limited tax information exchange with foreign revenue authorities.

The United States led this effort. And the results have been a spectacular success, at least from the U.S. Treasury's and the IRS perspective.

First, U.S. prosecutors persuaded the Swiss government to release the names and account records of nearly 5,000 alleged tax evaders from Swiss banking giant UBS. But that was just the beginning. The United States also forced Switzerland to sign a TIEA.

The U.S.-Switzerland TIEA isn't that bad, as TIEAs go. It only obligates Switzerland to release information if U.S. investigators give Swiss authorities a specific name or names of suspected tax evaders. The agreement doesn't allow the IRS to engage in "fishing expeditions" and ask for account records of unnamed U.S. taxpayers in one or more (or all) Swiss banks. (Earlier this year, the IRS tried, but failed, to get the account records of 52,000 unnamed UBS depositors via a so-called "John Doe" subpoena.)

To get off the OECD's most recent grey list, Switzerland signed this TIEA and 11 other TIEAs with high-tax countries. All the TIEAs require Switzerland to lift bank secrecy laws in tax investigations of named individual taxpayers. None of them permit fishing expeditions by revenue authorities.

Austria, another country with strict bank secrecy laws, completed a similar process. The OECD dutifully removed it from the grey list.

Smaller Jurisdictions Easier to Bully

But the devil, again, is in the details. Numerous smaller jurisdictions also find themselves on the grey list. And because they lack the diplomatic clout of Switzerland or Austria, it's much harder for them to get off.

Case in point is a small independent low-tax jurisdiction that, for the moment, will remain nameless. I recently had the opportunity to review internal government correspondence on its progress in meeting the OECD's demands. This jurisdiction already has signed, or is about to sign the requisite dozen TIEAs. But it's still on the OECD grey list, because it hasn't been able to come to terms with the U.S. Treasury Department.

In negotiations with this jurisdiction, the U.S. Treasury has demanded a super-TIEA. The proposed agreement would allow IRS authorities to automatically enter the jurisdiction to conduct interviews and gather evidence. It would also authorize use of the John Doe subpoenas for the same purpose.

Naturally, this jurisdiction doesn't want to sign that broad of an agreement. However, if it fails to do so, the United States may prevent the OECD from removing this nation from the grey list. Forget the fact that this country has complied with all the OECD's demands. If it doesn't submit to IRS blackmail, it may stay on the grey list.

By the way, you might be wondering: what's the world's largest tax haven with the highest degree of secrecy?

Surprise, surprise: it's the United States.

If you're a non-resident alien investor, you can arrange your U.S. investments so that you pay little if any U.S. tax. Except in the case of Canada, the IRS won't tell your home country about the income you earn in the United States. And you can still set up essentially anonymous banking relationships, perfectly legally.

Why Isn't the United States on the OECD Grey List?

That's a no-brainer: it's a matter of might makes right. And it shows how the game really works, behind the scenes. The devil, after all, is in the details.

WHERE ARE THE REAL MONEY LAUNDERING HAVENS?

Mark Nestmann, *The Sovereign Individual*, November 2003

For over a decade, governments worldwide, along with organizations such as the Organization for Economic Cooperation and Development (OECD) and its bastard stepchild, the Financial Action Task Force (FATF), have conducted a full-court press on small offshore financial centers (OFCs) alleged to be "money laundering havens."

We have documented these efforts — the FATF's infamous "blacklist" and, after the events of September 11, 2001, the notorious "USA PATRIOT Act," along with similar anti-OFC vendettas carried out in other high-tax countries.

The truth is that there is far more money laundered in OECD member countries than in the OFCs that they are targeting. For proof, you need to read between the lines of the statistics trotted out to justify the crackdown on OFCs. For instance, the FATF quotes the World Bank as stating that between US$500 billion and US$1.5 trillion is laundered each year. But every U.S. government agency that has studied money laundering has concluded that OFCs do not attract a disproportionate share of laundered funds.

Instead, laundering predominates in the world's largest economies — all members of the OECD. Indeed, about half of global money laundering activity is in the United States. The crackdown on OFCs due to their alleged involvement in "terrorism" doesn't hold water, either. To date, virtually all the funds used in last September's attacks on the United States have been traced to either OECD countries or in a handful of Islamic countries.

Why then, are the OECD, FATF and many governments trying to eliminate OFCs? The crackdown has very little to do with fighting money laundering or terrorism and everything to do with collecting taxes. As we've documented in recent issues, the OECD's spurious onslaught against OFCs alleged to engage in "harmful tax competition" has been completely discredited due to the refusal of the world's largest OFC — again, the United States — to participate in this effort. The FATF's vendetta against OFCs should also be discredited, for the same reason — its most important member is the single largest source of laundered funds.

There are signs that the attack against OFCs may abate, at least temporarily. This is due to infighting between the FATF and the largest (and by far the richest) of all "multilateral" organizations, the International Monetary Fund (IMF). Now, we are hardly fans of IMF taxpayer-financed bailouts of third-world countries. Indeed, IMF aid directly contributes to money laundering, since much of it, as U.S. Treasury Secretary Paul O'Neill recently observed, winds up stashed by the corrupt leaders of recipient governments in offshore bank accounts!

The IMF and the FATF have been trying to forge a joint approach to fight terrorist financing, but the IMF's Board (some members of which are blacklisted countries) is now insisting on a year's moratorium on the FATF's next blacklist as the price of the IMF's co-operation. The FATF has responded by temporarily suspending its blacklist. OFCs can breathe a little easier, if not for long.

Since most laundering occurs in OECD countries, does that mean they should take even more draconian measures than they have already — more seizures, less financial privacy, more restrictions on cash transactions, etc.? Not at all.

These approaches have been spectacularly unsuccessful. Indeed, the percentage of funds "laundered" in OECD economies is about the same today as it was two decades ago when the "War on Laundering" began.

What, then, is the answer to the laundering "crisis" in OECD countries? We have suggested that the real problem is that laundering laws are designed principally to punish crimes where there is no identifiable victim, such as drug offenses. Decriminalization or partial legalization would be far preferable from a civil liberties standpoint than providing governments even greater powers to incarcerate and seize property.

In contrast, where there is an identifiable victim of fraud or other wrongdoing, the legal tools needed for effective deterrence are already in place. They just need to be more effectively employed.

Acts of War
Robert E. Bauman JD, April 2009

I happen to hold to the old fashioned notion that America's national sovereignty is the foundation of our freedom as a people and of our individual liberty.

Sovereignty is the status, dominion, supreme authority and independent power held and exercised by a government. In America the prevalent founding theory was that the people rule as sovereign. Indeed, we gained our sovereignty by a famous revolution that stirred much of the world to emulate our system of government.

If that be true, then sovereignty rests strictly with the American people. We cannot allow foreign countries or international organizations to make decisions and impose policies that should be our own exclusive province. And that is true of every other sovereign nation.

End of History?

Robert Kagan, the noted author and a senior associate at the Carnegie Endowment for International Peace, writing in *The New Republic* (The End of the End of History, April 23, 2008) noted that "For three centuries, international law, with its strictures against interference in the internal affairs of nations, has tended to protect autocracies. Now the democratic world is in the process of removing that protection, while the autocrats rush to defend the principle of sovereign inviolability."

He quoted "…no less an authority than Henry Kissinger [who] warned that 'the abrupt abandonment of the concept of national sovereignty' risked a world unmoored from any notion of international legal order."

The New Autocracy

"Autocracy" used to be defined as a government in which one person has uncontrolled or unlimited authority over others, as in the government by an absolute monarch.

But I suggest, based on the outcome of the infamous G-20 London meeting last week, that the "new autocracy" should be defined as government imposed on the majority of the people by an elite group of politicians and their allied activists who think they know what is best for everyone else.

Their righteous certainties include plans for economics, politics, trade, international relations, but also for our lives — prescriptions that determine the extent of our freedom and liberty, our privacy, even our right to earn and accumulate wealth and private property.

Illegitimate Acts

What raised my concern was the utter disregard shown by the leaders of the G-20 countries, including President Obama, for American sovereignty, as well as the sovereignty of other nations as well.

Put aside Mr. Obama's mistaken surrender of the theoretical control of our national currency, our financial and banking systems and our economy to some newly formed, nebulous international groups. That betrayal is bad enough in and of itself.

Acts of War

But Mr. Obama, the world conciliator who likes to contrast himself as a man of peace, compared to his bellicose predecessor, Mr. Bush, didn't blink an eye in his endorsement of a frontal attack just short of war aimed at numerous independent jurisdictions that the G-20 scornfully calls "tax havens."

It seems this new American leader never considered what he (or the millions of Americans he represents), would do if the United States similarly was threatened with an organized global boycott, blacklisted as a financial pariah, subjected to trade and banking restrictions, and punishment was promised for foreigners who dared to do business with America.

Yet that is what the president of the United States (and the other G-20 London delegates) have decreed is to be the fate of a fluctuating number of countries (and British colonies) that arbitrarily have been smeared by a blacklist drawn up by a non-government group known as the Organization for Economic and Community Development (OECD).

(I would suggest, based on its overt selective hostility towards some communities, the last word of its name be change to the more appropriate, "Destruction.")

Far less serious international acts between and among nations have produced not only border conflicts, but all-out prolonged military actions.

PREPOSTEROUS LAW
Robert E. Bauman JD, *Offshore Confidential*, April 2014

When I studied law at Georgetown University Law Center I was taught that, except in rare cases, a nation's laws do not have legal effect beyond a country's borders.

True, some laws, such as U.S. tax laws, apply to a U.S. person individually without regard to where they may live or earn income. That's why a U.S. person living or earning offshore is still obliged to file an annual IRS Form 1040 and pay income taxes owed.

But the IRS — now armed with odious Public Law 111-147, known as the "Foreign Account Tax Compliance Act" or FATCA — claims the imperial power to control and set rules for every "foreign financial institution" in the world.

Not since the Roman Empire has such an imperious claim been made. In this article, Ted Bauman, my son and editorial associate, explains where FATCA stands now and what you need to know and do.

Thinking Americans, who are concerned with foreign banking, their investments abroad, as well as their personal and financial privacy, realize the ideologues and bureaucrats who control the U.S. government — especially the Internal Revenue Service — are prejudiced against all offshore financial activity by U.S. persons.

At the heart of this ingrained prejudice is a basic lie promulgated by the government and its financial enforcers: that "offshore" with tax evasion are one and the same.

Add to that prejudice, the arbitrary imposition of a complex U.S. tax code that virtually no one understands.

This unjust bias is intensified by the IRS attitude that violates one of the basic rules of law implied in the U.S. Constitution — that individuals are presumed innocent until proven guilty. Instead, the IRS operates in reverse.

In the last year, we have discovered the supposedly impartial IRS has quietly discriminated against conservative political groups. The crowning example of this official bias and prejudice is FATCA — a law that regards every American active offshore as a potential criminal. It is a law that destroys financial privacy without apology.

The IRS makes the preposterous claim that enforcement of FATCA might produce additional tax revenues of $8 billion over 10 years. This is laughable. Non-government experts say FATCA would be lucky to produce $1 billion. Meanwhile, estimates of the cost of implementing FATCA run into hundreds of billions of dollars, plus at least $10 billion per year to administer the additional filing and enforcement requirements. It's hardly cost-effective.

When the Democrats controlled the White House and both houses of the U.S. Congress, Obamacare was not the only fraud perpetrated on America. As a savvy member of The Sovereign Society Freedom Alliance or as a subscriber to *Sovereign Confidential* (now titled *The Bauman Letter*), you will be well aware of the threat of FATCA.

CHAPTER EIGHT: TAX HAVENS: INTERNATIONAL ASSET ACQUISITION   465

In March 2010, FATCA was rammed through without hearings as a rider on the so-called "Hiring Incentives to Restore Employment (HIRE) Act," one of several of President Obama's multi-billion dollar "shovel-ready" bailouts.

As Ted explains below, this unprecedented law imposes a 30% tax on U.S. transactions with any offshore banks or other financial institutions that fail to turn over information to the IRS about U.S. persons and their accounts. As with most major U.S. legislation, a careless U.S. Congress delegated the power to write FATCA rules to the government agency charged with enforcing the law, the beloved IRS.

In effect, the IRS is demanding that foreign banks act as financial spies on their Americans account holders, just as the PATRIOT Act requires U.S. domestic banks to spy on clients and report "suspicious activity" to the U.S. Treasury FinCEN crimes unit.

It might be some small comfort if these were stupid, unthinking IRS-Obama policies. But in my opinion, these are calculated to keep American investors — along with their cash and assets — at home, where they can be controlled (and their assets confiscated) at will by government.

In effect, FATCA is a not-so-subtle form of soft currency controls. FATCA is a threat that includes the possible confiscation of private pension and retirement plans — not to mention a Cyprus-like "bail-in" wealth tax that could be imposed overnight on all U.S. domestic accounts.

American Citizens Abroad has launched an international campaign to repeal FATCA, which they describe as "misconceived" and "dangerous for the U.S. economy." This campaign complements a U.S. drive to repeal FATCA led by the Coalition for Tax Competition, of which The Sovereign Society is a founding member.

Full implementation of FATCA has been delayed several times until July 1, 2014, largely because of the enormous requirements for new software, reporting and banking systems, costing billions at the expense of bank clients.

Another reason for delay was the firestorm of anti-FATCA American public opinion, not only from the international financial and banking industry, but also from foreign governments — but only at first. Now those same foreign governments see a tax collector's advantage in an international web of FATCA agreements as a means to track their taxpayers worldwide.

Even the United Nations is in on the act now. A U.N. "Conference on Global Taxation Governance" in 2002 in Mexico, proposed a worldwide system of international taxes to be collected and administered by the U.N. Then President George W. Bush refused to agree.

The only true solution to this outrageous power grab is the repeal of FATCA. U.S. Senator Rand Paul (R-KY) has introduced a bill that will do just that. The Senator called FATCA a "violation of sovereign nations' laws and individual privacy."

But until the majority party in the U.S. Senate and the occupant in the White House are changed, we are forced to live with the law.

FATCA Timeline

Date	Year	Event
March	2010	FATCA is signed into law as part of the Hiring Incentives to Restore the Economy (HIRE) Act.
July	2011	IRS issues guidance that delays implementation by providing additional time for foreign financial institutions (FFIs) to meet FATCA requirements.
February	2012	IRS issues guidance for FFIs to report imformation on certain account holders to their national tax authorities, which then must provide information to the U.S.
September	2012	IRS issues plans for FFIs to report directly to the IRS.
January	2013	Final FATCA regulations issued.
February	2013	IRS delays part of FATCA for six months.
April	2014	Deadline for FFIs to submit certain documentation extended to June 30.
July	2014	U.S. banks and FFIs will begin to withhold on all U.S.-source payments to accounts at non-compliant FFIs.
January	2015	Withholding on transfers to previously exempt non-compliant FFIs begins. Monitoring on accounts with balances or values of more than $1 million begins.
December	2015	FFIs must perform first annual review of individual accounts worth more than $1 million.
July	2016	U.S. banks and FFIs begin withholding on all recalcitrant individual and entity accounts that existed prior to July 1, 2014.
December	2016	U.S. banks and FFIs' ability to rely on old W-8 forms expires.
January	2017	Withholding on gross proceeds payments made to all recalcitrant accounts.
March	2017	FATCA reporting will include gross proceeds on sales or redemption of property.
June	2018	Requirement begins that once every three years, the responsible FFI officer must certify to the IRS is in compliance with FATCA.

Don't Believe the Smear… Offshore Tax Havens Are Legal
Robert E. Bauman JD, *The Sovereign Investor Daily*, April 2013

During the 1980 U.S. presidential election debate, Ronald Reagan uttered that now famous phrase that served to bring Jimmy Carter's veracity into question: "There you go again."

If Reagan were still with us, he would likely use the same phrase to describe the latest political and journalistic smear campaign against offshore financial havens, which claim that these activities are corrupt and even anti-American.

The latest attacks are also another attempt to drive a nail in the coffin destroying financial privacy.

Showing complete disrespect for the privacy of the individuals and their business activities, the Washington, D.C.-based International Consortium of Investigative Journalists (ICIJ) laid bare the assets of 120,000 offshore companies and trusts, implying that because they were "cloaked in secrecy," each one was tarred with the same brush. All were suspect.

Last Sunday, *The Washington Post* joined the crusade with a lurid story targeting offshore financial centers with alleged links to tax evasion (of course), massive frauds, murder, and jailed crooks, such as Bernie Madoff and Allen Stanford, (about whom I warned you years ago). Most of these new claims were based on nothing more than guilt by association.

This latest attack is simply an extension of a long running war led by the tax collectors of major nations, including the IRS, and spearheaded by the Organization for Economic Co-operation and Development (OECD).

The 86 international journalists involved in the ICIJ investigation bragged that their revelations could be bigger than Wikileaks' Cablegate. It is also one of the biggest thefts of documents in investigative reporting.

ICIJ did admit that sometimes "there are legitimate reasons for housing a company offshore."

We live in an age of propaganda, hyped up so-called news reporting, where facts are so distorted they become lies — an age of calculated political demagoguery, in which so-called leaders and the media deal in double speak.

One of my literary heroes, the late George Orwell, aptly wrote: "During times of universal deceit, telling the truth becomes a revolutionary act."

The Sovereign Society has been following that revolutionary course for 15 years now, telling the truth — even in an age where fact and fiction are blurred.

Here are a few of those truths:

- It is legal to have and use an offshore bank account.
- It is legal to create and donate assets to an offshore asset protection trust or family foundation.
- It is legal to form and operate an international business corporation.
- It is legal to acquire dual citizenship and a second passport.
- It is legal to voluntarily end U.S. citizenship and thereby remove yourself from the U.S. tax system.
- It is legal to purchase offshore life insurance and annuities that allow deferred taxes and it is legal to invest in offshore mutual and hedge funds, precious metals and real estate.
- It is legal to leave the U.S. and move to a foreign land, to retire or to make your home there.
- And it is still legal to transfer your cash and assets out of the U.S. into safer tax havens such as Uruguay, Panama, Switzerland, Liechtenstein or Hong Kong.

Thanks to the success of propaganda from OECD and politicians, such as Michigan Senator Carl Levin, the general public has come to think of "tax havens" as enclaves of shadowy international intrigue, where rich folks hide their cash.

One of America's leading tax policy experts, Daniel J. Mitchell, senior fellow at the Cato Institute in Washington, points out: "We are all beneficiaries of tax havens in ways you might not expect."

Tax competition from offshore financial centers has lowered taxes around the globe. There is even a moral case for tax havens.

Dan notes: "They play a critical role in protecting people who are subject to religious, ethnic, sexual, political, or racial persecution. Most of the world's population lives in regimes that have inadequate human-rights protections, and people with assets often are targets of oppressive governments."

These journalists obviously don't care about privacy or human rights. Their false thesis is simple — anything associated with financial activity offshore is bad, secretive, wrong, and evil.

If you want to know the true facts about tax havens, our web site is your best choice for fair and balanced offshore information.

For further information about legal offshore financial centers, tax-free banking, investment and legal possibilities, I recommend my book, *Where to Stash Your Cash Legally: Tax Havens of the World.*

THE IRS'S NEW OFFSHORE SETTLEMENT TAX: ARE THEY GETTING REASONABLE?

Ted Bauman, *The Sovereign Investor Daily*, December 2014

The United States is unique in many ways; some great, some OK … and some terrible. One of the latter is the fact that our government taxes its citizens and permanent residents on the income they earn *everywhere* on the planet … not just inside our own borders. (Unless you're a corporation, in which case you aren't taxed unless you bring your foreign earnings home.)

In the "old days," this "global taxation" system was something only we expatriates had to worry about. For example, I was legally required to file a U.S. tax return for every year I lived in South Africa, even though I earned all my income in South Africa, and ended up owing no U.S. tax thanks to the Foreign Earned Income Exclusion. If I had made more money, I would also have been required to file an FBAR, a separate Treasury Department report.

And like a lot of my fellow expats, I didn't file all those returns, partly because I didn't know I had to, and partly because I didn't think the IRS really cared about little ol' me.

As many of us now know, however, failure to file tax returns on foreign income DOES matter to the Internal Revenue Service … A LOT.

And until recently when they revised their offshore settlement tax, the stick the IRS used to punish non-filers was so big and mean that it scared many people from doing so. But that changed this year …

The "I Was Clueless" Defense

From 2009, when its war on offshore "tax evaders" began, until June 2014, the IRS regarded anyone and everyone who failed to report foreign income as a tax cheat, with no exceptions. As Jeffrey Neiman, a tax lawyer and former prosecutor in Fort Lauderdale, Florida puts it, "if Al Capone and Mother Theresa had an overseas bank account, they were treated the same" by the IRS. That applied equally to expatriates and to U.S. residents who had offshore financial assets and income of some kind.

Under the 2009 regime, if you caught up on your taxes and reporting voluntarily, the IRS required you to pay any back taxes, interest and a "miscellaneous offshore penalty" equal to 27.5% of your undisclosed foreign financial assets. The advantage of coming clean on your own was that you avoided the 50% offshore penalty inflicted on those caught by the IRS through their own investigations ... and you avoided prosecution and possible jail time.

Under the old program, 45,000 people came forward to pay $6.5 billion in back taxes, fines and penalties, in exchange for reduced fines and penalties and, in most cases, avoidance of prosecution.

Still, having to hand over 27.5% of your hard-earned foreign financial assets just because you didn't know you had to file your U.S. returns was the "cruel and unusual" punishment the U.S. Constitution forbids. Or so thought IRS Taxpayer Advocate Nina E. Olson, who issued a report in January this year slamming the IRS for "disproportionately burdening those who make honest mistakes" — in other words, expats like me who were just clueless, not criminals.

Not All Carrot

Under the IRS's revised Offshore Voluntary Disclosure Program, announced in June to coincide with the activation of the Foreign Account Tax Compliance Act (FATCA), U.S. taxpayers who are able to certify that their past failure to comply with U.S. tax law was "non-willful" can get off with just back tax, interest and a reduced "offshore penalty" of 5%. They also have to file three years' back 1040s and six years' back FBARs. For expats who lived outside the U.S. entirely during a given tax year, there is no penalty at all.

Just as important, the new program expands IRS offshore amnesty to U.S.-based taxpayers with foreign accounts who didn't know about their reporting requirements. They weren't previously covered.

But it's not all wine and roses.

If the IRS catches you before you can out yourself and settle your bills, you'll get socked with a 50% penalty in addition to back taxes and interest. Ouch. Very ouch.

Don't Wait

Although I probably don't have to spell it out to you, here's my advice: If you think you might have a tax issue involving foreign income and/or financial assets, get a good tax lawyer IMMEDIATELY and start the voluntary disclose process. That way the IRS will treat you like Mother Teresa.

After all, you *know* you don't want them to treat you like Al Capone.

Chapter Nine

Special Places for Business & Profits

Good Places to Do Business 472

Regional Destination

1) Caribbean & Latin America

Panama: Privacy & Profits Offshore 474

Panama Fast-Track Residence 480

The Island of Nevis: Privacy & Fast Service 486

The Bahamas: Offshore Haven Diminished 491

Oriental Republic of Uruguay: Welcome to the New Switzerland 497

Bermuda: The "Cadillac" of Offshore Banking 509

The Truth about the Cayman Islands 515

British Virgin Islands: IBC Headquarters 523

U.S. Virgin Islands — Little-Known American Tax Haven 527

Belize: Tarnished Caribbean Gem 534

2) Europe

Andorra: Troubled Mountain Tax Haven 539

Austria — Unique European Banking Secrecy 546

Principality of Liechtenstein: World's First Tax Haven 554

Principality of Monaco: For the Ultra Wealthy 563

Campione d'Italia: Where Taxes Are Non-Traditional 567

3) Asia

    The Cook Islands: Far Out 570

    The Republic of Singapore 574

    Hong Kong: A Far East Offshore Haven 580

Editor's Note:

The people in the countries and territories we name in this chapter have an acute business sense about what you need — expert banking, reliable professional assistance, instant worldwide communications, privacy and a well-developed code of laws and courts to support high-stakes financial activity.

Not all offshore havens are equal.

We tell you which ones are best and which to avoid. Here you will learn the secrets of the rich who are not famous, and do not wish to become so.

We show you ways and explain means, so that you can join them in profiting offshore.

GOOD PLACES TO DO BUSINESS
The Business Haven Report, 1997, Scope Books

What follows is a general description of the characteristics of those nations or territories that have tailored their laws to be hospitable to foreign businesses. Many of these areas also impose no taxes on foreign citizens who live in or have their businesses based in these states.

Imagine living in a large estate with servants to handle all the mundane chores. Imagine running your own business, setting your own hours, having plenty of money to do what you want when you want to do it. Imagine traveling and entertaining. Imagine being wealthy.

A dream? Not at all.

A life like that is well within your reach if you are willing to work hard and make the right business choices. The first, and most important, decision is to locate your business in a nation that caters to international business — a "business haven" if you will.

But what, exactly, is a business haven?

Chapter Nine: Special Places for Business & Profits

A business haven is a place — it may be a country or a region-where an individual, partnership, company, or corporation is given significant incentives to establish an active business. Because the government or ruling body of a business haven wants to attract new businesses, it offers the owners of businesses major advantages to locate their enterprises there. Such inducements might be tax free situations, tax holidays (for example, several years tax-free for specific operations), long-term, low-interest loans for new businesses, reduced rents for factory space, or other vital benefits.

In addition to these factors, many business havens also offer well-educated, highly motivated workforces at compensation rates well below those of the major industrialized nations. Thus, low overhead coupled with major incentives results in increased profitability.

While some countries qualify as business havens because of their pro-business policies, in many cases a business haven may be found in a particular part of a country. Often these areas go by the name of "free zones" or similar designations. They are found throughout the world.

The opportunities are limited only by your imagination. Think of all the kinds of businesses citizens of industrialized countries take for granted, from fast-food restaurants to convenience stores, to telecommunications firms to small specialty manufacturers and quiet bed and breakfast resorts.

Countless businesses are candidates to start new or relocate in a business haven. Of course you would need to carefully scrutinize the business haven you are considering to make sure that the business you are proposing would be successful there, but if it's not, simply choose one that is or consider a different business haven.

However, a few words of caution are necessary.

1. Thoroughly research any business haven both for the inducements it offers and any potential drawbacks. Write to the embassy of the country or unit that oversees the business haven and ask for all the information they can send you. Many business havens have special agencies that act as liaisons between the government of the business haven and entrepreneurs or corporations that would like to establish a business there. These agencies can streamline paperwork and put you in touch with the people who will provide you with the facts you'll need to make a sound decision.
2. Visit the business haven before making any commitments. See if the facts you have learned hold up under personal investigation. See if you like the area and the lifestyle you will be living there.
3. Before signing any agreements, have your attorney review them care- fully. Your attorney should have experience with international business relations. Don't agree to any contracts unless you are entirely satisfied. Remember: everything is negotiable. It won't hurt to ask.

4. Assess your potential overhead (be sure to include all your costs) and expected income carefully. Be certain that your venture is worth your investment of time and money.

5. If you are entering into the venture with partners, discuss their business attitudes and goals, and make sure that they match yours. It's not unusual for partners to find it more difficult to deal with each other than with the representatives of a business haven. This is especially true if your partner is from the country in which the business haven is located. Above all, remember that the choices you make in establishing a business will affect the business overall profitability.

Decisions based on first-hand experience can be the difference between a business that achieves great success and one that remains mediocre in performance.

Business havens offer entrepreneurs and corporations a marvelous chance to begin an enterprise with significant economic incentives and advantages on foreign soil. If you wish to expand your business, start a new business, or begin a new life in a different part of the world, exploring the opportunities presented by business havens is an option you must consider.

CARIBBEAN & LATIN AMERICA

PANAMA: PRIVACY & PROFITS OFFSHORE
Robert E. Bauman JD, *Offshore Confidential*, 2015

As far back as the 1920s Panama adopted statutes promoting offshore banking and business. To this day it continues to welcome offshore investors, financial business and foreign retirees. Its contentious relationship with the U.S. makes its government far less subservient to Washington, which can be a very good thing.

Along with the old millennium, 96 years of official United States presence in the Republic of Panama officially ended at midnight, December 31, 1999. Panama finally got what its nationalistic politicians had demanded for much of the last century — full Panamanian control over its famous inter-oceanic Canal. The Canal handover marked a major transition in the nation's history, but equally important, Panama's established offshore financial center is rapidly attaining world class tax haven status.

When most people hear "Panama" they think of one of the great technical wonders of the world, the Panama Canal. But the country is not so well known for what it has become in the last 20 years — after Miami, it is Latin America's second major international banking and business center, with strong ties to Asia and Europe, and a special relationship with the United States that, however contentious, continues apace.

New Era: Panama Revisited

In September 2000, I returned to Panama for the first time in 20 years. It's a very different place than I remember during my many visits in the 1970s when I served in the U.S. House of Representatives as the ranking Republican on the Panama Canal subcommittee.

My visits then were made during U.S. legislative implementation of the Carter-Torrijos Panama Canal treaty negotiations. Upon my return in 1999 I marveled at the modern skyscrapers, first-class hotels and restaurants, excellent digital Internet and other international communications, as well as the reduced American (as in U.S.) ambiance. Now there are many relatively well-priced buys on condos and other real estate, some of it a byproduct of the U.S. government exodus. Downtown Panama City, the balmy, tropical capital on the southern, Pacific end of the Canal, suggests Los Angeles or Miami, except arguably more locals speak English here than in some parts of South Florida.

Yes, Panama also has a long history of government corruption that has improved somewhat. This hasn't seemed to affect the regulated banking sector.

Privacy, Profits and No Taxes

For offshore investors and entrepreneurs, the Panama question is: "What's in it for me?"

Best answer: "If you move with care and make wise choices — major profits, no taxes and, best of all, maximum, statutorily guaranteed privacy."

In many ways the Republic of Panama is ideally suited for the offshore investor who wants to enjoy the increasingly rare privilege of strong, legally guaranteed financial privacy and no taxes, corporate or personal.

Unlike Bermuda and the Cayman Islands, Panama pointedly refused to sign the OECD memorandum of understanding which would have committed it to imposing taxes on offshore investors and banking. Panama has adopted more than 40 laws protecting foreigners' financial and investment rights, including the Investments Stability Law (Law No. 54), which guarantees foreign and local investors equal rights.

Panama's central location in the Americas makes it a natural base for world business operations. Most importantly, and in spite of its history, Panama isn't directly under the thumb of the United States. And unlike the British Overseas Territories of Bermuda and the Cayman Islands, it isn't under the control of the Foreign Office in London.

Among the current 83 banks [2010 figure] the major players are over 50 multinational banks representing thirty countries that primarily do offshore business. Banking alone accounts for about 11 percent of the nation's GNP.

Most major world banks have full-service branch offices in Panama, with representation from Japan, Germany, Brazil and the U.S. Like Wall Street or the City in London, Panama City's business district high-rises bear the logos of Citibank, HSBC, Lloyds, Bank of Tokyo, Republic National, Banc de Paris, Credit Lyonnais, the International Commercial Bank of China and Dresdner.

Admittedly, it's taken time for the banking sector's reputation to recover from the aftermath of the brutal 1989 U.S. military invasion ordered by the then President George Bush. In that invasion's aftermath nearly every financial institution in Panama was under suspicion of drug money activity.

Reasserting Financial Privacy

Since then Panama's bankers have reasserted the sanctity of their banking secrecy laws. Students of banking history realize that, along with Luxembourg and Liechtenstein, Panama adopted specific tax haven legislation as far back as the 1920s.

A central part of the long tax haven tradition has been attractive statutory guarantees of financial privacy and confidentiality. Violators can suffer civil and criminal penalties for disclosure.

There is no requirement to reveal beneficial trust or corporate ownership to Panama authorities and no required audit reports or financial statements. Bearer shares are permitted. Panama has no double-taxation agreements and no tax information exchange agreements with other countries.

Offshore banking and creation of international business corporations (IBCs) are major revenue sources. But to claim Panama has cleaned up its dirty money act would be too optimistic. In U.S. government circles a bank account in Panama raises immediate suspicion about the account holder.

But that's also true of accounts in Bermuda, the Cayman Islands, Nevis, the Channel Islands and anywhere else in the world the IRS can't readily stick its official nose into private financial activity.

The economic health of Panama depends on financial facilities with safeguards sufficient to ensure legal compliance. In June 2000, the OECD's Financial Action Task Force (FATF) placed Panama on a blacklist of 15 countries alleged to be tolerant of money laundering. Panama's Congress unanimously approved a strong anti-money laundering law in line with FATF recommendations. In June 2001 the nation was removed from the FATF blacklist. That law covers all crimes and brings all financial institutions under the supervision of the government banking agency.

The Yankee Dollar

While "dollarization" is debated as a novel concept elsewhere in Latin America, since 1904 the U.S. dollar has been Panama's official paper currency. (The local equivalent is the balboa, and there are Panamanian coins that circulate along with U.S. coins.)

Panama has no central bank to print money and Juan Luis Moreno-Villalaz, an economic adviser to Panama's Ministry of Economy and Finance notes: "In Panama… there has never been a systemic banking crisis; indeed, in several instances international banks have acted as the system's lender of last resort. The Panamanian system provides low interest rates on mortgages and commercial loans. Credit is ample, with 30-year mortgages readily available. These are unusual conditions for a developing country and are largely achieved because there is no exchange rate risk, a low risk of financial crises, and ample flow of funds from abroad."

He might have added that Panama has been the continued recipient of loans and credits from the International Monetary Fund and other world lending institutions.

Welcome Bankers

Panama grew as an international financial center after enactment of Decree No. 238 of July 1970, a very liberal banking law that also abolished all currency controls. The law exempts offshore business in Panama from income tax and from taxes on interest earned in domestic savings accounts and offshore transactions. In 1999, a comprehensive new Banking Law was enacted and it has accelerated Panama's growth as a leading world offshore finance center.

The 1999 law uses the guidelines of the Basle Committee on Banking Supervision requiring all banks with unrestricted a domestic or international commercial banking license to maintain capital equivalent to at least 8 percent of total assets. In 2001, Panama submitted to an IMF assessment that found it "largely complied" with 23 of the 25 Basle principles that set international standards.

Government investigative powers and tighter general controls have increased, bringing Panama in line with regulatory standards found in European and North American banking centers. Although confidentiality is reaffirmed in the new law, a prima facie case of illicit financial conduct can launch an investigation of possible criminal conduct. The law also permits foreign bank regulators to make inspection visits to any of their domestic banks with branches in Panama.

Another major business and financial attraction at the Atlantic end of the Canal is the booming Colon Free Zone (http://www.colonfreetradezone.com/freezone-colon.html), a major tax-free transshipment facility, the second largest free trade zone in the world after Hong Kong.

IBCs and Foundations

Panama has a host of liberal laws favoring trusts, international business companies and holding companies. In 1995 it enacted Law No. 25, a new private foundation statute modeled after the popular family wealth protection and estate planning vehicle long used in Liechtenstein. That law allows the tax-free family foundation to be used for investment, tax sheltering, commercial business and private activity, with the founder retaining lifetime control. Foundation assets are not counted as part of the founder's estate for death tax purposes, and Panama does not recognize the often restrictive inheritance laws of other nations.

Some argue that the Panamanian private foundation law is only a clone of the Liechtenstein law, recommending the real thing if this device interests you. Then too, Panama is a civil law nation without some of the English-U.S. common law legal precedents and traditions that make trusts somewhat easier to operate in the U.S. and U.K.

Panama's IBC Law 32 of 1927, is modeled after the U.S. State of Delaware's corporation friendly statutes. There are about 350,000 IBCs registered in Panama, second only to Hong Kong's 400,000 IBCs. A Panama IBC can maintain its own corporate bank account and credit cards for world management of investments, mutual funds, precious metals, real estate and trade. Tax-free corporate income can be spent for business purposes worldwide and the IBC allows avoidance of your home country zoning, labor, manufacturing, warranty, environmental and other restrictions.

However suspect it may have been in the past, the Republic of Panama is fast becoming one of the major financial crossroads of the world. Base your business here and you're connected everywhere.

World Class Retirement Haven

Spring-like weather year-round…a low, low cost of living…safety…security…peace of mind…beautiful landscapes — mountainsides covered with flowers, planted with coffee…cascading waterfalls…stone bridges over clear, sparkling rivers…that's Panama.

Foreign retirees who move to Panama benefit from one of the most attractive retirement *pensionado* programs available anywhere in the world today. In addition to benefits such as importing household goods tax free and paying no local taxes on foreign earned income, retirees get significant discounts on everything from movie tickets to medical and dental treatment, public transportation and airfares, even your utility bills. And a 20-year moratorium on real estate taxes if you buy. This is an excellent opportunity, both as an investment…and as your retirement, second, or vacation home.

Panama is an anomaly in Central America.

It's very affordable — a full-time, live-in maid costs $120 a month and first-run movies cost $1.50. It's the safest place in Central or South America (the Pinkerton Global Intelligence Agency recently gave Panama its highest rating for tourist safety).

And it's the most developed place south of the United States, home to some of the top companies in the world, including many of the world's leading banks, and other giants such as Federal Express, Kodak, DHL, Sears, Price Costco, and Bell South.

In 1998, the country's total overnight visitor count was 431,000 — 100,000 of whom came from the United States. To put this in perspective: Panama gets about as many American tourists in a year as Disneyland sees in three days! Panama has a long way to go before it can rival its northern neighbors Mexico and Costa Rica, for example, as a tourist destination. But this is good news for investors because it means prices are still very low.

The truth is, Panama offers more and better amenities than better known retirement spots like Mexico and Costa Rica, but costs and crime rates are far lower. And in Panama, would-be retirees and foreign residents find that there is much less red tape to wade through, and less interference from local authorities.

What are the qualifications for the *pensionado* program? Not a lot. You must be in good health and AIDS-free. You must have an up-to-date passport from your country of residence and a verifiable monthly guaranteed income of at least $1,000. (For more on residence and visas, see Charter Two.)

This Central America nation is still booming. A $5.25 billion expansion of the canal is well underway. Also, $1.9 billion is being invested in a new Panama City metro system and two Panamanian ports, Balboa and Colon, were Latin America's two busiest last year.

Panamanian GDP in 2012 was estimated to be between 7% and 7.5%. The middle class is growing. Higher wages and subsidized loans mean families are buying homes in the Panama City suburbs that spread beyond the Bridge of the Americas and out towards Tocumen International Airport.

Panama is still an international real estate buyer's dream. The Panamanian people are friendly and welcoming. The climate is warm and you can enjoy big city life, quiet rural countryside or beachfront without much travel.

Panama offers special laws, including its popular *pensionado* program, that provide residence plus retiree price discounts on everything from health insurance to restaurants. There are also special programs in designated tourism zones that waive income taxes on rental income and encourage investment in and construction of tourism facilities. A new 2012 program grants immediate residence to foreigners starting new businesses.

Panama remains the world's best, all-round offshore haven thanks to all the other investor-friendly policies and opportunities it offers: its asset protection friendly laws, a strong anti-money laundering law, a territorial tax system with tax exemptions for foreigners, an array of useful statutory legal entities and a host of qualified offshore professionals and bankers.

Panama's central geographic location makes it a natural base for world business operations. There are more than 80 banks in the country today. The major players are the 56 multinational banks that represent 30 countries primarily conducting offshore business.

In 2009, all Panamanian banks held an official $75 billion in total assets. Their liquidity was impressively high at an average of 30%. They had virtually no exposure to the kinds of investments that undermined U.S., U.K. and other national banking systems in 2008.

Contacts:

Rainelda Mata-Kelly JD
Suite 406-407, Tower B, Torres de las Americas
Punta Pacifica, City of Panama
Mailing address:
P.O. Box 0818-00534, Panama City, Republic of Panama
Tel.: (+ 507) 216-9299
When calling from the USA or Canada, dial:
Tel.: (011 507) 216-9299
Email: rmk@mata-kelly.com
Web: www.mata-kelly.com

For local real estate agents and information:
Margaret Summerfield
Director, Pathfinder International
Panama City, Republic of Panama
Email: msummerfield@pathfinderinternational.net

Panama Fast-Track Residence
Robert E. Bauman JD, *Offshore Confidential*, February 2013

Panama has opened its doors ever-wider for those looking for financial independence, personal liberty and unique investment opportunities. Panama offers an expedited path to greater freedom and profits in a friendly country just a two-hour flight away from Houston or Miami.

Second Rebirth Offers Great Opportunities

Panama is currently undergoing one of its periodic "rediscoveries" by the outside world.

Even the U.S. State Department said: "International indexes generally rate Panama as one of the best countries in Latin America for business and investment."

From 2005 to 2010, Panama's economy averaged 8% growth annually. In 2011, it was up 10.6%. In 2012, it neared 9% and so far, in 2013, it has grown by over 10%, the fastest growth in all of Latin America. Accounting for purchasing power, it is one of the five richest countries in mainland Latin America. It is also the 11th fastest growing economy in the world, ahead of China (7.8%), Brazil (1.3%) and the United States (2.2%).

From 2006 to 2010, poverty was reduced by 10% in Panama, while unemployment dropped from 12% to less than 3% in 2011. One major real estate developer told me: "Now we can't find enough workers. There is no unemployment." All this and inflation has remained in the 5% to 6% range. Growth has been augmented by the Panama Canal expansion project that began in 2007 and is scheduled for completion by 2014. Canal capacity will more than double, allowing passage of ships too large to traverse the existing waterway, with the U.S. and China among its major users. Some 15,000 ships, carrying 5% of the world's seagoing cargo, already pass through the canal every year producing over $1 billion in revenue.

At the heart of Panama's strong economy lies its well-developed service sector, which accounts for more than three-quarters of the country's GDP. This sector includes all Panama Canal operations and logistics, the Colon Free Trade Zone (second only to Hong Kong in trade volume), insurance, container ports, flagship registry, tourism and, of course, finance.

The country has more than 80 well-regulated banks, 50 of which are multinationals, that collectively hold an estimated $100 billion in assets, with liquidity impressively high at an average 30%, far better than in the U.S.

Panama City is the largest offshore and regional banking center south of Miami, serving all of Central and South America.

On the Fast Track

As I have previously said many times, the radical restrictions imposed in the U.S. by the PATRIOT Act, the Exit Tax and the Foreign Account Tax Compliance Act (FATCA) are driving wealth from the United States. For years, Americans have been subjected to laws that restrict and punish successful people for the offense of having worked hard and achieved success. Now, Panama is providing a convenient way out.

On May 16, 2012, then President Martinelli signed an order that created a new category of "Immediate Permanent Resident" aimed at attracting foreign nationals to Panama.

Executive Order 343 created a new category for foreigners from selected countries "that maintain friendly, professional, economic, and investment relationships with the Republic of Panama" making them eligible for immediate residence and eventual citizenship.

John Gaver, president of the conservative group, Action America, commented: "Panama is creating a huge magnet for foreigners with either skill or money to move to Panama and work or start a business at a time when the U.S. government is making it increasingly punitive for those same people to stay in the United States."

Under this new immigration category, qualified applicants will be able to engage in professional and economic activities, establish businesses and have the right to work in Panama — permissions that, in the past, have been difficult to obtain. After five years they will be eligible to apply for full citizenship.

This grants immediate residence and a "*cédula*," the national identification card issued to all Panamanians, not only to the qualified foreign individuals, but also to dependent spouses, children under 18, family members with disabilities and dependent parents. Children ages 18 to 25 can be included if they are students.

Visa applications are made to the National Immigration Service (NIS), but subsequent work permits are governed by commercial and labor laws administered by the Ministry of Labor, with foreigners barred from some professions. Experience shows applicants will need to be represented by a qualified Panamanian attorney, especially if they do not speak Spanish.

In addition to the fast-track residence program for foreigners looking to work in Panama, there is also a new "Professional Residence Permit" that makes it easy to qualify for residence without making a major financial investment or proving pensioner status.

Apart from the usual good conduct domestic police report, applicants for this visa need to have a bachelor, masters or doctorate degree, provided his or her intended profession in Panama is not one of those protected by legal restrictions for Panamanians only. Because of these limitations, this visa is mainly available to those in teaching or research positions.

Rainelda Mata-Kelly JD, a leading Panama immigration attorney and a senior member of The Sovereign Society Council of Experts, can assist applicants who wish to qualify for this new, quick residence category and in obtaining work permits.

Other visas available include:

The "investor visa" (*inversionista*) is issued to those who invest at least $160,000 in a permitted business and hire a minimum of five permanent Panamanian employees. It is granted provisionally for two years. Upon renewal an identification card (*cedula*) is issued. After five years, the holder is eligible to apply for citizenship. A similar visa is available for those who invest in agricultural projects.

An "immigrant visa" for those who want to become citizens of Panama is provisionally granted for one year, after which a petition for permanent residence must be filed. If approved, a permanent residence permit and a Panamanian identification card (*cedula*) are issued. After five years, the holder is eligible to apply for full citizenship.

Open for Business

There are also many possibilities for foreigners who want to do business in Panama. And the conditions for commerce are about to get even better.

After four years of stalling by President Barack Obama because of U.S. labor union objections, a U.S.-Panama Free Trade Agreement (FTA), signed in 2007 by President George W. Bush, was finally approved by the U.S. Congress and signed into law in October 2011.

The government of Panama does impose some limitations on foreign business ownership, as in the retail and media sectors where ownership must be Panamanian, but foreign retailers have been able to work through franchise arrangements. Currently about 55 professions are reserved for Panamanian nationals including medical practitioners, lawyers, accountants and custom brokers. The government also requires foreigners in some sectors to obtain explicit permission to work.

Under the FTA, Panama gives U.S. service suppliers substantial access to its markets, including financial services, express delivery and certain professional services previously reserved to Panamanians. They also agreed that U.S. portfolio managers can provide management services to both mutual funds and pension funds in Panama. U.S. insurance suppliers are permitted to operate as a branch or subsidiary.

If you are interested, Panama's Ministry of Commerce and Industry is responsible for promoting foreign investment. Proinvex (toll free from U.S., (888) 453-8257) is the agency that provides foreign investors with information, expedites specific projects, leads investment-seeking missions abroad and supports foreign investment missions to Panama.

Panama has established several export-processing zones that offer special tax and other incentives for manufacturers located there, including call centers. Companies pay basic user fees and a 5% dividend tax or 2% of net profits if there are no dividends. The zones also offer employees tax-free status, special immigration privileges and license and customs exemptions for manufacturers who locate there. Investment incentives are available equally to Panamanian and foreign investors. There are also special tax breaks for investing in tourist facilities. Tourist numbers exceeded two million in 2011.

To be sure, all is not perfecto in Panama.

The *2013 Heritage Foundation/Wall Street Journal Index of Economic Freedom* complains of "institutional shortcomings that weaken the rule of law" and that "anti-corruption laws seem to have little impact, and the judicial system remains vulnerable to political interference." Few Panamanians would disagree.

Dealing with bureaucracy in any country is tedious, but Panama adds the Latin "*mañana*" factor. Depending on the agency, permits, approvals and plans can take weeks, when days should be sufficient. It helps to have a local partner or know someone with influence — and a well-placed invitation to lunch or dinner never hurts. The pace is much faster when dealing with international agencies, such as the

Panama Canal or the busy Colon Free Trade Zone.

The *Heritage Index* also noted: "In other areas…the competitiveness of the economy is sustained by a continued high degree of openness to global commerce. Previous pro-growth reforms, including a simplified business start-up process and the reduced corporate tax rate, have enhanced the commercial environment and contributed to solid economic expansion over the past five years. The service-oriented economy continues to be a vibrant international business.

Miami South

Life in Panama is a far more modern experience than many expect. Panama City, the balmy, tropical capital on the southern, Pacific end of the Panama Canal, suggests Miami, except arguably more locals speak English here than in some parts of South Florida.

The city has thousands of modern condominiums and more than 100 sky-scrapers, new first-class hotels (two new Westins) and restaurants, plus excellent high-speed Internet and other global communications.

If you speak Spanish it helps, but Panama City is a world crossroads in every sense — people, commerce, business, goods, services and available products. Malls offer any high-end fashionable store you can find in New York or London, and every fast food or low cost retail outlet you find in Columbus, Ohio or Portland, Maine. Small cars dominate in traffic but dealerships sell anything you can afford.

The country, after almost a century of what amounted to American military occupation, is in many ways "Americanized," but not enough to dilute its distinctive friendly Latin flavor. Expats from the U.S., Europe, Asia, and the world live, work and play here providing a unique mix that is never dull. And an hour's drive away are the Pacific coast beaches, a few more hours are beautiful, cool mountain towns such as El Valle and Bouquete.

For reliable local real estate agents in all parts of Panama, contact:

Margaret Summerfield, Director, Pathfinder International
Panama City, Panama
Email: msummerfield@pathfinderinternational.net

Panama's Low-Tax Surprise

Unfortunately, Americans carry the obligation to pay U.S. taxes on their backs like a tortoise carries his shell. Wherever they go, they still must pay Uncle Sam his due.

But new arrivals coming to Panama to invest or work will be pleasantly surprised at the low taxes they will encounter. The system is territorial, so only earnings from within Panama are taxable. If you are employed by an international company, you may be able to structure your pay so that some can be paid offshore. The personal income tax is a sliding scale starting at 7% above the first $9,000, to a maximum rate of 27% only on Panama-source income. Capital gains are taxed at the same rate. For property held for two years or more not owned by someone in the real estate business, a flat tax of 10% applies to any gross profits.

Taxable income includes wages, salaries, business profits, pensions/bonuses, and income from copyrights, royalties, trademarks, stock sales, bonds and securities.

Deductions are allowed for in-country medical expenses, donations to charities, interest paid on home mortgages, education expenses and loans for home improvements.

Unlike the U.S., there are no inheritance taxes in Panama. There are taxes on gifts of Panamanian properties made between living persons (*inter vivos*). The tax rate depends on the degree of relationship between the donor and the recipient, but there is no gift tax on property owned outside Panama.

Property Taxes

Properties with a registered value of $30,000 or lower are exempt from property taxes. Properties of higher value are taxed as follows: 1.75% from $30,000-$50,000; 1.95% from $50,000-$75,000; and 2.1% above $75,000.

If you buy or build a residential property in Panama, you may be exempt from property tax for up to 20 years, if the construction permit was issued by Sept. 1, 2006, and if the occupancy permit issued and improvements were registered by Sept. 1, 2007. On houses or apartments where the construction permit was issued after Sept. 1, 2006, the following exemptions apply:

- Value up to $100,000: 15-year exemption
- Value from $100,000 to $250,000: 10-year exemption
- Value over $250,000: 5-year exemption

The exemption is transferable to any new buyer during the exemption period. The land is not exempted and would continue to incur property tax if its value is above $30,000.

Real estate transfer taxes in Panama are paid by the seller at a rate of 2% of the updated registered value of the real property, or the sale price, whichever is higher. The updated value is the registered value, plus 5% per year of ownership.

If the property is bought by a corporation, it is customary for the shares of the company to be sold instead of the title to the property, with the tax paid on the face value of the shares, rather than the assets in the company being transferred. Normally that would be $10,000, the stated value of the issued share capital. That would amount to a tax of $500 (5%).

Make Your Move

I have visited Panama many times since my first visits as a U.S. congressman in the turbulent 1970s, so many that I can't count them all.

Since Vasco Nunez de Balboa (1475-1519), the first European to set foot in Panama in 1510, the isthmus and its peoples have welcomed foreigners from all over the world; many thousands have stayed, intermarried and made and lost fortunes. Few countries can boast so romantic a history, so pleasant a climate, so friendly a people, and so dynamic and modern an economy.

Panama is still the ideal location for retirement, a second home, an offshore bank account or any number of legal, asset protection structures — and now it has a new mechanism that welcomes foreigners for employment, business and investment. The Republic Panama is a proud nation that will welcome you — as it always has me.

THE ISLAND OF NEVIS: PRIVACY & FAST SERVICE

Robert E. Bauman JD, *The Passport Book*, 2014

If there is one haven country that has all the things needed for smooth offshore financial operations, it's the two-island Federation of Saint Christopher (locally called "St. Kitts") and Nevis (pronounced *KNEE-vis*).

It's in the Leeward Islands in the eastern Caribbean, located 225 miles east of Puerto Rico and about 1,200 miles south of Miami. Each tropical island is a volcanic mountain rising over 3,000 feet from the sea, with about 75% of the total population living on St. Kitts. The islands' balmy, virtually unchanging weather, splendid beaches and accommodations have made them popular vacation spots, offering a wide range of recreational amenities. Visitors to St. Kitts & Nevis tend find the islands' pace to be more leisurely even than that of other Caribbean holiday spots.

The British first settled the islands in 1623, but control was disputed with the French until 1783, when the British prevailed. Independence was achieved on September 19, 1983, and the federation is now a member of the British Commonwealth. It is a parliamentary democracy based on the Westminster model, but the constitution of St. Kitts & Nevis allows either island to secede upon a referendum vote.

In August 1998, defying international pleas, residents of the seven-mile-long island of Nevis voted on whether to secede from St. Kitts and become the smallest nation in the Western Hemisphere. Approval of two-thirds of the island's voters was required for secession. The vote was 2,427 for secession and 1,418 against, falling just short of the two-thirds required.

The vote was the culmination of a struggle that began with Britain's colonization in 1628. In 1882, Britain stripped Nevis of its legislature and wed it to St. Kitts. When the islands became independent in 1983, Nevis reluctantly joined in a federation with neighboring St. Kitts, but Nevisians insisted on a constitutional clause allowing them to break away. After years of complaining that they are treated like second-class citizens by the federal government, the seat of which is located on St. Kitts, they invoked that right with the failed 1998 referendum. Nevis retains the right to secede, and proponents vow that they will try again.

Leading, if Small, Offshore Financial Center

Nevis, which has its own Island Assembly, has a no nonsense banking and business privacy law that even the U.S. government can't crack. Its pro-offshore laws have existed for over two decades — so there is plenty of experience and precedent in the local courts — and the legislative assembly keeps the applicable laws current. There are well-established offshore financial service companies that can do what you want, and some have convenient U.S. branch offices.

The Nevis independence movement owes much to its success as the business-friendly "Delaware of the Caribbean." Over the last two decades, its parliament has adopted and constantly updated excellent offshore corporation, trust and limited liability company laws, augmented by strict financial privacy. There are no exchange controls and no tax treaties with other countries. As a matter of official policy, the government does not exchange tax or other information with any other foreign revenue service or government. Unsuccessful moves by the St. Kitts-based government to take over the Nevis financial sector have spurred secession.

Home of the Asset Protection Trust

Building on their reputation for statutory corporate cordiality, in 1994, the Island Assembly adopted the Nevis International Trust Ordinance, a comprehensive, clear and flexible asset protection trust (APT) law. This law is comparable — and in many ways superior — to that of the Cook Islands in the South Pacific, already well known as an APT world center.

The Nevis law incorporates the best features of the Cook Islands law, but is even more flexible. The basic aim of the law is to permit foreign citizens to obtain asset protection by transferring property titles to an APT established in Charlestown, Nevis. In 2010 Nevis adopted a complete revision and updating of all of its laws, the first since 1961.

Nevis simply is taking advantage of the worldwide growth in medical, legal and professional malpractice lawsuits. Legislative and judicial imposition of no-fault personal liability on corporate officers and directors has become a nasty fact of business life. A Nevis trust places personal assets beyond the reach of foreign governments, litigious plaintiffs, creditors, and contingency fee lawyers.

Under the 1994 law, the Nevis judiciary does not recognize any non-domestic court orders regarding its domestic APTs. This forces a foreign judgment creditor to start all over again, retrying a case in a Nevis court with Nevis lawyers. A plaintiff who sues an APT must first post a US$25,000 bond with the government to cover court and others costs before a suit will be accepted for filing. In addition, the statute of limitations for filing legal challenges to a Nevis APT runs out two years from the date of the trust creation. In cases of alleged fraudulent intent, the law places the burden of proof on the foreign claimant.

This small, two-island country's greatest assets are its considerable natural beauty and Nevis as a financial center. To exploit potential tourism, the government has agreements with foreign-owned hotel and condominium developments. St. Kitts is a popular tourist destination, with white sand beaches, deep sea fishing, golf, tennis, and casino gambling. Since 1994, the federation has been part of the Association of Caribbean States (ACS) trading bloc of over 60 million people.

Fast Tax Haven Citizenship for Sale

St. Kitts & Nevis's excellent citizenship program was established and is governed by the Citizenship Act of 1984 (Section 3). It is the older of the two existing such programs and offers the benefits of visa-free travel to over 90 countries. The Citizenship Act provides for persons to be registered as non-voting citizens if "the Cabinet is satisfied that such a person has invested substantially in the country."

Under 2006 changes to the citizenship-by-investment regulations, to qualify for St. Kitts & Nevis citizenship, you must invest at least US$350,000 in designated real estate, plus pay considerable government and due diligence fees besides real estate purchase taxes. Or you can contribute to the Sugar Industry Diversification Foundation in the amount of US$200,000 (for a single applicant). Using the charitable contribution is an easier route for most applicants because it allows a set cost and avoids further expenses associated with owning real estate in a foreign country. Plus, you don't have to live in St. Kitts and Nevis to secure your second citizenship, so buying real estate could just be an additional burden if you're not interested in spending time there.

Under the 2006 official contribution options, now in effect, there are four categories:

- Single applicant: US$200,000 investment required, inclusive of all fees
- Applicant with up to three dependents (i.e., one spouse and two children below the age of 18): US$250,000
- Applicant with up to five dependents (i.e., one spouse and four children): US$300,000
- Applicant with six or more dependents: US$400,000

In each category, the total amount includes all government and due diligence fees. (As we go to press the rumor is that these fees soon may be doubled.)

The real estate option requires the purchase of a condominium or villa from an approved list of developers with a minimum investment of US$350,000. Transaction costs add 10% to the purchase price, i.e., at least US$35,000, and likely US$50,000 or more, as real estate prices are now on a relatively high level in St. Kitts & Nevis. Add government fees of US$35,000 for a single person.

Processing time for charitable contribution applications takes up to three months and dual nationality is permitted, with no residency requirement. Using the real estate option lengthens the average processing time from four to 12 months or longer. The real estate cannot be re-sold until five years after purchase.

The St. Kitts & Nevis passport is well regarded internationally and the program has been carefully managed with very few passports issued. St. Kitts & Nevis citizens enjoy a passport with an excellent reputation and very good visa-free travel to many nations. For visa-free travel throughout Europe, a St. Kitts & Nevis passport can be combined with a residence permit in a European Union country.

A visa-waiver agreement between the European Union and St. Kitts & Nevis is now in force providing for visa-free travel for EU citizens and for the holders of all passports issued by St. Kitts & Nevis, between their territories for stays not to exceed three months. This allows visa-free access throughout the 28 EU countries, and by extension to the Schengen travel area that includes Switzerland, Liechtenstein, Norway and Iceland.

Contacts

Government:

Government of Saint Christopher (St. Kitts) & Nevis: http://www.gov.kn

Nevis Government Information Service: http://www.queen-citynevis.com

Ministry of Finance, Nevis Offshore Financial Services
P.O. Box 689, Main Street
Charlestown, Nevis, West Indies
Tel.: + (869) 469-1469
Email: info@nevisfinance.com
Web: http://www.nevisfinance.com

Nevis Services Ltd.
545 Fifth Avenue, Suite 402
New York, NY 10017
Tel.: 212-575-0818
Email: nevisservices@nevisserv.com
Web: http://www.morningstarnev.com/nevis_services.htm

Embassy of St. Kitts & Nevis
3216 New Mexico Avenue, NW
Washington, D.C. 20016
Tel.: (202) 686-2636
Web: http://www. stkittsnevis.org

There is no American Embassy in St. Kitts & Nevis. The nearest U.S. Embassy is located in Bridgetown, Barbados, Wildey Business Park, Wildey, St. Michael, Barbados:
Tel.: 246-436-4950
Web: http://barbados.usembassy.gov

Residence & Immigration Professionals:

The Minister of Finance of Dominica appoints official foreign agents to administer the application process on behalf of the government. One of these appointed official agents is Mark Nestmann, a senior member of The Sovereign Society Council of Experts. Mark is a qualified professional who assists those interested in acquiring residence and citizenship in Dominica, St. Kitts Nevis and other countries. Henley & Partners Ltd. also is an official agent.

Mark Nestmann LL.M., President
The Nestmann Group, Ltd.
2303 N. 44th St. #14-1025

Phoenix, Arizona 85008
Tel.: (602) 688-7552
Email: service@nestmann.com
Web: http://www.nestmann.com

Henley & Partners Ltd.
Christopher Willis, Managing Partner
Henley & Partner Caribbean Ltd
Sugar Bay Club, Zenway Boulevard
Frigate Bay, St Kitts, West Indies
Tel.: +1 869-465-6220
Email: christopher.willis@henleyglobal.com
Web: https://www.henleyglobal.com/citizenship-dominica-citizenship

THE BAHAMAS: OFFSHORE HAVEN DIMINISHED
Robert E. Bauman JD, *The Passport Book*, 2014
& *Where to Stash Your Cash*, 2015

The Bahamas is the financial haven country nearest to the U.S., just minutes from Miami by airplane or a few hours by boat, 744 air miles from New York City.

During the 20th Century, these islands off the southeast coast of the U.S. blossomed into a major tax and asset protection haven, especially for nearby Americans and Canadians seeking tax exemption and well-crafted laws allowing IBCs, trusts, offshore banking and insurance — all wrapped in maximum financial privacy protected by law.

Because so many Americans used The Bahamas as their favorite offshore tax haven, the islands came under heavy pressure from the U.S. government and the IRS because of suspected tax evasion, drug smuggling and money laundering. In 2000, the government adopted U.S.-demanded laws that disrupted past cozy arrangements with Americans, but also diminished the islands role as an offshore financial center. The final nail in the tax evasion coffin was a Tax Information Exchange Agreement with the United States.

It's still a nice place to retire, vacation, or to have a second home, but more secure and batter banking, investment, tax and asset havens can be found elsewhere.

The nation consists of over 700 islands, only 22 inhabited. The main islands are Grand Bahama, Andros, Eleuthera, Abaco, and New Providence Island, site of the capital, Nassau. The second largest city is Freeport, on Grand Bahama. Eighty-five percent of the Bahamian population is of African heritage. About two-thirds of the population resides on New Providence Island. Many Bahamians' ancestors arrived on these islands when they served as a staging area for the slave trade in the early 1800s. Others accompanied thousands of British loyalists who fled the American colonies during the Revolutionary War.

Arakawa Indians inhabited these islands when Christopher Columbus arrived in 1492, but they remained largely unexplored by Europeans until 1717, when they came under control of the British Crown. Because of the American Revolution, in 1776, the islands were briefly in American hands, followed by Spanish control in 1781. In 1783, they again became British territory, remaining so until independence was declared on July 10, 1973. The Bahamas is a member of the British Commonwealth and a parliamentary democracy based on the Westminster model. Since independence, the nation has acquired a deserved reputation for official corruption and government venality, although this has lessened markedly in recent years.

Low-lying limestone or coral islets with sandy beaches, the Bahamian archipelago provides year-round recreational opportunities on land and in the water. The variety of its marine habitats assures a broad range of prospects for enthusiasts of deep-sea and reef fishing, diving, and sailing. Some of the islands' regattas and powerboat races draw participants and spectators from around the globe. The subtropical climate, warmed by the Gulf Stream, allows dry land activity around the calendar as well, including golf, polo, cricket, and tennis.

Over a quarter of a million people live in this archipelago, the oldest offshore money haven in the Americas. An independent nation since 1973, its origins as a money haven date to 1908 when the Royal Bank of Canada opened a branch in Nassau. Today, tourism, hotel, resort, and convention industries are doing well and the islands are a retirement haven for the very wealthy, many of them prominent U.S. and European expatriates.

The Bahamas is one of the wealthiest Caribbean countries with an economy heavily dependent on tourism and offshore banking. Tourism together with tourism-driven construction and manufacturing accounts for approximately 60% of GDP and directly or indirectly employs half of the archipelago's labor force. Steady growth in tourism receipts and a boom in construction of new hotels, resorts, and residences had led to solid GDP growth in recent years, but tourist arrivals have been on the decline since 2006 and will likely drop even further in 2009. Tourism, in turn, depends on growth in the US, the source of more than 80% of the visitors.

Financial services constitute the second-most important sector of the Bahamian economy and, when combined with business services, account for about 36% of GDP. However, since 2000, when the government enacted new regulations on the financial sector, many international businesses have left The Bahamas. Manufacturing and agriculture combined contribute approximately a tenth of GDP and show little growth, despite government incentives aimed at those sectors. Overall growth prospects in the short run rest heavily on the fortunes of the tourism sector.

Being close to the U.S. has advantages, but also can cause problems for offshore business and banking, especially if privacy is a major concern. The U.S. and Bahamian dollar are equal in value. Since 2000, 200 of 223 private banks in The Bahamas have closed and 30,000 international business companies have been stricken from the official register. Bahamian banks with U.S. branches find it difficult to avoid U.S. government pressures when Washington wants information. And since 2003, there has been a Tax Information Exchange Agreement between Washington and Nassau.

Keeping Money Clean

Anti-money laundering laws have been toughened to make violations punishable by a possible sentence of 20 years in jail and/or a US$100,000 fine for each instance. A "Currency Declaration Act" requires reporting of all cash or investment transfers, in or out of the islands, in excess of US$10,000. Offshore financial trustees and attorneys are now required to maintain records of beneficial owners of offshore trusts and international business corporations. Previously, professional attorney-client privilege rules prevented revealing such information

The Banks and Trust Companies Act authorizes government bank inspections and requires reports of "suspicious activities." New account applicants must show a valid passport and other official identification as well as business references, and banks have a legal duty to identify "beneficial owners" of accounts.

The Drug Trafficking Act of 1986 makes money laundering a crime and an extraditable offense. The U.S.-Bahamian "Mutual Legal Assistance Treaty" (MLAT) requires cooperation between Washington and Nassau in all financial investigations. The Bahamas has similar treaties with Canada and the U.K.

The Bahamas levies no taxes on capital gains, corporate earnings, personal income, sales, inheritance, or dividends. Tax freedom is available to all resident corporations, partnerships, individuals, and trusts. The International Business Companies Act of 1990 permits cheap, fast incorporation. Incorporation costs include registered agent, nominee directors and nominee officers, which can total up to US$1,500-$2,400. (Keep in mind that the U.S. and Bahamian dollar are equal in value.) Corporations can also be formed with bearer shares. The Bahamas are one of the few jurisdictions in which a company can act as a nominee director.

The government and the local financial community are pushing hard to establish the islands as an international securities trading center with emphasis on emerging countries' investments. Locals want closed-end funds to be listed and traded on the Bahamian Stock Exchange, but at far less cost and with greater privacy guarantees than are available in the U.S.

Washington Pressure

Instead of fighting back and telling these outsiders to "buzz off," the FNM government rapidly pushed through Parliament, over strong minority opposition, a host of statutory changes that substantially weakened the very financial privacy and asset protection that had attracted to the islands tens of thousands of offshore bank accounts, international business companies and asset protection trusts. These new laws admittedly were drafted with the direct assistance of "financial experts" from London and Washington, D.C. The government also said it had accepted "a generous offer" of technical assistance from the U.S. Treasury Department, no doubt including IRS agents.

This capitulation to Washington's demands echoed a crisis in the early 1980s when the late Prime Minister, Lynden O. Pindling, accused of drug dealing, was confronted by an angry U.S. government that threatened sanctions against The Bahamas. Although Pindling was cleared, he was forced to grant U.S. law and drug enforcement officers diplomatic immunity and free passage through the archipelago, plus some limited access to secret offshore banks of some accused criminals.

The Progressive Labour Party (PLP) parliamentary opposition rightfully argued that repeal or change of most of the offshore laws that brought huge investments and assets to The Bahamas would indeed result in capital flight, as individual offshore bank accounts were closed and financial activity fled elsewhere.

Subsequently, many private banks and offshore financial firms announced their departure, citing the new laws as reason for their exodus. PLP opposition members of parliament called on the government to resign over the OECD and FATF debacle, claiming that the blacklisting was directly related to the government's prolonged inability to deal with drug trafficking. Privately, Bahamian sources said government figures were implicated in numerous questionable, but highly profitable, financial activities, a situation the U.S. was holding over their heads unless they acted as Washington demanded.

In May 2002, the PLP opposition won control of parliament and a new PLP Prime Minister, Perry Christie, took office. All these new laws became a major political issue with the PLP, charging they had damaged the offshore financial community. Although Perry and the PLP promised to review and reverse many of these laws, they failed to do so. Indeed, they went ahead with the U.S. Tax Information Exchange Agreement initiated by the defeated FNM government.

Since then the FNM has regained political control and all the laws that drove away much of the offshore business remain in place.

New Laws, Amendments to Old Laws

Among the many laws, the "Evidence Act 2000" removed the requirement that requested evidence could not be released to another country until a court proceeding had begun in the requesting nation. Evidence can now be released for foreign preliminary investigations. This law appears to permit Bahamian enforcement of U.S. civil forfeiture orders. Another law allows confiscation of cash and assets under a U.S.-style civil forfeiture procedure that permits freezing of bank and other accounts. Still another law empowers Bahamian courts to extradite criminal suspects during investigations before trial. It should be noted that The Bahamas already had in force mutual legal assistance treaties with the U.S., U.K. and Canada.

Money Laundering

Existing anti-money laundering laws were toughened to make violation punishable by a possible sentence of 20 years in jail and/or a US$100,000 fine for each instance. A "Currency Declaration Act" requires reporting of all cash or investment transfers, in or out of the islands in excess of US$10,000. The Central Bank also has broad powers to regulate offshore banks, their registration, operation and reporting. The law allows foreign bank inspectors to conduct on-site and offsite examinations of the accounts in bank branches or subsidiaries located in The Bahamas.

The Bahamas "financial intelligence unit" was modeled after the U.S. Treasury Financial Crimes Enforcement Network (FinCEN). Opposition members of parliament criticized the FIU's powers as far too broad, charging there are no provisions to prevent political "fishing trips" or "witch hunts" by government police. This unit can request ("order" might be a better word) a bank to freeze any funds suspected of being part of criminal activity for up to 72 hours, while a secret "monitoring order" is sought by police to confiscate money or block transactions. In such cases, all other financial confidentiality laws are waived. The FIU issued U.S.-style rules requiring "suspicious activity reporting" by all financial institutions.

Still other laws require all banks to verify the true identity of customers for whom Bahamian intermediaries open accounts. Bahamian banks now use special U.S. cash flow analysis software to detect possible money laundering. Offshore financial trustees and attorneys are required to maintain records of beneficial owners of offshore trusts and international business corporations. Previously, professional attorney-client privilege rules prevented revealing such information.

IBCs Under Fire

Until 2002, IBCs had not been required to disclose the identities of shareholders or other detailed business information unless under a court order. Now, the right of IBCs to issue and use bearer shares has been repealed and all IBCs are required to submit to the government the true identities and addresses of directors. There are currently more than 100,000 international business corporations in The

Bahamas, with about 16,000 added each year. Secrecy of ownership undoubtedly was a large factor in attracting these IBCs and now that has ended.

Conclusion

Even though The Bahamas is still an offshore tax haven, it remains in considerable internal governmental and political turmoil. The mass exodus of so many Bahamian financial community members speaks volumes about those who judge events first hand. The best financial and investment climates are those that enjoy some degree of predictability and that's not The Bahamas.

My advice is to scratch The Bahamas off your list of offshore tax and asset haven nations. Things may change someday but if you were thinking of using the islands as a base of offshore operations, forget it.

Contacts

Government:

Government of the Bahamas: http://www.bahamas.gov.bs

Securities Commission of The Bahamas
Charlotte House, Charlotte Street
P.O. Box N-8347, Nassau, The Bahamas
Tel.: +1-242-397-4100
Email: info@scb.gov.bs
Web: http://www.scb.gov.bs

Central Bank of The Bahamas
P.O. Box N-4868, Nassau, The Bahamas
Tel.: +242-322-2193
Web: http://www.centralbankbahamas.com

Embassy of The Bahamas
2220 Massachusetts Ave. NW
Washington, D.C. 20008
Tel.: 202-319-2660
Email: bahemb@aol.com
Web: http://www.embassy.org/embassies/bs.html
List of Consulates: http://www.embassy.org/embassies/bs-other.html

United States Embassy
42 Queen Street, Nassau, The Bahamas
Tel.: + (242) 322-1181 or after hours: + (242) 328-2206
Email: acsnassau@state.gov
Web: http://nassau.usembassy.gov

Bank:

Bank of The Bahamas Limited
1st Floor Claughton House, Shirley & Charlotte Streets
P.O. Box N-7118, Nassau, The. Bahamas
Tel.: 242 397 3000
Email: Dianne.bingham@BankBahamas.com
Web: www.bankbahamas.com

Attorneys:

Higgs & Johnson
Chancery Court, The Mall
P.O. Box F 42519
Freeport, Bahamas
Tel.: 1-242-351-5050
Email: freeport@higgsjohnson.com
Web: www.higgsjohnson.com
Offices in Nassau, Lyford Cay, Marsh Harbor and the Cayman Islands.

McKinney, Turner & Co.
Oakbridge House, #13 West Hill St.
P.O. Box N-8195
Nassau, Bahamas
Tel.: +242-322-8914

ORIENTAL REPUBLIC OF URUGUAY: WELCOME TO THE NEW SWITZERLAND

Robert E. Bauman JD, *Offshore Confidential*, March 2012

For centuries, Switzerland has been the sanctuary of choice for wealthy people from many nations.

Now amid the growing crackdown on Swiss private banking, many wishing to maintain financial freedom are flocking to places such as Singapore and Hong Kong, which still offer some of the world's most private accounts.

But these Asian countries are not the only places that welcome Americans and their money. There are other low-tax financial oases that provide sound banking systems and far greater financial privacy than anything you'll find in the U.S., not to mention numerous attractive investment possibilities.

I have traveled the world in search of the perfect offshore base — both for investment purposes and for lifestyle — and I believe I have found one of the best in Uruguay.

Earlier this year, I was fortunate to visit Uruguay for the first time with 50 Sovereign Society members, and I was impressed.

It is for good reason this country's nickname is the "Switzerland of South America."

I have researched and written about Uruguay for years, established reliable professional contacts there and have paid close attention to developments in this impressive country.

But nothing prepared me for the way this tiny country — South America's smallest Spanish-speaking nation — encapsulates everything you might need as a second or retirement residence and for investment, banking and an offshore financial base.

Now, having seen the country, met its people and enjoyed their hospitality, this latest special report is a sequel that reflects firsthand knowledge and reinforces my judgment that this is definitely an extraordinary country you should visit and consider making your offshore home and financial base.

The Jewel of Latin America

You know you're not in America as soon as your plane lands at Montevideo's sun drenched, gleaming, white, ultra-modern Carrasco International Airport.

Unlike the long, mind-numbing lines that snarl the U.S. Immigration and Customs process at just about every American airport these days, you are whisked through the Uruguayan entrance routine in a matter of minutes. Outside, you are greeted by bright sunshine and a brisk breeze off the South Atlantic Ocean.

Welcome to Uruguay. Spend a few days here and you will no doubt be impressed by the friendly citizens, and soon you will also realize that this is not just a place to invest and bank, but you might also want to live here.

Uruguay has escaped the rigid class society that exists in much of South America.

There are no ethnically defined boundaries. An estimated 88% of the people here are of European descent, principally Italian and Spanish. Other immigrant groups include Portuguese, Armenians, Basque, Germans, and Irish, making the country somewhat like the ethnic melting pot the U.S. once was.

North American and European expats don't stand out as foreigners; tall, fair, or blue-eyed people are assumed to be Uruguayans. And Uruguayans show unlimited, un-Latin patience, both in person and on the road.

High-Ranking and Happy

Before you begin to plan your move, though, there are several details you should know…

Uruguay, which is about the size of Washington state, lies east of both the Uruguay River, separating it from Paraguay, and the huge, 137-mile wide estuary of the Río de la Plata.

Uruguay had the 25th highest quality of life index in the world in 2011, and ranked first in quality of life/human development in Latin America.

The Economist ranked Uruguay 17 out of 167 countries on the 2014 Democracy Index. *Reader's Digest* ranked it ninth most "livable and greenest" place in the world and first in the Americas.

According to Transparency International, in 2011 out of 182 countries, Uruguay ranked 25th and is the second-least corrupt country in Latin America, behind Chile. It was the highest rated country in Latin America (and 26th in the world) on the latest Legatum Prosperity Index, based on factors that help drive economic growth and create happy citizens.

But on top of all these accolades, Uruguay offers much more, making it what might be the best offshore residence for you. For one, it is still a tax haven. Uruguay definitely has now earned its "Switzerland of Latin America" title.

An Investor-Friendly Country

Uruguay has an export-oriented, agricultural and services-based economy with a well-educated workforce and high levels of social spending. Political and labor conditions are among the freest in Latin America.

Foreign and local investors are treated equally under the law and there are no limitations on foreign business ownership. At the same time, there are no currency-exchange controls or forced currency conversion.

In fact, foreign currencies are used freely, including dollars and euros. And there are no taxes or restrictions on transferring money in or out of the country. Most bank accounts are denominated in U.S. dollars, and dollars are also used for real estate and major business deals.

The Uruguayan economy is ideal for foreign expatriates, retired or otherwise. There is very little poverty, a high standard of living and large middle class. It also has the most equitable income distribution in Latin America, which equals a low crime rate and a very livable society.

If you do want to invest actively, start a company or do business, Uruguay offers an extremely positive environment.

Consider this: If you had packed up and moved to Uruguay a decade ago, you would have missed a lot — including the U.S. housing bubble and the property market crash.

Meanwhile, property values in Uruguay appreciated substantially.

You also would have missed the world recession — which went right past Uruguay, the only Latin American country to have escaped the global economic crisis unscathed.

A Strong and Growing Economy

Unlike the faltering powerhouses of the Americas and Europe, the Uruguayan economy expanded during the global recession. In 2011, Uruguay's gross domestic product was $52.02 billion in 2011, with per capita GDP at $15,400, the highest in South America.

Economic growth averaged 8% annually during 2004-08, slipped in 2008-09 to 2.6% during the world financial crisis, but rebounded to 8.5% in 2010 and 6% in 2011. Construction is booming in the country and, last year, a record three million tourists visited Uruguay.

Uruguay is also South America's leader in direct foreign investment with more than $10 billion coming into the country in 2010. The previous year, it became the first nation in the world to provide every school child with a free laptop and wireless internet.

While Uruguay provides the perfect environment in which to invest and do business, it is not a country where you should look for cheap retirement. Its first-world living standards come with first-world prices in some items.

However, if you plan to be in South American paradise for a few months every year, you should consider investing in local property. Foreigners are not required to become residents to own real estate, establish a corporation or to do business in Uruguay.

Montevideo: One of the World's Safest Cities

Montevideo, Uruguay's capital, is an attractive, modern city and among the safest in the world.

As a first-time visitor, I was immediately impressed by its cleanliness and charming mix of old and new architecture.

The traffic here is leisurely and the skyline is punctuated by a relatively few skyscrapers. Visitors will also enjoy its small boutiques, museums and a lively Ciudad Vieja (Old City). There is much to be said for this city of 1.3 million — about half of Uruguay's total population.

Especially appealing is the "*Rambla,*" miles of gleaming, spacious promenade and beaches, teeming with thousands of strollers and bronzed sun bathers.

Visitors will also enjoy the beautifully restored *Teatro Solís,* the city's venerable opera house, which opened in 1878. Here, black-tie crowds still turn out for world-class orchestras from around the globe. Down the same street, local folks gather at a tiny tango club, where the singing and dancing goes on until dawn.

The city's fine-dining establishments are nearby, along with dozens of casual *parrillas,* whose giant grills and blazing wood fires attract Montevideo's meat-lovers.

And if you're serious about living here, the most suitable apartments for the expat community conveniently face the Montevideo city golf course on the *Rambla.*

The average price for a 2,500 square foot apartment in this area is about $550,000. New construction prices are higher, closer to $750,000.

A smaller apartment of about 1,800 square feet, in an equally good section of the city, would cost you around $350,000.

It is also worth highlighting the fact that Uruguay offers not only financial, but physical security. You feel safe walking the streets and byways of Montevideo, Punta del Este… or anywhere else in this unusual country.

Worry-Free Property Investments

I stayed for several days in Punta del Este, South America's premier beach resort. I also traveled further along the Atlantic coast to La Berra and Jose Ignacio (according to locals, the next Saint-Tropez) — where the beach areas are so exclusive that Brad Pitt and Angelina Jolie shopped for groceries unrecognized.

Punta del Este is a town with miles of sandy beaches and blue waters, along with the country's hottest nightclubs, the best casinos and shows, and the highest concentration of fine restaurants, not to mention its world-renowned property market.

This is Uruguay's answer to Newport, Rhode Island. Bridge night s and cocktail parties are part of the routine. Many foreign and local people of wealth make their home here, and I saw several of the many international cruise ships that regularly visit the harbor.

As a South Atlantic Ocean-side resort, Punta del Este has a great deal of "old money," which makes it a more established re-sell market.

Prices are not cheap because of international demand, but your investment is safer and you'll be able to find a buyer whenever you want to cash out. There are more than 70 new developments in Punta del Este — all without mortgages. It's a cash business that is owner/developer financed.

The lowest starting price on the peninsula is around $300,000. Historically, property in Punta del Este has increased in price and holds value well. The rental market is strong during the peak summer season (January to March), with returns in the 3% to 4% range.

Don't miss Punta del Este's neighboring small town of La Barra. Real estate here is highly sought after and you'll pay between $600,000 and $800,000 for property. In the maze of narrow, European style streets, you will find art galleries, shops and restaurants. La Barra is well worth the investment.

An Easy Way to Invest Directly

One of most profitable investment opportunities is Uruguay is real estate. Many foreigners purchase second or vacation homes that return strong rental income when not in personal use.

One of the easiest ways to invest directly for profit is to buy farmland. This is a safe, turnkey investment with high appreciation potential and good returns.

Uruguay is ideal for agricultural pursuits. It is estimated that 46.4% of soils worldwide now have depleted biological functions, and 15% of that total is in Latin America. The causes are water and wind erosion, changes in soil composition and physical degradation.

However, almost all of the soil in Uruguay is non-degraded and productive. The climate is temperate and there is rainfall year-round. The country also sits atop the world's largest aquifer, a wet underground layer of permeable rock from which ground water can be extracted.

These factors all combine to make the country a competitive producer and exporter with no government interference in the market. Principal crops include soybeans, wheat, rice, cattle and sheep ranches and dairy farms. Forestry includes growing eucalyptus and pine and there are many vineyards, olives groves and fruits.

Foreign investors may work directly or have a farm management company handle all aspects of operation. There is also an active market for crop-land rental.

Overall, the Uruguayan property market has been safe and stable. For example, farmland prices have increased in value by a multiple of eight times since 2002 to a current average of $2,100 per hectare (although in real terms, and taking 1998 as the starting point, prices tripled).

All of Uruguay's land was mapped some decades ago, and each plot was rated according to its productivity. The rating system is called CONEAT and it assigns a numerical rating to all land. The rating can be accessed by anyone, online, making it very easy to determine the fair value of land in this transparent market. Most of the prime agricultural land lies along the western edge of the country, near the Uruguay River near the Argentine border.

Never buy without knowing the CONEAT rating. An agronomist can tell which crops are best under any given rating. And for the non-farmer investor, investing in farmland is easy: Uruguay has widespread expertise to help manage a farm, and the decisions are simple: you will usually plant what the global market dictates, typically soybeans in the summer and wheat in the winter.

Insider tip: If you are buying land for recreational, development or personal use, then you do not need a high CONEAT rating. If the rating is high, the land may be overpriced for your purposes.

Banks and Banking

Sixty-one years ago, in the wake of World War II, Uruguay was described as the "Switzerland of the Americas" in a 1951 *New York Times* article. It earned that name because of its popularity as a haven for capital and precious metals fleeing Europe at the time, and for its adoption of Swiss-inspired banking laws and customs.

Uruguay's banking system is solid, appealing to global investors and depositors who seek a safe haven and tax advantages. Since January 1, 2008 almost 400 banks have failed in the U.S. Meanwhile, Uruguay's banks have operated without problems.

Unlike too many offshore financial institutions in other parts of the world, banks in Uruguay welcome American clients, and most offer e-banking.

Uruguay's banking reputation has made it an important regional financial center for the southern continent. There are 11 private banks, totally or partially owned by American, Canadian, European and Brazilian financial institutions, plus the government's central bank, Banco de la República (BROU) that strictly supervises all the banks.

Financial Privacy Guaranteed by Law

Unlike the U.S., where the PATRIOT Act has destroyed financial privacy, Uruguay protection is based on a bank secrecy statute that forbids banks to share information — and that includes the government of Uruguay and foreign governments.

The only exceptions are cases of alimony, child support or alleged crimes, including tax evasion and fraud. Even then, information can be shared only after obtaining a court order. In the case of foreign tax crime, the information can only be shared if a tax-exchange treaty exists.

BROU also enforces the country's strong laws that protect financial privacy and, yes, banking secrecy. Uruguay does not automatically exchange tax or banking information with any government.

However, it is important to note that the country complies with the Organization for Economic and Community Development's standards for tax information exchange requests by having tax treaties with a handful of countries.

Uruguay is a respected sovereign state. Criminals and tax evaders are not welcome here.

Opening a Bank Account

One third of all bank accounts in Uruguay are held by foreigners, including many thousands of Brazilians and Argentineans.

There are no exchange controls or capital restrictions. Unlike neighboring Argentina, Uruguay has no political need, nor history of, forced conversion of currencies or of freezing or confiscation of deposits. The government guarantees bank insurance on deposits only to a maximum of $2,500, but bank failure is unknown here in recent years.

To open an account, you will need two IDs (passport and driver's license), proof of home address, and a reference letter from your home bank. You must also indicate the estimated amount of funds that will be deposited into and transferred out of the account monthly.

A personal interview is required and incoming funds must show proof of origin. A clean, non-criminal, personal record is required and you must and sign an IRS Form W-9.

Processing usually requires about two weeks and English-speaking account managers are assigned to non-Spanish speakers.

Bank financing is also available to foreign residents, with proof of income. A first or second mortgage on U.S. property is often accepted to finance local bank loans, as long as the bank can arrange for a back-to-back loan with its U.S. branch.

The country's interest rates are a nice bonus at around 7.5%. Banks offer up to 4.5% on various types of accounts. That means your money can earn up to 30 times more than it does in a U.S. bank account, where minimums are about 0.25%.

A Tax Haven by Any Measure

Uruguay's government does not want the country labeled as a "tax haven." However, by any measure, this is, in fact, an offshore tax haven that imposes very few taxes on foreign residents.

There is a territorial tax system here. Personal income tax only applies to Uruguayan-source income, including rental earning from properties in Uruguay. There is a flat tax of 12% on interest and dividend income from abroad.

However, resident foreigners are credited with any income tax paid to other countries, to avoid double taxation (Uruguay does this unilaterally; no double taxation treaty is necessary). Otherwise, income from abroad is not taxed.

So, if a resident foreigner already pays tax on income from another country, which Americans must, Uruguay does not tax you again. It is also worth noting that while Uruguayan banks may exchange information with some foreign governments upon proof of tax evasion or fraud, no agreement exists with the U.S. or Canada.

Three Types of Income Taxes

If you remain in Uruguay for more than 183 days in one year, the law presumes Uruguay is your tax domicile and you may become liable for all of the same taxes a local citizen would be required to pay.

So, which tax rates would you pay in Uruguay as a foreigner in residence? Although you will pay far lower rates than in the U.S., Uruguay levies the following taxes:

- **On assets:** Citizens face a small tax on offshore deposits, securities and loans. The rate is 0.07% to 0.5%. This tax, known as "IP," is being phased out in annual steps and will end in 2017. It will not affect anyone who gets citizenship after 2017.

- **On income:** Uruguay taxes three types of income generated outside of the country — interest on deposits, interest from loans to a foreign company and dividends. The tax is a flat 12%.

However, I repeat, if you already pay income tax abroad on any of these three types of income, you will not have to pay additional taxes in Uruguay. This means you avoid double taxation.

Any other type of income generated abroad, such as salary, capital gains on the sale of shares or property, pensions, lease income, or any other type of offshore income are all untaxed.

- **Job-related taxes:** If you decide to work in Uruguay, the personal income tax rate ranges from 10% to 25%, with a maximum overall effective rate of 18%.

Beneficial Uruguayan Taxes

Here's an example of just how good Uruguayan taxes could be for a U.S. citizen living there.

If you earn $1 million a year and bring $100,000 a year into Uruguay, the country taxes only 70% of that $100,000. There is also no tax on the first $800 of income you "earn" each month… so this further reduces the Uruguay tax burden.

Of that $100,000 you bring into the country each year, you'll face taxes on only $60,400. At a flat rate of 12%, you'll pay just $7,248 in taxes.

Compare this with what the IRS would take from $100,000 of annual income — $25,000. Even if it does not want to be called a "tax haven," it's clear that Uruguay is a low-tax jurisdiction for foreign residents.

Uruguay, like most countries in Latin America, imposes a value added tax (VAT) of 22% for most goods, and 10% for certain basic goods. It applies to imports (with exceptions) and to the sale of goods and services. A luxury tax is included in the cost of some specific goods, such as automobiles, alcoholic beverages, gasoline and tobacco. Unlike the U.S., these sales taxes are included in the higher price of an item; taxes are not added at the register.

Property taxes: The municipal property tax ranges between 0.25% and 1% of the market value of a property. It averages about 0.5% of the property value — but less on rural properties. There is also a school tax of some 0.1% to 0.2% of the market value that doesn't apply to rural properties.

The *transfer of real estate* is taxed at a rate of 2% of the assessed value of the property, paid by both parties in a transaction. Often, the "assessed value" is equal to half the market value of a property, or less. Uruguay does not tax the sale (partial or total) of bearer shares in a company that owns real estate.

The 25% *corporate tax* in Uruguay is levied on corporate profits generated within the country, regardless of your nationality. This includes branches or subsidiaries of foreign companies. There is a 7% tax on *distribution of dividends*.

The *capital gains tax* rate is 12% for individuals, 12% for foreign corporations, and 25% for Uruguayan corporations.

Tax Breaks for Investors and Businesses

Numerous businesses are eligible for special tax incentives and subsidies. For example, investments in tourism, including hotels and resorts, are exempt from import duties on equipment and materials. Such businesses are also exempt from corporate income tax and from capital/assets tax for 10 years.

This is what partly explains the $10 billion direct foreign investment figure.

Certain projects of "national interest" are also exempt from these taxes, including tourism, fishing, agro-industries, dairy products, and mining.

At the same time, Uruguay has thirteen "free trade zones" in the country, where foreign companies operate free of corporate and import taxes. That is, 0% income tax and no tax of any kind.

In our tour, we visited Uruguay's main free zone, Zonamerica, near Montevideo's international airport. This is an impressive, privately owned, modern commercial home to many global companies, such as Sabre, RCI, Tata and Merck, employing 7,000 workers.

These areas are used for imported product storage, assembly and distribution for introduction into Uruguay or export to other regional countries. These zones also are home to financial services firms such as Merrill Lynch, KPMG, Deloitte, as well as many other types of services, all tax free.

On July 1, 2007, a major tax law took effect that reaffirms the principle that taxes there are imposed only on a territorial basis — that is, the government taxes only income produced within, or brought into the country, not offshore income earned and retained elsewhere. That's important for foreign persons who may wish to live in Uruguay but have assets and income elsewhere.

Quick, Easy Residence

The immigration law of Uruguay states that residence is granted to those "who show intent to reside in Uruguay." That intent is evidence in the first instance by coming to the country and establishing your new home there.

Uruguay has a foreigner-friendly, open immigration policy, although, as with any official bureaucracy, it takes time; 12 to 18 months on average to obtain permanent resident status after coming to the country and applying. That said, you are a temporary resident, with a national ID card, from the day you apply.

After three to five years from arrival, one can apply for citizenship and a passport.

The government also requires that a temporary resident working towards citizenship must physically reside in Uruguay for at least six months during each year.

Importantly, the law in Uruguay, as in the United States, allows its citizens to hold dual or multiple citizenships. New citizens are not required to surrender their home country passport.

Documentation

Necessary foreign documents that must accompany a residence application include:

- Birth certificate;
- Marriage certificate (if applicable);
- Police record from country of origin, or country that issued your passport, as well as any countries where you lived in the last five years;
- Documented proof of sufficient income consistent with your living standard.
- All four documents must be stamped officially at a Uruguayan Consulate.

Proof of income can be shown by a foreign pension, mutual fund or retirement fund income, income from property leases abroad or in Uruguay, dividends or interest, or an employment contract in Uruguay. All such income must be received within Uruguay, so a local bank account must be opened.

There is also a special law (Act 16,340) that allows pensioners, including a spouse and minors, faster access to a Uruguayan passport, within six months from obtaining residency (although you must wait for the three years (from arrival) for citizenship.

The applicant, under this law, must prove a minimum monthly income of $1,500 and make an investment or buy property in Uruguay valued at $100,000, which cannot be resold for a period of 10 years. Those eligible may also import a vehicle duty free.

The "passport" granted under this law appears the same as the official one issued to any citizen of Uruguay, but in fact is only a "travel document" that identifies your home country citizenship and Uruguayan residency.

Uruguay offers one of the best and most complete offshore experiences I have found, providing quality of life, good infrastructure, profitable investments, beautiful beaches, personal safety, friendly banking and a broad welcome mat for foreigners, both as new residents and eventual citizens.

If you are looking for a beautiful and secure second home with solid banking and financial institutions, as well as a high-quality and affordable lifestyle, Uruguay is just the place.

Contacts

Government:

Embassy of Uruguay
1913 I (Eye) Street NW
Washington, D.C. 20006
Tel.: (202) 331-1313
Email: uruwashi@ uruwashi.org
Web: http://www.embassy.org/embassies/uy.html
List of Consulates: http://www.embassy.org/embassies/uy-other.html

United States Embassy
Lauro Muller 1776, Montevideo 11200, Uruguay
Tel.: + (598) 2 1770-2000
Email: MontevideoACS@State.gov
Web: http://uruguay.usembassy.gov/

Attorney:

Juan Federico Fischer Esq.
Managing Partner, Fischer & Schickendantz
Rincón 487, Piso 4, Montevideo 11000 Uruguay
Tel.: (+598) 2 915-7468 ext. 130
Email: jfischer@ fs.com.uy
Web: www.fs.com.uy

BERMUDA: THE "CADILLAC" OF OFFSHORE BANKING

Robert E. Bauman JD, *Where to Stash Your Cash*, 2015

This mid-Atlantic island is the world's leading place for "captive" self-insurance companies used by businesses and also for re-insurance companies; it offers excellent asset protection trusts and IBCs. Its respected banks have worldwide branches and investment services. But as a U.K. overseas territory, ultimately Bermuda is forced to take orders from London.

The "crown jewel of the Atlantic" and a world-class offshore center, Bermuda is located in the mid-Atlantic, 750 miles southeast of New York City and 3,445 miles from London. The island (69,839 people, 21 square miles) has a long history as a low-tax and banking haven. In the past, this has been a world-class financial outpost, not to mention a very pleasant place to visit or live in any season. But recently the government has experienced enough budget deficit problems that Fitch Rating Service reduced its bond rating.

The islands were first settled in 1609 by shipwrecked English colonists heading for Virginia. Bermuda has remained in British hands ever since and today is a British overseas territory with internal self-government.

The British Westminster system confers an immensely important constitutional right on each U.K. overseas territory, that of the right to declare independence. Until 2004, most local political leaders avoided the issue of Bermuda's possible independence from the United Kingdom. But then-Prime Minister Alex Scott called for a national debate on the subject, looking towards the possibility of ending London's control over the island. A referendum on independence was defeated in 1995 but sporadic independence talk continues. Independence is a possibility, but a remote one.

With a GDP of over US$6 billion, despite four years of recession and a public debt of $US1.4 billion, Bermuda enjoys the fourth highest per capita income in the world (US$86,000), about 70% higher than that of the U.S. Its economy is primarily based on providing financial services for international business and luxury facilities for tourists.

Because of its liberal regulatory laws, a number of U.S. re-insurance companies relocated to the island following the September 11, 2001, U.S. terror attacks and again after Hurricanes Katrina Rita, and Wilma in 2005, contributing to the expansion of a growing international business sector.

Tax-Free Business, Expensive Real Estate

Bermuda imposes no corporate income, gift, capital gains, or sales taxes. The income tax is extremely low — 11% on income earned from employment in Bermuda. More than 13,000 international business corporations call Bermuda home. They are drawn by the island's friendly, tax neutral environment, established business integrity and minimal regulation.

More than 60% of these companies operate as "exempted," meaning their business is conducted outside Bermuda (except for the minimal contacts needed to sustain an office on the island). Since Bermuda does not levy direct taxes, there are no double tax treaties with other jurisdictions. There is a tax treaty with the U.S. which exempts insurance premium payments from U.S. franchise taxes, and grants tax breaks to U.S. companies holding conventions in Bermuda.

Bermuda is also home to more than 600 "collective investment schemes" (mutual funds), unit trusts and limited partnerships. Under the strong protective umbrella of the U.K. Copyright Act of 1965, also applicable in Bermuda, many collective investment schemes with intellectual property and software interests use the island as a legal home port. With a statutory structure for protection, Bermuda has also become a center for offshore trust creation and management. The island offers a wide variety of trusts to meet every need, including offshore asset protection.

The "jewel of the Atlantic" is also a great place to live, but be aware of tough real estate restrictions. Demand for homes is high and supply short. In general, non-Bermudians are permitted to own only one local property. Acquisition is allowed only after careful background checks, (at least one bank reference and two or more personal references). Out of 20,000 residential units on the island, only 250 detached homes and 480 condominiums qualify for non-Bermudian purchasers based on government set values.

The average cost of a single-family home in 2013 was $1.1 million; a typical price for a modest two-bedroom, single-family house without water views was US$1.65 million. The average price of a condominium was above US$1 million.

In addition to the purchase price of a home or condominium qualified for sale to non-Bermudians, there is a 25% government upfront purchase tax on homes and 18% on condominiums. Purchase licenses are granted by the Department of Immigration and require six months or more for approval.

The buyers tend to be rich and famous. Aging rock star David Bowie owns property on the island, while former Italian Prime Minister Silvio Berlusconi and Texan Ross Perot, the one-time U.S. presidential candidate, are neighbors. International celebrities such as former New York Mayor Michael Bloomberg, a local land owner, can pass almost unnoticed on the island, a luxury unavailable on the streets of Manhattan or London.

Canadians currently have a special interest in buying on the island because Canadian tax laws make living abroad particularly attractive. The Immigration Department reports that citizens of more than 80 different countries work on the island, with the U.K. providing the most, followed by Canada, Portugal, the U.S., the Philippines, and workers from the Caribbean.

There are about 8,000 work permit holders on the island, a large number out of so small a population. Employers must apply to the Department of Immigration when they want to hire a non-Bermudian, showing proof that no suitably qualified islander is available. An estimated 8,000 registered U.S. citizens live in Bermuda, many of them employed in the international business community.

In recent years, friction has grown between native Bermudians and expatriates who come here for employment in the financial sector, the argument mainly based on disparities between wages. This has led to restrictions on the total number of expatriates allowed and their length of stay, and it is a continuing local political issue.

Business and Banking

Over many decades, Bermuda has achieved a global reputation as a world-class business center. It has set high standards with the best laws and infrastructure with continuing improvements based on experience. There is a spirit of cooperation between business and government in support of the offshore sector. Bermuda as an offshore financial center dates to the 1930s, but began to grow significantly after 1960, initially concentrating on Canada, the U.K. and countries in the sterling area. When Bermuda moved to the Bermuda dollar on a par with the U.S. dollar in 1970, focus shifted from the U.K. to the United States.

Such extensive worldwide finance and insurance activity requires a highly sophisticated banking system. Bermuda provides this with up-to-date services and fiber-optic connections to the world. The four local banks clear more than US$3 billion daily. Under the Banking Act of 1969, no new banks can be formed or operate in Bermuda unless authorized by the legislature. The chances of that happening are slim. However, international banks may form exempted companies engaged in non-banking activities and many have done so.

Bermuda's three banks follow very conservative, risk averse policies. They hold an average of 85% of customer liabilities in cash and cash equivalents. The Bank of Bermuda, founded in 1889, has assets exceeding US$5 billion and offices in George Town, the Cayman Islands, Guernsey, Hong Kong, the Isle of Man, Luxembourg, and an affiliate in New York City. The Bank of Bermuda is owned by HSBC. Butterfield Bank (founded in 1859) also has offices in all of those tax havens, except the Caymans.

Perhaps the biggest local banking news in years occurred in 2003 when the world's second largest bank, HSBC, purchased control of the Bank of Bermuda for US$1.3 billion. Many Bermudans opposed the sale. Since then several national divisions of HSBC have been charged with money laundering and paid billions in fines, none involving the Bank of Bermuda.

The Bermuda dollar circulates on par with the U.S. dollar. U.S. currency is accepted everywhere. There are no exchange controls on foreigners or on exempt companies, which operate freely in any currency, except the Bermuda dollar.

Unlike Panama, the Cayman Islands or The Bahamas, Bermuda has no bank secrecy laws officially protecting privacy, but bank and government policies make it difficult to obtain information in most cases. To do so requires judicial process.

A 1988 tax treaty with the U.S. allowed for governmental exchange of limited information in certain cases, but a more recent Tax Information Exchange Agreement (TIEA) with Washington opened the door to free exchange of information with the IRS. Bermuda also has signed a FATCA agreement with the U.S. The island has a total of 80 treaty partners, including 41 bilateral TIEAs and is one of 76 co-signatories of the EU Multilateral Convention on Mutual Administrative Assistance in Tax Matters.

For your personal and business purposes, a Bermuda bank account can offer a tax-free means for global financial activity and vast investment possibilities. If you have need for an offshore-based business locale, Bermuda, with its IBC creation laws and its modern digital Internet connections, is a very good choice.

Foreign Tax Evasion a Crime

Bermuda has toughened the provisions of the 1998 U.S.-Bermuda tax treaty. It also upgraded anti-money laundering laws, as well as financial management laws governing the chartering and operation of banks and trust companies. These laws were seen as Bermuda's calculated response to demands from the Foreign Office in London, the OECD and FATF.

The rewrite of the 1986 U.S.-Bermuda tax agreement in 1998 toughened the existing agreement at Washington's request. It clarified and expanded the types of information that Bermuda can now give the IRS "relevant to the determination of the liability of the [U.S.] taxpayer." For the first time, Bermuda also permitted on-site inspections of records by foreign tax authorities.

The Proceeds of Crime Act fiscal offenses list was broadened to include tax fraud. In effect, this meant that by proxy, American tax laws and their enforcement mechanisms were adopted by Bermuda.

Most importantly, the fraudulent evasion of foreign taxes was made a crime, a major reversal of prior Bermuda policy and law. This made Bermuda the first major offshore financial center (and the first British overseas territory) to adopt such legislation. Together, these laws allow the U.S. IRS and the U.K.'s Inland Revenue (as well as other nations' tax collectors) to pursue their alleged tax-evading citizens with the assistance of Bermuda prosecutors and courts.

Bermuda is an "approved jurisdiction" of the U.S. IRS for tax reporting purposes under the IRS Qualified Intermediary (QI) program. That means that the island's banks, investment advisors and other financial services that deal in U.S. securities agree to disclose to the IRS the names of their U.S. clients, or to impose a 30% withholding tax on investment income paid to such U.S. persons. This agreement was said to show IRS approval of Bermuda's stricter know-your-customer and suspicious activity reporting rules.

Service Economy

Because of the large number of international companies that conduct insurance operations from Bermuda, the island does not rely as heavily on personal offshore services and banking as do most other havens. In 2014, more than 15,000 international businesses maintained registration in Bermuda and more than 4,000 of these were local.

Total income generated by international companies exceeded US$2 billion. In the past the number of business permits surged as the island promoted itself as an e-commerce haven and opened its shores to licensed investment services providers for the first time. There is no income tax in Bermuda and international companies pay vastly reduced corporate taxes compared to the United States and Europe.

The Bermuda Stock Exchange, established in 1971, was intended as a domestic equities market. With the growth in international financial business, the exchange was restructured into a for-profit entity owned by the Bermuda banking institutions. It offers fully electronic clearing, settlement and depository services. The BSX has become the world's largest offshore fully electronic securities market offering a full range of listing and trading opportunities for global and domestic issuers of debt, equity, depository receipts, insurance securitization and derivative warrants.

Politics

Its strict laws have led the government to claim that the island is "the business leader among the British Overseas Territories," ready to meet and exceed international financial standards and regulation, but its international popularity has made it a target.

Even before Barack Obama became the U.S. president, Bermuda was made the target of anti-tax haven American politicians led by former U.S. Senator Carl Levin (D-MI). Barack Obama as an Illinois senator joined Levin in sponsoring anti-tax haven legislation that would have revoked long-standing U.S. offshore corporate tax breaks. As a presidential candidate, Obama repeatedly denounced tax havens as places where he claimed rich Americans engaged in tax evasion. U.S. companies that re-incorporated in Bermuda were Obama's special target.

The reason companies did this is easy to understand. Under U.S. tax law, a corporation pays 40% or more in federal and state taxes, one of the two highest corporate taxes in the world. Once that company changes its corporate registration to Bermuda, its profits from foreign operations are tax-free if the funds are kept offshore outside the U.S. It's easy for U.S. politicians to demagogue this issue, rather than do the hard work of reforming tax laws and lowering U.S. corporate taxes.

President Obama proposed abolition of this offshore corporate tax break, but without any compensating reduction in the U.S. 35% tax. Obama wanted to tax all worldwide income of corporations with main operations based in the U.S. He also proposed reducing the U.S. corporate tax to 28%, but only if the added revenue produced was earmarked for Obama spending programs.

As a result of the announced legislative intentions of Obama and his congressional allies, beginning a growing number of U.S. companies decide to move from Bermuda to Ireland or Switzerland as part of a search for "a more stable environment." In a sense, Bermuda was being made to pay the price for being too cozy with Washington in the past.

Some major British corporations that previously had moved their corporate headquarters from the U.K. to Bermuda began to have second thoughts. Reacting to heavy handed attacks by the U.K. Labor Party government on tax havens and concerned about what London might do, these companies moved to Switzerland where a network of over 70 double tax treaties offers a more secure tax environment

In spite of all the political noise Bermuda remains a good, basic, no-tax asset protection jurisdiction for the location of offshore trusts, IBCs and it is a leader for all types of insurance. Its banks are first-class.

Conclusion

Bermuda remains a good, basic, no-tax asset protection jurisdiction for the location of offshore trusts, IBCs and is great for insurance. Its banks are first-class. But its willingness to cooperate with tax-hungry governments in Washington and London has diminished what was formerly a policy of strict financial privacy.

Contacts

Bermuda Corporation Registry
30 Parliament Street
Hamilton HM 12m, Bermuda
Tel.: + 441 297-7753
Email: slowe@gov.bm
Web: www.roc.gov.bm

Bermuda Monetary Authority
BMA House 43 Victoria Street
Hamilton HMJX, Bermuda
Tel.: +441-295-5278
Email: info@bma.bm
Web: http://www.bma.bm

Bermuda's interests in the U.S. are represented by the Embassy of the U.K.:
3100 Massachusetts Avenue NW
Washington, D.C. 20008
Tel.: (202) 588-7800
Web: https://www.gov.uk/government/world/organisations/british-embassy-washington

United States Consulate General
Crown Hill, 16 Middle Road
Devonshire DV03, Bermuda
Tel.: +1- 441 295-1342 or after hours: + 441 235-3828
Email: HamiltonConsulate@state.gov
Web: http://hamilton.usconsulate.gov

The Truth about the Cayman Islands

Robert E. Bauman JD, *Where to Stash Your Cash*, 2015

The Cayman Islands, described famously as "a sunny place for shady people," is the world's sixth largest international banking center in terms of liabilities and asset. For decades it was the jurisdiction of choice for tax free international banks and businesses that wanted ironclad secrecy guaranteed by law. But a sea change in international rules on tax evasion and reporting of foreign accounts has ended Cayman's absolute secrecy.

Under extreme pressure from London and Washington, this British overseas territory weakened, but did not end, its still-formidable financial secrecy laws. The Caymans remain an efficient, tax-free OFC for offshore bank accounts, trusts, international business corporations, hedge and mutual funds, captive and other insurance.

Its name may be a red flag for foreign tax collectors and anti-tax haven politicians everywhere but it has weathered the political storm, as well as the occasional hurricane.

Let's face it: the major reason the Cayman Islands originally became a world-renowned tax-free haven was its strict bank and financial privacy — not just privacy, but near absolute secrecy. Guaranteed by law and zealously enforced by local courts, foreigners of all sorts doing business here were shielded from scrutiny — unless it was shown that they were engaged in overtly criminal acts. Even then, a lengthy judicial process often was needed to pierce this wall of secrecy.

Secrecy was for sale and the Caymans sold it well. But that was the old Cayman Islands before it was forced, under orders from its colonial masters in London, to compromise its bank and financial secrecy, and instead to become a potential proxy tax collector for other nations.

Many of Caymans' 54,000 residents do not agree with what has happened to them. Michael Alberga, a leading senior Caymans lawyer sees the world as practicing "economic terrorism" against the Caymans. He says "We were simply practicing pure capitalism; few or no taxes and little regulation and asking to be left alone."

Government & History

The Cayman Islands is a parliamentary democracy with judicial, executive and legislative branches. The present 1972 constitution provides for governance as a British Dependent Overseas Territory, meaning ultimate power rests with London.

Christopher Columbus discovered the islands in 1503 and named them Las Tortugas, after the giant turtles that he sighted in the surrounding seas. The islands were later renamed Caymanas, from the Carib Indian word for a crocodile.

The territory consists of three islands in what was known as the British West Indies, Grand Cayman (76 sq. mi.), Little Cayman (10 sq. mi.) and Cayman Brac (14 sq. mi.). Administered by Jamaica from 1863, they remained a British dependency after 1962 when Jamaica became independent. Grand Cayman is located directly south of Cuba, approximately 500 miles south of Miami, Florida. The capital, George Town, is located on Grand Cayman and serves as the center for business and finance.

Prince Philip, Duke of Edinburgh, the husband of Queen Elizabeth II, who rules the British Commonwealth and is Cayman Islands Head of State, is known for his off-the-cuff remarks. During a 1994 royal visit to the Cayman Islands Philip asked one of hosts whether he was "descended from pirates".

Until the mid-1960s there were less than 8,000 Caymanians with most engaged in farming, fishing, turtling, and boat building. Many men served as merchant seamen on ocean-going ships. It was a place where everyone knew each other. In 1952, an aircraft runway was built and the next year Barclays Bank opened a branch on Grand Cayman. Cayman's status as an international offshore financial center grew out of the foresight of the island's early legal practitioners and a friendly government. Together they drafted and enacted laws to take advantage of the absence direct taxation on the income or wealth of individuals and corporations.

The Cayman Islands is an English-speaking, common-law jurisdiction with no direct taxation on income, profits, wealth, capital gains, sales, estates or inheritances. Described as being "one of the more mature jurisdictions … in terms of regulatory structure and culture," the traditionally impenetrable confidentiality of the Cayman Islands ended finally in 2001, when it signed a tax information exchange treaty with the United States. Among other things, that treaty gave the U.S. Internal Revenue Service permission to examine accounts of Cayman financial institutions.

World Leader by the Numbers

Banks: The Cayman Islands is the sixth largest offshore banking center in the world, after New York, London, Tokyo, Singapore and Hong Kong. Regulated by the Cayman Islands Monetary Authority (CIMA), there were 210 banks in 2014, (74 of them U.S. branches), including 40 of the world's 50 largest banks. Assets and liabilities were reported as US$1.503 trillion and US$1.524 trillion respectively in June 2014.

Captive Insurance: Cayman is the second largest captive insurance base, after Bermuda, with assets worth US$60 billion and a total of 764 companies licensed; it is the number one jurisdiction for healthcare captives. With 257 companies, medical malpractice liability represents 34% of captive licenses in 2014, largest business area within the insurance sector. The second largest line of insurance business is workers' compensation, which accounts for 167 companies. As of June 2014 total premiums were US$12.3 billion and total assets US$54.9 billion. Most captives were from North America, with 90% originating there.

Trusts, Mutual and Hedge Funds: As of 30 June 2014 there were 141 active trust licenses and the trust sector is thought to manage more than US$500 billion. With 11,296 mutual funds with over US$1.8 trillion in net assets in 2014, this has been a growth sector since the 1997 opening of the Cayman Islands Stock Exchange. The Cayman Islands have emerged as the predominant registration base for hedge funds; as of 2014, there were more than 10,000 hedge funds registered here with assets exceeding US$800 billion. Cayman dominates offshore hedge funds with 85% of the world market.

Companies: As of January 2041 there were 95,530 registered companies operating through the islands. Thousands of closed-end funds exist here, plus the latest financial schemes or special purpose vehicles for structured finance dreamed up by cutting edge lawyers and investors, as the unfortunate 2001 Enron scandal showed. (Enron's creative managers formed 692 Cayman subsidiary IBCs used to conceal company debts, leading to the company's collapse and damaging the Cayman's reputation.)

The Caymanian dollar is fixed against the US dollar at CI$1.00 to US$1.20. There are no exchange controls. Cayman is an expensive jurisdiction with an established commercial and professional infrastructure in place and a flexible approach to regulation, within a strong desire to maintain respectability. It has excellent communications facilities and extensive professional services.

Companies Law

Until recently, a business could only be conducted in the Cayman Islands by: 1) a CI citizen or a resident foreigner who had a Residence Certificate, or; 2) a company licensed to do business or to trade within the Cayman Islands. The law now allows exempted companies and limited partnerships that locate in a "special economic zone," if they are registered with the Registrar of Companies for this purpose.

Under the former CI law "exempted" CI companies or exempted limited partnerships could not engage in trade other than business outside the Cayman Islands. Under the 2011 "SEZ Law" this restriction remains but now, even if a business has a physical presence in the CI, it is legally deemed to be outside the CI for tax purposes. The SEZ law also ends in certain cases the requirement that local companies had to have 60% CI share control; beneficial ownership and at least 60% of its directors were Caymanians.

Offshore business accounts for roughly 30% of the territory's gross domestic product of nearly US$3.5 billion. Many of the world's most reputable companies, including many American companies, do business through subsidiaries registered in the islands, to take advantage of the favorable, tax-free laws. The Caymanians enjoy a standard of living comparable to that of Switzerland with a per capita GDP of US$43,800 a year.

Politics as Usual

The Caymans, even more than Bermuda, became a major punching bag for U.S. politicians, especially after it was revealed that the defunct Enron Corporation used the islands for its numerous tax avoiding subsidiaries. Hollywood movies, such as the 1993 film *The Firm*, adopted form a John Grisham novel, falsely depicted the islands as a sinkhole of fetid corruption awash in billions of illicit cash.

Many U.S. firms have fully legal tax-saving subsidiaries registered in the Cayman Islands, including big energy companies such as El Paso Corp., Transocean Inc. and GlobalSantaFe Corp. Most U.S. companies have corporate units offshore for strategic, financial and tax reasons and they make no attempt to hide them because they are a fully legal means of avoiding U.S. taxes.

In both the 2008 and 2012 presidential campaigns, candidate Barack Obama made his hostility toward offshore jurisdictions clear. He repeatedly scored points with crowds when he said: "There's a building in the Cayman Islands that houses supposedly 12,000 U.S.-based corporations. That's either the biggest building in the world or the biggest tax scam in the world, and we know which one it is."

It made no difference to Obama that a similar corporate registration building in Wilmington, Delaware, home of his running mate, U.S. Vice President, Joe Biden, houses more than 50,000 American corporations as a means legally to escape state taxes in other American states.

Ugland House, on South Church Street near the center of George Town, is indeed home to Cayman's largest law firm, Maples and Calder that serves as registered agent for all the 12,000 legal corporations that it represents.

The issue was retreaded in the 2012 presidential campaign when Democrats attacked Republican nominee, Mitt Romney, who had legal tax-reducing investments based in the Cayman Islands. This sort of unwanted publicity has made the Caymans the stereotypical media "tax haven" — but objective reality denies that false image.

Money Laundering Crackdown

The truth is that Cayman has adopted a large number of modern laws in response to the international pressure for clean offshore financial centers. But, fortunately for the islands clients, the prevailing attitude in Cayman remains highly protective of strict financial confidentiality in the absence of demonstrated criminality.

As far back as 2001, the Cayman Islands was praised by the OECD Financial Action Task Force for its efforts to conform to 40 FATF recommendations in a code of good practice governing money laundering. The islands adopted anti-money laundering regulations and amendments to laws governing the Monetary Authority, Proceeds of Criminal Conduct, Banks and Trust Companies, Companies Management and it required compulsory licensing for financial firms.

The Cayman Islands now has tax information exchange relationships with 81 jurisdictions, including 35 TIEAs, one with Washington. There is a separate tax agreement with the U.S., implementing FATCA. In 2015, with the approval of the U.S. IRS, the government opened a unique online Automatic Exchange of Information Portal that allows CI financial institutions to file required FATCA Notifications and Reports with the CI tax Information Authority. Cayman happens to be the jurisdiction with the highest number of financial institutions registered with the IRS under FATCA.

Anthony Travers, one of the Cayman Island's most respected senior attorneys and former Chairman of the Cayman Islands Stock Exchange, exposed the lie in arguments that exalt increased tax transparency at the expense of financial privacy. Calling them "the purest nonsense" he points out that Tax Information Exchange Agreements have failed to generate any discernable revenue but that any tax revenues generated by FATCA for the benefit of the U.S. and U.K. Treasuries will not even cover the huge cost of enforcement.

The Cayman Islands rightfully view themselves at the forefront of the fight against money laundering in the Caribbean. Drug money laundering was made a serious crime in 1989 and so-called "all crimes" anti-money laundering legislation took effect in 1996 that encouraged reporting of suspicious transactions by providing a safe harbor from liability for those who report suspected crimes.

In 2000, the government announced what its politicians repeatedly had said they would never do. They reached an agreement with the OECD on the issue of future "transparency." The government officially embraced the OECD's demand for an end to the Caymans' traditional bank and financial secrecy, guaranteeing it would provide financial information about Caymans' clients to foreign tax collecting authorities when warranted by evidence. In return for this major change, the OECD did not include the Caymans on the OECD blacklist of tax havens allegedly engaged in "harmful tax practices."

Within three weeks of the OECD deal, all the primary legislation necessary to address every one of the FATF's concerns was on the CI statute books. A few weeks more, and additional anti-money laundering rules were introduced to complete the legislative framework.

The Cayman Islands now has a legal regime considerably tougher than that in many of the FATF's 29 member countries. The laws allow the Cayman Islands Monetary Authority to obtain information on bank deposits and bank clients without a court order and also allow sharing tax information with foreign investigators.

It is now a crime for bankers to fail to disclose knowledge or suspicion of money laundering. Previously, it had been a crime for financial sector workers to disclose any private financial information without a court order. The Caymans government even went so far as to guarantee that it would stop island financial services providers from "the use of aggressive marketing policies based primarily on confidentiality or secrecy."

But there are limits. As with the British Virgin Islands, the Caymans are one of a group of British Overseas Territories that have resisted demands from London that they implement more transparency reforms in the form of a public registry of beneficial corporate and trust ownership. The Caymans has judicial procedures that allow discovery of ownership in cases where that is required.

Recommendation

We have visited the Cayman Islands and met with financial and legal experts. We came away greatly impressed by what we heard and saw.

Regardless of the end of financial secrecy, enormous amounts of money have flowed through these islands over many years. That has created an impressive financial and professional community from which you and your businesses can benefit. These professionals can provide first-class investment advice, a variety of offshore legal entities, trusts and IBCs, annuities and insurance, mutual and hedge funds in which to invest.

If you value financial privacy and are considering or have financial dealings in the Cayman Islands, as with any British overseas territory haven, plan accordingly. But focus on what the Caymans have to offer — even if everything these days is out in the open.

Contacts

Government:

The Cayman Islands are part of the consular district administered by the U.S. Embassy in Kingston, Jamaica:

United States Embassy
142 Old Hope Road, Kingston 6, Jamaica, West Indies
Tel.: + (876) 702-6000
E-mail: KingstonIRC@state.gov
Web: http://kingston.usembassy.gov

U.S. Consular Agent in the Cayman Islands
150 Smith Rd., Smith Road Center Unit 202B
George Town, KY1-1010 Grand Cayman, Cayman Islands
Tel.: + (345) 945-8173
Email: usconsagency@gmail.com
Web: http://kingston.usembassy.gov/service/consular-agents.html
A U.S. Consular Agency is also available in Montego Bay, St. James

Cayman Islands Monetary Authority
P.O. Box 10052, Elizabethan Square
Grand Cayman, KY-1001, Cayman Islands
Tel.: + 345-949-7089
Web: http://www.cimoney.com.ky

Cayman Islands Department of Tourism
Miami (305) 599-9033, New York (212) 889-9009
Houston (713) 461-1317, Chicago (630) 705-0650
Web: http://www.caymanislands.ky

Cayman Islands Immigration Department
P.O. Box 1098GT, 94A Elgin Avenue
George Town, Grand Cayman, Cayman Islands
Tel.: + (345) 949-8344
Web: http://www.immigration.gov.ky

The Cayman Islands are represented in the United States by the Embassy of the United Kingdom:
3100 Massachusetts Avenue NW, Washington, D.C. 20008
Tel.: 202-588-6500
Web: https://www.gov.uk/government/world/organisations/british-embassy-washington

Recommended Law Firm:

Travers Thorp Alberga, Attorneys at Law
Michael Alberga, Managing Partner
Harbour Place, 2nd Floor, 103 South Church Street
George Town, Grand Cayman KY1-1106
Tel.: +1-345-949-0699
Email: malberga@traversthorpalberga.com
Web: www.traversthorpalberga.com

Real Estate Contact for general questions, agents, listings:

Cayman Islands Real Estate Brokers Association (CIREBA)
PO Box 1977, Grand Cayman, KY1-1104, Cayman Islands
Tel.: 1 (345) 949-7099
Email: cireba@candw.ky
Web: www.cireba.com

British Virgin Islands: IBC Headquarters

Robert E. Bauman JD, *Where to Stash Your Cash*, 2015

"BVI" as it is known, has a little more than 31,000 people — but more than 400,000 registered IBCs, second only to Hong Kong in total number. That's because the BVI specializes in creating, servicing and promoting offshore corporations for every purpose. The BVI can truthfully say, "IBCs R Us." And don't overlook their asset protection trusts, international limited partnerships and insurance. But remember: they take orders from London.

The British Virgin Islands consists of more than 60 islands, only 16 inhabited, at the eastern end of the Greater Antilles in the Caribbean, 25 minutes flying time east of Puerto Rico. Its economy is closely integrated with the nearby (to the west) U.S. Virgin Islands.

First inhabited by Arawak and later by Carib Indians, the Virgin Islands were settled by the Dutch in 1648 and then annexed by the English in 1672. The islands were part of the British colony of the Leeward Islands from 1872-1960 and were granted autonomy in 1967.

The capital, Road Town, located on Tortola, is the financial center and the seat of government and courts. As a British overseas territory, the BVI has a long history of political stability with a measure of self-government, but London calls the shots. There is a ministerial system of government headed by a chief minister, with an executive council chaired by the U.K. appointed governor and a legislative council.

The BVI is one of the world's most popular offshore jurisdictions for registering international companies and is a growing, but much lesser force in offshore hedge funds (currently about 2000), trust administration and captive insurance markets. The currency, since 1959, has been the U.S. dollar and there are no exchange controls.

The economy, one of the most stable and prosperous in the Caribbean, is highly dependent on tourism, generating an estimated 45% of the national income. Almost one million estimated tourists, mainly from the U.S., visit the islands each year. The economy is one of the most stable and prosperous in the Caribbean. International financial services produce 50% of the GDP.

IBCs R Us

The BVI adopted its successful International Business Company (IBC) Act in 1984. The Act was superseded by the BVI Business Companies Act 2004, which removed the distinction between 'offshore' and 'onshore' companies. Well over

500,000 have registered by 2015, the government said. That figures out to be more than 17 companies for every one of the BVI's 32,600 people.

Hong Kong and Latin America have been the main sources of clients, which is ironic, since Hong Kong leads all jurisdictions in registration of offshore corporations. (Many of BVI's Hong Kong clients are newly rich Chinese seeking to avoid taxes on the mainland.)

The IBC Act allows quick and cheap formation of tax-free corporations to hold assets and execute offshore transactions. The IBCs are used as holding companies, for consultancies, royalty income, foreign real estate, equipment leasing and ownership of moveable assets, such as airplanes and yachts.

The BVI has significant mutual fund and captive insurance sectors. Banking activity is, by design, minor. The BVI has tried hard to exclude money laundering, mostly with success, and has a relatively good reputation.

In 2013, the BVI received $92 billion in foreign direct investment, the fourth largest world amount, more than that which Brazil and India received combined. That was up 40% compared to 2012, continuing a trend that began after the 2008 economic crisis began. Unlike most countries where FDI is used by companies on new acquisitions and projects, most of the BVI money was transferred quickly in and out of the country or moved through the treasury accounts of large firms incorporated there.

The adoption of a comprehensive insurance law in 1994, which provides a blanket of confidentiality with regulated statutory process for investigation of criminal offenses, made the BVI even more attractive to international business. Because of traditionally close links with the U.S. Virgin Islands, the BVI has used the US dollar as its currency since 1959.

Ultimately, the financial industry here is under indirect control of the British government in London. The Labor Party during its control that ended in 2010 forced changes relaxing financial privacy and permitting international exchange of tax information. The islands now have in place a Tax Information Exchange Treaty (TIEA) with the United States and 24 other countries. In 2013, the BVI Premier announced the decision to negotiate an intergovernmental agreement with the U. S. to implement FATCA.

There is no statutory duty of confidentiality or privacy under BVI laws. However, confidentiality is imposed under the British common law and also may be imposed by contract. A breach, or threatened breach, of confidence is actionable in court, which may grant an injunction or award damages for an actual breach. Several laws waive confidentiality for criminal investigations.

In the past, one of the major attractions for BVI corporate registration was that true beneficial ownership was not a matter of public record. That has now changed. Under pressure from the Labour government in London, the BVI colonial government enacted numerous laws that compromised this former strict corporate privacy. In 2002, the BVI signed a tax information exchange agreement with the United States. The BVI has adopted the Article 26 OECD guidelines for tax information exchange.

Anti-money laundering laws cover reporting of suspicious activities and apply know-your-customer rules. The use of bearer shares (freely transferable corporate shares with the owner designated only as "bearer") has been so restricted that they remain "bearer shares" in name only.

In 2015 the BVI government again refused to establish a public central registry of beneficial corporate owners, in spite of pressure from London to adopt this as an anti-money laundering and tax evasion measure. It argued that BVI judicial procedures are adequate to discover ownership in cases where that is required. The only corporation documents on public record are the Memorandum and Articles of Association of each company. Names of directors are not public, much like the incorporation privacy laws of the State of Delaware after which they are patterned.

In 2014, as in the case of Luxembourg, BVI bank records stolen by the far left, anti-tax haven International Consortium of Investigative Journalists revealed that two BVI companies had 21,000 clients from mainland China and Hong Kong who were using the BVI as a tax haven, many of them relatives of, or members of the Communist Chinese ruling elite. In response, the BVI proposed a new law holding a person who publishes in any media unauthorized information on BVI companies may be fined up to US$1 million or jailed for up to 20 years.

BVI companies are not subject to withholding tax on receipts of interest and dividends earned from U.S. sources. There are no capital gains or asset taxes. Use of a standard domestic BVI corporation can be more profitable than an IBC, particularly if one wants to take advantage of the BVI double tax treaties in effect with Japan and Switzerland. The U.S. canceled a similar BVI tax treaty more than a decade ago.

The BVI hobbled somewhat as an offshore center because of its status as a U.K. offshore territory under the control of the government in London. That's where its orders come from and it follows them. But the colonials are growing restless. With the past attacks on tax havens coming from London, BVI folks fear their economic lifeline could disappear. The revenue from registering foreign companies has paid for a community college and a hospital. But if you need an IBC to conduct your worldwide business, the British Virgin Islands will provide it efficiently — and all the service and maintenance you will ever need. They also offer trusts and limited partnerships.

Contacts

Ministry of Finance
3rd Floor West Atrium, Central Administration Building
33 Admin Drive, Road Town, Tortola, BVI VG1110
Tel.: (284) 494-3701 ext. 2144
Email: finance@gov.vg
Web: http://www.finance.gov.vg

BVI Finance
Cutlass Tower, 4th Fl
Road Town, Tortola, BVI
Tel.: 1 284 468 4335
Email: info@bvifinance.vg
Web: http://www.bvifinance.vg

Government of the Virgin Islands
33 Admin Drive, Road Town, BVI VG1110
Tel.: 284-468-3701
Web: http://www.bvi.gov.vg

BWI is represented in the United States by the Embassy of the United Kingdom:
3100 Massachusetts Avenue NW
Washington, D.C. 20008
Tel.: 202-462-1340
Web: https://www.gov.uk/government/world/organisations/british-embassy-washington

The U.S. has no Embassy in the BVI. The nearest is:

United States Embassy Barbados
Wildey Business Park, Wildey, St. Michael, BB 14006
Tel.: 246-227-4000
Email: bridgetownacs@state.gov
Web: http://barbados.usembassy.gov

The U.S. Consular Agent in Antigua is closest to the BVI and can also assist in some limited, non-emergency cases.

U.S. Consular Agency
Suite #2, Jasmine Court, Friars Hill Road, St. John's, Antigua
Tel.: + (268) 463-6531
Cell: + (268) 726-6531
Email: ANUWndrGyal@aol.com
Web: http://barbados.usembassy.gov/consular_agents2.html

U.S. Virgin Islands — Little-Known American Tax Haven

Robert E. Bauman JD, *Where to Stash Your Cash*, 2015

It's not well known, but under a unique special U.S. federal income tax arrangement applying only to the U.S. Territory of the Virgin Islands, it is possible for U.S. nationals and others who make the islands their main residence to enjoy substantial U.S. personal and business tax benefits. These lower taxes make the islands an offshore tax haven option for very wealthy U.S. citizens, entrepreneurs and foreign nationals seeking U.S. citizenship.

The Virgin Islands of the United States, as their name is officially styled, constitutionally are "an unincorporated territory" of the U.S. With the Caribbean Sea to the south and the Atlantic Ocean to the north, the Virgin Islands offer a variety of deep sea and coastal fishing. Their tropical climate and minimal industrial development assure an abundance of unspoiled reefs for divers and snorkelers, with sandy beaches ringing deep coves. The large number of isolated, secure anchorages in the U.S. Virgin Islands and the British Virgin Islands just to the east has made the chain a center for yachting. A thriving charter-boat industry in the Virgin Islands draws tens of thousands of visitors annually for crewed sailing adventures.

After their discovery by Columbus in 1493, the islands passed through control by the Dutch, English and French. In 1666, St. Thomas was occupied by Denmark, which, five years later, founded a Danish colony there to supply the mother country with sugar, cotton, indigo, and other products. The Danes secured control over the southern Virgin Islands of St. Thomas, St. John, and St. Croix during the 17th and early 18th centuries. Sugarcane, produced by African slave labor, drove the islands' economy during the 18th and early 19th centuries. By the early 17th Century, Danish influence and control were established and the islands became known as the Danish West Indies. That political status continued until Denmark sold the islands to the U.S. for US$25 million in 1917.

The islands have a strategic value for the U.S. since they command the Anegada Passage from the Atlantic Ocean into the Caribbean Sea, as well as the approach to the Panama Canal.

U.S. citizenship status was conferred on the V.I. inhabitants in 1927. Although they do not vote in U.S. presidential elections, residents are represented by a non-voting Delegate in the U.S. House of Representatives.

Little-Known U.S. Low-Tax Paradise

The United States Virgin Islands (USVI) lie 1,100 miles southeast of Miami, Florida — and it's one of the most impoverished jurisdictions under the American flag. But most Americans only know the islands as a vacation venue with beautiful resort hotels, white sandy beaches and blue lagoons.

The four principal islands — St. Croix, St. John, St. Thomas, and Water Island — have a population of about 104,170 (2014 est.). Per capita income in the territory is only US$14,500. That's less than half the average in the continental United States and $10,000 less than in Mississippi, the poorest American state. Island resident racial composition is black 76%, white 15.6%, Asian 1.4%, other 4.9%, mixed 2.1%; 17.4% self-identify as Latino.

In addition to poverty, the USVI has another unusual distinction. They have been, until now, America's very own "offshore" tax haven. So much so, that the low-tax hating OECD denounced the USVI as the U.S. version of "unfair tax competition."

What upset the OECD was the territory's prohibition against U.S. and local ownership of USVI "exempt companies," although this was required by the U.S. Congress in the U.S. Internal Revenue Code. The USVI was removed from the OECD "unfair tax" black list in 2002, but the OECD continued to criticize the islands for being America's own tax haven.

In 2009, when the G-20/OECD issued its list of tax havens allegedly deficient in tax information exchange, surprisingly, the USVI appeared on the "white list" of "good" offshore financial centers, even though the United States and President Barack Obama vocally, led the G-20 attack on all tax havens. But perhaps more importantly, the U.S. finances most of the budget of the OECD staff that authors the black list.

The islands — St. Croix, St. Thomas, St. John and Water Island — have been territorial possessions of the United States since they were purchased from Denmark in 1917. They are overseen by the U.S. Department of the Interior. The Naval Services Appropriation Act of 1922 (Title 48 U.S.C. § 1397) provides in part: "The income tax laws in force in the United States of America ... shall be held to be likewise in force in the Virgin Islands of the United States, except that the proceeds of such taxes shall be paid to the treasuries of said islands."

USVI residents and corporations pay their federal taxes on their worldwide income to the Virgin Islands Bureau of Internal Revenue (BIR), not the U.S. IRS. In the U.S. Virgin Islands, the average corporate tax rate is just 3.37%.

Persons who are born in the USVI or those who become naturalized U.S. citizens in the USVI, for purposes of U.S. federal gift and estate taxes, are treated as nonresidents of the U.S. Since the USVI has no estate or gift taxes, this means that upon death the estates of such persons owe zero U.S. or territorial estate or gift taxes as long as they are domiciled in the USVI at the time of death or at the time of making a gift and have no U.S. assets. (As with any other nonresidents of the U.S. for gift and estate tax purposes, assets located within the U.S. are subject to federal estate and gift tax.)

Generous Package

To attract outside investment, the USVI Economic Development Commission (EDC) grants generous tax relief packages that include a 90% credit against U.S. federal income taxes. This tax grant package, which is offered for a period of 10 to 30 years depending on the business location within the USVI (with possible 10-year and then five-year extensions), is available to USVI chartered corporations, partnerships and limited liability companies.

The tax credit applies to income from USVI sources including fees for services performed in the USVI, and certain related income, such as sales of inventory and dividends and interest from non-U.S. sources received by banking and finance companies based in the USVI.

For many years, a few U.S. investors with business activities ranging from petroleum production, aluminum processing, hotel and other tourism activities, to transportation, shopping centers, and financial services, have taken advantage of USVI tax laws and enjoyed income with very little taxes. As a result of the EDC marketing campaign to attract corporations, about 100 companies qualified for the program in between 2002 and 2004, employing nearly 3,100 people.

The tax benefit program began paying dividends almost immediately after tax wise hedge fund managers started moving to the USVI in 1995. The islands' tax revenue doubled from US$400 million to US$800 million in a five-year period ending in 2005. The increase effectively erased a US$287.6 million budget deficit for the territory. The EDC program was worth about US$100 million annually to the local economy. A USVI government spokesperson said that the EDC was crucial in lifting the territory from a dire financial crisis to a fiscal year surplus in excess of US$50 million.

Paradise Almost Lost

All went well until the early 2000s when the IRS noticed a rapid increase in the number of high net worth individuals moving to the USVI — based on the increasing amount of taxes that the BIR counted as tax-exempt income the USVI. The IRS discovered copies of what it perceived to be "marketing materials" from various EDC beneficiaries seeking additional investors; the federal and local statutes did not limit the number of investors to one beneficiary.

In 2003, the IRS raided a financial services firm, Kapok Management, in St. Croix, accusing the firm of sheltering income for dozens of partners who were living on the U.S. mainland, not in the USVI. In 2004, a Massachusetts life insurance executive who used this same fake resident ruse, pled guilty to federal tax evasion in St. Croix.

But in 2009, after a two-month trial in the USVI federal district court, the IRS lost a big case when a jury acquitted 99 Kapok defendants of conspiracy, attempted tax evasion and fraud charges. The original indictment accused Kapok of fraudulently abusing the Virgin Islands' economic development program designed to promote local economic development and employment through the use of tax credits.

The IRS claimed authority to go back as far as it wants and examine tax years without regard to the usual three-year IRS statute of limitations. In the 2015 Sanders case referenced below, the U.S. Tax Court expressly held that the IRS must abide by the three-year limitations statute in USVI cases.

But the U.S. IRS keeps on trying.

In 2015, the U.S. Tax Court ruled that the IRS could not assess alleged tax deficiencies against a deceased USVI man accused by the IRS of participating in a tax avoidance scheme. The Tax Court rejected the IRS argument, ruling that Travis L. Sanders, who paid taxes to the USVI Bureau of Internal Revenue from 2002 to 2004, was not a true resident and therefore was obligated to pay federal income tax. The case centered on IRS claims that Sanders was not a USVI resident, but the Tax Court disagreed, saying Sanders met his federal tax obligations through USVI Bureau of Internal Revenue filings and that the test of residence depends on an individual's intentions and length of stay. *Estate of Travis L. Sanders, Deceased et al. v. Commissioner of Internal Revenue*, Case number 4614-11, U.S. Tax Court. 144 TC —, No. 5, Dec. 60,222.

The case is important also because the IRS has kept examinations of hundreds of USVI taxpayers in limbo since the early 2000s, ignoring the three-year limit. USVI observers fear now that *Sanders* has cut off IRS attacks on the transactions that qualified the income for the USVI 90% tax credit, the IRS will step up attacks on USVI residence, trying to define questionable residence as tax fraud. The islands' tax practitioners hoped that the IRS would drop its crusades against USVI taxpayers after the IRS resounding defeat in the 2009 Kapok case. Now they hope the *Sanders* case will cause the abandonment of hundreds of stale but never decided IRS examinations of USVI taxpayers from the early 2000's.

Strict Six-Month Residence Requirement

In 2004, U.S. Senator Charles Grassley (R-Iowa) drafted legislation to impose a strict six-month residency requirement and limited the territory's tax benefits only to income earned exclusively within the islands. (The 1986 legislation had provided that the territory's tax benefits applied to USVI and income connected with a USVI trade or business, but also directed the IRS to issue special regulations to define "source" and "effectively connected income" for this purpose. But the diligent IRS went 18 years without issuing these regulations.)

Grassley slipped his changes into a major tax bill without any hearings, and with no notice to the USVI delegate to Congress, the governor, or the U.S. Interior Department, all of whom were stunned to learn what had happened. This major change was imposed without any testimony, territorial input, and certainly without any consideration or understanding of the critical importance of the territory's Economic Development Program to its impoverished economy. The Congressional Joint Committee on Taxation estimated in a wild guess that Grassley's legislation would increase federal revenue by US$400 million over a 10-year period.

IRS Terror

In a reign of tax terror after the 2004 insurance executive case, the IRS opened about 250 audits on individuals who filed as USVI residents and on businesses that were beneficiaries of the economic development program. Many of these individual audits were of persons who had no economic development credits and made no tax exemption claims on their returns. The IRS and the U.S. Department of Justice also brought the Kapok case mentioned above. At that point everyone who lived in the USVI had to wrestle with the six-month residency requirements whether they were being audited or not.

After the 2004 residence changes were adopted, about 50 hedge funds managers and other financial services companies either halted activities temporarily or withdrew from the islands. The islands' finance sector boom withered, crushed by the IRS and Grassley with a combination punch of the law and subsequent IRS rules that are still unclear with regard to income eligible for tax credits.

Residence Rules

The old, pre-Grassley rules required a person to be a bona fide USVI resident on the last day of the tax year, "looking to all the facts and circumstances," similar to the "domicile" test for estate and gift tax purposes. There was no "number of days" test and no requirement that a person be a resident for all or most of the year to file as a resident for that year.

The rules now require a resident to be present physically in the USVI at least 183 days, or roughly six months, every year. The IRS did set up four alternative ways to meet the physical presence test of the new residency requirement: 1) spend no more than 90 days in the United States during a taxable year; 2) spend more days in the USVI than in the U.S. and don't have more than $3,000 in earned income from the U.S.; 3) average 183 days a year over a rolling three-year period, or; 4) meet a "no significant connection" test. This last test means no house, no spouse, no minor kids and no voting registration in the United States — and no number-of-days counting requirement.

The residence rules also require a "bona fide resident" to have a "closer connection" to the USVI than anywhere else — considering where you vote, what address you use, the location of the closet in which most of your clothes hang, where you have homes, where you bank and where your family lives. Finally, "a bona fide resident" must have a tax home in the USVI — which is usually your principal place of business.

The number of financial firms and other service businesses that once made the USVI their corporate home now has fallen by half from more than 80 several years ago.

The IRS also drafted an intrusive form for island residents it says is needed to prove valid residency. IRS Form 8898 requires those who stop filing tax returns with the IRS, in order to file them in the USVI, to list where their immediate family lives, where their cars are registered and where they hold driver's licenses.

The former chief executive officer of the EDC has said: "In the States, they definitely see that they are losing taxes when some of their taxpayers move elsewhere. All of the people everywhere are competing for the same business. What's wrong with the Virgin Islands attracting some of those people?"

In fact, the betrayal of the USVI by the federal government, assures only one thing — that Americans seeking legal tax breaks will instead find them in secure tax havens such as Panama, Belize, the Channel Islands, Singapore and Hong Kong.

Something for Everyone

Notwithstanding all of the above, tax breaks could still be yours — but it is an absolute necessity that, to qualify, a person actually live and make their main residence in the USVI.

The USVI offers two types of benefit programs that are either fully or partially exempt from USVI taxes and U.S. federal income taxes as well.

One type is a USVI corporation (or partnership or LLC) that qualifies for the benefits of the Economic Development Program for its USVI business activities. Most beneficiaries of this program are in one of three areas — hotels, manufacturing, and service businesses serving clients outside the USVI. But benefits are also available for businesses engaged in transportation, marinas, large retail complexes, medical facilities and recreation businesses. Most of the service businesses that have obtained benefits are engaged in fund management, general management and financial services activities.

The beneficiaries that do qualify are fully exempt from most local taxes including the gross receipts tax (otherwise 4%), property taxes (otherwise 0.75%) and excise taxes on raw materials and building materials. Beneficiaries also get a 90% credit against their USVI income taxes (although for C corporations the credit is equal to 89% of taxes). Beneficiaries also enjoy a special customs duty rate of one percent. They are exempt from U.S. federal income taxes on their USVI operations. The 90% credit also applies to dividends or allocations to a beneficiary's USVI bona fide resident owners — which is why it is so critical to meet the residence requirements.

Strict Requirements

To qualify for these great benefits, a business must employ at least 10 people full-time (32 hours a week) and must make a minimum capital investment of $100,000 (or more). Beneficiaries must also provide health and life insurance and a retirement plan to employees and must purchase goods and services locally, if possible.

For non-U.S. foreign persons, generous exemptions are available through the use of the second type of tax-free entity, a USVI exempt company. The USVI is the only jurisdiction in the world where a non-U.S. person can establish a tax-free entity under the U.S. flag. These exempt companies are used as holding companies for portfolio investments, for the ownership of aircraft that are registered with the U.S. Federal Aviation Administration, or as captive insurance companies. There are a number of other offshore tax-planning structures that can take advantage of USVI exempt companies. Up to 10% of the shares of an exempt company can be owned by U.S. residents and up to 10% can be owned by USVI residents.

The USVI also has a research and technology park at the University of the Virgin Islands, and technology businesses can also benefit from world-class connectivity through Global Crossing, AT&T's underwater cables on St. Croix.

Close By

Moving your residence to the USVI is no more difficult than moving from one U.S. state to another. The USVI has a well-developed infrastructure. The legal system is subject to the U.S. Constitution and is part of the Third Circuit U.S. Court of Appeals. The U.S. court system, postal service, currency, and customs and immigration agencies serve the islands. There is no restriction against maintaining a second home elsewhere inside or outside of the United States, so long as you maintain your principal residence in the USVI.

This unique American tax haven is limited, but certainly worth considering for any high net-worth foreign person considering U.S. naturalization, or any current U.S. citizen willing to relocate to a warmer climate legally to avoid burdensome taxes.

The benefits are particularly beneficial for businesses with a global, rather than a U.S., focus because certain foreign source (but not U.S.) dividends and interest are treated as effectively connected income for tax credit purposes and owners of such a business do not have to spend 183 days in the USVI as long as they are in the United States for no more than 90 days annually and have a closer connection to the USVI and a USVI tax home.

Obviously, the USVI tax exemptions are unique in that they require a foreign or U.S. person to reorder their personal and business lives in a major way. It means moving and establishing a personal residence and/or business headquarters in the USVI. However, this is a comparatively small price to pay to gain the substantial tax savings that can result from such a move.

Contacts

Government:

U.VI Economic Development Authority: http://www.usvieda.org

Office of the Governor: http://www.governordejongh.com

USVI Bureau of Internal Revenue
9601 Estate Thomas
Charlotte Amalie, St. Thomas, V.I. 00802
Tel.: (340) 715-1040
Web: http://www.viirb.com

U.S. Virgin Islands Net: http://www.usvi.net

Recommended Attorney:

Marjorie Rawls Roberts, PC, LLB, JD, AB
P.O. Box 6347, St. Thomas, U.S.V.I. 00804
Tel.: +340-776-7235
Email: jorie@marjorierobertspc.com
Web: http://marjorierobertspc.com

BELIZE: TARNISHED CARIBBEAN GEM
Robert E. Bauman JD, *Offshore Confidential*, 2015

Belize, the only English-speaking nation in Central America, two decades ago adopted a series of excellent offshore laws allowing asset protection trusts, IBCs, maritime registration, insurance, banking — plus maximum financial privacy. Its parliament, courts and government are very pro-offshore and cultivate foreign business and investments. An unusual feature is a special, tax-free retirement residence program for foreigners. But having said all that, this is definitely a Third World country, with all the problems that entails.

In the Caribbean region after Panama and Nevis, until recently Belize was a close third for banking privacy, low and no taxes and a business-friendly government. It was on everyone's list of possible offshore financial bases, but in 2014 times changed in Belize. In 2014 there were at two major fraud investigations by the US SEC involving Belize-based US and Canadian persons.

As a result, the entire Belize banking sector was in crisis. CIBC First Caribbean International Bank has closed down and Atlantic Bank was dropped by Bank of America as a correspondent, meaning it was denied access to the US banking system and to dollar transactions. The one major bank, Bank of Belize International, dropped many US clients and refused new ones. Much stricter "know your customer" rules were imposed. Until this cloud of questionable banking practices is lifted, you are advised to bank elsewhere.

Even before this crisis, having visited Belize twice, I can attest that it's definitely "Third World," but people are very friendly and oceanfront real estate is still relatively cheap. Belize is one of the few remaining independent nations that, until the recent banking crisis, was proud to hold itself out as a tax and asset protection haven, a status is still enjoys, despite scandals.

Belize is the only English-speaking country in Central America. Its mixed population of 304,000 includes descendants of native Mayans, Chinese, East Indians and Caucasians. Independent since 1981, its language came from its colonial days when it was known as "British Honduras."

Situated south of Mexico and to the east of Guatemala, Belize is on the Caribbean seaboard. It has the largest barrier reef in the Western Hemisphere and great deep-sea diving. To the east, there's a sprinkle of Caribbean tropical islands included within the nation's borders. A few years ago, American television viewers discovered Belize as the locale for one of the first reality TV shows, "Temptation Island."

Belize retains many of the colonial customs and features familiar in places such as the Cayman Islands and Bermuda, although it is far less developed. The first settlers were probably British woodcutters, who in 1638, found the valuable commodity known as "Honduran mahogany." Bananas, sugar cane and citrus fruit are the principal crops. Like many small countries dependent on primary commodities, Belize recognized the benefits of introducing offshore tax haven financial services to boost its income.

Clean Money Problems

American government officials have had a case of nerves over Belize. Some feared that the sleepy little capital town of Belmopan would become a prime site for U.S. tax evasion and money laundering. As it turned out, SEC stock fraud was the eventual problem in 2014. But the Belizean government has cooperated with the U.S. in the SEC cases and in drug and money laundering cases, although extradition from Belize is still difficult. The nation's clean money reputation was boosted by adoption of a strong anti-money laundering law that was supposed to be enforced vigorously.

In 1992, the Belize National Assembly enacted modern legislation seeking to make the country a competitive offshore financial center. Drafters combed tax haven laws worldwide and came up with a series of minimal corporate and tax requirements that could well fit your business needs. The new laws include the Trust Act, which allows a high level of asset protection, great freedom of action by the trustee and no taxes on income earned outside Belize. There is also a statute allowing the creation of international business companies that can be formed in less than a day for less than $1000. You only need one shareholder and/or director, whose name can be shielded from public view.

There are no local income taxes, personal or corporate and no currency exchange control. Since1990 when the International Business Companies Act became law foreigners have registered about 5,000 IBCs. That's a relatively small number compared to a place like the British Virgin Islands, but the number is growing. Belize is also home to major growth in the shipping registry business. Other laws favor offshore insurance companies, limited liability partnerships and banking.

Over the last decade, the government of Belize has carefully and systematically established the nation as an offshore haven that welcomes foreign investment and foreign nationals. It has enacted a series of laws crafted to protect financial privacy and promote creation of offshore trusts and international business corporations (IBCs). It has an attractive special residency program aimed at retirement bound foreign citizens.

Offshore Industry Expands

In spite of OECD's carping, Belize's small offshore industry continued to grow, providing financial services to a largely nonresident clientele. These services include international business company and offshore trust formation and administration; international banking services, including foreign currency bank accounts and international VISA cards; fund management, accounting and secretarial services; captive insurance; and ship registration.

A sympathetic government continues to work closely with the Belize Offshore Practitioners Association in drafting future legislation covering offshore banking, captive insurance, limited duration companies, protected cell companies and limited partnerships. All professional trust providers now must register with and be licensed by the government.

The Belizean banking sector is small but secret by force of law. Now there are only three commercial banks. Privacy protection here rivals even that of air-tight Nevis. In 2009, Belize was placed in the OECD "gray list" of those countries allegedly failing to meet international standards concerning tax information exchange. It has indicated that it will do so.

Some banking clients here have complained to me about a Third World attitude on the part of Belize bankers, with slow service and failure to protect client privacy due to sloppy work.

Tax Free Residence

A good example of a Belize welcome of offshore persons is the Retired Persons Incentive Act that is implemented by the Belize Tourism Board. The program, which resembles the popular *pensionado* program in Panama, is designed to attract foreign retirees and foreign capital.

Known as the "qualified retired persons" (QRP) Program, the law offers significant tax incentives to those willing to become permanent residents, but not full citizens. The program is aimed primarily at residents of the U.S., Canada and the U.K., but is open to all.

A "qualified retired person" is exempted from all taxes on income from sources outside Belize. QRPs can own and operate their own international business based in Belize exempt from all local taxes. Local income earned within Belize is taxed at a graduated rate of 15 45% and QRPs need a work permit in order to engage in purely domestic business activities. For QRPs, import duties are waived for personal effects, household goods and for a motor vehicle or other transport, such as an airplane or boat. There is no minimum time that must be spent in Belize and QRPs can maintain their status so long as they maintain a permanent local residence such as a small apartment or condo.

To qualify for the QRP Program, an applicant must be 45 years of age or older and prove personal financial ability to support oneself and any dependents. A spouse and dependents (18 and younger) qualify along with the head of household at no extra fee. Initial fees for the program are US$700, plus US$100 for an ID card upon application approval. Minimum financial requirements include an annual income of at least US$24,000 from a pension, annuity or other sources outside Belize.

For more information about the QRP Program, contact the following agency:

Belize Tourism Board
64 Regent Street, P.O. Box 325
Belize City, Belize
Tel.: 501-227-2420
Toll-free (from US): 1-800-624-0686
Email: info@travelbelize.org
Web: https://btb.travelbelize.org/btb/tourism-in-belize/belize-retired-persons-incentive-program

Conclusion

In spite of British, U.S. and OECD pressures, Belize is not about to enact income or corporate taxes that would drive away foreign investors and residents. In this relatively impoverished country, the offshore sector is a needed and highly valued source of foreign capital that has strong government support. Any modifications to offshore laws are likely to be minimal and mainly window dressing to mute foreign critics.

The offshore professional sector in Belize certainly is not comparable to a highly developed nation such as Panama as an offshore haven. Its laws offer a full array of offshore entities for asset protection and as investment vehicles, trusts, IBCs and limited liability companies. Its weakness is its small and under siege banking community, but you can just as easily locate your Belize IBC bank account in Vienna or London, where private banking is an art.

Contacts

Government:

Government of Belize: http://belize.gov.bz

Belize Embassy
2535 Massachusetts Avenue NW
Washington, D.C. 20008
Tel.: (202) 332-9636
Email: ebwreception@aol.com
Web: http://www.embassyofbelize.org

Belize travel information office (New York City): 1 (800) 624-0686

United States Embassy
Floral Park St.
Belmopan, Cayo, Belize
Tel.: + (501) 822-4011
Email: embbelize@state.gov
Web: http://belize.usembassy.gov

Banks:

Belize Bank International Ltd.
The Matalon Business Center
Coney Drive, 2nd Floor, Belize City, Belize CA
Tel.: + (501) 227-0697/227-1548
Email: services@BelizeBankInternational.com
Web: https://www.belizebankinternational.com

Licensed Domestic Banks:
https://www.centralbank.org.bz/financial-system/regulated-institutions/domestic-banks

EUROPE

ANDORRA: TROUBLED MOUNTAIN TAX HAVEN
Robert E. Bauman JD, *Where to Stash Your Cash*, 2015

The Principality of Andorra, nestled high in the Pyrenees, between Spain and France, is a low-tax jurisdiction for very wealthy foreigners who enjoy winter sports. It's difficult to become a citizen, but establishing residence is fairly easy. There are no income taxes (yet) and banking privacy still exists, but this tiny country is under international siege due to charges of massive money laundering by one of its major banks.

High and Jagged

This tiny, mountainous country is without many taxes, a military or poverty. It has only been accessible from France or Spain by motor vehicles over mountainous roads in long journeys, depending on weather conditions. The country's standard of living is high, the cost of living relatively low, but growing, and the scenery delightful.

According to legend, Charlemagne, Emperor of the Holy Roman Empire, in 748AD gave Andorra its name and its independence. Gazing over the mountain region newly wrested from the Moors of Spain, the Bible-quoting emperor is said to have exclaimed, "Wild valley of hell, I name you Endor!" (The valley of Endor, at the foot of Mount Thabor in the Holy Land, was the campsite of the Israelites during the war against the Canaanites. Old Testament: 1 Sam. 28:20)

With political and economic stability, no labor strikes, virtually no unemployment and the lowest crime rate in Europe, and banking secrecy perhaps too strict for its own good, remote Andorra could be your haven to get away from the modern world's problems.

Bargain Isolation

Until the end of World War II, Andorra was a time capsule of traditional European mountain life. Napoleon, who was busy elsewhere, declined to invade the diminutive joint principality, said: "Andorra is too amazing. Let it remain as a museum piece."

In the last four decades, the country has been transformed from a traditional pastoral and farming economy to one of commerce and year-round tourism. The population has increased from 5,500 in 1945 — the same as in the 1880s — to around 85,458 in 2014. Only about 14,000 are citizens, the rest resident foreigners. Most of the others have moved here for work opportunities or to escape onerous taxes in their home countries.

Andorra has an amazing 11.6 million visitors annually, mainly skiers, but many more bargain hunters for low tax discount goods and cigarettes.

Geography, Government

Andorra consists of 185 square miles, about one-fifth the size of the smallest American state, Rhode Island. Andorra's rugged terrain consists of gorges and narrow valleys surrounded by mountain peaks that rise higher than 9,500 feet above sea level.

It is an independent nation-state and is governed by 28 elected members of the General Council. Until 1993, the President of France and the Bishop of Seo d'Urgel (Spain), as co-princes, were responsible for Andorra's foreign affairs and judicial system. These "co-princes" could veto decisions by the General Council. They controlled the judiciary and police, but did not intrude into Andorra's affairs, except in 1933, when French gendarmes were sent in to maintain order after the judiciary dissolved the General Council. For the next 60 years, demands for independence were a repeated political refrain.

In 1993, Andorrans voted to sever their feudal links with both France and Spain. The country subsequently gained a seat in the United Nations as the third-smallest member-state. While citizenship is a daunting prospect — it can only be attained by marrying an Andorran and being a resident in the principality for at least 25 years — the number of resident foreigners in Andorra demonstrates just how attractive the country is as a tax haven. Seventy percent of the people who live in Andorra are resident foreigners and these immigrants are demanding more political rights.

Andorra established formal links with the European Union in 1991. After two years of tough negotiations, Andorra signed its first ever international treaty by joining the EU customs union, the first non-EU member country to do so. Andorra now applies the common EU external tariff and trade policy. This allows free transit of its goods (except for farm products) within the EU market. Andorra adopted the euro in 2002 and signed a monetary agreement with the EU in 2011 making it effectively subject to the monetary policy of the European Central Bank.

Duty Free

Andorra's simple, pastoral life of a half century ago is gone. Instead, it has become the shopping mall of the Pyrenees because of its duty-free tax status. The country is exempt from the EU's value added taxes, making it a sort of "Mall of Europe." More than 11 million visitors a year — mostly day-trippers — invade Andorra. They pour over the border and head for shops along the central valley road. On weekends, traffic jams are a prelude to the jostling, shopping, crowd-packed streets of Andorra la Vella, the capital.

Until recently Andorra's citizens and residents paid no taxes on personal income, capital gains, capital transfers, inheritance or profits. There is no sales tax or VAT. Until 2011 there were no taxes for resident companies or individuals other than modest annual registration fees, municipal rates, property transaction taxes, some minor sales taxes and a sliding scale capital gains tax introduced in 2007.

A law imposing a corporate income tax of 10%, initially on non-resident entities, is now in force as is a government imposed 10% tax for non-residents on local-sourced income — so much for foreign investment. This tax is being extended to resident individuals who have incomes of €30,000 (US$33,000) or more per year. Since 84% of Andorrans earn less than that each year, this was a popular "soak-the-rich" measure affecting only the wealthy minority.

There is also talk of the introduction of a value added tax to be followed by extension of the income tax of non-resident individuals and corporations, but these plans have met with verbally violent opposition from the many foreign residents here. Nominal local property taxes pay for municipal services — average annual rental property tax varies from around US$120 for an apartment to US$240 for a house of any size.

Little known outside of the skiing and financial communities, this small European tax haven saw some startling, double-digit rises in real property values in recent years, prior to the 2008 global recession. Buyers come from an active local market, second homebuyers looking for ski condos and international buyers who want to establish residence in a leading tax haven. A 2-3-bedroom condo here can sell for US$500,000, approximately half the cost of similar digs in Monaco.

In 2009, for the first time in seven centuries, the government of Andorra opened up investment in resorts and other businesses to foreign investors. Along with lifting this curb on foreign investment, the government paid the usual lip service of now wanting to be seen as an "investment haven" and not a "tax haven."

Residents

A second residence in Andorra won't alter your domicile of origin for the purposes of home nation inheritance or estate taxes. But if you're granted a passive residence in Andorra, you have the right to protection under the law, certain benefits from the health and social security systems, the right to a driver's license and the right to own and register resident-plate vehicles. Resident status does not confer the right to vote, nor does it allow local commercial activity, such as owning or running a business.

If you're looking for residence status, there are two categories of permits — both of which are difficult to obtain — those that give the holder the right to work in Andorra and those that don't allow employment.

To encourage immigration of high-net-worth individuals, often retired persons, the government grants "Passive Residence Permits" called *residencias* that are subject to a quota determined periodically according to the "economic and social needs of the Principality of Andorra."

Otherwise, long term residence is only possible to those with work permits, which are controlled by quotas. It is possible to get around this system by owning a nominee company, which is relatively expensive, but the government watches closely, and any kind of suspicious activity or competition against locals can bring rapid expulsion.

Due to the high ratio of foreigners to Andorrans in the principality, the government uses selective methods of admitting new residents. Residence permits, *residencias*, are available to applicants, retired or otherwise, who have an address in the principality and who genuinely wish to reside in Andorra and become an active community member.

The applicants must prove private income sufficient that he/she need not seek local employment. Once the applicant is accepted, a *residencia* is issued for one year, renewable after the first year for a period of three years. Applying for a *residencia* is a lengthy procedure and must be conducted in the official language, Catalan. Applications are handled by the Immigration Department of the Police. Tel.: + (376) 826-222).

Anyone in Andorra who is not a resident is considered a tourist — but there's no legal limit on the period of stay. Tourists can even rent or purchase a property for personal use for as long as they wish. So it's easy to live in Andorra, "perpetual traveler" style, without an official residence permit.

The annual quota for non-work permits in recent years has ranged from 200 to 500. The earlier you apply, the better your chance of success. Applicants must also show availability of sufficient economic means to permit residence in Andorra without having to work throughout the period of passive residence.

Bank Secrecy

Andorra has no exchange controls and bank secrecy is strict — but nowhere near as strict as it used to be. The principality has five banks with combined assets of about 16 billion euros, or US$17 billion, an integral part of the economy of Andorra.

We say "was strict" because in 2015 a major money laundering scandal erupted. Criminal investigators for the U.S. Treasury Department Financial Crimes

CHAPTER NINE: SPECIAL PLACES FOR BUSINESS & PROFITS   543

Enforcement Network (FINCen) published a report accusing Banca Privada d'Andorra (BPA) of laundering hundreds of millions of dollars on behalf of some of the world's most powerful criminal gangs from Russia, China, Mexico and elsewhere. The bank president was arrested, a board member ousted, with suspect funds impounded and others "semi-frozen." HSBC, Bank of America, Citigroup and Deutsche Bank provided access to U.S. financial system to Banca Privada d'Andorra with correspondent-banking relationships; all are reconsidering ties. The U.S. Department of the Treasury's Financial Crimes Enforcement Network (FinCEN) in 2015 named BPA as a foreign financial institution of primary money laundering concern pursuant to the USA PATRIOT Act. Banco de Madrid, BPA's Spanish subsidiary, filed for bankruptcy less than a week after the US announcement. The BPA owners have sued FinCEN.

Like other Andorran banks, BPA had weathered the euro debt crisis, emerging from it with a €20.5 million profit in 2013. In PBA took control of Banco Madrid making it the first Andorran bank to get a Spanish banking license. Spain had been investigating in Banco Madrid, for more than a year before the 2015 U.S. Treasury report. FinCEN's announcement came as a shock for the small country, which was trying to shed a long-standing reputation as a tax haven.

The *Wall Street Journal* reported: "Some rival bankers suggested that PBA's aggressive pursuit of clients had, in fact, long raised concerns within a close-knit financial community, in which a small number of extended families dominate the banking industry. BPA was evidently considered something of a black sheep."

In spite of claims by some offshore hucksters claiming inside contacts at Andorran banks, even before this scandal, the government of Andorra no longer allowed numbered and coded accounts without identifying and recording the true owners. Foreigners and their legal entities may open and operate bank accounts with fewer restrictions than imposed in Switzerland, for example, but the foreign party must justify the need for a local bank account by establishing residence in the country or by buying a condominium.

Until 2009, bank secrecy laws prevented giving bank account information to foreign governments. Since then the Andorran government has applied the OECD standard for tax information exchange, providing information in individual cases where evidence of foreign tax evasion is alleged by a government with which Andorra has a tax treaty. In 2016 Andorra had 18 TIEAs with other countries including neighboring France and Spain, as well as Monaco, Liechtenstein, Austria and the Netherlands, although none yet with the United States or the United Kingdom.

Under pressure from the OECD, France and Spain, Andorra already had adopted a broad definition of the crime of "money laundering." That includes having an account here that has not been declared to the tax authorities of the country where the account owner lives and is taxed. If an official foreign tax authority, such as the U.S. IRS, tells the Andorran government that one of its nationals is suspected of foreign tax evasion in Andorra, banking secrecy is automatically suspended.

The local Andorran judge orders the Anti-Money Laundering Police Unit to demand information about the person from all five banks in Andorra on all present and past accounts held in the banks or in money management or investment vehicles. That information is turned over to the foreign tax authorities before the suspect is ever charged or tried, much less convicted.

Locals quietly admitted that, as deposits fled, the country was, and is, financially bleeding to death. The PBA scandal deepened the wound. They predict that sooner or later most of the banks will disappear. No country with a population of 85,000 needs five banks. The banks here made all their profits from the business of nonresident clients, the vast majority being Spaniards. Now the bank secrecy is gone and foreigners are closing their accounts.

Interestingly, Andorra's two major banks, Andorra Credit Bank and Andbank (Andorra) have offices in Panama and other leading offshore financial centers. It appears that while these banks were founded in Andorra, they now look elsewhere for clients and funds, a trend that an Andbank official in Panama confirmed to us.

Andorra has been home to thousands of bank accounts belonging to prudent Spaniards. Annually, an estimated 10% of the billions of euros that escape Spanish regulation and taxes are thought to be funneled through Andorran accounts. Perhaps 1,500 tax exiles from the U.K. have residences here also.

All five local banks had until now a worldwide network of foreign correspondents and some foreign branches. With no exchange controls, accounts can be held in up to 20 foreign currencies and traded in any quantity at the rate quoted in Zürich. Exchange rates for clients are some of the best in Europe.

A Local Opinion

A longtime American friend who has lived in Andorra for many years and is himself a former Swiss banker, told us that "...the banks now require anyone opening an account here to appear in person. Lawyers can no longer open accounts for them. U.S. persons who reside here are not allowed to hold or buy any American securities in their local bank accounts. Since the adoption of strict American anti-money laundering and anti-terrorism laws, the banks here unanimously agreed to forbid any investments in, or holding of, U.S. securities.

The banks are frank to say they don't want to waste excessive time and money in reporting to the IRS and the SEC. When the new U.S. laws took effect a few years ago the banks made resident Americans here sell all their U.S. investments or close their accounts."

My friend also observed that in his opinion all these recent tax increases condemn Andorra to implode because "…two real attractions for foreigners — no income tax and banking secrecy — have been eliminated. What remains is a very ugly place to live with a proposed low initial tax rate that may not be low enough to attract a very appealing class of new residents."

Economy

If the PBA scandal was not enough, slower growth in Spain and France has dimmed Andorra's current prospects. In 2010 and 2011, a drop in tourism contributed to a contraction in GDP and a deterioration of public finances, prompting the government to implement several austerity measures.

The GDP in 2012 was US$3.163 billion with a per capita GDP of US$37,200. To bring in new revenue and diversify sources of economic growth, the government approved a 2012 law opening investment to foreign capital.

The country has developed summer and winter tourist resorts, with more than 250 restaurants and over a thousand retail and wholesale shops. There are about 300 hotels, ranging from elegant to simple. Some have double rooms available for as low as US$50 per night. Tourism employs a large portion of the labor force.

During the winter, skiers flock to Andorra's slopes. High peaks separate six deep valleys and though the Pyrenees lack the famous Alpine altitudes, they are breathtakingly steep and far less expensive to visit. The Andorran government encourages upscale tourism at its popular ski resorts, attractive because of comparatively low prices. Ski areas are state of the art and bountiful snowfall guarantees weekend visitors from throughout Europe. Hikers use the lifts in the summer.

In the past, Andorra's thriving tourist industry hastened the country's economic transformation. Former shepherds — now wealthy investors — import cheap Spanish and Portuguese labor to support a building boom, which transformed Andorra's central valley into a string of shops and condominiums. Don't get the idea, however, that all the land is developed. Only 8% of Andorra's land is both suitable and zoned for development. One can still find small villages in which to live. Many have less than 100 inhabitants and offer absolute peace and quiet.

With all this pending bank controversy, Andorra is not the best place for an offshore bank account.

Contacts

Government:

Andorran Tourism Board: http://visitandorra.com/en

Embassy of Andorra
2 United Nations Plaza, 27th Floor, New York, NY 10017
Tel.: (212) 750-8064

Email: contact@andorraun.org
Web: http://www.embassy.org/embassies/ad.html

The Andorran Permanent Representative to the United Nations is accredited as Andorra's ambassador to the United States. The U.S. Ambassador to Spain is also accredited as ambassador to Andorra. U.S. Consulate General officials in Barcelona are responsible for the conduct of relations with Andorra.

United States Embassy
Serrano 75, 28006, Madrid, Spain
Tel.: + (34) 91-587-2200
Email: amemb@embusa.es
Web: http://madrid.usembassy.gov

U.S. Consulate General
Paseo Reina Elisenda de Montcada 23, 08034 Barcelona, Spain
Tel.: + (34) 93-280-2227
Web: http://madrid.usembassy.gov

Real Estate:

Servissim
(Private Client services /residence permits/ property sales / rentals)
Avinguda Sant Antoni, Edifici Rossell, Baixos, La Massana - Principality of Andorra Tel.: + (376) 737-800
Email: maite.servissim@andorra.ad
Web: http://www.servissim.com/index.cfm

Banks:

Andbank: http://www.andbank.com/comercial/en
MoraBanc: http://www.morabanc.ad
Banca Privada d'Andorra (BPA): https://www.bpa.ad/eng
Banc Sabadell d'Andorra: https://www.bsandorra.com/en
Crèdit Andorrà: https://comercial.creditandorragroup.ad/ca

Austria — Unique European Banking Secrecy
Robert E. Bauman JD, *Where to Stash Your Cash*, 2015

The Austrian Republic is not a haven in the sense of low taxes, but it is a "banking haven." That's because this nation still has some of the strongest financial privacy laws in the world, although they have somewhat weakened. The basic privacy guarantee has constitutional protection that can be changed only by a national referendum of all voters.

For a very few select of the foreign wealthy, Austria also offers low-tax residence for those who can qualify. The Austrian Republic has long been a bastion of banking privacy strategically located on what was once the eastern European border of countries dominated by Communist Russia, the Soviet Bloc. From the end of World War II in 1945 to the collapse of Soviet Communism in 1992, with the Soviet Union and the United States locked in armed confrontation, Austria served as a willing Cold War financial and political go-between for both

West and East

With a population of 8.3 million, Austria covers approximately 75% of the eastern Alps. It borders on Germany, Liechtenstein, Switzerland, Italy, Slovenia, Hungary, Slovakia and the Czech Republic. German is the official language. Most people, especially the younger generation, speak English.

Vienna was once the center of power for the multinational Austro-Hungarian Empire created out of the realms of the Habsburgs by proclamation in 1804. It was the second largest country in Europe after the Russian Empire and one of the world's great powers. But as a losing combatant Austria was reduced to a small republic after its defeat in World War I. Following annexation by Nazi Germany in 1938, and occupation by the victorious World War II Allies in 1945, Austria's status remained unclear for a decade. A 1955 treaty ended the Allied occupation, recognized Austria's independence and forbade unification with Germany. Austria joined the European Union in 1995.

Since World War II, two parties usually have dominated Austrian political life: the conservative Austrian People's Party (ÖVP) and the center-left Social Democratic Party of Austria (SPÖ). Despite the philosophical differences between the two, these parties historically have worked together in a "Grand Coalition." That coalition persists in the form of a ruling government by the two major parties, but divisions have grown due to issues of an aging population, an influx of illegal immigrants, and the global and EU economic problems.

Austria, with its well-developed market economy, skilled labor force, and high standard of living, is closely tied to other EU economies, especially Germany's. Its economy features a large service sector, a sound industrial sector, and a small, but highly developed agricultural sector.

Austria is one of the ten wealthiest countries in the world in terms of GDP per capita. The 2014 GDP was US$386.9 billion, with US$45,400 GDP per capita. Following several years of solid foreign demand for Austrian exports and record employment growth, the international financial crisis of 2008 and subsequent global economic downturn led to a sharp, but brief, recession. Austrian GDP contracted 3.9% in 2009 but saw positive growth of about 2% in 2010 and 2011, but it fell to less than 1% in 2013-14.

The international financial crisis of 2008 caused difficulties for Austria's largest banks, whose extensive operations in central, eastern, and southeastern Europe suffered large losses. The government provided bank support, including, in some instances, nationalization to stabilize the banking system. This high banking exposure to central and Eastern Europe continues.

Austria may be a good place for you to do business. Its capital gold reserves rank third in the western world. It is industrialized and developed with a large service sector.

Austria always has had close links to eastern European countries and has benefited from these links since the collapse of the Soviet Union in 1993. Many businesses have relocated from Eastern Europe to Austria in recent years. Among the major Austrian companies is the Red Bull drinks label and Swarovski crystal. Worldwide, Austria has the highest number of graduates from secondary education; the workforce is reliable and highly motivated. Industrial labor problems are almost non-existent.

Secrecy: It Is the Law

When Austrian national banking laws were officially re-codified in 1979, the well-established tradition of bank secrecy was already two centuries old. During that time, Austrian bank secrecy and privacy produced two major types of so-called "anonymous accounts."

These accounts usually required no account holder identification, no mailing address and no personal references. Just deposit funds and use the account as you pleased, all done anonymously. Both the *Sparbuch* bank account and the *Wertpapierbuch* securities account have been abolished, victims of the European Union's fixation with destroying financial privacy wherever possible.

Notwithstanding the demands of the EU, current Austrian bank secrecy laws forbid banks to "disclose secrets which have been entrusted to them solely due to business relationships with customers." This prohibition is waived only in criminal court proceedings involving fiscal crimes, with the exception of petty offenses. The prohibition does not apply "if the customer expressly and in writing consents to the disclosure of the secret."

The Austrian Federal Constitutional itself does not recognize explicitly the right of privacy, but section 1(1) of the 2000 Austrian Data Protection Act does have constitutional status recognizing protection of personal data as an individual fundamental right. This special law guarantees and raises banking and financial privacy to a constitutional level and it only can be changed by a majority vote in a national referendum, a highly unlikely event. The Data Protection Commission (*Datenschutzkommission*) is responsible for enforcing the DP Act and decides complaints.

All major political parties support financial privacy as a longstanding national policy. As a member EU country, until 2009 Austria strongly opposed EU demands for compulsory withholding taxes and financial information sharing. In 2009, in a change of policy under pressure from the G-20 countries and the EU, Austria agreed to apply Article 26 of the "OECD Model Tax Convention." The government of Austria refused to agree to start sharing personal bank account information with other countries until similar rules were applied to financial centers such as Switzerland, that are not part of the 28-nation EU bloc. It was the first time that Austria, long known for its strict banking secrecy, had made such a commitment, after refusing for a decade.

As discussed before, OECD Article 26 recognizes "tax evasion" as a valid basis for foreign tax agency inquiries concerning their citizens with offshore accounts. Under the OECD procedure, foreign tax authorities wishing to take advantage of tax information exchange agreements must supply evidence of their suspicions (e.g., names, facts, alleged tax crimes) to the requested government. If there is sufficient probable cause to believe tax evasion has occurred, the requested government must supply the information.

In spite of an OECD demand that each country signs at least 12 tax information exchange agreements (TIEAs) with other nations, Austria has signed TIEAs only with Gibraltar, Andorra, Monaco and St. Vincent & the Grenadines, all in 2009, with Jersey in 2012 and none since. A foreign government must prove "foreseeable relevance" as well as request specific information on a specified account. The requesting country must prove that it has exhausted all local and domestic means of obtaining the information before applying to the Austrian authorities. Account holders are given notice of any requests and can appeal any decisions concerning the account. In practice this means there is no automatic exchange of information.

Austria was one of three EU nations exempted from the 2005 EU tax directive information sharing plan, (along with Belgium and Luxembourg). At that time, all three nations, joined by non-EU member Switzerland, declined to share tax information, but agreed to collect the 35% EU withholding tax on interest paid to nationals of EU member states. Foreign nationals of non-EU nations, including U.S. persons, are not subject to this EU withholding tax. Today all four countries, with variations in procedures, have surrendered to OECD Article 25 exchanges.

Stocks and Bonds

Until the world recession that began in 2008, the Austrian stock market had one of the world's best performance records in years. It benefited in part from the eastern European expansion boom that began in the 1990s after the East-West Iron Curtain disintegrated and its formerly Communist-dominated eastern European neighbors turned to free market polices.

Nonresidents are not subject to restrictions on securities purchased in Austria and they can be transferred abroad without restrictions or reporting. Nonresidents can purchase an unlimited amount of bonds and/or stocks on the condition that the money used for purchase is in either foreign currency or Euros. When securities are sold, the cash proceeds can be freely converted and exported without restrictions.

Taxes

Taxes are comparatively low; corporate income tax is 25% and has been since 2005. The highest personal income tax rate is 50%. All resident companies and permanent establishments of non-resident companies are subject to corporate income tax. Resident companies are liable for tax on their worldwide income. Non-resident businesses are taxed on their Austrian-sourced income only. Dividend income is exempt from corporate income tax when the shares are held by a private foundation. Income from interest and capital gains from the selling of shares are subject to an interim tax of 12.5%.

Austrian tax authorities found a way to profit from their attractive banking haven status — the government levies a 25% tax on the total bank interest earned. Foreigners can avoid the 25% tax on bond interest because no tax is withheld if a declared nonresident is the bank account holder. Interest paid on investments held in non-bearer form in Austrian banks, such as certificates of deposit, is also exempt from the withholding tax. Interest on convertible bonds, however, is subject to a withholding tax of 20% at the payment source.

Unfortunately, an American citizen bondholder is subject to capital gains tax in the U.S. on the full capital gain, despite the Austrian tax. A double taxation treaty between the U.S. and Austria eases this hardship. If you file a request with the IRS, the Austrian tax will be partly repaid, diminishing the net tax burden to 10%. The remaining 10% tax can offset part of the U.S. capital gains tax ordinarily imposed. The double taxation agreement does not apply to Austrian interest and dividends, which remain fully taxable in the U.S.

The Austrian government's decision to reduce the corporate tax rate from 34% to 25% in 2005 led to a 30% increase in new investment projects. In addition to cutting corporate taxes to one of the lowest levels in the EU, the reforms also reduced the tax burden on multinational firms using Austria as regional headquarters.

Austria also offers significant tax concessions to holding companies, foundations and certain other investment incentives, all successfully designed to attract foreign capital.

My Sovereign Society colleague, Mark Nestmann, who lived in Vienna for three years, offers this first hand observation: "Austria offers major advantages including a stable economy, safe banks and, for foreign investors, virtually no taxes. Austria is also a popular expatriate haven. If you have sufficient wealth to support yourself, it is one of the world's top havens for residence — although unfortunately it is difficult to obtain a residence permit. Austria welcomes foreigners but it doesn't promote itself as an investment or residential haven, so you'll have to take the first step if you are interested in investing or living here."

Live Income Tax-Free

Austria is also a desirable place to live. Mercer's, a human resources consultancy, rates Austria's historic capital of Vienna as the most desirable city in the world in which to live.

Because of its diminutive size, Austria does not accept many new resident aliens. Indeed, limiting immigration has become a major political issue, giving rise to the conservative Freedom Party that opposes further immigration. In response to an influx of immigrants from Eastern Europe, Turkey, and Africa, Austria enacted legislation in 2005 significantly restricting immigration. The country admits only about 8,000 immigrants annually, with the majority being foreigners married to Austrian nationals. In practice, it is difficult for non-EU nationals to obtain legal residence in Austria without an expensive and time-consuming application process.

An Austrian passport is one of the world's most desirable travel documents. It not only permits you to live or work in any of the 28 EU countries without obtaining a visa, but also allows visa-free travel to more countries than almost any other travel document.

It is not widely known, but a wealthy foreigner who can qualify to become a resident of Austria also may qualify for a unique tax break — 100% of annual income completely free of taxes! This preferential tax treatment, called a *Zuzugsbegünstigung*, used to be ready and waiting at the obliging Ministry of Finance.

A foreigner who is a new Austrian resident can qualify if the person meets all the following requirements:

- Had no residence in Austria during 10 years prior to application
- Doesn't engage in any business activity within Austria
- Can prove sufficient income from outside sources
- Agrees to spend a minimum of US$70,000 in Austria each year
- Has a residence and intends to stay in Austria for at least six months (183 days) each year

When all those conditions are met, a foreigner may be able to live tax-free in Austria. All income from foreign pension or retirement funds, dividends and interest from foreign investments and securities or any offshore businesses outside Austria are tax exempt.

In most cases, officials grant a tax break of at least 75% of potential tax liability — but a good local lawyer may be able to negotiate a 100% reduction. If you have foreign income taxable in your home country and there is no double taxation agreement between Austria and your country, the Ministry of Finance may grant you a zero tax base, or a special circumstances ruling, but only after you establish your residence in Austria.

Although Austria does not have an economic citizenship program per se, statutory law does allow the granting of citizenship to a foreign person if he or she is judged to contribute in some extraordinary way, including economic, to the interests of Austria. However, this is a very difficult way to acquire citizenship and may require a year to process at a minimum.

Applicants are approved on a case-by-case basis and must be willing to invest or make a charitable contribution of at least US$2 million in an approved project in Austria. Investment proposals are submitted to the Office of Economic Development. Those that provide export stimulation or local employment receive preference. Representation by a knowledgeable Austrian lawyer is essential, and is likely to cost considerably more than US$50,000. Fees of €250,000 (US$325,000) or more apply, depending on the case and the number of persons in an application, as each case is handled on an individual basis. The Nestmann Group and Henley & Partners can provide details on these possibilities.

Is Austrian residence status for sale to the very rich?

To be frank, yes. If you are a reputable and wealthy foreigner, there will be few obstacles to becoming a resident. Residency gives you the best of both worlds — life in an extremely desirable location, but without the high taxes Austrian citizens must pay.

Once in residence, you could apply for citizenship, but that would defeat the purpose. As an Austrian citizen, you'd be liable for full taxation. The only additional advantages would be having an Austrian passport and the right to purchase as much real property as you wish, which is otherwise very difficult for a foreigner merely residing in Austria.

Even with its agreement to share tax information using the OECD standard, Austria's financial and banking privacy laws provide much great security than most other countries. As a result, it's wise to keep Austria near the top of your potential banking list, especially if your major area of business interest lies in eastern Europe or Russia.

CHAPTER NINE: SPECIAL PLACES FOR BUSINESS & PROFITS 553

Contacts

Government:

Ministry of Finance: https://english.bmf.gv.at

Embassy of Austria
3524 International Court NW,
Washington, D.C. 20008
Tel.: (202) 895-6700
Email: consularsection@austria.org
Web: http://www.austria.org

United States Embassy
Boltzmanngasse 16 1090, Vienna, Austria
Tel.: + (43-1) 31339-0
Email: ViennaUSEmbassy@state.gov
Web: http://vienna.usembassy.gov

U.S. Consular Section
Parkring 12a, 1010 Vienna, Austria
Email: ConsulateVienna@state.gov
Web: http://vienna.usembassy.gov

Recommended Bank:

Wiener Privatbank SE
Parkring 12, 1010 Vienna, Austria
Phone: +43 1 534 31 -0
Web: https://www.wienerprivatbank.com

Because of FATCA restrictions, Wiener Privatbank does not accept bank investment accounts applications directly from U.S. persons. The two Sovereign Society associates listed below act as intermediaries for opening Wiener Privatbank accounts and can assist you.

Robert Vrijhof, President
Weber, Hartmann, Vrijhof & Partners
Schaffhauserstrasse 418, CH-8050 Zürich, Switzerland
Contact: Julia Fernandez
Tel.: 01141-44-315-77 77
Email: info@whvp.ch
Web: http://www.whvp.ch

Eric N. Roseman
President and Chief Investment Officer
ENR Asset Management, Inc.
1 Westmount Square, Suite 1400
Westmount Quebec, H3Z 2P9 Canada

Tel.: 1-877-989-8027 / 1-514-989-8027
Email: eric@enrasset.com
Web: www.enrassetmanagement.com

Recommended offshore vault for storage of precious metals and other valuables:

DAS SAFE
Auerspergstrasse 1, A-1080, Vienna, Austria
Tel.: +43 1 406 61 74
Email: info@dassafe.com
Web: http://www.dassafe.com

Recommended Consultant on Residence and Citizenship:

The Nestmann Group
Renngasse 12/16, 1100 Vienna, Austria
Tel.: + (43) 1 587 57 95 60
Email: service@nestmann.com
Web: http://www.nestmann.com

Henley & Partners
Klosbachstrasse 110, 8024 Zürich, Switzerland
Tel.: +41 44 266 22 22
Heiligenstädter Lände 29, 1190 Vienna
Tel.: +43 1 532 0 777 77
Web: https://www.henleyglobal.com

Principality of Liechtenstein: World's First Tax Haven

Robert E. Bauman JD, *Where to Stash Your Cash*, 2015

This tiny principality, the world's 6th smallest country in territory, is a constitutional monarchy that has graced the map of Europe since 1719. Within the last century it has transformed itself into a major offshore financial center. Among all the world's OFCs, Liechtenstein has adopted some of the most drastic recent changes, abolishing near absolute financial privacy and ending their past refusal to share client information with any other government.

Major Changes in Oldest Tax Haven

Tiny Liechtenstein (16 miles long and 3.5 miles wide with a population of 36,700) is nestled in the mountains between Switzerland and Austria. It has existed in its present form since January 23, 1719, when the Holy Roman Emperor, Charles VI, granted it independent status.

In the past, the worlds wealthy could do business here quietly, protected by near absolute secrecy and financial privacy laws. It also offered global banking and investment direct access through its cooperative neighbor, Switzerland. The Swiss franc is the local currency and, in many respects, except for political independence, Liechtenstein's status is that of a de facto province integrated within Switzerland.

With asset protection laws dating from the 1920s, a host of excellent legal entities designed for wealth preservation and bank secrecy guaranteed by law, at one time this tiny principality had it all. But that secrecy made it a prime target for outside pressure from the OECD, the U.S. and other major high tax countries.

Under pressure, Liechtenstein more than blinked, it folded.

In the not too distant past, one had to be a philatelist to know the Principality of Liechtenstein even existed. In those days, the nation's major export was exquisitely produced postage stamps, highly prized by collectors. Until the 1960s, the tiny principality subsisted on income from tourism, postage stamp sales and the export of false teeth.

In the last 60 years, its tax free financial privacy propelled Liechtenstein to top rank among the world's wealthiest nations. This historic Rhine Valley principality grew into a major world tax and asset haven, posting the second highest per capita income level in the world, after Monaco; US$134,617 in 2013, according to the World Bank — higher than Germany, France and the United Kingdom.

Absolute Monarchy

The Prince of Liechtenstein, Johannes "Hans" Adam Ferdinand Alois Josef Maria Marco d'Aviano Pius Fürst von und zu Liechtenstein, rules the government in a constitutional monarchy as head of state. In a 2003 referendum, Hans-Adam II won an overwhelming majority in favor of changing the constitution to give him powers greater than any other European monarch. The Prince ("Fürst" in German) owns LGT banking group, has a family fortune of $7.6 billion and a personal fortune of about $4.0 billion.

Liechtenstein's ruling Prince has the right to dismiss governments and approve judicial nominees. The Prince may also veto laws simply by refusing to sign them within a six-month period. Tempering this authority is the fact that the signature of 1,500 Liechtenstein citizens on a petition is sufficient to force a referendum on the abolition of the monarchy, or any other change in the law.

In 2004 Prince Hans-Adam II has ceded day-to-day rule of the country to his son, Prince Alois, now 47, while he remains the official head of state. This was seen as the first step towards the eventual full succession of power to Prince Alois.

Financial Center

Liechtenstein's economy is well diversified and it is, for its small size, one of the most heavily industrialized countries in Europe.

Still, financial services provide a third of GDP. Its 16 locally owned banks, 60 law firms and 250 trust companies employ 16% of the workforce. Its licensed fiduciary companies and lawyers serve as nominees for, or manage, more than 80,000 legal entities, most of them owned and controlled by nonresidents of Liechtenstein.

Although only 16% of workers are in the financial sector, financial services account for 30% of the gross national product, with industry and manufacturing trade (4%), general services (25%) and agriculture and households (5%). Forty-six percent of the workforce is employed in the industrial sector and 40% of employees work in other service activities, such as trade, hotels and restaurants, transport and public administration. About 12,000 workers commute daily from Austria and Switzerland. GDP has grown as much as 10% annually in recent years and unemployment stays below 2%.

Liechtenstein has positioned itself as "an oasis of political and economic stability" amidst the chaos of European debt crisis and despite significant pressure to tighten control over tax evaders. Leaders of this nation have distanced themselves from the "tax haven" label.

Liechtenstein was one of the first nations in the world to adopt specific offshore asset protection laws, as far back as the 1920s. Indeed, Liechtenstein's unique role in international circles was not so much as a banking center, but as — that hated phrase — a tax haven.

The nation still acts as a base of operations for foreign holding companies, private foundations, family foundations and a unique entity called the *Anstalt* (i.e., establishment). The banks and a host of specialized trust companies provide management services for thousands of such entities. Personal and company tax rates are low, generally under 12% for local residents.

Any company domiciled in Liechtenstein is granted total exemption from income tax if it generates no income from local sources. Low business taxes — the maximum tax rate is 20% — and easy incorporation rules have induced many holding companies to establish nominal offices in Liechtenstein providing 30% of state revenues. Foreign-owned holding companies are a major presence in Liechtenstein, with many maintaining their accounts in Swiss banks

Liechtenstein is independent, but closely tied to Switzerland in a customs union. The Swiss franc is the local currency and Liechtenstein's status is that of a de facto province operating within Switzerland. Liechtenstein banks are integrated into Switzerland's banking system and capital markets. Many cross-border investments clear in or through Swiss banks.

Reputation

For the most part, Liechtenstein had an impeccable reputation with government regulators stressing the professional qualifications and local accountability of its well-trained financial managers. Liechtenstein's reaction to outside demands for stronger anti-money laundering laws and combatting foreign tax evasion has been in keeping with its conservative history.

In 2001, Liechtenstein was removed from the Financial Action Task Force (FATF) blacklist after it adopted tough anti-money laundering laws that covered "all crimes;" created a Financial Intelligence Unit (FIU); imposed much stricter "know-your-customer" and suspicious activity reporting laws; eased its historic, strict financial secrecy; and abolished the rights of trustees and lawyers not to disclose the identity of their clients to banks where funds are invested.

Liechtenstein's longstanding tax haven status was the source of criticism by the OECD, which placed the principality on its questionable, 41-nation FATF "harmful tax practices" blacklist because of its low taxes.

Stolen Names

Until 2008, Liechtenstein managed to stay on the good side of the self-appointed international busybodies who make it their duty to attack tax havens and, most especially, demand an end to bank secrecy.

It was then revealed that the German government illegally had bribed a disgruntled former Liechtenstein bank employee, Heinrich Kieber, to gain confidential bank information he had stolen from LGT Bank in Liechtenstein with 1,400 names of foreigners with LGT accounts.

The German secret police paid Kieber €5 million (US$7.9 million) for the stolen data, containing about 1,400 "client relationships," 600 of them Germans, a major haul for German tax collectors. Germany shared the information with the governments of Britain, France, Italy, Spain, Norway, Ireland, Netherlands, Sweden, Canada, the U.S., Australia and New Zealand.

Liechtenstein's billionaire royal family manages and controls LGT Bank and LGT Group. Banking secrecy and the government's refusal to share financial information, except in criminal cases, used to be one of Liechtenstein's leading selling points. LGT Bank and Liechtenstein authorities rightfully advanced the theory that high tax governments were using the stolen DVD and misinformation to scare people away from the principality and from its banks, which is what indeed happened.

After this highly publicized incident, the high tax governments of the G-20, assisted by the OECD, began a coordinated year-long "surrender now" phase in their decade long anti-tax haven campaign.

The worldwide publicity about the stolen bank list and the pressure from neighboring Germany, the G-20 countries and the OECD, seriously hurt the principality's financial bottom line. Liechtenstein's banking industry suffered a 60% drop in profits in 2009, in part due to the global economic downturn, but also because of questions about its future as a leading tax haven. Assets under management by the principality's 15 banks were down 22%. (Unlike in most other countries, Liechtenstein's banks did not ask for or require any government bailout support).

Liechtenstein was removed from the OECD black list of uncooperative tax havens in 2009 after it agreed to reveal foreign tax dodgers. Yielding to the pressure, the country all but eliminated its banking secrecy laws That scandal plus tough markets and a rise in value of the Swiss franc (Liechtenstein's official currency since 1924) slashed assets managed in the country from a 2007 peak of CHF171 billion (US$177 billion) to CHF117 billion (US$121 billion) at the start of 2012. In 2012, ratings agency Standard & Poor's confirmed its AAA rating for Liechtenstein, citing "stable and conservative policies…which we expect to continue."

Less Secrecy Guaranteed by Law

Bloomberg News reported: "Liechtenstein, a principality once fabled for its banking secrecy laws, is losing its perch as one of the world's top tax havens for the richest people on Earth."

The reason was and is clear: the principality has abandoned its strict bank secrecy laws, the main attraction for many foreigners in decades past. Until 2009, there was a near-total absence of any international treaties governing double taxation or exchange of information, with the one exception of a double tax agreement with neighboring Austria, primarily to cover taxes on people who commute across the border for work.

In 2009, Liechtenstein was one of the first acknowledged tax havens to adopt OECD tax information exchange standards that cover alleged foreign income tax evasion. As part of that major change in policy, the principality began negotiating tax information exchange treaties with other nations. In 2008, Liechtenstein and the United States signed a tax information exchange treaty that provides for direct cooperation between the two countries tax and judicial authorities. By 2015, Liechtenstein had signed 85 tax information exchange agreements, including one with the U.S.

Liechtenstein's financial secrecy statutes historically were considered even stronger than those in Switzerland. In almost every case of lawsuits or official requests it refused to divulge client information. The adoption of the OECD tax information exchange standard ended that tradition. Nevertheless, Liechtenstein claimed that it still would enforce its strict confidentiality law, with criminal penalties for unauthorized information release. In its promotional advertising, Liechtenstein keeps up the pretense of having strict bank secrecy.

Banks keep "know your customers" records of clients' identities, but supposedly these may not be made public except by judicial or official government order. Financial secrecy is also said to extend to trustees, lawyers, accountants and to anyone connected to the banking industry. All involved are subject to the disciplinary powers of Liechtenstein's Upper Court. A court order or an officially approved request showing cause from a foreign government still is required to release an account holder's bank records. Creditors seeking bank records face a time-consuming and costly process.

Big Bucks Banking

Liechtenstein's banks have no official minimum deposit requirements, but their stated goal is to lure high net-worth individuals as clients. Opening a discretionary portfolio management account generally requires a minimum of CHF1 million (US$1.34 million).

Trusts and limited companies registered here must pay an annual government fee of 0.1% of capital. Most banks also charge an annual management fee of 0.5% of total assets under their supervision. Bank, investment and professional fees here are at the top of the world scale.

If you're considering opening an offshore bank or investment account, Liechtenstein may be worth a comparative look if the level of your wealth permits it. The principality has benefits many other OFCs lack, including a strong economy, rock-solid (Swiss) currency, political stability and ease of access, plus a few added attractions of its own. The government guarantees all bank deposits against loss, regardless of the amount involved, even though there have been no recent bank failures.

Rob Vrijhof, senior partner in a leading Swiss investment firm and a senior member of The Sovereign Society's Council of Experts, for years has done considerable business in Liechtenstein on behalf of international investors. He has witnessed a noticeable cleaning up of suspect practices, together with a new willingness to accommodate legitimate foreign banking and investment. He says, "I recommend Liechtenstein unreservedly — if you can afford it."

Foundation/Trust/Corporation Options

Liechtenstein is known worldwide among lawyers for its highly original and innovative legal entities created by statute, some of them copies of other countries' laws.

Liechtenstein law allows limited liability companies (LLCs), but does not provide for formation of international business corporations (IBCs) as they are known elsewhere. Over the years, the country's legislators have been highly inventive when it comes to unusual and useful legal entities fashioned to serve special financial needs.

Government regulation of the *Anstalt* (see below), foundations, companies and trusts is extremely strict. This is primarily accomplished through training and regulation of managers, not by prying into the internal affairs of the entity or its holdings. As a result, business management services available in Liechtenstein are excellent in terms of quality, if somewhat slow in execution.

The *Anstalt*

Liechtenstein is perhaps best known for the *Anstalt*, sometimes described in English as an "establishment" (the German word's closest English equivalent). The *Anstalt* is a legal entity unique to Liechtenstein and is something of a hybrid somewhere between the trust and the corporation with which Americans are familiar.

The *Anstalt* may or may not have member shares. Control usually rests solely with the founder, or with surviving members of his or her family. Both have the power to allocate the profits as they see fit.

The law regulating *Anstalt* formation is extremely flexible, allowing nearly any kind of charter to be drafted. Depending on the desired result, *Anstalts* can take on any number of trust or corporation characteristics. They can be tailored to meet specific U.S. tax criteria, the basis for an IRS private letter ruling recognizing your *Anstalt* as either a trust or corporation.

Only limited information about those involved with an individual *Anstalt* or company appears on public records. The beneficial owners of a company do not appear by name in any register and their identity need not be disclosed to the Liechtenstein authorities.

On the other hand, diligent inquisitors may discover members of the board of directors by searching the Commercial Register. At least one member of the board must reside in Liechtenstein. Unlike U.S. corporations, the shares of a Liechtenstein company do not have to disclose the names of shareholders.

The Family Foundation

Liechtenstein's concept of a "foundation" is unique. Although Americans associate a foundation with a non-profit, tax-exempt organization, in Liechtenstein a foundation is an autonomous fund consisting of assets endowed by its founder for a specific, non-commercial purpose. The purpose can be very broad in scope, including religious and charitable goals.

One of the more common uses is as a so-called "pure family foundation." These vehicles are dedicated to the financial management and personal welfare of one or more particular families as beneficiaries. The foundation has no shareholders, partners, owners, or members — only beneficiaries. It can be either limited in time or perpetual.

The foundation and a beneficiary's interest therein cannot be assigned, sold, or attached by personal creditors. Only foundation assets are liable for its debts. If engaged in commercial activities, the foundation's activities must support noncommercial purposes, such as support of the family. Unless the foundation is active commercially, it can be created through an intermediary. The founder's name need not be made public. Foundations may be created by deed, under the terms of a will, or by a common agreement among family members.

A family foundation can sometimes be more useful than a trust, since it avoids many restrictive trust rules that limit control by the trust creator. On the issue of cost, a simple family foundation located here may cost US$30,000, while the same entity in Panama, where the law was copied in 1995, can cost as little as $15,000.

If you are interested in exploring the creation of a foundation, I recommend you obtain top quality tax and legal advice, both in your home country and in Liechtenstein.

Hybrid Trusts

You can use a Liechtenstein trust to control a family fortune, with the trust assets represented as shares in holding companies that control each of the relevant businesses that may be owned by the family. This legal strategy brings together various family holdings under one trust umbrella, which, in turn, serves as a legal conduit for wealth transfer to named heirs and beneficiaries.

Liechtenstein's trust laws are practical and interesting due to the country's unusual combination of civil law and common-law concepts. In 1926, the Liechtenstein Diet adopted a statutory reproduction of the English-American trust system. They even allow trust grantors to choose governing law from any common law country.

This places the Liechtenstein judiciary in the unique position of applying trust law from England, Bermuda, or Delaware (U.S.A.) when addressing a controversy regarding a particular trust instrument.

Even though it is a civil law nation, a trust located in Liechtenstein can be useful in lowering taxes, sheltering foreign income and safeguarding assets from American estate taxes. The law allows quick portability of trusts to another jurisdiction and accepts foreign trusts that wish to re-register as local entities. The trust instrument must be deposited with the Commercial Registry, but is not subject to public examination.

In 2009, revisions and updates of existing 70-year-old statutes by Parliament produced a new Foundation Act and amendments to the Law on Persons and Companies.

It is worth noting that some of the best life insurance, annuities and private placement polices are issued by companies in Liechtenstein, although they are usually purchased through Swiss based companies.

Taxes

In 2011, Liechtenstein adopted a first ever flat annual tax of 12.5% on the net earnings, including earnings from interest, of family foundations, trusts and corporations. The result of this new tax has been the re-domiciling of a number of Liechtenstein trusts, foundations and companies to Panama and other financial centers where no tax is imposed.

Low business taxes — the maximum tax rate is 20% — and easy incorporation rules have induced many holding or so-called letter box companies to establish nominal offices in Liechtenstein, providing 30% of state revenues.

The principality participates in a customs union with Switzerland and uses the Swiss franc as its national currency. It imports more than 90% of its energy requirements. Liechtenstein is a member of the European Economic Area, an organization that serves as a bridge between the European Free Trade Association and the EU.

Contacts

Government:

Embassy of Liechtenstein
2900 K Street NW, Suite 602B
Washington, D.C. 20007
Tel.: (202) 331-0590
Web: www.liechtensteinusa.org

The U.S. has no Embassy in Liechtenstein; the U.S. Ambassador to Switzerland is accredited to Liechtenstein.

United States Embassy
Sulgeneckstrasse 19, CH-3007 Bern, Switzerland
Tel.: + (031) 357-70 11
Email: bernacs@state.gov
Web: http://bern.usembassy.gov

U.S. Consular Agency Zürich
Dufourstrasse 101 3rd floor, Zürich, Switzerland
Mailing Address: Postfach 5266, 3001 Bern, Switzerland

Tel.: + (043) 499-29 60
Email: Zurich-CA@state.gov

Recommended Attorneys & Trust Company:

First Advisory Group
Dreikönigstrasse 12, CH-8002 Zürich, Switzerland
Tel.: +41 22 319 37 90
Web: http://www.firstadvisorygroup.com
Other locations include Geneva, Hong Kong, Panama, Singapore, and Vaduz

Recommended US SEC-registered financial advisor:

Robert Vrijhof, President
Weber, Hartmann, Vrijhof & Partners
Schaffhauserstrasse 418, CH-8050 Zürich, Switzerland
Tel.: 011 41-44-315 77 77
E-mail: info@whvp.ch
Web: http://www.whvp.ch

PRINCIPALITY OF MONACO: FOR THE ULTRA WEALTHY

Robert E. Bauman JD, *Where to Stash Your Cash*, 2015

Monaco is a tax haven for the exceedingly wealthy — and great wealth is what it takes to afford living here. It is home to many millionaires and billionaires from around the world, many of them retired and enjoying the good life.

The 1.08 square miles of Monaco on the French Riviera is home to over 33,000 people, but this unique and ancient principality is not for everyone. If you want to make this your permanent home, it helps to have more than a modest amount of money and an assured income for life. And it doesn't hurt to know the Prince and his royal family.

Monaco, in general, is for individuals who have already made their money — people who want to practice the art of living while others mind the store for them; people who want to spend time on the Riviera. If tax avoidance is the only goal, there are cheaper places to do it.

Many residents are just upper class people who have decided to retire in Monaco. They are drawn to the pleasant atmosphere, Mediterranean climate and leisure. Monaco has all the facilities that wealthy people consider necessary: country clubs, health clubs, golf and tennis clubs. Indeed, Monaco may have a small population and area, but it has all the services and cultural activities of a city the size of San Francisco.

Monaco's prices are expensive, but no worse than London, Paris, or Geneva. These days, there are as many Italian restaurants as there are French ones. Long before the euro, money of any kind was the European common currency in this principality.

Monaco is high profile. The world remembers Grace Kelly, the Hollywood film star, who married Prince Rainier in 1956. The international spotlight followed her until she died in a tragic car accident in 1982. During his long rule, Prince Rainier III worked hard to expand the economic and professional scope of the country. Few recent monarchs can claim credit for extending their dominions by one-fifth without conquest. But, by land filling the sea, the Prince managed to expand his tiny principality by 23% in his long reign beginning in 1949. This land expansion mirrored the late Prince Rainier's determination to make this a dynamic modern mini state.

Monaco is stable and any major changes are unlikely to come from inside. In 1997, the Principality celebrated its 700th anniversary of life under the rule of the Grimaldi family.

Three months after the death of his father, Prince Rainier III, on April 6, 2005, Prince Albert II formally acceded to the throne on July 12, 2005. The Grimaldi children had wild personal reputations and the details of their private lives constantly appeared in the gossip columns of the European press. As they have aged, things have calmed down, although Prince Albert has acknowledged paternity of a child born to an African airline hostess and another born to California woman.

Monaco has also been at the heart of a remarkable economic development based around trading, tourism and financial services in a tax friendly environment. Monaco manages to generate annually over US$8 billion worth of business. The state has an annual income of €593 million (US$800 million), carries no debts and possesses unpublished liquid reserves of at least US$1.8 billion.

The Principality is no longer just a frivolous playground for the rich, although its government is funded primarily through casino gambling proceeds. Ever since Monaco's famed casino opened in 1856, the tourism industry has been booming. It currently accounts for close to 25% of the annual revenue. But Monaco is now a modern economy participating at a global level in a diverse range of sectors.

Some people may find Monaco's police presence a little severe. The Principality has the lowest crime rate of any highly urbanized area in the world. This physical security is, of course, one of its great advantages.

Significant Tax Benefits for Residents

Undeniably, there are tax benefits to be gained from a move to Monaco. The authorities do not like the Principality to be known as the tax haven that, in fact, it is. It's a low-tax area rather than a no-tax area, but still a haven. Since

1869, there have been no income taxes for Monegasque nationals and resident foreigners — one of the main attractions for high net worth individuals. There are no direct, withholding or capital gains taxes for foreign nationals, except for the French, who because of a bilateral tax treaty with Paris, cannot escape the clutches of the French tax system. There are first-time residential registration taxes, but no ongoing real estate taxes.

Banking

The principality is a major banking center and has successfully sought to diversify into services and small, high-value-added, nonpolluting industries. The state has no income tax and low business taxes and thrives as a tax haven both for individuals who have established residence and for foreign companies that have set up businesses and offices.

There are corporate and banking advantages, too. Confidentiality is good as far as business records go and the same can be said for the banking services. The Bank of France is responsible for the Monegasque banking system and carries out regular inspections. The banking services in Monaco are not as comprehensive as they could be. There is a strong anti-money laundering law. The normal minimum for opening a bank account is €300,000, about US$400,000. Banking secrecy is strict, but the government exchanges information about French citizens with neighboring France and in 2009 it announced its intention to abide by OECD standards governing exchange of tax information in cases of alleged foreign tax evasion.

Residency and Citizenship

It is actually much easier to obtain a residency permit here than many might suppose. A clean record, solid bank references and a net worth of US$500,000 should do it. Fees for establishing residency are likely to cost in the US$10,000 to $20,000 range.

The Principality has offered financial and fiscal concessions to foreign nationals for a long time. These have been restricted by the Conventions with France in 1963 and, more recently, by agreements with France after pressure from the EU. And here lies the major concern. Monaco isn't likely to initiate changes. But the rest of Europe, especially France, which has always exhibited a jealous dog-in-the-manger attitude towards the Principality, might pressurize it into getting into line.

If you're on the move already, stability may not be an important issue. However, you might be looking for a base and would do well to consider Monaco. The lifestyle is attractive, but is not everybody's cup of tea. If you are contemplating a move purely for financial or fiscal reasons, you might, depending on your specific requirements, do better elsewhere.

Once there, keep a low profile. Foreign nationals who are resident are afraid to make any public criticisms of the country. Why? If the authorities consider you a troublemaker, they can issue a 24-hour notice of expulsion. There's no one to appeal to and you'll be out the door.

Contacts

Government:

Embassy of Monaco
3400 International Dr. NW, Suite 2K 100
Washington, D.C. 20008
Tel.: (202) 234-1530
Email: info@monacodc.org
Web: http://www.monacodc.org

Diplomatic representation of the U.S. to Monaco is handled by the U.S. Embassy in Paris:

United States Embassy
2 Avenue Gabriel, 75382 Paris Cedex 8, France
Tel.: + (33) 1-4312-2222
Web: http://france.usembassy.gov

U.S. Consulate General at Marseille is located at:
Place Varian Fry, 13286 Marseille Cedex 6, France
Tel.: 01 43 12 47 54
Web: http://marseille.usconsulate.gov

Banks:

Crédit Foncier de Monaco (CFM)
Web: https://www.ca-indosuez.com/monaco/fr

For a list of additional banks: http://www.monaco-privatebanking.com/en

Legal, Tax, & Accounting Advisors:

Moores Rowland Monaco
2 Avenue de Monte-Carlo, B.P. 343 98006
Tel.: +377 97 97 00 22
Email: mr@mri.mc
Web: http://www.mri.mc

CAMPIONE D'ITALIA: WHERE TAXES ARE NON-TRADITIONAL

Robert E. Bauman JD, *Where to Stash Your Cash*, 2015

This little bit of northern Italy is an enclave completely surrounded by Switzerland and it's one of the least-known residential tax havens in the world. But you must buy a condo or home to become a resident. In the past, foreigners who could afford to live here and foreign-owned businesses paid few taxes. It may be Italian territory, but everything here is Swiss — auto license plates, currency, postage, communications and banking, but the taxes are Italian.

"Commune di Campione," as the Italians call it, on the shores of beautiful Lake Lugano, is distinguished by its uniqueness; a little plot of Italian soil, completely surrounded by the southern Swiss canton of Ticino. Although in the middle of Swiss territory, it is an Italian commune (municipality) of the Province of Como, an enclave separated from the rest of Italy by Lake Lugano and mountains; eleven miles north of the Swiss/Italian border town of Chiasso and five miles by road from Lugano, Switzerland, a beautiful scenic drive around the lake.

We have visited Campione and recommend its beauty. It is a very pleasant place to live, located in the heart of one of the best Swiss and nearby Italian tourist areas of Lombardy. The region boasts lakes, winter sports, and the cultural activities of Milan, Italy, are only one-hour south by auto.

Until his death in 777 AD, Campione was the private land of one Sr. Totone Campione, after whom it is named. He willed it to the Archbishop of the Milan. Over ensuing centuries his testamentary bequest endured a tug of war for control between Italy and Switzerland. At one point it was part of the Austrian empire. After the fall of Napoleon, the 1815 Congress of Vienna rejected the Swiss claim and it remained part of the "Kingdom of Lombardy" (Northern Italy) until 1861, when it was awarded to the Kingdom of Italy. Detached geographically from the rest of Italy, it has remained sovereign Italian soil ever since.

There are no border controls and complete freedom of travel. Home to less than 3,000 people (including about a thousand foreign residents), this mountainside village uses Swiss banks, currency, postal service, and telephone system. Even automobile license plates are Swiss. All that's needed to become an official resident is to rent or buy property here, although formal registration is required. However, living here is very expensive; you might have to pay US$750,000 for a very small townhouse. Foreigners may buy real estate without restrictions, unlike in Switzerland.

Real estate prices are well above those in surrounding Ticino. Condominiums range from US$5,500 to $6,500 per square meter, and broker fees add a 3% commission. The real estate market is very small, hence the extremely high prices. This small market is served by a few local real estate agents, some of whom operate rather unprofessionally and some even without a license. A foreign buyer has to be very careful. If you are interested in establishing your residence in Campione and purchasing real estate there, you should be represented by a competent lawyer from the beginning. (See the end of this section for reliable professional contacts in the area we recommend.)

Corporations

Corporations registered in Campione have some advantages over Swiss companies. They use Swiss banking facilities and have a mailing address that appears to be Swiss, while escaping Switzerland's income and withholding taxes. Corporations are governed by Italian corporate law and can be formed with a minimum capitalization of about US$1,000.

Corporations can be owned and directed entirely by foreigners, a status Swiss law limits to some degree. Corporate registrations are usually handled by Italian lawyers in nearby Milan, and fees are modest. As part of Italy, EU business regulations do apply to Campione businesses, as do Italian corporate taxes, which can be high.

The official currency is the Swiss franc, but the euro is accepted as well. All banking is done through Swiss banks, which gives its residents additional financial privacy.

Taxes

A famous casino did generate substantial revenue, which is among the reasons local residents enjoyed some special tax concessions. Until 2006, there were clear tax advantages to living in Campione. But when gambling was made legal in Switzerland, the casino, which was Campione's only major income source, declined. To make up the deficit some Italian personal income and corporate taxes were levied. But Campione is still exempt from Italian VAT.

Tax advantages only apply to private persons residing in Campione, and not to companies domiciled or managed from there. Residents of Campione do not pay the full Italian income tax.

Based on a special provision in Italian law, the first CHF200'000 (US$205,000) of income is exchanged into euro, the official currency in Italy, at a special exchange rate. This results in a lower effective income and consequently a lower tax rate is applied. Other than this special concession, the Italian tax laws and tax rates apply.

Taxation of an individual's income in Italy is progressive. In 2013 the tax rate for an individual was between 23%-43%. In addition to direct taxation there is also a regional tax of 1.2%-2.03% and a municipal tax of 0.1%-0.8%. The standard rate of Italian corporate tax in 2013 was 27.5%. In addition, local tax is imposed at a rate of 3.9%, bringing the effective tax rate to 31.4%.

There is no local inheritance or gift taxes but inheritances of spouses and direct descendants are subject to an Italian inheritance tax at a rate of 4% on the amount exceeding €1,000,000 per beneficiary (US$1,326 million). Transfers to brothers or sisters are taxed at 6% on the amount exceeding €100,000. Income from interest of foreign bonds paid through an Italian bank is taxed at a special, reduced rate of 12.5%. Capital gains taxes range from 12.5% to 27.5%.

To say that the Italian authorities are less than zealous in collecting taxes in Campione is an understatement. Unlike Switzerland or Italy, at this writing, Campione has no tax treaties, but Italy has signed 97 double taxation treaties, and exchanges tax information under OECD Article 26.

Residence

To obtain a Campione residence permit, you must buy an apartment or a house. There is very rarely an opportunity to rent. Clearance from the Italian police, as well as approval by the local Campione authorities is also required. While residence permits are issued by Italian authorities, as we said, access to the territory of Campione is governed by Swiss visa regulations.

This means that the passport you hold should allow you to enter Switzerland without a visa, otherwise you will have to apply for a Swiss visa beforehand. A passport is required for entry into Switzerland but a visa is not required for U.S. citizens for stays of up to 90 days.

Obtaining facts about Campione is much more difficult than for other tax havens because the enclave does not promote itself. There is no central office of information. Outsiders are not unwelcome, but no one readily volunteers news about this secret haven. A personal visit is mandatory for anyone seriously interested in making this their home.

Contacts

Government:

Amministrazione Comunale, Comune di Campione d'Italia
Tel.: 031 27 24 63
Email: protocollo@comunecampione.ch
Web: http://www.comune.campione-d-italia.co.it

Tourist Guide:

Azienda Turistica
Corso Italia n. 2
22060 Campione d'Italia
Tel.: 004191 649 50 51
Email: aptcampione@ticino.com
Web: http://www.campioneitalia.com

Real Estate:

AGENCY c/o DOMTVUOJ s.r.l.
Campione d'Italia, Via Antonio Bezzola 2
Tel.: +41 (0) 91 649 63 45
E-mail: info@immowehner.com
Web: http://www.elitehomeseurope.com/campioneditalia-real-estate

Residence & Citizenship Assistance:

Henley & Partners
Klosbachstrasse 110, 8024 Zürich, Switzerland
Tel.: +41 44 266 22 22
Web: http://www.henleyglobal.com

ASIA

THE COOK ISLANDS: FAR OUT

Robert E. Bauman JD, *Where to Stash Your Cash*, 2015

Way out in the South Pacific (in the middle of nowhere) are the Cook Islands — home to a very modern set of offshore financial laws that may be just what you need: iron-clad asset protection trusts, IBCs, limited liability partnerships and a very strict financial privacy law that protects your personal business. But some people don't like too much distance between themselves and their assets and — let's face it — for most people these islands are very far out.

Independent but Dependent

If you're researching the more esoteric part of the world of offshore asset protection, you'll soon hear about the Cook Islands. Since a quarter of a century ago when the government first began adopting (and updating) a series of wealth and asset-friendly laws in 1981, the Cook Islands — though small in population and remote from the rest of the world — have come to play a definite role in offshore financial circles.

A broad net of 15 coral islands in the central heart of the South Pacific, the Cook Islands are spread over 850,000 square miles, southwest of Tahiti and due south of Hawaii. The islands occupy an area the size of India, with a declining population (12,000+), no bigger than an American small town. Local time is 10 hours behind GMT, with 9:00 am in Hong Kong being 3:00 pm the previous day in the Cook Islands. This geographic location gives the Cook Islands a strategic advantage in dealing with both the Asian and American markets.

Indirectly, the islands are part of the British Commonwealth by virtue of their unique association with nearby New Zealand. From 1901 to 1965, this was a colony of New Zealand and NZ still subsidizes the CI government. The New Zealand subsidy has become a sore point in both nations. The islanders even enjoy dual New Zealand and Cook Islands citizenship. There is a written CI constitution with a Westminster-style parliament elected every four years by universal suffrage. The legal system is based on British common law and closely reflects that of New Zealand and other Commonwealth jurisdictions.

Planned Offshore Center

The Cook Islands' offshore industry was the result of the government's official collaboration with the local financial services industry. Financial services now rank second only to tourism in the economy. Despite some 50,000 visitors a year to the capital island, Rarotonga, the Cook Islands have remained largely unspoiled. Cook Islanders have their own language and enjoy a vigorous and diverse culture, though most speak English. The New Zealand dollar is the local currency, but most offshore transactions are in U.S. dollars.

This is a micro-state with macro aspirations, but the grasp may have exceeded the reach. Their checkered history of high finance has been marked by some scandals, sponsored by fast-talking American, U.K. and New Zealand expatriates. It's no secret that certain American asset protection attorneys have played a large role in advising the government on asset protection issues, actually drafting statutes for the island's parliament.

Constantly teetering on the brink of bankruptcy, the CI government is chronically in debt, much of it a result of bad decisions. Two-thirds of the workforce is on the government payroll, financing an old fashioned spoils and patronage system that would make an American big-city political boss blush. In the 1980s and 1990s, the country lived beyond its means, maintaining a bloated public service and accumulating a large foreign debt. Subsequent reforms, including the sale of state assets, the strengthening of economic management, the encouragement of tourism, and a debt restructuring agreement, have rekindled investment and growth.

Tailored Wealth Protection

But don't let the deficits and the distance put you off. There is much here to cheer the hearts of knowledgeable offshore financial enthusiasts.

Existing statutes meticulously provide for the care and feeding of IBCs, including offshore banks, insurance companies and trusts. All offshore business conducted on the Cook Islands must be channeled through one of the five registered trustee companies. A comprehensive range of trustee and corporate services is offered for offshore investors. The government officially guarantees no taxes will be imposed on offshore entities. Thousands of foreign trusts, corporations and partnerships are registered here, protected by an exceedingly strong financial privacy law, although that has been tempered by the adoption of the OECD Article 26 standards for the exchange of tax information among governments. In 2009, the Cook Island's government welcomed the G-20 call for more transparency in tax information and adopted necessary amendments to its tax laws to conform to the new standard.

The Development Investment Act requires all foreign enterprises (those with more than one-third foreign ownership) to first obtain approval and register their planned activities with the Cook Islands Development Investment Board. There are various incentives and concessions for tariff protection; import duty and levy concessions; tax concessions by way of accelerated depreciation; allowance for counterpart training; and recruitment of Cook Islanders from overseas.

Updated Laws

The Cook Islands systematically has adopted a series of new anti-money laundering, financial reporting and anti-financial-crime laws. These laws were sufficient to get them removed from the Financial Action Task Force blacklist, which was their stated objective.

The laws liberalize the extent to which local financial institutions are obligated to disclose information and override all other laws, making compliance with anti-money-laundering laws and standards paramount. However, the law instituted a procedure which provides due process before any information can be released, including a formal request to the Financial Intelligence Unit showing reasonable grounds to believe that money laundering or criminal activities have taken place. This ensures that any information disclosed is done through proper channels with legal justification. This procedure is also used for tax information exchange requests from foreign governments.

International companies incorporated here have a great deal of flexibility in corporate structure with provisions for ease of administration and maximum benefit in global commercial transactions. Incorporation can be completed within 24 hours.

In 1989, by an amendment to the International Trusts Act 1984, the Cook Islands introduced the asset protection trust (APT). This legislation at the time was considered cutting edge and has since been copied and adopted by other offshore centers. The Cook Islands also has laws allowing international banking and insurance business to be conducted tax free, also with strong privacy protections. Both government and trust companies here constantly develop new products to meet the complexities of the offshore world.

Strict Confidentiality

Strong financial and banking secrecy provisions apply in the offshore regime, requiring government officials as well as trustee company and bank employees to observe strict secrecy backed by criminal sanctions. The official registrar records of foreign companies and of international trusts are not open for general search, with defined exceptions under the Financial Transactions Reporting Act of 2004 and the Proceeds of Crimes Act of 2003.

In a major American legal case, the U.S. government tried to force the repatriation of funds under a Cook Island trust and lost, even though the Americans who created the trust for a time were jailed for contempt of court. Not even a federal court could crack the Cook Island trust laws. See the decision known as the "Anderson case" (*FTC* vs. *Affordable Media LLC*, 179 F. 3rd 1228, U.S. Ct. of Appeals, 9th Cir. 1999).

In 2009, the OECD listed the Cook Islands as one of the tax havens committed to the internationally agreed tax information exchange standard but one that had not yet substantially implemented it. The CI government says it is committed to the OECD Article 26 standard and will implement it.

Conclusion

Don't let those thousands of miles of distance scare you. Your offshore attorney is a lot closer to you and he or she should know how to use the Cook Islands and their asset protection laws to your benefit.

Contacts

Ministry of Finance & Economic Management: http://mfem.gov.ck

Puai T. Wichman Esq., Managing Director
Ora Fiduciary (Cook Islands) Limited
Global House, P.O. Box 92, Avarua, Rarotonga, Cook Islands
Tel.: (+682) 27047
USA Direct Tel.: (734) 402-7047
Email: puai@oratrust.com or info@oratrust.com
Web: http://oratrust.com

Capital Security Bank
P.O. Box 906, Centrepoint, Avarua, Rarotonga, Cook Islands
Tel.: 682 22505
Email: info@csb.co.ck
Web: https://www.capitalsecuritybank.com

THE REPUBLIC OF SINGAPORE
Robert E. Bauman JD, *Where to Stash Your Cash*, 2015

Singapore has fashioned itself into a major international financial center — but it's not exactly an offshore tax haven. It has traded its ancient Oriental image for towers of concrete and glass and rickshaws have been replaced by high-tech industry. Singapore appears shockingly modern, but this is an Asian city with Chinese, Malay and Indian traditions from *feng shui* to ancestor worship as part of daily life. These contrasts bring the city to life, but foreigners may want to avoid talking about local politics.

With his death in 2015, Singaporeans are asking whether the house that its founder, Lee Kuan Yew built, modern Singapore and his vaunted "Singapore model," will survive him, or has the sleek Asian financial hub outgrown the father-knows-best style of government?

The Republic of Singapore (population 5.46 million) has the distinction of its 277-square miles being a small island, a state and a city — all in one. Located just a few steamy miles north of the Equator, it has Malaysia and Indonesia as close and sometimes uneasy neighbors. The climate is hot and very humid, with rainfall of over two meters (about seven feet) annually.

Colonial Singapore gained its independence from Great Britain in 1965. Lee Kuan Yew became its autocratic leader and served until 1990, when his son, Lee Hsien Loong, now in office, replaced him in his official capacities. Until his death at the age of 91 in 2015, the father remained the power behind his son's throne and their one-party state does not tolerate dissent or opposition. There are no jury trials. Civil matters, such as alleged libel or slander, can escalate into criminal issues with serious consequences, especially for political opponents. It has been called "a utopian police state." But as The Economist observed: "Under him Singapore, with no natural resources, was transformed from a tiny struggling island into one of the world's richest countries."

Draconian laws keep crime (and freedom) to a minimum, but the enforced stability attracts massive foreign investment. Moreover, as visitors can attest, the streets are very clean, since spitting or littering can land you in jail. Clean streets are a tradeoff for individual political freedom. And as recent local election results suggest, opposition to such restrictions is increasing. With the death of Lee Kuan Yew, there may be a chance for greater freedom.

Offshore Financial Center

As a city, Singapore routinely tops world rankings. In 2014 it placed fourth in the Global Financial Centers index; it is the best city for "transportation and infrastructure," according to PricewaterhouseCoopers; the best place in the world to do business, according to the Economist Intelligence Unit; in a virtual deadlock with Hong Kong for first place in the 2015 Index of Economic Freedom. Rather as Hong Kong's prosperity was based on being Chinese but not entirely part of China, Singapore has flourished by being in South-East Asia, but not of it.

But as *Salon* says: "But if money is free in Singapore, people are not. Speech, expression and assembly are all tightly controlled; the justice system is notoriously harsh. Migrant workers are treated poorly; labor organizers are deported. There is no minimum wage, and the Gini co-efficient for inequality is among the highest in the developed world."

"Singapore is improving," its defenders insist. But Reporters Without Borders in 2014 ranked it 151st of 180 nations in press freedoms, down from 135 in 2012. *The Economist* magazine's rigorous Democracy Index ranked it with Liberia, Palestine and Haiti.

Nevertheless, Singapore has grown into a world offshore financial haven, certainly comparable to Hong Kong and way ahead of its neighbor, fledgling Labuan in nearby Malaysia. Singapore has cultivated a sophisticated private banking sector, offering discreet financial services aimed at luring wealthy clients. Many Swiss banks have been here for several years and in 2015 it was reported that BNP, Credit Suisse, Morgan Stanley and UBS all were trying to hire more private bankers in Singapore to service wealthy mainland Chinese clients. As does Hong Kong, it sees itself as a second financial gateway to expanding China, the eventual colossus of the East.

Free trade and export zones weren't invented in Singapore, but they were perfected here. Tax incentives and low labor costs pulled in industries and multi-national corporations, making Singapore the No. 1 location for multinationals' headquarters in East Asia.

In recent years, Singapore has emerged as the financial service center for African and Middle Eastern sovereign wealth funds wanting to put oil and natural resource money to work in Asia, as well as for Western money seeking investments in Southeast Asia.

Modern infrastructure, developed capital markets, an educated workforce, comparatively stable political institutions and a low crime rate are added attractions. Singapore is viewed as highly developed with some of the best investment potential in Asia and with some of the lowest levels of economic corruption. It has attracted investors seeking profits as well as those seeking safety outside the U.S. dollar.

Singapore is reportedly the world's fourth-largest foreign exchange center after London, New York and Tokyo, and is home to many businesses, multinational corporations, banks and financial investment companies. It holds the world's ninth-largest foreign exchange reserves, impressive for a small country. The currency is the Singapore dollar and it has become a safe haven currency, similar to the Swiss franc.

Singapore also provides investors the ability to access other regional markets. A number of companies with direct ties to Myanmar, Vietnam, Thailand and other neighboring economies are listed on the Singapore Exchange, providing a convenient way to invest in regional growth.

Singapore has become a financial melting pot attracting foreign corporate foot soldiers and investors. That benefits key Singapore industries such as banking as well as tourism and real estate. Regional business travelers and tourists now visit for shopping, casinos and finance.

Singapore has attracted major investments in pharmaceuticals and medical technology production and actively seeks to establish itself as Southeast Asia's financial and high-tech hub.

It has a highly developed and successful free-market economy. In spite of political repression, it enjoys a remarkably open and corruption-free environment, stable prices, and a per capita GDP ($62,400 in 2013) higher than most developed countries. The economy depends heavily on exports, particularly in consumer electronics, information technology products, pharmaceuticals, and on a growing financial services sector.

The common language is English. Most Singaporeans are Asian, with commerce dominated by ethnic Chinese. Malays make up 15%, with a mix of Indians, Thais, Vietnamese, Laotians and a very small number of Europeans. Europeans hold most management positions and are generally well regarded. In Singapore, state regulation has created a paradise, if you like high-rise buildings, crass materialism and minimal personal freedom.

Many Swiss banks, such as Bank Julius Baer, have expanded their operations in Singapore to capitalize on the new business opportunities. In 2013 the Swiss National Bank opened a small branch in Singapore, being the first non-Asian official central bank to do so. The number of private banks operating in Singapore has nearly doubled to 35 in the past seven years, according to officials. The Singapore Monetary Authority estimates that assets held by banks in Singapore has grown 20% each year since 2000 to more than US$800 billion in 2014.

Taxes

Singapore is not necessarily a tax haven. The government supports welfare state programs of free schools, low-fee universities, childcare, socialized medicine and subsidized housing.

But as competitors, the two Asian financial hubs of Singapore and Hong Kong have kept personal and corporate taxes among the lowest in the world to attract more foreign investment. Top individual income tax rates are 20% in Singapore and 17% in Hong Kong, compared with 35% at the federal level in the United States.

The two Asian financial centers also have simpler taxation systems than the U.S. and other countries. Businesses make an average of three tax payments per year in Hong Kong and five in Singapore, compared with 11 in the U.S. and a global average of 28.5 per year. The tax codes are also more transparent so that many small businesses don't require a tax consultant or adviser.

The corporate tax rate in Singapore is 17% and the GST (goods and services or VAT) tax applies only when annual sales exceed S$1 million (US$782,000). Dividends and capital gains earned from foreign subsidiaries/branches are tax exempt. There is no withholding tax on dividend distribution by Singapore based companies. The withholding tax on interest is 15 % and on royalties 10%.

Personal income tax rates are some of the lowest globally and based on residence. Individuals pay tax ranging at rates of 0% to 20% and amount ranging from $0 to $42,350.

There are no capital gains or inheritance taxes. Under a territorial tax system income from offshore sources are tax exempt; only income earned in Singapore is taxed. Non-residents are taxed on Singapore net income after expenses at 15% for employment income and 20% for director's and consultant fees.

Foreigners can incorporate with a single shareholder, one resident director with a local address, and a minimum paid up capital of S$1 within 48 hours. Self-registration isn't permitted but for foreign individuals or entities, professional firms provide company formation and local nominee directors. Work visas are available for foreigners for employment, entrepreneurs or short-term for attending to business.

Modern infrastructure, developed capital markets, an educated workforce, comparatively stable political institutions and a low crime rate are added attractions. Negatives are a high cost of living for employees, (the city's cost of living index is the highest in the world), mandatory filing of audited accounts of a foreign parent company, and mandatory designation of an active local secretary.

We visited Singapore for a legal conference and personally saw how local trust laws have been updated on a par with leading offshore trust nations, such as Bermuda or Panama. Singapore strengthened its bank secrecy laws, originally patterned after the strict privacy laws in Switzerland, and more recently including Swiss-like compromises on strict bank secrecy.

Under pressure from the G-20 major nations, the government joined other OFCs and adopted the OECD standards governing the exchange of tax information among nations. It honors bona fide requests for tax information. Instead of signing separate TIEAs, it amended existing double tax agreements with other countries to include information exchange provisions and Singapore is now officially on to the OECD "white list."

Immigration

The government actively recruits wealthy businesspersons as residents. For those active in offshore finance, the island city-state wants to establish itself as Asia's newest private banking hub by luring the super-wealthy away from places such as Hong Kong and even Switzerland.

The government allows foreigners, especially Europeans, who meet its wealth requirements, to buy land and become permanent residents. The goal is to attract private wealth from across Asia, as well as riches that Europeans and other Westerners are moving out of Switzerland and European Union nations to avoid new tax and reporting laws there.

Singapore, which occupies an area about half the size of the city of Houston, Texas, has added about one million people since 2004 with government encouragement to make up for a declining birth rate. This has contributed to crowded transportation and more competition for jobs, housing and places in schools, fueling voter anger that led to the ruling party's smallest electoral win in 2011 since independence in 1965.

Foreigners and permanent residents make up more than a third of the island's 5.4 million population. The majority of new citizens come from countries other than China, nearly half from Southeast Asia. The surge of new arrivals from China was part of a government immigration push that almost doubled Singapore's population to 5.4 million since 1990.

The government has made it more expensive for companies to hire overseas workers by raising taxes and in 2012 it increased salary thresholds and required better educational qualifications for some categories of foreigners.

Tensions over immigration are problems in many nations, but most of Singapore's population was already ethnic Chinese, many born of earlier Chinese immigrants. Some locals now blame mainland Chinese for driving up real-estate prices, stealing the best jobs and clogging the roads with flashy European sports cars.

The government reacted by adjusting immigration downward. New permanent residents have decreased two-thirds since 2008, when 80,000 applications were accepted and the number of people granted citizenship has remained level at about 18,500 a year. But in spite of the growing complaints, Singapore remains the third-most desirable immigration destination for affluent Chinese after the United States and Canada, according to a survey by the Bank of China.

Political Change

The year 2012 saw an increased civic activism sweeping this highly politically controlled island. Many of the loudest vocal activists are young, wired and cynical about the government's argument that it alone can maintain the prosperity and social harmony that has transformed this resource-starved island into one of the most advanced economies.

Activists say some opposition started in the 1990s, but was seen in 2011 when the governing People's Action Party lost six seats in the 87-member Parliament. The PAP has dominated politics since 1959 and is headed by Prime Minister Lee Hsien Loong, the son of the late Lee Kuan Yew, Singapore's founding father. The PAP support in the most recent 2011 election dropped to a historic low of 60%, down 6 points from the previous election, but the PAP got more than 90% of the seats.

Public rallies have demanded repeal of the anti-subversion law coinciding with the 25th anniversary of Operation Spectrum, a crackdown on activists that led to the arrest of 22 student leaders, lawyers and teachers grabbed in nighttime raids and forced, in what they alleged were harsh interrogations, to confess to an anti-government plot.

Over the years, legal advocates here claim more than 2,600 people have been arrested under the Internal Security Act, which allows the authorities to imprison suspects without trial.

Based on the past 50 years of local history, no one is predicting any huge public agitation or the end of Singapore's one party rule, but political types do say increasingly people are dropping traditional reluctance to challenge Singapore's paternalistic leaders and their "autocratic light" style of governance.

Contacts

Government:

Government of Singapore: http://www.gov.sg

Monetary Authority of Singapore: http://www.mas.gov.sg

Embassy of the Republic of Singapore
3501 International Place NW

Washington, D.C. 20008
Tel.: (202) 537-3100
Email: singemb_was@mfa.sg
Web: http://www.mfa.gov.sg/washington

United States Embassy
27 Napier Road, Singapore 258508
Tel.: + (65) 6476-9100
Email: singaporeacs@state.gov
Web: http://singapore.usembassy.gov

Professional Assistance:

Singapore & Hong Kong

Sovereign Society recommended banks in Singapore & Hong Kong usually do not accept accounts directly from individual U.S. persons, but require an intermediary to submit account applications. The banks may require account applicants to appear personally at their offices as part of the application process.

Below is contact information for our designated intermediary, Josh Bennett, Esq., an expert attorney in offshore asset protection, U.S. offshore taxes and reporting requirements. He also acts as contact for Trident Corporate Services that provides incorporation, trust creation and related business and banking services in both Hong Kong and Singapore and in many other OFCs worldwide.

Josh N. Bennett, Esq.
440 North Andrews Avenue
Fort Lauderdale, FL 33301
Tel.: (954) 779-1661
Email: josh@joshbennett.com
Web: www.joshbennett.com

HONG KONG: A FAR EAST OFFSHORE HAVEN
Robert E. Bauman JD, *Where to Stash Your Cash*, 2015

Gateway to China

If you're doing business in China (or anywhere in Asia), you should consider Hong Kong as your base of operations, a place to obtain financing, do your banking, create the corporate or trust entities you may need to succeed in a very tough market — especially in China.

The huge mass of 1.4 billion people living in China are experiencing some of the most rapid, although highly uneven, economic growth in recent world history. For some of the population, living standards have improved dramatically and this has increased room for personal choice, yet political controls remain tight. In 2009, the per capita GDP was only US$6,000.

Over the three years through the end of 2007, China's gross domestic product (GDP) growth has exceeded 9% annually. In 2008, as China commemorated the 30th anniversary of the Communist takeover and its historic economic reforms, the global economic downturn began to slow foreign demand for Chinese exports for the first time in many years. The government vowed to continue reforming the economy and emphasized the need to increase domestic consumption in order to make China less dependent on foreign exports for GDP growth in the future.

The recession that began in 2008 only slowed expansion; the 2008 GDP was valued at US$9 trillion. Beijing's channeled four trillion yuan (US$586 billion) as stimulus into the mainland economy and Hong Kong benefitted as well. In 2009, a wave of money flooding into Hong Kong from mainland China and the rest of the world propelled property and stock prices even as the economy faltered with a shrinkage of 6.5% in 2009 and unemployment was at a three-year high.

Hong Kong's pre-recession expansion spurred massive domestic consumer demand for every imaginable commodity and service, from thousands of high-rise apartment and condo blocs, to millions of automobiles — and for all sorts of financial services. All this rapid growth turned the eager eyes of world business towards the obvious profits to be made in China.

But with only a rudimentary, struggling financial system consisting of banks, stock markets and financial exchanges controlled by the Communist government and the military, the domestic economy lacks the experience and controls Western nations take for granted. Indeed, many of the existing financial institutions in China are loaded with billions in non-performing, politically allocated loans, thousands of shaky investments, all of it permeated with corruption.

To add to this certainty, accept the fact that, at present, there is no true "rule of law" or reliable judicial system in China, in the sense the Western world understands such basic safeguards. This means doing business in China lacks the legal protection foreign investors take for granted everywhere else.

Gateway to the World

This mainland financial situation has served to accentuate and expand the role that Hong Kong has played with great success since the Communist revolution took control of China in 1949 — that of China's financial window and conduit to the rest of world. Hong Kong's position as the most important international financial services center in Asia, specifically, the gateway through which capital is most likely to flow out from China, appears unassailable.

Hong Kong is situated ideally — legally part of, but also different and somewhat apart from China. In Hong Kong, you can find what struggling mainland China sorely lacks — the legal, financial and investment expertise and experience that can provide you with a sensible approach to investing and doing business in China.

And that's where the profits will be — if you are prudent and careful in your approach. If you want to deal in China, unless you have longstanding family or business ties there, you are best served working with a Hong Kong based partner who has first-hand knowledge of the Chinese market.

Hong Kong is proof that "money talks." China has too much invested in Hong Kong to destroy it all in a fit of rigid political ideology. Today, 30% of Hong Kong bank deposits are Chinese and China accounts for 22% of all its foreign trade (including cross-border trade), 20% of the insurance business and over 12% of all construction. More than 2,000 Chinese-controlled entities now do business in Hong Kong, many of them "red chip" stocks, the value of which have declined steeply in the last year. China has long employed Hong Kong as a convenient financial window to the world. It serves as their banker, investment broker and go-between in what is now a multi-billion annual trade flow. In the past 17 years, some US$200 billion of direct foreign investment has flooded into China — 60% of which came from, or through, Hong Kong.

In the 12 years since it passed from British to Chinese rule, Hong Kong has tried to remained a bastion of civil liberties unknown in mainland China, under an arrangement known as "one country, two systems." The result was the continuation of a freewheeling press, an independent judiciary and a well-oiled bureaucracy. [*Editor's Note:* Those more liberal policies changed in 2015 when the Communist rulers in Beijing clamped down on anti-Communist journalists, censoring publications, inspiring violence against opposition leaders, including murder and kidnapping, and rejecting massive student protests supporting free elections of HK officials.]

Despite their wrong-headed attitudes regarding Hong Kong democracy, the leaders of the People's Republic of China should realize that they have an enormous vested interest in Hong Kong's economic health. They want Hong Kong to keep running at full steam, but on their own terms.

But many democracy advocates and civil libertarians in Hong Kong are increasingly anxious about whether laissez-faire Hong Kong can maintain its independence from Beijing's authoritarian grip and its distinct identity as an amalgam of Western and Chinese sensibilities. In 2008, Beijing postponed promised direct elections until 2017 for the chief executive and 2020 for the full legislature. Its critics say China is wielding a heavier hand in Hong Kong's affairs.

World-Class Financial Sophistication

In a strange twist of world economic fate, the clampdown by the European Union and the OECD on tax havens in the West operated to the benefit of other tax havens such as Hong Kong. An added factor: wealthy account holders from the Middle East started shifting cash towards Asia and away from Europe and the United States in the wake of the September 11, 2001 terrorist attacks.

Asian banks, many of them based in Hong Kong, were sitting on more than US$2 trillion of reserves in early 2009. Funds have been continuously pouring money into emerging markets and Hong Kong has been a major beneficiary if this global trend. No leading Asian banks were caught in the bank near-collapses in 2009, so no bailouts were needed.

World Leader

By almost any measure, Hong Kong is one of the world's leading financial and economic powerhouses. In total cash and assets, it is the world's third wealthiest financial center, after New York and London.

Hong Kong, described as a "barren rock" more than 150 years ago, is a great world-class city. It has no natural resources, except one of the finest deep water ports in the world. A hardworking, adaptable and well-educated workforce of about 3.5 million, coupled with entrepreneurial flair, is the bedrock of Hong Kong's productivity and creativity. There is a Chinese phrase that describes Hong Kong well, Zhong Si He Bing, literally meaning "combination of east and west."

Hong Kong is the world's 9th largest banking center, 6th largest foreign exchange center, 11th largest trading economy, busiest container port and is Asia's second biggest stock market. With low taxes and a trusted legal system, international banking and business flow in and out, sure of stability and a high degree of financial privacy.

Long known as a world free market business center, as a measure of its collective wealth, Hong Kong's seven million residents, in 2008 enjoyed a per capita GDP of US$43,800. That impressive GDP figure is higher than that enjoyed by the citizens of Germany, Japan, the United Kingdom, Canada and Australia.

Hong Kong is still regarded by foreign firms as a highly advantageous location from which to do business. Almost 80% of foreign firms based in Hong Kong surveyed said they felt that it was an advantageous location for them, due to advanced telecommunications networks, a free trade environment, low taxes and effective regulation. On an industry basis, according to the survey results, the financial services sector was the most positive overall.

A major attraction for offshore business has been Hong Kong's relatively low 17.5% business tax rate. The ceiling for taxes on personal income and unincorporated businesses is 16%. Hong Kong's status as one of the world's top trading centers for stocks, bonds, commodities, metals, futures, currencies and personal and business financial operations long has meant that such transactions could be conducted there with a high degree of sophistication. That's still true and in 2009 the city's 154 licensed banks held in excess of US$400 billion in assets.

Hong Kong as a Business Base

In Hong Kong, there is no specific legal recognition of an international business company (IBC). Hong Kong has a territorial tax system which also applies to "territoriality of profits." If profits originate in or are derived from Hong Kong, then profits are subject to local tax. Otherwise, they are tax-free, regardless of whether the company is incorporated or registered there. Interestingly, IBCs and all other foreign corporations generally may open a Hong Kong bank account without prior registration under the local business statute. This can save charges for auditing and annual report filing and removes the annoyance of having to argue with the Inland Revenue Department about the territoriality of the business.

On the other hand, one must be careful not to transact any taxable local business, because doing that without local registration is against the law. In cases where local business does occur, tax authorities generally are lenient, usually requiring local registration and payment of unpaid tax. But in some cases, IBCs have been forced to register as a listed public company at considerable expense.

Hong Kong offshore companies require by law a local resident company secretary, who usually charges about US$500 per year for filing a few documents with the Company Registry. Annual auditing by a CPA starts from about US$500 for companies with few transactions and can easily reach 10 times as much for a mid-size operational offshore trading company.

Hong Kong Corporations

There are more companies — over 500,000 — registered in Hong Kong than anywhere else in the world. (Here, they are called "private limited companies" and are identified with a "Ltd.," not an "Inc.") It is also home to the largest community of multinational firms in Asia. This is due, first, to the territory's colonial roots, which have for the past 150 years made it the natural hub in Asia for British companies and, second, to its consistent and longstanding reputation for openness, simplicity of operation and institutional familiarity.

In Hong Kong, there is no specific legal recognition of an international business company (IBC) per se as there are in some offshore financial havens. The law recognizes only the one corporate Ltd. form. Companies must have a minimum of one director and two shareholders. Shareholders or directors do not have to be residents of Hong Kong and they can be individual persons or corporations. Company incorporation does require a registered office in Hong Kong and a Hong Kong resident individual or Hong Kong corporation to act as the secretary. Hong Kong companies must be audited each year.

Hong Kong offshore companies require by law a local resident company secretary, who usually charges about US$500 per year for filing a few documents with the Company Registry. Annual auditing by a CPA starts from about US$500 for companies with few transactions and can easily reach 10 times as much for a mid-size operational offshore trading company.

Financial Privacy

Until recently Hong Kong's banking laws did not permit bank regulators to give information about an individual customer's affairs to foreign government authorities, except in cases involving fraud. Hong Kong never had specific banking secrecy laws like many other asset and tax haven nations such as Switzerland, Panama and Luxembourg.

As a matter of local custom, Hong Kong banks always requested a judicial warrant before disclosing records to any foreign government. Access is much easier for the local government, but there are few double taxation agreements with countries other than the People's Republic of China. At this writing that will soon change since tax information exchange agreements are now being negotiated with several nations, under pressure from the OECD and the G-20, of which China is a member.

At the April 2009 meeting of the G-20 in London, at which a major attack was launched on all tax havens, the Organization for Economic Cooperation and Development (OECD) excluded Hong Kong and Macao, its sister Chinese SAR, from a list of jurisdictions that have "not yet substantially implemented" internationally agreed tax standards. Under pressure from China's president, the OECD instead acknowledged that the two Special Administrative Regions of China "have committed to implement the internationally agreed OECD tax information exchange standard."

Hong Kong's chief executive Donald Tsang sought to distinguish his city-state from the world's other tax havens. "Indeed our tax rates are low but this does not mean we harbor irregularities in our system," he said. In 2009 his government adopted legislation liberalizing the exchange of tax information with foreign governments. Hong Kong and Macao's willingness to embrace greater transparency, after years of resistance, underscored their fear of being tarred as *bei sui tin tong* or "tax evasion heavens," as tax havens are known in Cantonese.

There is an MLAT with the United States. Anti-money laundering laws and "know-your-customer" rules have made the opening of bank accounts for IBCs more difficult, but no more so than in other countries these days. Account applicants must declare to the bank who the "true beneficial owner" of an IBC or a trust is, with supporting documentation. Proof must be shown for all corporate directors and shareholders of the registering entity and any other entities that share in the ownership.

Which Direction?

If you do intend to make Asia your business investment target, keep in mind lessons other foreigners have already learned the hard way. Pick your Asian business partners (and business investments) carefully, avoiding the inefficient Chinese state-owned enterprises. Stick to those with solid basics like marketing, distribution and service. Guard technology from theft. And remember, a series of small ventures gets less government attention and red tape than big showcase projects that often produce demands for graft. Many foreign business investors have been burned by crooked bookkeeping, few shareholder controls, sudden government rule changes and systemic corruption.

Only recently, as China's economy has become more westernized, did Beijing finally begin to address the need for laws guaranteeing the right for citizens and foreigners to own and transfer private property. So, in dealing with China, remember: "Caveat emptor!"

Most importantly, keep a sharp eye not on the government's hype, but on what's really happening in China. All this uncertainty means that offshore financial activities by foreign citizens can prosper, but without immediate assurance of success. Unless the "New China" is definitely your sphere of intended business activity, you may want to look elsewhere for your Asian financial haven in places such as Singapore or Malaysia.

Contacts

Hong Kong SAR government: http://www.gov.hk/en/residents

Hong Kong Trade Development Council: http://www.tdc.org.hk

Hong Kong Government Economic and Trade Office
1520 18th Street NW
Washington, D.C. 20036
Tel.: (202) 331-8947
Email: hketo@hketowashington.gov.hk
Web: http://www.hketousa.gov.hk/usa/index.htm

U.S. Consul General
26 Garden Road, Hong Kong
Tel.: + (852) 2523-9011 or + (852) 2841-2211
Email: acshk@state.gov
Web: http://hongkong.usconsulate.gov

Chapter Ten

Personal & Digital Privacy Secrets

The War Against Privacy 588
Your Privacy Is Compromised in the U.S. Mail 590
Surveillance? Who Cares? 592
Your Internet Address Isn't Private 594
The Internet Never Forgets 596
Beat the Data Thieves with These Privacy Measures 597
Government Surveillance: A Greater Threat Than Terrorism 599
A 600,000 Cubic Foot Blimp May Be Spying on You 601
Become Invisible to NSA Snooping: Beat the Government's Plan to Steal Your Privacy 603
The NSA's Latest Attempt to Hack Your Computer 615
MIT Just Made It Easier to Find You 617
U.S. Authorizes Back Door "Roving Wiretaps" 619
Does the Constitution Mean Anything Anymore? 620
The United States: An Informer's Paradise 623
Defend Your Privacy: Helpful Tools to Prevent Government Spying 628
Leftist Lies Attack Your Right to Privacy 630
Using Attorney-Client Privilege Effectively 632
Identity Theft: Ways to Protect Yourself 637
Escaping the Matrix: A Privacy-Protection Guide for Our Brave New World 642
Say Goodbye to Financial Freedom, America 653
Sorry, the Police Can Still Steal Your Property 655

Editor's Note:

Reading this chapter your blood may figuratively boil as you discover the enormous degree to which your personal privacy has been compromised by big government, big business, big banking and the Internet.

The right to privacy is not even mentioned explicitly in the U.S. Constitution.

But to survive in a modern world where most of us are forced to live in financial glass houses, maximum privacy is still essential.

In this chapter, we reveal the cold, hard facts about how anti-privacy forces, led by the government and police, try to strip you of your privacy and sometimes your wealth, constantly engaging in stealthy technological dirty work done without your knowledge or consent. Nothing is sacred any more — not your mail, email, phone calls, and certainly not your Internet surfing.

Unless you take the precautions we describe, you may be naked before the world.

Your Editor wishes to thank Mark Nestmann, not only for his many contributions to this chapter and book, but especially for his review and updating of the content of this chapter on privacy, a topic on which he is a recognized expert.

THE WAR AGAINST PRIVACY
John Pugsley, *The Sovereign Individual*, August 1999

Like you, I am distressed at the amount of information about my private affairs that is collected, archived and traded by business. Even more so, I am outraged about the covert surveillance of my financial and personal life that is carried out by government. The decision of my wife and me to move offshore was strongly influenced by our desire to protest the destruction of personal privacy in the United States. While we're not doing anything that we know to be illegal, we don't like being spied upon.

I'm a bit embarrassed to admit that when I was young I was a spy for the U.S. government — sort of. In the 1950s, I was drafted into the Army and served my two years as a "Morse Code Interceptor." My job was to sit at my short-wave radio and listen for encrypted Morse-code messages being transmitted by government agencies and military units throughout Europe, Russia and the Middle East. I eavesdropped on the British, the French, the Germans, the Israelis, the Russians and anyone else who was using the airwaves. Eight hours wearing headphones and typing out an endless series of scrambled letters wasn't the sexy side of espionage, but I was definitely a spy.

In those days, despite the fact that all governments monitored each other's radio traffic and everyone knew that everyone did it, covert surveillance of neighbor nations was illegal according to international treaties. As one British gentleman had sniffed, "Gentlemen do not read other gentlemen's mail." As recently as 40 years ago, it was presumed that even governments had the right to privacy. My, how times have changed.

Today, governments have dropped the pretense. Government-to-government espionage is an enormous industry.

Neither the public nor governments see any moral issue relative to government espionage, notwithstanding the hullabaloo Congress and the media make of special cases such as the theft of U.S. nuclear secrets by the Chinese. Friendly nations still fuss a bit when their allies are found snooping, but no one sees any moral issue involved in spying on friend or foe.

Spying on private citizens, however, is another matter. One of the major issues being debated today is the extent to which individuals have a right to privacy. Privacy is losing. Governments and businesses are both aggressively accumulating immense data banks on private citizens. Most data is gathered by assembling information given out by the person in the normal course of daily activities, such as making a credit card purchase, registering a car, applying for insurance, etc.

A growing amount, however, is gathered by covert means. For example, it is probable that the U.S. National Security Agency records and scans every long-distance phone call, fax, and e-mail sent or received in the United States. In addition, all financial transactions conducted through commercial financial institutions are recorded and open to scrutiny by the Feds.

Surveillance is even further advanced in Europe. Over 150,000 cameras throughout the United Kingdom transmit round-the-clock images of public areas to 75 constabularies. The United States isn't far behind. Big Brother really is watching.

Nor is lobbying likely to turn this trend around. I agree with author David Brin who argues that cameras on every lamppost are coming, as surely as the new millennium. They can't be stopped by all the agitation, demonstration or legislation we can muster. Although we might delay the growth of government surveillance by blocking this bill or that law, the public is overwhelmingly convinced that government needs to snoop in order to catch criminals. It's hard to conceive that most people miss the irony. "I'm from the government, and I'm here to help — by watching you."

It seems probable that the vestiges of privacy that citizens still cling to will become extinct in the not-too-distant future. While privacy advocates still refer to the "right" to privacy, that concept is likely soon to become as passé as the old belief that sovereign governments shouldn't spy on one another. The masses are being brainwashed into believing that there is no moral case for a right to privacy.

How tragic. The moral right to privacy is so clear.

The late physicist and teacher Andrew Galambos argued that all conflicts were property conflicts and could be quickly resolved with what he referred to as the "universal can-opener," which was to simply ask the question, "Whose property is it?" Applying Galambos' argument, the privacy issue boils down to a question of property rights.

Does information about your personal life belong to you, to someone else, or to everyone? Are your affairs your property or public property?

In private financial dealings, we take it for granted that revelations we make to our banker or broker do not then become his property, to be given out or sold at his discretion. In this light, we take it for granted that our private communications and activities are our property and morally can be used only with our consent. How can it be otherwise?

The moral rights to property and privacy do exist. The problem facing the sovereign individual is how to defend privacy in a world that believes otherwise. This is an ongoing task for anyone seeking to become a sovereign individual and one of the major issues of our lifetimes.

YOUR PRIVACY IS COMPROMISED IN THE U.S. MAIL

Robert E. Bauman JD, *The Sovereign Individual*, December 1997

The U.S. Congress imposed a government monopoly over first class mail delivery in 1872. This monopoly facilitates surveillance by requiring the delivery of most correspondence by a single carrier.

While it ordinarily requires a search warrant to open first-class mail, the monitoring and opening of mail without a search warrant by police, intelligence agencies and the U.S. Postal Service is legal or condoned under various circumstances. For instance, all packages sent from "source areas for the distribution of narcotics and/or controlled substances" might be inspected by drug-sniffing dogs.

Court testimony from federal agents indicates that every major city in the United States is considered such a "source area." The Postal Service also sells change-of-address information to direct marketing companies (and provides it to government agencies) and has an established intelligence unit to target for surveillance persons engaged in "suspicious mailing patterns." Mail surveillance programs carried out by or with the cooperation of the Postal Service include mail covers, intelligence agency "mail taps," and opening of mail.

Mail Covers

The monitoring of mail by a government agency is a "mail cover." The mail is only monitored, not opened; no warrant is required. The investigating agency records the address, sender, return address, meter number, place and postmark date and class of mail for all mail delivered to the target address.

Mail covers can be extended indefinitely. International correspondence is a frequent target of mail covers. At one time the IRS photocopied all correspondence between Switzerland and the United States. It matched the postal codes on the envelopes with the names and addresses of Swiss banks and audited persons who had received correspondence from these banks. Many account holders were subsequently prosecuted for income tax evasion.

Intelligence Agency Mail Taps

The courts have ruled that opening mail requires probable cause of criminal wrongdoing. But according to testimony before Congress from Professor Mel Crain of San Diego State University, while employed by the CIA, "I found myself extensively involved in mail tapping of American citizens.

The letters were opened, reproduced, and sent on their way without interrupting mail flow or their opening in any way being detected." Targets were chosen, according to the National Center for Security Studies, "on [the agents'] own interpretation of current events" This operation was curtailed in the 1970s in the wake of the Watergate scandal, although unofficial reports of illegal mail opening by U.S. intelligence agencies continue. In the meantime, the CIA built a database of 1.5 million persons whose names were listed in the illegally opened correspondence. Portions of this list may have been merged with the federal anti-terrorist databases.

The FBI also illegally opened mail during this period from a list of about 600 "subversives," mostly opponents of the War in Vietnam. However, only about 25 percent of the mail that was opened came from persons on this list. As with the CIA, individual FBI agents used their "judgment" to determine what other mail to open.

Opening Mail

The U.S. Postal Service may allow mail to be detained while a law enforcement agency decides if it has probable cause to examine the contents. However, the definition of probable cause is remarkably broad, as the following example, taken from documents filed in federal court, demonstrates:

The Chicago division of the U.S. Postal Inspection Service has implemented an Express Mail Profile program at the air mail facility at Chicago O'Hare International Airport. This program consists of a physical profile of express mail parcels which have been mailed to or from locations within the Northern District of Illinois. Targets were cities and/or areas of the United States which have been identified by law enforcement personnel as being source areas for the distribution of narcotics and/or controlled substances.

After the packages are identified, they are placed in front of DEA dogs trained to sniff out the smell of drugs. If the dogs "alert" to the presence of drugs, the packages are then opened for inspection. Should drugs be found, the package is delivered to the address, and the recipient arrested. The positive reaction of the dogs, according to the affidavit, provides probable cause for the packages to be opened. Many packages opened contain no drugs, only cash, which in some cases may be seized if it contains narcotics residues. Packages may then be re-sealed and delivered to the addressee with no indication a search has occurred.

Mail Drops

Mail drops or mail receiving services are available in many countries.

A mail drop may facilitate privacy when receiving or sending sensitive correspondence, but may be compromised. International investors can use mail drops outside their domestic jurisdiction to defeat mail covers of their international correspondence.

Law enforcement agencies associate mail drops with criminal activity. Some advertisements for mail drops in privacy-oriented publications are a ploy to get your name and address, which is cross referenced with lists of missing or wanted persons. This is known as "reverse skip tracing."

SURVEILLANCE? WHO CARES?

John Pugsley, *The Sovereign Individual*, December 2002

Does anyone really care that they are being watched by the government?

As I sat in the boarding area waiting for my flight to be called, I found myself studying the faces of fellow passengers. Light ones, dark ones, speckled, hairy and hairless, long noses or petite, balanced and lopsided, densely made up or freshly scrubbed.

I wasn't the only one in the room looking at faces. The surveillance camera sat there taking in the same facial nuances. Was it piping its pictures to a government computer where facial recognition software was looking for matches? I wondered if anyone else among the passengers had any thought about being watched, either by the cameras or me.

Surveillance is everywhere. Airports. Train stations. Malls. Department stores. Although private owners install many surveillance cameras, increasingly they are installed by local, state and federal agencies. And cameras are just one means of surveillance. More insidious are the covert eavesdropping techniques of telephone, e-mail and fax wiretaps ordered by federal and state authorities. They jumped 20% in the past two years, with more to come. In the aftermath of the September 11th attacks, roughly half of America's states introduced electronic surveillance bills.

What do Americans think about this? The majority thinks it's just keen.

A Harris Poll showed that 86% of the more than 1,000 adults polled supported the use of facial-recognition technology; 63% supported expanded camera surveillance on streets and public places; 63% supported monitoring of Internet discussions and chat rooms; and 54% supported more monitoring of cell phones and e-mails.

Another poll conducted by ABCNEWS.com asked, "Do you personally feel that the government's anti-terrorism efforts are intruding on your civil liberties?" Eighty percent of respondents said no, the government efforts were not impinging on their freedoms.

Why should we be surprised?

The vast majority of Americans have no clear sense of the meaning of "civil liberties." For an intrusion to gain the attention of the average citizen, a SWAT team must be knocking at the door. With the exception of the inconvenience of having your shoes sniffed at the airport, snooping goes unnoticed.

Most people think their civil rights are unaffected by the new surveillance laws because most of them have not felt any effect. While their phones may be tapped and their images scrutinized as they walk through the mall, they sense nothing. Even most of us who are sensitive to the erosion of privacy feel no immediate consequences — yet.

It's akin to Frederick Bastiat's parable of "that which is seen and that which is not seen" in economic events. The passerby sees the bakery window broken by a vandal, and thinks of the good fortune of the glazier whose business will profit from making a new one. The observer even thinks that this will be good for the community, as the glazier will then spend his profits with the tailor for a new suit, and the good fortune will trickle down. What is not seen, of course, is that the poor baker must now spend the money he had saved for a new suit on a new window, and that the community in toto is poorer by the amount of property destroyed.

So it is with the average individual regarding the loss of privacy. What is seen is the added security from terrorists (a negligible if not completely imaginary security, to be sure). What is not seen is the dramatically lowered security from the threat of government (an extremely real threat).

History testifies that a citizen's risk from street crime or terrorism pales in comparison to the numbers killed by authoritarian governments. As noted by R. J. Rummel in his sobering book, *Death by Government*, "The mass murder of their own citizens or those under their protection or control by emperors, kings, sultans, khans, presidents, governors, generals, and other such rulers is very much part of our history." In the 20th century alone he tallies 169,202,000 murdered by government.

Yet the masses continue to believe that government is there to protect them.

When younger, I was certain that all individuals were educable, and that they could easily be convinced of their own right to the fruits of their labors. After all, it's obvious, isn't it? From there it should be simple to prove that the state is an imposter posing as their protector.

Alas, it's not so. The masses do not change their views simply through logical persuasion. They are more attracted to bread and circuses (or baseball and sitcoms in today's world) than to critical thinking. There is little hope that the masses will suddenly awaken to the danger of omnipotent government, so the cameras and wiretaps will undoubtedly proliferate.

The real question facing those of us seeking to become sovereign individuals is how to best insulate ourselves from popular ignorance and the concomitant threat to our personal liberty.

History suggests the answer is for individuals to continuously search for our own personal security. As for changing the course of society, the best way to change the direction of a running herd is not to try to convince them they're heading toward danger, but to run in the right direction yourself, and have confidence that by protecting yourself you'll set an example. The thoughtful members of the crowd will follow you.

Meanwhile, technology in the form of the expanding Internet and science in the form of the biology of human behavior will, hopefully, awaken the younger generations to the ultimate destiny of the species, which is individual sovereignty.

YOUR INTERNET ADDRESS ISN'T PRIVATE

Marc Nestmann's Blog, 2009
(www.nestmann.com)

If you're reading this posting you're probably sitting in front of your computer without anyone gazing over your shoulder. It's therefore easy to believe that what

CHAPTER TEN: PERSONAL & DIGITAL PRIVACY SECRETS   595

you do on the Internet — browsing, chatting, e-mailing, or whatever — is private. Don't believe it. Your Internet Service Provider (ISP) can monitor every email message you send, every web page to which you surf, and every chat session you initiate. If police demand this information, your ISP must turn over a record of everything you've done online. And now, thanks to a ruling by U.S. District Court Judge Richard Jones in Seattle, you have no right to keep your "Internet identity" anonymous. That opens the door to even greater privacy invasion.

Jones issued the ruling in dismissing a class-action lawsuit against Microsoft stemming from the company's practice of collecting the "Internet Protocol addresses" (IP addresses) of consumers who download automatic updates from the company. Your IP address is a unique number that represents your publicly visible identity on the Internet. But because the address identifies your computer — and not you personally — according to Jones, you have no "expectation of privacy" in the address. That means any Website can legally collect your IP address, unless they've promised not to do so.

Moreover, it's relatively easy for Websites, police, or anyone else to combine your IP address with other information to determine your identity. That means if you don't want details of what you do on your computer divulged to the highest bidder, or anyone armed with a subpoena, you need to take precautions to anonymize it.

The easiest way to do this is to use a "virtual private network" (VPN). Essentially, the VPN acts as an intermediary (called a proxy) between your PC and the Website to which you're connecting. That Website records the IP address of the proxy, not of your PC. This lets you use the Internet virtually anonymou't track your web surfing, either.

The only way anyone could recover your IP address would be by comparing the logs from the VPN and the logs from the Website in question. That's a little like looking for a needle in a haystack. What's more, a well-designed VPN will be configured so that it's impossible to retrieve a meaningful log to connect to individual subscribers.

There are many VPN services available. I prefer services that don't have networks installed in the United States to avoid possible compromise under legislation such as the USA PATRIOT Act. The service that I use is http:// www.cryptohippie.com. Its only U.S. presence is to authenticate connections to Cryptohippie servers in other countries. None of Cryptohippie's servers are in the United States.

If you already have a VPN that you're satisfied with, keep using it. But if not, and you value your online privacy, give the "Road Warrior" VPN a try.

The Internet Never Forgets
Marc Nestmann's Blog, 2009

Web-savvy employers and universities are increasingly employing a new tactic to screen applicants: conducting online research to unearth photos, blog entries, or other "digital dirt" you might prefer to keep private.

Indeed, companies are springing up to dig up Internet postings that might be of interest to employers, government agencies, or whoever else might be interested. For instance, you can view Web pages that were modified months or even years ago through the Internet Archive, also known as the Wayback Machine, at http://www.archive.org.

But that doesn't mean you can't obscure your digital trail. While I normally suggest that anyone interested in privacy avoid posting information to the Internet about themselves, if data you don't want others to see is already there, here are a few suggestions on how to cope:

Delete, delete, delete. Start by deleting any photo, personal profile, or personal description on any social networking or dating Website that is even mildly embarrassing. For instance, I suspect Sergey Brin, the co-founder of Google founders, might prefer not to have this photo of him in drag immortalized. While Sergey may be wealthy enough not to care, you may not be.

Unfortunately, most social networking sites create archives in which your photos may reside permanently, even if you delete them from your profile. Someone with a link to the original photo — or using the Internet Archive — might be able to find it.

Do a search of yourself on Google. Look for any links back to potentially incriminating or embarrassing posts or photos. Unfortunately, Google won't remove content itself, but merely will refer you to the Webmaster posting the content. If you can't figure out who's in charge of a Website, search for the owner at www.whois.net. Contact the owner of the site and ask that comments by or about you be deleted. In most cases the owner has no obligation to remove the content, but it may do so if you persist or threaten legal action.

Set up a Google alert for yourself. You'll receive a daily e-mail update of the latest updates of whatever topic — yourself in this case — that you choose. This is a great way to monitor what others are saying about you online.

Create favorable content about yourself. You can do this in many ways. For instance, create a professional Website and/or professional blog. For blogs,

Wordpress, LiveJournal and TypePad all have high Google page ranks. You can also create a Wikipedia entry for yourself. To further ensure these sites are at the top of any Google search of your name, use title tags and headers to highlight information about you that you want people to see. Don't forget to create a Google profile that contains the information about yourself you wish to highlight. You can also leave comments on blogs and Websites you respect under your own name.

Use social networking sites intelligently. It's almost impossible to permanently eliminate content you post to social networking sites, even if you unsubscribe. However, you can also use these sites to your advantage, especially if you're setting up a profile for the first time. Websites like Facebook, MySpace, LinkedIn, Flickr, and Twitter are a good place to begin.

You don't even need to use these sites. Just create a profile and add the content you want people to see. Websites that let you create a unique link with your name in it are especially useful (e.g., LinkedIn). Those pages will show up ahead of most other sites that might contain content you don't want others to view.

Use protection. There's no such thing as an Internet condom, but you can hire companies that will contact sites that have published material pertinent to your character. One that has good reviews — although I haven't used it personally — is http://www.trackur.com.

Just don't forget that once you've posted something on the Internet, it's very difficult to permanently delete it. So before you hit the "post" button, be absolutely certain that whatever you're about to send into cyberspace belongs there.

BEAT THE DATA THIEVES WITH THESE PRIVACY MEASURES

Ted Bauman, *The Sovereign Investor Daily*, December 2014

You probably know the feeling.

It's the early hours of the morning. You're in bed, but a strange feeling has wakened you. You sense a presence in your house. Cautiously, trying your utmost to be silent, you creep downstairs and peer into the gloom of your living room. A curtain is flapping in the breeze, broken glass sparkling on the moonlit floor. Something of yours — a TV, perhaps — is gone.

Almost everyone who has experienced property crime will tell you that the loss of physical things isn't the real blow. It's the sense that the sanctity of home and hearth has been "violated" that really hurts.

That could be happening to you right now, in the middle of the day, even as you sit alone in your comfortable home ... because if thieves aren't hacking into your house, they can too easily violate your privacy online.

Passwords Won't Secure Your Internet Privacy

The Centre for International Governance Innovation (CIGI) recently surveyed Internet users in 24 countries, and found that 64% of respondents are more worried about their privacy since Edward Snowden blew the lid on National Security Agency (NSA) spying. Large numbers of people are updating their passwords more frequently and avoiding websites and software that might put their data at risk.

If only that were enough. The CIGI report noted that more than 750 million people around the world have taken steps to improve their privacy since Snowmen's revelations ... but that these steps would make "little difference to the NSA's ability to gather data on them or to defy the surveillance techniques of large firms."

Indeed, passwords are of little consequence to a determined hacker — especially one that isn't hacking into your computer, but rather into the mainframe of a company or government agency with whom you do business, where your password is stored along with millions of others.

Strong passwords are essential, of course, and regular changes to them are important. (Indeed, a password manager I use has recently added a feature that can change all of your passwords with one click.) But passwords can only protect you from garden-variety data theft. They're like burglar bars on your home — important, but once they're compromised, you're completely exposed. You need more than passwords to be truly secure.

Protecting Yourself from Digital Burglary

Here are three ways to get started on a sound personal privacy strategy:

1. **An Alarm System:** Most reputable websites now have a feature that alerts you by email or text message or both whenever someone logs into your account. Such alerts can also be set for transactions above a certain amount. I've saved myself money on more than one occasion after getting such an alert and calling my bank immediately to stop the transaction ... even while I've been overseas.

2. **Play Your Cards Close to Your Chest:** Every good poker player knows that the secret to success is to limit the information about you available to the other players. The same goes with digital security. Don't do business with websites or use "apps" that ask for more information than is reasonably required. This is especially true of "free" services that essentially want information about you so they can sell it to someone else. Don't participate in surveys, submit reviews or participate in other aspects of websites that aren't strictly necessary.

3. Encrypt, Encrypt, Encrypt: Above all, turn your data into a form that's useless to anyone who doesn't have the key to unlock its meaning. As I've stressed before and will surely do again, use solid encryption software and, where appropriate, a secure browsing setup like TOR. It's not that they are impossible to hack … but they are so hard to crack that almost all potential digital burglars will move on to another victim.

It's Entirely Up to You

The U.S. Congress has one again demonstrated its lack of concern for the wishes of the American people by recently endorsing the very government surveillance that Edward Snowden revealed. A provision of the recent omnibus spending bill, inserted quietly at the last minute, stipulates that "any nonpublic telephone or electronic communication" sent by or among Americans that's intercepted by intelligence agencies can be stored for five years, if it was obtained illegally.

With people like Congress looking after your interests, you might think that you're on your own when it comes to protecting your privacy. Essentially you are. In the New Year, however, I'm going to become your partner in defeating the data burglars …. so stay tuned!

Government Surveillance: A Greater Threat Than Terrorism
Ted Bauman, *The Sovereign Investor Daily*, January 2015

The man sat on the floor, awkwardly wedged into the far corner of his apartment, his knees drawn up under his chin. The faltering light from the dirty window barely illuminated the book balanced on his knees. Periodically he bent closer to see the words as he scrawled out his thoughts with a dull pencil.

This was the only way he could express himself beyond the scrutiny of government surveillance that sought to know and record his every thought and action.

You may recognize this scene, one of the most arresting from George Orwell's dystopian fiction classic, *Nineteen Eighty-Four*. Winston Smith was breaking the law by seeking privacy outside the range of the "telescreen" in his apartment.

In an irony that would no doubt give Orwell grim satisfaction in his own prescience, Britons today are being pursued and prosecuted under an Act of Parliament designed to curb terrorism … for failing to pay a license fee for the televisions in their own homes.

Big Brother is Watching You

Orwell wrote soon after the invention of the television, which he envisaged as having evolved into an all-seeing two-way surveillance and propaganda device — the telescreen. It subjected viewers to constant hectoring demands for obedience, and reported their every move to Big Brother, the avatar of the all-seeing surveillance state.

The fact that the novel is set in a future (and fictional) Britain only heightens the irony of recent revelations in the UK. The government of Tory Prime Minister David Cameron has been using surveillance powers designed for the "War on Terrorism" to ferret out Britons who have not paid their hated "TV License," a £145.50 ($220) annual tax imposed on every home containing a set in the country.

Her Majesty's government clearly takes this odious little tax very seriously ... so much so that the BBC is using the Regulation of Investigatory Powers Act (RIPA) — designed to catch terrorists and Internet criminals — to track down people who dodge the license fee.

About 200,000 people were prosecuted for failing to buy a TV license between 2012 and 2013. More than 50 of those were sent to prison, and many others received penalties of up to £1,000 and a criminal record.

We can assume that none of them were terrorists — just ordinary subjects who dislike stupid taxes.

Freedom is Slavery

Orwell wrote with extraordinary perception and clarity, taking as his central theme the ways in which government's attempts to serve its citizens are inevitably turned against us. Any policy, program or technique developed to "protect our freedoms" will be used to achieve the opposite.

Orwell would recognize the absurd irony of the situation in Western countries following the recent atrocities in Paris targeting the satirical newspaper *Charlie Hebdo*. In response to these terror attacks, David Cameron has effectively launched a war against encryption, deeming private communication too great a threat to afford to keep as it prevents government from tracking and monitoring potential terrorists.

After loud protestations for "freedom of speech" following a terrorist attack on a magazine, our leaders barely pause for breath before demanding even greater surveillance powers than they already have — powers that, as Winston Smith knew, turn us all into self-censoring drones, fearful of saying or doing something that might offend Big Brother.

Today anti-terrorism laws are being used to enforce petty taxes. How will the new rules and capacities that inevitably emerge from the "*je suis Charlie*" hysteria in Paris be deployed? We can imagine, as Orwell surely would, that the end result will be the opposite of the stated intention: Freedom will indeed become slavery.

"You're On Your Own"

The more I research and write about personal and financial privacy, the more I turn instinctively to this phrase. In a world where government is the principal enemy, no one but ourselves will meet our needs for sovereign independence of thought and action. It is truly up to us.

Every bit of information about you out there in the cloud — the details of your lives and finances, triumphs and defeats, plans and dreams — is a target. If otherwise law-abiding Britons can go to jail over a petty tax, courtesy of surveillance powers grabbed in the name of fighting terrorism, imagine what can and will happen if the government decides to turn its attention to *you*.

This is why, now more than ever, you need to take concrete steps to secure your privacy … not just from crooks, but from the greatest enemy of freedom there is: the government.

By using techniques of encryption (while it's available), secure end-to-end communication and identity masking, you can become a free and sovereign man or woman, because you control the knowledge available about you.

But you've got to start now … before it's too late.

A 600,000 Cubic Foot Blimp May Be Spying on You

Ted Bauman, *The Sovereign Investor Daily*, January 2015

In the summer of 1849, Austrian Field Marshall Joseph Radetzky did something no one had done before: He bombed a city from the air.

His target was Venice, then in rebellion against the Habsburg crown. During the siege, he launched a fleet of unmanned linen balloons, carrying bombs made from canister shot and gunpowder, timed to drop over the besieged city.

Radetzky told Emperor Franz Joseph that the effect on the people of Venice was "frightful." Indeed, Radetzky's balloons had done little physical damage, but had a substantial effect on the morale of the city's defenders. As the 19th century wore on, fear of attack by airships became a constant theme in popular literature. By World War I, the mere mention of the word "Zeppelin" was enough to cause panic in the streets of London.

A prevailing theme in the literature of the era and the minds of the people was that these aerial monsters would always be deployed by one's enemies. So it says a lot about the current atmosphere in the U.S. that the overwhelming public reaction to the deployment of massive Army blimps over Interstate 95 in Maryland has been fear and rejection…

Government Surveillance: From Zeppelin to JLENS

The blimps launched just outside Baltimore in December — known as Joint Land Attack Cruise Missile Defense Elevated Netted Sensor Systems (JLENS) — are the largest ever sent aloft. At 80 yards long with a total volume of around 600,000 cubic feet, they're the size of three Goodyear blimps. They will float at 10,000 feet, about one-third as high as an airliner. They're also expensive. The two prototype airships have cost almost $3 billion so far.

Officially, the blimps will deploy a sophisticated radar system that can spot and track aircraft, missiles, ships or even ground vehicles in a circular area, ranging from New York to North Carolina and from halfway to Bermuda to the Ohio Valley. They are meant to replace the Air Force radar planes currently used for this purpose.

But JLENS isn't technically limited to radar. If equipped with high-resolution cameras, they can see and record everything for miles, in extraordinary detail. In Kabul, for example, residents are used to seeing the U.S. military's tethered blimp — called the Persistent Ground Surveillance system — hovering above the city, capturing video of daily life below.

Blimps are ideal platforms for mass surveillance. As Ginger McCall, associate director of the Electronic Privacy Information Center (EPIC), says, "There's something inherently suspect for the public to look up in the sky and see this surveillance device hanging there. It's the definition of persistent surveillance." Not only can the blimps potentially see everything you're doing — they can be seen seeing you. That speaks volumes.

Like Radetzky's balloons and Count von Zeppelin's dirigibles, the main effect of the big blimps will be psychological. As Ed Herlik, a former Air Force officer and technology analyst, explains: "If you put a camera in a sky over an area where you expect a lot of unrest, the area will calm down."

Stay Calm, but Get Ready to Go

Does the U.S. government expect unrest in an area the size of Texas centered on Washington, D.C.? If our rulers are smart, they should.

They incur debt on our behalf at a terrific rate. They use those borrowings to increase their capacity to monitor and control us, and to undertake ruinous foreign wars. They indulge in wholesale corruption, sanitized as "campaign finance." And they resolutely refuse to listen to the wishes of the majority of Americans, who don't want any of these things.

As we advise our *Freedom Alliance* members, you can expect a lower level of public service and amenities in countries that aren't as rich as the U.S. The upside is that the governments of those countries also can't afford to spend $3 billion on massive surveillance blimps parked atop their capital cities, even if they wanted to.

From where I stand, our slide towards a corrupt, oligarchic U.S. society, held in check by mass technological surveillance and unaccountable bureaucracy, is well under way. It's not a theoretical issue anymore — and neither is the need to do something about it.

Don't put all your eggs in one basket. Begin making steps to establish second residency in another country, and start preparing for a life elsewhere ... where there aren't any blimps hovering overhead.

BECOME INVISIBLE TO NSA SNOOPING: BEAT THE GOVERNMENT'S PLAN TO STEAL YOUR PRIVACY
Ted Bauman, *Offshore Confidential*, September 2014

In the late 1980s, when I was a student at the University of Cape Town, the South African system of apartheid was in its death throes.

It was hard to tell that at the time, of course: the police state was everywhere — on your phone line, in your mail, in your workplace, watching your movements.

They even made it into my bedroom — the ultimate private space.

Like most South African university students, I was active in the anti-apartheid movement. I attended rallies, got tear-gassed, and participated in strategy meetings. I wrote political pamphlets that were posted anonymously around the university and the neighborhoods where students gathered at night to drink and watch live music. I taught undergraduate courses where my views — liberty and equal rights for all, regardless of color — were in plain view.

But none of that brought the security police to my door. They came because of a private and personal issue: my girlfriend wasn't white.

Under the Group Areas Act, it was a crime for a "non-white" person to live in an area reserved for "white" people. My girlfriend was classified "colored" (mixed-race) under apartheid law. Both postgraduate students, we lived in a flat in the City Bowl section of Cape Town.

The police had much bigger fish to fry than Group Areas violations. Nevertheless, somehow or other I had come to their attention. So they came to my door one fine spring day and demanded to search my home. (No search warrants needed in those days.)

After going through my library, writing down the titles of political tracts and photographing political posters on the walls, the police moved on to our bedroom. Using a riding crop — a sort of "swagger-stick" carried by police colonels — they rifled through our clothing drawers.

Their leader, a typical Afrikaner with a big belly and a thick snorr (mustache), lifted one of my girlfriend's undies and slowly looked up at me. He said nothing, merely putting the clothing back in the drawer and closing it slowly.

As they prepared to leave, the squad leader turned back, and said, in the classic affectation of a TV police detective, "one more thing."

I knew then I was done for.

"We know all about you, Mr. Bauman. We know you spoke to X yesterday for 20 minutes on the phone, and what it was about. We know about your pamphlets. We know what you're teaching our kids at that communist shithole of a university up on Devil's Peak.

We even know what rubbish you're writing to your family back in the States. We can deal with that. But this arrangement of yours" — he gestured around the flat — "is a step too far. Best see to it. Good day."

I can't say I was stunned, since I had it coming, as it were, but I was deeply shaken. I assumed I would be deported forthwith.

I wasn't. Instead, life went on, albeit under a cloud of uncertainty that changed everything. I assumed everything I did and said was monitored and recorded somewhere.

Since I wanted to continue living in South Africa, which had become my home, I had little choice but to withdraw from open political activity, shut my mouth, and hunker down like Winston Smith from George Orwell's *1984*.

My experience all those years ago turned me into a staunch defender of civil liberties and privacy. It also prompted me to learn many techniques to conceal my online identity and to become "invisible" to the prying eyes and ears of the government and others.

In what follows, I'm going to share them with you, so you too can appear to be "off the grid" … while still being on it.

You're Being Controlled Through Uncertainty

I now understand that the South African security police didn't deport me in 1988 because they didn't have to. All they had to do to neutralize me was create the uncertainty that comes with knowing you are being watched at all times … and therein lies an important lesson for anyone living in the heavily surveilled America of 2014.

As all of us who exercise our rights to financial and personal freedom know, there's no more effective way to shape people's behavior than to create uncertainty about what you're allowed to do and whether the government is watching you while you do it.

Whether it involves finance, politics or even personal behavior, the knowledge that what you do and say is being monitored by those in positions of power has a strong inhibiting effect.

The adoption of the abhorrent Foreign Account Tax Compliance Act (FATCA), which has prompted many people to close offshore accounts because it turns foreign banks into IRS spies, is one excellent example.

The typical response to those who point out the dangers of pervasive surveillance is "if you haven't done anything wrong, you have nothing to worry about." But that misses the point entirely.

The U.S. has so many laws and regulatory agencies with enforcement powers that it's literally impossible to know the legal definition of "wrong" in every case.

And that's how they control you. If you don't know what can get you into trouble, a prudent person will tend to restrict their own behavior to what they know to be "OK." We talk about this constantly when it comes to offshore banking and finance.

Indeed, one of the reasons we publish *Offshore Confidential* and related titles is to alert you to things that are perfectly legal, but little-known and therefore feared. Letters from our subscribers confirm that the biggest obstacle to true freedom isn't always the law — it's the fear that comes with not knowing what can get you into trouble.

Don't Kid Yourself: Big Bro is Really Watching

If you think concerns about privacy are for other people — or just plain tinfoil-hat paranoia — I've got news for you: you are in grave danger. The government is spying on you constantly, often using the private sector to do it.

Let's review a couple of the worst cases.

Thanks to Edward Snowden and Glenn Greenwald, we all know now about the shenanigans at the National Security Agency. Under the USA PATRIOT Act, the NSA is authorized to demand access to all call records from telephone service providers such as Verizon, AT&T or Sprint.

The cell companies have to surrender any information in their systems, both within the U.S. and between the U.S. and other countries on an "ongoing, daily basis." That includes our calls and emails.

Maybe that's why the NSA is building a data storage center in Utah five times the size of the U.S. Capitol building, with its own power plant that will reportedly consume $40 million a year in electricity.

Then there's the Federal Bureau of Investigation (FBI). Also thanks to the PATRIOT Act, the FBI makes liberal use of National Security Letters (NSLs), an "administrative subpoena" that allows its agents to seek information considered "relevant" to investigations into "international terrorism or clandestine intelligence activities."

NSLs usually prevent the recipient from telling anyone — even a spouse — that the FBI has requested the information. In this way, just by accusing you of "terrorism," the FBI can learn just about anything it wants from anyone with whom you do business — your bank, your cell company, even your own company — and you won't know anything about it, because they're not allowed to tell you they've been asked.

And lest you think this is a concern to just "terrorists" … an audit covering only 10% of FBI investigations between 2002 and 2007 found that agents had violated NSL rules more than 1,000 times. Many NSLs involved requests for information that FBI agents aren't allowed to obtain. NSLs have been abused for drug investigations and even banking and tax investigations.

My favorite snoop is the Treasury Department's Financial Intelligence Center (FinCEN) unit. FinCEN nicely illustrates why government isn't the only concern when it comes to your privacy. Although FinCEN can't just demand to see your records, its arcane rules create enough uncertainty that banks will proactively hand them over if they have the slightest suspicion that you're up to no good.

Under FinCEN's "Operation Choke Point," legal business activities — such as running an online business that accepts credit cards — can "flag" you as a "threat," prompting your bank to send everything to FinCEN voluntarily. Everything your bank knows about you — your identity, financial history, and complete details of your banking activity — is at risk.

Of course, the uncertainty here is intentional — a feature, not a bug. When people know that FinCEN and other government agencies can get their records easily, they avoid activities that could be construed as suspicious — even if they are perfectly legal. That's the point.

But still … why should you worry, you may ask, if you haven't done anything wrong? And doesn't the Constitution protect you?

No.

As every schoolchild knows, there are three check-and-balance branches of the U.S. government: the executive, legislative and judiciary. But the U.S. government has seemingly sprouted a fourth branch: the national security state.

The Central Intelligence Agency (CIA) was recently forced to admit that it deliberately hacked into the computers of U.S. Senate Intelligence committee researchers working to compile a report on CIA torture in the years after 9/11.

Like its Roman forebear, the U.S. Senate is an enormously important institution, designed as a constitutional check on the executive and judicial branches of government. As representatives of the sovereign states, senators are typically accorded a great deal of deference. And yet the CIA thought it could get away with spying on the very Senate committee charged with its oversight.

If the hallowed Senate can't trust the U.S. security state to refrain from spying on it, Constitution or no, then we shouldn't either. We should assume that whether the USA Freedom Act or any other legislation passes, we are on our own when it comes to preserving our privacy.

And Not Just the Feds

Back in the old days, the word most often associated with government surveillance was "wiretap." It evokes images of fedora-hatted G-men with old-fashioned headphones listening in on a bad guy's phone calls from a van across the street.

These days, the word "wiretap" rarely makes an appearance. That's because the government itself no longer needs to do anything technical to obtain information about you.

It orders the companies that provide us with communications, banking, commercial or other services to hand over whatever they have stored on their servers. All it takes is a National Security Letter, FinCEN directive or some other secret, extra-judicial demand and it's all handed over to the government.

That's because we wiretap ourselves 24/7, 365 days a year. Everything we say and do, online and offline, is recorded and stored somewhere. The GPS chip in your smartphone allows for close tracking of your location, right down to the aisle you're walking down in Target. Your credit cards and loyalty cards are tracking your specific purchases. Amazon knows more about you than most of your friends and relatives. The Nest thermostat in your house is tracking your movement in the house, and when you're away.

All that digital-age convenience … and all that risk.

The Government Won't Protect You ...

NSA whistleblower Edward Snowden's bombshell revelations about domestic NSA spying emerged just over a year ago. The initial reaction was widespread shock and consternation at the extent of the U.S. government's invasion of its citizens' privacy.

A year later, however, very little has changed — except that the public debate has been brought largely under control by the powers-that-be.

Predictably, once the initial flurry of indignation subsided, the mainstream press stopped reporting on the issue and the backroom deal-making began.

The major players are the Senate, White House and the very agencies responsible for these outrages — the CIA and NSA.

As a result, Congressman Jim Sensenbrenner's signature "reform" legislation, the appropriately named USA Freedom Act, has been stalled in Congress for months.

Although the Senate recently passed a beefed-up version, House Republicans continue to object to attempts to narrow the scope of who and what the NSA can monitor, and also to the creation of an independent Privacy Advocate for the secretive court that oversees the NSA.

Given the upcoming elections — and the decrepit state of respect for America's Constitutional values — it's highly unlikely that the Senate bill will be taken up by the House anytime soon.

Six Key Steps to Protecting Yourself

Many of the key elements to a strong personal privacy strategy should be common sense. The big challenge is to secure your communications so that you can be sure everything you say and do online is truly private. Fortunately, the year since Edward Snowden's revelations has seen the introduction of some new powerful tools to help you to do just that. Let's look at some of the most promising. All of them are legal, inexpensive and relatively easy to execute.

Imagine how you'll feel when the fear tactics of the NSA, FBI and IRS have no effect on you ... because you'll be invisible!

Let me show you how you too can "disappear" for the electronic landscape.

#1 Your Cellphone is Sharing All Your Secrets

Let's start with the gadget many of us use more than any other: the cellphone.

A lot of security and privacy options depend on what you want and need to use a cellphone for.

If you just want a phone for outgoing and incoming calls from trusted contacts, use a cellphone that isn't registered in your name, but rather in the name of a hard-to-track LLC or other structure. Pay cash for prepaid calling and Internet access cards so the number can't be linked to your banking details. Activate your phone as well as any calling and Internet cards at a pay phone. Don't give out your real name, phone number or any other personal information when you activate the phone. Make sure the phone is set to prevent your number from showing up in the recipient's "Caller ID." In this way, your outgoing calls will be untraceable to you.

But what about snooping directly on the content of your calls and texts? They won't know it's you if you follow the advice in the previous paragraph, but a dedicated snoop could simply grab the contents of your calls and texts out of the ether, by listening in wirelessly.

Here's where encryption comes in. There's a new service I can recommend called Silent Circle, which offers encrypted calling and text plans, as well as data security for when you use your cellphone as a "smartphone" for email and web browsing. When a Silent Circle subscriber makes a phone call, sends a text or video chats with another Silent Circle member, that transmission is secured and encrypted end-to-end. You can use Silent Circle from an iPhone, Android device, iPad or even from a Windows or Apple computer.

How does Silent Circle achieve this? By focusing on the physical security of their servers, networks and equipment. The company owns, controls and even custom builds their own equipment, and employs NSA-level security measures to prevent intrusion. They have built their own backbone for their encrypted communications service, and unlike most telecoms companies, they don't share their dedicated network with third parties.

The next level up for cellphone security and privacy is to get a phone that's almost impossible to hack. That's because, even if you use a service like Silent Circle, you're still vulnerable to physical or software bugs that can be planted on your phone remotely. To beat that threat, I recommend a Blackphone, a self-described "anti-NSA" phone. It's preconfigured for privacy with simple tools that anyone can use, and it won't allow you to install vulnerable third-party "apps." It offers a level of security and data you certainly won't get with anything else … it's practically unhackable.

If you don't want to spring for a Blackphone, which goes for about $650, use an Apple iPhone rather than an Android-based phone. Because their operating system is tightly controlled by Apple, and not open-source, Apple iPhones are invulnerable to the most common forms of hacking.

But remember none of these steps matter if you don't switch your calling plan away from one of the main call companies and use something designed for maximum privacy, like Silent Circle, instead.

#2 The Trick to Keeping Your Inbox Private

Email is an important and challenging electronic privacy issue. It's the tool most of us use often, and critical for sensitive but complicated transactions like banking and investing.

The key to protecting your email is to use encryption. As with cellphone encryption, email encryption scrambles the contents of your messages. They can be unscrambled only with an "encryption key" that you set and share with your trusted contacts. To date, the NSA and other agencies have not been able to crack 128-bit encryption, which is the highest standard.

But whatever you do ... don't use commercial encryption software, especially from large vendors such as Symantec. That's because we must assume they have NSA-friendly "back doors" built in. One of Snowden's revelations was that the NSA made secret deals with developers of the most common "closed-source" encryption software that such companies use.

Instead, look to "open-source" applications. An open-source program is one that allows any programmer to look at the code, unlike "closed-source" software (like Windows). Open-source encryption code can be examined by anyone with the skills, and so any hacks planted by someone will inevitably be discovered.

GNU Privacy Guard (GnuPG), which I recommend for advanced users, is a free encryption program that Edward Snowden used to communicate with journalists Glenn Greenwald and Laura Poitras when making his bombshell revelations. GnuPG is based on the "Pretty Good Privacy" (PGP) software developed in the 1990s by encryption pioneer Phil Zimmermann. The program converts your email messages into unreadable gibberish that only the intended recipient of your message can decode. It also lets you encrypt files on your hard drive so only you can access them.

But installing and using PGP can be challenging, which is why tech giants Google and Yahoo recently announced a joint encrypted email system, due out next year, that will be based on PGP. (It will almost certainly be free.) Google in particular has an incentive to develop such a system — if it doesn't, it will watch its privacy-conscious user base evaporate.

There are two critical aspects to the new Google-Yahoo system. First, your local Internet Service Provider (ISP) — which in most parts of the country is Comcast, AT&T or another cable company — won't be able to decipher your emails since they won't have the encryption keys. Neither wiretaps nor court orders will be able to pry the content of your communications out of them. Second, neither Google nor Yahoo will be able to access or surrender your communications for the same reason — they won't have your encryption key either.

A similar initiative is ProtonMail, which is also free. I personally use ProtonMail because, being a Swiss company, it's far less likely to succumb to pressure from government than Google or Yahoo.

Like the envisaged Yahoo-Google joint venture, ProtonMail separates the encrypted message from its encryption key. All the encryption takes place on your computer and the receiver's computer. Neither message nor key are stored on ProtonMail's servers, so there's no way for government to get their hands on them, even with a court order against ProtonMail or your ISP.

ProtonMail has the edge over the Yahoo-Google venture, in my opinion, because they've placed all their servers in Switzerland, which has some of the world's toughest privacy laws. That's why there's a waiting list — demand for ProtonMail is so high that there aren't enough available servers in Switzerland to accommodate it. But the group is currently raising money to build more.

#3 An Easy Fix for Your Biggest Weakness

Passwords are critical to online security. But they are also one of the biggest weak spots in most of our privacy-protection arsenals.

One thing you can do is use two-factor authentication for Facebook, Google, Dropbox, Apple ID, Microsoft, Twitter and other accounts. Whenever you log in, you'll also need to enter a special code that the site texts to your phone. I've done this with many of my accounts. This is free, easy and particularly worthwhile for any finance related accounts.

I recently started using a secure password generation and management software, called Dashlane, which works across multiple devices, such as my home PC, laptop and cellphone. An annual subscription costs $30.

It was getting to the point where I had so many passwords to remember that it was seriously cutting into my productivity. And I was at risk, because the natural tendency when you have a lot of passwords to remember is to re-use them on multiple sites.

Dashlane not only remembers all your passwords, but will also generate super strong and unique ones and automatically fill them into login fields with the click of a button.

Although I use Dashlane, there are other services, such as LastPass. I regard them as interchangeable — the core of their business model is watertight security over your encrypted passwords, so they have a powerful incentive to get it right: one slip-up is the end of them.

Of course, there are some simple things you can do, too when it comes to passwords. For example, you can lie when setting up password security questions, such as "your mother's maiden name." You can even lie about your own name when setting up accounts with any online commercial site, like Amazon!

#4 How to Browse Anonymously on the Internet

The next most important aspect of electronic privacy is your online activity. There are two aspects to this: the technology you use and your own browsing habits.

The first thing to know is that you should use only Google Chrome or Firefox — never Microsoft Internet Explorer. That's because unlike IE, those browsers are easily customizable. With Chrome or Firefox, you can customize for privacy to your heart's content.

For example, on my personal Google Chrome installation I use the following "extensions," which are all free and can be found on Chrome's web store.

- AdBlock: prevents most tracking cookies.

- AVG Privacy Fix: analyses all my online activity and makes recommendations for security improvements that can be activated with a single click.

- Collusion: shows what information websites silently send and receive to and from other websites that I never directly visit, so I can stop it.

- HTTPS Everywhere: encrypts my web traffic on most sites.

- IBA Opt-Out: prevents Google and other sites from tracking my browsing habits for advertising purposes.

Both Chrome and Firefox allow "anonymous browsing windows" that achieve most of these things in completely private, browsing sessions. Both browsers also disable Java and Flash by default, since both of these products are known to be a security risk.

While I use Chrome myself, many people prefer Firefox because unlike Google, it is a nonprofit company that uses open-source software. My personal opinion is that if you are concerned enough about privacy, you should just go straight to a browser that is set up as part of a Virtual Private Network. A VPN is a private, encrypted, password protected system.

For the more technically-minded, you can use the Tor Browser, which is free, open-source, and operated through distributed computers rather than a central server. This means it can't be "hacked" or invaded at any central point. Tor is based on a browser interface and is instantly available once Tor is installed.

Tor has become much easier to use and more secure since the Snowden revelations emerged, but it remains a browser to use primarily when you are concerned about privacy rather than for everyday surfing. It isn't as customizable and doesn't have as many bells and whistles as Chrome or Firefox, but it can do the main things easily — banking, secure email, online chats, and so on.

#5 Making Yourself Invisible Online

There are a number of tips and tricks that can help you maximize your privacy online. Here are some of the most important.

- Avoid surfing the Net while signed into the major social media. That includes Facebook, Google (including Gmail and YouTube), LinkedIn and so on. If you're logged in, those companies will be able to track most sites you visit for marketing purposes.

- Enter as little information as possible in your social media profiles. Delete photos of friends or family members online from social networking sites — especially Facebook. They help investigators reconstruct your social network. Don't accept "friend" invitations from strangers on services such as Facebook, LinkedIn, Twitter or Skype.

- To scrub information about you that is available online, use a service such as http://www.reputation.com to remove personal information from websites that market it.

- Never fill in unnecessary or optional information in online forms. Use fictitious information for your name, etc. unless it is absolutely necessary to provide accurate information. In your email software settings, make sure the default "From" field is something other than your name.

- Wipe your browser of "cookies" every time you close it. All browsers can now be set to do this automatically.

- Turn off Geolocation, which tells the Internet where your browsing session is located.

#6 How to Keep Out Hardware Invaders

So much of the business of today's life is conducted on the computer. Yet we rarely think about the machine itself as a source of privacy risk. For those who really want to go the extra mile, here's how you can eliminate that risk, which is minor but still exists.

Most people know that you should be using a "firewall" such as ZoneAlarm or Malwarebytes. They both come in free versions, and annual subscriptions that include anti-virus definitions cost less than $50. (I use Malwarebytes. But they're both good.)

A firewall prevents your PC from contacting an address on the Internet without your knowing about it. Most spyware, malware and "bots," like keystroke loggers, work this way. With a firewall installed, you have to choose to allow an outgoing connection, giving you time to find out whether it's a malicious one.

Similarly, you should use full disk encryption (FDE) software, like the one I use (DiskCryptor) that make the entire contents of your hard drives unintelligible without a decryption password. Microsoft's built-in version, BitLocker, is actually pretty good too.

But what about the hardware in your computer — the hard disks, motherboards, Ethernet cards and other physical parts? They can also pose a risk. To beat this, I've been using self-built computers running Microsoft Windows for decades. (Unfortunately, you can't build Apple computers yourself.) I make computers myself from parts I buy off the shelf.

But even if that's not something you want to do yourself, there's nothing stopping you from having one built by a local tech shop.

Even big chains such as Best Buy or Computer Warehouse can do this for you. A customized computer can run any software you like and do anything any other computer can do. And they are often cheaper and more reliable than brand-name machines such as Dell or HP.

The reason I suggest this is that Snowden's revelations included the shocking news that the NSA and other government agencies have been working secretly to create vulnerabilities in computer hardware manufactured in the U.S.

For example, the NSA has secretly modified U.S.-made computer parts such as Cisco Ethernet cards (which connect your PC to your modem or router) to enable snooping. Similarly, the NSA, FBI and other agencies have been putting pressure on U.S. hardware and software manufacturers to deliberately leave "back doors" into their products to facilitate the same thing.

To beat this, the next time you upgrade your Windows-based computer, consider having your local computer store assemble one for you out of parts that come from generic manufacturers outside the U.S.

As paradoxical as it may seem, parts from Taiwan or China are less likely to contain backdoors that the U.S. government can access, so you're more secure using them. Any good computer tech can advise you on the parts you need and get them for you.

There are two other hardware related issues you need to know about:

1. Always do particularly sensitive work on a computer that's never been connected to the Internet — preferably one that has no wireless or Ethernet capacity at all. Install strong file encryption software on it. You can use such as a so-called "Air Gap" computer to create documents, spreadsheets and other sensitive records. When you want to transfer a file, encrypt the file on the secure "air gap" computer and transfer it to your Internet-connected computer, using a USB stick. To decrypt something, reverse the process.

2. Before you dispose of a computer (or cellphone), get rid of all the personal information it stores. Use a wipe utility program to overwrite the entire hard drive. Then dismantle the machine and smash it to bits with a hammer — especially the hard disk.

A Final Word

So you've composed a private document on an air gap computer you had custom-made for yourself. Your "air gap's" hard disk and the contents of your file are encrypted. You transfer it to your Internet machine, also custom-made, and send it by encrypted email within a VPN, to a friend with a similarly secure setup. You send the password she needs to decrypt it via encrypted text using message Silent Circle.

With all that encryption going on, your message will be safe — as long as everyone involved follows the protocols and advice I've set out in this report.

And yet, I'd be lying if I said that a dedicated adversary can never find a way to discover your secrets. (After all, there's always the rack … or rather its modern counterparts.) The critical thing is to make it as difficult as possible to invade your privacy. Multiple levels of encryption and other privacy tricks make you so hard to hack that government and other snoops will just move on to the next person.

THE NSA'S LATEST ATTEMPT TO HACK YOUR COMPUTER

Ted Bauman, *The Sovereign Investor Daily*, February 2015

Sometimes I wonder just how bad the news about government spying can get. The answer was in my inbox this morning. I quickly ran out of superlatives: Awful. Terrible. Appalling. Dreadful.

The article in question reported that for most of the last two decades, the National Security Agency (NSA) has been deliberately infecting the "firmware" that runs most common hard drives, including those made by Seagate, Western Digital, IBM, Toshiba, Samsung and Maxtor. There's a 99% chance that the computer you're using has one of those in it. Mine has four.

The malware campaign, called "Equation," has infected tens of thousands of public and private computers in more than 30 countries. And it allows the NSA to read everything on those machines at will.

Unless you've done one simple thing to thwart them…

NSA Surveillance: A Big, White Lie

So how does the NSA get away with this sort of thing? By lying and abusing its legal authority.

According to Kaspersky Labs, a highly-respected Russian anti-malware outfit, ex-NSA sources confirmed that agents pose as software developers to trick hard drive manufacturers into supplying source code, which they would then modify and deploy. Even worse, the agency often simply keeps a copy of the code when it does mandatory "code audits" on behalf of Pentagon procurement departments.

Hacks like this — which basically make the entire world's information grid vulnerable to U.S. government spying — are why Phil Zimmermann, creator of email encryption software Pretty Good Privacy (PGP) and now president and co-founder of secure cellphone company Silent Circle, says: "Intelligence agencies have never had it so good."

But the good times depend on computer users ignoring the one thing that can make even a wide-open computer useless to the NSA or other spies.

Your Keys to the Digital Kingdom

Imagine a world where you could leave your house, your car, even your safe unlocked at all times. All you'd need is a technology that would make the things inside those places unusable to a thief. The lock on your front door would be redundant, because nobody could use your property even if they got their hands on it.

The technology needed to make your digital property secure — even if the front door is pried open by hacks like "Equation" — already exists. In fact, it's been around even longer than Equation ... since June 5, 1991, to be exact. That's the day Phil Zimmermann released encryption software PGP to his friends, who then distributed it worldwide.

PGP and the many encryption programs that are its progeny make anything stored on your computer, or transmitted by email, instant message and voice-over-internet — anything digital — unusable to a spy or thief. They turn digital information into useless gibberish that can be unlocked only with a special key. The NSA could walk right in and rummage around, but would be unable to read a thing.

Relying on Inaction

The NSA isn't the only gang trying to break open digital doors. Also in my inbox this morning was a report on a group of hackers who may have stolen $1 billion from more than 100 banks in 30 countries, the "biggest bank heist in history."

Both the NSA and the digital bank robbers rely on one thing to get away with their misdeeds: That their targets don't use good encryption.

As amazing as it seems in this day and age, the banks targeted by the hackers relied on old-fashioned "locks" on their digital front doors — passwords — but failed to encrypt the client information and account details stored behind them. Once the banks' passwords were compromised, the hackers could pillage at will, often by stealing a few cents at a time from millions of accounts, making them virtually undetectable for long periods.

It's just that sort of inaction that the NSA and other privacy vampires need in order to remain in business.

In Us We Trust

The easiest way to get started on the route to digital sovereignty is to explore some of the options freely available here. You could have your hard drive protected in the time it takes to read this article.

The "Equation" revelations prove that our own government is prepared to lie and cheat in order to steal our privacy from us. Imagine what they would do if they were really motivated … say by an executive order to implement wealth confiscation.

It'd be too late then to write your Congressman. But if you were using good encryption to protect your digital assets, it wouldn't matter.

That's because you'd be able to exercise a "Veto of One," the ultimate goal of every sovereign individual.

MIT Just Made It Easier to Find You
Ted Bauman, *The Sovereign Investor Daily*, February 2015

Some years ago, *The New York Times* used bulk search records mistakenly published online by America Online (AOL) to identify a woman living in Lilburn, GA — just down the road from me — solely from the pattern of her web queries.

That was the first time I can recall "metadata" receiving serious public attention as a threat to our personal privacy. Since then, it's become a matter of serious concern to many people.

"Metadata" is the information surrounding our electronic activity. Unlike actual content, like our emails or bank account numbers, metadata in isolation is anonymous. It's like the postmark of origin and destination address on a letter. Even if the names of the sender and received aren't visible on the envelope, it doesn't take much to figure out *who sent what to whom* ... and from there, to speculate about *why*.

Now researchers at the Massachusetts Institute of Technology have developed a method to determine an individual person from just four pieces of secondary information — metadata such as location or timing of credit card purchases, for example.

And it's accurate 90% of the time. That's bad news if you care about your privacy. But there's a way to beat it.

Private Eyes No Longer

Ever since Sir Arthur Conan Doyle started writing Sherlock Holmes mysteries, it's been fun to follow fictional detectives as they use their skills to infer names and facts from apparently unrelated information. We admire the intelligence and lateral thinking involved to catch the bad guy. It's a long but captivating process, helpfully concluded just before the end of each story, TV show or movie.

But now an army of private and public agencies is going way beyond the limitations of the individual human brain to deduce all sorts of things about all of us from the digital trail we leave behind.

Now, the MIT study in question didn't actually identify the individuals associated with those four pieces of metadata. But they did demonstrate that it's easy to do so when you combine that metadata with other easily-obtainable information, like location information captured by smartphone apps for Facebook, Twitter or Foursquare.

The Wall Street Journal reports, for example, that "Last November ... ride-share company Uber disclosed it had combined its customer records of late-night trips in major cities with local crime reports to calculate the likelihood that its weekend riders were visiting prostitutes."

Ouch. Especially given the fact that Uber is known to be able to identify specific users from their customer records.

Of course, there are deeper implications.

Hiding in Plain Sight

Metadata enables the private sector and government to track your movements and purchases, even if the data has been stripped of identifiers specific to you, like your credit card numbers. But there's a way to beat that ... one that takes advantage of a technology I predict you'll be using soon.

Earlier this year I wrote a report for *Offshore Confidential* subscribers in which I described a way to achieve far greater data and personal security than possible when using physical credit and debit cards. It involves smartphone-based payment systems such as Apple Pay.

Although iPhones can be a privacy risk — one that can be mitigated with some smart adjustments — their one great advantage is that the new Apple Pay app uses a technology called "tokenization," which completely masks your personal identity and banking information. When you transact, that information is converted into an encrypted form that nobody can read — not even Apple, or your bank. The encrypted "token" is unique to each transaction, so it can't be tracked from place to place and from time to time.

Outwitting the Spies

In a testament to the power of the market, companies like Apple are increasingly being forced to meet the popular demand for fully encrypted, anonymous means of communication and transacting.

It's a tricky path for some of them, like Google, who also want to make money from the data they collect about us. But for companies like Apple who aren't in the business of selling customer data to third parties — or giving it to the government — digital anonymity is a major attraction for privacy-minded customers.

I'm always suspicious of things that seem too good to be true. Someday Apple Pay and similar tokenization technologies may be found wanting. But for now, the pragmatist in me is willing to give them a try.

So should you.

U.S. Authorizes Back Door "Roving Wiretaps"

Robert E. Bauman JD, *The Sovereign Individual*,
December 1998, updated 2010

If you're the U.S. Attorney General, head of the U.S. Department of Justice, and you can't persuade legislators to openly pass laws that curtail civil liberties, you have another option: Hide the same laws in other, less controversial legislation. Wait until that law has passed both the House and the Senate and is sent to a conference committee to iron out minor differences between the two versions. Persuade the conferees to insert the controversial provision into the conference bill. Then quietly pass the revisions without public debate. This was the back-door approach used by the U.S. Department of Justice in 1984 to bring about the largest expansion in civil forfeiture laws in U.S. history.

And in 1998 it repeated the performance. Without debate or notice, U.S. lawmakers approved a proposal long sought by the FBI that dramatically expanded the authority of police to conduct "roving wiretaps" (i.e., tapping any and all phones potentially used by a criminal suspect). (Congress rejected this very same idea when the matter was openly debated as part of the1996 Anti-Terrorism bill).

The law, which allows police to tap any telephone used or located near a wiretap target, was added to the Intelligence Authorization Conference report during a closed-door meeting. Then, without debate, both the House and Senate approved it.

Previously, police had to demonstrate that a target was switching telephones for the specific purpose of avoiding surveillance. Now, they need only show that the target of a wiretap's actions could have the effect of thwarting interception from a specific facility.

When the FBI originally requested roving wiretap authority, it acknowledged that less than one percent of the conversations it recorded were relevant to its investigations. In other words, 99 percent of the time, police are listening in on irrelevant conversations. The vast majority of these conversations involve participants neither suspected nor accused of any wrongdoing. Roving wiretap authority will makes it even more likely innocent third parties will be drawn into the government's surveillance net.

Say, for instance, you're unknowingly meeting with the target of a roving wiretap in your home or office. Your phone number is added to the list of target phones, not for a single day, but potentially for as long as the investigation continues — perhaps weeks, months or years.

Investigators are supposed to ignore conversations that are not directly relevant to the authorized wiretap. But of course they don't.

The safest course of conduct: Don't say anything on a telephone that you don't want to hear played back in a courtroom.

Does the Constitution Mean Anything Anymore?

Robert E. Bauman JD, *Sovereign Society Offshore A-Letter*, 2007

When I was 15-years-old, I swore my first oath to support and defend the United States Constitution serving as a young page boy in the House of Representatives. Later, as a Member of Congress (and as a Republican and a conservative), I took that same oath to the Constitution, by which every congressman and senator currently serving has also supposedly sworn their allegiance.

So knowing that, how can we explain the U.S. Congress passing a new law that virtually repeals the guarantees against unreasonable search and seizure in the Fourth Amendment of the Bill of Rights?

My answer: cowardly fear. It's not fear of the "terrorism boogeyman" — but fear of not getting reelected! Politics rules, to Hell with principle!

The minority Republicans in Congress, sheep that they are, went along with President Bush's demand for even greater police power over all of us. But the real hypocrites were the Democrats that now control both Houses.

I am always nervous when I find myself in agreement with *The New York Times*, but they said it right:

"It was appalling to watch over the last few days as Congress — now led by Democrats — caved in to yet another unnecessary and dangerous expansion of President Bush's powers, this time to spy on Americans in violation of basic constitutional rights. Many of the 16 Democrats in the Senate and 41 in the House who voted for the bill said that they had acted in the name of national security, but the only security at play was their job security."

Congressmen Who Attacked the PATRIOT Act Now Support Wiretapping

These are the same Democrats that have been loudly attacking (as they should be attacking), the befuddled U.S. Attorney General Gonzales for violating civil rights using the PATRIOT Act. And they also attacked President Bush for his secret wiretapping when it was revealed late last year.

As *The Times* noted the law "…would allow the government to intercept, without a warrant, every communication into or out of any country, including the United States. Instead of explaining all this to American voters — the minimal benefits and the enormous risks — the Democrats have allowed Mr. Bush and his fear mongering to dominate all discussions on terrorism and national security."

According to neutral observers, the new law gives the U.S. government virtually unchecked power to secretly wiretap all our phone calls and spy on and read our emails, faxes or other electronic communications without any court order and no due process of law.

This is a radical, subversive departure from American legal traditions. As an attorney, I see this new wiretap surveillance law as yet another abandonment of the rule of law and a violation of due process in America.

Gone is the requirement that laws must relate to legitimate government interests and may not result in unfair or arbitrary treatment of an individual. Now impartial judges are replaced by faceless bureaucrats and anti-terror police who will decide our fate.

What Happens When Fear Rules Congress

In 1757, Edmund Burke wrote: "No passion so effectively robs the mind of all its powers of acting and reasoning as fear."

Fear as a decisive factor in political and national life is nothing new in history. But President Bush has made fear his trademark. He constantly uses the fear factor to get his way, describing threats that are amorphous, shadowy, unclear, yet perceived as very real, the threat of terrorism.

Politicians too often have employed fear as a controlling and guiding principle to achieve their dubious ends. Such politicians offer themselves as protectors. National leaders have touted their remedies against alleged foreign invasions, barbaric tribes, hated minorities, Communists, drugs and a host of other manufactured threats.

Now the fear of the hour is terrorism. Yes, the threat is real and it must be guarded against, but not by surrendering all our freedoms.

If a member of Congress does not support whatever the proposal may be, he or she is accused of being "soft" on terrorism. Nearly six years after 9/11, and with the miserable track record of Attorney General Gonzales, a majority in Congress rolls over and proclaims: "We are against the terrorists, too!" — even as they vote to trash the Bill of Rights.

Why Spy on Just the Terrorists?

And don't think for a moment that Big Brother's police will limit this unchecked surveillance law to anti-terrorism alone. Just as they have done with the PATRIOT Act, this vast power will be used to spy on anyone they wish, whether alleged IRS tax evaders or SEC violators.

No one is safe from trumped up charges based on eavesdropping on our phone calls, reading our emails and monitoring our other communications.

When we at The Sovereign Society recommend offshore financial havens for placement of bank accounts or asset protection trusts, or suggest countries for a possible foreign residence, the existence of the rule of law always is a major factor in our choice.

Sacrificing Liberty AND Safety

Of course, we know that in the United States anti-terror laws have seriously compromised what we used to know as the rule of law. So who is winning — freedom or terrorism?

This raises the question: Just how far are Americans willing to go in surrendering their liberty and their privacy? How much are we willing to pay for this promised, illusory defense? Are we willing to become Fortress America with Big Brother watching and listening to all that we say and do? Americans had better put aside these politically inspired fears, and start asking and answering that question — before we enjoy neither safety nor liberty.

The United States: An Informer's Paradise
Robert E. Bauman JD, *The Sovereign Individual*, 1997, updated 2010

Most Americans know little or nothing about the widespread domestic use of police informants — and few government and police officials are willing to talk openly about this big, dirty secret.

For people outside the U.S., an accurate knowledge about how the U.S. government uses informants in its international operations is essential to avoid entrapment and worse. What happens in the U.S. has a disturbing tendency to be exported elsewhere. It could be you being investigated or charged with crimes you didn't commit because an informant pointed the finger at you.

Increasingly informants are being used by U.S. police agents in so-called "white collar" international business and finance cases. "Money laundering" is one of the favorite charges pursued. Shrouded in secrecy, informers don't want publicity about their nasty work. They want lenient treatment for past crimes, money rewards and sometimes revenge.

Despite constant government efforts to keep the public in the dark, the bright sunlight of publicity has exposed the squirming mass under the rock. In numerous U.S. money laundering cases, informants have played an important role.

It's Happening in America

The informant scandal is so serious it prompted federal appeals court judge Stephen S. Trott of Boise, Idaho, head of the Criminal Division of the U.S. Department of Justice under President Reagan, to warn, "The integrity of the criminal justice system is at stake. There needs to be better control and supervision of informants." He said the current use of informants "… reminds me of a movie I saw in which the characters played a game they called TEGWAR — an acronym for 'The Exciting Game Without Any Rules.'"

And yet, in the wake of the 1995 Oklahoma City bombing, President Clinton quickly demanded that Congress pass legislation greatly increasing police wiretapping, FBI surveillance and the expanded use and protection of government informants. According to press reports, a key part of what the President wanted was a national network of paid informants, or so-called "human intelligence sources."

Fortunately, congressional civil rights advocates, on the left and right, managed to thwart the worst excesses Clinton wanted, but many of his dubious proposals found their way into law under the guise of "anti-terrorism" controls. Unfortunately many of these same police powers were granted in the PATRIOT Act of 2001.

15,000 "Wild, Out-of-Control" Informants

Michael Levine, a retired 25-year veteran of both U.S. Customs and the Drug Enforcement Agency (DEA), estimates there are currently at least 15,000 informers on federal payrolls, not counting many thousands more paid by state and local police. His estimate does not include more than 10,000 informants who claim money rewards each year for reporting fellow taxpayers to the IRS, or the nearly 1,000 so-called "controlled informants" the IRS pays to inform on others, some of them tax accountants.

Levine, retired in 1990, charged that informants, earning three or four times more in government pay than the DEA and FBI agents who are supposed to be their bosses, have literally taken over most criminal investigations. Says Levine: "Our rights as citizens and the U.S. Constitution are now in the hands of 15,000 wild, out-of-control informants. If you get in their way they will take you down, and government agents are ignorant enough or lazy enough to let them do "

Protests Are Few

In this era of sound bites and media-oriented "get tough on crime" politics, few elected officials dare to decry loss of constitutional protections. The late U.S. Representative Henry J. Hyde was a courageous exception. In the 1996 book Forfeiting Our Property Rights (Cato Institute, Washington D.C.), the then Chairman of the U.S. House Judiciary Committee attacked government use of "an army of well-paid secret informers," whom he described as "a motley crew of drug pushers, ex-cons, convicts, prisoners and other social misfits."

Hyde stated bluntly: "They have a strong incentive to lie, and they often do. Informants, by their very nature, are not normal, gainfully employed, honest, upright citizens. Rather they are, or have been, involved in drug or other serious criminal activity, and their motivation is to save their own skins."

Typical is the 1996 New York federal district court case in which Emad A. Salem, the unsavory main government witness in New York's World Trade Center terrorist bombing conspiracy trial, admitted he lied, testifying he was promised more than US$1 million by the government for his assistance as the principal informer in the case. Similarly, informants in the Miami federal case against ex-Panama dictator Manuel Noreiga were paid over US$4 million and spared hundreds of years of potential prison time.

Informing — A Big Business

Individual informants do receive princely sums from the U.S. Treasury, a grotesque example of tax dollars at work. Like U.S. lawyers, informers are sometimes paid on a contingency fee; the total value of property they finger for successful forfeiture determines how much money the government pays into their personal bank accounts. So-called "cooperating witnesses" receive 25 percent of the value of property seized by the government in any one case, with a maximum cap of US$250,000.

Secrecy Is the Rule

Although the Sixth Amendment, part of the U.S. Constitution's Bill of Rights, guarantees an accused person the right "to be confronted with the witnesses against him," courts have held this is not absolute and usually applies at trial, but not always in preliminary stages of investigation and indictment. These rulings supporting the so-called "informant's privilege," allow secret accusers to avoid risk of exposure by having to testify in public. Instead, a police officer seeking a search warrant simply repeats before a magistrate, or testifies before a grand jury about what he was told by "a reliable informant."

The highly unfair result: most criminal defendants never find out who accused them of wrongdoing, unless prosecutors decide an informant's testimony at trial is essential to convict. Prosecutors, police and federal agents defend this system, arguing informants are indispensable in organized crime, terrorism and white-collar crime cases.

It's the War on Drugs, Stupid!

The driving force behind the massive use of informants originally was the much-touted "war on drugs." Informants are often the key to drug arrests and property confiscation under civil asset forfeiture laws, a valuable cash cow for police. Law enforcement officials keep most of the cash and property seized, and the funds go directly into police budgets, salaries and other perks.

Phantom Police Informers

In his book, *The Best Defense*, Harvard law professor Alan Dershowitz offers some little-known rules he says "govern the justice game in America today." Rule IV is, "Almost all police lie about whether they violated the Constitution in order to convict 'guilty defendants."

That is certainly accurate when it comes to the use and/or manufacture of police informers. It is now commonplace for police lacking a "reliable informant" on which to base a request for a search or arrest warrant, to invent them.

Lying by police to support questionable criminal charges against suspects has gone on for years in New York City, according to a report of the Mayor's commission investigating police corruption. After 1993-94 hearings, the Mollen Commission concluded New York police routinely made false arrests, invented informers, tampered with evidence and committed perjury on the witness stand. "Perjury is the most widespread form of police wrongdoing," the report stated, noting it even has a well-known nickname among the court house cognoscenti — "testilying."

Early on the morning of October 2, 1992, millionaire Donald Scott was shot to death by a member of a 27-man police drug squad as they broke into his rural ranch home. A subsequent five-month investigation by the Ventura County district attorney found police had lied to a judge to obtain the search warrant, based on a false tip by an informant that Scott was growing marijuana.

The report also concluded police hoped to confiscate Scott's ranch and turn it over the National Park Service, a federal agency to which Scott has repeatedly refused to sell his land. No charges were brought against the police and no one was disciplined for Scott's death.

America is Under Surveillance

The official incompetence, corruption and criminal conduct associated with informants might be understandable if these were isolated examples, but such events are widespread. Studies show the major groups who suffer as a result are African-Americans, Latinos, Arabs and Asians, including international travelers.

In 1992 in the Memphis, Tennessee, airport, 75 percent of the travelers stopped by police on informant tips were black, yet only four percent of the flying public is black. CBS television's "60 Minutes" reporters checked out DEA airport operations in New York, Atlanta and other cities, with a well-dressed black male undercover reporter buying a plane ticket with cash. Within minutes of each purchase, DEA agents accosted the reporter and confiscated all his money; ticket clerk informers turned him in on the spot every time.

DEA operates permanent surveillance in designated hotels in New York, Miami, Los Angeles and other cities considered scenes of likely drug activity. Hotel employees are paid to act as informers and report "suspicious" guests and people with too much or too little luggage, guests who pay room bills in cash or make multiple long distance phone calls.

The IRS too

A new federal rewards program dishes out cash to people who turn in friends, relatives and employers for fudging their tax returns.

For years the IRS grudgingly paid stingy rewards to squealers who brought it mostly small cases; during 2004 and 2005, 428 informants received a total of $12 million — only 7% of the paltry $168 million all their leads brought in. But in 2006, hoping to entice insiders to rat out big-dollar cheats and corporate tax shelters and games, Congress directed the IRS to pay tipsters at least 15% and as much as 30% of taxes, penalties and interest collected in cases where $2 million or more is at stake.

The gambit seems to be working very well. The IRS continues to get thousands of small case tips a year. But in fiscal 2009, ended Oct. 30, the IRS Whistleblower Office also logged big case leads on 1,900 taxpayers, up from 1,246 in fiscal 2008, the first full year the new law was in effect. Dozens of these tips involve purported tax losses of $100 million or more. Sure, those are just allegations. But informants "often provide extensive documentation to support their claims," the Whistleblower Office noted in a report. The Treasury Inspector General for Tax Administration, in a separate report, added up all the 2008 tips and found that $65 billion in unreported income was alleged.

In June 2007, Bradley C. Birkenfeld — motivated in large part, he now acknowledges, by the new reward law — came to U.S. officials with documents in hand and laid out how his former employer, UBS AG, helped wealthy Americans hide money offshore.

So far the investigation he triggered has produced a $780 million payment to the U.S. government from UBS, Switzerland's largest bank; an unprecedented agreement by the Swiss to finger 4,450 U.S. taxpayers with secret UBS accounts; and criminal investigations of more than 150 American UBS clients. That, in turn, helped pressure 14,700 taxpayers to make "voluntary" disclosures of previously undisclosed offshore kitties during a special program earlier this year, yielding extra billions in tax for the Treasury. "The entire game has changed on international tax evasion," crows IRS Commissioner Douglas Shulman.

Threats to Civil Liberties

The late Congressman Hyde believed that "most Americans don't realize the extent to which our constitutional protections have been violated and diminished in recent years." Neutral observers, libertarians like the Cato Institute, political conservatives like Hyde and Judge Trott, joined with liberals and others on the Left such as Professor Dershowitz and the American Civil Liberties Union (ACLU).

They believed unchecked police informant use constitutes a serious danger to individual liberty.

While the public only learns about major informant cases that go wrong, there are thousands of accused persons fingered by a "friend" for a crime they did not commit. Carefully controlled use of informants has a place in proper law enforcement, but what kind of justice is it when prosecutors boast of charges against a businessman whose employee or associate settles a score with an anonymous accusation of criminal conduct?

Betrayal is an essential element in the government police-informant game, but the repeated betrayal of basic constitutional principles guaranteeing our freedom is the real menace to society. In a 1928 dissent in an early wiretapping case, the late Supreme Court Justice Louis D. Brandeis warned: "The greatest dangers to liberty lurk in the insidious encroachment by men of zeal, well-meaning but without understanding."

U.S. government agents may boast of cleverly turning criminals into instruments of law enforcement, but in this crude process law officers have become willing co-conspirators in crime — and too often, criminals themselves.

Defend Your Privacy: Helpful Tools to Prevent Government Spying
Ted Bauman, *The Sovereign Investor Daily*, March 2015

What do you do when someone tells you "no"?

Do you accept it and move on? Continue your attempts at persuasion? Or ignore the answer and do what you want regardless?

If you're the governments of the U.S. and U.K., you make the third choice. You do what you want and congratulate yourself on a job well done.

That's the message the rest of the world will take away from the news that the National Security Agency (NSA) and its British counterpart, the Government Communications Headquarters (GCHQ), stole the master encryption keys for most of the world's cellphones — including yours. They wanted them, so they just took them, violating numerous laws and treaties in the process.

Washington and London now have some explaining to do, especially to the Netherlands, where the theft took place.

But you have some work to do as well ... to beat these privacy thieves at their own dirty game.

Stealing the Master Key

The privacy of your mobile communications — voice calls, text messages and Internet access — depends on an encrypted connection between your cellphone and your wireless carrier's network. This encryption uses keys stored on the SIM, a tiny chip inserted into your phone.

In April 2011, the NSA and GCHQ created a Mobile Handset Exploitation Team (MHET) to steal the keys that would unlock this encryption. The MHET targeted a Dutch company called Gemalto that makes these chips. Among its clients are AT&T, T-Mobile, Verizon, Sprint and some 450 wireless network providers around the world. By hacking the email and Facebook accounts of employees at Gemalto and its clients, the MHET was able to steal Gemalto's master encryption keys. They even created a program that would steal the keys automatically.

With these stolen keys, the NSA and GCHQ can monitor mobile communications without warrants, wiretaps or approval from telecom companies and governments, leaving no trace of their actions. They can just vacuum up cellular signals out of the air and listen to any or all of the communications they intercept.

Key Weakness: Single-Tier Encryption

The reason this NSA/GCHQ hack works is because your cell communications are encrypted by your wireless carrier using keys that they possess. With the keys, anyone can listen in to your calls, texts or emails. You have no control over the matter — unless you take steps to protect yourself.

As numerous observers have noted, the implications of wholesale compromise of master cell encryption keys go well beyond the NSA and GCHQ. After all, if they can steal these keys, so can other countries. Naturally, criminals and fraudsters would love to get their hands on them too: Imagine how much money you could make if you had access to cell calls made around Wall Street.

But the Gemalto hack may be about much more than cellphones. The company is a global leader in digital security, producing banking cards, mobile payment systems, building security devices and identification cards. Among its clients are Visa, MasterCard, American Express, JP Morgan Chase and Barclays. It also provides chips for luxury cars, including those made by Audi and BMW.

Oh, and one other client: the U.S. government, which uses Gemalto technology in its electronic passports.

Assume the Worst and Prepare

You should assume that your cellphone is insecure and that someone is listening in on your communications. Time will tell whether the same is true of your credit cards, passport and car as well.

But there is a simple way to prevent government spying on your cellular communications. Rather than rely on your cellphone company's SIM card-based security, use secure communications software that encrypts your calls, texts and emails with a private key that only you and your contacts know.

You can encrypt your voice calls by using encrypted Voice over Internet Protocol (VoIP) apps such as Signal, RedPhone and Silent Phone. These work by turning your calls into encrypted Internet data, bypassing cell networks entirely. Apps such as TextSecure and Silent Text similarly encrypt your text messages. Email services such as Gmail are already encrypted, but you can double down by adopting a specialist service such as Proton Mail.

If you use these encryption apps, governments may still be able to intercept your communications, but listening to them would be impossible without targeting you specifically with time-consuming high-tech codebreaking efforts. And even then they would probably fail.

So what are you waiting for? Secure your cell communications quickly and simply. I have.

Leftist Lies Attack Your Right to Privacy

Robert E. Bauman JD, *The Sovereign Investor Daily*, February 2012

The constant lies of Left-wing radicals, both American and foreign, continue without cease.

An example of this radical campaign of falsehoods appeared today under the byline of one Scott Cohn, identified as "Senior Correspondent, CNBC." The arresting title of his article: "*Ranch House Near Reno is a Thriving Tax Haven, and It's Not Alone.*" You can read it for the full details of Cohn's distortions and slanted reporting, but one would suspect a "senior" reporter would have some integrity and concern for the truth. Not this guy.

Given that CNBC has become the broadcast mouthpiece of American leftists and the chief cheerleader for Barack Obama, Cohn's article is still an unbalanced smear of the State of Nevada and its laws that permit incorporation of businesses without having a public record of the true "beneficial owners."

Cohn wrongfully equates business ownership privacy with money laundering, tax evasion and criminal conduct — for none of which he offers any proof.

Anti-Privacy Conspiracy

For the last decade the U.S. and international radicals have fought to abolish financial and personal privacy with the specious argument that government has the right to know everything about your finances. This position is endorsed by President Obama and radical Democrats in the U.S. Congress who adopted the horrendous Foreign Account Tax Compliance Act (FATCA).

As part of their anti-freedom campaign these Leftists demand public and government access to all financial accounts of U.S. and others citizens, wherever located in the world — including the States of Nevada and Delaware.

The anti-privacy campaign began in 1990 with the Financial Action Task Force (FATF), a 33-nation offshoot of the Organization for Economic Cooperation and Development (OECD) in Paris. Both are public relations operations on behalf of the major welfare, high tax governments known as the "G-7."

Using their alleged war on dirty cash as cover, the FATF proclaimed what it calls "recommendations" it insists countries must convert into national laws. It began issuing these "rules" in 1990, revised them in 1996 and is still at in 2012.

Behind FATF's smoke screen about fighting money laundering and terrorism lies complete and utter destruction of financial and personal privacy for everyone. The true FATF objective is handing welfare state tax collectors complete access to every citizen's financial lives.

War on Drugs Excuse

The original justification for FATF's anti-privacy assaults was claimed to be waging the "war on drugs." We were all supposed to surrender our financial privacy as governments pawed through millions of our accounts in hopes of finding one drug lord. Since the terror attacks of 9-11, 2001 the FATF cry justifying its latest demands has been "anti-terrorism."

What FATF wants is an end to private beneficial ownership of corporations, trusts, foundations and partnerships. FATF claims legal entities including corporations, trusts, foundations and partnerships, and limited liability companies "can be exploited for money laundering or terrorist financing purposes."

FATF's solution to this non-problem — allow government and tax collectors carte blanch access to all records of all legal entities. The FATF assumption seems to be that privacy per se is bad and Big Brother government has an unlimited right to know all.

This decade old FATF lie was what CNBC's Cohn repeated today in his slanted article about Nevada's laudable privacy laws.

Left's Intent: Destroy Financial Privacy

This OECD, leftist, Big Brother anti-tax haven pressure is a smoke screen for welfare state tax collectors aiming for complete destruction of financial and personal privacy for everyone, (just as the so-called PATRIOT Act already has done in the U.S.)

For these anti-freedom dictators abolishing bank secrecy is not enough. They also want to end lawyer-client privilege, plus the imposition of a global system of total tax information exchange among all nations.

For citizens of the United States all this is an academic discussion — under the Draconian terms of the 2001 PATRIOT Act, financial privacy is already dead. The government has the power to obtain financial information in secret about anyone — and to confiscate your wealth.

Small wonder that many millions of Americans do business offshore to take advantage of the strong privacy laws in places such as Switzerland, Panama, Singapore, Austria and Luxembourg.

The Real Issue: Liberty

Of course the spurious cry by those who advocate ever increased government surveillance of not just our finances, but every aspect of our lives, is the old saw: *"If you aren't doing anything wrong, what do you have to hide?"*

It is absolutely wrong to characterize this debate as "clean money versus dirty cash" or "security versus privacy."

The true issue is the fundamental right to privacy.

Privacy is an inherent human right. True privacy is a basic requirement for maintaining the human condition with dignity and respect. The real choices in this debate are personal freedom and liberty versus government control of our lives and our fortunes.

Tyranny, whether it arises under threat of terrorist attack, alleged solutions to money laundering problems or under any form of unrelenting domestic authoritative scrutiny, is still tyranny.

Liberty requires security without intrusion — security plus privacy. Widespread surveillance, whether by police or nosey bureaucrats, in whatever form it takes, is the very definition of a police state.

And that's why we should champion privacy, both personal and financial, even when we have nothing to hide.

USING ATTORNEY-CLIENT PRIVILEGE EFFECTIVELY
Mark Nestmann & Robert E. Bauman JD,
The Sovereign Individual, 1999, updated 2010

It's an established right recognized and protected by law. But unless you understand how it works and exercise that right, your private business could become a matter of public record.

In the United States it's known as the "attorney-client privilege." In the United Kingdom, it's called the "solicitor client privilege." At times, you may hear it referred to as an "attorney's duty of confidence."

In each instance, the phrase describes a long-established rule that establishes a legal and ethical duty binding an attorney not to divulge confidential communications from a client. It also gives a client the right to refuse to disclose, and to prevent others from disclosing, "confidential communications" between the client and his attorney.

Attorney-client privilege has evolved as a means to encourage clients to make complete disclosure when seeking legal advice, without fear that their attorney might inform others. It encompasses verbal and written communications, including letters, records, an attorney's notes, research, and the legal work product developed for a client.

Effective use of this privilege is crucial to preserve the privacy of any asset protection plan, estate plan or any other confidential legal matter. And when "going offshore" requires professional legal assistance, you should understand what this privilege means and how to use it.

Your attorney cannot divulge information protected by the privilege unless you give your consent or he is so ordered by a court. For you to gain this protection, it is always best to establish a formal representation agreement in writing with an attorney before discussing confidential matters.

Exceptions & Waivers

Attorney-client privilege is narrower than generally perceived.

For example, your identity and fee arrangements are not protected. In addition, an attorney, as a licensed member of the bar, is an "officer of the court." While your attorney must pursue your best interests, his actions are constrained by professional rules of conduct. For instance, your attorney cannot knowingly assist you in perpetrating a fraud or other illegal act.

If your attorney delegates responsibilities to others, usually the privilege extends to these persons also. Typically, this may include other lawyers in the firm, a secretary or legal aides. But the privilege does not attach to work an attorney does at the direction of another person on your behalf, such as your accountant.

The privilege is also waived if you disclose information your attorney conveyed to you in confidence or that you conveyed to him. If you hire an attorney to prepare a legal opinion, your engagement letter should stipulate that release of the opinion letter does not waive your privilege concerning any other communications between you. Include a statement to this effect with any information you might disclose about your estate or asset protection plan.

To guard against waiver, it is best not to discuss legal matters with a spouse or business partner, unless you are confident the relationship will remain permanent. Many states recognize a "spousal privilege" that allows a wife or husband called as a witness to refuse to answer questions relating to communications between them. However, this protection is dissolved by divorce and does not extend to unmarried partners.

Offshore Privilege Limited

In the United States, an attorney has no duty to disclose to authorities' suspicion that a client may have in the past engaged in criminal activities. However, he must report immediately any knowledge of a client's planned future criminal acts.

In contrast, solicitors and attorneys in the United Kingdom, Switzerland and some other countries are required to notify police if they suspect a client may be engaged in certain illegal activities relating to "money laundering." A similar Canadian requirement is now pending.

In the United Kingdom, this includes any suspicion that a client may be evading taxes. In the U.K. barristers and solicitors are forced to serve as the government's "independent financial investigators" under the terms of the Criminal Justice Act and Money Laundering Regulations. The law states that any such disclosure "will not be treated as a breach of the solicitor's duty of confidence."

These rules by extension apply in principle to attorneys practicing in all U.K. Overseas Territories. However, many of the OTs, including the Cayman Islands and Bermuda have enacted similar local laws, as have the Crown Dependencies of Jersey, Guernsey and the Isle of Man.

Attorneys in Switzerland who act as asset managers are required to notify a central authority if they suspect a client is engaged in money laundering. But an attorney asset manager need not notify authorities of suspected money laundering after an initial contact with a prospective client, if that individual is not accepted as a client. Swiss attorneys acting in other capacities are not subject to these rules.

Compromised Privilege

The attorney-client privilege can be compromised in numerous other ways.

As an "anti-money laundering" tactic, U.S. law is unique in requiring attorneys to report to the government one or more "related" cash payments made to them by a client that, in aggregate, exceeds US$10,000. Courts have consistently upheld these requirements as superseding attorney-client privilege.

In the United States — and elsewhere — the attorney-client privilege does not apply where:

- you involve your attorney in a criminal conspiracy, even if the attorney isn't aware of it. This may include efforts to defeat a judgment or hide assets from legitimate creditors.
- your attorney becomes an informant against you.
- you sue your attorney and the attorney in good faith releases documents in his own defense.
- you file bankruptcy and the court-appointed trustee waives the privilege.
- the government serves your attorney with a valid warrant allowing eavesdropping on conversations between you and your attorney.
- your attorney is under criminal investigation and his files are subpoenaed by a grand jury.

The privilege may be partially waived if:

- a person who is not a client of the attorney participates in a conversation between you and your attorney.
- a court issues a subpoena to your attorney to obtain your name and address or to review your fee arrangements.
- your attorney possesses documents relating to your case that he did not prepare.
- your attorney prepares your income tax return.
- you testify under oath that you are acting on the advice of your attorney.
- you review privileged documents prior to testifying concerning those documents.

High-Tech Risks Abound

Modern technology may compromise attorney-client privilege.

According to the American Bar Association, "confidential" communications between an attorney and client via e-mail are protected by the privilege. But e-mail is easily monitored. The solution is to encrypt confidential messages with encryption software such as PGP or a similar program.

Similarly, it is illegal to monitor cellular or cordless telephone calls, but these electronic communications often travel via unencrypted radio waves and are easily monitored. This security problem is so serious that state bar associations have warned attorneys that use of unencrypted cellular or cordless phones to discuss sensitive client matters may violate attorney client privilege. The solution is to use only the latest generation of cordless phones and digital cellular phones that digitally encrypt transmissions sent through the air.

Attorneys Under Attack

The worldwide proliferation of tough anti-money laundering and civil forfeiture laws has placed attorneys "under the gun." As a potential client, you must be aware of these challenges.

In the United States, attorneys face possible "criminal liability" just for providing alleged "routine legal services." They are advised by a former federal prosecutor to "conduct client conferences as if each client is an undercover agent or a government informant (as he or she may be)." The risk is illustrated by the conviction of a California attorney whose prosecution was based solely on routine legal services for a client who later testified against him in exchange for a reduced sentence.

To avoid criminal liability, some attorneys in the United States insert language in offshore asset protection instruments that eases compliance with certain forfeiture or repatriation orders. An asset protection guidebook recommends insertion of language defining circumstances under which trustees of "asset protection trusts" must convey trust assets to U.S. regulatory agencies.

Attorneys "Know Thy Client"

We have discussed "know your customer" requirements that U.S. based offshore financial planners must follow to avoid criminal liability for their actions. Similar precautions now apply to U.S. based attorneys and increasingly to attorneys in other countries.

An attorney's main defense against civil or criminal liability for subsequent wrongdoing by a client is to obtain full facts about a client and his finances. If you contact an attorney for such advice, expect a thorough grilling about your personal and professional background and your offshore motives.

Conversely, you should make an effort to "know your lawyer." Call the bar offices to determine if an attorney is a member in good standing of the state and local bar. Inquire whether he or she has been the subject of bar disciplinary actions — usually a matter of public record. Check court calendars to see if an attorney has been a defendant in civil cases or has judgments recorded against him. This information is available through your local clerk of court's office or with help from a private investigator.

Make the Most of It

You can strengthen your own attorney-client privilege protection by using a domestic attorney working in tandem with another attorney located offshore in the haven nation where you plan to do business. You retain the offshore attorney, who in turn retains an attorney in your home country to assist him. Under this plan, the foreign attorney is the client of the domestic attorney. For example, your offshore attorney can establish a foreign asset protection trust, working with a domestic attorney to insure compliance with domestic tax and reporting requirements.

Even if a domestic creditor pierces the attorney-client privilege between the offshore and domestic lawyers, the most he could learn would be the name and address of the offshore lawyer and the fee arrangements. This dual strategy obviously adds additional costs, but it can be a very powerful enhancement of attorney-client privilege.

IDENTITY THEFT: WAYS TO PROTECT YOURSELF
Mark Nestmann, *The Sovereign Individual*, 2003, updated 2010

"He that filches from me my good name robs me of that which not enriches him and makes me poor, indeed." — Iago in Shakespeare's "Othello"

Each year a staggering number of Americans have their good name stolen by "identity thieves Approximately 15 million Americans were victimized by some sort of identity-theft related fraud in the 12 months ending in 2006, according to a survey by Gartner, Inc. That's up 50% from the 12-month period ending in 2005.

Expatriates and others away from home for extended periods are particularly vulnerable. Nor is the problem limited to the United States — in recent months, gigantic ID thefts have been uncovered in Canada and in Russia.

If you're an American, all someone needs to impersonate you is your name and Social Security number (SSN), plus one or two other easy-to-find pieces of information such as your birth date, mother's maiden name or residential address. Millions of people have access to this information. Anyone you've ever borrowed money from probably has a record of your SSN. Under federal law, banks and brokers must keep your SSN on file. Employers must have it to withhold Social Security taxes. Other businesses can ask for it at their discretion, and many do — doctors, hospitals, utility companies, insurance companies, etc.

Most ID theft victims are liable for no more than US$50 per fraudulent account. But a much larger loss is denial of credit and employment, or even arrest, as impostors misuse their identities. Many victims spend thousands of dollars in legal fees and spend years cleaning up the mess. Nor is it practical to count on help from police. Because ID theft victims often live outside the state, or even the country, where the theft occurs, investigations often hit jurisdictional "brick walls." Preventing identity theft is much easier than recovering from it after it occurs.

Why Expatriates Are Vulnerable

Because they may not check their mail frequently, expatriates and others away from home for extended periods are especially vulnerable to ID theft. ID thieves begin by filing a change-of-address form with the Postal Service to forward your correspondence to a new address. Of particular interest is correspondence from banks, brokers, credit card companies, etc. They use these account numbers to buy goods or services on your credit. They open new credit card accounts, using your name, birth date and SSN.

ID thieves may order checks or debit cards and use them to drain your bank account, or open new accounts and write bad checks. They can also set up phone or cellular service, take out auto loans, make false insurance claims or even file for bankruptcy — all under your name.

None of these activities will necessarily come to your attention, because the person conducting these transactions is supposedly "you." Indeed, your first inkling of a problem may come when you are detained or arrested at a U.S. border crossing.

Identity Theft — How It's Done

Most ID thefts are "inside jobs." The perpetrator has access to credit or other records useful for ID theft. Members of fraud rings continually seek to employment at with access to such data, often as temporary workers or cleaning staff.

Other common sources of ID theft include:

- Duping a person out of information required for ID theft. One clever scam involves falsified tax forms purportedly from the IRS to gather private data.

- Dumpster/mailbox diving. ID thieves examine discarded trash and unlocked mailboxes for credit card and bank statements or pre-approved offers of credit.

- Burglary and robbery. A wallet, purse, glove compartment or file cabinet can be a gold mine for ID thieves.

- Someone you know. Family members, household employees and visitors to your home can pilfer to confidential documents.

- Computer hacking. It is relatively simple for someone to hack into an unsecured home PC or business computer to retrieve personal information: addresses, credit card numbers, etc.

Make Yourself a "Hard Target"

No magic bullets exist to prevent ID theft, because it's such a simple crime to commit. However, by adhering to the following suggestions, you'll become a "hardened target" to impersonation.

Basic strategies:

1. Check your credit records at least annually. Federal law requires credit bureaus to give consumers one free copy of their credit report annually. For more information, see http://www.annualcreditreport.com, call toll-free (877) 322-8228

or download the written request form at https://www.annualcreditreport.com/cra/requestformfinal.pdf.

2. Never disclose personal information unless you have initiated the contact. Identity thieves often pose as bank representatives or government employees to obtain your SSN, mother's maiden name or financial account information.

3. Guard your SSN. Don't disclose it unless you are applying for credit, dealing with the IRS or the Social Security Administration or (in some states) applying for a driver's license. Never have your SSN imprinted on stationary or checks. Don't carry any document in your wallet or glove compartment that lists your SSN. Keep the card itself in a safety deposit box.

4. When using a credit card, don't let it out of your sight. This guards against an employee surreptitiously reading the information in the card's magnetic stripe using a device called a "skimmer." If you can't keep watch on your credit card during the entire transaction, use cash.

5. Pay attention to billing cycles. A missing bill could mean a thief has taken over your account and changed your billing address.

6. Put passwords on your credit card, bank and phone accounts to prevent unauthorized changes of service. Avoid easy-to-learn passwords (e.g., your birth date, the last four digits of your SSN, etc.).

7. Use credit cards wisely. Minimize the number that you carry and keep the lowest credit practical credit limits. Cancel inactive accounts; unused accounts still appear on your credit report, and can be used by thieves.

8. Guard your residential address. Use a post office box or mail receiving service to receive your mail. Ask companies that provide services at your residential address to bill to a secured address.

9. Buy a crosscut shredder. Bank and credit-card statements, receipts, old tax forms, pre-approved offers of credit, etc. should go into it.

10. Get off commercial mailing lists. Write to the Direct Marketing Association's Mail Preference Service, P.O. Box 9008, Farmingdale, NY 11735 and ask to be removed from all commercial mailing lists. https://dmachoice.org.

11. Opt out of pre-approved credit card offers. Call 1 (888) 5OPT OUT. You will need to disclose your SSN to use this free service.

12. Lock up sensitive information. Keep credit card records, bank records, etc. in a locked safe bolted, or even better, embedded, in the floor.

13. Use common sense. If it seems too good to be true, it probably is.

14. Learn more about ID theft. Reliable sources of free information include: Identity Theft Resource Center (www.idtheftcenter.org) and Privacy Rights Clearinghouse (www.privacyrights.org).

Advanced Strategies

The preceding strategies are sufficient for most members. However, expats and anyone else scoring higher than 50 points on our ID theft vulnerability quiz (see below) should seriously consider taking the following additional precautions. (Downside: These advanced strategies may lead to inconvenience, particularly if you need credit quickly).

1. Notify credit bureaus and card issuers not to authorize credit extensions over the phone. This forces credit card issuers to obtain written authorization before they give someone a card in your name. Also, it gives you a sample signature to compare to your own.

2. Join a credit report monitoring service such as Trusted ID (https://www.trustedid.com). You'll be asked to provide substantial additional information to "insure the accuracy" of their records. However, you're under no obligation to give a credit monitoring service any more information than they need to identify you. This means providing only your SSN, a non-residential contact address, plus whatever information you want them to correct (if any). Don't complete the rest of the multi-page questionnaire that will likely be included with your membership kit.

3. Place a credit freeze on your credit bureau account. This action "locks" your credit file, prohibiting new extensions of credit being issued in your name. When you sign up for a credit freeze, you're assigned a PIN with which you can lift the freeze when necessary. Most states now authorize credit freezes. Major credit bureaus such as TransUnion and Equifax now offer credit freezes in all 50 states.

What to Do If You Suspect ID Theft

1. Call the three credit bureaus. Place a "fraud alert" on your file and have them send you copies of your reports. Review them for fraudulent activity or inaccuracies.

2. Contact local law enforcement. They must take a report and give you a copy of it, although they may not have the resources to investigate. You'll need the report to "prove" to credit grantors that you reported a crime to authorities.

3. Notify creditors who have opened fraudulent accounts in your name. Start with a phone call and follow up with a certified letter. Request copies of all application and transaction information.

4. Notify your bank. If necessary, cancel your checking and savings accounts and obtain new account numbers.

5. Contact the Federal Trade Commission's Identity Theft Hotline at 1(877) ID-THEFT. Link: http://www.ftc.gov/bcp/edu/microsites/idtheft.

A Quiz to Protect Yourself from ID Theft

Are you at risk for ID theft? Take this quiz (adapted from one at www.privacyrights.org) to learn how vulnerable you are.

1. I receive frequent offers of pre-approved credit (5 points). Add five points if you don't shred these offers before discarding them.
2. I carry my Social Security card in my wallet or glove compartment (10 points). Add 10 points if you carry your driver's license, military ID or any other documents containing your SSN there.
3. My driver's license has my SSN printed on it (10 points).
4. I receive mail in an unlocked mailbox (5 points).
5. I use an unlocked mailbox to drop off outgoing mail (10 points).
6. I do not shred banking and credit information when I discard it (10 points).
7. I provide my SSN whenever asked (10 points). Add 5 points if you provide it orally without checking who might be listening.
8. I use my SSN as an employee or student ID number (5 points).
9. I have my SSN printed on my employee badge that I wear at work or in public (10 points).
10. I have my SSN and/or driver's license number printed on personal checks (10 points).
11. I am listed in a Who's Who guide (5 points).
12. I have not ordered a copy of my credit report in at least two years (20 points).
13. I do not believe that people would look in my trash looking for credit or financial information (10 points).
14. My name is listed in U.S. credit bureau files and I live outside the United States (15 points).

Scores: 100+ points: High risk. Carefully follow the precautions listed in the accompanying article to reduce your vulnerability. 50-100 points: Average risk; higher if you have good credit. 0-50 points: Low risk. Keep up the good work and don't let your guard down now.

Escaping the Matrix: A Privacy-Protection Guide for Our Brave New World

Robert E. Bauman JD, *Offshore Confidential*, September 2013

In a memorable scene from a memorable film, Neo, Keanu Reeves' character in *The Matrix* awakens after a lengthy interview with Morpheus to find himself inside an egg-like cocoon, covered in goo, with tubes protruding from his body. He's in a chamber full of similar occupied cocoons stretching into the distance.

Neo got there after taking a red pill that Morpheus promised would reveal The Truth. He had the option of taking a blue pill to remain where he was. Morpheus had carefully explained the consequences of his decision: Everything he thought about reality would be proved false. If he took the red pill, he would never be the same again. He would shift into an unfamiliar, terrifying reality he could not possibly conceive beforehand. Which pill will you take?

Our Modern-Day Matrix

Other than semi-crazed conspiracy theorists, few people genuinely believe that the reality we perceive is an illusion. We are flesh and blood, and the things we see and touch are real.

Nevertheless, like Neo before the red pill, we inhabit an illusion. Although not as profound as Neo's, this illusion is a critical constraint on our personal liberty.

Our illusion — our Matrix — consists of a carefully crafted narrative in which we are made to believe that we are free individuals joined together in a democratic society, in which we are able to shape the conditions of our freedom through conscious political choice. In this Matrix, we are able to maintain our privacy, albeit within certain boundaries set by the need to maintain an orderly society.

And yet, we are not really free. We are not permitted our privacy.

Instead, we are constrained, watched and manipulated by official forces that present themselves as the guarantors of our liberty. These forces include the familiar — the out-of-control government — and the less familiar: the private institutions and individuals that collaborate with government to maintain and profit from this illusion.

Sovereignty, Individuals and Information

At least since Thomas Hobbes, the idea of the "sovereign individual" has been fundamental to Western political philosophy. Basically, individual sovereignty means the same thing as the sovereignty of nations: the right to make all decisions concerning the conduct and disposal of one's self and one's possessions. It was this philosophy that gave birth to The Sovereign Society 15 years ago.

At its core, the current debate over spying by the U.S. National Security Agency (NSA) is a contest over the relationship and limits of state and individual sovereignty. The state maintains that its sovereignty extends into our own sovereign sphere. Many of us disagree. The specific issue at dispute is information.

As we know very well, the governments of nation-states cherish the information they possess. They go to great lengths to protect that information, and to obtain information from other governments ("spying"). Under President Obama, the U.S. government has relentlessly pursued and harshly punished individuals who had exposed "sovereign" information — such as Thomas Drake, Bradley Manning and Edward Snowden.

At the same time, the U.S. government has dramatically expanded its own claims to the "sovereign information" possessed by each of us as individuals. At first, this search for information was generally understood to be aimed at non-U.S. persons, who are not protected by U.S. constitutional provisions, such as the Fourth Amendment.

In recent months, however, thanks to Mr. Snowden, we have learned that our government wants private information about U.S. citizens as well. Essentially, the U.S. government claims the right to access information about *us*, without our permission or, until recently, without our knowledge.

In other words, our government asserts the right to spy on us.

Government Spying: The Enemy of Your Dignity and Liberty

Most of us accept the obligation to report certain designated information to the government, as The Sovereign Society often reminds us, and we will abide by those rules in the understanding that this is essential to the orderly management of our society, and thus to our own prosperity.

That concession emphatically does not mean we have surrendered our right to privacy, however.

Privacy is an inherent human right and a requirement for maintaining the human condition with dignity and respect. Liberty requires both physical and informational security without intrusion by the state — security plus privacy.

For that reason, all of us should champion privacy, both personal and financial, even when we have nothing to hide. All of us should be appalled and angry at the current behavior of the U.S. government, regardless of our political leanings. Consider some of this "official" behavior:

- The U.S. Department of Homeland Security (DHS) routinely abuses laws designed for immigration enforcement purposes to extract private information, including passwords, from U.S. residents before they have officially crossed into U.S. soil at airports and land borders. A similar law was used by U.K. authorities to detain and rifle through the possessions of David Miranda, partner of journalist Glenn Greenwald, but few people are aware that such conduct is common at the U.S. border as well. Customs and Border Protection, part of the DHS, conducted electronic media searches on 4,957 people from October 1, 2012, through August 31, 2013 — *15 a day* — close to the average for the previous two years. Ominously, U.S. lawyers, journalists and political activists who support the right to personal privacy and political dissent have been deliberately targeted for border searches and seizures of electronic information.

- The NSA has routinely collected telephone, texting (SMS), email, VOIP (i.e., Skype), instant messaging and location "metadata" in order to discern the activities, interests and intentions of individual U.S. residents. To accomplish this, the NSA and FBI have forced U.S. corporate providers of email, web and cloud data-storage services to allow access to their systems, essentially by asking these private companies to "look the other way" while government agents hack into them. This has destroyed the credibility of the U.S. cloud-computing industry overseas. Fifty-six percent of 500 industry respondents in a recent survey said Edward Snowden's disclosures would cause them to lose non-U.S. business, a cost of up to $50 billion in revenues.

- The NSA has worked for years to force purveyors of cryptographic software to build, in secret, "backdoor" keyholes that allow it to access encrypted data. Almost all of the major encryption products developed and produced in the U.S. should now be assumed unsafe. The NSA has deliberately weakened the encryption standards developed by the National Institute of Standards and Technology (NIST) and adopted by developers around the globe. This has devastated the U.S. encryption-software industry, once the world's leader.

- According to the German daily, *Der Speigel*, the NSA developed a system called TRACFIN to hack into VISA's credit-card transaction network to target customers in Europe, the Middle East and Africa, and has also hacked into the Society for Worldwide Interbank Financial Telecommunication (SWIFT) system, which I have exposed in the past. Although there are no reports — so far — that this TRACFIN system has been deployed inside the U.S., there is no reason to think it hasn't been, especially considering who is in charge. In any case, it is similar to PRISM, a clandestine mass electronic-surveillance, data-mining program operated by the NSA since 2007.

- The attitude of NSA Chief Gen. Keith Alexander, the "Cowboy of the NSA," has been described by a former intelligence official as: "Let's not worry about the law. Let's just figure out how to get the job done … a lot of things aren't clearly legal, but that doesn't make them illegal." A generous interpretation might be that the general intends for Congress to decide when legal boundaries have been crossed. Given that both he and Director of National Security James Clapper have perjured themselves before our elected representatives on the activities and capabilities of the NSA, this would appear naïve in the extreme.

- A recent review of U.S. government documents reveals that there are 72 categories of U.S. citizens and residents that are to be considered "extremists" and "potential terrorists." By far, the majority of these categories relate to legitimate political viewpoints. Given that the NSA's own standards require only a "reasonable suspicion" of "terroristic" intentions to prompt a privacy-invading information search, most of us are probably eligible targets.

Uncle Sam, Inc. Wants YOU — *and* Your Money

As I stated above, a serious commitment to liberty — beyond the self-serving rhetorical type — requires us to dispense with the notion that we have nothing to worry about if we have nothing to hide. Even if you are personally willing to allow the government to rifle through your finances, communications and personal records, you should care that it is doing this to people who do mind and are protected by the Fourth Amendment.

The sad truth is that the U.S. government is completely out of control when it comes to respecting the right to individual privacy. Things have become so bad that the author of the despicable PATRIOT Act, U.S. Rep. James Sensenbrenner (R-WI) recently submitted an *amicus curiae* brief in a case brought by the American Civil Liberties Union (ACLU) against the NSA. In it, Sensenbrenner argues that Congress never intended the PATRIOT Act to permit the NSA's collection of records of every telephone call made to, from and within the United States. As he put it:

> "The proper balance has not been struck between civil rights and American security. A large, intrusive government — however benevolent it claims to be — is not immune from the simple 5 truth that centralized power threatens liberty. Americans are increasingly wary that Washington is violating the privacy rights guaranteed to us by the Fourth Amendment."

Sadly, as Founder James Madison warned us, we should expect governments to behave this way. History teaches that those we allow to manage our collective affairs will inevitably seek to acquire ever more power, all the while believing their intentions noble and true.

In the "good old days," virtuous citizens, including many captains of industry, pushed back against this arrogant tendency. Sewell Avery, for example, in the 1930s, while the CEO of retailer Montgomery Ward, refused President Franklin Roosevelt's order to settle a labor dispute, and was physically carried out of his office by two National Guardsmen. Today, however, the burden of resistance increasingly seems to have fallen to an odd coalition of committed conservative defenders of personal freedom, such as myself, and younger civil libertarians like Edward Snowden, the late <u>Aaron Swartz</u>, <u>Glenn Greenwald</u>, U.S. Rep. <u>Justin Amish</u> (R-MI), Kentucky Senator <u>Rand Paul</u> and others.

Where are the sage "establishment" voices of yesteryear? Frankly, they are nowhere to be found. Aside from the leaders of tech-industry companies forced to collaborate in these obscenities, none of the major U.S. business and industry associations have commented publicly on these matters. Even the Tea Party has been largely silent. (The National Rifle Association has supported the ACLU's lawsuit against the NSA, but was careful to specify that it was concerned mainly about future breaches of privacy — not necessarily those being conducted right now.)

Two intertwined processes have effectively operated to silence the historical voices of individual liberty in the U.S.

First, both major political parties have become increasingly "tribal," placing their own electoral fortunes above the good of the country. Leading figures of both parties are either complicit in violations or unwilling to take firm positions on civil liberty issues. Both parties, of course, are guilty of supporting abominations such as the 2001 PATRIOT Act, and of neglecting Congress' core oversight duties in respect of the NSA and other intelligence agencies. Republicans and Democrats are equally guilty in the destruction of our constitutional liberties, and have applied their energies to bait-and-switch tactics designed to get Americans to votes for party "brands," rather than for what is right. Their reluctance to go against the "security first" trend is reflected in the vast lobbying, think-tank, and activist networks supporting the two parties.

Second — and more sinister — is that, to an underappreciated extent, contemporary U.S. captains of industry are an increasingly integral part of the surveillance state itself. They depend on generous taxpayer-funded government contracts for their companies' profits and their own bonuses and stock options. For them, collaboration with a liberty-destroying government goes beyond public support for outrageous laws; it involves massive profits, at our expense as well as huge, selective campaign contributions.

Indeed, the really unprecedented feature of the current situation is the extent to which government and U.S. industry have joined forces, the former to extend its power, and the latter to profit. Consider that companies such as General Dynamics, Hewlett-Packard, AT&T, and many others provide significant intelligence-related services to the American Surveillance State, totaling more than $1 trillion.

That sort of money has serious sway in Washington, D.C.

Naturally, Washington politicians are joining in on the fun. For example, since 2006, Congressman Mike Rodgers (R-MI), chairman of the Permanent Select Committee on Intelligence, has received more than $425,000 in campaign contributions from the companies listed above — despite having no serious opposition to his re-election. His voting record and his actions as committee chairman reflect this: He is one of the prime enablers of civil-liberty violations in Congress. The record of Democrats such as Senator Dianne Feinstein (D-CA), whose husband's company does millions of dollars' worth of security-related work for the government, is no better.

There is Hope!

Sadly, no matter how unhappy we may be at these violations of our constitutional liberties, there is little prospect that they will be addressed politically anytime soon. The bipartisan consensus in favor of the growing surveillance state is built on the solid foundation of widespread public ignorance of, and/or apathy about, the destruction of our freedoms.

So for all intents and purposes, you are on your own versus Thomas Hobbes' "Leviathan." What can you do to protect yourself and your privacy?

I will tell you how.

I will divide possible personal responses — all of which are legal, inexpensive and relatively easy to execute — into two categories: privacy protection strategies and secure communications strategies.

Safeguard Your Privacy

Protecting your privacy essentially means limiting other parties' access to information about you. Obviously, for each of us there is a great deal of information to be protected. But with a surprisingly few steps, you can keep most of it relatively private.

One privacy protection often overlooked is the attorney-client privilege supported by law. That simply means that once you hire an attorney, anything you discuss with him or her cannot be revealed, with few exceptions.

Privacy-protection strategies vary depending on from whom you're trying to protect it. There is a difference between people who know you already — friends, family, business associates, companies you do business with and so on — and people who don't know you, but might want to for some reason.

Existing Contacts

For the former category (existing contacts), you have much more control; the key is to limit sharing of personal information to what others absolutely need to know, and to place "firewalls" between detailed facts (such as your physical address or phone number) and the information that you give to third parties.

For example:

- Share sensitive personal facts only with a few close, trusted family members and friends. Never, ever discuss personal matters with casual acquaintances.

- Conceal your home address by using a mail drop — you might even consider using a forwarding mail drop in a foreign country with strict privacy laws. Have utility bills, credit cards and home deliveries made in a corporate or other entity name, and do the same with motor-vehicle registration. Get an unlisted phone number and don't disclose it to anyone.

- Never discard sensitive personal correspondence in the trash unless it has been shredded and mixed. Your trash is public property and can be searched by anyone. Shred receipts, credit offers, credit applications, insurance forms, physician statements, checks, bank statements, expired charge cards and similar documents when you don't need them any longer.

- Enter as little information as possible in your social media profiles — preferably just your name.

- Delete your photos from social-networking sites (especially Facebook) and dating sites. If you don't delete your photos, mark your profile as "private." Don't post photos of friends or family members online; this helps investigators reconstruct your social network. To minimize information about you available online, consider a service such as www.reputation.com to remove personal information from websites that market it.

- Don't accept "friend" invitations from strangers on services like Facebook, LinkedIn, Twitter or Skype.

- Run background and due-diligence checks on all prospective personal and business employees. Never leave sensitive information around when workers are in your home.

- Always password-protect your home PC and your cellphone.

- Keep important documents in a safe-deposit box or, better still, in a secure safe in your home.

Third Parties

To ward off privacy attacks form unknown third parties, the strategies above apply, along with several others:

- Use cash in transactions whenever possible.

- Refuse to provide your ZIP code when buying with a credit card unless absolutely necessary.

- Never use your Social Security number as an identifier if it can be avoided.

- Use one or more domestic bank accounts for minimal operating cash; bank the bulk of your cash in the name of appropriate legal entities (LLCs, trusts, family foundations) in selected offshore banks in more than one country with strong financial privacy laws and sound banking systems.

- Acquire a well-recognized second passport and use it when traveling outside the U.S. (U.S. passports must be used to leave or re-enter the U.S.)

- Use a prepaid cellphone, not registered in your name, for most purposes. Pay in cash when purchasing prepaid calling and Internet-access cards. Activate your phone at a pay phone — not with a phone connected to you in any way. Don't give out your real phone number when you activate the phone.

- If you have a personal, permanent phone, deactivate the GPS facility unless it's absolutely necessary to leave it on.

- When you go out, take only the identification, credit and debit cards you need. Leave your Social Security card at home. Make a copy of your Medicare card and blackout all but the last four digits on the copy.

- Never fill in unnecessary or optional information in online forms. Use made-up information for your name, etc. (my personal favorite is "A. Lincoln"), unless it is absolutely necessary to provide accurate information. In your email-software settings, make sure the default "From" field is something other than your name.

- Only use laptops when traveling, and wipe them clean when not using them.

- Make sure websites are safe and authentic before sharing information with them. Make sure any online accounts are properly configured for optimum privacy. Read and act on those privacy notices that come with statements.

- Use a password manager that will not only remember all your passwords, but will generate super strong and unique ones and automatically fill them into login fields with the click of a button. LastPass is an excellent and free choice.

- Use two-factor authentication for Facebook, Google, Dropbox, Apple ID, Microsoft, Twitter and other accounts. Whenever you log in, you'll also need to enter a special code that the site texts to your phone.

- Set up a Google alert for your name at www.google.com/alerts. This involves telling the Google search engine to look for your name, as well as what kinds of web pages to search, how often to search and what email address the search-engine giant should use to send you notifications.

- Lie when setting up password-security questions, like "your mother's maiden name."

- Close old online (and offline) accounts if you are not using them.

- Opt out of marketing "cookies," using services like PrivacyFix or OptOut. Wipe your browser of "cookies" every time you close it. CCleaner is a good software for this task.

- Use anonymous browsing windows whenever possible, preferably on Google Chrome or Firefox.

- Be especially careful with Adobe Flash Player (AFP). You can configure AFP to minimize tracking as well as other settings using a virtual control panel at https://www.macromedia.com/support/documentation/en/flashplayer/help/index.html. If you use Firefox, install the "Better Privacy" add-on. You can download it at https://addons.mozilla.org/en-US/firefox/addon/betterprivacy.

- Before you dispose of a computer or cellphone, get rid of all the personal information it stores. Use a wipe-utility program to overwrite the entire hard drive.

Securing Your Communications

Protecting your communications is significantly more difficult than protecting personal information, like your address, bank details and so on. If you want to communicate at a distance, you are going to have to send information through a channel or channels over which you have no, or only limited, control — including the U.S. mail. Like the spies of yesteryear, to keep things secret you are going to have to use codes and/or encryption.

Unfortunately, existing strategies for protecting electronic communication are currently in a state of disarray. As we have recently learned, thanks to Edward Snowden and Glenn Greenwald, the NSA has deliberately built weaknesses into most publically available encryption technologies, and we frankly do not know which of them are truly secure and which are compromised.

The shocking detention of journalist Glenn Greenwald's partner, David Miranda, by U.K. authorities using laws designed to combat terrorism is evidence that even directly delivering electronic information by hand is no longer fool proof. For the time being, we must assume that the only truly secure communication is verbal, face to face with people whom you trust. Nevertheless, there _are_ things you can do to stop adversaries less determined than the NSA.

Start with the obvious: Use password protected wireless in your home and office. Unplug your webcam and/or microphone when not using it. Never use the telephone for sensitive communication. I always assume someone is listening when I speak on the phone and act accordingly.

Above all, use the strongest encryption available to you. Do not use commercial encryption software, especially from large vendors such as: Symantec or BitLocker. Most encryption products from large U.S. (and probably EU and Israeli) companies have NSA-friendly "back doors" built in. Proprietary "closed-source" software is easier for the NSA to manipulate than open-source software.

Open source software using public-domain encryption must be compatible with other implementations to be effective. The NSA is far less likely to try to install secret backdoors in open-source encryption software, since it is more likely to be discovered given the many people working on it.

Use the Tor Browser. TOR is a sophisticated service based on a browser interface that allows most users to use the web entirely anonymously. TOR is similar to a Virtual Private Network, but has the advantage of being instantly available once TOR is installed.

If you have something really important to share, use an "air gap." This is a computer that has never been connected to the Internet that also has strong file encryption software installed. You can use such a computer to create files (documents, spreadsheets, what have you). When you want to transfer a file, you encrypt the file on the secure "air gap" computer and carry it to your Internet-connected computer, using a USB stick. To decrypt something, reverse the process.

While it is true that the NSA and other government agencies can, and do, target users of the strategies above, it is difficult work for them. The harder it is for your computer to be compromised, the more work and risk it would take to do so, deterring all but the most determined adversaries.

For additional advice on privacy protection, I turned to Mark Nestmann. Mark is a senior member of The Sovereign Society Council of Experts. For 27 years, he has written books, articles and published newsletters concerning privacy. Here are his three suggestions:

1. **Use encryption software.** Protect yourself by using the GNU Privacy Guard (GnuPG) encryption program (www.gnupg.org). GnuPG is based on the "Pretty Good Privacy" or PGP software developed in the 1990s by encryption pioneer Phil Zimmerman. The program converts your e-mail messages into unreadable gibberish that only the intended recipient of your message can decode. It also lets you encrypt files on your hard drive, so only you can access them.

2. **Use a virtual private network.** There's a remarkably simple way to make it virtually impossible for police, the NSA, or any other three-letter agency to monitor your Google searches or online activities. You go "dark." You make yourself invisible — at least when it comes to what you do from the privacy of your own computer screen. All you need, to do that, is something called a "virtual private network," or VPN.

There are many VPN services available, but the one I personally use and highly recommend is called Cryptohippie, and specifically the "Road Warrior" program. It's an ideal for someone like me who travels globally and needs secure communication wherever I go. But even if you don't move beyond the dining room table, this software goes a long way to protecting your from the snoops.

I'll spare you the (frankly) boring details about how it all works and what makes it the best in the business. You can learn more about them at their site: www.cryptohippie.com.

3. **Avoid surfing the Net while signed in to the major social media.** That includes Facebook, Google (i.e. Gmail, YouTube), LinkedIn etc. I don't have the space here to explain why, but basically, if you're logged in, those companies will be able to track major (and many minor) sites you visit ... from major news portals, to pages of a more risqué nature. For more information, visit www.nestmann.com.

The Ultimate Solution

In the end, the only lasting solution to the problem of privacy and securing communications is a change in the political conditions that have allowed it to become so compromised.

Until the recent exposure of the secret NSA spying on all Americans, U.S. and international radical leftist elements had fought to abolish financial and personal privacy on many fronts. This is the plan of President Obama and radical Democrats in the U.S. Congress, who adopted the horrendous Foreign Account Tax Compliance Act (FATCA).

This attack on personal and financial privacy was, in part, a smoke screen for more welfare state taxes. But for these anti-freedom ideologues, abolishing privacy is only the start. They also want to end lawyer-client privilege, expose all forms of private-property ownership and they are well along in imposing a global system of automatic tax information exchange among all nations.

Under the unconstitutional PATRIOT Act, financial privacy in America is already dead. The government has the power to obtain financial information in secret about anyone and to confiscate your wealth.

The real choices in this debate are personal freedom, liberty versus government control of our lives and our fortunes. Tyranny, whether it arises under threat of terrorist attack, solutions to alleged tax evasion or under any form of unrelenting domestic authoritative scrutiny, is still tyranny.

I repeat: Liberty requires security without government intrusion — security plus privacy. Widespread surveillance, whether by police or bureaucrats, in whatever form it takes, is the very definition of a police state.

We have the constitutional and legal means to make changes in our government at the ballot box, and to save America. If an informed majority fails to act, we will be condemned to tyranny.

Start by protecting your privacy in the ways that are still possible.

Say Goodbye to Financial Freedom, America

Ted Bauman, *The Sovereign Investor Daily*, May 2014

In the Old South, a black man seeking to eat at a restaurant or shop at a whites-only store might have been told, "Your money's no good here." In other words — "We don't care if you have money to spend, YOU aren't welcome here." Thankfully, those days are over.

But an increasing number of Americans are hearing something with a similar meaning when they try to open a bank account. I've written before about how the Foreign Account Tax Compliance Act (FATCA) has resulted in thousands of Americans abroad being told by foreign banks to take their money and leave. Now we're being told the same thing here at home — by American banks on American soil.

You already know your financial freedom is at threat from wealth confiscation by the government. But now there's another reason you should convert it into gold, or gems, or stamps, or foreign real estate … in fact, you may have no choice.

The reason is that our old friend, the U.S. government, has adopted a "stop and frisk" policy towards private financial transactions. Just as the New York City Police routinely (and unconstitutionally) stop, question, and frisk certain categories of residents going about their business on the streets of that city, Uncle Sam is now doing the same to tens of thousands of "suspicious" bank accounts — perhaps including yours and mine.

New Program Threatens Your Financial Privacy

The Financial Fraud Enforcement Task Force (FFETF), a group including representatives of the Department of Justice, the Federal Trade Commission and the Federal Deposit Insurance Corporation, has launched its own version of stop-and-frisk with a program called "Operation Choke Point." Under it, the Feds "frisk" banks by sending a blanket subpoena for financial information on all clients who could "potentially" be up to no good. If they find something suspicious, they investigate those clients further. No crime need be committed; it's the exact reverse of innocent until proven guilty.

The theory behind Operation Choke Point is the same as "stop and frisk": by casting a wide dragnet over banks and their customers, innocent as well as guilty, ne'er-do-wells will find it increasingly difficult to launder money or commit fraud. So how do the Feds determine the size and shape of their financial dragnet? The same way the NYPD does: by "profiling" all bank customers and targeting those classes they consider suspicious.

The FFETF looks at the size and frequency of transactions, especially when cash is involved; the percentage of transactions that result in a refund to a third party; and the type of business the account-holder conducts. That last criterion is critical.

To understand why, consider that there are entire industries — perfectly legal lines of business — that find it almost impossible to get banking services in the U.S. because the banks are afraid of what the Feds *might* do. Marijuana growers and retailers in Colorado and Washington. Anyone involved in Southern California's pornographic film industry. Small businesses all over the country that operate primarily in cash. Escort services in Nevada. These are all licensed, regulated, tax-paying enterprises — and all are routinely told by banks, "Your money's no good here."

To that profiling list and in addition to the pattern of transactions I mentioned earlier, Operation Choke Point has added online merchants who transact small amounts by credit card, online gambling enterprises and payday lenders, with more inevitably to come.

Of course, the FFETF isn't telling banks not to open accounts for these businesses. That would be illegal! Instead, they and other regulators, such as the Financial Crimes Enforcement Network (FinCEN), are careful to leave just enough uncertainty in their rule-making to keep the banks nervous and off-balance. That way the banks do the Feds' dirty work for them — by refusing to do business with entire classes of enterprises and individuals for fear of "getting into trouble." It's the same way the IRS has convinced millions of Americans that moving their money offshore to establish financial freedom is somehow "wrong."

Establishing a Frightening Precedent

What a nifty trick! By insinuation and vague threats, the Federal government is able to force tens of thousands of legitimate account holders out of the financial system. As I said above, this is exactly what FATCA does to American account holders who dare to do business with foreign banks.

Mine may be an old-fashioned interpretation, but I'm pretty sure the United States was founded precisely to escape this unaccountable, high-handed approach to governance. The Financial Fraud Enforcement Task Force — and FATCA, FinCEN and the rest — interferes in the private affairs of U.S. residents without following the due process of law, or involving the judiciary, the only branch of government empowered to determine guilt or innocence.

The men who gave their lives at Concord, Bunker Hill, Trenton and Valley Forge, who we honored this past weekend, would surely not have done so had they known this would be the result of their sacrifice. But as I said in my contribution to *Sovereign Investor Daily* last week, tyranny has a way of starting small and growing in reach until it ensnares those who are convinced they have "nothing to worry about."

So next time the cops start violating the rights of the weak, as on the streets of New York City, or on America's borderlands, remember that they're just setting a precedent that will ultimately be used against you.

Sorry, the Police Can Still Steal Your Property
Ted Bauman, *The Sovereign Investor Daily*, January 2015

My father Bob has long warned *The Sovereign Investor Daily* readers about "civil asset forfeiture" — a legal provision that permits government to act against *inanimate objects* suspected of involvement in criminal activity — such as houses, land or money — independently of any criminal charges against the property's owners. They can take your belongings, whether or not you have done anything wrong.

In a reversal of the principle of "innocent until proven guilty," it's up to the owners of seized property to prove that it is "innocent." If they're unable — or can't afford — to do so, such unlucky individuals simply lose their stuff, and police get to sell it for a profit or use it for themselves. It's abused to such an extent that there's a growing groundswell of demand for reform.

So it's great news that Attorney General Eric Holder has suspended federal participation in certain forms of asset forfeiture, right? Not so fast …

Making Every Cop a Criminal

Federal, state and local governments initially adopted civil asset forfeiture as a tool against organized crime and drug smuggling.

Like most of government's good intentions, however, asset forfeiture hasn't lived up to its promise. Instead it's become a multi-billion-dollar business, targeting innocent and defenseless people who can't afford to challenge the cops. For this reason, only a tiny fraction of cases ever get to court, and few victims are ever charged with a crime.

Asset forfeiture is much-beloved by America's police. It allows every cop, from FBI agent to traffic patrolman, to seize whatever they deem suspect and use it to increase their ability to dominate us. Indeed, some commentators have identified a self-reinforcing cycle in which seized assets are used to invest in greater surveillance capacity, which results in more asset seizures. Very entrepreneurial of our police.

Hold the Hallelujahs

Noting that the practice has expanded massively since 9/11, The Washington Post recently published a highly-praised series on asset forfeiture, including a hard-hitting op-ed piece by two of its original architects, damning the practice.

Seemingly in response, outgoing Attorney General Eric Holder announced earlier this month that he was "suspending" federal government participation in certain forms of asset forfeiture. The provision in question is known as "adoption," in which a federal agency takes over an asset forfeiture case from a state or local government in order to direct it to more lenient federal courts, in return for a share of the proceeds.

Cue much rejoicing from a curious mixture of quasi-libertarians and Democrat loyalists who compulsively praise anything the administration does, even if they don't really understand it. But the jubilation is misplaced.

As Radley Balko, a Cato Institute scholar who focuses on policing abuses, puts it: "adoption ... makes up only 14 percent of the equitable sharing program, which itself only makes up 22 percent of overall federal forfeiture receipts. Using the six-year figures, the new policy at most will restrict about 3 percent of all federal forfeiture revenue."

Indeed, knowledgeable experts confirm Balko's assessment that Holder's announcement is a fig leaf. Besides covering only, a small fraction of federal forfeiture activity, it did nothing to address state forfeiture laws, which account for the greatest amount of forfeiture activity by far.

Despite the limited reach of Holder's action, "law enforcement" officials across the nation are up in arms, warning of Armageddon if they are prevented from stealing from us with impunity. That's understandable, given that forfeited assets have been used to fund police pension funds, office furniture, Christmas parties and other items apparently essential to our liberty.

If All Else Fails ... "Take Your Things and Go"

I advise you to look up your state's asset forfeiture laws so as to know how to best defend yourself against this insanity should the need arise. But be aware that challenging these cases is often costly, and litigants rarely get all their money back. Needless to say, you also should contact your state and local elected officials and demand an end to this legalized theft.

But there is another way to prepare for this madness. As they used to say back in South Africa, sometimes there is nothing left to do but "vat jou goed en trek" — take your things and go. It's hard to tell whether we've reached that stage yet, but unless you prepare now, you'll have nowhere to go when the time comes.

Chapter Eleven

Unchain Your Personal and Civil Liberties

Protect Your Wealth by Keeping a Low Profile 658
Four Steps to a Low Profile 661
Family Security Protection Check Points 663
You Can Protect Yourself from Identity Theft—Here's How! 665
Security Checklists for Business People 667
Learn to Read People 668
10 Mistakes to Avoid When World Traveling 670
How to Avoid Scams, Frauds and Swindles 674
What You Don't Know About Foreign Laws Can Hurt You 685
Ways to Make Travel More Private 686

Editor's Note:

Here we explain how the personal safety of people of wealth can be compromised.

Kidnapping is not just for government officials anymore. You and your family could be the target of terrorists willing to use you as pawns to obtain cash.

But don't despair. In these pages, the experts tell you exactly how to protect your family, your cash and yourself.

PROTECT YOUR WEALTH BY KEEPING A LOW PROFILE
Nicholas Pullen, April 1998, Scope Books

There is an old Chinese proverb: The nail that sticks out is the first to be knocked down.

In the modern world it is the wealthy that must make sure they don't stand out.

That's because in today's world, it is distinctly dangerous to be wealthy, outstanding and successful. Your wealth — the fruit of your talents and creativity, the reward for hard work and sacrifice — exists in an increasingly hostile and unstable climate.

In today's world, wealth and those who have accumulated it are used for target practice. If you have visible wealth, you are a visible target — easily hit. If you don't take adequate precautions, it may only be a matter of time before you show up on some predator's radar screen. There is no shortage of predators out there constantly looking for an opportunity to get their hands on your wealth.

Big Government: In the first instance, your wealth is aggressively targeted by tax-hungry governments.

Poor performing economies, sprawling bureaucracies and wasteful welfare programs don't come cheap. To foot the bill, governments and their tax officials expend huge resources in an effort to turn as much of your private wealth as possible into government wealth.

The U.S. government is particularly aggressive in its pursuit of private wealth. It actually has a policy directing its investigative agents and prosecutors to actively seek out high-profile and successful people. More is likely to fall from a wealthy man's pockets when he is turned upside down and shaken than a poor man's. Unfortunately, other western governments are following suit.

Deep-Pocket Litigation: The growing litigation culture directly threatens the wealthy. Courts in the U.S. increasingly operate on a deep-pocket theory — like star-struck puppies, other western nations are again following suit.

As far as the "justice" system as the twenty-first century is begins, if you've got cash — you are fair game. Unscrupulous litigants can, quite literally, select affluent targets at their leisure and then make speculative claims, spurious allegations, allude to imagined grievances and point to exaggerated or non-existent damages in the hope of being awarded a bumper payout from a jury.

This is the age of the litigation lottery. More and more greedy and malevolent individuals are finding it pays to play. For wealthy people who must pay to launch defenses against spurious lawsuits or be found guilty by default (and face a heavy fine and possibly worse), the situation isn't particularly encouraging.

Sharks Always Circling: Finally, as outlined in an example below, the world is full of unscrupulous individuals who are only too keen to launch predatory attacks on the wealthy. Those in most danger from the criminal classes — robbers, con men, fraud artists and other parasites — are those wealthy individuals who haven't taken sufficient precautions to protect themselves from opportunists.

Unprotected rich people are little more than sitting ducks just waiting to be bagged.

Blend In: The key to successful wealth defense is the adoption of a low profile lifestyle. Blend into the background and avoid being noticed. If predators don't see you, it is highly unlikely they'll be able to single you out for attack. If the nail isn't standing out for all to see, there is no opportunity to hammer it.

It's extremely foolhardy for high net worth individuals to adopt a high profile. It is suicidal and reckless to make ostentatious displays of success and wealth. Tax investigators, opportunist litigants and parasites spend their whole lives looking for just these signs of excess — the signs of an ideal target.

And, once they've spotted wealth, they never stop thinking of methods to separate it from its owner. Parasites are all around. Constantly watching and listening, unseen in the shadows, waiting for the chance to strike.

Aim for Invisibility

Sensible people, as well as striving to be invisible to all governments, must also strive to be invisible to those they encounter on a casual basis in day to day life — these people can be as dangerous as your government. Invisibility means not attracting the attention of anybody — your neighbors, the people with whom you work, the girl at the check-out register, the authorities — anybody.

By adopting a few low-profile methodologies, you'll give yourself the type of insurance you can't buy from some slick talking guy in a suit.

- Blend in like a chameleon. Appear normal. Don't do anything that sets you apart from the crowd. In a nutshell, invisibility is the art of appearing as the gray man. Who is the gray man? He's Mr. Average. Unspectacular. Unworthy of note. Unlikely to attract attention. Unlikely to stand out to predators.

- Adopt an air of genteel poverty or modest success. Dress down. Don't be outspoken — this attracts attention. Appear humble. Arrogance breeds resentment. Fade into the background. Don't strive to be the center of attention.

- Don't be the local celebrity. Shun media exposure. Don't have your photograph leaping out of the newspapers. Keep your activities cloaked in privacy. It may seem like fun to be the life and soul of the community but it can prove expensive. Learn to distrust publicity. Lose your ego. It's better than losing your wealth to a malicious litigant who takes a speculative potshot.

- Don't spend money recklessly. This gets you noticed. Great rolls of notes and lavish spending sprees breed resentment. Don't be a big shot at the casino. Avoid lavish displays.

- Don't drive top-of-the range, luxury vehicles or exotic sports cars. Tax men in particular notice these status symbols with alarming regularity. They often log the details and launch investigations into the registered owners on the basis of their sightings.

- Avoid gold, platinum or black credit cards. Even to the uneducated eye these signal money. Stick with the standard issue card.

- Be seen to live comfortably, not ostentatiously. Palatial homes equipped with all the latest security systems invite closer attention. A comfort able, discreet home doesn't get noticed. A comfortable home doesn't invite speculation or investigation.

- Avoid strutting around town like a peacock dripping with gold jewelry. Similarly, you may love your wife or girlfriend but bedecking her with diamonds and pearls means she will be an irresistible lure to predators for more than one reason.

- Avoid any situation where you may be likely to come under the scrutiny of any authority figure, official representative or police officer. These are the very last people you want taking an interest in your affairs and activities. The best way of avoiding them permanently is never to arouse their curiosity. Observe all laws, even minor ones. Don't get into arguments. Don't annoy your neighbors. Live the life of an ordinary, moderately successful, law-abiding citizen and you're likely to be left alone.

- Keep your mouth shut. Never tell anybody your business. Never mention your wealth, activities or any success you have enjoyed. Loose lips sink ships. More people have fallen foul of their own slack jaws than for any other reason.

Today's friend, wife, lover or colleague is tomorrow's government informer. Trust no one. If nobody knows your business, they can't tell anybody about it.

- Sometimes it is helpful to appear slightly stupid. A little play-acting and a little misinformation means many predators will pass you by. Feigned stupidity is an excellent smokescreen. Remember, there is always someone watching, listening and waiting. There is always someone waiting for an opportunity to strike. A scrap of information, a glimpse of wealth, and the sharks will circle. Your wealth is their target.

Take steps to protect it — adopt a low profile today.

Four Steps to a Low Profile
Patrick O'Connor, *You Are the Target*, 1997, Scope Books

None of us can afford the luxury of being indifferent to security in this day and age.

Indifference means your head could wind up on the criminal chopping block. We must realize that we are the only certain guardians of our own and our family's security. Others will take care of themselves — or perhaps be making plans to "take care of us" in a most undesirable way.

STEP 1: Always Be Security Conscious

Behavior that is unthinking or born of a momentary personal arrogance destroys sound personal security procedures. The approach to security should be as professional and business-like as the approach to a chosen career. That is the only reasonable way to guard against harm to yourself and your family or loss of your personal and business assets.

Explore the positive steps that can and should be taken to reduce your personal target profile. Begin by developing a low personal profile. Remember collaboration with the enemy is one of the worst offenses and when you advertise your target potential, that is exactly what you are doing.

Obviously, if your life attracts the media, a low personal profile may be difficult or impossible to achieve. Moderate behavior is the key to an effective low personal profile. Develop a list of things that call attention to yourself in public and eliminate them. We all developed habits that call unnecessary attention to ourselves.

STEP 2: Avoid the Habitual Routines

This is one of the most important aspects of personal security.

Studies of rapists, muggers, assassins, robbers and kidnappers prove the incredible dangers posed by their victims' habits. Living in a predictable way can be the perfect scenario for predatory criminals.

You can alter your routine. Do grocery shopping with your spouse on Wednesday if the usual day is Saturday. At work vary your lunch time and the place you eat. Reporting to your office every day at the same time is a common error. When leaving home notify a trusted person of your destination; make arrangements for a second phone call to verify arrival.

Arrange code words to alert your wife or a friend of trouble by phone. In the office, adopt silent emergency signals. The cash room of a major department store has a code system by which a supervisor regularly greets employees with a cheery "Hello." The response must be a bright, "Hello, Mr. Powers." If the response is anything else, the supervisor takes immediate emergency measures.

Whether your car is parked in a public place or in a locked garage it is a target for bombing, bugging or disabling. Transmitters can be attached in seconds. These can emit a signal picked up and traced over several miles. An explosive device can be clamped to the underside a car in seconds.

A cellular phone should be carried in your car so you can summon help or report trouble. After looking for bugs and explosives, check tires, lights, the horn and be sure your petrol tank is full and not leaking. A flat tire or a slow leak can place you in a critical and vulnerable position.

It is imperative to avoid anyone who may be following you. Professional followers have a number of techniques designed to fit specific needs. They may use several vehicles including helicopters. Changing taxis and often doubling back on yourself can throw off pursuers off your tail. If you are in your car and feel threatened by followers, lead them into a congested traffic area if possible, stop the car, get out and walk away quickly leaving the car where it is.

Police say victims of crimes are often accomplices in their own demise. Private security consultants caution customers that imprudent or showy conduct is the catalyst in random criminal activity.

Your safety checklist should include a check of cosmetic features. Do you consistently overdress for surroundings? Do you wear inappropriate or unnecessary jewelry? These are signposts to criminals seeking a target. Avoid flashing inordinate amounts of cash or wallets filled with credit cards. Carry only cash you need and don't flash a roll of bills. Use the credit card you need and keep the others safely concealed. A minimum conscious effort provides great personal security by denying criminals information.

Personal conversation should be guarded in public. If you maintain a moderate appearance and conservative conduct, why negate it all with loose conversation. Professional criminals make an excellent living capitalizing on overheard conversations.

STEP 3: Avoid Dangers, Known & Unknown

Strangers about which we know little or nothing should be assumed to be dangerous until proven otherwise. That sounds stringent until examined under the light of effective security. It doesn't offend anyone and it keeps us from compromising ourselves by keeping people at a safe arm's length until their background and character are known to us. The same approach is correct for strange places, venues about which we know little or nothing.

They are the types of places that we find ourselves at an unguarded moment. When there is even the slightest doubt about a place, avoid it. There never is a good reason for putting yourself in an area of potential jeopardy.

STEP 4: Make Your Home Secure

Every residence should be penetration proof. Only residents should be able to come and go at will. This means there must be a security system and security procedures which will vary with single- or multi-unit dwellings.

FAMILY SECURITY PROTECTION CHECK POINTS

Patrick O'Connor, *You Are the Target*, 1997, Scope Books

Practical things you can do now — today — to protect your family, at home and away at school. What to tell your children, plus a school security check up.

Security Begins at Home

- Be certain outside doors, window, and screens, especially those children's rooms, are locked securely.

- Keep children's room doors open so you can hear any unusual sounds; or install an intercom or video camera system in their rooms.

- Make sure your residence is not readily accessible from the outside and that the alarm system is functional.

- Never leave young children unattended at home or anywhere else. Be certain they are always in the care of a responsible person.

- Instruct your family and domestic staff that doors and windows must be locked and that strangers are never to be admitted.

- Instruct young children how to telephone the police and test their knowledge with a trial call.

- If you leave pre-teenage children at home with a sitter at night, keep the house well-lit inside and out.

- During an extended absence, avoid indications you are away. Close garage doors and cancel newspaper delivery. Install day-night, light-sensitive controls on appropriate light systems.

- Never advertise family activity routines. To acquaint themselves with a family's habits, would-be intruders often have victims under surveillance prior to acting.

- Instruct your family, especially the children, your staff and business associates never to provide information to strangers.

- Avoid providing personal details in response to inquiries from publications such as business directories, social registers, or community directories. Always demand a caller's identification and double-check by calling them back at their office before talking at length.

Security Tips to Tell Your Children

- Always travel in groups or pairs.
- Walk along heavily traveled streets and avoid isolated areas whenever possible.
- Refuse automobile rides from strangers and never go with strangers anywhere on foot. Never accept any gifts, food, candy, drinks, or money from strangers. Refuse requests for help from strangers.
- Use municipal or private play areas with recreational activity supervision by responsible adults and readily available police protection.
- Immediately report anyone who molests or annoys you to the nearest person of authority.
- Never leave home or a hotel without telling you parents where you are going and who will be with you.
- Instruct your children never to disclose your residential address without your permission, especially over the Internet.

Minimum Security Rules for Your Child's School

- Never release a child except to his/her parents during school hours. A teacher or school official must confirm parents' approval before release of a child to any person other than the parent.
- Confirm the caller's identity when phone requests are made concerning a child's activity or a request is made that the child be permitted to leave during school hours. If a parent calls, check the request by a return telephone call and have the child positively identify the parent's voice. When appropriate, the caller

should be asked identifying questions such as the child's date of birth, courses being studied, names of teachers and classmates and other facts known only to the parents. When in doubt, do not release the child.

- Be alert to suspicious persons loitering in or near school buildings or grounds. If such persons can provide no logical explanation for their presence, notify police immediately. Obtain the identity and full description of the suspect person.

- School personnel must ensure that adult supervision is provided in schools and recreational areas at all times.

Security Questions for Your Child's School Administrator

- Are thorough background checks done before hiring school staff, including maintenance people?
- While children are in school is a qualified nurse on duty at all times?
- Describe procedures followed when a child is injured at school. How is parental notification given?
- To what hospital is a child transported in the event of injury?
- What police and fire station has supervision over the school?
- How many and what kind of security personnel are available on the school premises? Where is their office?
- Is a special background check made on all security personnel before hiring?

You Can Protect Yourself from Identity Theft—Here's How!

Mark Nestmann, *The Sovereign Investor Daily*, February 2008

In one of my recent blog posts, I described the rapidly increasing risk that identity theft poses to every American.

Fortunately, you can take a simple and nearly foolproof precaution that will virtually guarantee that you won't become a victim. It takes about 15 minutes to implement this recommendation. Just don't count on credit bureaus, banks, or merchants to tell you about it though, for reasons I'll describe in a moment.

What you need to do is to place a "credit freeze" on your credit file. A credit freeze, in effect, places an electronic padlock on your credit report. No one can review your credit report until you remove the padlock. And if a company can't review your credit report, it's very unlikely to issue you (or an impostor) credit.

The best news: all three major credit bureaus now offer credit freezes to anyone who requests it! The service is often free, although in some states, you will need to pay a nominal fee (normally, $10).

To freeze your credit file, send a letter via certified mail to the following addresses (visit each website to confirm the mailing address):

- Experian Security Freeze, P.O. Box 9554, Allen, TX 75013
  http://www.experian.com/consumer/security_freeze.html
- Equifax Security Freeze, P.O. Box 105788, Atlanta, GA 30348
  http://www.equifax.com/help/credit-freeze/en_cp
- Trans Union Consumer Protection Center, P.O. Box 380, Woodlyn, PA 19094
  http://www.transunion.com/fraud-victim-resource/protected-consumer

The letter should state your full name, address, Social Security number, and that you wish to place a "security freeze" on your credit file. (Credit bureaus don't use the phrase "credit freeze," although that's what it is.) In addition, enclose a copy of a government issued identification card, such as a driver's license, state or military ID card, etc., and one copy of a utility bill, bank or insurance statement, etc.

Why aren't credit bureaus, banks, and merchants shouting from the rooftops the benefits of a credit freeze? The reason is simple. Anyone who places an "electronic padlock" on their credit file won't be able to make an impulse purchase by obtaining "instant credit" at an electronics store, car dealership, etc.

Impulse buyers are the most lucrative prospects of all for any retailer, because they want to buy "now," and aren't that concerned about price. Sales personnel are trained to say something like, "Don't worry about what it costs—you won't need to make any payments until next year!"

With a credit freeze in effect, you won't be able to make an impulse purchase. Instead, you'll need to contact the credit bureau to remove the padlock from your credit file. This costs $10 and a few minutes of your time online or over the phone.

The biggest practical drawback to a credit freeze is that an increasing number of companies demand access to credit reports to establish service. For instance, you may find banks, phone companies, landlords, and even your employer want access to your credit report when you set up service or open an account. On the other hand, companies that have an existing relationship with you can continue to access your credit file, even with a credit freeze in effect.

In addition, if you're planning a major purchase—buying a home, for instance—and require financing for that purchase, you'll want to remove the credit freeze from your credit file.

Is giving up the ability to purchase a big-ticket item with "instant credit" worth virtual total protection from identity theft? Only you can answer that question, but for me, the choice is clear:

"Freeze me!"

SECURITY CHECKLISTS FOR BUSINESS PEOPLE
Patrick O'Connor, *You Are the Target*, 1997

Service, manufacturing or retail, every business has its soft spots and choke points. Do you know where your business vulnerabilities are?

The four most common targets for security violations:
1. Your physical person
2. Your loved ones, including family, home and possessions
3. Your business
4. Your employees

The two most serious challenges to security:
1. Your own indifference
2. Hostile outside forces

The two guiding principles when considering security:
1. Eliminate all vulnerabilities.
2. Never knowingly create or invite a threat.

Security check points for service-oriented businesses:
- Keep a minimum amount of cash on hand.
- Keep all valuable papers and records in a secure place within a restricted area.
- Release papers and records only on a qualified and controlled basis. Pin-point responsibility at all times.
- Screen all visitors and potential clients within a reception area separate and apart from work and office areas.
- Designate specific responsibility for day-end premises lock up.
- Periodically test premises and telephones for electronic spying apparatus.

- Caution employees to avoid shop talk outside the office except in controlled business situations.
- Screen new employees thoroughly and avoid the use of temporary help for confidential or critical assignments.
- Provide intelligent security when the premises are vacant.

Additional security check points for manufacturing businesses:
- Assign portable equipment and collect it daily.
- Keep a running inventory of raw materials.
- Distribute raw materials on a sign-out basis.
- Maintain daily inventory records of manufactured goods in a secure place.
- Promulgate and enforce specific entrance and departure procedures for all employees.
- Adopt responsibility and assignment rules for stationary machinery.
- Have uniformed security personnel on duty and highly visible at all times.

Additional check points for retail businesses:
- Display expensive items in the most controlled manner possible.
- Make frequent but irregularly timed bank deposits depending on cash flow.
- Employ uniformed store guards.
- Keep inventories well secured.
- Establish individual responsibility for cash drawers.

Learn to Read People
Perpetual Traveler 2, 1997, Scope Books

 A little intuition and practical savvy can help you avoid some of life's worst pitfalls — other human beings bent on making trouble for you. You can stop them before they even start if you know how to read the telltale signs.

 People who are born and live in other cultures have unique ways of expressing themselves through body language. Before traveling internationally, always familiarize yourself with local customs in the countries you will visit.

 As Groucho Marx used to say, "When in Rome, do as the Romanians do!" Every good guide book contains an introductory lesson on possibly offensive body language to be avoided. Fail to heed such useful advice and you may cause a social crisis that not only deeply offends local people but also brings unwanted negative attention to yourself.

Once while visiting the Temple of the Emerald Buddha in Bangkok, one of Thailand's most holy shrines, I saw a woman insult every Thai within sight. She accomplished this when she sat in front of the statue of Buddha with the soles of both of her feet pointing directly at the shrine. In Thailand, it is highly insulting to show anyone the soles of your feet, much less Buddha. Thais present angrily whispered among themselves, until someone finally asked the woman to leave the shrine. Her ignorance had transformed the traditionally friendly Thais into menacing adversaries.

She is probably still wondering what all of the fuss was about.

As in Thailand, the soles of your feet are an insult in most Arab nations. In many Moslem countries, a man who sits with crossed legs is indicating he is gay. Finger signs mean different things in different places. Making a circle by putting your forefinger and thumb together means "perfect" or "thanks" in most countries.

In Greece, however, it invites homosexual advances. The two-finger sign ("bull") that expresses disbelief in the U.S., in Italy is a private signal that the wife of a man with whom the signal sender is speaking is having an extramarital affair.

In any country a good indication of a conversation partner's honesty of expression can be seen in his or her body language. Read some books on this subject if you are frequently involved in conferences where clues to the true feelings of your opponents or colleagues may be helpful.

Someone who fidgets while talking is probably nervous. If one stands with arms crossed over the chest it may mean a negative or defensive attitude, even more so if a person sits with arms crossed on the chest.

When you learn how to read others, you also learn how not to reveal your own attitudes through body language.

Reading facial expressions is trickier. People are usually more aware and in control of their facial expressions than of their body language. As a defense mechanism some people constantly present a poker face to the world. A hint: someone who is less than truthful may respond to an accusation with a fleeting facial expression of feigned surprise or astonishment. If the look lasts a bit too long, he's probably a phony. Test yourself on this in a mirror. The insincerity revealed is quite obvious once you attuned to its meaning.

So when you go abroad, learn how to look before you leap.

10 Mistakes to Avoid When World Traveling
Paul Terhorst, December 1997, Scope Books

Don't believe all those old wives tales about travel precautions you've heard repeatedly.

Take it from a veteran traveler who learned the truth from hard experience.

After 16 years living and investing all over the world I thought I could be most helpful to you by exposing some bad advice you may hear — advice that travel agents, credit card vendors, tour guides, innkeepers and others want you to hear because it's in their interest.

Below are the Ten Worst Offshore Travel Tips — advice you're likely to hear about traveling and investing abroad that you can feel comfortable ignoring.

1. **The American Express Card, Don't Leave Home without It.** An ad campaign for American Express many years ago and bad advice. One time I was in London during a period of stable exchange rates. I charged several items each day on a Diners, American Express, Visa, and MasterCard. When I got the bills back in the U.S., I checked the exchange rates. Diners, Visa, and MasterCard were all close. But American Express stepped three percent on every exchange rate. Why pay American Express three percent of your monthly expenditures? I cut up the card.

2. **Don't Drink the Water.** This tip is okay as far as it goes. But then the guidebooks remind you that "water" includes ice, and advises you not to put ice in drinks. This is an example of "developed world-centric" thinking. In rich countries bars and restaurants buy ice machines and connect them to the tap water. But in Third World countries bars and restaurants buy their ice from ice plants. I've been in some of those ice plants, and in each case the host has pointed out the water purifier. The last thing these ice people want is dirty water jamming up their plant. So the ice is probably okay. On a hot day you're probably running a greater risk of dehydration than you are of getting sick from eating ice.

3. **Buy Cheap Countries.** This is bad advice and the reason why is quite complicated. It sounds reasonable enough — buy low, sell high, right? Why shouldn't you buy cheap countries? Well, first of all, when I say cheap, I don't mean stocks are cheap, but that the country is cheap to you — the visitor. A beer or a taxi ride or a local hotel room is cheap. The only way a country can be cheap, with only a few exceptions that I can think of, is to have an undervalued currency. So cheap means a foreign currency is cheap.

So why is expensive good and cheap bad? Because of a paradigm shift. The old model, most notably in Japan and Western Europe, particularly Germany, in the 1950s, was to undervalue the currency. That way those countries could produce things cheaply. Years later, after booming exported growth and the expansion of internal markets, the market revalued those currencies.

The new paradigm today is to skip directly to the expensive currency phase. To heck with building factories, taking advantage of low cost labor, improving manufacturing techniques, becoming the low cost producer, then watching your currency go up in value. In every case — Brazil, Argentina, Russia, Hungary — countries which have overvalued their currencies, or revalued their currencies, have met with initial success under this new paradigm:

- Inflation disappeared.
- Money poured in from Wall Street and Western Europe.
- Stock markets soared.
- Real estate and other assets soared.

So why am I telling you all this?

Because PTs are in a unique position to take advantage: PTs travel and they have money to invest in speculative, turnaround situations. As a PT all you need to do is note when a given country becomes very expensive, very quickly. There's your opportunity.

Expensive is Good, Cheap is Bad.

So where's the next opportunity likely to be?

Well, it's got to be a cheap country right now: Indonesia, the Philippines, even Burma or Vietnam, none of which are tied to the old model, are viable possibilities. Here's what I'm saying—but don't be premature — wait until these countries purposefully and dramatically overvalue their currency.

Bide your time, continue your travels. Keep your eye out for newly expensive, especially very expensive places. When you see a big change… there's your opportunity. This is the new paradigm and you can do very well from it.

4. **Pack Your Fodor's Guide.** Over the years, I think I've seen all the guidebooks and the best for travelers are the *Lonely Planet* guide book series. I'm talking here about travelers versus tourists. I define "travelers" as people who move around within the country at large rather than within carefully defined, guided, tourist groups. Lonely Planet guidebooks have the best maps, details on transportation, and lists of hotels in all price ranges.

They're very specific. For example, they tell you precisely how to take the train from Bangkok to Chiang Mai in Thailand. Go to the station, through the black door on the right, to the left toward a desk marked "Foreigners." Believe me this depth of illumination can help you avoid all sorts of confusion and mistakes. Contact Lonely Planet Publications, www.lonelyplanet.com.

5. **Avoid Countries in Turmoil.** No one went to Iraq during the Kuwaiti war. Then again, I guess not many people go to Iraq under any circumstances. But deciding whether or not to go to a country in turmoil depends on the turmoil. If you're in a country shortly after a coup, for example, you're safer than any place on earth. After many years being around it, my view is that turmoil is good. It's exciting and provides all kinds of benefits to the traveler who's in a position to take advantage.

For example, in 1989 I was in Argentina, a country in turmoil with massive inflation. I got up one morning and decided to buy a pair of leather Adidas tennis shoes. I had seen the shoes the day before at 2,000 pesos. With the peso at 100 to the dollar, that was about US$20, a good price. By the time I got to the store the peso was at 200, so the shoes were now only US$10. The merchant guaranteed the 2,000-peso price for an hour while I raced downtown to change money. By the time I got to the exchange dealer the peso was at 500. The shoes wound up costing only US$4.

6. **Check Home for Messages Every Now and Again.** Calling home is old fashioned. Computers, email and the Internet provide the modern traveler with a direct line to the wider world. Using the Internet, you can have your messages forwarded to you. You can operate bank and broker accounts and check that transactions were recorded properly. You can purchase plane tickets. During 1995–96, Vicki and I were on the go for over a year. All the while we were in constant touch, via e-mail, with family and friends. I don't think we would have been comfortable traveling for that long without having our small computer along.

7. **Enjoy Exotic, Native Culture in Tahiti.** The principal argument I have with this advice is that Tahiti is one of the world's most expensive tourist destinations. Now you may have your own reasons for going to Tahiti. But westerners, in general, are terrified of visiting inexpensive countries. Tourism to Mexico plummeted after the 1994 devaluation. Travel agents and airlines are already bracing for a huge drop in tourism to Thailand and Malaysia this season, because of the devaluations there.

Why do people avoid countries that become cheap? They feel uncomfortable. They assume they can't get the luxury they want. They don't know how to tip, think that they're unfairly taking advantage, whatever. There's no reason for this. Visit countries when you want to go, whether they're cheap or not. If a country is cheap—you can take advantage and cut some deals. In the South

Pacific, consider going to Bali, Malaysia, or Fiji instead of the much more expensive Tahiti.

8. **Beware of Dictatorships or Corrupt Countries.** When I first moved to Argentina in 1981, it was a military dictatorship. People in the U.S. were screaming about lack of rights. But the streets of Buenos Aires were safe. I'm not supporting dictatorships. But dictatorships are often very safe for tourists. Under a military dictatorship the guys in the streets with the guns are often protecting you. Another point here: there seems to be little correlation between investment results and whether a country is a dictatorship or not, or whether it's very corrupt or not.

9. **Take Traveler's Checks.** They're Safer than Cash. They're also expensive and obsolete. It's difficult to replace them, unless you have a purchase voucher, and if your checks are lost in your luggage, the purchase voucher is often lost too. But that's if you lose them. If you don't lose them, you're sure to get a lousy exchange rate and pay exchange fees. You're sure to have to present your passport to cash them.

A better way to travel is with plastic — cash machine cards, credit cards. ATMs work just as well in Thailand or Argentina as they do at home. They also have higher limits on withdrawals, charge no exchange fees, and offer very favorable exchange rates. Personally, I prefer debit cards. With these you can go into a bank and get more money than from the machines, and you don't pay the cash advance fee credit cards charge.

10. **If You Get in Trouble Abroad, Get Help from the U.S. Consulate.** One specific piece of advice for Americans-avoid U.S. consulates. Remember: the people there don't work for you. They work for the government of the United States. And like all government types they have only contempt for those who propose making work for them.

If you're in trouble abroad, the person to ask for help is the owner of your hotel or apartment hotel.

He's a big man in town, because he owns significant real property, and you're his customer. He probably speaks some English. He's working for you, your interests coincide, you both want to get you out of trouble.

If you must go to a government office, use the British or Canadian consulates. They speak English and for some reason seem to have a more compassionate attitude toward needy travelers than their U.S. counterparts.

Finally, I want to leave you with the sense that life is an adventure, and that travel, and living abroad, and investing abroad are part of that adventure, and a wonderfully exciting part.

How to Avoid Scams, Frauds and Swindles
Robert E Bauman JD, *Offshore Confidential*, February 2012

Scams are everywhere and the world of offshore finance and investment is especially littered with them.

Call it fraud — and that's where we come in. Our expert advice has guided thousands of people through the world of swindlers and cheats over the years, and we're proud of that.

Still, I never ceased to be amazed at how easily so many people can be taken in.

On numerous occasions, I've been asked whether some outlandish offshore "investment" guaranteeing 20% returns monthly is likely to be reliable. (My response: *Are you kidding?*)

Or whether an offshore bank with nothing more than a web page, no physical office address and no listed officers, is a good place to stash cash. (My response: *Puh-leez!*)

One of The Sovereign Society's major warnings over the past 15 years has been to guard against frauds of all sorts. And that goes especially for offshore frauds, in which many are touted on slick looking Internet web sites.

A recent study contradicted the common perception that most scam victims are vulnerable senior citizens. Instead, it found that while older people were most often the targets of cons, it is those aged between 35 and 44 who are most likely to fall for them.

This study also showed that men and women are equally likely to be the victims of scams — although women were more likely to be caught by miracle health scams, while men were more likely to be the victims of investment cons.

However, if you are careful and know the score, you don't have to get hurt.

The Ponzi Scheme

This scam is a good place to start, and was brought back into the headlines recently by the swindler Madoff and his $18 billion rip-off.

A Ponzi scheme is basically a fake investment operation that pays its existing investors with cash from new investors, rather than from any actual investment profit.

It originated with Charles Ponzi, an Italian immigrant who arrived in Boston in 1903 with $2.50 in his pocket. Ponzi soon found that honesty was not necessarily the quickest way to get rich.

In 1919, he hit upon his big idea. He discovered that international reply coupons had the same nominal value in every country, although they were much cheaper in Europe than in the U.S.

Ponzi set up a "Securities Exchange Company" and promised investors they would double their capital in 90 days. Fools responded in droves and most of these "investors" lost everything.

In August 1920, Ponzi's bubble burst and he spent three and a half years in federal prison for mail fraud and another seven years on state larceny charges. He died in 1949 in Rio de Janeiro, as poor as when he arrived in Boston.

There's a Sucker Born Every Minute

The persistent Nigerian letter fraud is one that most of us are aware of nowadays. But here are two examples of my past fraud alerts that were issued well before any official action was taken to stop them. These frauds included the since-closed Millennium Bank, as well as Robert Allen Stanford and his now defunct Stanford Financial Group and Caribbean banks.

There is a historical dispute whether circus impresario P.T. Barnum, actually made the well-known statement that "a sucker is born every minute," but those words have come to epitomize a certain type of credulous individual who will fall for just about anything if a quick buck is promised.

Just imagine some shady type, who slips out of a dark alley, sidles up to you and whispers: *"Pssst! Buddy! I can get ya' 20%-a-month return if you give me your money."* That's roughly what the U.S. Securities and Exchange Commission in 2009 said happened to at least 375 investors since 2004, after two U.S. residents, now in jail, cheated them in a $68 million Ponzi scheme. They offered ridiculously high interest CDs issued by Millennium Bank, which they controlled from Saint Vincent and the Grenadines, a poorly regulated tax haven.

The Millennium Bank scandal was easy to predict. Attracted by what should have been unbelievable promises of such high returns, several Sovereign Society members and readers asked me whether I thought they should entrust their cash to Millennium Bank.

In less than 24 hours of due diligence, I told them: "Absolutely not!"

I discovered a major Millennium Bank claim was simply a lie. Their web site claimed that: *"Millennium Bank is a subsidiary of United Trust of Switzerland S.A., a Swiss-registered private trust company established in 1931. United Trust of Switzerland S.A.'s extensive experience in financial services provides Millennium Bank with a solid foundation..."*

The Swiss banking agency web site told me the so-called "United Trust of Switzerland S.A" did not exist. It was neither registered as a financial institution as required by Swiss law, nor did it appear in the trade registry of Swiss corporations. In other words, Millennium Bank was a fraud. A banking contact in Zürich told me: "Unless we missed something… this bank is a sham…"

That was in 2006. The big question for me is this: What took the U.S. SEC and the government of Saint Vincent and the Grenadines so long (three years) to stop this obvious fraud?

Beware of Dazzling Offshore Deals

Some folks seem to check their judgment at the border when it comes to dazzling offshore deals touted on slick Internet sites offering high returns on investments (20% a month guaranteed).

Whether it's greed or temporary insanity, these deluded folks send large amounts of money to unknown persons based on nothing more than web site promises, often without even knowing the names or addresses of those who want your cash. Wire that cash and it's likely you'll never see it again, much less a 20% return on it.

My experience is that many elderly people are far more cautious about falling prey to fraudulent investment schemes. Perhaps because they have been around longer and have learned that human nature does not always translate into goodness and honesty.

A large part of the U.S.'s total population of 311.8 million is in "the senior age demographic." Those who are 65 years and older comprise 13% of the population. By 2030, with a huge influx of baby boomers, the senior population will swell to 20%.

As the attorney charged with due diligence investigations at The Sovereign Society, I often encounter elderly people who ask for my advice. Often, I must tell them they are about to be scammed. Money is always involved.

According to a 2011 study by the MetLife Mature Market Institute, elderly victims of financial abuse suffer an estimated $2.9 billion in annual losses. But data collected by the Federal Trade Commission (FTC), the government agency charged with protecting consumers against "unfair or deceptive" trade practices, indicates that seniors are in better shape than other age groups.

Fraud, as defined by the FTC, covers most cases involving stranger — induced scams: fake credit card schemes, lottery and prize promotions, pyramid clubs and phony investment sales. These are typically sold through the Internet, telemarketing or direct mail. Elder-care experts say such scams are only a small part of the financial crimes committed against the senior population.

1. Offshore Scams and Frauds Avoid Offshore Problems

In the last decade, under relentless international pressure, there has been a real, self-imposed reform of offshore financial centers, with a tightening of laws and rules to protect against fraud.

But one problem for the offshore investor is that similar credit rating information on foreign companies is not always available.

Although some countries (Canada, the U.K.) have strict accounting and disclosure standards, others do not. That makes your own personal due diligence inquiries all the more necessary.

An important point to remember is that a non-U.S. foreign promoter may have little knowledge of U.S. tax or reporting laws. The best offshore professionals will tell you that you need expert American professional tax and reporting help to evaluate any offshore plans or investments.

However, too many U.S. attorneys and CPAs have limited knowledge of U.S. offshore tax laws. We can help you by recommending experienced professionals who know what needs to be done. Refer to Appendix A for the listing of The Sovereign Society's Council of Experts.

a) Tax Haven Scam

I am surprised at the number of people who ask me with all sincerity how they can become a criminal. These unthinking folks want to know about the best tax haven to hide their money "to avoid paying U.S. taxes."

One of the most persistent scams foisted on U.S. persons is the claim that offshore tax havens can be used by U.S. persons to avoid taxes. The harsh truth is that the U.S. is only one of four countries in the world that imposes income and estate taxes on citizens and residents based on their worldwide income — regardless of where they live.

While many high-tax countries tax the worldwide income of their residents, they do not tax the income of their non-resident citizens. Thus, a citizen can escape from a high tax country (other than the U.S.) by moving to a low tax country. And, in many countries of the world, income earned by a trust or corporation that is domiciled in another country is not subject to tax by the owner of the corporation or by the grantors or beneficiaries of the foreign trust.

While there are some limited exemptions and exceptions for U.S. persons working outside the country, the tax law often subjects a U.S. person to far more harsh tax treatment on their foreign entities than on domestic entities.

As many Sovereign Society members know, the U.S. government intimidates and extorts other countries into divulging information about the financial affairs of

U.S. citizens in their countries. A horrendous example of this IRS extraterritorial overreach is the Foreign Account Tax Compliance Act (FATCA).

An offshore bank account is an essential asset protection and investment tool, but you need to understand and comply with all U.S. IRS offshore reporting requirements. We can recommend professionals and SEC qualified offshore banks and foreign investment firms that will make sure you are in compliance with all U.S. tax and reporting laws.

b) Foreign Bank Account Scam

Some offshore "advisors" will claim that money in a foreign bank account is protected from creditors. That works only if you are able to keep your foreign account a total secret and commit perjury on your U.S. tax return and other reports. These shady advisors whisper about "numbered accounts" in Andorra or Panama banks, where there will be no record of your ownership of the account. **DO NOT BELIEVE IT.**

Yes, many reputable offshore financial centers, such as Switzerland, Panama and Singapore, have financial privacy guaranteed by law. That's far better than the U.S., where the dubious PATRIOT Act has abolished all financial privacy. But even in these and other offshore financial centers, tax information exchange agreements (TIEAs) exist that honor official IRS requests.

U.S. tax law now imposes on U.S. persons duplicate reporting requirements of offshore accounts on your annual IRS Form 1040, as well as the annual FBAR report due on June 30. Failing to tell the truth is a federal crime.

As I explained in your *January 2012 Special Report* the Foreign Account Tax Compliance Act (FATCA) imposes further individual reporting, starting with the April 2012 income tax filing.

As far as transferring funds to an offshore account, each transaction of $10,000 or more is reported automatically by banks to the U.S. Treasury's FinCEN unit and they also must be reported by travelers leaving or entering the U.S. on customs forms.

c) Abusive Trusts

Although this sort of nonsense has died down in recent years, there were promoters, some of whom are now in federal prisons, who claimed they could set up a special trust that would protect assets from all creditors, including the IRS, eliminating income, estate and gift taxes.

These trusts were said to give you complete control over investments and use of the trust funds.

A common sales pitch was that these were the same "secret trusts" used by the Rockefellers, Mellons, Kennedys and other wealthy families, who were able to avoid taxes with their little known trusts. These entities were sold under beguiling names such as "constitutional trust," "pure trust," "patriot trust" and "common law trust." Similar tax exempt claims were made for a "corporation sole" if you obtained a license as a clergyman and for people claiming to be "sovereign citizens."

A decade ago, the IRS, CIA and FBI formed a special joint task force to track down and eliminate what they called "abusive" trusts. The anti-abusive trust campaign put a number of the promoters in jail, many operating offshore in places such as Panama, Costa Rica and Canada.

d) Tinker Toy Legal Network

Slick promoters will try to sell you a complex series of trusts or a foreign limited liability company (LLC) or international business company (IBC) — or all three.

Confronted by such a dubious proposal, you should always seek the impartial opinion of an international tax expert.

In fact, U.S. court decisions strictly interpret the obligations of a U.S. person actively involved in an offshore corporation. These cases attribute "constructive ownership" to the involved U.S. person as an individual, or find that actual control exists based on a chain of entities linking the U.S. person to the offshore corporation.

For U.S. persons who control shares in an offshore IBC, there are major limitations on U.S. tax benefits that would otherwise be available to a corporation formed in the U.S. That is because the offshore corporation is probably listed on what is known as the IRS "per se" list of foreign corporations, which appears in IRS regulations. The listed corporations are barred from numerous U.S. tax benefits.

Such scams are offered by some lawyers and "incorporation services" that advise inexperienced clients to set up an IBC, or an offshore trust, and link them to a Nevada or Wyoming corporation as the unlisted owner. This network of legal entities is claimed to provide secrecy, legal insulation and reduce or avoid taxes. Ultimately, it will achieve none of these objectives. Instead, the result may be serious penalties.

e) Passport Fraud

Beware of passport fraud. It's worldwide and it can not only cost you huge sums of money, it can land the unwary person in jail.

There is a little-known but lucrative underground black market in forged passports. In 2008, U.S. government security agencies uncovered a criminal ring in Thailand that produced counterfeit passports and other travel documents, including hundreds of fake U.S., Malaysian, Singapore, French, Spanish, Belgian, Maltese and Japanese passports sold on the world black market.

Even legal passports can go astray. In recent years, thousands of official passports have been stolen or lost in France, Australia, Finland and Belgium. In 2005, the U.K. admitted that in the prior year more than 10,000 British passports were lost, stolen or disappeared.

A few years ago, a U.S. State Department official was indicted for fraudulently helping foreigners obtain preferential treatment "green cards."

Ten years ago, had you read the classifieds in the respectable journal, The Economist, you would have seen an advertisement that promised to provide a "European Union passport, fully registered and renewable" for only $19,500. Of course, it was a fraud.

Certainly, the most important consideration when evaluating the usefulness of an alternative citizenship and a second passport is that it is legal in every respect. That may seem obvious, but the proliferation of passport fraud operations, especially on the Internet, requires a reminder.

In this age of instant communication, it takes only hours, certainly no more than a few days, before customs and immigration officials worldwide know when a passport is called into question and, when caught, illegal passport holders go straight to jail.

If you are interested in obtaining dual citizenship and the second passport that comes with that enhanced status, you can learn about every aspect of what is required in the latest edition (2011) of my book, *The Passport Book*.

2. Investment and Other Frauds

a) Email Scams

Most everyone knows that email is a great convenience — but it can also be a major headache. If you are not careful, one email can cost you thousands of dollars, if not more.

Phishing is a word invented to describe attempts to acquire information such as usernames, passwords, credit card and bank details by masquerading as a trustworthy entity in an email. Fake emails pretending to be from popular social websites, auction sites, online payment processors, banks or IT administrators are commonly used to lure the unsuspecting public.

Here is the golden rule: Never give out important personal information to anyone that you don't know well and trust. Make sure that you protect yourself at all times. Remember, the reason that you get so many of these emails is because gullible people fall for them every day.

Here are the top five scams for February 2012, according to the Scam Trends website:

1. Your correct tax information is essential: Identity thieves targeted consumers with bogus emails, claiming a W-2 form was not submitted and provided a link to a site for you to input your information. The link directed taxpayers to a malicious site that harvested that information, such as Social Security numbers and addresses, which were later used to hack into bank accounts.
2. USPS Delivery Failure Notification (This is definitely not from the Post Office.)
3. American Airlines: Your order has been completed (Open the zip file and you are caught!)
4. Have you seen what this person is saying about you? (Twitter users targeted with malware).
5. Penalty for the failure to file income tax returns.

For tips on reducing the odds of becoming a victim of an online financial scam, check online for The Top 10 Looming Computer Security Threats of 2012. If you use technology you must know how to combat the ways it can be used against you.

b) Gold Scams

For years The Sovereign Society has recommend buying gold as part of a balanced portfolio. When we first recommended gold in 1999, it was at less than $300 an ounce. Recently gold hit a record high above $1900 an ounce and predictions are that it will go higher.

There are many ways to invest in gold, including bullion, certificates and coins. Most people depend on an investment advisor or company to help them. But you need to make certain the person or company you choose is licensed by your state securities administrator.

Be aware that the U.S. Mint's American Eagle Gold Bullion Coins are the only gold coins guaranteed by the U.S. government in terms of purity, weight, and content. They're available from precious metal or collectible coin dealers, certain banks, and brokerage houses.

If you're considering investing in gold, do your homework first. Check with the U.S. Mint. The Federal Trade Commission is another useful source for information on protecting yourself against scam artists, who are touting coins and precious metals as safe investments.

Andy Hecht, the editor of *Trade Hunter*, and one of the most sought-after commodity traders in the world, has warned against the media ads for companies offering cash for gold. He says many businesses, including some jewelry stores, now operate like pawn shops. They pay cash up front to buy old jewelry and gold. The problem is that they only pay $380-$400 per ounce for gold, a fraction of the metal's market value. The same is true for other precious metals.

We have all heard the phrase — Buyer beware.

c) Nigerian Scams

A year or so ago, I was contacted by someone who had seen my Internet writings about passports.

This credulous U.S. citizen, hunting the web for a second passport and dual citizenship, made contact with "*a woman in Nigeria*," who claimed she could provide (for a substantial fee) an official passport of an unnamed nation. The gentleman was then surprised when, after wiring the fee, no passport arrived, and (Surprise!) the Nigerian lady no longer responded to his e-mails. He turned to me for advice on what he might do.

Of course, I couldn't help him lock the barn door once the proverbial horse had been stolen. I didn't say so, but I did wonder how anyone could not know about the millions of dollars lost in the notorious Nigerian scams.

Just Say "No!"

The most famous "Nigerian scam" (also known as "advance fee fraud" and the "419 fraud") has been around for several years and has bilked many thousands out of countless millions of dollars.

I recall talking, over a period of months, with an elderly Sovereign Society member in an effort to convince him that he was a victim of this scam. He was truly convinced by a skillful con man that he stood to gain hundreds of thousands of dollars if he would just send his new, unseen friend a few thousand. I finally talked him out of it, but it took some effort.

This type of scam is generally referred to as the "Nigerian scam," because of its prevalence in the region, particularly during the 1990s.

Here, the emailer requests help in the transfer of a substantial sum of money. In return, the sender offers a "commission," usually several million dollars. The scammers then request that money be sent to pay for some of the costs of the transfer. If money is sent, the scammers either disappear or try to get more money with claims of continued problems with the transfer.

This scam is not limited to Nigeria and is used by crooks in many countries. The origins of this scam are debated, some suggest it started in Nigeria during the 1970s; others say its origins go back hundreds of years to other confidence scams such as the late 19th century Spanish prisoner scam, also known as the advance-fee scam.

All of these scammers play on human greed, hoping the commission offered will entice the recipient to risk sending thousands of dollars to a stranger. Official U.S. government warnings about this scam have been issued by the FBI, FTC, the Treasury and, one of the best, by the U.S. State Department African Desk. I urge you to read it.

Intelligent Financial Decisions Begin with Your Own Due Diligence

"Due diligence" can be defined as, *"The care that a prudent person might be expected to exercise in the examination and evaluation of risks affecting a business transaction."*

Here at The Sovereign Society, we try to keep you straight on tax and other financial matters. But a good dose of your own common sense is also helpful. The due diligence process should be used to investigate any potential financial matter, including investments, banking and the hiring of professionals.

Sadly, this process is too often ignored, usually when an individual's good judgment is suspended after a slick sales barrage of glittering promises of immediate financial gain.

My Eight Rules for Sound Due Diligence:

1. **Conduct your own due diligence.** Don't rely on appearances, fancy offices, nice suits and power lunches. You're seeing what others want you to see and hearing what others want you to hear, and it could be a lie. Always ask for and check references.

2. **Do comparison shopping.** As a "come on" some promoters charge prices half or even less than those of competitors for similar offshore services. A careful comparison of the competition's fees and the costs associated with the involved services may suggest that the only way the low-price promoter can survive is to dip into the funds he has under management.

   Obtain certified financial statements of a company's assets and liabilities and check the standing with the offshore official regulatory or licensing agency. We can recommend experienced offshore professionals, both in the U.S. and foreign countries, who charge reasonable fees. Please check the end of this report for contact details.

3. **Obtain independent advice on any proposed legal structure or investment.** Get competent counsel, both in the U.S and the offshore country, who is responsible to you, and only you, with the experience to realistically evaluate the deal. Remember, it's legal to find ways to avoid certain taxes. Tax evasion, however, is a criminal offence.

4. **Ignore tantalizing promises of easy profits.** The best opportunities require hard work, significant risk and time. Easy money and promoters like Bernie Madoff, who guarantee unrealistic profits (more than 12%-15% annually, or consistent profits without significant variation in returns), are sure signs of a con.

5. **Don't rely on secrecy.** Dealing with an offshore promoter who claims that he can help you "hide money" from tax authorities is an invitation to blackmail. The slick promoter knows that, if you break the law, you're unlikely to ask a court to help return your assets when they disappear.

6. **Diversify.** Don't put all your eggs in one basket. Prudent investors diversify investments in stocks, bonds, mutual funds, currencies, and precious metals. And they employ more than one independent wealth adviser. We can recommend solid wealth managers and reading *The Sovereign Investor* as the starting **point.**

7. **Keep informed.** Hiring a firm in the U.S. or offshore to build a legal structure or manage your wealth is only the start. You're always responsible for your own wealth. So keep up to date with financial and world events — and keep an eye on those you employ.

8. **If it's too good to be true, it probably isn't true.** Applying this truism is the most important precaution of all. Unrealistic profits, barely believable promises or vague feelings that you're being "led on" are all indications that whatever deal you're being "pitched" is best avoided.

Tip: You might be surprised what you can find using the Google search engine — but you should always go much farther than that. It may be a well-worn platitude, but it's the truth: "There's no such thing as a free lunch."

Contacts

If you have questions about investments or possible frauds, refer to Appendix A to find the members of The Sovereign Society Council of Experts who can help. They also can provide contacts in many foreign countries.

Other Information Sources:

Offshore Alert newsletter, highly recommended: www.OffshoreAlert.com

Offshore Frauds: http://www.quatloos.com/offshore_planning_scam.htm

U.S. State Department: Nigerian Fraud:
http://www.state.gov/www/regions/africa/naffpub.pdf

Internet Scams, Identity Theft, and Urban Legends:
http://www.scambusters.org

What You Don't Know About Foreign Laws Can Hurt You

Mark Nestmann, *The Sovereign Individual*, 2002

As if increasing threats against English-speaking tourists aren't bad enough, there's an often overlooked threat when you travel internationally: that of being arrested or even jailed for something that's perfectly legal where you live.

Here's a rundown of some laws of which you should be aware. But for the most definitive information, consult the embassies or consulates of the countries to which you will be traveling to learn more about what regulations might apply.

- **Credit cards.** In some countries (Greece is one) you can be arrested for overextending the credit limit on your credit card. Make certain you have adequate credit limits before you leave.

- **Motor vehicles.** Be careful how you drive and, if you rent a vehicle, where you drive it. In some countries — Mexico is one — even a passenger of a vehicle involved in an accident may be temporarily detained, and occasionally, even jailed. Make certain that you obtain temporary auto insurance. In Mexico, you can be arrested if you don't have it. If you rent a vehicle, it may be illegal to leave the country where you rented it. In Austria, for instance, drivers attempting to enter countries listed as "prohibited" on the car rental contract may be arrested, fined and even charged with attempted auto theft.

- **GPS devices.** The use of global positioning system devices is subject to special rules and regulations in many countries. A U.S. citizen was imprisoned in Russia on charges of espionage for using a GPS device to confirm proper operation of newly installed telecommunications equipment. While he was released after 10 days, using a GPS device in a manner deemed to compromises Russian national security can result in a 20-year prison term.

- **Cell telephones.** Many countries require a permit to import a cellular telephone. Russia again has some of the strictest laws. To obtain permission to bring in a cellular telephone, you must sign an agreement for service from a local cellular provider. That agreement and a letter of guarantee to pay for the cellular service must be sent to a government agency, along with a request for permission to import the telephone. In Panama, a government granted phone monopoly will require you to rent a cell phone while there.

- **Laptop computers.** Laptops are commonplace these days, and most countries permit you to freely cross a border with one in your possession. There may be restrictions on how you use your laptop, particularly if you plug it in to the national telecommunications system. For instance, some countries that monitor telecommunications prohibit the use of encryption programs. Others permit laptops to be imported, but will confiscate them when you leave the country, particularly if the laptop contains encryption software or software that uses encryption, which is standard in all Internet browsers.

- **Prescription drugs.** Bringing a sufficient quantity of prescription drugs into a country for your use while you are there is almost never a problem. But this is not always the case; in Bahrain, for instance, you must obtain a license from the Health Ministry to import prescription drugs. Even if imported pharmaceuticals are permitted, keep your medication in its original container and carry a copy of your prescription with you.
- **Firearms.** Bringing a firearm (and in some cases merely ammunition) across an international border can result in a long prison sentence and the confiscation of the luggage, vehicle or boat in which it was found. In Mexico, for instance, dozens of Americans are incarcerated for the crime of bringing a licensed U.S. firearm into the country. In several cases, the firearms were even declared to the border inspector — but the persons carrying it were still arrested, tried and imprisoned.

If you are arrested or detained in a foreign country, you can usually turn to your local embassy or consulate for at least limited assistance. Most countries, including the United States, have ratified the Vienna Convention on Consular Relations, which requires ratifying states to permit consular officers to have access to imprisoned nationals of their country.

The Convention also provides that the foreign law enforcement authority shall inform the local consulate or the arrest of a national "without delay" (no time frame specified), if the national requests such notification.

Consular services available to prisoners generally include: visiting the prisoner as soon as possible after notification of the arrest; providing a list of local attorneys to help the prisoner obtain legal representation; providing information about judicial procedures in the foreign country; notifying family and/or friends, if authorized by the prisoner; relaying requests to family and friends for money or other aid; providing loans to destitute prisoners; arranging dietary supplements; and arranging for medical and dental care if not provided by prison.

Ways to Make Travel More Private

Mark Nestmann, *The Sovereign Individual*, November 2002

When you travel, from the time you book your ticket to the time you return home, computers, sensors, transmitters and cameras surround you, all collecting data. Much of this data collection is supposedly justified to fight the "War on (Some) Terrorists;" all of it is intrusive.

Monitoring is most pervasive if you're traveling by air, but governments also monitor travel by rail, bus and even private vehicles, with the United States (as usual) leading the way. Meet the wrong "profile," have the wrong passport stamp or make the wrong comment to a security guard, and you could be fined or even land in prison.

There are still ways to make traveling more private, although the era of anonymous travel is mostly over. Here are suggestions to increase travel privacy.

- Pay cash (except for air travel). Cash is untraceable, but if you purchase your airline tickets with cash, this automatically marks you for further attention.
- Small is beautiful. Fly on small airlines. Rent vehicles from small local operators. Stay in small local hotels. Avoid rental and hotel chains that will keep records of your stay in a database that is often posted to a national or international computer system.
- Don't get your passport stamped. This may require a special request to customs officials, which may or may not be honored. Some countries (Cuba and Switzerland are two) do not automatically stamp passports.
- Beware of importing electronic equipment without prior authorization. In most countries, it's legal to bring cellular telephones and laptops in for your personal use, but not always. For instance, in Russia, the unauthorized importation of a cellular telephone is a criminal offense.
- Consider indirect routing. If your final destination is a country that you'd rather not have identified in computerized records, don't fly there, but to a nearby country. Then take a train or rent a car to your final destination. Example: Fly to Germany to visit Switzerland, Liechtenstein, Austria or Luxembourg.
- Consider air charters or private planes. Air charter and general aviation companies rarely search their passengers or inspect their luggage. However, tickets can cost 10 times or more as much as tickets on commercial airlines. Since October 2002, U.S. air charter companies operating planes heavier than 95,000 pounds (about 130 seats) have had to comply with the same security regulations as commercial airlines. Smaller charters will not be required to comply with these regulations. In Europe, the cutoff is 100,000 pounds.

Tips for Clearing Airport Security

- Check your luggage and minimize carry-ons. Avoid carrying on sharp objects or anything that could be used as a weapon. Wear non-metallic clothing and tennis shoes, not leather shoes. Place any metal items you bring with you in your carry-on luggage that is x-rayed. Items that commonly set off the detectors include cell phones, car alarm transmitters, pagers, key rings, watchbands, pens, coins, glasses, metal buckles and candy wrapped in foil.
- Do not lock checked luggage. Airline and security personnel are notorious for stealing cash and other valuable items from checked luggage. But new rules

allow security personnel to search your luggage without asking you open it for them.

- Don't interfere with a search or even raise your voice. Assaulting a screener is a federal crime in most countries. In the United States, assault is defined as including fear of imminent physical assault. Under the new Aviation and Transportation Security Act, it carries a penalty of up to 10 years in prison, a fine, or both. Yelling at the screener could land you in federal prison!
- Keep batteries in your laptop. If you carry on your laptop, you may be asked to "boot it up" at security. Be sure to charge your battery.
- Keep controversial reading material in your checked luggage. Or leave it at home. In several cases, individuals carrying books with provocative titles or illustrations in carry-on luggage have not been permitted to board their flight. In one case, when security personnel discovered a book by Karl Marx in a passenger's carry-on luggage, they arrested him! "After September 11, you can't travel with books like this," said the arresting officer.

Private Rail, Bus and Auto Travel

All forms of ground transportation are much more private than air transportation. Amtrak, the U.S. rail carrier now requires a photo ID to board its trains. Bus carriers on some interstate routes now require photo ID as well. Outside the United States, air and bus travel is more private except when crossing borders, other than EU borders across which IDs are no longer systematically checked.

- To avoid showing up in rental car databases, rent from a small, local firm. If you rent a car in most countries, you will need to show a driver's license (or international driving permit) and credit card. Do not list your home address on the agreement — use a mail receiving service instead. (This address should match that on your driver's license.) Read the agreement to make certain that your rental vehicle will not be tracked by a GPS satellite, as is becoming increasingly more common.
- Avoid toll roads. If you must use them, pay tolls with coins, never with an automated payment voucher system.
- Don't volunteer information. Finally, and most important: the best way to protect your privacy, at home, in the air or on the road, is to maintain a private attitude. Never give out your Social Security number (or its equivalent if you're not a U.S. resident). When in doubt — try to "blend in" with the crowd and keep your mouth shut! Do terrorists use these techniques to avoid detection? Perhaps.

But "terrorism" is now so broadly defined that anyone who participates in a concerted effort to effect political change can arguably be labeled as a terrorist. Don't let "fear of terrorism" prevent you from protecting your privacy.

Appendix A

The Sovereign Society's Council of Experts

A Rolodex of International Expertise at Your Fingertips

Robert E. Bauman JD, Editor and Legal Counsel
The Sovereign Society
Address: 55 NE 5th Avenue, Suite 200, Delray Beach, FL 33483 USA
Tel.: (888) 245-3882
Email: sovereignconfidential@sovereignsociety.com
Web: www.sovereignsociety.com

Ted Bauman, Editor of *The Bauman Letter* and Plan B Club
The Sovereign Society
Address: 55 NE 5th Avenue, Suite 200, Delray Beach, FL 33483 USA
Tel.: (888) 245-3882
Email: sovereignconfidential@sovereignsociety.com
Web: www.sovereignsociety.com

Jeff Opdyke, Executive Editor
The Sovereign Society
Address: 55 NE 5th Avenue, Suite 200, Delray Beach, FL 33483 USA
Tel.: (866) 584-4096
Email: sovereigninvestor@sovereignsociety.com
Web: www.sovereignsociety.com

Tax and Asset Protection

Erika Nolan, CEO and Managing Partner
1291 Group of the Americas
Address: Sterling House, 16 Wesley Street, Hamilton, Bermuda, HM11
Tel.: (+441) 295-3492
Email: erika.nolan@1291americas.com
Web: www.1291americas.com

Gideon Rothschild, JD, CPA, Chair of Trusts & Estates and Asset Protection Practices
Moses & Singer LLP
Address: 405 Lexington Avenue New York, N.Y. 10174 USA
Tel.: (212) 554-7806
Email: grothschild@mosessinger.com
Web: http://www.mosessinger.com

Josh N. Bennett, Esq., P.A.
Address: 440 North Andrews Avenue, Fort Lauderdale, Florida 33301 USA
Tel.: (954) 779-1661
Mobile: (786) 202-5674
Email: josh@joshbennett.com
Web: www.joshbennett.com

Juan Federico Fischer, Esq., MBA, Managing Partner
Fischer & Schickendantz
Address: Rincón 487, Piso 4 - C.P: 11.000, Montevideo, Uruguay
Tel.: (+598) 2915 7468 x 130
Mobile: (+598) 99-925-106
Email: jfischer@fs.com.uy or info@fs.com.uy
Web: http://www.fs.com.uy

Marc-André Sola, Founder & Managing Partner
1291 Group Switzerland
Hottingerstrasse 21
P.O. Box 1369
8032 Zürich, Switzerland
Tel.: +41 44 266 21 41
Email: info@1291Switzerland.ch
Web: www.1291Switzerland.ch

APPENDIX A: COUNCIL OF EXPERTS

Mark Nestmann, LL.M., President
The Nestmann Group, Ltd.
Address: 2303 N. 44th St. #14-1025, Phoenix, Arizona 85008
Tel.: (602) 688-7552
Email: service@nestmann.com
Web: http://www.nestmann.com

Michael Chatzky, Esq., President
Chatzky & Associates, Estate Planning and Asset Protection
Address: 6540 Lusk Boulevard, Suite C121, San Diego, CA 92121 USA
Tel.: (858) 457-1000
Email: mgchatzky@aol.com
Web: http://chatzky-alc.com

Rainelda Mata-Kelly, LL.M., Panamanian Lawyer
Law Offices Rainelda Mata-Kelly
Address: P.O. BOX 0818-00534, Panama City, Republic of Panama (Suites 406-407, Tower B, Torres de las Americas, Punta Pacifica, City of Panama)
Tel.: (+507) 216-9299
Email: rmk@mata-kelly.com
Web: www.mata-kelly.com

Offshore Banking and Investing

Daniel Zurbrügg, CFA, Managing Director & Partner, Investments and Client Relations, Co-Founder
Swiss Infinity Global Investments GmbH
Address: Gartenstrasse 23, CH-8002 Zürich, Switzerland
Tel.: +41 44 315 77 77 or +41 44 200 2310
Email: info@swissinfinity.ch
Web: www.swissinfinity.ch

Dominique J. Spillmann, Partner and CEO
Swisspartners Advisors Ltd.
Tel.: +41 58 200 0 801
Contact Form: http://www.swisspartners.com/structure/en/contact.php
Web: www.swisspartners.com

Eric N. Roseman, President and Chief Investment Officer
ENR Asset Management, Inc.
Address: 1 Westmount Square, Suite 1400, Westmount Quebec, H3Z 2P9 Canada

Tel.: (877)-989-8027 or (514) 989-8027 or (514) 989-0009
Email: eric@enrasset.com
Web: www.enrassetmanagement.com

Geoff Anandappa, Investment Portfolio Manager
Stanley Gibbons Investment
UK Address: 399 Strand, London, WC2R 0LX
Tel.: 0845 026 7170
Email: ganandappa@stanleygibbons.com or investment@stanleygibbons.com
Web: http://investment.stanleygibbons.com

Rich Checkan, President & COO
Asset Strategies International, Inc.
Address: 1700 Rockville Pike, Suite 400, Rockville, MD 20852
Tel.: (800) 831-0007 or (301) 881-8600
Email: infoasi@assetstrategies.com
Web: www.assetstrategies.com

Robert Vrijhof, President & Senior Partner
Weber, Hartmann, Vrijhof & Partners, Ltd.
Assistant: Ms. Julia Fernandez
Address: Schaffhauserstrasse 418, CH-8050 Zürich, Switzerland
Tel.: 01141-44-315 77 77
Email: info@whvp.ch
Web: http://www.whvp.ch

Van Simmons, President
David Hall Rare Coins
Address: P.O. Box 6220, Newport Beach, CA 92658
Tel.: (800) 759-7575 or (949) 567-1325
Email: van@davidhall.com or infor@davidhall.com
Web: www.davidhall.com

The professionals listed below assist our members in opening bank and other financial accounts in the countries indicated.

(The banks listed accept U.S. clients as of the date of publication, but individual bank policies may change.)

Australia

Dwyer Lawyers
Terry Dwyer Esq.
Address: Suite 4, Level 2, CPA Australia Building, 161 London

Circuit, Canberra City 2601, Australia
or GPO Box 2529, Canberra City Act 2601, Australia
Tel.: +61 02 6247 8184
Email: terence.dwyer@dwyerlawyers.com.au
Web: http://www.dwyerlawyers.com.au

Canada

Royal Bank of Canada (RBC)
Robert (Bob) Spicer, Investment & Retirement Planning
Address: 1 West Mount Square, Westmount Quebec, H3Z 3B5
Canada
Tel.: (514) 874-5523
Email: bob.spicer@rbc.com
Web: http://www.rbc.com/country-select.html
Minimum Balance: US$50,000

People's Republic of China

Jeffrey Y.F. Chen Esq.
Address: 3A, Yunhai Garden Office Tower
118 Qinghai Road, Shanghai, 200041, China.
Tel.: (86) 21 52281952
Mobile: (86) 13916089368
Email: lawyer_chen@lawyers.cn

Please note that banks in mainland China do not accept account applications from foreign individuals or from corporations unless they have registered subsidiaries located in China. Mr. Chen advises on investments, business or other matters concerning China.

The Cook Islands

Ora Fiduciary (Cook Islands) Ltd.
Puai T. Wichman Esq., Managing Director
Address: Global House, P.O. Box 92, Avarua, Rarotonga, Cook Islands
Tel.: +682 27047 or U.S. (734) 402-7047
Email: puai@oratrust.com or info@oratrust.com
Web: http://oratrust.com
Mr. Wichman provides introduction to these Cook Island banks:
ANZ Banking Group Limited
Bank of the Cook Islands Limited
Capital Security Bank Cook Islands Limited
Westpac Banking Corporation

New Zealand

David A Tanzer & Assoc., PC.
David A Tanzer, Esq.
Tel. + (64) 9 353-1328
Email: Datlegal@aol.com
Web: http://www.davidtanzer.com

Republic of Panama

Banks in Panama require an introduction from a local professional for foreigners seeking to open bank accounts.

Law Offices Rainelda Mata-Kelly
Rainelda Mata-Kelly, LL.M.
Address: P.O. BOX 0818-00534, Panama City, Republic of Panama (Suites 406-407, Tower B, Torres de las Americas, Punta Pacifica, City of Panama)
Tel.: (+507) 216-9299
Email: rmk@mata-kelly.com
Web: www.mata-kelly.com

Banvivienda
Banco Panameño de la Vivienda, S.A.
Address: Ave. La Rotonda & Boulevard Costa del Este, Panamá
Tel.: (+507) 306-2000 or (+507) 306-2100 or (+507) 300-4700
Web: https://www.banvivienda.com/en

Multibank Inc.
Address: Vía España No. 127, Edif. Prosperidad, Apdo 0823-05627, Panamá, Rep. of Panamá
Tel.: (+507) 294-3500 ext. 1530
Web: https://www.multibank.com.pa/en/default.html

UniBank
Address: Edificio Grand Bay Tower, Avenida Balboa Piso N° 3, Panamá, Rep. de Panamá
Tel.: (+507) 297-6000 or (+507) 297-6006
Email: ideas@unibank.com.pa
Web: https://www.unibank.com.pa/en/index.html

Scotiabank

Address: Punta Pacifica Branch - Centro Commercial Plaza, Pacifica, #9, Rep. de Panamá
Tel.: (+507) 297-5200 or (+507) 215-5450 or (+507) 215-5457
Web: http://www.scotiabank.com/pa/es/0,,3784,00.html

Singapore & Hong Kong

The Sovereign Society recommended banks in Singapore and Hong Kong do not accept accounts directly from individual U.S. person but require an intermediary to submit account applications. The banks may require account applicants to appear personally at their offices as part of the application process. Below is contact information for our designated Singapore and Hong Kong intermediary, Josh Bennett, Esq., an expert attorney in offshore asset protection, U.S. offshore taxes and reporting requirements. He also acts as contact for Trident Corporate Services that provides incorporation, trust creation and related business and banking services in Singapore and Hong Kong and in many other OFCs worldwide.

Josh N. Bennett, Esq., P.A.

Address: 440 North Andrews Avenue, Fort Lauderdale, Florida 33301 USA
Tel.: (954) 779-1661
Mobile: (786) 202-5674
Email: josh@joshbennett.com
Web: www.joshbennett.com

Oriental Republic of Uruguay

Fischer & Schickendantz

Juan Federico Fischer, Managing Partner
Address: Rincón 487, Piso 4 - C.P: 11.000, Montevideo, Uruguay
Tel.: (+598) 2915 7468 x 130
Mobile: (+598) 99-925-106
Email: jfischer@fs.com.uy or info@fs.com.uy
Web: http://www.fs.com.uy

Banco Itau

Andrea Tejeira, Account Executive
Address: Pedro Berro 1039, 11300 Montevideo, Uruguay
Tel.: +598 2916 0127 x 505
Email: atejeira@itau.com.uy
Web: https://www.itau.com.uy/biu/index.htm
Retail banking only—Minimum Balance: US$2,500

Appendix B

About the Authors

Robert E. Bauman JD, legal counsel to The Sovereign Society, is a former member of the United States House of Representatives from Maryland, (1973–1981). He is also a former federal official and Maryland state senator, member of the Washington, D.C. Bar, and a graduate of Georgetown University Law Center (1964) and the G.U School of Foreign Service (1959) in Washington, D.C.

In 1998, Bob helped found The Sovereign Society. He served as the editor of the Society's first publication, *The A-Letter*, the predecessor to its flagship letter, *The Sovereign Investor*. In 2008, Bob founded and serves as chairman of The Sovereign Society's *Freedom Alliance*, an elite personal information service that provides members with inside news about protecting their wealth and freeing themselves from unnecessary taxes and government oversight. He also was the founding editor of *Offshore Confidential*, a monthly in-depth special report service that focused on offshore opportunities and events, and now contributes to *The Bauman Letter*. In many of Bob's publications, he provides priceless recommendations and shares access to his wealth of offshore professional and banking contacts worldwide.

Bob is also the author or co-author of numerous books and reports, including *Forfeiting Our Property Rights*, The Cato Institute, Washington, D.C. (1995, with Hon. Henry Hyde) and publications of The Sovereign Society, including; *The Passport Book: Complete Guide to Offshore Residence, Dual Citizenship and Second Passports*; *Where to Stash Your Cash Legally: Offshore Financial Centers of the World*; *Lawyer Proof Your Life: A Do-It Yourself Guide to Saving Money, Saving Time and Avoiding Lawsuits*; *Forbidden Knowledge: Inside Information They Don't Want You to See*.

Bob has authored articles and reviews for *The Cato Institute* and *The New York Times, Washington Post, Los Angeles Times, Baltimore Sun, The Wall Street Journal, National Review, The Advocate, Human Events* and made appearances on *National Public Radio* (NPR), *The News Hour* (PBS), *CNN*, *20/20* (ABC), *Nightline, World News* (ABC), *Today Show* (NBC) and *Good Morning America* (CBS).

Ted Bauman joined The Sovereign Society in 2013 and serves as the editor of *The Bauman Letter* and Plan B Club. As an expat who has traveled to over 60 countries, Ted specializes in asset protection and international migration issues.

Born in Washington, D.C. and raised on Maryland's Eastern Shore, Ted emigrated to South Africa as a young man. He graduated from the University of Cape Town with postgraduate degrees in Economics and History. During his 25-year career in South Africa, Ted served a variety of executive roles in the nonprofit sector, primarily as a fund manager for low-cost housing projects. During the 2000s, he worked as a consultant, researching and writing extensively on finance, housing and urban planning issues for clients as diverse as the United Nations, the South African government and European grant-making agencies. He also traveled extensively, largely in Africa, Asia and Europe.

In 2008, Ted returned to the U.S., where he served as Director of International Housing Programs for Habitat for Humanity International, based in Atlanta, Georgia. During that time he extended his travels to Latin America and the Caribbean. He continued to research and write on a variety of topics related to international development. In 2013, Ted left Habitat for Humanity to work full-time as a researcher and writer.

Ted has been published in a variety of international journals, including the *Journal of Microfinance, Small Enterprise Development and Environment and Urbanization*, as well as the South African press, including the *Cape Times, New Internationalist, Cape Argus*, and *Mail and Guardian*. More recently, he co-authored the book *Where to Stash Your Cash Legally: Offshore Financial Centers of the World* and co-edited the book Forbidden *Forbidden Knowledge: Inside Information They Don't Want You to See* with his father Robert Bauman.

Harry Browne was the author of 11 books. His first book, *How You Can Profit from the Coming Devaluation*, was published in 1970. Browne's warnings proved to be accurate when the dollar was devalued twice and his recommended investments rose many times over. Ten more books followed, and from 1974 to 1997. He also published Harry Browne's Special Reports, a newsletter covering the economy, politics, and investments. His book, *Fail-Safe Investing*, explains in detail how set up a permanent portfolio.

Michael Chatzky specializes in federal and international taxation and wealth protection with an emphasis on business, estate and asset protection planning. For over 36 years, Michael has assisted clients in establishing a wide variety of wealth preservation structures, many of which contain valuable tax saving features. A highly sought-after speaker at wealth protection seminars, Michael is known for his detailed knowledge and uncanny ability to quote page and paragraph on any current tax law in question. Michael regularly shares his expertise on the usage of foreign trusts, limited partnerships and other entities as wealth protection vehicles through numerous published articles, lectures and appearances on radio and television. His practice is currently located in the San Diego, California office of Chatzky & Associates.

"P.T. Freeman" is the pseudonym of a former U.S. citizen living in a Caribbean country and doing business throughout the world, including countries subject to U.S. sanctions.

Vernon K. Jacobs CPA, CLU is an independent tax accountant and consultant who focuses on offering tax services for U.S. persons with offshore investments or entities and for non U.S. persons who have tax obligations in the U.S. He also provides consulting and research services involving international tax matters for other CPAs and tax professionals. Additionally, he is the President of Offshore Press, Inc., Editor and publisher of the online International Wealth Protection Monitor and Research Library, co-author of *The Controlled Foreign Corporation Tax Guide* and co-author of *Risk Management for Amateur Investors*.

Marshall J. Langer JD, is co-author of *U.S. International Taxation and Tax Treaties* (Matthew Bender Inc. New York) and author of several books, including The Tax Exile Report. Of counsel, Shutts & Bowen, London and Miami; Professor of Law, LL.M. International Tax, St. Thomas University School of Law, Miami, FL.

Vincent H. Miller is founder and president of the International Society for Individual Liberty (ISIL). He is also a member of The Sovereign Society Council of Experts.

Daniel J. Mitchell is a leading expert on tax reform and supply-side tax policy. Prior to joining the Cato Institute, he was a senior fellow with The Heritage Foundation, and an economist for Senator Bob Packwood and the U.S. Senate Finance Committee. He also was Director of Tax and Budget Policy for Citizens for a Sound Economy. His articles can be found in such publications as *The Wall Street Journal*, *The New York Times*, *Investor's Business Daily*, and *Washington Times*. He is a frequent guest on radio and television and a popular speaker. He holds BA and MA degrees in economics from the University of Georgia and a Ph.D. in economics from George Mason University.

Mark Nestmann BA, LL.M, for more than 27 years, has helped over 9,000 customers and clients successfully protect their assets and financial privacy. Fans include well-known free thinkers, such as former U.S. Congressman and presidential candidate Ron Paul, as well as Dr. Gary North and Dr. Mark Skousen.

Mark was the original editor for The Oxford Club and one of the founders of The Sovereign Society. His consulting firm, The Nestmann Group, provides asset protection and international tax planning services with a focus on second citizenship and tax planning for expatriation. His work has been featured in notable media including *The Washington Post*, *The New York Times*, *ABC News*,

Barron's, *Bloomberg News*, *Business Week*, and *Forbes*. He is also the author of The Lifeboat Strategy — widely considered the gold standard in American-client asset protection and financial privacy resources. He holds a Master of Law (LL.M.) in international tax law from the University of Vienna.

Erika Nolan is the CEO of the 1291 Group of the Americas. The Bermuda-based company specializes in tailored asset protection and tax/estate planning solutions, as well as unique asset management options. The 1291 Group of the Americas caters to the U.S & Latin American markets and works with professionals and private individual investors. The firm is also a SEC-registered investment adviser and offers full asset management services.

Prior to her role with the 1291 Group, Erika was the Executive Publisher for The Sovereign Society and Dent Research, divisions of Agora Publishing, for 16 years. She is the co-author of *The Offshore Advantage — The Beginner's Guide to Going Offshore and The Insured Portfolio*. In addition, she has written dozens of financial and asset protection articles for *The Sovereign Investor* and *Offshore Confidential*. Erika is sought after speaker at international financial conferences around the world. Erika is a member of the Young Presidents' Organization's Florida chapter, the world's premier peer network of chief executives and business leaders. She travels extensively throughout Europe and South America.

Jeff Opdyke is the investment director and executive editor at The Sovereign Society. Jeff has been investing directly in the international markets since 1995, making him one of the true pioneers of foreign trading. His passion is finding the renegade plays "on the ground" in overseas markets and uncovering those explosive trends long before they become mainstream.

Jeff is the editor of *Jeff Opdyke's Total Wealth Insider* newsletter. For his 25,000 subscribers, he finds proven investments … from global stocks to emerging-market investments and foreign currency plays that most people will never hear about. In addition to profitable investment picks, Jeff also provides his subscribers with the latest updates on offshore banking havens, international tax strategies and asset protection secrets from experts around the globe. He is also the editor of the *Frontline Investor*, a weekly advisory that shows his subscribers how investing "in country" can result in far greater returns than you could ever find in stagnant American markets.

As our investment director, Jeff also has his hands in other Sovereign Society services, such as being the editor of *Precision Profits*, a weekly advisory that uses seasonal-based stock patterns to routinely deliver triple-digit gains. He is also the editor of *Uncommon Fortunes*, a service designed to keep subscribers informed about the hottest collectibles markets, bring them into the world of some of the most successful investors, who are shieling their money from Wall Street volatility and government intrusion.

Prior to writing his own investment letter, Jeff spent 17 years with *The Wall Street Journal*, writing about investing and personal finance, including the *Journal's* nationally syndicated "Love & Money" column. His work has been published in upward of 80 newspapers nationwide and he is also the author of six books, including his newest publication *Replay: Your Second Change to Invest in the American Dream*. When not traveling the globe, he lives in Louisiana with his family… and attends every LSU football game he can.

Nicholas Pullen writes widely on offshore opportunities and individual liberty and authored *The Internationalist Blueprint*.

John Pugsley was a founder of Common Sense Press and a co-founder of The Sovereign Society. He authored many books on economics, investing and politics. His first book, *Common Sense Economics* (1974), sold over 150,000 hardcover copies and predicted the inflation that followed U.S. abandonment of the gold standard in the early 1970s. In 1980, his second bestseller, *The Alpha Strategy*, warned against coming U.S. deficits, giving investors a practical plan for self-protection. For a decade beginning in 1988, he published *John Pugsley's Journal*, a newsletter of political, economic and investment ideas.

Gideon Rothschild JD, CPA is a nationally recognized authority on the use of offshore trusts and other planning techniques for wealth preservation. Gideon focuses his practice in the areas of domestic and international estate planning and asset protection, including the use of sophisticated estate planning techniques in the representation of high net-worth individuals.

His clients include professionals, real estate developers and owners, closely-held business owners and directors of publicly held companies. He practices estate administration and represents clients in taxpayer disputes at the federal, state and local levels. Gideon is an adjunct professor at The University of Miami School of Law Graduate Program, and a Fellow of The American College of Trust and Estates Counsel. He has lectured frequently on asset protection and estate planning to professional groups including the American Bar Association, the New York State Bar Association, and the American Institute of Certified Public Accountants.

Eric N. Roseman is the founder, president and chief investment officer of ENR Asset Management, Inc. based in Montreal, Canada. ENR Asset Management Inc. currently manages US$373 million dollars in global assets and is registered as an Investment Advisor with the United States Securities and Exchange Commission. Prior to his position at ENR Asset Management, Mr. Roseman studied at McGill University and earned his Bachelor of Arts in political science in 1989. He soon after launched The Impartial Global Mutual Fund Investor, which ranked many of the world's top-performing money-managers, including interviews, until 2007. In 1991, Mr. Roseman began advising non-Canadian investors, including the non-resident founder of Canada's largest mutual fund company in the 1990s, and in 1996, established private banking relationships for international clients in Denmark, Austria and Switzerland. In 1995, he joined Agora Publishing — the largest investment publishing company in America. Mr. Roseman also joined an Agora sister company, The Sovereign Society, in 1997 as a founding contributing editor and later became founder and editor of *Commodity Trend Alert* in 2003. From 2007 to 2010, he was the Investment Director of The Sovereign Society. In 2005, the company began advising U.S. investors following registration with the SEC.

Since 1991, Mr. Roseman has employed a global asset allocation approach to investing, offering traditional and non-traditional investment programs. ENR's largest investors include one of Switzerland's largest insurance intermediaries, several European private banks, multinational corporations and high net-worth U.S. investors. In 1998, he co-launched the Momentum Emerald Fund with London-based Momentum Asset Management UK, a multi-manager boutique later sold to Pioneer Investments in the early 2000s. Additionally, since 1995, Mr. Roseman has spoken at public investment seminars and conferences, including The Sovereign Society, Agora LLC, The World Money Show, and has appeared in numerous editorials, including *The New York Times*, *The Globe & Mail* and *The Montreal Gazette*. He also serves on the Board of Investment Advisors for The Oxford Club and the Board of Governors for The Sovereign Society.

Shannon Crouch Sands is a graduate of Loyola College, Baltimore, Maryland. She worked for Agora Publishing, one of the largest financial newsletter publishers in the United States, before moving to The Sovereign Society in 1999 to manage operations and publishing activities. She has traveled in Europe, Asia, the Caribbean, and Central America and is the co-author of *Offshore Investments That Safeguard Your Cash*.

Jocelynn Smith has spent her career immersed in the financial industry. Prior to joining The Sovereign Society in December 2014, she acquired her Series 7 and 63 licenses while working for a top-ranked brokerage firm and spent more than a decade as a stock market analyst. In the past, she has specialized in options analysis, trading strategies and options education.

She has appeared on *Fox Business News* and *Bloomberg*. In addition, she had been regularly quoted in publications such as *Reuters*, *MarketWatch*, *BusinessWeek*, *Wall Street Journal Online*, *Forbes* and the *Associated Press*, as well as contributed articles to *Stock, Futures and Options* (SFO) and *Option Trader* magazine. She is also a *New York Times* and *USA Today* best-selling author with more than 10 books published.

Marc-André Sola started his first company at the age of 20 and has since founded, or co-founded, a number of businesses in different fields and in multiple countries. Mr. Sola has served as the managing partner with 1291 Group Switzerland and its predecessors since 2000. Prior to his current engagement,

Marc has held various senior positions in the financial industry, such as CEO of an international U.S. registered investment advisory firm in Switzerland. During his career, Marc has advised clients from all over the world and has built up a vast experience in finding or tailoring solutions in banking and insurance.

Mr. Sola holds a Masters of Law degree from the University of Zürich and serves on the board of various companies. He specializes in insurance and retirement planning, as well as tailored asset protection and estate and tax planning solutions. For over 20 years, he has been advising clients from all over Europe, North & South America, the Middle East, Asia, and Africa. Mr. Sola is a sought after speaker at international investment, asset protection and estate planning conferences worldwide. Furthermore, he has published a variety of professional articles and co-authored the book, *The Insured Portfolio*, published by John Wiley & Sons (2010). He is a member of YPO (Young Presidents Organization), Zürich Chapter.

John Sturgeon JD, is a U.S. lawyer who advises clients on their offshore moves and assists them in reorganizing their business and personal lives.

Paul Terhorst was a successful CPA for Peat Marwick, an international accounting firm. He was able to retire at age 35. His book, Cashing in on the *American Dream —How to Retire at Age 35* (Bantam Books, 1988), tells how he did it.